**07**

LOS ANGELES

**Where to Stay and Eat
for All Budgets**

**Must-See Sights
and Local Secrets**

Ratings You Can Trust

Fodor's Travel Publications   New York, Toronto, London, Sydney, Auckland
www.fodors.com

FODOR'S LOS ANGELES 2007
Editor: Jennifer Paull

Editorial Production: David Downing, Tom Holton
Editorial Contributors: Kristina Brooks, Kathy Bryant, Matthew Flynn, Roger J. Grody, Lina Lecaro, Kathy A. McDonald, Laura Randall, Kastle Waserman
Maps: David Lindroth, *cartographer*; Rebecca Baer and Bob Blake, *map editors*
Design: Fabrizio La Rocca, *creative director*; Guido Caroti, *art director*; Moon Sun Kim, *cover designer*; Melanie Marin, *senior picture editor*
Production/Manufacturing: Robert Shields
Cover Photo (Oscar attendees enter the Kodak Theatre for the 75th Annual Academy Awards in Los Angeles): Mark J. Terrill/Associated Press Wide World Photos.

COPYRIGHT

SPECIAL SALES

This book is available for special discounts for bulk purchases for sales promotions or premiums. Special editions, including personalized covers, excerpts of existing books, and corporate imprints, can be created in large quantities for special needs. For more information, write to Special Markets/Premium Sales, 1745 Broadway, MD 6-2, New York, New York 10019, or e-mail specialmarkets@randomhouse.com.

AN IMPORTANT TIP & AN INVITATION

Although all prices, opening times, and other details in this book are based on information supplied to us at press time, changes occur all the time in the travel world, and Fodor's cannot accept responsibility for facts that become outdated or for inadvertent errors or omissions. So **always confirm information when it matters,** especially if you're making a detour to visit a specific place. Your experiences—positive and negative—matter to us. If we have missed or misstated something, **please write to us.** We follow up on all suggestions. Contact the Los Angeles editor at editors@fodors. com or c/o Fodor's at 1745 Broadway, New York, New York 10019.

PRINTED IN THE UNITED STATES OF AMERICA

10 9 8 7 6 5 4 3 2 1

Be a Fodor's Correspondent

Your opinion matters. It matters to us. It matters to your fellow Fodor's travelers, too. And we'd like to hear it. In fact, we *need* to hear it.

When you share your experiences and opinions, you become an active member of the Fodor's community. That means we'll not only use your feedback to make our books better, but we'll publish your names and comments whenever possible. Throughout our guides, look for "Word of Mouth," excerpts of your unvarnished feedback.

Here's how you can help improve Fodor's for all of us.

Tell us when we're right. We rely on local writers to give you an insider's perspective. But our writers and staff editors—who are the best in the business—depend on you. Your positive feedback is a vote to renew our recommendations for the next edition.

Tell us when we're wrong. We're proud that we update most of our guides every year. But we're not perfect. Things change. Hotels cut services. Museums change hours. Charming cafés lose charm. If our writer didn't quite capture the essence of a place, tell us how you'd do it differently. If any of our descriptions are inaccurate or inadequate, we'll incorporate your changes in the next edition and will correct factual errors at fodors.com *immediately*.

Tell us what to include. You probably have had fantastic travel experiences that aren't yet in Fodor's. Why not share them with a community of like-minded travelers? Maybe you chanced upon a beach or bistro or B&B that you don't want to keep to yourself. Tell us why we should include it. And share your discoveries and experiences with everyone directly at fodors.com. Your input may lead us to add a new listing or highlight a place we cover with a "Highly Recommended" star or with our highest rating, "Fodor's Choice."

Give us your opinion instantly at our feedback center at www.fodors.com/feedback. You may also e-mail editors@fodors.com with the subject line "Los Angeles Editor." Or send your nominations, comments, and complaints by mail to Los Angeles Editor, Fodor's, 1745 Broadway, New York, NY 10019.

You and travelers like you are the heart of the Fodor's community. Make our community richer by sharing your experiences. Be a Fodor's correspondent.

Happy traveling!

Tim Jarrell, Publisher

CONTENTS

CLOSEUPS

MAPS

ABOUT THIS BOOK

Our Ratings

Sometimes you find terrific travel experiences and sometimes they just find you. But usually the burden is on you to select the right combination of experiences. That's where our ratings come in.

As travelers we've all discovered a place so wonderful that its worthiness is obvious. And sometimes that place is so unique that superlatives don't do it justice: you just have to be there to know. These sights, properties, and experiences get our highest rating, **Fodor's Choice,** indicated by orange stars throughout this book.

Black stars highlight sights and properties we deem **Highly Recommended,** places that our writers, editors, and readers praise again and again for consistency and excellence.

By default, there's another category: any place we include in this book is by definition worth your time, unless we say otherwise. And we will.

Disagree with any of our choices? Care to nominate a place or suggest that we rate one more highly? Visit our feedback center at www. fodors.com/feedback.

Budget Well

Hotel and restaurant price categories from ¢ to **$$$$** are defined in the opening pages of their respective chapters. For attractions, we always give standard adult admission fees; reductions are usually available for children, students, and senior citizens. Want to pay with plastic? **AE, D, DC, MC, V** following restaurant and hotel listings indicate whether American Express, Discover, Diner's Club, MasterCard, and Visa are accepted.

Restaurants

Unless we state otherwise, restaurants are open for lunch and dinner daily. We mention dress only when there's a specific requirement and reservations only when they're essential or not accepted—it's always best to book ahead.

Hotels

Hotels have private bath, phone, TV, and air-conditioning and operate on the European Plan (aka EP, meaning without meals), unless we specify that they use the Continental Plan (CP, with a continental breakfast), Breakfast Plan (BP, with a full breakfast), or Modified American Plan (MAP, with breakfast and dinner) or are all-inclusive (including all meals and

most activities). We always list facilities but not whether you'll be charged an extra fee to use them, so when pricing accommodations, find out what's included.

Many Listings

★	Fodor's Choice
★	Highly recommended
✉	Physical address
✛	Directions
⌖	Mailing address
☎	Telephone
🖷	Fax
⊕	On the Web
✉	E-mail
✆	Admission fee
☉	Open/closed times
Ⓜ	Metro stations
🖦	Credit cards

Hotels & Restaurants

🏨	Hotel
🛏	Number of rooms
⌘	Facilities
ⵒⵔⵍ	Meal plans
✕	Restaurant
☌	Reservations
🛆	Dress code
⌇	Smoking
⌘⌇	BYOB
✕🏨	Hotel with restaurant that warrants a visit

Other

☕	Family-friendly
🔢	Contact information
⇨	See also
✉	Branch address
☞	Take note

WHEN TO GO

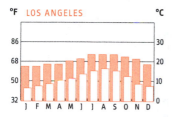

°F LOS ANGELES °C

Almost any time of the year is the right time to go to Los Angeles; the climate is mild and pleasant year-round. Contrary to popular belief, Los Angeles does have seasons. Winter brings crisp, sunny, unusually smogless days from about November to May. Although this takes in the rainy season, December to April, the storms are usually brief, and afterward the skies are brilliant. Of course, the nearby mountains are glorious in winter, perfect for skiing. However, dining alfresco, bike riding, sailing, catching a concert under the stars—these are the domain of Los Angeles summers. Summers are virtually rainless, leading to the occasional days of air-quality alerts. Prices skyrocket and reservations are a must when tourism peaks from July through early October.

Climate

Southern California is a temperate area: the Pacific Ocean is the primary moderating influence. In addition, mountains along the north and east sides of the Los Angeles coastal basin act as buffers against the extreme summer heat and winter cold of the desert and plateau regions.

Mild sea breezes and winds from the interior can mix to produce a variety of weather conditions; an unusual aspect of the Los Angeles climate is the pronounced difference in temperature, humidity, cloudiness, fog, rain, and sunshine over short distances. Rule of thumb, particularly in spring and summer, is that the San Fernando Valley (Burbank, North Hollywood, Sherman Oaks, Van Nuys, etc.) will be hotter than the Beverly Hills/Hollywood/Mid-Wilshire/downtown area, while the coastal areas (Malibu, Santa Monica, Venice, etc.) will be cooler. Late spring brings "June gloom," when skies tend to be overcast until afternoon.

i **Forecasts** **Weather Channel Connection** ☎ 900/932−8437 95¢ per minute from a Touch-Tone phone ⊕ www.weather.com.

WHAT'S WHERE

When Dorothy Parker described Los Angeles as "72 suburbs in search of a city" a half century or so ago, it was probably true; today the world at large tends to think of Los Angeles as *several* cities: L.A. proper, West Hollywood, Beverly Hills, Santa Monica, and more. It's hard to tell the real cities from areas that are really handy geographic and postal designations. For instance, West Hollywood is a city, but Hollywood is not (though some residents would like it to be).

To get a handle on the geography of L.A., picture yourself heading north from Los Angeles International Airport (LAX). Barring bad traffic you soon reach the coastal area of Santa Monica, from which two major thoroughfares run more or less due east into downtown. Sunset Boulevard winds around the upscale residential areas of Bel Air and Beverly Hills before hitting the legendary West Hollywood commercial stretch known as the Sunset Strip. Sunset then passes through Hollywood and ends downtown near Chinatown and Dodger Stadium. The other major street, south of Sunset, is Wilshire Boulevard, which takes you from Santa Monica through Westwood, UCLA's college village, past Beverly Hills's famous shopping district, through the financial Wilshire district, and into the city center.

The major neighborhoods listed below appear the same order they appear in the Exploring chapter, starting with downtown in the center and fanning out toward Pasadena and the city's outskirts.

DOWNTOWN LOS ANGELES

Downtown L.A. feels like it should be the city's center, but it hasn't yet reached critical mass. It's got spectacular modern architecture in the swooping Walt Disney Concert Hall and the stark Cathedral of Our Lady of the Angels. The Music Center and the Museum of Contemporary Art make downtown the closest thing L.A. has to an arts hub. Olvera Street, Chinatown, and Little Tokyo ground the neighborhood in the city's historic and ethnic past. Businesspeople flood downtown's cluster of skyscrapers and offices. But who lives here? Adventurous young people, artists, immigrants, and a concentrated homeless population. In short, it's a neighborhood in transition—and it's well worth getting out of your car to explore, even if you don't think so at first sight.

HOLLYWOOD	Glitzy and tarnished, good and bad, fun and sad—Hollywood is just like the entertainment business itself. But they don't make many movies or TV shows here anymore—they *once* made movies and TV shows here. After a serious decline, the neighborhood has slowly been improving over the past decade. This brand of urban renewal mixes new with vintage: restorations of old movie palaces plus splashy new developments such as the Hollywood & Highland entertainment complex. With a keen eye and your street smarts about you (stay where the lights are bright), you can enjoy the reminders of the area's romantic past, like the Walk of Fame, Grauman's Chinese Theatre, and the Hollywood Bowl.
WEST HOLLYWOOD	West Hollywood's an area for urban indulgences—shopping, restaurants, nightspots—rather than sightseeing. Its main arteries are the Sunset Strip (Sunset Boulevard), shorthand for longstanding clubs and cruising past boffo billboards, and Melrose Avenue, lined with shops punk, precious, and postmodern.
BEVERLY HILLS, CENTURY CITY & THE WESTSIDE	Go for the glamour, the restaurants, and the scene. This is the L.A. that gives East Coasters material for snarky jokes: plastic surgery, scads of sushi spots, and a parade of custom cars inching down the congested Westwood corridor along legendary streets like Sunset, Wilshire, and Santa Monica boulevards. The phrase "conspicuous consumption" is just the tip of the overprivileged iceberg. Beverly Hills is particularly good for a look at wretched or ravishing excess; Rodeo Drive is the best-known of its terrific outdoor shopping areas. But don't overlook the Westside's cultural attractions—especially the dazzling Getty Center.
SANTA MONICA, VENICE & MALIBU	First and foremost Santa Monica wants you to know that it's *not* Los Angeles and it plays by a different set of rules. That being said, the vibe here is what sets this city apart from L.A. proper. Stereotypical beach scenes play out almost every day, with skateboarders riding the rails, kids shrieking on the pier, and bikini babes on the sand. It's also a study of have and have-nots; while real estate is breathtakingly expensive, the community is quite liberal and supports a large homeless population. Venice, just south of Santa Monica along the coast, is a more raffish mix of artists, beach freaks, and yuppies, most of whom you'll see on the Venice Boardwalk.

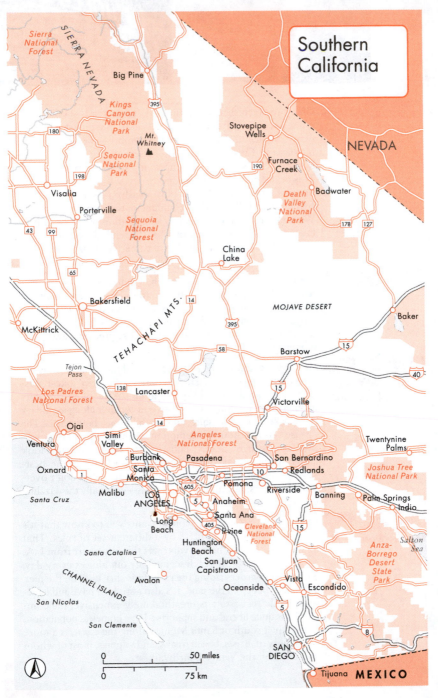

Southern California

NEVADA

MEXICO

	If you're not into shopping or "the scene," take a leisurely drive up PCH (you know, the Pacific Coast Highway) with the Eagles blaring on the stereo. Life is good in Malibu where the beach is king. The rich and famous hide away in their residential "Colony," but the rocky coves and amazing surf are open to all. And you can get a look at an extravagant residence of a different kind at the Getty Villa Malibu, modeled after an Italian country home and stuffed with antiquities.
SAN FERNANDO VALLEY	Referred to simply as "the Valley," the San Fernando Valley is the undisputed center of TV and film production. It's also got a hard-to-beat rep for tackiness and soulless urban sprawl. Entertainment types don't want to admit that they live here . . . but they do. The main sightseeing draws are tied into the Industry: Universal Studios Hollywood, studio tours at Warner Bros., and television-show tapings at NBC.
PASADENA AREA	Like Santa Monica, Pasadena feels like it's part of L.A. but is actually a separate city. (You've probably seen the main drag on TV, during the Tournament of Roses Parade on New Year's Day.) It's a quiet, genteel area to visit, with outstanding Arts and Crafts homes and a pair of exceptional museums: the Norton Simon and the Huntington estate in San Marino.
LONG BEACH, SAN PEDRO & PALOS VERDES	The peninsula of Palos Verdes and the port cities of San Pedro and Long Beach are far from the commotion of stars and stargazers. You'll likely come here only if you're interested in specific sights, like the aquariums or the art deco *Queen Mary* ship.
ORANGE COUNTY & CATALINA ISLAND	For decades, Orange County was equated with Disneyland—that is, if visitors didn't assume Disneyland was in L.A. But these days, the beach communities are getting just as much attention, even if they aren't quite as opulent as seen on TV. Coastal spots such as Huntington Beach, Newport Harbor and the Balboa Peninsula are perfect for chilling out in a beachfront hotel. Laguna Beach is wonderfully well-rounded, with an arts festivals and nature preserves as well as its beach. A short boat ride away is Catalina Island, with its pocket-size town and large nature preserve.

QUINTESSENTIAL L.A.

Car Culture

"Car culture" is not an oxymoron. Angelenos spend an enormous amount of time driving, and this influences far more than the city's legendary web of freeways and sprawling layout. Morning radio shows better be good, as they have to distract impatient drivers from rush-hour traffic jams. Joan Didion famously wrote about the hypnotic pull of the freeways. Commercial architecture started playing to drivers as early as the 1920s. First, business owners tried buildings that could be easily "read" and identified by people in passing cars—one great example of this is the hot-dog-shaped Tail O' the Pup hot dog stand. Later, big plate-glass windows became popular so that drivers would get a tempting look at the illuminated store or restaurant interiors. There are the drive-through fast food spots, too, with their deep roots in convenience and pop culture. You'll see plenty of vintage cars on the road, from tenderly restored 1950s Chevys driven by car-clubbers to ironic, grungy, '70s Pontiacs. And let's face it: cars are one of the ways locals categorize and label each other, just as with clothes or music.

How about you? A convertible may cost more to rent, but what better place to drive one. If you've got green concerns, you can rent an ecofriendly hybrid vehicle, the wheels of choice for Cameron Diaz and Leonardo DiCaprio. Or maybe you'd like to splurge on a trendy sportscar, a knockout classic, or something exotic like a Maserati . . .. Whatever your pleasure, there are plenty of rental companies that can set you up.

If you want to get a sense of local life, start by familiarizing yourself with these key influences. These are a few of the aspects that define L.A.—and they're elements to take pleasure in, even if you're here for just a day.

The (Entertainment) Industry

The Industry with a capital "I." It's the topic of most conversations you'll overhear; it leaves fingerprints all over local economics and politics; and it keeps local bloggers and gossips in a frenzy. Box office receipts grab headlines in the local newspapers and there's a constant stream of much-hyped opening weekends. Film awards season lasts longer than all the winter holidays put together. Sure, it's possible to have a conversation about the latest Salman Rushdie novel or an upcoming baseball trade. But sooner or later, it all comes back to the multiplex.

A massive chunk of the world's entertainment is developed, written, filmed, edited, distributed, and sold here. So why does it seem so difficult to find the heart of the In-dustry? Because most of it goes on behind closed doors. If you want a closer look, become a Method tourist! For instance, all movies start with an idea and ideas start with writers. Writers drink coffee. So spend some time at one of the city's many Coffee Bean & Tea Leaf cafés and there you'll see most of the WGA (Writers Guild of America) at work. You could do a fly-by at one of the major agencies, like CAA (Creative Artists Agency) on Wilshire Boulevard for now, but soon to move to Century City—and the nearby restaurants and take-out spots where assistants and agents scurry at lunch. But if you want to see some action, you'll likely have to pay for it, by hitting Warner Bros. Studios in the Valley or signing up as a TV audience member with Audiences Unlimited (⇨ Nightlife & the Arts chapter).

QUINTESSENTIAL L.A.

The Beaches

There's something of a disconnect when it comes to L.A.'s beaches. Although hitting the beach is an integral part of life here, the coastline and the exclusive communities that front it somehow seem a bit removed from the rest of the city. Access to some beaches can be confusing (we're talking about you, Malibu), parking can be limited, and public services differ significantly. Unlike places like Miami, where the beach is basically an extension of the city, part of its "living room," the L.A. coast can feel like an entity unto itself. Each beach also has a distinct character, shaped by the surf quality (calm versus serious waves), the landscape, the facilities, and the beachgoers themselves. Do a little investigation before you commit to a certain beach: does it have what you're looking for? ⇨ See the Sports & the Outdoors chapter for info. Also, keep in mind that the water quality can vary greatly depending on weather and other conditions—for instance, storms can make things pretty mucky.

IF YOU LIKE

Scenic Drives

See Los Angeles the way it was designed to be seen: from behind a steering wheel! Plan your cruising times to avoid rush hour, then gas up, get your music ready, and hit the road.

- **Santa Monica Boulevard, Beverly Hills to the beach.** Santa Monica Boulevard is one of the most congested streets in all of L.A., and that's saying a lot, so choose your driving time here carefully. Starting in Beverly Hills and going southwest, you'll pass the Peninsula hotel on your left, a classic example of BH luxury. As you cross the Beverly Hills city limit, you'll see a country club and across from it, the Westfield Century City outdoor mall, built on what was once a studio backlot. Cruising toward the beach, you'll whip by about 1,000 Coffee Bean & Tea Leafs, indie movie theaters, and stores that may lure you to pull over and stop every five minutes—just like a native. Keep going all the way down Santa Monica Boulevard until the Pacific Ocean stares you in the face.

- **Pacific Coast Highway, Santa Monica Beach to Zuma Beach.** It's time to coast on the coast—but stay alert because PCH can be a treacherous drive, especially at the evening rush hour from 4 to 7 PM. You can merge onto the PCH in Santa Monica at the California Incline from Ocean Avenue. Shoot right; the Pacific Ocean and the beaches will be glistening just outside your window. It's tempting to stop near here, but turning across the traffic and then getting back on PCH heading north is really tough. Hold off until you're returning south. Better yet, wait until you reach Zuma Beach, past Point Dume. This is a great place to take a break, stretch your legs, and watch the surfers.

- **Malibu Canyon, Malibu to the Valley.** Curves, tunnels, and gorgeous vistas will clamor for attention on a drive through Malibu Canyon. From the PCH, turn onto Malibu Canyon Road, which is right by the Pepperdine University campus. As on the PCH, stay alert and take your time in this mountain pass; you'll get unbelievable views of the ocean and craggy mountains. There are several turnoffs where you can stop for photos, but *be careful* since local drivers speed though the canyon like it's the Amalfi Coast. Malibu Canyon morphs into Las Virgenes Road, which will dump you at the Ventura Freeway or 101.

- **Mulholland Drive.** Few roads in L.A. are as legendary, or as curvy, as Mulholland Drive. On a clear day, this route can't be beat for awesome views of the San Fernando Valley and the Santa Monica Mountains. But be careful while driving, since Angelenos use Mulholland as a key artery, not a scenic drive, and slow-mo drivers are not appreciated. There are several clearly marked pullouts dotted along the drive where you can park, soak up the views, and think David Lynch thoughts. Start your Mulholland drive from Mulholland's intersection with the 405 freeway. Head east on Mulholland for several miles, winding your way past Coldwater Canyon, Laurel Canyon, and the Hollywood Bowl. Mulholland finally hits Cahuenga Boulevard, right by Highway 101 Sunset is a spectacular time to be up here, but the traffic gets bad at rush hour and the vista parks close at dusk, so start your drive at least half an hour before sunset.

IF YOU LIKE

The Beach

We can't say it enough: all L.A. beaches are not alike. Sure, you can easily find the classic broad, flat, sand-in-your-bikini spots crammed with shrieking teens or ripped guys playing volleyball. Boardwalks and buzzing piers, check. But you can also seek out small, quiet, rocky coves or an estuary with excellent bird-watching. Getting to the beach takes time and sometimes a parking fee, so think about what you're looking for before you get behind the wheel. Surfing or swimming, a busy scene or tranquility, lots of facilities or a relatively untouched landscape? Some beaches are a little tricky to find, like those at Robert H. Meyer Memorial State Beach, but the payoff is that they're not as crowded. And remember to call the beach conditions hotline, especially in the days following a storm. Here are a few favorites, running north to south.

- **Malibu Dream: Zuma Beach.** At the north end of Malibu, Zuma delivers mostly pristine waters, killer surf, family gatherings, and gorgeous sunsets. Well-organized parking and bathrooms make things easy.

- **Surfing First: Malibu Lagoon/Surfrider.** Simply put, one of the best-known surfing spots in the world, with three point breaks. This is also where the Surfrider Foundation, a major environmental organization, took shape.

- **Baywatch Beach: Santa Monica State Beach.** This long stretch of sand is packed on the weekends and wide open on weekdays. Recent efforts have resulted in clearer water on most days, dolphin sightings, and fewer cigarette butts in the sand.

- **Freaky Beach: Venice City Beach.** Steroid-style muscle-men and -women, sandside vendors, breakdancers, and skaters give this spot its own grimy, lively character. Bring your tiny bathing suit, slather on the lotion, and join the parade.

- **OC in L.A.: Manhattan Beach.** Million-dollar condos, low-fat bodies, blondes everywhere, and why is no one at work on a weekday? Here you'll also find well-maintained, sandy beaches, volleyball courts, and a great bike path. Parking is mostly metered on the street so bring plenty of quarters.

Shopping Outdoors

Certain shopping strips are some of the rare places where walking in L.A. is actively encouraged. These are the perfect antidote to that SoCal standby, the megamall, since they're mostly known for independent boutiques. It's lovely to feel the sun on your shoulders in between stops, and there's always great people-watching, too. Charge!

- **Rodeo Drive, Beverly Hills.** We just had to start with this, the best-known name for serious shopping. Ro-*day*-o is crammed with international clothing designers and major jewelry houses. Nearby Wilshire and Beverly boulevards have plenty of temptations too. Whether or not you run into a snooty salesperson, don't be intimidated and step inside the exclusive stores to admire the plush interiors (like Ralph Lauren) and avant-garde design (like Prada).

- **Melrose Avenue, West Hollywood.** The Melrose of yore can still be seen between Highland and North Fairfax avenues: punky holes-in-the-wall, edgy streetwear, and many, many piercings. But farther west, toward La Cienega, things get fancier and pricier, with sleek home decor boutiques and $100 T-shirts instead of vinyl pants and brothel creepers.

- **Montana Avenue, Santa Monica.** Can everyone on a single street be this fit and beautiful? Here they can—it's celluloid L.A. to the nines! Montana distills the rosy-glow lifestyle, from organic bread to carrot juice, yoga studios to Kiehl's skincare. Take the walk and shop the shops for understated but expensive clothes, children's gear, and jewelry.

- **Third Street Promenade, Santa Monica.** This pedestrian zone is a longstanding favorite, though it's pretty vanilla. Most of the stores and cafes are familiar chains, but the fountains and street performers help make for a busy and kid-friendly scene. It also tends to keep going later than most L.A. hangouts. There's ample parking in nearby, clearly marked structures.

- **Abbot Kinney Boulevard, Venice.** Off the beach but still infused with the laid-back Venice vibe, this strip of cafés, boutiques, and yoga studios has become increasingly cool. The shops lean more toward art and design, with the occasional surfwear or fancy-food store thrown in. Make sure you save time for tea and a pastry on the outdoor patio at Jin Patisserie, an outstanding bakery that combines an Eastern aesthetic with a Western sweet tooth.

- **Santee Alley, Downtown.** Now that you've browsed lizard handbags at Ferragamo, browse lizards, turtles, and faux Ferragamo bags at Santee Alley in the fashion district of downtown. This area comes alive on weekends, when swarms of shoppers crowd into a narrow alley that's packed with goods just waiting to be seized by authorities. Watch your wallet, dress down, and be sure to sample some of the vendor snacks like sweet corn on the cob and chorizo. Avoid coming on a warm day, though, since this alley can get Cartagena-hot. There's usually plenty of street parking.

IF YOU LIKE

Stadium Sports

So what if the Rams haven't played here for decades and the Dodgers have lost some of their oomph. Don't pass up the chance to spend a few hours cheering in L.A.'s spectacular sports venues.

- **Staples Center.** The Lakers might have internal personality issues, but the pro basketball team is full of star power. Jack Nicholson has been a fan for years; now it's your turn to get a seat in one of the country's premier sports palaces. This complex gives you great sight lines, shipshape interiors, and better-than-most food options. And when the Lakers are away, you can always catch the second-best Clippers, a concert, or a high-energy Kings hockey game.

- **Dodger Stadium.** There are some that still scorn the Dodgers for leaving Brooklyn. But once you see this 1962 stadium and its stunning locale, you might not blame them for packing their bags. Dodger Stadium sits in Chavez Ravine, an area that was once a tight-knit Mexican community, controversially bulldozed to make way for the stadium. A summer nighttime game may be the best time to come, when you'll see the twinkling lights of downtown. They've recently installed new seating, field boxes with tabletops, and most importantly, cup holders. Be sure to get a frozen malt and some of the best hot dogs on the West Coast.

- **Rose Bowl Stadium.** If your allegiance lies with UCLA, trek to Pasadena to the Rose Bowl, the home of Bruin football. This stadium is tucked into Arroyo Seco, a natural bowl surrounded by gorgeous mountains and parks. Take in a game or the occasional concert as it was meant to be experienced: with 92,000 other fans. Or you could hit the regular swap meet, the largest in the country.

GREAT ITINERARIES

CLASSIC L.A.: STARS, CARS & VISTAS

A car is virtually a necessity in L.A. (public transit is sparse and taxis are expensive and not that convenient). If renting a car, this is the perfect place to make it a convertible. Play for local sympathy and say you hail from a cold place and need solar therapy!

Day 1: Beverly Hills & the Getty Center

Make like the Clampetts and head straight for the riches of Beverly Hills. Many of the stereotypes about Angelenos are rooted here. Hey, you're a visitor, you're allowed to indulge in some gawking! Do a bit of driving along Sunset Boulevard, perhaps dipping into Bel Air to see some of the over-the-top mansions. Then stretch your legs with shopping, real or window, on Rodeo Drive and Wilshire Boulevard.

Next up: a bird's-eye view of the city from the Getty Center in Brentwood. Wander among the stunning, travertine marble-clad pavilions and explore the gardens. And then there's the art, including exceptional European paintings and antique French furniture. But it's hard to tear your eyes from the view, especially at sunset. As the day winds down, splurge on a posh meal in Beverly Hills or West Hollywood.

Day 2: Culture Vulture

Follow your artsy preferences to today's destination—but wherever you end up, you're sure to defeat the old joke that L.A. is a cultural vacuum. The newest major museum is the revamped Getty Villa Malibu, dedicated to Greco-Roman antiquities. As with the Getty Center, the gardens and views are almost as mesmerizing as what's in the galleries. If you're a serious museum fan, consider the cluster along Museum Row, especially the LACMA. Or, you could drive inland to the Pasadena area to see the art and enormous gardens of the Huntington estate, plus the impressive European and Asian exhibits at the Norton Simon. Let your hair down at night (and rest your museum-fatigued feet) at a live-music or comedy club.

Day 3: Hit the Beach!

Some cities have snow days but L.A. has beach days: parents pack up the car, make lunch, cancel lessons, and take the kids to the beach. Take a page from the locals and spend a day just enjoying the sun and sand. Before you pack your picnic, do some planning and pick a beach that suits your needs (⇨ *see* If You Like Beaches *and the* Sports & the Outdoors chapter). Remember to bring cash for parking and, as Murphy's Law insurance, some books or games in case the water's too cold for much swimming. If you end up in Venice, you might want to rent bikes to ride along the boardwalk, and also spend an hour browsing in Abbot Kinney Boulevard's funky boutiques. If you're in Santa Monica, there's always the pier, with its old-school amusement-park rides.

Day 4: Downtown Bound

Pick a weekday to venture downtown—and wear comfortable shoes because unlike other parts of L.A., downtown is best explored on foot. Start at the Cathedral of Our Lady of the Angels (couldn't they

GREAT ITINERARIES

just call it COLA?). You can see the Music Center, with the shining Walt Disney Concert Hall, on the way to the Museum of Contemporary Art. Not far from here is the Grand Central Market, where you might pick up a tamale or fresh fruit juice while eyeing the produce. Hop back in the car for the short drive to the grand Union Station; zip across to Olvera Street for a browse through the crafts market and perhaps an early Mexican dinner. Do you still have time for a performance at the Disney concert hall? Or a drink at the Millennium Biltmore (retro) or Downtown L.A. Standard (cutting-edge)? Hurry, back to the car!

Logistics: Downtown has some sketchy blocks, so use common sense. If you don't like the look of a certain street, turn around. There's also a DASH shuttle bus for short hops between sights.

Day 5: Hurray for Hollywood

Over breakfast, check the Calendar section of the *Los Angeles Times* for showtimes at the old movie palaces like Grauman's Chinese or the El Capitan. (The Arclight is another top film spot.) Once you're in Hollywood, pay your respects to your favorite celluloid stars at their plaques on the Walk of Fame. Hit the Hollywood & Highland complex for a great view of the "Hollywood" sign and perhaps lunch at Vert. If you're a major movie buff, you may want to tour the complex's Kodak Theatre, where the Academy Awards are held, or spend an hour at the Hollywood Museum. Music fans should make time for the awesome Amoeba Records shop. If you'd like to do some funkier shopping, or try a low-key place for dinner, drive east on Sunset Boulevard to Los Feliz or Silver Lake. Somewhere in the day, take time out for a flick—it's Hollywood, after all.

L.A. WITH CHILDREN

When planning a trip to L.A. with kids, do your best to keep freeway time to a minimum. Stick to one general area per day rather than trying to cross the city more than once. Santa Monica, with its beach access and bike trails, is a good base for families. If you have older children, the Hollywood day described in the itinerary above may be suitable, too.

Day 1: Get Sandy

Get acclimated on your first day with a beachfront ride, picking up the oceanfront bike trail near the Santa Monica Pier. Follow the concrete path south to Venice Beach, grab a boardwalk snack, and take in the waves of magicians, body builders, and street artists. Pedal back up to Santa Monica for an evening at the Third Street Promenade.

Day 2: Theme Park Time

The Disneyland Resort, in Orange County, is likely top of your list; see the Orange County & Catalina Island chapter for tips on how to get the most out of a stint at these parks. If you're coming here, it's best to spend the previous night nearby and get an early start at the parks, rather than trying to drive down from L.A. the same day. If you've already done Disney, consider Knott's Berry Farm (also in OC, lots of coasters), Universal Studios Hollywood, or Six Flags Magic Mountain (for thrill rides).

Day 3: Green Spaces, Urban Places

Recover from the rides—and all the lines for the rides—with a few hours in Griffith Park, exploring its well-marked trails, zoo, and museums. Children's activities include pony rides, a 1926 merry-go-round, and the Griffith Park Southern Railroad, a miniature train that takes young riders past fabricated scenes of the Old West. Alternatively, you could head to Will Rogers State Historic Park, a good place for picnicking and hiking.

If you'd like to squeeze in a museum, the Page Museum at the La Brea Tar Pits may be best, especially if you have younger children. But look into the Getty Center, too—it's quite kid-friendly with its gardens and special children's programs. If your kid loves sports, find out what's on at the Staples Center, Dodger Stadium, or Angel Stadium Anaheim and go for a game.

ON THE CALENDAR

	There's always something going on in L.A., but Angelenos look forward to certain events with extra anticipation. Here are the best picks; if you plan to visit during one of the major events, book well in advance.
WINTER January 1	The annual **Tournament of Roses Parade and Football Game** (☎ 626/449–7673) takes place in Pasadena on New Year's Day, bringing flower-decked floats, marching bands, and equestrian teams, followed by the Rose Bowl game.
January	Hit the **L.A. Auto Show** (☎ 213/741–1151 ⊕ www.laautoshow.com) at the Los Angeles Convention Center to size up hundreds of vehicles, from classics to experimental concept cars.
January–March	Point Vicente Park on the Palos Verdes Peninsula is known as the best place for **whale-watching** during the gray whales' annual migration south to Mexico.
January–June	The **Eclectic Orange** (☎ 949/553–2422 ⊕ www.eclecticorange.org) festival in Orange County presents cutting-edge and music, dance, and theater performances in various venues throughout the county.
February	The red carpet rolls out at Hollywood's Kodak Theatre for the **Academy Awards** (⊕ www.oscar.com). Oscar betting pools run hot and heavy.
	Los Angeles's large Chinese-American community brings in the **Chinese New Year** (☎ 213/617–0396) with a parade, beauty pageant, and street fair.
	African-American History Month (☎ 323/758–4358) celebrations include films, exhibits, performances, and more. Events take place throughout Los Angeles.
	The **Pan African Film and Art Festival** (☎ 323/295–1706 ⊕ www.paff.org), the world's largest African-American film festival, screens more than 100 films, organizes children's events, and hosts a spoken wordfest with poets and storytellers.
Mid-February	Long Beach buzzes with both bagpipes and reggae in February. The **Queen Mary Scottish Festival** (☎ 562/499–1650) brings pipe bands, Highland dancing, and performances by Scottish theater groups.
	The two-day **Ragga Muffins Festival** (☎ 562/436–3661 ⊕ www.bobmarleydayfestival.com) has become the largest reggae festival on the West Coast.

Early March	The **Los Angeles Marathon** (☎ 310/444–5544 ⊕ www.lamarathon. com) involves thousands of runners, plus bicyclists and in-line skaters, dozens of bands and musical groups, and a million spectators.
SPRING Late March	**Pasadena Custom Rod Show** (☎ 626/256–6618) shows off more than 500 of California's finest hot rods, customized cars, and antique and classic vehicles.
	Thousands of designers, architects, manufacturers, and visitors descend on West Hollywood's Pacific Design Center for **Westweek** (☎ 310/657–0800 ⊕ www.pacificdesigncenter.com), an event that showcases the latest in design. The Avenues of Art and Design host DesignWalk in conjunction with Westweek; showrooms, shops, restaurants, and art galleries stay open late for special exhibits, tastings, and performances.
Late March–April	The centuries-old Catholic tradition of the **Blessing of the Animals** (☎ 213/485–8225) is kept alive at El Pueblo de Los Angeles; animals of every kind and their owners come for a blessing on Holy Saturday, the day before Easter.
April	The **Toyota Grand Prix** (☎ 562/981–2600 ⊕ www.lbgp.com) in Long Beach, the largest race car competition in North America, draws top competitors from all over the world.
	More than 50 interior and exterior designers transform an estate for the **Pasadena Showcase House of the Arts** (☎ 626/578–8500 ⊕ www.pasadenashowcase.org).
April–June	On with your bodkin for the **Renaissance Pleasure Faire** (☎ 800/523–2473 ⊕ www.renfair.com), a festival of Elizabethan-theme revelry. At this writing, the fair's southern California location was still to be determined.
May 5	On **Cinco de Mayo** (☎ 213/485–9777), Mexico's victory over the French is celebrated with food, mariachi music, and folk dancing.
Mid-May	North Hollywood's **NoHo Theatre & Arts Festival** (☎ 818/508–5155 ⊕ www.nohoartsdistrict.com) puts on more than 120 live theater presentations in one weekend, plus storytelling, art exhibits, music, cultural booths, and children's events.
	Artists have always lived in Venice, drawn by its ocean views and easygoing lifestyle, and the **Venice Art Walk** (☎ 310/392–9255) provides the chance to tour their studios and see their work.

ON THE CALENDAR

Late May	On Memorial Day weekend, St. Nicholas Church in Northridge hosts the **Valley Greek Festival** (☎ 818/886–4040), with traditional Greek music, dancing, and tons of food.
SUMMER June	To experience a true movie palace, sign up for one of the **Last Remaining Seats** (☎ 213/623–2489 ⊕ www.laconservancy.org), organized by the Los Angeles Conservancy. Classic films are shown in the opulent, historic theaters on Broadway in downtown L.A.
Late June	**Christopher Street West's Gay & Lesbian Pride Celebration** (☎ 323/323–8302) brings a two-day explosion of sequins, dancing, and floats.
	One of the country's premier air shows, the **Van Nuys Airport Aviation Expo** (☎ 818/909–3529) includes aircraft and educational displays, live entertainment, and spectacular aerobatics.
June–September	June marks the opening concert of the **Hollywood Bowl** (☎ 323/850–2000 ⊕ www.hollywoodbowl.org season), which includes the famed Playboy Jazz Festival. Pack a picnic and join music lovers nearly every night for a concert presented by the Los Angeles Philharmonic Orchestra.
July	The **Los Angeles Latino International Film Festival** (☎ 323/469–9066 ⊕ www.latinofilm.org) presents more than 70 feature films, documentaries, and short subjects at the Egyptian Theatre.
	The **Lotus Festival** (☎ 213/485–8745), celebrating Asian and Pacific culture, is held each year in Echo Park, which boasts the largest lotus bed outside of China.
	Some of the world's finest jazz, pop, and R&B performers play at the **Old Pasadena Jazz Festival** (☎ 818/771–5544 ⊕ www.omegaevents.com).
Late July	Ever wonder how seriously Angelenos take their cars? Head to the annual **Blessing of the Cars** (⊕ www.blessingofthecars.com); as with the Blessing of the Animals, people arrive for a blessing, but in this case they bring pre-1968 autos.
July–August	Laguna's **Festival of the Arts and Pageant of the Masters** (☎ 800/487–3378 ⊕ www.foapom.com) shows the works of 160 artists in a juried show, along with a unique pageant where art masterpieces are depicted as tableaux vivants.
August	L.A. teams up with the cities of Hermosa Beach, Manhattan Beach, and Redondo Beach to host the **International Surf Festival** (⊕ www.surffestival.org) in early August. The weekend includes all kinds of competitions, from surfing to volleyball to sand-castle building.

		The **Long Beach Jazz Festival** ☎ 562/424–0013 (⊕ www. longbeachjazzfestival.com) lures internationally recognized musicians.
		L.A.'s Japanese community celebrates the summer season with **Nisei Week** (☎ 213/687–7193 ⊕ www.niseiweek.org), a Japanese festival featuring Taiko drummers, kimono-clad dance troupes, marching bands, and arts-and-crafts fairs.
		At San Pedro's **Taste in San Pedro** (☎ 310/832–7272 ⊕ www. tasteinsanpedro.com), local restaurants dish up food and wine.
		The **African Marketplace and Cultural Faire** (☎ 323/734–1164 ⊕ www. africanmarketplace.org), in Exposition Park, highlights the various cultures in the African-American community with readings, a big-band jam, and more.
	Early September	The **Los Angeles City Birthday Celebration** (☎ 213/485–9777) commemorates the city's 1781 founding with historical reenactments, demonstrations, and art exhibits.
	Mid-September	The **Los Angeles County Fair** (☎ 909/623–3111 ⊕ www.lacountyfair. com), in Pomona, hosts entertainment, exhibits, livestock, horse racing, food, and more.
		Olvera Street gets even livelier than usual during the weekend-long **Mexican Independence Day** (☎ 213/625–5045) festival, with arts-and-crafts exhibits, historic displays, and occasional carnival rides.
		A gaggle of galleries organize an annual **ArtCrawl** (☎ 323/666–7667) through their spaces in Los Feliz, Silver Lake, and Echo Park.
		San Pedro's three-day **Lobster Festival** (☎ 310/366–6472 ⊕ www. lobsterfest.com) serves up thousands of steamed crustaceans; there are also live bands and contests.
FALL Late September		Watts fills with music during the **Watts Towers Day of the Drum and Jazz Festival** (☎ 213/847–4646). It's held at the Watts Art Center Amphitheater, next to Simon Rodia's Watts Towers, on the last weekend in September.
	September–October	The **L.A. International Short Film Festival** (☎ 323/851–9100 ⊕ www. lashortsfest.com), held in September or early October, screens hundreds of short films.
		Offered one day yearly in September or October, the West Adams Heritage Association Tours takes visitors on the **Living History Cemetery Tour** (☎ 323/732–2774) at the Angelus-Rosedale Cemetery in

ON THE CALENDAR

	West Adams. People portray inhabitants of the cemetery, including film stars and civic leaders; it sells out well in advance, so plan ahead.
October	The **Los Angeles Bach Festival** (☎ 213/385–1345 ⊕ www.fccla.org/music.htm) mounts a series of concerts in the Gothic First Congregational Church building.
	Pasadena stages the world's most comprehensive event dedicated to the American Arts and Crafts movement, **Craftsman Weekend** (☎ 626/441–6333 ⊕ www.pasadenaheritage.org). You can tour historic homes, ogle Arts and Crafts antiques, and attend lectures.
	The **Hollywood International Film Festival** (☎ 310/288–3040 ⊕ www.hollywoodawards.com) includes a few film premieres, plenty of screenings and celebs, and workshops.
	Calabasas Arts and Crafts Festival (☎ 818/878–4242) features 200 nationally known artists and craftspeople displaying their works, children's art activities, a beer garden, international foods, music, dancing, and performances.
	American Film Institute's Los Angeles Film Festival (☎ 323/856–7707 ⊕ www.afi.com) brings together films and stars from all over the world.
	The **Industry Hills Pro Rodeo** (☎ 626/961–6892 ⊕ www.industryhillsprorodeo.org), held in the City of Industry mid-month, includes a professional rodeo, a petting zoo, and pony rides.
Late October	West Hollywood's **Halloween and Costume Carnival** (☎ 800/368–6020) draws more than 400,000 participants to Santa Monica Boulevard for a wildly imaginative costume competition, musical acts, and stand-up comedy.
Early November	Look for faces painted like skeletons in honor of **Dia de los Muertos** (☎ 213/625–5045), the Mexican celebration honoring the dead. Held at the historic El Pueblo de Los Angeles on Olvera Street, the event features beautifully decorated altars, entertainment, and a solemn procession.
	The **Beverly Hills Flower & Garden Show** (☎ 310/285–2524), held at the 1927 neo-Gothic Greystone mansion, gives guided tours through the home and gardens, which are decked with floral exhibits, food vendors, and demonstrations. It's a rare chance to see the mansion's interior.

Late November	Pasadena's **Doo Dah Parade** (☎ 626/440–7379), a fun-filled spoof of the annual Rose parade, features the Lounge Lizards, who dress as reptiles and lip-synch to Frank Sinatra favorites, and drag cheerleaders from West Hollywood.
	Song and candlelight are the hallmarks of **Las Posadas** (☎ 213/625–5045), a traditional Mexican event depicting the journey of Joseph and Mary. The procession starts at the Avila Adobe and continues on to Olvera Street.
	For the **DWP Light Festival** (⊕ www.ladwp.com), the city's Department of Water and Power puts up spectacular light displays in Griffith Park. Drive by after twilight, but avoid the evening rush hour, especially on weekends.
	Newport Beach celebrates Christmas on the ocean with more than 200 festooned boats at the **Newport Harbor Christmas Boat Parade** (☎ 949/729–4400 ⊕ www.christmasboatparade.com).

Exploring Los Angeles

WORD OF MOUTH

"The Getty is awesome. . . . The grounds are beautiful, and the views immense. Take a book and just meander through the grounds and bask in the sun. It is very peaceful and serene."

—Heavens

"The Grove is just a retail mall, but the Farmers Market has been around since the 1930s. This is a great place to get lunch . . . unlike your typical mall food court, this is real food."

—Lisa Oh

"Beverly Hills is much different [from] West Hollywood. WeHo is all Paris Hilton and BH is all Elizabeth Taylor. You will find the lifestyle of BH to be much quieter than in West Hollywood."

—aschie30

www.fodors.com/forums

Revised &
Updated by
Matthew Flynn
& Kastle
Waserman

LOS ANGELES IS AS MUCH an idea as it is a physical city. It sprawls across 467 square mi; add in the surrounding five-county metropolitan area, and you've got an area of more than 34,000 square mi. Contrary to popular myth, however, that doesn't mean you have to spend all your time in a car. In fact, getting out of your car is the only way to really get to know Los Angeles. We've divided the major sightseeing areas into 10 driving and walking tours that take you through the various entertainment-industry-centered, financial, beachfront, wealthy, and fringe neighborhoods and minicities that make up the vast L.A. area. But remember, no single locale—whether it be Malibu, downtown, Beverly Hills, or Burbank—fully embodies Los Angeles. It's in the mix that you'll discover the city's character.

Looking at a map of sprawling Los Angeles, first-time visitors are sometimes overwhelmed. Where to begin? What to see first? And what about all those freeways? Here's some advice: relax. Begin by setting your priorities—movie and television fans should first head to Hollywood, Universal Studios, and a taping of a television show. Beach lovers and outdoorsy types might start out in Santa Monica or Venice or Malibu, or spend an afternoon in Griffith Park, one of the largest city parks in the country. Those with a cultural bent should probably make a beeline for the twin Gettys (the center in Brentwood and the villa near Malibu), the Los Angeles County Museum of Art (LACMA), or the Norton Simon Museum. And urban explorers might begin with downtown Los Angeles.

KNOW YOUR ROAD

As for the freeways—breathe deeply and embrace the traffic. The freeways are well marked, for non-rush hour travel they're still the best route from one end of the city to the other. Here are a couple of tips: most freeways are known by a name and a number; for example, the San Diego Freeway is I-405, the Hollywood Freeway is U.S. 101, the Ventura Freeway is a different stretch of U.S. 101, the Santa Monica Freeway is I-10, and the Harbor Freeway is I-110. It helps, too, to know which direction you're traveling; say, west toward Santa Monica or east toward downtown Los Angeles. Distance in miles doesn't mean much, depending on the time of day you're traveling: the short 10-mi distance between the San Fernando Valley and downtown Los Angeles might take an hour to travel during rush hour but only 20 minutes at other times.

DOWNTOWN LOS ANGELES

For the past few decades, Los Angeles has continually tried to reinvent its downtown area, cultivating new businesses, attractions, yuppie lofts, and cultural landmarks to create a core for a city that is in many ways decentralized. Valiant efforts to bring the suburban-bound masses back to the city center—including the stunning Walt Disney Concert Hall, the Cathedral of Our Lady of the Angels, and the world's most expensive, but still limited, subway—have yielded mixed results. The changes may not happen as quickly as the city's movers and shakers might like, but downtown L.A. is keeping its place as the cultural and historic heart of the city, and its pulse is slowly getting stronger.

What to See

Angels Flight Railway. The turn-of-the-20th-century funicular, dubbed "the shortest railway in the world," operated between 1901 and 1969, when it was dismantled (but saved) to make room for an urban renewal project that saw total redevelopment of the Bunker Hill district. In 1996, 27 years later, Angels Flight returned with its two original orange-and-black wooden cable railway cars cabling people up a 298-foot incline from Hill Street (between 3rd and 4th streets) to the fountain-filled Watercourt at California Plaza. Due to a fatal accident in 2001, the railway remains closed indefinitely. ⌗ *351 S. Hill St., between 3rd and 4th Sts., Downtown* ☎ *213/626–1901.*

★ ❷ **Bradbury Building.** Designed in 1893 by a novice architect who drew his inspiration from a science-fiction story and a conversation with his dead brother via a Ouija board, the office building is a marvelous specimen of Victorian-era commercial architecture. Originally the site of turn-of-the-20th-century sweatshops, it now houses somewhat more genteel firms beyond the pink marble staircases. The interior atrium courtyard, with its glass skylight, wrought-iron balconies, and caged elevators, is frequently used as a movie locale (*Blade Runner* was filmed here). The building is open daily 9–5 for a peek, as long as you don't wander beyond the first-floor landing. ⌗ *304 S. Broadway, southeast corner Broadway and 3rd St., Downtown* ☎ *213/626–1893.*

❶ **Broadway.** From the late 19th century to the 1950s—before malls and freeways—Broadway was the main shopping and entertainment street downtown. Photos taken during those glory days show crowded sidewalks and lights ablaze on movie marquees. Most of the historical character of Broadway has suffered dramatically over the years, but it hasn't disappeared completely, thanks to renovations and restoration from the Los Angeles Conservancy. The **Million Dollar Theater** (⌗ 307 S. Broadway, Downtown)

WALKING WITH EXPERTS

The **Los Angeles Conservancy** (213/623–2489, www.laconservancy.org) regularly conducts Saturday-morning walking tours of downtown architectural landmarks and districts. Tours begin at 10 AM, last about 2½ hours, and are offered rain or shine. Reservations are required. Call for schedule and fees.

MATTHEW'S TOP 5

- **Farmers Market** since it's such a great place to see food, culture, and generations swirling around the melting pot.

- **The Gettys,** both Brentwood and Malibu. Outstanding art, vistas, and all-around style.

- **Rodeo Drive,** L.A. in a nutshell. Glamorous, sunny, over the top, and ready for prime time.

- **Santee Alley** as the anti-Rodeo Drive. A feeling of barely organized chaos, and part of L.A. most visitors don't get to see.

- **Walt Disney Concert Hall** is like Disney's *Fantasia* come to life as contemporary architecture—thrilling.

A GOOD TOUR

Numbers in the text correspond to numbers in the margin and on the Downtown Los Angeles map.

Begin a downtown tour by heading north on **Broadway** ❶ from 8th or 9th Street. Somewhat scruffy but with some neat old storefronts and a buzzing street energy, Broadway demonstrates downtown's changing times. At the southeast corner of Broadway and 3rd is the **Bradbury Building** ❷, with a fascinating interior court. (You can park behind the Bradbury Building on Spring Street for about $6.) Across the street is the **Grand Central Market** ❸—once you've made your way through its tantalizing food stalls, you'll come out the opposite side onto Hill Street.

Cross Hill Street and climb steps up a steep hill to Watercourt, a plaza with cafés and cascading fountains. (Unfortunately, the **Angels Flight Railway** won't be able to save you the hike, because it's out of service.) Next, walk toward the glass pyramidal skylight topping the **Museum of Contemporary Art (MOCA)** ❹, half a block north on Grand Avenue.

Across from MOCA glimmers the swooping stainless-steel skin of the **Walt Disney Concert Hall,** one of the performance venues along Grand that make up the **Music Center** ❺. Heading north, you'll spot the stark concrete bell tower of the **Cathedral of Our Lady of the Angels** ❻. The concert hall and the cathedral are a fascinating architectural odd couple, one all silvery curves, the other all sharp angles. It's well worth stepping inside the cathedral to see the delicate alabaster used instead of stained glass.

Now walk south on Grand to 5th Street, where you'll find two of downtown's historical and architectural treasures: the **Millennium Biltmore Hotel** ❼, an atmospheric 1920s stunner, and the **Richard J. Riordan Central Library** ❽, also from the 1920s and now smartly renovated for the digital age. Take a breather behind the library in the tranquil Maguire Gardens. Across 5th Street are the **Bunker Hill Steps** ❾, a monumental stairway with a stream spilling down its center.

Return to your car, and drive north on Broadway to 1st Street. Make a right turn here and drive a few blocks to **Little Tokyo** and the expanded **Japanese American National Museum** ❿. **The Geffen Contemporary** ⓫ art museum, an arm of MOCA, is a block north on Central.

From Little Tokyo, turn right (north) from 1st onto Alameda Street. As you pass over the freeway, you'll come to the next stop, **Union Station** ⓬, on the right. Street parking is limited, so your best bet is to park in the pay lot at Union Station (about $5). After a look inside this grand railway terminal, cross Alameda to **Olvera Street** ⓭, a pedestrian zone crammed with craft and food stalls—lots of kitsch, a few treasures.

Driving from Union Station, turn right on Alameda and then immediately left on Cesar Chavez Avenue for three blocks. At Broadway, turn right to **Chinatown.** Reverse your route on Broadway from Chinatown; cross back over the freeway, and at Temple Street make a left. Look to the right as you drive down Temple to see the back of **City Hall of Los Angeles** ⑭. Head out of downtown Los Angeles (take Los Angeles Street south to 11th Street, turn right—west—onto 11th toward Figueroa, then turn left—south—onto Figueroa Street) past **Staples Center** ⑮ with its flying saucer-esque roof to **Exposition Park,** site of three good museums: the **California Science Center** ⑯, the **Natural History Museum of Los Angeles County** ⑰, and the **California African-American Museum** ⑱. (Heading out here, though, is worthwhile only if you're planning to hit one or more of the museums.)Adjacent to Exposition Park is the **University of Southern California (USC)** ⑲, its park-like campus a distinct contrast to its grittier surroundings. The school's got its share of snarky nicknames, like University of Spoiled Children, but there's no arguing with its strong academics and fierce athletics . . .not to mention that marching band. Return to downtown at night for a performance at the Music Center or East West Players in Little Tokyo, and after the show take in the bright lights of the big city at BonaVista, the revolving rooftop lounge atop the **Westin Bonaventure Hotel & Suites,** or take your chances of getting a rooftop seat at the **Downtown L.A. Standard** hotel.

■ **TIP**→ A convenient and inexpensive minibus service— DASH, or Downtown Area Short Hop—has several routes that travel past most of the sights on this tour, stopping every two blocks or so. Each ride costs 25¢, so you can hop on and off without spending a fortune. Special (limited) routes operate on weekends. Call DASH (☎ 808−2273 from all Los Angeles area codes) for routes and hours of operation.

🕑 **TIMING TIPS**→ Weekdays are the best time to experience downtown, when the area is bustling with activity and restaurants are open for lunch. On weekends you may be able to find street parking, but you might keep asking yourself, "Where did everyone go?" Seeing everything included on this tour in one day will require running shoes, stamina, and careful timing. Spread it over two days if possible, especially if you plan on spending time in the museums. Minus a few nightspots, downtown is best (and safest) to visit during the day. Keep in mind that some museums are closed Monday.

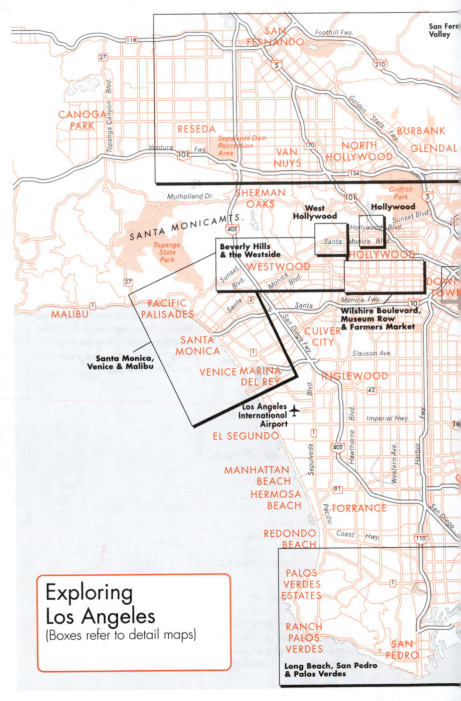

Exploring Los Angeles
(Boxes refer to detail maps)

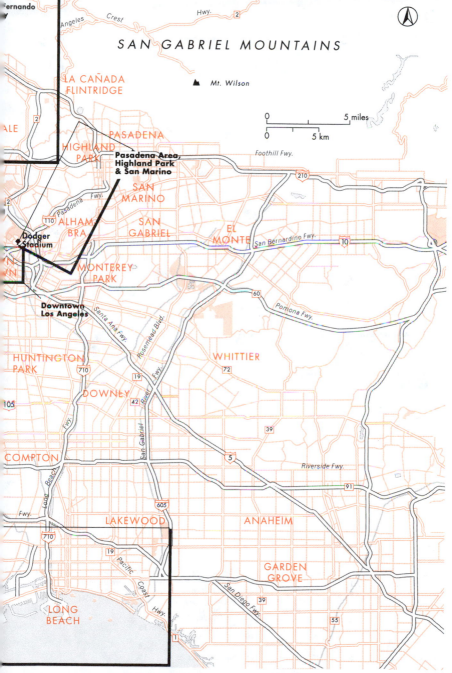

SAN GABRIEL MOUNTAINS

LA CAÑADA FLINTRIDGE

PASADENA

HIGHLAND PARK

Pasadena Area, Highland Park & San Marino

SAN MARINO

ALHAMBRA

SAN GABRIEL

EL MONTE

Dodger Stadium

MONTEREY PARK

Downtown Los Angeles

HUNTINGTON PARK

DOWNEY

WHITTIER

COMPTON

LAKEWOOD

ANAHEIM

GARDEN GROVE

LONG BEACH

Mt. Wilson

ernando

Angeles Crest Hwy.

Foothill Fwy.

San Bernardino Fwy.

Pomona Fwy.

Santa Ana Fwy.

Rosemead Blvd.

Pasadena Fwy.

River Fwy.

San Gabriel

Long Beach Fwy.

Riverside Fwy.

Pacific Coast Hwy.

San Diego Fwy.

0 5 miles
0 5 km

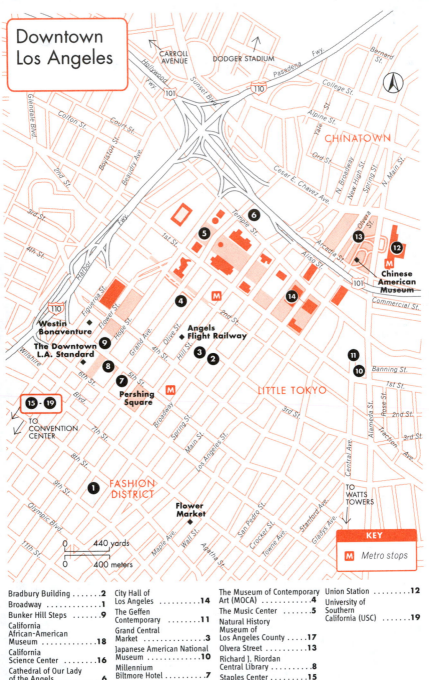

Downtown Los Angeles

CARROLL AVENUE

DODGER STADIUM

CHINATOWN

Chinese American Museum

Westin Bonaventure

The Downtown L.A. Standard

Angels Flight Railway

LITTLE TOKYO

Pershing Square

15 - 19

TO CONVENTION CENTER

FASHION DISTRICT

Flower Market

TO WATTS TOWERS

KEY

M *Metro stops*

0 — 440 yards
0 — 400 meters

now rents for filming and special events. The **Orpheum** (✉ 842 S. Broadway, Downtown) hosts special events and concerts. Shops and businesses catering to a mostly Mexican and Central American immigrant community have moved into the old movie palaces; between 1st and 9th streets you'll find mariachi and *banda* music blaring from electronics-store speakers, street-food vendors hawking sliced papaya sprinkled with chili powder, and fancy dresses for a young girl's *quinceanera* (15th birthday).

9 **Bunker Hill Steps.** A fountain stream spills down the center of this monumental staircase into a small pool at its base. (If you're not inclined to walk up, hop on the escalator parallel to the stairs.) The stream originates at the top of the stairs where Robert Graham's nude female sculpture *Source Figure* stands atop a cylindrical base. The figure's hands are open, as if to offer water to the city. Halfway up there's a coffeehouse where you can fortify yourself before tackling the remaining climb. ✉ *5th St. between Grand Ave. and Figueroa St., Downtown.*

18 **California African-American Museum.** A 2005 renovation opened up exhibit space and improved lighting dramatically here. Works by 20th-century African-American artists and contemporary works of the African diaspora are the backbone of this museum's permanent collection. Its exhibits document the African-American experience from Emancipation and Reconstruction through the 20th century, especially as expressed by artists in California and elsewhere in the West. Special musical as well as educational and cultural events are offered the first Sunday of every month. ✉ *600 State Dr., Exposition Park* ☎ *213/744–7432* ⊕ *www.caamuseum.org* ✉ *Free, parking $6* ☼ *Wed.–Sat. 10–4.*

16 **California Science Center.** Clusters of interactive exhibits illustrate the relevance of science to everyday life, from bacteria to airplanes. Tess, the 50-foot animatronic star of the exhibit "Body Works," dramatically demonstrates how the body's organs work together to maintain balance. Other kid-friendly, hands-on exhibits challenge you to construct earthquake-resistant structures and match actual brains with their animal owners. A cavernous Air and Space Gallery includes the *Gemini 11* space capsule that gave us our first view of Earth as a sphere. The latest addition: the Apollo Soyuz command module and the story behind the first joint space project between the United States and the Soviet Union. An IMAX theater shows large-format releases. ✉ *700 State Dr., Exposition Park* ☎ *213/744–7400* ⊕ *www.casciencectr.org* ✉ *Free, except for IMAX, prices vary; parking $6* ☼ *Daily 10–5.*

OFF THE BEATEN PATH

CARROLL AVENUE – The 1300 block of Carroll Avenue in Angelino Heights, designated a historical monument in one of Los Angeles's oldest neighborhoods, has the city's highest concentration of Victorian houses. Look for the Sessions House (No. 1330) and the Haunted House (No. 1345)—the latter seen in Michael Jackson's *Thriller* video. To get to Carroll Avenue from downtown, take Temple Street west to Edgeware Road, turn right onto Edgeware, and go over the freeway. Carroll Avenue is on the left. ⊕ *www.laconservancy.org.*

A Guide to SoCal Freeway Driving

SURE, THE VEINS OF ASPHALT crisscrossing L.A. look innocent enough from your plane window. But down on the ground, those freeways can turn into a slow-moving mess of cars and cantankerous commuters jockeying for position. So how do you survive and conquer SoCal freeway driving if you're not a native?

Pick a lane. The car pool lane, the "fast lane," the truck lane, the merge lane—this isn't your typical freeway. First of all, keep out of the two far right lanes. The California Department of Motor Vehicles restricts buses and trucks to these two truck lanes, which run slower than the regular speed of traffic. To drive at least the speed limit, get yourself in the middle lane. If you're ready to bend the rules a bit, the fourth lane moves about five miles over the speed limit. Newbies should stay out of the far left lane (the one that's next to the car pool lane). Speeds here range from 75 to 90, and besides that, you've got to deal with car-pool-lane mergers.

And what about that car pool lane—also known as the diamond lane? Use it if you have two or more people in your car and it's moving faster than the speed of traffic; if Bus 187 to Pasadena is in it, don't. If traffic is light, stay in the main lanes. This gives you the freedom to change lanes when needed: car-pool lane entrances and exits are miles apart.

Speed, with caution—but we didn't tell you that. Sure, you shouldn't go faster than the posted 65 or 55 mph. Easy to say, hard to do—especially when everyone else seems to be doing it and getting away with it. If you want to keep up with the speed of traffic and avoid the prize of a speeding ticket, 70 to 74 mph is a good target range. If, however, you notice that you're passing lots of cars—slow down!

Can't we all just be friends? Here's how to avoid causing road rage: Don't tailgate. Don't flail your arms in frustration. Don't glare at the driver of the car you finally have a chance to pass. And above all, don't fly the finger. Road rage is a real hazard.

Use your signal correctly. Here, signaling is a must. Because of all the different lanes, people may try to merge into the same spot as you from three lanes away. Protect yourself and your space by always using your signal. And don't forget to turn your signal off when the lane change is complete.

Get a freeway map. The small, laminated maps that just cover the jumble of freeways are indispensable if you merge onto the wrong freeway, get lost, or get stuck in traffic and want to find an alternative route. Nearly every gas station sells them; you can get a decent one for a few bucks.

Don't pull over on the freeway. Short of a real emergency, never, ever, pull over and stop on a freeway. So you took the wrong ramp and need to huddle with your map—take the next exit and find a safe, well-lighted public space to stop your car and get your bearings.

—Sarah Sper

⑥ Cathedral of Our Lady of the Angels. Controversy surrounded Spanish architect José Rafael Moneo's unconventional, costly, austere design for the seat of the Archdiocese of Los Angeles. But judging from the swarms of visitors and the standing-room-only holiday masses, the church has carved out a niche for itself in downtown's daily life. Opened in 2002, the ocher-concrete cathedral looms up by the Hollywood Freeway. The plaza in front is relatively austere, glaringly bright on sunny days; a children's play garden with bronze animals helps relieve the stark space. Imposing bronze entry doors, designed by local artist Robert Graham, are decorated with multicultural icons and New World images of the Virgin Mary. The canyonlike interior of the church is spare, polished, and airy. By day, sunlight illuminates the sanctuary through translucent curtain walls of thin Spanish alabaster, a departure from the usual stained glass. Artist John Nava used residents from his hometown of Ojai, California, as models for some of the 135 figures in the tapestries that line the nave walls. Make sure to go underground to wander the bright, somewhat incongruous, mazelike white-marble corridors of the mausoleum. Free guided tours start at the entrance fountain at 1 on weekdays. There's plenty of underground visitor parking; the vehicle entrance is on Hill Street. ■ TIP➔ **The café in the plaza has become one of downtown's favorite lunch spots, as you can pick up a fresh, reasonably priced meal to eat at one of the outdoor tables.** ⊠ *555 W. Temple St., Downtown* ☎ *213/680–5200* ⊕ *www.olacathedral.org* ⊡ *Free, parking $3 every 20 min, $14 maximum* ⊙ *Weekdays 6:30–6, Sat. 9–6, Sun. 7–6.*

FodorsChoice
★

Chinatown. Los Angeles's Chinatown is much smaller in size and scope than San Francisco's, but this downtown sector near Union Station still represents a slice of Southeast Asian life. The neighborhood is bordered by Yale, Bernard, Ord, and Alameda streets, but North Broadway is the heart—during Chinese New Year, giant dragons snake down the street. Unfortunately, many longtime establishments have closed as new generations leave for the suburbs, but in the past couple of years, new stores and cafés have slowly returned to the once-thriving neighborhood. Artists are now taking advantage of the available space and opening galleries along Chung King Road, a faded pedestrian passage behind the West Plaza shopping center between Hill and Yale. Most galleries are open in the afternoon and early evenings from Wednesday through Saturday. One Asian holdout, the **Empress Pavilion** (⊠ 988 N. Hill St. ☎ 213/617–9898), still buzzes with activity as one of Chinatown's best restaurants.

Chinese American Museum. This intimate museum highlights the struggles, milestones, and achievements of Chinese-Americans, especially those living in Los Angeles. Housed in the oldest "Chinese building" in the city, the exhibits are straightforward and simple. They range from local contemporary Chinese artist Cindy Suryiani's mixed-media installation of rice scrolls and pup-

> **WORD OF MOUTH**
>
> "I get so tired of the 'there's nothing to do downtown' line. Believe me, there is plenty to do. If you need to see the beach, leave after 9:30 or 10 in the morning, and return after 7 or so at night, and there will not be any commuter traffic." —mlgb

pets addressing Americanism to historical photographs of L.A.'s original Chinatown, full of dirt streets and paper lanterns. One exhibit follows the evolution of Chinese neighborhoods, as the immigrants tried to re-create familiar urban landscapes, resulting in the various versions of Chinatown. ⊠ *425 Los Angeles St.* ☎ *213/626–5240* ⊕ *www.camla.org* ⊠ *$3 suggested donation* ⊙ *Tues.–Sun. 10–3.*

⑭ City Hall of Los Angeles. This gorgeous landmark 1928 building reopened in 2001 after four years of extensive renovation—which included getting the Lindburg Beacon back in action. The revolving spotlight, inaugurated by President Calvin Coolidge from the White House via a telegraph key, was used from 1928 to 1941 to guide pilots into the Los Angeles airport. During the latest renovation, a worker discovered the discarded light in a city warehouse; now it's back on top of the hall's 13-story tower. There are free weekday tours of the beautifully detailed building at 10 and 11, which sometimes include a visit to the observation deck atop the tower. Reservations are strongly recommended. ⊠ *200 N. Spring St., Downtown* ☎ *213/978–1995.*

Downtown L.A. Standard. There has always been a place to stay downtown—but nothing as trendy, loud, or hip as the Standard. This in-your-face cool hotel is housed in the former Standard Oil Headquarters. Stop by and take in the 1950s architecture dressed up with contemporary interior design that would make Hugh Hefner grin. A crowded rooftop lounge and bar with fantastic views makes the perfect after-theater hangout—provided you can get in. ■ **TIP→** **Even if you can't make it past the rope, look up at the nearby skyscrapers, which serve as screens for video projections from atop the hotel.** ⊠ *550 S. Flower St.* ☎ *213/892–8080* ⊕ *www.standardhotel.com.*

Exposition Park. Originally developed in 1880 as an open-air farmers' market, this 114-acre public space hosted Olympic festivities in 1932 and 1984 in conjunction with the adjacent Memorial Coliseum and Sports Arena. The park includes a lovely sunken rose garden and three museums, the **California African-American Museum, California Science Center,** and the **Natural History Museum of Los Angeles County.** Unfortunately, though, the park and neighborhood become sketchy at night, so it's wise to leave once the museums close. ⊠ *Between Exposition and Martin Luther King Jr. Blvds., Exposition Park.*

OFF THE BEATEN PATH

FASHION DISTRICT – Few street scenes in Los Angeles are more entertaining than the downtown blocks around Los Angeles and 7th streets, where a mélange of retailers, wholesalers, and manufacturers sells clothing, fabrics, accessories, textiles, and an occasional iguana. Hawkers try to coax you to enter shops for children's clothing, men's suits, discounted designer dresses, and yard goods. A clutch of retail shops and street vendors occupy **Santee Alley** (⊠ Santee St. and Maple Ave. from Olympic Blvd. to 12th St.) and the **Cooper Building** (⊠ 860 S. Los Angeles St. ☎ 213/627–3754), but the heart of the district is the **California Market Center** (⊠ 110 E. 9th St. ☎ 213/630–3600), a trade market housing 1,500 showrooms. The market opens to the public the last Friday of each month from 9 to 5 for its "Friday Sample Sale." The **Downtown Property Owners Association** (☎ 213/488–1153 ⊕ www.fashiondistrict.org) sponsors a team of security officers in bright yellow shirts who can provide maps, info, and assistance.

★ **⑪ The Geffen Contemporary.** Back in 1982, Disney Concert Hall architect Frank Gehry transformed a warehouse in Little Tokyo into a temporary space for the **Museum of Contemporary Art (MOCA)** while it was being built a mile away. The Temporary Contemporary—and its large, flexible space, antiestablishment character, and lively exhibits—was such a hit that it remains part of the museum facility. Now called the Geffen, it houses a concise sample of MOCA's permanent collection, spanning the years from the 1940s to the present, and usually one or two temporary exhibits that evoke grins from even the most stuffy museumgoers. ✉ *152 N. Central Ave., Downtown* ☎ *213/626–6222* ⊕ *www.moca-la.org* 💳 *$8, free with MOCA admission on same day and on Thurs.* 🕐 *Mon. and Fri. 11–5, Thurs. 11–8, weekends 11–6.*

❸ Grand Central Market. Handmade white-corn tamales, warm olive bread, dried figs, Mexican fruit drinks . . . hungry yet? This mouthwatering gathering place is the city's largest and most active food market. The butcher shops display everything from lambs' heads to pigs' tails; the produce stalls are piled high with locally grown avocados and heirloom tomatoes. Stop by **Del Rey**, at stall A7, for a remarkable selection of rare chilies and spices. Even if you don't plan to buy anything, the market is a great place to browse and people-watch. ✉ *317 S. Broadway, Downtown* ☎ *213/624–2378* ⊕ *www.grandcentralsquare.com* 💳 *Free* 🕐 *Daily 9–6.*

❿ Japanese American National Museum. What was it like to grow up on a coffee plantation in Hawaii? How difficult was life for Japanese-Americans interned in concentration camps during World War II? These questions are addressed by changing exhibits at this museum in Little Tokyo. Insightful volunteer docents are on hand to share their own stories and experiences. The museum occupies an 85,000-square-foot adjacent pavilion as well as its original site in a renovated 1925 Buddhist temple. ✉ *369 E. 1st St., at Central Ave., next to Geffen Contemporary, Downtown* ☎ *213/625–0414* ⊕ *www.janm.org* 💳 *$8, free Thurs. 5–8 and 3rd Thurs. of month* 🕐 *Tues., Wed., and Fri.–Sun. 10–5.*

Little Tokyo. The original neighborhood of Los Angeles's Japanese community, this downtown area has been deserted by most of those immigrants, who have moved to suburban areas such as Gardena and West Los Angeles. Still, Little Tokyo remains a cultural focal point. Nisei Week (a nisei is a second-generation Japanese) is celebrated here every August with traditional drums, dancing, a carnival, and a huge parade. Bounded by 1st, San Pedro, 3rd, and Central streets, Little Tokyo has dozens of sushi bars, tempura restaurants, karaoke bars, and trinket shops selling transformer robots, lanterns, and Hello Kitty tchotchkes. On 1st Street you'll find the only strip of intact buildings from the early 1900s. Look down when you get near San Pedro Street, and you'll see the art installation "Omoide no Shotokyo" ("Remembering Old Little Tokyo"). Embedded in the sidewalk are brass inscriptions naming the original businesses, quoted reminiscences from Little Tokyo residents, and steel time lines of Japanese-American history up to World War II. The **Japanese**

American Cultural and Community Center (✉ 244 S. San Pedro St., Downtown ☎ 213/628–2725) presents traditional and contemporary cultural events. Through the center's basement you can reach the James Irvine Garden, a serene sunken garden where local plants mix with bamboo, Japanese wisteria, and Japanese maples.

⑦ Millennium Biltmore Hotel. The Beaux-Arts Biltmore, opened in 1923, is a creation of the architecture firm Schultze and Weaver, which also built New York City's Waldorf-Astoria. The lobby has the feel of a Spanish palace, and the ornate Rendezvous Court is a civilized retreat for afternoon tea. The Academy Awards were held here in the 1930s and '40s, and the hotel has also been seen in many films and TV shows, including *Chinatown, Commander in Chief,* and *Austin Powers: Goldmember.* ✉ 506 S. Grand Ave., Downtown ☎ 213/624–1011 ⊕ www. thebiltmore.com.

④ The Museum of Contemporary Art (MOCA). The MOCA's permanent collection of American and European art from 1940 to the present divides itself between two spaces: the linear red-sandstone building at California Plaza and the **Geffen Contemporary,** in nearby Little Tokyo. Likewise, its exhibitions are split between the established and the cutting-edge. Heavy hitters such as Mark Rothko, Franz Kline, Susan Rothenberg, Diane Arbus, and Robert Frank are fixtures, while at least 20 themed shows rotate through annually. It's a good idea to check the schedule in advance, since some shows sell out, especially on weekends. The museum occasionally closes for exhibit installation. ✉ 250 S. Grand Ave., Downtown ☎ 213/626–6222 ⊕ www.moca.org ✉ $8, free on same day with Geffen Contemporary admission and on Thurs. ☉ Mon. and Fri. 11–5, Thurs. 11–8, weekends 11–6.

FodorśChoice ★

MUSEUM OF NEON ART (MONA) – In the Renaissance Tower office building, you'll discover one of the world's few tributes to the art of neon— a form of lighting that evolved from advertising status to fine art in less than half a century. The art moves, hisses, and flashes, bringing the entire room to life. Some of the larger signs from the museum's collection can be seen in full glowing splendor at **Universal Studio's City Walk.** ■ **TIP→ In spring and summer MONA organizes popular nighttime double-decker bus tours that visit historic and contemporary neon signs throughout the city, plus a stop for a snack or two at the iconic Canter's Deli on Fairfax.** ✉ 501 W. Olympic Blvd., enter on Hope St., Downtown ☎ 213/489–9918 ⊕ www. neonmona.org ✉ $5, free 2nd Thurs. of month 5–8, bus tour $45 ☉ Wed.–Sat. 11–5, Sun. noon–5; 2nd Thurs. of month 11–8.

OFF THE
BEATEN
PATH

★ ⑤ The Music Center. L.A.'s major performing arts venue since its opening in 1964, the Music Center is also now downtown's centerpiece. Home to the Los Angeles Philharmonic, the Los Angeles Opera, the Center Theater Group, and the Los Angeles Master Chorale, the Music Center is also a former site of the Academy Awards. The center's latest star is the **Walt Disney Concert Hall,** designed by Frank Gehry. Opened in fall 2003, the gorgeous stainless-steel-clad structure soars lyrically upward, seeming to defy the laws of engineering. Because nearby residents complained of glare, the gleaming founder's wing was recently buffed to a matte finish. But on the plus side, nighttime illumination was added in

FodorśChoice ★

2006, giving a stunning glow to the steel curves. Inside the main hall, the seating completely surrounds the stage, a ceiling of Douglas fir billows overhead, and an enormous pine-clad organ branches out across an entire wall. The carpet, named "Lily" (also designed by Gehry), is a wild collage of petals inspired by Lillian Disney's love of flowers. The only thing better than touring the hall is attending a performance of the Philharmonic or the Master Chorale in this magnificent space. For more experimental works, check out REDCAT, CalArts's 266-seat theater.

The largest of the center's four theaters is the **Dorothy Chandler Pavilion,** named after the philanthropic wife of former *Los Angeles Times* publisher Norman Chandler. The **Ahmanson,** at the north end, is a flexible venue for major musicals and plays. In between these two sits the round **Mark Taper Forum,** a surprisingly intimate 700-seat theater mainly showing experimental works. ⊠ *135 N. Grand Ave., at 1st St., Downtown* ☎ *213/972–7211, 213/972–4399 for tour information* ⊕ *www.musiccenter.org* ⊡ *Free* ⊙ *Free tours Tues.–Fri. 10–1:30, Sat. 10–noon.*

☾ **⑰ Natural History Museum of Los Angeles County.** With more than 3½ million specimens, this is the third-largest museum of its type in the United States after the Field Museum in Chicago and the American Museum of Natural History in New York. It has a rich collection of prehistoric fossils and extensive bird, insect, and marine-life exhibits. Brilliant stones shimmer in the Gem and Mineral Hall. An elaborate taxidermy exhibit shows North American and African mammals in detailed replicas of their natural habitats. Exhibits typifying various cultural groups include pre-Columbian artifacts and a display of crafts from the South Pacific. The Times-Mirror Hall of Native American Cultures delves into the history of Los Angeles's earliest inhabitants. The Ralph M. Parsons Discovery Center for children has hands-on exhibits. ⊠ *900 Exposition Blvd., Exposition Park* ☎ *213/763–3466* ⊕ *www.nhm.org* ⊡ *$9, free 1st Tues. of month* ⊙ *Weekdays 9:30–5, weekends 10–5.*

★ ☾ **⑬ Olvera Street.** This busy pedestrian block tantalizes with piñatas, mariachis, and fragrant Mexican food. As the major draw of the oldest section of the city, known as **El Pueblo de Los Angeles,** Olvera Street has come to represent the rich Mexican heritage of L.A. It had a close shave with disintegration in the early 20th century, until the socialite Christine Sterling walked through in 1926. Jolted by the historic area's decay, Sterling fought to preserve key buildings and led the transformation of the street into a Mexican-American marketplace. Today this character remains; vendors sell puppets, leather goods, sandals, serapes (woolen shawls), and handicrafts from stalls that line the center of the narrow street. The quality of what

WORD OF MOUTH

"The most obvious is Olvera Street, a small two or three block park located across the street from Union Station in Downtown L.A. It's a bit chintzy in my opinion, and there isn't a whole lot to see. So, go on a weekend, when they usually have musicians and vendors who make it an enjoyable experience."
–Big_Money_D

you'll find ranges from Tijuana-style "junkola" (donkey-shape salt and pepper shakers) to well-made glassware and pottery. Then there are those paintings on black velvet: tacky or artistic? Up to you. On weekends, the restaurants are packed as musicians play in the central plaza. The weekends that fall around two Mexican holidays, Cinco de Mayo (May 5) and Independence Day (September 16), also draw huge crowds.

■ TIP➜ **To see Olvera Street at its quietest, visit late on a weekday afternoon, when long shadows heighten the romantic feeling of the passageway.** For information, stop by the **Olvera Street Visitors Center** (⊠ 622 N. Main St., Downtown ☎ 213/628–1274 ⊕ www.olvera-street.com), in the Sepulveda House, a Victorian built in 1887 as a hotel and boardinghouse. The center is open Monday–Saturday 10–3. Free 50-minute walking tours leave here at 10, 11, and noon Tuesday–Sunday.

Pelanconi House (⊠ W-17 Olvera St., Downtown), built in 1855, was the first brick building in Los Angeles. It has been home to La Golondrina restaurant since 1930. **Avila Adobe** (⊠ E-10 Olvera St., Downtown), built in 1818 and furnished in the style of the 1840s, is considered the oldest building still standing in Los Angeles. This graceful, simple adobe with a traditional interior courtyard is open daily 9–3.

Another landmark, the **Italian Hall building** (⊠ 650 N. Main St., Downtown), isn't open to the public, but it's noteworthy because its south wall bears a controversial mural. Famed Mexican muralist David Alfaro Siqueiros shocked his patrons in the 1930s by depicting an oppressed worker of Latin America being crucified on a cross topped by a menacing American eagle. The anti-imperialist mural was promptly whitewashed but was later restored by the Getty Museum.

At the beginning of Olvera Street is the **Plaza,** a wonderful Mexican-style park with plenty of benches and walkways, shaded by a huge Moreton Bay fig tree. On weekends, mariachis and folkloric dance groups often perform. Two annual events particularly worth seeing are the Blessing of the Animals and Las Posadas. On the Saturday before Easter, Angelenos bring their pets (not just dogs and cats but horses, pigs, cows, birds, hamsters) to be blessed by a priest. For Las Posadas (every night between December 16 and 24), merchants and visitors parade up and down the street, led by children dressed as angels, to commemorate Mary and Joseph's search for shelter on Christmas Eve.

NEED A BREAK?

Dining choices on Olvera Street range from fast-food stands to comfortable sit-down restaurants. The most authentic Mexican food is at **La Luz del Dia** (⊠ W-1 Olvera St., Downtown ☎ 213/628–7495), which has traditional favorites such as chiles rellenos and pickled cactus, as well as handmade tortillas patted out in a practiced rhythm by the women behind the counter. **La Golondrina** (⊠ W-17 Olvera St., Downtown ☎ 213/628–4349), midblock, has a delightful patio.

Pershing Square. The city's cultures come together in one of the city's oldest parks, dating to 1866. It's no time capsule, though; in the 1990s architect Ricardo Legorreta and landscape architect Laurie Olin introduced colorful walls, fountains, and towers, which unfortunately have not aged well. Usually, the square comes across as rather grim and neglected. From mid-November to mid-January, though, an outdoor ice rink is open. ✉ *Bordered by 5th, 6th, Hill, and Olive Sts.* ☎ *No phone* ⊕ *www. laparks.org* ✉ *Free* ☉ *Daily.*

8 **Richard J. Riordan Central Library.** Still known locally as the Central Library, this facility was renamed to honor the former mayor of Los Angeles. Major fires in the 1980s closed the library for six years, but today, at twice its former size, it's the third-largest public library in the nation. The original building, designed by Bertram Goodhue, was restored to its 1926 condition, with the pyramid tower and a torch symbolizing the Light of Learning crowning the building. On weekdays it can feel more like a megabookstore than a library as students rush the halls with sacks of CDs and books. On the second floor, in the Cook rotunda, take a look at Dean Cornwell's murals depicting the history of California as well as card files from precomputer days. Also on the second floor, take in the **Getty Gallery**'s literary exhibits. The Tom Bradley Wing, named for another mayor, has a soaring eight-story atrium. The library offers frequent events and special exhibits. There are also a gift shop and a small cafeteria-style restaurant. ✉ *630 W. 5th St., at Flower St., Downtown* ☎ *213/228–7000, 213/228–7168 for tour information* ⊕ *www. lapl.org* ✉ *Free* ☉ *Mon.–Thurs. 10–8, Fri. and Sat. 10–6, Sun. 1–5; docent tours weekdays at 12:30, Sat. at 11 and 2, and Sun. at 2.*

NEED A BREAK? **Cafe Pinot** (✉ *700 W. 5th St., Downtown* ☎ *213/239–6500*), in the Maguire Gardens just behind the Central Library, is a great stop for a tranquil meal or an afternoon dessert and latte at the bar. A complimentary shuttle runs to the Music Center for evening performances.

15 **Staples Center.** If you're prone to extravagance, you'll find much to tempt you at this plush arena, from the luxury suites and private club levels to the humidor. It's home to the ice hockey team the Los Angeles Kings and to the Lakers, the Clippers, and the Sparks, all basketball teams. Food choices vary by stadium location, so be sure to take a lap before making your final choice. The center also hosts ice shows, tennis, and superstar performers like Bruce Springsteen, Rod Stewart, and Madonna. ✉ *1111 S. Figueroa St., Downtown* ☎ *213/742-7340* ⊕ *www. staplescenter.com.*

 12 **Union Station.** Built in 1939, Union Station was the key entry point into Los Angeles prior to LAX. Designed by City Hall architects John and Donald Parkinson, it combines Spanish colonial revival and art deco styles into a whole that's one of the country's last great rail stations and one of the most striking structures in L.A. The waiting hall's commanding scale and enormous chandeliers have provided the setting for so many films and TV shows that you may feel you've been here before. The station's restaurant, **Traxx,** is a great place for lunch, evoking a time when travel and style went hand in hand. ✉ *800 N. Alameda St., Downtown.*

19 **University of Southern California (USC).** There's more to this private university than mascot Tommy Trojan and the legendary marching band. Its parklike inner-city campus dates to 1880, its film school is George Lucas's alma mater, and it fosters a fanatical cross-town rivalry with

UCLA. Join a free weekday campus tour, taking in the more notable of its 191 buildings, like the Romanesque **Doheny Memorial Library; Widney Alumni Hall,** a two-story 1880 clapboard; and **Mudd Memorial Hall of Philosophy,** which contains a rare book collection of missives from the 13th through 15th centuries. ⊠ *Guest Relations, 615 Childs Way, University Park, adjacent to Exposition Park* ☎ *213/740–6605* ⊕ *www.usc.edu/visit* ⊙ *Call for tour schedule and reservations.*

OFF THE BEATEN PATH

WATTS TOWERS OF SIMON RODIA – The jewel of rough South L.A. is the legacy of Simon Rodia, a tile setter who emigrated from Italy to California and erected one of the world's greatest folk-art structures. From 1921 until 1954, without any help, this eccentric man built the three main cement towers, using pipes, bed frames, and anything else he could find. He embellished them with bits of colored glass, broken pottery, and more than 70,000 seashells. The towers still stand preserved, now the centerpiece of a state historic park and cultural center. ⊠ *1727 E. 107th St., Watts, (take I–110 to I–105 east; exit north at S. Central Ave., and turn right onto 108th St., left onto Willowbrook Ave.)* ☎ *213/847–4646* ⊠ *Gallery free, tours $5* ⊙ *Gallery Tues.–Sat. 10–4, Sun. noon–4; tours Tues.–Sat. 11–2:30.*

Westin Bonaventure Hotel & Suites. In 1976 John Portman designed these five shimmering cylinders in the sky, with nary a 90-degree angle. Sheathed in mirrored glass, the now-dated building once looked like a science-fiction fantasy; this emblem of postmodern architecture has been featured in more TV shows and movies than any other L.A. building. The only elevator open to the public rises through the lobby roof to soar up to the panoramic restaurant L.A. Prime Steakhouse, on the 35th floor. ⊠ *404 S. Figueroa St., Downtown* ☎ *213/624–1000* ⊕ *www.westin.com/bonaventure.*

HOLLYWOOD

Hollywood, like much of Los Angeles, is as much an idea as it is a place. Since the 1920s, Hollywood has lured us with its carefully manufactured images promising showbiz glitz and glamour. As visitors, we just want a glimpse of that sexy sophistication, a chance to say, "I was there!" Reality check: the magic of Hollywood takes place, for the most part, on soundstages that are not even in Hollywood anymore and in non-descript film-processing labs and editing bays. Go to Beverly Hills and look at jewelry-store windows if you want glitz. Hollywood is really a working town. Sure, many of the people involved in the concept of Hollywood—actors, directors, writers, composers—are among the highest paid and most celebrated workers in the world. But they'll often refer to their movie, TV, and recording studios as factories where they put in long hours.

And for many years, that factory wasn't even in a very good part of town. After the radio networks closed their Hollywood headquarters and the opulent movie theaters shut down in the '50s, the neighborhood slid into decay. But since 2000, Hollywood has been undergoing a massive face-lift, reaching back to the glamour of the '20s, '30s, and '40s. These days, much of Hollywood's sparkle can be found within walking distance of the current home of the Academy Awards, the Kodak Theater, part of the Hollywood & Highland entertainment complex. Neighboring 1920s Grauman's Chinese Theatre plays its part as the quintessential movie palace. Two other renovated golden-age cinemas on Hollywood Boulevard, the 1926 El Capitan Theatre and the 1922 Egyptian Theatre, are prime examples of successful Hollywood remakes.

By mixing old and new, Hollywood is trying to keep one foot in the golden age. With all the renovations, some critics have accused Hollywood of overgentrifying, as giant shopping strips and luxury apartment high-rise structures began dwarfing such classic landmarks as the Formosa Café. But redevelopment has progressed only sporadically, and there's still a high quotient of grit and faded kitsch here. As you walk along the Hollywood Walk of Fame to find tributes to your favorite stars, you're likely to encounter more than a few panhandlers. Off the main drag spread blocks of down-at-the-heel buildings. And the occasional costumed superhero not sanctioned by Marvel comics heckles passersby for souvenir photos.

What to See

Arclight/Cinerama Dome. Film buffs and preservationists breathed a sigh of relief when the Arclight complex opened its doors and rewrote the book on cushy moviegoing. With plush stadium seating, reserved seats for some showings, state-of-the-art sound, an usher who welcomes you and introduces the film, and snack bars that cook up their own fresh caramel corn, the Arclight justifies its high ticket prices ($11–$14, depending on the hour you go). Built next to the restored geodesic Cinerama Dome, a curved-screen architectural icon, the complex also caters to film lovers with special director's Q&A nights as well as exhibits of movie costumes and photography throughout the lobby. Even though there are 14 other theaters in the complex, many films sell out quickly. Your best chance at prime seating is to order tickets online and to choose a seat in advance. A printed receipt allows you to walk directly into the theater and avoid the lines. Weekend nights have an especially hip buzz as film enthusiasts and industry power couples linger in the soaring lobby. Buy your tickets in advance, and arrive early for the show before the show. Parking is $2 in the adjacent garage with a movie ticket purchase and validation. ⊠ *6360 Sunset Blvd., at Vine St., Hollywood* ☎ *323/464–4226* ⊕ *www.arclightcinemas.com.*

OFF THE BEATEN PATH

BARNSDALL PARK/HOLLYHOCK HOUSE – The panoramic view of Hollywood alone is worth a trip to this hilltop cultural center. After many years of closure as the buildings were repaired and retrofitted after the 1994 Northridge earthquake, this arts center is coming back into its own. On the grounds is the famous Hollyhock House, designed by architect Frank Lloyd Wright between 1919 and 1923. It was commissioned by philanthropist Aline Barnsdall to be the centerpiece of an arts community on the hill, complete with theaters and an actors' dorm. While Barnsdall's project didn't turn out quite the way she planned, the park now hosts the L.A. Municipal Art Gallery and Theatre, which provides exhibit space for visual and performance artists; affordable art classes for children and adults are also taught here. A film chronicling the Holly-

A GOOD TOUR

Numbers in the text correspond to numbers in the margin and on the Hollywood map.

Start off by driving up into the Hollywood Hills on Beachwood Drive (off Franklin Avenue, just east of Gower Street) for an up-close look at one of the world's most familiar icons: the HOLLYWOOD sign ❶. Follow the small sign pointing the way to the LAFD Helispot. Turn left onto Rodgerton Drive, which twists and turns higher into the hills. At Deronda Drive, turn right and drive to the end. The HOLLYWOOD sign looms to the left. Turn around and retrace your route down the hill and back to Beachwood for the drive into Hollywood.

Make a right (west) at Franklin Avenue, and prepare to turn left at the next light, Gower Street. Stay on Gower, driving through the section known as **Gower Gulch,** where small B-picture "Poverty Row" studios once stood. Radio broadcasts with Edgar Bergen and Charlie McCarthy originated at the CBS studio, on the northwest corner. At the southeast corner is the old Columbia Pictures studio (*Gilda, All the King's Men, Born Yesterday, From Here to Eternity, The Caine Mutiny*), now known as **Sunset-Gower Studios,** where major television shows are taped.

At Gower and Santa Monica Boulevard, look for the entrance to **Hollywood Forever Cemetery ❷**, half a block east on Santa Monica. Here you can pay your respects to Rudolph Valentino or two of the Ramones if you're so inclined. (Those three markers get a lot of lipstick kisses.) If you visit the cemetery, retrace your route back to Gower Street and turn left to drive along the western edge of the cemetery flanking Gower. Abutting the cemetery's southern edge is **Paramount Pictures ❸**. The famous gate Norma Desmond (Gloria Swanson) was driven through at the end of *Sunset Boulevard* is no longer accessible to the public, but a replica marks the entrance on Melrose Avenue: turn left from Gower Street to reach the gate.

Next, drive west (right off Gower) on Melrose for three blocks to Vine Street, turn right, and continue to the world-famous intersection of **Hollywood and Vine ❹**. Across the street is the **Capitol Records Tower ❺**, which resembles a stack of 45 rpm records. A few steps east of the intersection on Hollywood Boulevard stands the ornate, restored Pantages Theatre. A block west on **Ivar Street** are the former homes of novelists William Faulkner and Nathanael West.

Drive west along Hollywood Boulevard. Stop along the way to look at the bronze stars that make up the **Hollywood Walk of Fame ❻** or to visit the **Hollywood Wax Museum, Guinness World of Records,** or **Ripley's Believe It or Not Museum**—all shrines to Hollywood camp. Metered parking is fairly easy to find. If not, small lots just north and south of the boulevard have reasonable hourly rates.

At Hollywood Boulevard and Las Palmas Avenue is Hollywood's first movie palace, the striking **Egyptian Theatre ❼**. Farther west, on

Highland Avenue just south of Hollywood Boulevard, is the **Hollywood Museum** 🟠, one of the best places to see movie memorabilia. Continue west on Hollywood Boulevard until you see the giant, Babylonian-theme, hotel-retail-entertainment complex **Hollywood & Highland** 🟠, which includes the 3,300-seat Kodak Theatre, home of the Academy Awards.

Next to Hollywood & Highland is **Grauman's Chinese Theatre** 🟠, a genuinely kitschy monument to Hollywood history. The elaborate pagoda-style movie palace is still the biggest draw along Hollywood Boulevard. Also on the north side of the boulevard and west of Grauman's is the **Hollywood Entertainment Museum** 🟠, which covers small-screen as well as big-screen history. From the museum, cross Hollywood Boulevard and loop back east past the **Hollywood Roosevelt Hotel** 🟠, a spot that's both historic and newly hot. In the next block, the Disney folks have impeccably restored the El Capitan Theatre's elaborate facade. Several blocks north of the boulevard on Highland Avenue is the **Hollywood Heritage Museum** 🟠, which focuses on the early days of moviemaking, and the **Hollywood Bowl** 🟠, the beloved outdoor concert venue. If you're visiting during the summer concert season, look into getting a ticket for an evening show.

■ **TIP**➜ If you're on Hollywood Boulevard after the stores close, you'll get an after-hours show; as part of the city's ongoing beautification efforts, many of the shops' pull-down security doors are painted with portraits of the stars named on the Walk of Fame.

For a spectacular Cinemascope view of the glittering city lights, from Hollywood to the ocean, head up to the **Griffith Observatory,** perched on a promontory in Griffith Park. From Hollywood Boulevard, go north on Western Avenue, which becomes Los Feliz Boulevard. Take a left on Vermont Avenue and follow the signs that lead you into the park and up the hill to the observatory. The observatory itself is due to reopen in spring 2006, so for now you can just get views of the skyline, not the stars.

⊗ **TIMING TIPS**➜ **Plan to spend the better part of a morning or afternoon taking in Hollywood. Hollywood Boulevard sometimes attracts a rough collection of homeless people and runaways; if you've got children in tow, stick to a daytime walk. Later in the evening, you can return to Hollywood for a cabaret performance at the Roosevelt Hotel's Cinegrill, a movie at the Chinese or the Egyptian, or a summertime concert at the Hollywood Bowl.**

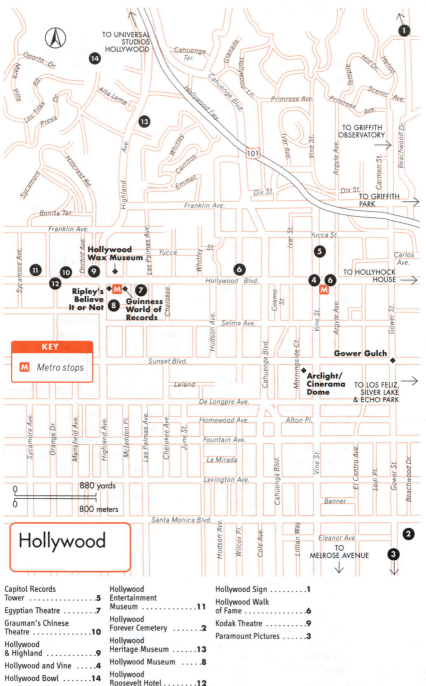

Hollywood

hock House runs daily in the lobby of the Municipal Art Gallery—but better yet, join a docent tour of the building. Wright dubbed this style "California Romanza" (romanza is a musical term meaning "to make one's own form"). Stylized depictions of Barnsdall's favorite flower, the hollyhock, appear throughout the house in its cement columns, roofline, and furniture. The leaded-glass windows are expertly placed to make the most of both the surrounding gardens and the city views. ✉ *4800 Hollywood Blvd., Los Feliz* ☎ *323/644–6269* ⊕ *www.hollyhockhouse. net* ✉ *$2, gallery $5* ⊙ *Museum Wed.–Sun. noon–5, Fri. noon–8:30; Hollyhock tours Wed.–Sun. hourly 12:30–3:30.*

★ ❺ **Capitol Records Tower.** The romantic story about the origin of this symbol of '50s chic is that singer Nat King Cole and songwriter Johnny Mercer suggested that the record company's headquarters be shaped to look like a stack of 45s. Architect Welton Becket claimed he just wanted to design a structure that economized space, and in so doing, he created the world's first cylindrical office building. On its south wall, L.A. artist Richard Wyatt's mural *Hollywood Jazz, 1945–1972* immortalizes musical greats Duke Ellington, Billie Holiday, Ella Fitzgerald, and Miles Davis. The recording studios are underneath the parking lot; all kinds of major artists, including Frank Sinatra, the Beatles, and Radiohead, have filled the echo chambers with sound. At the top of the tower, a blinking light spells out "Hollywood" in Morse code. Due to tightened security, the building is not open to the public. ✉ *1750 N. Vine St., Hollywood.*

OFF THE BEATEN PATH

CHEMOSPHERE HOUSE – Perched high up off Mulholland overlooking the Valley is the Chemosphere House, shaped like a flying saucer and with the futuristic stylings of the 1960s. Design by the late architect John Lautner, who studied under Frank Lloyd Wright, the Chemosphere House is held together with special glues used at the request of the original owner, who worked with a chemical company. Now owned by the publisher Benedikt Taschen, the Chemosphere is an awesome sight for architecture fans of the mod era. Directions: go north up Laurel Canyon, east on Mulholland, right on Torreyson Drive. Turn left up the narrow unmarked road where the Chemosphere House sits at the top. Please do not disturb the residents. ✉ *7776 Torreyson Dr.*

❼ **Egyptian Theatre.** Hieroglypics in Hollywood, why not? Impresario Sid Grauman built Hollywood's first movie palace in 1922; the Egyptian-theme theater hosted many premieres in its early heyday. In 1992 it closed—with an uncertain future. Six years later it reopened with its Tinseltown shine restored. The nonprofit American Cinematheque now hosts special screenings and discussions with notable filmmakers, and on weekends you can watch a documentary about Hollywood history (*Forever Hollywood*, $7). Walk through the lines of giant palm trees to the theater's forecourt and entrance. Backstage tours of the theater are available once a month. Films, primarily classics and independents, are shown in the evening. ✉ *6712 Hollywood Blvd.* ☎ *323/466–3456* ⊕ *www.egyptiantheatre.com* ✉ *$9; call for tour reservations and times.*

NEED A BREAK?

During Hollywood's heyday, the **Pig 'n Whistle** (✉ 6714 Hollywood Blvd., Hollywood ☎ 323/463–0000) was the place to stop for a bite before or after seeing a movie in the Egyptian Theatre, next door. After extensive restoration, the

Griffith Park

WITH SO MUCH of Los Angeles paved in cement and asphalt, 4,100-acre Griffith Park stands out as a special place. It's the largest municipal park and urban wilderness area in the United States. On warm weekends, there are parties, barbecues, mariachi bands, and strolling vendors selling fresh fruit. Joggers, cyclists, and walkers course its roadways, and golfers play its four municipal courses. Within the park there are three tennis courts, horse stables, a collection of vintage locomotive and railroad cars called Travel Town, and pony rides. L.A.'s oldest **merry-go-round** (☎ 323/665-3051) continues to spin here, playing a fabulous Stinson calliope. It's open weekends 11–5, and it costs $1.50 There's also the 6,100-seat **Greek Theatre** (☎ 323/665-1927 ⊕ www.greektheatrela.com), where Tina Turner and the Gipsy Kings have performed.

The park was named after Col. Griffith J. Griffith, a mining tycoon who donated 3,000 acres of land to the city for the park in 1896. Additional donations and land purchases by the city expanded the park to its present size. The park has been used as a film and television location since the early days of motion pictures. One early Hollywood producer advised, "A tree is a tree, a rock is a rock, shoot it in Griffith Park!" Since then, those trees and rocks have appeared in countless films and television shows.

One of the park's most famous filming sites is the **Griffith Observatory and Planetarium.** Overlooking Hollywood and downtown, this art deco landmark off Vermont Avenue was immortalized in *Rebel Without a*

Cause. After many years of renovation, the observatory was due to reopen in 2006. The silver-screen cowboy Gene Autry created the **Autry National Center** (✉ 4700 Western Heritage Way, at Zoo Dr. ☎ 323/667-2000 ⊕ www.autry-museum.org), an impressive museum that traces the history of the American West and Western moviemaking. Open Tuesday–Wednesday and Friday–Sunday 10–5, Thursday 10–8. Admission is $7.50.

Not far from the museum, at the junction of the Ventura Freeway (Highway 134) and the Golden State Freeway (I–5), is the 80-acre **Los Angeles Zoo** (☎ 323/644-4200 ⊕ www.lazoo.org). You'll need good walking shoes for this as distances are compounded by plenty of construction detours. You'll see tigers, lions, and bears along with a few rare glimpses of endangered species such as the California condor. In 2005, the zoo opened a new sea lion exhibit; currently, a new children's discovery center is in the works.

Griffith Park is accessible in several places: off Los Feliz Boulevard at Western Canyon Avenue, Vermont Avenue, Crystal Springs Drive, and Riverside Drive; from the Ventura/134 Freeway at Victory Boulevard, Zoo Drive, or Forest Lawn Drive; from the Golden State Freeway (I–5) at Los Feliz Boulevard and Zoo Drive. The park is open from 5 AM to 10 PM. The **ranger station** (☎ 323/913-7390) is on Crystal Springs Drive, near the merry-go-round.

historic restaurant is back, with overstuffed booths, dramatic paneled ceilings, and attentive service.

★ **Grauman's Chinese Theatre.** This fantasy of Chinese pagodas and temples is a place only Hollywood could turn out. Although you have to buy a movie ticket to appreciate the interior trappings, the courtyard is open to the public. Here you'll find those oh-so-famous cement hand- and footprints. This tradition is said to have begun at the theater's opening in 1927, with the premiere of Cecil B. DeMille's *King of Kings,* when actress Norma Talmadge accidentally stepped into wet cement. Now more than 160 celebrities have contributed imprints for posterity, including some oddball specimens, such as one of Jimmy Durante's nose and Betty Grable's legs. Recent inductees include Christopher Walken and Adam Sandler. The main theater itself is worth visiting, if only to see a film in the same seats as hundreds of celebrities who have attended big premieres here. You could also take a tour of the theaters and VIP lounge. If it's movies you want, six more theaters are next to the Hollywood & Highland complex with all the modern movie-going comforts. You may have to wade through the crowd of tourists and performance artists on the sidewalk for the front box office, but there's easy access to the upper theaters from the Highland parking garage through the elevators near the Kodak Theater. ✉ *6925 Hollywood Blvd., Hollywood* ☎ *323/461–3331, 323/463–9576 for tours* ⊕ *www.manntheatres.com.*

Griffith Observatory. High on a hillside overlooking the city, the Griffith Observatory is one of the most celebrated icons of Los Angeles, as much for the spectacular views as for the academic astronomy shows in the planetarium theater, the free telescope viewings, and the astronomy exhibits in the Hall of Science. You might recognize the observatory and grounds from such movies as *Rebel Without a Cause* and *The Terminator.* ■ **TIP**➜ At this writing, the planetarium was due to open in late 2006 after several years of renovations. Its new incarnation will double the exhibit space, double the theater size, and add a café, classroom, and bookstore. If you're determined to see some stars, there's a modest satellite facility near the zoo. ✉ *2800 E. Observatory Rd., Griffith Park* ☎ *323/664–1191* ⊕ *www.griffithobservatory.org.*

Guinness World of Records. Saluting those who have gone the extra mile to earn placement in the *Guinness Book of Records,* this museum's exhibits include replicas and photographs of endearing record breakers that include such oddities as the most-tattooed human and the world's heaviest man. An interactive simulation theater allows guests to sit in moving, vibrating seats while viewing a film to actually "experience" the force of a record being broken, and educational monitors give a hands-on approach to

BLONDE AMBITION

Keep an eye out for pictures of billboard queen Angelyne. This cartoonish blonde bombshell (and one-time candidate for governor) is a lively representative of Hollywood; having made a name for herself primarily by plastering her picture on giant murals around the city, she's a classic example of being famous for being famous.

trivia pursuit. ⊠ *6764 Hollywood Blvd., Hollywood* ☎ *323/463–6433* ⊕ *www.guinnessattractions.com* ☒ *$10.95* ⊗ *Daily 10 AM–midnight.*

★ ❾ **Hollywood & Highland.** Now an extremely busy tourist attraction (read: not a lot of locals), this hotel-retail-entertainment complex was a swaggering play to bring glitz and attention back to Hollywood. The design pays tribute to the city's film legacy with a grand staircase leading up to a pair of magnificent 33-foot-high elephants, a nod to the 1916 movie *Intolerance*. (Something tells us that the reference is lost on most visitors.) ■ **TIP→** **Pause at the entrance arch, Babylon Court, which frames the HOL-LYWOOD sign in the hills above for a picture-perfect view.** There are plenty of clothing stories and eateries—and you may find yourself ducking into these for a respite from the crowds and street artists. On the sidewalk below you could encounter everything from a sidewalk evangelist to a guy dressed as Spiderman posing for pictures. If you want avoid the crowds, your best bet is to get there before noon. A Metro Red Line station provides easy access to and from other parts of the city, and there's plenty of underground parking accessible from Highland Avenue. ⊠ *Hollywood Blvd. and Highland Ave., Hollywood* ⊕ *www.hollywoodandhighland. com* ☒ *Parking $2 with validation* ⊗ *Mon.–Sat. 10–10, Sun. 10–7.*

❹ **Hollywood and Vine.** The mere mention of this intersection inspires images of a street corner bustling with movie stars, hopefuls, and moguls arriving on foot or in Duesenbergs and Rolls-Royces. In the old days this was the hub of the radio and movie industry, and film stars like Gable and Garbo visited their agents' office buildings at these fabled cross streets. The famous intersection has hope to relive that golden era, but for now it comes alive only after dark as a place for theater and nightlife. The **Pantages Theatre** (⊠6233 Hollywood Blvd.) brings in Broadway shows such as the *Lion King, Hairspray,* and *Mama Mia*. Across the street is the opulent **Henry Fonda Music Box Theatre** (⊠ 6126 Hollywood Blvd. ⊕ www.henryfondatheater.com), built in the 1920s with an open-air palazzo. Pop-music concerts and small theater productions are both put on here. Just north on Vine, the **Avalon Theater** (⊠1735 N. Vine St. ⊕www. avalonhollywood.com) hosts rock concerts and dance nights in the space where the 1950s TV show *This Is Your Life* was recorded; it's now a rental venue for rock shows and dance clubs. Even the Red Line Metro station here keeps up the Hollywood theme, with a *Wizard of Oz*–style yellow brick road and giant movie projectors decorating the station.

NEED A BREAK? Stop at **Hollywood and Vine** (⊠ 6263 Hollywood Blvd. ☎ 323/464–2345) for a hearty (and somewhat pricey) meal or cocktail. The handy location makes it perfect for taking in a bite after a show; for panoramic people-watching on the famous corner, be sure to grab a table near the floor-to-ceiling windows.

❶❹ **Hollywood Bowl.** Summer-evening concerts have been a tradition since 1922 at this amphitheater cradled in the Hollywood Hills. The Bowl is the summer home of the Los Angeles Philharmonic, but the musical fare also includes pop and jazz. A new shell arrived in 2004, improving the acoustics. Evoking the 1929 shell structure, the new shell ripples out in a series of concentric rings. The 17,000-plus seating capacity ranges from boxes (where alfresco preconcert meals are catered) to concrete bleachers in the rear. Some prefer the back rows for their romantic appeal. Come early for a picnic in the grounds. Before the concert, or during the day, visit the **Hollywood Bowl Museum** (☎ 323/850–2058) for a time-capsule version of the Bowl's history. The micophone used during Frank Sinatra's 1943 performance is just one of the pieces of rare memorabilia on display. Throughout the gallery, drawers open to reveal vintage programs or letters written by fans tracing their fondest memories of going to the Bowl. Headphones let you listen to recordings of such great Bowl performers as Amelita Galli-Curci, Ella Fitzgerald, and Paul McCartney, and videos give you a tantalizing look at performances by everyone from the Beatles to Esa-Pekka Salonen. Be sure to pick up a map and take the "Bowl Walk" to explore the parklike grounds of this beautiful setting. ✉ *2301 N. Highland Ave., Hollywood* ☎ *323/850–2000* ⊕ *www.hollywoodbowl.com* ✉ *Tickets $1–$100, museum free* ☉ *Museum Tues.–Sat. 10–4:30; July–mid-Sept. concert nights, 10 AM–8:30 PM; grounds daily sunrise–sunset, call for performance schedule.*

⓫ Hollywood Entertainment Museum. You'll have to look hard to find this museum, as it's underground in a strip mall that seems to be in a constant state of renovation, but once inside you get an eyeful of small- and big-screen history. Famous props are a strong suit. The entire sets of the *Cheers* bar and Mulder's office from *X-Files* have landed here; you can even sit in the *Starship Enterprise* captain's chair from *Star Trek*. Other collections focus on early television and film cameras and makeup by Max Factor, the first cometics designed for film. To get the most out of this place, take a docent-led tour—the enthusiastic guides give an in-depth look at costume making, storyboarding, and set design. ✉ *7021 Hollywood Blvd., Hollywood* ☎ *323/465–7900* ⊕ *www.hollywoodmuseum.com* ✉ *$12* ☉ *Daily 10–6.*

★ ❷ Hollywood Forever Cemetery. With its revived grounds and mediagenic approach, this celebrity-filled cemetery (formerly the Hollywood Memorial Park) is well worth a visit. The lush gardens, lakes, and spectacular views of the HOLLYWOOD sign and Griffith Park Observatory (whose founder, Griffith J. Griffith, is buried here) make it a good spot for an afternoon walk; you can pick up a map of the grounds in the gift shop. Among the graves are those of Cecil B. DeMille, Douglas Fairbanks Sr., and Mel Blanc, voice of many Warner Bros. cartoon characters, whose headstone reads, "That's all, folks!" Film and music fans flock here to find their recently departed idols, including King Kong's love Fay Wray and punk rockers Johnny Ramone and Dee Dee Ramone (buried under his given name Douglas Glenn Colvin). The large Grecian tomb in the center of the lake belongs to philanthropist William A. Clark Jr., founder of the Los Angeles Philharmonic. Inside the Cathedral Mausoleum is Rudolph Valentino's crypt, stained red from many lipstick kisses. For years, a mysterious "Lady in Black" visited Valentino's tomb on the anniversary of his death. In summer, films starring Valentino and other interred residents are screened on the mausoleum's outer wall, and the grounds become quite a party scene. Private and group tours are available by appointment. The cemetery also has a kiosk in the main office with video memorials and digital scrapbooks of those buried here. ✉ *6000 Santa Monica Blvd., Hollywood* ☎ *323/469–1181* ☉ *Daily 8–5.*

13 **Hollywood Heritage Museum.** This unassuming building across from the Hollywood Bowl is a trove of memorabilia from the earliest days of Hollywood filmmaking. A must for Cecil B. DeMille fans, the museum gives a thorough history of his career. A recent acquisition: large sections of the original stone statue props from *The Ten Commandments*. A documentary tracking Hollywood's golden era is worth sitting down and taking in. The building itself is the restored Lasky–DeMille Barn, designated a California State Historic Landmark in 1956. ⊠ *2100 N. Highland Ave., Hollywood* ☎ *323/874–2276* ⊕ *www.hollywoodheritage. org* 💲 *$8* ☉ *Weekends 11–4.*

Hollywood High School. Surely no other high school has such a stellar alumni list. Such names as Carol Burnett, Carole Lombard, John Ritter, Lana Turner, and Sarah Jessica Parker did their time here. While you cannot enter the school grounds, it's easy to imagine the pre-celebs struggling over an algebra equation or being asked out to the prom. You can also see the mural *Diversity in Entertainment,* by famed local painter Eloy Torrez. ⊠ *1521 N. Highland Ave., Hollywood.*

★ **8** **Hollywood Museum.** Lovers of Hollywood's glamorous past will be singing "Hooray for Hollywood" when they stop by this gem of cinema history. It's inside the Max Factor Building, purchased in 1928. Factor's famous makeup was made on the top floors and a glamorous salon was hosted on the ground floor. After its renovation, this art deco landmark now holds more than 10,000 bits of film memorabilia. The extensive exhibits inside include those dedicated to Marilyn Monroe and Bob Hope and to costumes and set props from such films as *Moulin Rouge, Silence of the Lambs,* and *Planet of the Apes.* There's an impressive gallery of photos showing movie stars frolicking at such venues as the Brown Derby, Ciro's, the Trocadero, and the Mocambo. Hallway walls are covered with the stunning autograph collection of ultimate fan Joe Ackerman; aspiring filmmakers will want to check out an exhibit of early film equipment. The museum's showpiece, however, is the Max Factor exhibit, where separate dressing rooms are dedicated to Factor's "color harmony": creating distinct looks for "brownettes" (Factor's term), redheads, and of course, bombshell blondes. You can practically smell the peroxide of Marilyn Monroe getting her trademark platinum look here. You can also spy the

> ## KASTLE'S TOP 5
>
> - **Arclight/Cinerama Dome** as a blockbuster Hollywood movie experience—and the dome has vintage cool.
>
> - **Hollyhock House,** which recently reopened to the public. A great example of Frank Lloyd Wright's distinctive architecture.
>
> - **Huntington Library, Art Collections, and Botanical Gardens,** a trifecta of amazing things to explore. The themed gardens are so extensive you can forget you're in a city.
>
> - *Queen Mary* because it makes you feel like you've stepped back in time to the 1930s.
>
> - **Wayfarers Chapel** is off the beaten path, but worth the trip to see the all-glass church.

actual makeup cases owned by Lucille Ball, Lana Turner, Ginger Rogers, Bette Davis, Rita Hayworth, and others who made the makeup as glamorous as the starlets who wore it. ✉ *1660 N. Highland Ave., Hollywood* ☎ *323/464–7776* ⊕ *www.thehollywoodmuseum.com* 🎟 *$15* 🕓 *Thurs.–Sun. 10–5.*

⑫ Hollywood Roosevelt Hotel. In the local hotel world, the Roosevelt's something of a comeback kid. This historical landmark opened in 1927 and hosted the first Academy Awards that same year. It was a glamour magnet during Hollywood's golden age, but its reputation had recently slumped. A substantial face-lift (still ongoing at this writing) and a new nightlife scene turned things dramatically around. Now you're likely to need an insider connection to get into the celeb-filled club or the Tropicana poolside bar, where you can peek at the underwater mural by David Hockney. Though the new management tries to play down the ghost stories of the hotel's past, including sightings of Montgomery Clift, Clark Gable, and Carole Lombard, they did put a replica of the famous "Marilyn Mirror" in every room, modeled after the original, which sparked reports of the actress's ghostly reflection. ✉ *7000 Hollywood Blvd., Hollywood* ☎ *323/466–7000* ⊕ *www.hollywoodroosevelt.com.*

★ ❶ HOLLYWOOD Sign. With letters 50 feet tall, Hollywood's trademark sign can be spotted from miles away. The sign, which originally read HOLLYWOOD-LAND, was erected on Mt. Lee in the Hollywood Hills in 1923 to promote a real-estate development. In 1949 the "land" portion of the sign was taken down. By 1973, the sign had earned landmark status, but since the letters were made of wood, its longevity came into question. A makeover project was launched and the letters were auctioned off (rocker Alice Cooper bought the O, singing cowboy Gene Autry sponsored an L) to make way for a new sign made of sheet metal. Inevitably, the sign has drawn pranksters who have altered it over the years, albeit temporarily, to spell out HOLLYWEED (in the 1970s, to commemorate lenient marijuana laws), GO NAVY (before a Rose Bowl game), and PEROTWOOD (during the 1992 presidential election). A fence and surveillance equipment have since been installed to deter intruders. ⊕ *www.hollywoodsign.org.*

★ ❻ Hollywood Walk of Fame. Along Hollywood Boulevard runs a trail of affirmations for entertainment-industry achievers. On this mile-long stretch of sidewalk, inspired by the concrete handprints in front of Grauman's Chinese Theatre, the names are embossed in brass, each at the center of a pink star embedded in dark-gray terrazzo. They're not all screen deities; many stars commemorate people who worked in a technical field. The first eight stars were unveiled in 1960 at the northwest corner of Highland Avenue and Hollywood Boulevard: Olive Borden, Ronald Colman, Louise Fazenda, Preston Foster, Burt Lancaster, Edward Sedgwick, Ernest Torrence, and Joanne Woodward (some of these names have stood the test of time better than others). Since then, more than 1,600 others have been immortalized, though that honor doesn't come cheap—upon selection by a special committee, the personality in question (or more likely his or her movie studio or record company) pays about $15,000 for the privilege. To aid you in spotting celebrities you're looking for, they are identified by one of five icons: a motion-picture

WALK OF FAME LOCATIONS

Here are the sites of a few of the biggest stars along the Walk of Fame. Seeking out a particular star? Hit the directory on the Hollywood Chamber of Commerce's Web site, www.hollywoodchamber.net.

Charlie Chaplin: 6751 Hollywood Blvd.

Bette Davis: 6225 Hollywood Blvd.

Clark Gable: 1608 Vine St.

Cary Grant: 1610 Vine St.

Marlon Brando: 1765 Vine St.

Audrey Hepburn: 1652 Vine St.

Marilyn Monroe: 6774 Hollywood Blvd.

Bob Hope: 6541 Hollywood Blvd.

John Wayne: 1541 Vine St.

Alfred Hitchcock: 6506 Hollywood Blvd.

Billy Crystal: 6925 Hollywood Blvd.

Queen Latifah: 6915 Hollywood Blvd.

Tom Hanks: 7000 Hollywood Blvd.

Tom Cruise: 6912 Hollywood Blvd.

camera, a radio microphone, a television set, a record, or a theatrical mask. Contact the **Hollywood Chamber of Commerce** (✉ 7018 Hollywood Blvd. ☎ 323/469–8311 ⊕ www.hollywoodchamber.net) for celebrity-star locations and information on future star installations.

Hollywood Wax Museum. Looking for stars? You can spot celebrities past (Mary Pickford, Elvis Presley, and Clark Gable) and present (Angelina Jolie, Russell Crowe, Keanu Reeves, and Nicolas Cage), or at least their waxy likenesses, here in this museum that pays tribute to Hollywood's favorites. A short film on Oscar winners is shown daily. The lighting is purposely kept low to give the wax figures a more lifelike appearance, but some look downright spooky. Be especially cautious when entering the Horror Chamber, where figures of serial slashers and horror favorites from *Nightmare on Elm Street, Friday the 13th,* and *Texas Chainsaw Massacre* are animated to leap out to greet you. The creepiness is especially evident at night, when fewer visitors are around. ✉ *6767 Hollywood Blvd., Hollywood* ☎ *323/462–8860* ⊕ *www.hollywoodwax.com* ✉ *$12.95* ⊗ *Sun.–Thurs. 10 AM–midnight, Fri. and Sat. 10 AM–1 AM.*

NEED A BREAK?

Musso & Frank Grill (✉ 6667 Hollywood Blvd., at N. Las Palmas Ave. ☎ 323/467–5123), open since 1919, is the last remaining Old Hollywood watering hole. Come for dinner or just stop in for a martini and soak up some atmosphere. Expect high prices and some attitude. On the lighter side, the **Snow White Cafe** (✉ 6769 Hollywood Blvd., at Highland Ave. ☎ 323/465–4444), created by some of the original Disney animators and filled with murals of the film's characters, is a good stop for a quick bite.

CLOSE UP

L.A. on the Fast Track

1

ONCE UPON A TIME, Los Angeles had an enviable public transportation system known as the Pacific Electric Red Cars, trolleys that made it possible to get around this sprawling city without an automobile. In the mid-1900s, the last of the Red Cars disappeared, and Los Angeles lost itself in the car culture. Make no mistake, the car culture is here to stay; an afternoon in rush-hour traffic will drive that point home. But for the last few years, a sleek new rail system has emerged. You can now take a subway through parts of downtown Los Angeles, Hollywood, Pasadena, and North Hollywood.

The Metro Red Line subway, which is the most useful for exploring parts of the city, starts at downtown's Union Station, then curves northwest to Hollywood and on to Universal City and North Hollywood. The Blue and Green light rail lines are geared for commuters. The latest addition, the Gold Line, goes from Union Station up to Pasadena.

Though it takes some planning, using the Metro can spare you time you might otherwise spend stuck in traffic—if the stations are convenient, that is. For nuts-and-bolts information on riding the Metro Rail, see Smart Travel Tips. If you're worried about being caught in the subway during an earthquake, keep in mind that stations and tunnels were built with reinforced steel and were engineered to withstand a magnitude-8 earthquake.

The Metro Rail stations are worth exploring themselves, and you can sign up for a free docent-led **MTA art tour** (☎ 213/922–2738 ⊕ www.mta. net). You'll receive a free day pass to ride the rails as you visit the colorful murals, sculptures, and architectural elements of each station, designed to carry out themes of Los Angeles history. The Universal City station is next to the site of the Campo de Caheunga, where Mexico relinquished control of California to the United States in 1847, and the station features a time line of the area's past done in the traditional style of colorful Mexican folk art.

The North Hollywood station also celebrates local history: native Gabrielino culture, many immigrant communities, Amelia Earhart (a local), Western wear designer Nudie, and the history of transportation in Los Angeles County. The station at Hollywood Boulevard and Highland plays off Tinseltown fantasies, encouraging travelers to look beyond the subway station facade to concrete walls and mechanical ducts.

The Hollywood and Vine station has recycled film reels on the ceiling, original Paramount Pictures film projectors from the 1930s, and floor paving that looks like the yellow brick road from *The Wizard of Oz*. There are imposing, glass-clad columns juxtaposed with rock formations at the Vermont and Beverly station. The old Red Car trolley makes a guest appearance in the Hollywood and Western station. For a more information, call 213/922–2738 or visit the Web site: www.metro.net/about%5Fus/metroart/ma_docent.htm

Ivar Street. William Faulkner wrote *Absalom, Absalom!* while he lived at the old **Knickerbocker Hotel** (⊠ 1714 N. Ivar St., Hollywood), and Nathanael West wrote *The Day of the Locust* in his apartment at the **Parva Sed-Apta** (⊠ 1817 N. Ivar St., Hollywood).

★ ❾ **Kodak Theatre.** Follow the path of red-carpet Hollywood royalty to the home of the Academy Awards. While taking a half-hour tour of this famous setting isn't cheap, it's a worthwhile expense for movie buffs who just can't get enough insider information. The tour guides share plenty of behind-the-scenes tidbits about Oscar ceremonies as they take you through the theater. You'll get to step into the VIP George Eastman Lounge, where celebrities mingle on the big night and get a bird's-eye view from the balcony seating. (Be sure to ask how Oscar got his name.) The interior design was inspired by European opera houses, but underneath all the trimmings, the space has some of the finest technical systems in the world. Although you may not make it in for the Oscar show itself, you can always come here for a musical or concert performance by the likes of Alicia Keys or the Dixie Chicks. ⊠ 6801 Hollywood Blvd., Hollywood ☎ 323/308–6300 ⊕ www.kodaktheatre.com ☑ $15.

❸ **Paramount Pictures.** With a history dating to the early 1920s, this studio
Fodor'sChoice was home to some of Hollywood's most luminous stars, including
★ Rudolph Valentino, Mae West, Mary Pickford, and Lucille Ball, who filmed episodes of *I Love Lucy* here. The lot still churns out memorable movies and TV shows, including *Forrest Gump, Titanic,* and *Star Trek.* You can take a studio tour (reservations required) led by friendly guides who walk and trolley you around the back lots. As well as gleaning some gossipy history (see the lawn where Lucy and Desi broke up), you'll spot the sets of TV and film shoots in progress, including such hits as *Entertainment Tonight, Dr. Phil,* and *Everybody Hates Chris.* You can also be part of the audience for live TV tapings. Tickets are free; call for listings and times. ⊠ 5555 Melrose Ave., Hollywood ☎ 323/956–1777 ⊕ www.paramount.com/studio ☑ Tours $35.

Ripley's Believe It or Not. "Odditorium" is a good name for it—where else can you see a wreath of human hair, a sculpture of Marilyn Monroe made of shredded money, shrunken heads, and animal freaks of nature? You're asked to "believe it or not," and many of the curiosities may fail a strict authenticity test, but it's silly good fun for families. ⊠ 6780 Hollywood Blvd., Hollywood ☎ 323/466–6335 ⊕ www.ripleys.com ☑ $11.95 ☉ Sun.–Thurs. 10 AM–10:30 PM, Fri. and Sat. 11 AM–11:30 PM.

OFF THE BEATEN PATH **LOS FELIZ, SILVER LAKE, AND ECHO PARK** — Over the past few years, these neighborhoods east of Hollywood have become an intriguing mix of subcultures. Low rents drew artists and musicians to Los Feliz, then farther southeast to Silver Lake and, lately, Echo Park. Funky, independent boutiques, galleries, and cafés have followed in their wake. Los Feliz is the most gentrified, Echo Park the least. Silver Lake's namesake is a lovely oasis, and the neighborhood also has a cluster of modernist homes designed by Richard Neutra and R. M. Schindler. Echo Park's **Echo Lake** has a sprawling lotus bed; its slender **Sunset Art Park**, at 1478 Sunset Boulevard, gives a glimpse of "drive-by art." Musicians can brush up on their skills with $20 lessons at the **Silver Lake Conservancy of Music** (✉ 3920 W. Sunset ☎ 323/665–3363) founded by Flea of the Red Hot Chili Peppers. For a blast of the neighborhoods' creative energy, visit during late summer's **Sunset Junction Street Fair** (⊕ www.sunsetjunction. org), with concerts by alternative bands. There's also an annual Silver Lake Film Festival (⊕ www.silverlakefilmfestival.org), which showcases up-and-coming independent filmmakers. Both of these annual events bring together a crowd drawn from the arts, Latino, and gay communities. The easiest way to reach these neighborhoods is to drive east on Sunset Boulevard, then head north up Hillhurst or Vermont Avenue to Los Feliz, or continue southeast on Sunset to Silver Lake and Echo Park.

WILSHIRE BOULEVARD, MUSEUM ROW & FARMERS MARKET

The three-block stretch of Wilshire Boulevard known as Museum Row, east of Fairfax Avenue, racks up five intriguing museums and a prehistoric tar pit to boot. Only a few blocks away is the historic Farmers Market and The Grove shopping mall, a great place to people-watch over breakfast. Wilshire Boulevard itself is something of a cultural monument—it begins its grand 16-mi sweep to the sea in downtown Los Angeles. Along the way it passes through once-grand but now run-down neighborhoods near MacArthur Park; Mid-Wilshire, holding some of the city's first high-rise office buildings; the elegant old-money enclave of Hancock Park along with Miracle Mile and Museum Row; the showy city of Beverly Hills; and the high-price high-rise condo corridor in Westwood, before ending its march at the cliffs above the Pacific Ocean. The drive from downtown to the ocean can be traffic clogged; Wilshire is a major thoroughfare and tends to be busy all day long. ■ TIP→ Finding parking along Wilshire Boulevard can present a challenge any time of the day; you'll find advice on the information phone lines of most attractions. For avid urban explorers, the most interesting stretch historically is the boulevard's eastern portion, from Fairfax Avenue to downtown.

What to See

Bullock's Wilshire. This 1929 copper-trimmed, art moderne building just east of Vermont Avenue used to house Bullock's department store, the first Los Angeles store built to accommodate the automobile—it has a porte cochere and parking behind the building. Now listed on the National Register of Historic Places, it houses Southwestern University's law school library. ✉ *3050 Wilshire Blvd., Mid-Wilshire.*

❻ Craft and Folk Art Museum (CAFAM). A small but important cultural landmark in the city, CAFAM pioneered support of traditional folk arts. These days, it takes on a global scope, embracing contemporary crafts as well as long-established artisan work. The gallery space mounts rotating exhibitions where you might see anything from costumes of carnival celebrations around the world to Mennonite quilts. Shows slated for 2007 include found-object art by Ramona Otto and photographs of war-torn Africa by journalist Dan Eldon. ✉ *5814 Wilshire Blvd., Miracle Mile* ☎ *323/937–4230* ⊕ *www.cafam.org* 💲 *$5* ⊙ *Wed.–Sun. 11–5.*

A GOOD TOUR

Numbers in the text correspond to numbers in the margin and on the Wilshire Boulevard, Museum Row & Farmers Market map.

Start the day with coffee and fresh-baked pastries at the **Farmers Market ❶**, a few blocks north of Wilshire Boulevard at 3rd Street and Fairfax Avenue. Drive south on Fairfax Avenue to the **Miracle Mile ❷** district of Wilshire Boulevard. The black-and-gold art deco building on the northeast corner is a former May Company department store that now houses satellite exhibition galleries of the Los Angeles County Museum of Art (LACMA). Turn left onto Wilshire and proceed to Ogden Drive or a block farther to Spaulding Avenue, where you can park the car and set out on foot to explore the museums.

The large complex of contemporary buildings surrounded by a park on the corner of Wilshire and Ogden Drive is the **Los Angeles County Museum of Art (LACMA) ❸**, the largest art museum west of Chicago. Also in the park are the prehistoric **La Brea Tar Pits ❹**, where many of the fossils displayed at the adjacent **Page Museum at the La Brea Tar Pits ❺** were found. Across Wilshire is the **Craft and Folk Art Museum (CAFAM) ❻** and, back at the corner of Wilshire and Fairfax, the **Petersen Automotive Museum ❼**, which surveys the history of the car in Los Angeles.

From Museum Row and Miracle Mile, a drive east along Wilshire Boulevard to downtown gives you a minitour of a historical and cultural cross section of Los Angeles. At Highland Avenue you enter the old-money enclave that is the **Hancock Park** neighborhood. At Western Avenue the **Wiltern Theater ❽** stands across the street from the intersection's Metro station. The frequency of Korean-language signs in this area is a clue that you're now driving along the edge of **Koreatown.** If you'd like one more look at cool architecture, continue on Wilshire until it crosses Vermont Avenue toward downtown Los Angeles, and you'll pass the magnificent **Bullock's Wilshire** building. Otherwise, stick around Koreatown for some Korean barbecue.

⊙ **TIMING TIPS→** The museums open between 10 and noon, so plan your tour around the opening time of the museum you wish to visit first. LACMA is open Monday but closed Wednesday and has extended hours into the evening, closing at 8 (9 on Friday). The other museums are closed on Monday (except the Page). If you're on a tight budget, keep tabs on museum free days; for instance, on the second Tuesday of the month LACMA admission to all but ticketed exhibits is free. Set aside a day to do this entire tour: an hour or two for the Farmers Market and The Grove, four hours for the museums, and an hour for the Wilshire Boulevard sights.

1

1 **Farmers Market and The Grove.** In 1934, two entrepreneurs convinced
Fodor's Choice oil magnate E. B. Gilmore to open a vacant field for a bare-bones mar-
★ ket; a group of farmers simply pulled up their trucks and sold produce
off the backs. From this seat-of-the-pants situation grew a European-
style open-air market and local institution at the corner of 3rd Street
and Fairfax Avenue. The saying "Meet me at 3rd and Fairfax" became
a standard line for generations of Angelenos who ate, shopped, and spotted the stars who had drifted over from the studios for a breath of unpretentious air. Now the market includes 110 stalls and more than 20
counter-order restaurants, plus the landmark 1941 Clock Tower. In
2002 a massive expansion called The Grove opened; this highly con-
ceptualized outdoor mall has a Euro spin, with cobblestones, marble
mosaics, and pavilions. By afternoon, it bulges with shoppers and teens
hitting the movie theaters and chain stores such as Banana Republic,
Crate & Barrel, Barnes & Noble, and J. Crew. Los Angeles history gets
a nod with the electric steel-wheeled Red Car trolley, which shuttles two
blocks through the Farmers Market and The Grove. ■ **TIP→ The Grove
really dazzles around Christmas, with an enormous Christmas tree and a nightly
faux snowfall until New Year's Day.** ✉ *Farmers Market, 6333 W. 3rd St.;
The Grove, 189 The Grove Dr., Fairfax District* ☎ *Farmers Market 323/
933–9211, The Grove 323/900–8080* ⊕ *www.farmersmarketla.com;
www.TheGroveLA.com* ⊙ *Farmers Market weekdays 9–9, Sat. 9–8, Sun.
10–9; The Grove Mon.–Thurs. 10–9, Fri. and Sat. 10–10, Sun. 11–7.*

**NEED A
BREAK?** If you're feeling peckish, the Farmers Market is the place to be. Snag a snack
at one of the fruit stands or fresh bakeries, or for something more substantial,
hit the **French Crepe Company** (☎ 323/934–3113) for made-on-the-spot crepes,
waffles, salads, and sandwiches. In the middle of the Farmers Market is also
the longstanding favorite **Gumbo Pot** (☎ 323/933–0358), which steams with
Cajun goodies—gumbos, jambalaya, cornbread, and beignets.

Hancock Park. Highland Avenue marks the western perimeter of the
neighborhood called Hancock Park (which is east of the park of the same
name, home of LACMA and the La Brea Tar Pits). In the 1920s, wealthy
families came here to build English Tudor–style homes with East Coast
landscaping that defied local climate and history. Today Hancock Park
is a quiet, relatively suburban neighborhood whose residents frequently
venture out to the **Larchmont Village** shopping district to browse a collection of bookstores, antiques shops, and a Saturday farmers' market.
Neighbors are still up in arms about the **"House of Davids"** (✉ 304 S.
Muirfield, at 3rd St.), whose owner has installed 18 white statues of Michae-
langelo's *David* around his circular driveway. ✉ *Bordered by Wilshire
and Beverly Blvds., Highland Ave., and Wilton Pl., Mid-Wilshire.*

Koreatown. Although L.A.'s sizable Korean population is scattered
throughout the city, it's especially concentrated here, along Olympic Boulevard between Vermont and Western avenues, where you'll find Korean
specialty food stores and restaurants among many shops displaying
furniture, electronics, and other items. The **Korean American Museum**
(✉ 3727 W. 6th St., Suite 400, Miracle Mile ☎ 213/388–4229 ⊕ www.
kamuseum.org ☞ Free ⊙ Weekdays 11–6, Sat. 11–3) highlights the cul-

Wilshire Boulevard, Museum Row & Farmers Market

KEY

Ⓜ *Metro stops*

KOREATOWN

HANCOCK PARK

The Wilshire Country Club

Pan Pacific Park

Bullock's Wilshire

tural heritage of Korean-Americans. On the 4th floor of an office building, the museum is a modest but devoted reflection of the dedication to preserving cultural history. ⊠ *Bordered by Vermont and Western Aves., 8th St., and Pico Blvd., west of Downtown.*

★ ❹ **La Brea Tar Pits.** About 40,000 years ago, deposits of oil rose to the earth's surface, collected in shallow pools, and coagulated into sticky asphalt. In the early 20th century, geologists discovered that the sticky goo contained the largest collection of Pleistocene, or Ice Age, fossils ever found at one location: more than 600 species of birds, mammals, plants, reptiles, and insects. Roughly 100 tons of fossil bones have been removed in excavations over the last seven decades, making this one of the world's most famous fossil sites. You can see most of the pits through chain-link fences. Pit 91 is the site of ongoing excavation; tours are available, and you can volunteer to help with the excavations in summer. Statues of a family of mammoths in the big pit near the corner of Wilshire and Curson suggest how many of them were entombed: edging down to a pond of water to drink, animals were caught in the tar and unable to extricate themselves. There are several pits scattered around Hancock Park and the surrounding neighborhood; construction in the area has often had to accommodate them, and in nearby streets and along sidewalks, little bits of tar occasionally ooze up, unstoppable. The ⇨ **Page Museum at the La Brea Tar Pits** displays fossils from the tar pits. ⊠ *Hancock Park, Miracle Mile* ⊕ *www.tarpits.org* ✉ *Free.*

❸ **Los Angeles County Museum of Art (LACMA).** Since it opened in 1966, **Fodor'sChoice** LACMA has assembled an encyclopedic collection of more than 150,000 ★ works from around the world; its collection is widely considered the most comprehensive in the western United States. American, Latin American, Islamic, and South and Southeast Asian works are especially well represented. Other standout areas include costumes and textiles, decorative arts, European paintings and sculpture, photography, drawings, and prints. Architectural cohesiveness, on the other hand, is not LACMA's strong suit. The collections are spread through five disparate buildings on the main campus, plus another building two blocks away. Plans for a renovation, set to open by 2007, were announced in 2005.

Most of LACMA's buildings cluster around a courtyard. The museum equivalent of Art History 101, the Ahmanson building is the largest and most culturally diverse section of the complex. Its displays include ancient Mesoamerican artifacts, Chinese and Korean art, outstanding Islamic collections, and European painting and sculpture. There's also a stellar section on American art, stretching from the Federal-period landscape and genre paintings to frontier art to regional developments, such as California impressionism. Masterworks include George Bellows's *Cliff Dwellers,* Mary Cassatt's *Mother About to Wash Her Sleepy Child,* and Winslow Homer's *The Cotton Pickers.*

The Robert O. Anderson building covers 20th-century and contemporary art, where the European avant-garde (Picasso, Kandinsky, Magritte) meets American artists such as David Hockney and Ed Keinholz. Special exhibits are often mounted in the Hammer Building. The Pavilion for Japanese Art showcases Japanese drawings, paintings, textiles, and decorative arts; it's a particularly peaceful space, as it's mostly lighted by natural light and a fountain on the ground floor fills the building with the sound of flowing water. The Bing Center holds a research library, resource center, and film theater.

A pleasant stroll down the adjacent grassy courtyard along Wilshire leads you to the **LACMA West,** a streamlined building built in 1939. Inside is the Bernard and Edith Lewin Latin American Art Galleries. The Lewins, who started their collection with three Diego Rivera paintings they bought in the 1950s, eventually amassed the largest private collection of Latin American art in the world. In 1999 the Lewins donated more than 2,000 artworks from their collection to LACMA. Heavy on Mexican modern masters (Rivera, Tamayo, Orozco, Siquieros), the Lewins' collection also includes the work of Cuban artist Wifredo Lam, Chilean artist Roberto Mata, Guatemalan artist Carlos Merida, and Uruguayan painter Pedro Figari. Though LACMA West is on a continuously changing exhibit schedule, moving out gallery regulars to make way for large temporary exhibits, the Boone's Children's Gallery always maintains its art-making mission through art classes, interactive displays, and brightly colored decor. ⊠ *5905 Wilshire Blvd., Miracle Mile* ☎ *323/ 857–6000* ⊕ *www.lacma.org* ✉ *$7, free 2nd Tues. of month* ☉ *Mon., Tues., and Thurs. noon–8, Fri. noon–9, weekends 11–8.*

■ **TIP→** Temporary exhibits sometimes require tickets purchased in advance, so check the calendar ahead of time. In 2007, special shows will highlight Salvador Dalí and portraits by David Hockney.

NEED A BREAK? For a pop art–style meal, detour up Fairfax to **Swingers** (⊠ 8020 Beverly Blvd. ☎ 323/653–5858). Andy Warhol cow-print wallpaper, tartan vinyl booths, and a modern take on '50s greasy-spoon standbys turned this once average coffee shop into a hipster hangout.

② **Miracle Mile.** The strip of Wilshire Boulevard between La Brea and Fairfax avenues was vacant land in the 1920s, when a developer bought the parcel to develop into a shopping and business district. Nobody thought the venture could be successful, but the auto age was just emerging, and the strip became known as Miracle Mile. It was the world's first linear downtown, with building designs incorporating wide store windows to attract attention from passing cars. The area went into a decline in the 1950s and '60s, when high-rises began to break up its cohesiveness, but it's now enjoying a comeback, as Los Angeles's art deco architecture has come to be appreciated, preserved, and restored. The exemplary architecture includes the **El Rey Theater** (⊠ 5515 Wilshire Blvd., Miracle Mile ☎ 323/936–6400), now a sometime nightclub.

☜ ❺ **Page Museum at the La Brea Tar Pits.** This member of the Natural History Museum family is set, bunkerlike, half underground. A bas-relief around four sides depicts life in the Pleistocene era, and the museum has more than 3 million Ice Age fossils. Exhibits include reconstructed, life-size skeletons of mammoths, wolves, sloths, eagles, and condors. The fishbowl-like, glass-enclosed laboratory is a real attention getter—here you can watch paleontologists as they clean, identify, catalog, and piece together bits of fossils excavated from the nearby asphalt deposits. *The La Brea Story,* a short documentary film, is shown every 15–30 minutes. A hologram magically puts flesh on 9,000-year-old "La Brea Woman." ⊠ *5801 Wilshire Blvd., Miracle Mile* ☎ *323/934–7243* ⊕ *www.tarpits.org* ✉ *$7, free 1st Tues. of month* ☉ *Weekdays 9:30–5, weekends 10–5.*

❼ **Petersen Automotive Museum.** More than just a building full of antique and unusual cars, the Petersen proves to be a cool stop for everyone, not just gearheads. Lifelike dioramas and street scenes spread through the ground floor help to establish a local context for the history of the automobile. Rotating exhibits on the second floor may include those on Hollywood-celebrity and movie cars, "muscle" cars (like a 1969 Dodge Daytona 440 Magnum), motorcycles, and commemorating the Ferrari. You'll also learn about the origins of our modern-day car-insurance system, as well as the history of L.A.'s formidable freeway network. A children's interactive Discovery Center illustrates the mechanics of the automobile; there are also a gift shop and a research library. ⊠ *6060 Wilshire Blvd., Miracle Mile* ☎ *323/930–2277* ⊕ *www.petersen.org* ✉ *$10* ☉ *Tues.–Sun. 10–6.*

Fodor's Choice ★

❽ **Wiltern Theater.** Designated an official Hollywood landmark, this magnificent example of all-out art deco architecture is still used for performances. The 1930s zigzag design glows in brilliant turquoise; a giant chandelier hangs from the vaulted ceiling. A 2001–02 revamp cleared out the ground-floor theater seats to create an open floor; since its reopening the theater has been back on the circuit for major music and comedy acts. ⊠ *3790 Wilshire Blvd., at Western Ave., Mid-Wilshire* ☎ *213/380–5005* ⊕ *www.wiltern.com.*

WEST HOLLYWOOD

West Hollywood is not a place to see things (like museums or movie studios) as much as it is a place to do things—like go to a nightclub, eat at a world-famous restaurant, or attend an art gallery opening. Since the end of Prohibition, the Sunset Strip has been Hollywood's nighttime playground, where stars headed to such glamorous nightclubs as the Trocadero, the Mocambo, and Ciro's. Las Vegas eclipsed the Strip's glitter in the 1950s, but in the next decade the music industry moved into town, and rock clubs like the Whisky A Go-Go took root. While the trendiest nightclubs are orbiting elsewhere, today's Sunset Strip is still going strong, with club goers lining up outside well-established spots like the Viper Room and House of Blues.

But hedonism isn't all that drives West Hollywood. Also thriving is an important interior-design and art-gallery trade. West Hollywood has always attracted the mavericks and the disenfranchised, and in the 1980s, a coalition of seniors, gays, and lesbians spearheaded a grassroots effort to bring cityhood to West Hollywood, which was still an unincorporated part of Los Angeles County. The coalition succeeded in 1984, and today West Hollywood has emerged as one of the most progressive cities in southern California. It's also one of the most gay-friendly cities anywhere, with one-third of its population estimated to be either gay or lesbian. Its annual Gay Pride Parade is one of the largest in the na-

tion, drawing tens of thousands of participants each June. This driving
tour will help you capture some of the spirit of West Hollywood.

What to See

7 **Avenues of Art and Design** (☎ 310/289–2525 or 800/368–6020 ⊕ www.
visitwesthollywood.com). A concentration of design studios and art
and antiques galleries along Melrose Avenue, San Vicente Boulevard,
Robertson Boulevard, North Almont, and other streets around the Pacific Design Center has given rise to this catch-all designation. The galleries are very high-end, but it doesn't cost anything to look (sometimes
the window is as far as you can get; many of these studios are "to the
trade only"). ■ **TIP→** Periodically, usually on the first Saturday evening of
the month, several of the galleries host group-opening receptions, known as
Gallery Walks, to premiere new exhibits and artists. Contact the **West Hollywood Convention and Visitors Bureau** for information.

**NEED A
BREAK?**   Work in a photo op at **Tail O' the Pup** (✉ 329 N. San Vicente Blvd. ☎ 310/652–
4517), a hot dog stand that's shaped like its product. A local landmark, it has
been featured in several movies, including *LA Story*. And you just might spot a
celebrity or two breaking their diet on one of the specialty dogs, such as the
"Mexican Olé." Tail O' the Pup's main rival in the dog biz is **Pink's** (✉ 709 N.

A GOOD DRIVE

Numbers in the text correspond to numbers in the margin and on the West Hollywood map.

Begin a driving-loop tour of West Hollywood by heading west along **Sunset Boulevard** ❶ from Fairfax Avenue. On the north side of the street is the **Guitar Center**; if you have a moment, park and take in the RockWalk to size up your favorite rock star's handprints. Keep going west on Sunset, and as you enter the "Strip," the first block past Crescent Heights Boulevard, look up the hill to the right for a glimpse of the famous **Chateau Marmont** ❷ hotel. As you cruise down the boulevard, look up at the billboards, or "vanity boards," advertising the latest in everything from jeans to entertainment.

About three blocks west of the Chateau Marmont, you'll pass the landmark art deco masterpiece the Sunset Tower hotel, on the left. Built in 1929 and now back on the map after a revamp, the hotel counted many celebrities among its residents, including Clark Gable and Marilyn Monroe. Next up are two famous nightclubs on the **Sunset Strip** ❸: the Delta-inspired House of Blues, on the left, and the Comedy Store, on the right. (The legendary Ciro's nightclub used to occupy the Comedy Store spot.) Look to the left for the all-white Mondrian Hotel; its poolside SkyBar lounge still attracts a buzz.

Sunset Plaza ❹ is a good place to get out of the car and take a stroll, do some high-end window-shopping, or pass the time people-watching from a sidewalk café. Look for parking in the lot behind the shops, off Sunset Plaza Drive. The club scene picks up again along this stretch of Sunset, with the Viper Room, the Whisky A Go-Go, which has rocked since the '60s, and the Roxy, a Strip mainstay since 1972.

Doheny Drive marks the division between West Hollywood and Beverly Hills. From Sunset, turn left on Doheny to drive south to **Santa Monica Boulevard** ❺. At Santa Monica, turn left to continue the loop tour. From roughly Robertson Boulevard to La Cienega Boulevard, Santa Monica Boulevard is the commercial core of West Hollywood's large gay and lesbian community. (It also used to be part of Route 66.) A right turn at San Vicente Boulevard will bring you West Hollywood's most visible landmark, the **Pacific Design Center** ❻. There's public parking available at the PDC, and you can get out and walk back a block to Santa Monica Boulevard or head west on **Melrose Avenue.** This walkable section of town is known as the **Avenues of Art and Design** ❼, because of its many design studios and art galleries.

Plan to return to West Hollywood in the evening to check out the club scene along Sunset and Santa Monica boulevards.

⏱ **TIMING TIPS**→ **Traffic on Sunset and Santa Monica boulevards is heavy most of the time, especially at night and on weekends. Weekday afternoons are generally the easiest driving times. For street parking, bring plenty of quarters; parking on residential streets is by permit only.**

La Brea Ave. ☎ 323/931–4223 ⊕ www.pinkshollywood.com), where a line stretches down the block for massive dogs that reach 10 inches and are named for such celebrities as Ozzy Osbourne and Martha Stewart. Pink's is open until very late—3 AM on weekends.

❷ Chateau Marmont. If we had a dollar for every time a celebrity interview was conducted alongside the Marmont pool. . . . This secluded hotel, hidden in greenery off the Sunset Strip, has earned its stripes as a popular hideaway for industry actors, musicians, and writers. The ambience is chic without being frosty; most important, the hotel cultivates a sense of privacy. Stars such as Jim Morrison, Robert De Niro, Boris Karloff, Marilyn Monroe, and Dustin Hoffman liked this hotel so much that they moved in for long periods of time. In 1982 actor John Belushi checked out permanently here, of a drug overdose. Though most areas are strictly for guests, you can visit the main-floor lounge or outdoor patio for a meal or a cocktail. ⊠ *8221 Sunset Blvd., West Hollywood* ☎ *323/656–1010* ⊕ *www.chateaumarmont.com.*

Guitar Center RockWalk. Musicians and the fans who love them will want to stop by the Guitar Center on Sunset, where you can try out any musical instrument your heart desires as well as view memorabilia donated by some of the store's star customers——Led Zeppelin's set list, Jeff Beck's yellow Strat guitar, and KISS members' platform boots. A place that has provided essentials for virtually every band to have come out of Los Angeles since the 1960s, the store started paying tribute to its rock star clientele by creating a "RockWalk," out front. The concrete slabs are imprinted with the talented hands of Van Halen, Bonnie Raitt, Chuck Berry, Dick Dale, Def Leppard, Carlos Santana, KISS, and others. Two standouts are Joey Ramone's upside-down hand and Lemmy of Motörhead's "middle finger salute." Inductees are celebrated with a ceremony that's open to the public—check the Web site for details. ⊠ *7425 Sunset Blvd., West Hollywood* ☎ *323/874–1060* ⊕ *www.rockwalk.com* 🖾 *Free* ⊙ *Weekdays 10–9, Sat. 10–8, Sun. 11–7.*

Melrose Avenue. It may have shone brightest when the *first* George Bush was in the White House, but Melrose Avenue still has shopping clout. High-end stores such as Maxfield cluster at the western end, near the Pacific Design Center. Farther east, past North Fairfax Avenue and the high school, the boutiques get younger and funkier as Euro-brands get bumped for Wasteland and Aardvark's Odd Ark. Don't bother trying to hit the stores here early: shops usually don't start opening until noon.

| NEED A BREAK? | Pair a shopping high with a sugar rush at **Boule Pâtisserie** (⊠ 420 N. La Cienega Blvd., between Melrose Ave. and Beverly Blvd. ☎ 310/289–9977), a streamlined, Paris-influenced pastry place from acclaimed pastry chef Michelle Myers. The mouthwatering, handmade chocolates, sweets, and ice creams include unusual flavors, like chocolates laced with Scotch bonnet chiles and caramel cardamom sorbet. Or take your sweet tooth over to **Sweet Lady Jane** (⊠ 8360 Melrose Ave., at N. Kings Rd. ☎ 323/653–7145), where you can eat a sandwich or lemon bar while watching people jockey for the beautifully decorated cakes. |

6 **Pacific Design Center.** Cesar Pelli designed these two architecturally intriguing buildings, one sheathed in blue glass (known as the Blue Whale), the other in green (the Green Whale). Together, they house 150 design showrooms, making this the largest interior design complex in the western United States. Though focused on the professional trade (meaning only the pro decorators could shop the showrooms), the PDC has become more open over the past couple of years, with public events and some showroom access. The downtown Museum of Contemporary Art has a small satellite **MOCA Gallery** (☎ 310/289–5233 ⊕ www.moca. org) here that showcases current artists and designers and hosts exhibit-related talks. Three cafés on the premises are also open to the public. ✉ *8687 Melrose Ave., West Hollywood* ☎ *310/657–0800* ⊕ *www. pacificdesigncenter.com* ☿ *Weekdays 9–5.*

5 **Santa Monica Boulevard.** For many gay and lesbian visitors to southern California, Santa Monica Boulevard is the local Main Street of modern gay America. From La Cienega Boulevard on the east to Doheny on the west, it's the commercial core of West Hollywood's gay community, with restaurants and cafés, bars and clubs, bookstores, and other establishments catering largely to gays and lesbians. Twice a year, during June's Gay Pride Parade and on Halloween, in October, the boulevard becomes an open-air festival. ■ **TIP➔** **Santa Monica Boulevard is also prone to bad traffic, so if you need to get out of a jam, try Pico or Olympic boulevards, which run roughly parallel a bit further south.**

1 **Sunset Boulevard.** One of the most fabled avenues in the world, Sunset Boulevard began humbly enough in the 18th century as a route from El Pueblo de Los Angeles (today's downtown L.A.) to the ranches in the west and then to the Pacific Ocean. Now as it winds its way across the L.A. basin to the ocean, it cuts through gritty urban neighborhoods and what used to be the working center of Hollywood's movie industry. In West Hollywood, it becomes the sexy and seductive Sunset Strip, then slips quietly into the tony environs of Beverly Hills and Bel-Air, twisting and winding past gated estates. Continuing on past UCLA in Westwood, through Brentwood and Pacific Palisades, Sunset finally descends to the beach, the edge of the continent, and the setting sun.

4 **Sunset Plaza.** With a profusion of sidewalk cafés, Sunset Plaza is one of the best people-watching spots in town. Sunny weekends reach the highest pitch, when people flock to this stretch of Sunset Boulevard for brunch or lunch and to browse in the shops, which tend to be expensive and showy. There's free parking in the lot behind the shops.

> **WORD OF MOUTH**
>
> "One of the quintessential L.A. experiences is to drive Sunset Boulevard to the ocean, making stops all along the way. Some of the highlights include historical downtown, Hollywood, West Hollywood, Beverly Hills, Westwood, Bel Air, Brentwood, and Pacific Palisades. There are tons of sights to see on Sunset and just a few blocks to the north or south all along the route. (Dodger Stadium is one of them.) I always take my first time L.A. visitors on this trip and it's always a big hit."   –jayinla

⊠ 8600 block of Sunset Blvd., 2 blocks west of La Cienega Blvd., West Hollywood.

NEED A BREAK?

For a truly rocking meal, stop by the laid-back, low-lit **Duke's** (⊠ 8909 W. Sunset Blvd., at N. San Vicente Blvd. ☎ 310/652–3100) coffee shop, where autographed rock posters and glossies cover the walls. The menu here suits tight budgets, and the packed table arrangements increase your odds of rubbing elbows with a celebrity or a hungover local musician indulging in the greasy-spoon comfort food. Just remember, it's not polite to ask for autographs while they're eating. Note that Duke's closes at 3:30 PM on weekends. News junkies should hit **the Newsroom** (⊠ 120 N. Robertson Blvd., at Beverly Blvd. ☎ 310/652–4444), which streams current event headlines nonstop on several TVs hung around the café. It's also got a magazine stand and Internet access to distract you while you wait for a table (which could take a while during peak hours). The menu's health focused, with smoothies and vegetarian choices.

★ ❸ **Sunset Strip.** For 60 years the Hollywood nighttime crowd has headed for the 1¾-mi stretch of Sunset Boulevard between Crescent Heights Boulevard on the east and Doheny Drive on the west, known as the Sunset Strip. In the 1930s and '40s, such stars as Tyrone Power, Errol Flynn, Norma Shearer, and Rita Hayworth came for wild evenings of dancing and drinking at nightclubs like Trocadero, Ciro's, and Mocambo. By the '60s and '70s, the Strip had become the center of rock and roll: Johnny Rivers, the Byrds, the Doors, Elton John, and Bruce Springsteen gave legendary performances on stages at clubs like the **Whisky A Go-Go** (⊠ 8901 Sunset Blvd., West Hollywood ☎ 310/652–4202 ⊕ www.whiskyagogo.com) and **Roxy** (⊠ 9009 Sunset Blvd., West Hollywood ☎ 310/276–2222 ⊕ www.theroxyonsunset.com). Nowadays it's the **Viper Room** (⊠ 8852 Sunset Blvd., West Hollywood ☎ 310/358–1880), the **House of Blues** (⊠ 8430 Sunset Blvd., West Hollywood ☎ 323/848–5100 ⊕ www.hob.com), and the **Key Club** (⊠ 9039 Sunset Blvd., West Hollywood ☎ 310/274–5800 ⊕ www.keyclub.com), where you'll find on-the-cusp actors, rock stars, club-hopping regulars, and out-of-towners all mingling over drinks and live music. Parking and traffic around the Strip can be tough on weekends, but the time and money may be worth it if you plan to make the rounds—most clubs are within walking distance of each other.

BEVERLY HILLS & CENTURY CITY

If you only have a day to see L.A., see Beverly Hills. Love it or hate it, it delivers on a dramatic, cinematic scale of wealth and excess. Beverly Hills is the town's biggest movie star, and she always lets those willing to part with a few bills into her year-round party. Just remember to bring your sunscreen, sunglasses . . . and money for parking.

Boutiques and restaurants line the palm tree–fringed sidewalks. People tend to stroll, not rush. Shopping ranges from the accessible and familiar (Pottery Barn) to the unique, expensive, and architecturally stunning (Prada on Rodeo Drive). It's hard not to imagine yourself in a film since this locale has basically become a backlot itself.

Just a few blocks west on Santa Monica Boulevard is Beverly Hills's buttoned-down brother, Century City. If Beverly Hills is about spending money, Century City is about making it. This collection of glass office towers and a favorite outdoor mall is home to entertainment companies, law firms, and investment corporations. It's a peculiarly precise place, with angular fountains, master-planned boulevards, and pedestrian bridges connecting lawyers to their turkey tahini wraps. With two of Hollywood's key talent agencies, CAA and ICM, moving to Century City by 2007, the area will surely continue to heat up.

What to See

② **Beverly Hills Hotel.** Built in 1912, the Pink Palace is steeped in Hollywood lore. Greta Garbo, Howard Hughes, and other movie-industry guests kept low profiles when staying at this pastel landmark, while other film luminaries, notably Cecil B. DeMille, cut very visible deals in the **Polo Lounge**, which still makes a fantastic reservations-are-a-must lunch destination. ✉ *9641 Sunset Blvd., 1 mi west of Doheny Dr.* ☎ *310/276– 2251* ⊕ *www.thebeverlyhillshotel.com.*

NEED A BREAK? A longtime refuge from California's leaner cuisine, **Nate 'n' Al's** (✉ 414 N. Beverly Dr., at Brighton Way, Beverly Hills ☎ 310/274-0101) serves up steaming pastrami, brisket, and Larry King wearing his trademark suspenders. Or stop at **The Farm** (✉ 439 N. Beverly Dr. ☎ 310/273-5578) and grab a seat at one of the sidewalk tables. The restaurant is known for dishes such as ahi tuna appetizer, a lobster club with applewood-smoked bacon, and a luscious brownie sundae. Reserve a table on the patio, sit back with an endless glass of iced tea with mint, and take in the view; you'll have a good chance of a celeb sighting here.

Century City. This 280-acre mixed-use development of office buildings, a shopping center, hotels, an entertainment complex, and housing was built in the 1960s on what used to be the back lot of Twentieth Century Fox. (The studio is not open to the public.) The focal point of this complex is the pair of silvery triangular towers known as **Century City Towers** (✉ Ave. of the Stars and Constellation Blvd.). The **Westfield Century City** (✉ 10250 Santa Monica Blvd. ☎ 310/277–3898 ⊕ www. westfield.com/centurycity) open-air shopping center was under renovation at this writing, but it does have the city's best mall food court.

① **Greystone Mansion.** Doheny Drive is named for oilman Edward Doheny, the original owner of this 1927 neo-Gothic mansion of 46,000-plus square feet. Now owned by the city of Beverly Hills, it sits on 18½ landscaped acres and has been used in such films as *The Witches of Eastwick* and *Indecent Proposal.* Though you can't actually enter the mansion itself, the gardens are open for self-guided tours, and you can get an idea of the exquisite interior by peeking through the windows. Picnics are permitted in specified areas during hours of operation, and, sporadically, concerts are held in the mansion's courtyard on summer afternoons. ✉ *905 Loma Vista Dr., Beverly Hills* ☎ *310/550–4796* ⊕ *www. beverlyhills.org* ✐ *Free* ☉ *Daily 10–5.*

A GOOD TOUR

Numbers in the text correspond to numbers in the margin and on the Beverly Hills & the Westside map.

Begin a tour of Beverly Hills with a drive into the hills above Sunset Boulevard for a look at **Greystone Mansion ❶**, on Loma Vista Drive. Less than a mile west on Sunset is the landmark **Beverly Hills Hotel ❷**, otherwise known as the Pink Palace. Snap your postcard picture here, then duck around behind the hotel to Elden Way, where you'll find the **Virginia Robinson Gardens ❸**, the oldest estate in Beverly Hills and now open to the public for walking tours.

Across the street from the Beverly Hills Hotel is the pretty little triangular park named for the cowboy-philosopher Will Rogers, who was once honorary mayor of Beverly Hills. Turn south here onto **Rodeo Drive ❹** (pronounced ro-*day*-o). You'll pass through a residential neighborhood before hitting the shopping stretch of Rodeo south of Santa Monica Boulevard. Find a parking space, slide on your sunglasses (the better to subtly people-watch, my dear), and flex your credit card. At Rodeo Drive and Dayton Way you'll see the

aluminum sculpture *Torso*, by Robert Graham; installed in summer 2003, it ushered in the Walk of Style, the fashionista equivalent of Hollywood's Walk of Fame. Across Wilshire, the **Regent Beverly Wilshire ❺** hotel serves as a temporary residence for the rich, famous, and cultured. The **Museum of Television & Radio ❻** stands a block east of Rodeo, on Beverly Drive. A few blocks west of Beverly Hills is the high-rise office-tower and shopping-center complex known as **Century City.**

🕑 **TIMING TIPS➔** After a drive along Sunset Boulevard and a foray or two up into the hills for a look at the opulent homes, plan to arrive in the Golden Triangle of Beverly Hills at midday. Most stores open by 10 or 11, with limited hours on Sunday. (Some close on Sunday or Monday.) Park your car in one of several municipal lots (the first one or two hours are free at most of them), and spend as long as you like strolling along Rodeo Drive. The major routes in and out of Beverly Hills—Wilshire and Santa Monica boulevards—get very congested during rush hours.

★ ❻ **Museum of Television & Radio.** Revisit great shows of the past at this sleek stone-and-glass building, a sister to the Museum of Television & Radio in New York, entirely duplicating its collection of 100,000 programs spanning eight decades. Search for your favorite commercials and television and radio shows on easy-to-use computers, and then watch or listen to them in an adjacent room. There are special exhibits of television- and radio-related art and costumes, as well as frequent seminars with television and radio cast members. ✉ *465 N. Beverly Dr., Beverly Hills* ☎ *310/786–1000* 🌐 *www.mtr.org* ✉ *$10 suggested donation* 🕑 *Wed.–Sun. noon–5.*

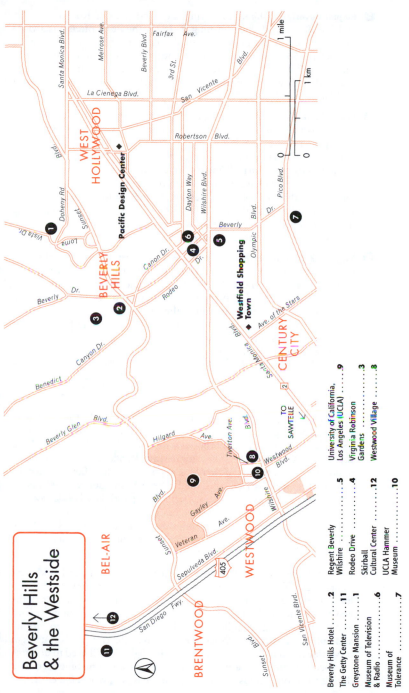

Beverly Hills & the Westside

BRENTWOOD

BEL-AIR

WEST HOLLYWOOD

BEVERLY HILLS

CENTURY CITY

WESTWOOD

Pacific Design Center

Westfield Shopping Town

TO SAWTELLE

1 mile

1 km

⑤ Regent Beverly Wilshire. Anchoring the south end of Rodeo Drive at Wilshire Boulevard since opening in 1928, the hotel often hosts visiting royalty and celebrities; it's where the millionaire businessman played by Richard Gere ensconced himself with the hooker (Julia Roberts) in the movie *Pretty Woman.* Step inside the Wilshire entrance to admire the opulent flower arrangement in this lovely, tranquil lobby. ✉ *9500 Wilshire Blvd., Beverly Hills* ☎ *310/275–5200.*

④ Rodeo Drive. The ultimate shopping street, Rodeo Drive is one of southern California's bona fide tourist attractions; here you can shop for five-digit jewelry or a $35 handbag. The arts of window-shopping and window displays play out among the retail elite: Tiffany & Co., Gucci, Armani, Hermès, Harry Winston, Prada, you get the picture. Several nearby restaurants have patios where you can sip a drink while watching fashionable shoppers saunter by. At the southern end of Rodeo Drive (at Wilshire Boulevard) is **Via Rodeo,** a curvy cobblestone street designed to resemble a European shopping area or a Universal Studio backlot—take your pick. ✉ *Beverly Hills.*

FodorsChoice ★

③ Virginia Robinson Gardens. The estate, the oldest in Beverly Hills, was owned by department store heir Harry Robinson and his wife, Virginia, who bequeathed it to Los Angeles County. The classic Mediterranean-style villa is surrounded by nearly six sloping acres of lush planted grounds. The collection of King palms is reported to be the largest grove outside the tree's native Australia. Fountains and falls flow through a grove of citrus and camellias. Call in advance to schedule a tour. ✉ *Address available when advance reservations are made, Beverly Hills* ☎ *310/276–5367* ✉ *Tours: $10.*

THE WESTSIDE

For some privileged Los Angelenos, the city begins west of La Cienega Boulevard, where keeping up with the Joneses takes on a meaning on an epic scale. Chic, attractive neighborhoods with coveted postal codes—Bel Air, Brentwood, Westwood, West Los Angeles, and Pacific Palisades—are home to power couples pushing power kids in power strollers. But conspicuous consumption has changed since the flashy '80s and dot-com '90s. Now the status game involves prestigious schools, yoga studios, holiday locales, and airspace rights to coastal views. But the Westside is also rich in culture—and not just entertainment-industry culture. It's home to UCLA, the monumental Getty Center, and the engrossing Museum of Tolerance.

What to See

⑪ The Getty Center. With its curving walls and isolated hilltop perch, the Getty Center resembles a pristine fortified city of its own. You may have been lured up by the beautiful views of L.A. (on a clear day stretching all the way to the Pacific Ocean), but the architecture, the uncommon gardens, and the fascinating art collections will be more than enough to capture and hold your attention. When the sun is out, the complex's rough-cut travertine marble skin seems to soak up the light. You'll need to do some advance planning, since parking reservations are sometimes required during vacation periods, but the experience is well worth the effort.

FodorsChoice ★

A GOOD TOUR

Numbers in the text correspond to numbers in the margin and on the Beverly Hills & the Westside map.

The major sights on the Westside are spread out, so choosing a starting point is arbitrary; the best strategy is to select one of the major attractions as a destination and plan your visit accordingly. A visit to the **Museum of Tolerance** 7 in the morning, for example, can be easily followed with lunch and shopping in Beverly Hills or Century City. Afterward you might drive through **Westwood Village** 8, home of the **University of California, Los Angeles** 9 campus and the Fowler Museum of Cultural History, stopping at the **UCLA Hammer Museum** 10. The Hammer has gotten quite zippy lately, so it's definitely worth a peek to see if the exhibits interest you. The vast **Getty Center** 11 offers the trifecta of art, architecture, and sweeping views at its hilltop perch in Brentwood. A visit here could easily eat up a few hours, as you wander around the grounds, have a bite at the cafe (the food's a cut above the average museum fare), and explore the galleries. About 2 mi north on Sepulveda Boulevard is the **Skirball Cultural Center** 12, which has a gallery exhibition on Jewish life.

For a less destination-oriented tour of the posh Westside, simply follow Wilshire Boulevard west out of low-rise Beverly Hills as it turns into a canyon of million-dollar condos.

Once past the San Diego Freeway (I–405), detour to the right onto San Vicente Boulevard and the upscale urban-village center of Brentwood. At the Santa Monica city line, turn right on 26th Street and follow it as it turns into Allenford Avenue. The route will loop you around to Sunset Boulevard. A left turn here will take you to Pacific Palisades and the ocean. A right leads back toward Beverly Hills and West Hollywood, past the Getty Center and Bel-Air mansions, all but invisible behind high walls and lush landscaping.

⏱ TIMING TIPS→ **Advance reservations are not essential but are well advised, for visits to the Museum of Tolerance, closed Saturday, and the Getty Center, closed Monday—so plan accordingly. Each museum merits at least a half day. If the Getty Center's on your list, try to get there relatively early, so that you can park close to the main complex. (Using the satellite parking lots means you'll have to take an extra tram ride.) In the evening and on weekends, the restaurants, cafés, and streets of Westwood Village and Brentwood's commercial district on San Vicente Boulevard come alive. The afternoon rush hour is predictably congested along Wilshire and Sunset boulevards.**

J. Paul Getty, the billionaire oil magnate and art collector, began collecting Greek and Roman antiquities and French decorative arts in the 1930s. He opened the J. Paul Getty Museum at his Malibu estate in 1954, and in the 1970s, he built a re-creation of an ancient Roman village to house his initial collection. When Getty died in 1976, the museum received an endowment of $700 million that grew to a reported $4.2 billion. The Malibu villa, reopened in 2006, is devoted to the antiquities. The Getty Center, designed by Richard Meier, opened in 1998. It pulls together the rest of the collections and museum's affiliated research, conservation, and philanthropic institutes.

Getting to the center involves a bit of anticipatory lead-up. At the base of the hill, a pavilion disguises the underground parking structure. From there you either walk or take a smooth, computer-driven tram up the steep slope, checking out the Bel Air estates across the humming stream of the 405 freeway. The five pavilions that house the museum surround a central courtyard and are bridged by walkways. From the courtyard, plazas, and walkways, you can survey the city from the San Gabriel Mountains to the ocean.

In a ravine separating the museum and the Getty Research Institute, conceptual artist Robert Irwin created the playful **Central Garden** in stark contrast to Meier's mathematical architectural geometry. The garden's design is what Hollywood feuds are made of; with Meier losing control of the garden, the two men sniped at each other during construction, with Irwin stirring the pot with every wild plant he chose and every loose twist his garden path took. The result is a refreshing garden walk whose focal point is an azalea maze (some insist the Mickey Mouse shape is on purpose) in a reflecting pool.

Inside the pavilions are the galleries for the permanent collections of European paintings, drawings, sculpture, illuminated manuscripts, and decorative arts, as well as American and European photographs. The Getty's collection of French furniture and decorative arts, especially from the early years of Louis IV (1643–1715) to the end of the reign of Louis XVI (1774–92), is renowned for its quality and condition; you can see a pair of completely reconstructed salons. In the paintings galleries, a computerized system of louvered skylights allows natural light to filter in, creating a closer approximation of the conditions in which the artists painted. Notable among the paintings are Rembrandt's *The Abduction of Europa,* van Gogh's *Irises,* Monet's *Wheatstack, Snow Effects, Morning,* and James Ensor's *Christ's Entry into Brussels.*

If you want to start with a quick overview, pick up the brochure in the entrance hall that guides you to 15 highlights of the collection. There's also an instructive audio tour ($3) with commentaries by art historians. Art information rooms with multimedia computer stations contain more details about the collections. The Getty also presents lectures, films, concerts, and special programs for kids and families. The complex includes a restaurant (reservations required), two cafeterias, and two outdoor coffee bars. ■ TIP→ **On-site parking is subject to availability and usually fills up by late afternoon on holidays and summer weekends, so try to come early in the day.** You may also take public transportation (MTA Bus 561 or Santa Monica Big Blue Bus 14). ✉ *1200 Getty Center Dr., Brent-*

wood ☎ 310/440–7300 ⊕ www.getty.edu ✉ Free, parking $7 ⊙ Tues.–Thurs. and Sun. 10–6, Fri. and Sat. 10–9.

★ ⑦ **Museum of Tolerance.** Using interactive technology, this important museum (part of the Simon Weisenthal Center) challenges visitors to confront bigotry and racism. One of the most affecting sections covers the Holocaust, with film footage of deportation scenes and simulated sets of concentration camps. Each visitor is issued a "passport" bearing the name of a child whose life was dramatically changed by the German Nazi rule and by World War II; as you go through the exhibit, you learn the fate of that child. Anne Frank artifacts are part of the museum's permanent collection. Interactive exhibits include the "Millennium Machine," which engages visitors in finding solutions to human rights abuses around the world, and the "Point of View Diner," a re-creation of a 1950s diner, red booths and all, that "serves" a menu of controversial topics on video jukeboxes. To ensure a visit to this popular museum, make reservations in advance (especially for Friday, Sunday, and holidays) and plan to spend at least three hours there. Testimony from Holocaust survivors is offered at specified times. Museum entry stops at least two hours before the actual closing time. A photo ID is required for admission. ✉ *9786 W. Pico Blvd., just south of Beverly Hills ☎ 310/553–8403 ⊕ www.museumoftolerance. com ✉ $10 ⊙ Nov.–Mar., Sun. 11–5, Mon.–Thurs. 11:30–4, Fri. 11:30–3; Apr.–Oct., Sun. 11–5, Mon.–Thurs. 11:30–4, Fri. 11:30–5.*

⑫ **Skirball Cultural Center.** This imposing concrete-and-steel complex, designed by Moshe Safdie, rises out of the Santa Monica Mountains above the San Diego Freeway (I–405). It contains conference and educational centers, but the big draw is the museum, where the core exhibition is "Visions and Values: Jewish Life from Antiquity to America." Twelve galleries use artifacts, building reconstructions, and multimedia installations to tell the story of the Jewish immigration experience. Highlights include a large collection of Judaica and a two-thirds-size replica of the torch of the Statue of Liberty. Children can participate in a simulated archaeological dig at the Discovery Center. ✉ *2701 N. Sepulveda Blvd., north of Brentwood ☎ 310/440–4500 ⊕ www.skirball.org ✉ $8 ⊙ Tues.–Sat. noon–5, Sun. 11–5.*

⑩ **UCLA Hammer Museum.** In the heart of Westwood, the Hammer emphasizes the here and now, luring in new museumgoers with splashy, eye-catching displays in the museum's glass entryway. (These bold murals and installations have been known to slow traffic on busy Wilshire Boulevard.) Focused on art and artists of our time, the museum bridges artistic expression with the city and the forward educational spirit of adjacent UCLA. The museum also incorporates selections from Armand Hammer's permanent collection with works by Claude Monet and Vincent van Gogh. Included in the collection is a powerful portrait by John Singer Sargent of Dr. Pozzi, a gynecologist of notable esteem and skill. ✉ *10899 Wilshire Blvd., Westwood ☎ 310/443–7000 ⊕ www.hammer.ucla.edu ✉ $5, free Thurs.; 3-hr parking $2.75 with validation ⊙ Tues., Wed., Fri. and Sat. 11–7, Thurs. 11–9, Sun. 11–5.*

⑨ **University of California, Los Angeles (UCLA).** With spectacular buildings such as a Romanesque library, the parklike UCLA campus makes for a fine stroll through one of California's most prestigious universities. In the heart of the north campus, the **Franklin Murphy Sculpture Garden** contains more than 70 works of artists such as Henry Moore and Gaston Lachaise. The **Mildred Mathias Botanic Garden,** which contains some 5,000 species of plants from all over the world in a 7-acre outdoor garden, is in the southeast section of the campus and is accessible from Tiverton Avenue. West of the main-campus bookstore, the **Morgan Center Hall of Fame** displays the sports memorabilia and trophies of the university's athletic departments. Many visitors head straight to the **UCLA Fowler Museum of Cultural History** (☎ 310/825–4361 ⊕ www.fmch. ucla.edu), which presents exhibits on the world's diverse cultures and visual arts, especially those of Africa, Asia, Oceania, and Native and Latin America. Museum admission is free; use parking lot 4 off Sunset Boulevard ($8). It's open Wednesday–Sunday noon–5.

Campus maps and information are available at drive-by kiosks at major entrances daily, and free 90-minute walking tours of the campus are given on weekdays at 10:15 and 2:15 and Saturday at 10:15. Call 310/825–8764 for reservations, which are required several days to two weeks in advance. The campus has cafés, plus bookstores selling UCLA Bruins paraphernalia. The main-entrance gate is on Westwood Boulevard. Campus parking costs $8. ⊠ *Bordered by Le Conte, Hilgard, and Gayley Aves. and Sunset Blvd., Westwood* ⊕ *www.ucla.edu.*

❽ **Westwood Village.** Laid out in the 1930s as a master-planned shopping district next to the UCLA campus, Westwood Village has lost some of its luster as locals opt for one-stop shopping centers and multiplexes. But the Village offers some terrific movie theaters, like the Mann Village, and casual eateries; on weekends, it still teems with students. ■ **TIP→ Look for the long line of students outside Diddy Riese Cookies at 926 Broxton Avenue, which bakes up L.A.'s best (and cheap) cookies late into the night.** Westwood is also the site of a cemetery with one of the world's most famous graves. Tucked behind one of the behemoth office buildings on Wilshire Boulevard is **Westwood Village Memorial Park** (⊠ 1218 Glendon Ave.). Marilyn Monroe is buried in a simply marked crypt on the north wall. For 25 years after her death, her former husband Joe DiMaggio had six red roses placed on her crypt three times a week. Also buried here are Truman Capote and Natalie Wood; Jack Lemmon and Billy Wilder are posthumous neighbors

SANTA MONICA, VENICE & MALIBU

The desirable, varied communities of Santa Monica, Venice, and Malibu curve along L.A.'s coastline. These high-rent areas hug Santa Monica Bay in an arc, from the ultracasual, ultrarich Malibu to the bohemian-seedy mix of Venice. What they have in common, however, is cleaner air, mild temperatures, often horrific traffic, and an emphasis on the beach-focused lifestyle that many people consider the hallmark of southern California.

Santa Monica—which, because of its liberal populace, has been dubbed the People's Republic of Santa Monica—is a pedestrian-friendly little city, about 8⅓ square mi, with a dynamic population of artists and writ-

CLOSE UP

Sawtelle Boulevard

THE FOUR BLOCKS on Sawtelle Boulevard between Olympic Boulevard and Missouri Avenue is filled with predominantly Japanese specialty stores, restaurants, and plant nurseries. A trip here makes for an interesting, out-of-the-ordinary trip from either Westwood or Santa Monica. In the 1920s, after a wave of Japanese immigrants arrived in L.A., Sawtelle began to resemble an authentic Japanese main street, rather than a touristy Little Tokyo. Although most establishments remain Japanese, the area also encompasses Chinese, Taiwanese, and Malaysian businesses. To reach Sawtelle from Westwood, head south on Westwood Boulevard, turn right on Santa Monica Boulevard, and take a left on Sawtelle. There's plenty of metered street parking, plus minimall lots near Olympic Boulevard. There are some great places for lunch, including **Mizu 212 Degrees** (✉ 2000 Sawtelle Blvd. ☎ 310/478–8979), a streamlined diner that serves shabu-

shabu (meat and vegetables you cook at your table in a boiling broth). If you're in the mood for a steaming bowl of Japanese noodles, head across the street to **Asahi Ramen** (✉ 2027 Sawtelle Blvd. ☎ 310/479–2231), a cash-only, casual spot. Pop into **Giant Robot** (✉ 2015 Sawtelle Blvd. ☎ 310/478–1819) to check out the house-produced 'zine and a sampling of T-shirts, books, and accessories seemingly plucked from the coolest areas of Tokyo. Just north, **Lollicup** (✉ 2012 Sawtelle Blvd ☎ 310/231–3522) serves up sweet Taiwanese beverages like milk tea with tapioca pearls (aka *boba*, or bubble tea). Save some time to explore the collection of bonsai at **Yamaguchi Bonsai Nursery** (✉ 1949 Sawtelle Blvd. ☎ 310/473–5444), next to the Chinese Baptist Church. This family business has been going strong since the 1950s; you can find bougainvillea bonsai germinated from a flowering plant on the property.

---

ers, entertainment folk, educators, and retired people, all attracted by the cooler, sometimes-foggy climate. Mature trees, Mediterranean-style architecture, and strict zoning have helped create a sense of place often missing from L.A.'s residential neighborhoods. This character comes with a price; real estate costs are astronomical.

Venice was a turn-of-the-20th-century fantasy that never quite came true. Abbot Kinney, a wealthy Los Angeles businessman, envisioned this little piece of real estate, which then seemed so far from downtown, as a romantic replica of Venice, Italy. He developed an incredible 16 mi of canals, floated gondolas on them, and built scaled-down versions of the Doge's Palace and other Venetian landmarks. Some canals were rebuilt in 1996, but they don't reflect the Old World connection quite as well as they could. Figures. Ever since Kinney first planned his project, it was plagued by ongoing engineering problems and disasters and drifted into disrepair. Three small canals and bridges do remain and can be viewed from the southeast corner of Pacific Avenue and Venice Boulevard. Another great glimpse of the canals can be caught when walking along Dell Avenue from Washington Street north to Venice.

Stargazing 101

GO AHEAD—GAWK! Lucy did it at the Brown Derby over William Holden, and now it's your turn. You're in Du-Par's coffee shop in Studio City and George Clooney is in the next booth, downing a short stack. This may not be the best time to run up and ask for an autograph—he's got syrup on his chin. But when is a good moment? And when will you have another opportunity to see the stars in their natural habitat? And . . . wait! George is about to split.

You decide to jump at the chance. Remain calm. Be polite, brief, and have the pen and paper ready if an autograph is part of your mission. When introducing yourself, mention that you're "visiting from . . ." It will buy you a lot of leeway. Don't blurt out anything about a celebrity's appearance; keep all comments about looks, height, and, heaven forbid, weight strictly to yourself.

If you're determined to see some celebs, skip the star maps and draw on the following tips:

1. Beverly Hills delivers. Plenty of stars go about their daily routines in the Technicolor back lot of 90210, so keep your eyes peeled. The Farm of Beverly Hills, on Beverly Boulevard, is a favorite lunch haunt, as is The Ivy, on Robertson Boulevard. The Grill on the Alley gets busy around Oscar time, but think twice before depriving an agent of his or her table.

2. Head for the hills. Stars spend the first half of the day doing lunch and the second part of the day working it off. Gyms are out and hiking is in, so put on your sneakers and hit the trails. Remember, avoid hiking alone or after sunset.

3. Charge! Stylists may get a lot of credit (or blame) these days, but stars will always shop. Hot spots include Montana Avenue in Santa Monica, Kitson on Robertston Boulevard, Fred Segal on Melrose Avenue, and The Grove at the Farmers Market shopping center.

4. When all else fails, head for the one place where stars must make an appearance: work. Book well in advance to attend a TV-show taping. Hide a snack in your pockets and make sure to bring a government-issued photo ID for admittance. **Audiences Unlimited** (☎ 818/753-3483 ⊕ www.tvtickets.com) is the best source for tickets to many television shows. For tickets and information about *The Tonight Show with Jay Leno*, contact **NBC** (☎ 818/840-3537). For *Jeopardy* and *Wheel of Fortune* tickets, get in touch with **Sony Studios** (☎ 800/482-9840). To get tickets to *The Price Is Right* and *The Late Late Show*, contact **CBS** (☎ 323/575-2458).

What about that famous L.A. nightlife? You've heard so much about the Sunset Strip, Bar Marmont, the clubs with the bouncers waiting to step in as the next Vin Diesel. Trying to predict the latest hot spot, though, is like trying to predict the next earthquake—nearly impossible. Even if you do hit the right place, your chances of brushing elbows with a celeb are slim; many places have private VIP rooms for the inner circle. You'll have better luck with daytime locales. Good luck, and remember to smile and say thank you.

—Matthew Flynn

By the late 1960s, however, anyone who wanted to live near the beach but couldn't afford to was attracted by the low rents in Venice, and the place quickly became SoHo-by-the-Sea. The trade-off was that the area was pretty run-down, and the remaining canals were stagnant and fairly smelly, but as the area's appeal grew and a more upscale crowd started moving in, these drawbacks were rectified. The Venice of today is a grudgingly thrown-together mix of old hippies, artists, architects, yuppies able to swallow inflated rents, and senior citizens who have lived here for decades. ■ **TIP**➡ **Abbot Kinney's namesake boulevard is now an especially cool place to hang out, where you can browse notable boutiques now roosting in the old bungalows, nibble on an exquisite pastry, or linger with laid-back locals over a beer.** Both Venice and Santa Monica have substantial numbers of homeless people, who live off foot traffic and community support.

North of Santa Monica, up the Pacific Coast Highway, past rock slides, rollerbladers, and cliffside estates, is Malibu. Home to blockbuster names like Spielberg, Hanks, and Streisand, this ecologically fragile 23-mi stretch of coastline can feel like a world of its own, with its slopes slipping dramatically into the ocean. In the public imagination Malibu is synonymous with beaches and wealth—but in the past couple of years there's been some friction between these two signature elements. Some property owners, such as billionaire music producer David Geffen, have come under attack for blocking public access to the beaches in front of their homes. ■ **TIP**➡ **All beaches are technically public, though; if you stay below the mean high-tide mark you're in the clear.** And everyone is welcome (with reservations) to the reimagined yet still intimate seaside Getty Villa and its collection of Greek, Etruscan, and Roman art and artifacts.

What to See

⑩ Adamson House and Malibu Lagoon Museum. The Rindge family, which owned much of the Malibu area in the early part of the 20th century, also originally owned this home. Malibu was quite isolated then, with all visitors and supplies arriving by boat at the nearby Malibu Pier (and it can still be isolated these days when rock slides close the highway). The Moorish Spanish–style structure was built in 1929. The Rindges had an enviable Malibu lifestyle, decades before the area was trendy. The house, covered with magnificent tile work in rich blues, greens, yellows, and oranges from the now-defunct Malibu Potteries, is right on the beach—high chain-link fences keep out curious beachgoers. Even an outside dog shower, near the servants' door, is a tiled delight. Docent-led tours provide insights on family life here as well as the history of Malibu and its real estate (you can't have one without the other). Signs posted around the grounds outside direct you on a self-guided tour, as well. There's pay parking in the adjacent county lot or in the lot at PCH and Cross Creek Road. ✉ *23200 Pacific Coast Hwy., Malibu* ☎ *310/456–8432* ⊕ *www. adamsonhouse.org* ✍ *$5* ☉ *Wed.–Sat. 11–3; last tour departs at 2.*

Bergamot Station. Named after a stop on the Red Trolley line that once shuttled between downtown and the Santa Monica Pier, Bergamot Station is now a depot for intriguing art. Industrial facades house more than a dozen art galleries, shops, a café, and a museum. The galleries cover many kinds of media: photography, jewelry, and paintings from somber

A GOOD DRIVE

Numbers in the text correspond to numbers in the margin and on the Santa Monica, Venice & Malibu map.

Look for the arched neon sign at the foot of Colorado Avenue marking the entrance to the **Santa Monica Pier** ❶, the city's number one landmark, built in 1906. Park on the pier and take a turn through **Pacific Park** ❷, an amusement park. The wide swath of sand on the north side of the pier is Santa Monica Beach, on hot summer weekends one of the most crowded beaches in southern California. From the pier, walk to Ocean Avenue, where **Palisades Park** ❸ provides panoramic ocean views. Three blocks inland is the **Third Street Promenade** ❹, a popular outdoor mall. If this whets your shopping appetite, head up a few blocks to Montana Avenue, another street thick with boutiques, particularly past 9th Street.

Retrieve your car and drive two blocks inland on Colorado to Main Street. Turn right and continue to Ocean Park Boulevard. There you'll find the **California Heritage Museum** ❺. The next several blocks south along Main Street are great for browsing.

Next stop: **Venice Boardwalk** ❻. Walk up Main Street through the trendy shopping district until you hit Rose Avenue. Ahead on the left you'll spot an enormous pair of binoculars, the front of the Frank Gehry–designed Chiat-Day Mojo Building. Turn right toward the sea. The main attraction of this dead end is the classic–odd boardwalk.

For the drive to Malibu, retrace your route along Main Street. At Pico Boulevard, turn west, toward the ocean, and then right on Ocean Avenue. When you pass the pier, prepare to turn left down the California Incline (the incline is at the end of Palisades Park at Wilshire Boulevard) to Pacific Coast Highway (Highway 1), also known as PCH. About 5 mi north is the recently reopened, spectacular **Getty Villa Malibu** ❼. Another 6 mi or so will bring you into Malibu proper. Park in the lot adjacent to the **Malibu Pier** ❽ and take a stroll out to the end for a view of the coast. Back on land, take a walk on **Malibu Lagoon State Beach** ❾, also known as Surfrider Beach. On the highway side of the beach is the Moorish **Adamson House and Malibu Lagoon Museum** ❿, a tiled beauty with a great Pacific view.

🕑 **TIMING TIPS→** If you've got the time, break your coastal visit into two excursions: Santa Monica and Venice on one excursion, and Malibu on the other. The best way to "do" L.A.'s coastal communities is to park your car and walk, cycle, or skate along the 3-mi beachside bike path. For this, of course, a sunny day is best; on all but the hottest days, when literally millions of Angelenos flock to the beaches, try to get started in the late morning. Places like Santa Monica Pier, Main Street, and the Venice Boardwalk are more interesting to observe as the day progresses. Try to avoid the boardwalk, beach, and back streets of Santa Monica and Venice at night, when the crowds dissipate. Avoid driving to Malibu during rush hour, when traffic along the PCH moves at a snail's pace.

to lurid. Inside a cavernous, steel-beamed warehouse, the **Santa Monica Museum of Art** (☎ 310/586–6488 ⊕ www.smmoa.org) showcases exhibits of emerging artists. It's open Tuesday–Saturday 11–6, with a $3 suggested donation. The museum also presents evening salons with artists, performers, and speakers. ⊠ *2525 Michigan Ave., Santa Monica* ☎ *310/829–5854* ⊙ *Galleries generally Tues.–Fri. 10–5, Sat. 11–5.*

⑤ California Heritage Museum. The real star of this small collection of decorative and fine arts is the 1894 Victorian house the museum occupies. The interior has been beautifully restored to represent four decades of design. Exhibits are informal and loose. ⊠ *2612 Main St., Santa Monica* ☎ *310/392–8537* ⊕ *www.californiaheritagemuseum.org* ☚ *$5* ⊙ *Wed.–Sun. 11–4.*

⑦ Getty Villa Malibu. Feeding on the cultures of ancient Rome, Greece, and Etruria, the remodeled Getty Villa opened in 2006 with much fanfare—and some controversy concerning the acquisition and rightful ownership of some of the Italian artifacts on display. The antiquities are astounding, but on a first visit even they take a backseat to where they're exhibited. This megamansion sits on some of the most valuable coastal property in the world. Modeled after an Italian country home, the Villa dei Papiri in Herculaneum, the Getty Villa includes beautifully manicured gardens, reflecting pools, and statuary. The largest and most lovely garden, the Outer Peristyle, gives you glorious views over a rectangular reflecting pool and geometric hedges to the Pacific. The new structures blend thoughtfully into the rolling terrain and significantly improve the public spaces, such as the new outdoor amphitheater, gift store, café, and entry arcade. Talks and educational programs are offered at an indoor theater. ■ **TIP**➡ Make reservations well in advance since this is one L.A. hot spot with long-term popularity, and talking your way in is out of the question. ⊠ *17985 Pacific Coast Hwy., Pacific Palisades* ☎ *310/440–7300* ⊕ *www.getty.edu* ☚ *Free, reservations required. Parking $7, cash only* ⊙ *Wed.–Sun. 11–4.*

Fodor'sChoice
★

⑨ Malibu Lagoon State Beach. Bird-watchers, take note: in this 5-acre marshy area you could spot egrets, blue herons, avocets, and gulls. (You'll need to stay on the boardwalks so as not to disturb the birds.) The signs listing opening and closing hours refer only to the parking lot; the lagoon itself is open 24 hours and is particularly enjoyable in the early morning and at sunset. Streetside parking is available at those times, but not at midday. ⊠ *23200 Pacific Coast Hwy., Malibu.*

NEED A BREAK?

The Sunset Restaurant and Bar (⊠ Off Pacific Coast Hwy., just north of Zuma Beach, 6800 Westward Beach Rd., Malibu ☎ 310/589–1007) is as close to the sand as you can get without being on the beach. This local secret serves up breathtaking views of the surf, dolphins, surfers, and celebrity locals taking a break on the protected patio—oh, and delicious chicken tempura sticks.

⑧ Malibu Pier. This 780-foot fishing dock is a great place to take in the sunset or to watch local fishermen reel up a catch. A pier has jutted out here since the early 1900s; storms destroyed the last one in 1995, and it was rebuilt in 2001. In 2004 private developers worked with the state and re-

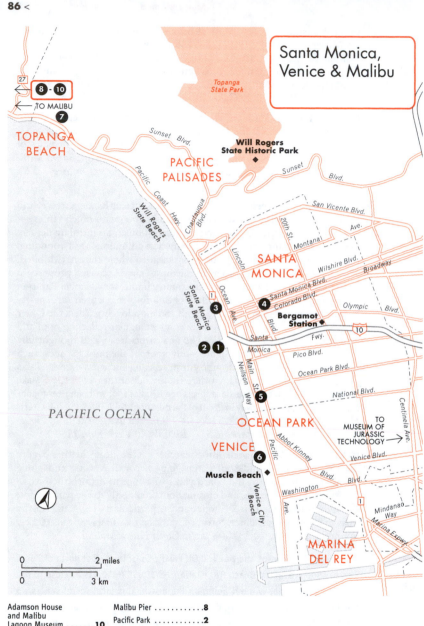

Santa Monica,
Venice & Malibu

Topanga
State Park

27

8 - **10**

TO MALIBU

7

TOPANGA
BEACH

Sunset   Blvd.

Will Rogers
State Historic Park

PACIFIC
PALISADES

Sunset   Blvd.

San Vicente Blvd.

Pacific   Coast   Hwy.

Will Rogers
State Beach

Chautauqua   Blvd.

20th St.

Montana   Ave.

Lincoln

SANTA
MONICA

Wilshire Blvd.

Broadway

Santa Monica
State Beach

Ocean   Ave.

1

3

4

Santa Monica Blvd.

Colorado Blvd.

Olympic   Blvd.

Bergamot
Station

Santa

10

2 **1**

Monica   Fwy.

Pico Blvd.

Main   St.

Neilson   Way

Ocean Park Blvd.

PACIFIC OCEAN

5

National Blvd.

Centinela Ave.

OCEAN PARK

Pacific

TO
MUSEUM OF
JURASSIC
TECHNOLOGY

VENICE

6

Abbot Kinney

Venice Blvd.

Muscle Beach

Blvd.   Blvd.

Washington

Venice City
Beach

Ave.

1

Mindanao
Way

Marina Espwy.

MARINA
DEL REY

0   2 miles

0   3 km

furbished the pier, yielding a bait shop, water-sport rentals, and a surfing museum. ⊠ *Pacific Coast Hwy. at Cross Creek Rd.* ⊕ *www.parks.ca.gov.*

OFF THE BEATEN PATH

MARINA DEL REY – South of Venice is the world's largest man-made small-boat harbor. So? If you're a fan of small boats (and some tony yachts), that's a big deal. Otherwise, this condo-laden, chain restaurant–lined development is a good place to ride bikes along the waterfront. There are a few man-made beaches, but you're better off hitting the larger (and cleaner) beaches up the coast. Call **Hornblower Dining Yachts** (⊠ 13755 Fiji Way, Marina del Rey ☎ 888/467–6256 ⊕ www.hornblower.com) in Fisherman's Village, to arrange marina and dining cruises.

Muscle Beach. Bronzed young men bench-pressing five girls at once, weightlifters doing tricks on the sand—Muscle Beach fired up the country's imagination from the get-go. There are actually two spots known as Muscle Beach. The original Muscle Beach, just south of the Santa Monica Pier, is where bodybuilders Jack LaLanne and Vic and Armand Tanny used to work out in the 1950s. When it was closed in 1959, the bodybuilders moved south along the beach to Venice, to a city-run facility known as "the Pen," and the Venice Beach spot inherited the Muscle Beach moniker. Efforts are under way to restore the original Muscle Beach, and bodybuilders continue to work out at the Venice location.

OFF THE BEATEN PATH

MUSEUM OF JURASSIC TECHNOLOGY – Don't bring the kids here expecting to see dinosaur bones. This fascinating, strange place, in a realm somewhere between a museum and an art installation, has a permanent collection of natural (and partly fictional) wonders such as a human horn and the "piercing devil" (a tiny bat that uses radar to fly through solid objects). Exhibits cover a grab bag of topics: old wives' tales, miniaturism, the culture of the mobile home. Head up to the second floor to the small, samovar-equipped tearoom for a free cuppa. The directions can catch you off guard as well; head east on Venice Boulevard several miles, past the 405 freeway, turn left onto Culver Boulevard, and take another quick left onto Venice Boulevard. The museum will be on your right. ⊠ *9341 Venice Blvd., Culver City* ☎ *310/836–6131* ⊕ *www.mjt. org* ✉ *$5 suggested donation* ☉ *Thurs. 2–8, Fri.–Sun. noon–6.*

❷ **Pacific Park.** Built on Santa Monica Pier, extending over the bay, this small amusement area harks back to the days of the grand Pacific Ocean Park (1957–67). Its attractions include a tame coaster, a large Ferris wheel, and a handful of rides that wildly satisfy the under-six crowd. ■ **TIP→** **This isn't squeaky-clean Disneyland, so expect real-world litter and watch your personal belongings. Since the pier is riddled with nails and splinters, opt for sneakers over flip-flops.** ⊠ *380 Santa Monica Pier, Santa Monica* ☎ *310/260–8744* ⊕ *www.pacpark.com* ✉ *Rides $2–$6, all-day pass $20* ☉ *Entire park daily May–Sept.; Oct.–Apr., selected rides and games Mon.–Thurs., entire park Fri. evening–Sun. evening; call for hrs.*

❸ **Palisades Park.** The ribbon of green that runs along the top of the cliffs from Colorado Avenue to just north of San Vicente Boulevard has flat walkways peopled by casual strollers, joggers, and the homeless. The rose gardens and the spectacular views of the Pacific (especially at sunset) are hard to beat.

① Santa Monica Pier. Eateries, souvenir shops, a psychic adviser, arcades, and **Pacific Park** are all part of this truncated pier at the foot of Colorado Boulevard below Palisades Park. The pier's trademark 46-horse Looff Carousel, built in 1922, has appeared in many films, including *The Sting*. Free concerts are held on the pier in summer. ⌧ *Colorado Ave. and the ocean, Santa Monica* ☎ *310/458–8900* ⊕ *www.santamonicapier.org* ⌧ *Rides $1* ☉ *Carousel May–Sept., Tues.–Fri. 11–9, weekends 10–9; Oct.–Apr., Thurs.–Sun., hrs vary.*

> ## WORD OF MOUTH
>
> "The Museum of Jurassic Technology in Venice (near Santa Monica) is a must-visit if you're a museum hound. Funky and strange, you'll find yourself scratching your head a lot."   —tracys2cents

Santa Monica Pier Aquarium. This small, interactive aquarium is tucked under the eastern end of the Santa Monica Pier along Ocean Front Walk and has the look of a homemade aquarium in a garage—not a bad thing, but some visitors are surprised not to find something more elaborate. Run by the Heal the Bay organization, which is credited with cleaning up Santa Monica Bay and the surrounding beaches, the tide-pool exhibits focus on the area's ecology. ⌧ *1600 Ocean Front Walk, Santa Monica* ☎ *310/393–6149* ⊕ *www.healthebay.org/smpa* ⌧ *$5 suggested donation* ☉ *Tues.–Fri. 2–5, weekends 12:30–5.*

★ **④ Third Street Promenade.** Stretch your legs along this pedestrians-only three-block stretch of 3rd Street, just a whiff away from the Pacific, lined with jacaranda trees, ivy-topiary dinosaur fountains, strings of lights, and branches of nearly every major U.S. retail chain. Outdoor cafés, street vendors, movie theaters, and a rich nightlife make this a main gathering spot for locals, visitors, and the homeless. It's fun to watch the mix of people here, from elderly couples out for a bite to skateboarders and street musicians. There's plenty of parking in city structures on the streets flanking the promenade. ⌧ *3rd St. between Wilshire Blvd. and Broadway, Santa Monica* ⊕ *www.thirdstreetpromenade.com.*

NEED A BREAK? If you're of legal drinking age, head up to Montana Avenue and drop by **Father's Office** (⌧ 1018 Montana Ave., between 10th and 11th Sts., Santa Monica ☎ 310/393–2337). Their business: barkeeping and turning out fantastic burgers with gussied-up fries (think aioli, not ketchup).

⑥ Venice Boardwalk. "Boardwalk" may be something of a misnomer—it's

really a five-block section of paved walkway—but this L.A. mainstay delivers year-round action. Bicyclists zip along and bikini-clad rollerbladers attract crowds as they put on impromptu demonstrations, vying for attention with magicians, fortune-tellers, a chain-saw juggler, and sand mermaids. At the adjacent Muscle Beach, bulging bodybuilders with an exhibitionist streak pump iron at an outdoor gym. Pick up some cheap sunglasses, grab a hot dog, and enjoy the boardwalk's show. You can rent in-line skates, roller skates, and bicycles (some with baby seats) at the south end of the boardwalk (officially known as Ocean Front Walk), along Washington Street near the Venice Pier.

1

OFF THE BEATEN PATH

WILL ROGERS STATE HISTORIC PARK – The humorist Will Rogers lived on this site in the 1920s and 1930s. His 187-acre estate is a folksy blend of Navajo rugs and Mission-style furniture. The ranch-house museum features Rogers memorabilia, and a short film presented in the visitor center highlights his roping technique and homey words of wisdom. Rogers was a polo enthusiast, and in the 1930s, his front-yard polo field attracted such friends as Douglas Fairbanks Sr. for weekend games. The tradition continues, with free weekend games scheduled April–October, weather permitting. The park's broad lawns are excellent for picnicking, and there's hiking on miles of eucalyptus-lined trails. From the Pacific Coast Highway, turn inland at Sunset Boulevard. Follow Sunset for about 5 mi to the park entrance. ⌧ *1501 Will Rogers State Park Rd., Pacific Palisades* ☎ *310/454–8212* ✉ *Free, parking $7* ☉ *Parking daily 8–sunset, house tours daily 10:30–3:30.*

THE SAN FERNANDO VALLEY

There are some Angelenos who swear, with a sneer, that they have never set foot in "the Valley." Some even claim they have no idea of its whereabouts. But without the dreaded Valley, the world would be without Disney, Warner Bros., Universal Studios, NBC, *Seinfeld, Desperate Housewives,* and a large chunk of pornography. In fact, nearly 70% of all entertainment productions in L.A. happen here. That means that some very rich entertainment executives regularly undergo sweltering summer temperatures, smog, and bumper-to-bumper traffic on their trek from their Westside and Malibu compounds to their less glamorous workplaces.

So what's in store for you? Well, besides the somewhat tired Universal Studios Hollywood, there's an archetypal urban sprawl. You might start wondering if there's a center to this maze of minimalls, gas stations, and midcentury tract homes. Nope. Instead, there are a dozen or so neighborhoods with names like Encino, Van Nuys, and Burbank; each has its own character if you look hard enough. One small jewel of the valley, Studio City, is rich with film history dating to 1920s silent movies. Its pedestrian-friendly strip along Ventura Boulevard has some of the tallest palms in L.A. and many interesting boutiques, antiques stores, and great nonchain outdoor cafés. But with so much to see on "the other side of the hill," your visit to the Valley is most likely best spent focusing on the entertainment industry aspect rather than searching for the diamond in the rough.

TIMING The Valley is surrounded by mountains, and the major routes to and from it go through mountain passes. During rush hour, traffic jams on the Hollywood Freeway (U.S. 101/Highway 170), San Diego Freeway (I–405), and Ventura Freeway (U.S. 101/Highway 134) can be brutal, so avoid trips to or from the Valley at those times. Expect to spend most of a day at Universal Studios Hollywood and CityWalk; studio tours at NBC and Warner Bros. last up to two hours.

What to See

 Disney Studios. Although tours of this film studio are not available, a peek from Riverside Drive shows you that Disney's innovations go beyond the big and small screens to fanciful touches of architecture (note

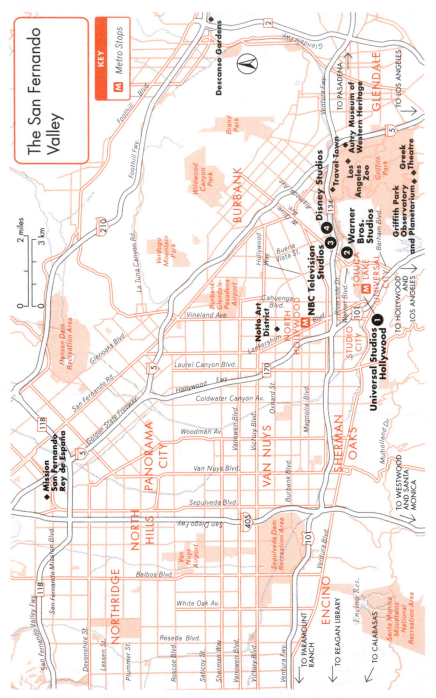

The San Fernando Valley

KEY

 Metro Stops

0 2 miles
0 3 km

the little Mickey Mouse heads mounted on the surrounding fence). On the Michael Eisner Building, designed by architect Michael Graves, giant figures of the Seven Dwarfs support the roof's gable. The Animation Building, meanwhile, has a cartoonish spin with an 85-foot-tall "Sorcerer's Apprentice" hat, red-and-white stripes, and the word ANIMATION in tall letters. You can see the colorful complex from the Ventura Freeway (Highway 134). ✉ *500 S. Buena Vista, Burbank.*

❸ NBC Television Studios. This major network's headquarters is in Burbank, as any regular viewer of *The Tonight Show* can't help knowing. An hour-long tour given on weekdays takes you onto the actual sets of shows like *Days of Our Lives* and *Access Hollywood.* If you'd like to be part of a live studio audience, free tickets are available for tapings of the various NBC shows. ✉ *3000 W. Alameda Ave., Burbank* ☎ *818/840–3537* 🖃 *Tours $7.50.*

NEED A BREAK?

Only in L.A. could a **Bob's Big Boy** (✉ 4211 W. Riverside Dr., at W. Alameda Ave., Burbank ☎ 818/843–9334) be classified a historical landmark. Built in 1949, this Big Boy stands as the best example of streamlined coffee-shop architecture in L.A. Its signature Big Boy Combo plate stacks a double-decker burger with fries and a salad, preferably with the rich blue cheese dressing. The best time to come is on Friday night in summer, when local car clubs flood the diner's parking lot to show off their restored hot rods. Weekends from 5 PM to 10 PM are car-hop nights, when waitresses will serve your burger and malt on 1950s-style window trays.

NoHo Arts District. Don't let the name fool you—this West Coast enclave bears little resemblance to its New York namesake. In fact, the name *NoHo* was spawned when the city, desperate to reinvent this depressed area, abbreviated the region's North Hollywood name. A square mile at the intersection of Lankershim and Magnolia in North Hollywood, the NoHo Arts District has slowly tried to transform itself into a cultural hot spot that includes several theaters showcasing aspiring young actors, dance schools, a comedy club, art galleries, boutiques, and restaurants. The results are mixed at best. The month of May brings the annual Theater and Arts Festival: free live theater performances, arts exhibits from an eclectic range of southern California's visual artists, music, an arts and crafts marketplace, dance showcases, and a children's area are all part of the fun. ✉ *Intersection of Lankershim Blvd. and Magnolia Blvd., North Hollywood* ⊕ *www.nohoartsdistrict.com.*

OFF THE BEATEN PATH

★

THE RONALD REAGAN PRESIDENTIAL LIBRARY AND MUSEUM – On 100 acres high up in the hills of Simi Valley is the final resting place of President Ronald Reagan along with an extensive museum that chronicles his early days as a Hollywood movie star, the two terms he served as governor of California, and his journey to the presidency. A massive new pavilion shelters the Air Force One plane that flew Reagan and six other presidents from 1973–2001, plus memorabilia from the flying White House and a new café. Give yourself a good three hours to get through it all; a guided tour is your best bet. Don't forget to step outside to take time to enjoy the spectacular views. The library holds more than 50 million pages of presidential papers, photographs, film, video, audio, and books. It takes at least half an

Laurel Canyon & Mulholland Drive

THE HILLS THAT SEPARATE HOLLYWOOD from the Valley are more than a symbolic dividing line between the city slickers and the suburbanites; the hills have a community in their own right and a reputation as a bohemian artists' hideaway for those who have been fortunate enough to make a living at their creative pursuits. The 2002 movie *Laurel Canyon* provided one view of the lifestyle of one kind of Canyon dweller—freethinking entertainment-industry movers and shakers who seek a peaceful refuge in their tree-shaded homes. By day they're churning out business deals and working on projects; by night they're living it up with private parties high above the bustle of the city streets.

Though you may not get to see all the goings-on inside these homes, you can use your imagination as you take a drive through Laurel Canyon and pass estates and party pads dating back to the silent film era, such as that of Clara

Bow, on to music icons of the '60s and '70s (including Brian Wilson and Frank Zappa). At the Canyon's halfway point is the **Canyon Country Store** (✉ 2108 Laurel Canyon Blvd. ☎ 323/654–8091), an institution of hippie-esque good vibes filled with household essentials and specialty foods that include vegetarian items and British imports. If you stop for dinner at **Pace** (✉ 2100 Laurel Canyon Blvd. ☎ 323/654–8583), below the store, there's a good chance of spotting a movie star on a low-key date. Because the restaurant is popular with the locals, make weekend reservations two weeks in advance.

A few steps away from Pace is the house once occupied by Jim Morrison. Take a drive up Lookout Mountain and you'll find yourself on the grounds that inspired resident Joni Mitchell to pen "Ladies of the Canyon." If you have time to cruise Mulholland Drive, you'll get breathtaking views that can help take you away from the city's relentless pulse.

---

hour to drive here from downtown L.A. ✉ *40 Presidential Dr., Simi Valley* ☎ *800/410–8354* ⊕ *www.reaganfoundation.org* ✉ *$12* ⊘ *Daily 10–5.*

Santa Monica Mountains National Recreation Area. The line that forms the boundary of the San Fernando Valley is one of the most famous thoroughfares in this vast metropolis. **Mulholland Drive** cuts through the Santa Monica Mountains National Recreation Area, a vast parkland that stretches along the top and west slopes of the Santa Monica Mountains from Hollywood to the Ventura County line. Driving the length of the hilltop road is slow and can be treacherous, but the rewards are sensational views of valley and city on each side and expensive homes along the way. The park incorporates several local and state parks, including Will Rogers and Malibu Lagoon. Large scenic portions of these oak-studded hills were owned at one time by such Hollywood stars as Ronald Reagan and Bob Hope. They provided location sites for many movies; the grassy rolling hillside continues to serve a stand-in for the Wild West. Sets at the **Paramount Ranch** back lot have been preserved and continue to be used as location sites. Rangers regularly conduct tours of the Paramount Ranch, where you can see sets used by *M*A*S*H* and *Dr. Quinn, Medicine Woman.* From Hollywood reach Mulholland Drive via Outpost Drive off Franklin Avenue or Cahuenga Boulevard west via Highland Avenue north. Keep an eye out for deer, raccoons, or a rare mountain lion. ✉ *401 W. Hillcrest Dr., Thousand Oaks* ☎ *805/370–2301* ✉ *Free* ☺ *Daily 9–5.*

★ ☼ ❶ **Universal Studios Hollywood.** Worn and a bit frayed around the edges, this special-effects-laden theme park delivers a handful of thrilling experiences at a steep price. A confusing layout, long lines in summer, and subpar food service make it fall short of its main rival, Disneyland, on almost every front. Still, hard-core entertainment junkies will find a few rides worth a thumbs up. ■ **TIP→** If you get here when the park opens, you'll likely save yourself from long waits in line—arriving early pays off.

The first-timer favorite is the tram tour, during which you can experience the parting of the Red Sea, an avalanche, a snowstorm, and a flood; meet a 30-foot-tall version of King Kong; be attacked by the ravenous killer shark of *Jaws* fame; survive an all-too-real simulation of an earthquake that measures 8.3 on the Richter scale, complete with collapsing earth; and come face to face with an evil mummy. The trams have sound and LCD systems, and the guided trip circles the 415-acre complex all day long. ■ **TIP→** This tram ride is usually the best place to start, since it's on the lower level of the park, which gets really crowded in the afternoon.

Many attractions are based on Universal films and television shows. The latest attraction, the bone-rattling roller coaster *Revenge of the Mummy—The Ride,* improves Universal's slate of attractions, though at the cost of replacing the longtime favorite *E.T.* flying ride. You can watch breathtaking stunts during the 20-minute *Spider-Man Rocks!* show. *Terminator 2: 3D* mixes 3-D effects with virtual reality and live action. *Jurassic Park—The Ride* is a short thrill ride through a jungle full of dinosaurs with an 84-foot water drop. The simulated warehouse fire in *Backdraft* is so real you can feel the heat.

Long lines form at *Back to the Future,* a flight simulator disguised as a DeLorean car that shows off excellent special effects, though it's a rough ride for your back and neck. *Shrek 4-D* reunites the film's celebrity voices to pick up where the movie left off in a 15-minute trailer of 3-D animation shown in an action simulation theater. At *Lucy: A Tribute to Lucille Ball,* a 2,200-square-foot heart-shape museum contains memorabilia from the *I Love Lucy* television show personally selected by Lucy's daughter, Lucie Arnaz. Throughout the park, costumed characters mingle with guests and pose for photos. Aside from the park, **CityWalk** is a separate venue, where you'll find a slew of shops, restaurants, nightclubs, and movie theaters, including IMAX 3-D. ✉ *100 Universal City Plaza, Universal City* ☎ *818/622–3801* ⊕ *www.universalstudios.com* ✉ *$56, parking $10* ☺ *Contact park for seasonal hrs.*

❷ **Warner Bros. Studios.** If you're looking for a more authentic behind-the-scenes look at how films and TV shows are made, head to this major studio center. There aren't many bells and whistles here, but you'll get a much better idea of production work than you will at Universal Studios. ■ **TIP→** The two-hour tours involve a lot of walking, so dress comfortably and bring plenty of sunscreen. You start with a short film on Warner Bros. movies and TV shows, then hop into a tour cart for a ride to the studio museum.

The archives here include costumes, props, and scripts from the studio's productions, including the sitcom *Friends* and the *Harry Potter* movies. Finally you'll visit the sets and soundstages, where you might spot a celeb or see a shoot in action—tours change from day to day depending on the productions taking place on the lot. Reservations are required. Call at least one week in advance and ask about provisions for people with disabilities; children under 8 are not admitted. Tours are given at least every hour, more frequently from May to September. ⊠ *3400 W. Riverside Dr., Burbank* ☎ *818/972–8687* ⊕ *www.wbsf.com* ✉ *$39* ⊙ *Weekdays 8:30–4.*

OFF THE BEATEN PATH

SIX FLAGS MAGIC MOUNTAIN – If you're a true thrill seeker looking for "monster" rides and breathtaking roller coasters, you'll find several of the biggest, fastest, and scariest in the world at this anti-Disney amusement park. The aptly named Scream, for instance, drops you 150 feet and tears through a 128-foot vertical loop. On X, you start with a climb of 200 feet before dropping headfirst at an 89-degree angle. Superman: The Escape is a 41-story coaster that hurtles you from 0 to 100 mph in less than seven seconds. On Riddler's Revenge, the world's tallest and fastest stand-up roller coaster, you stand for a mile-long 65-mph total panic attack. As at other theme parks, there are shows and parades, along with rides for younger kids, to fill out a long day. Weekends are peak times here, so be prepared to stand in line for the more popular rides. (In warm weather, be sure you have sunscreen and water.) If you really need to cool down and don't mind communal pools, you can hop over to its sister theme park, Six Flags Hurricane Harbor, right next door, and for $16.99 take a slippery cool trip down its massive waterslides. ⊠ *Magic Mountain Pkwy, off I–5, 25 mi northwest of Universal Studios and 36 mi outside L.A., Valencia* ☎ *661/255–4100* ⊕ *www.sixflags.com* ✉ *$60, parking $15* ⊙ *Mid-Mar.–mid-Sept., daily; mid-Sept.–early Mar., weekends; call for hrs.*

MISSION SAN FERNANDO REY DE ESPAÑA – An important member of a chain of 21 California missions established by Franciscan friars, Mission San Fernando was founded in 1797 and named in honor of King Ferdinand III of Spain. Today, as you walk through the mission's arched corridors, you may experience déjà vu—because you probably *have* seen it before, in an episode of *Gunsmoke, Dragnet,* or in any number of movies. Inside the mission, Native American designs and Spanish artifacts depict the mission's 18th-century culture. Look for the small museum and gift shop. To reach the mission, drive north on either the San Diego (I–405) or Golden State (I–5) Freeway. From I–405, drive east; from I–5, drive west. Exit at San Fernando Mission Boulevard. The mission is about a ½ mi from either freeway on the north side of the street. (A scenic but lengthy route back to L.A. is via Mulholland Drive, whose exit is about 15 mi, or 20 minutes, from the mission off I–405.) ⊠ *15151 San Fernando Mission Blvd., Mission Hills* ☎ *818/361–0186* ✉ *$4* ⊙ *Daily 9–4:30.*

PASADENA AREA

Although seemingly absorbed into the general Los Angeles sprawl, Pasadena is a separate and distinct city. Noted for its Tournament of Roses, seen around the world each New Year's Day, the city brims with noteworthy spots, from its gorgeous Craftsman homes to its exceptional museums, particularly the Norton Simon and the Huntington Library, Art Collections, and Botanical Gardens. Where else can you see a Chaucer manuscript and rare cacti in one place?

Between downtown Los Angeles and Pasadena, the Pasadena Freeway follows the curves of the arroyo (creek bed). This was the main road north during the early days of Los Angeles, when horses and buggies made their way through the countryside to the small town of Pasadena. In 1939 the road became the Arroyo Seco Parkway, the first freeway in Los Angeles, later renamed the Pasadena Freeway. The freeway remains a pleasant drive in non–rush hour traffic, with old sycamores winding up the arroyo in a pleasant contrast to the more common 10-lane freeways of Los Angeles.

To reach Pasadena from downtown Los Angeles, drive north on the Pasadena Freeway (I–110). From Hollywood and the San Fernando Valley use the Ventura Freeway (Highway 134, east), which cuts through Glendale, skirting the foothills, before arriving in Pasadena.

What to See

Castle Green. One block south of Colorado Boulevard stands the one-time social center of Pasadena's elite. This Moorish building is the only remaining section of a turn-of-the-20th-century hotel complex. Today the often-filmed tower is residential; local painter R. Kenton Nelson can often be spotted at work in his turret art studio along Raymond Avenue. The building is not open to the public on a daily basis, but it does organize seasonal tours on the first Sundays of December and June. ✉ *99 S. Raymond Ave., Pasadena* ☎ *626/577–6765* ⊕ *www.castlegreen.com.*

OFF THE
BEATEN
PATH

DESCANSO GARDENS – Getting its name from the Spanish word for "rest," this lovely oasis is a truly tranquil setting, shaded by massive oak trees. It's a sort of smaller, mellower version of the nearby Huntington complex. Once part of the vast Spanish Rancho San Rafael, these 160 acres were purchased by E. Manchester Boddy, publisher of the *Los Angeles Daily News*, in 1937. He developed the area into acres of lushly planted gardens and slopes covered in native chaparral as well as an elegant 22-room mansion, which now serves as a museum for watercolor paintings. A forest of California live oak trees makes a dramatic backdrop for thousands of camellias, azaleas, and a breathtaking 5-acre International Rosarium holding 1,700 varieties of antique and modern roses. The Japanese Tea House operates on weekends between February and November: its Zen garden is a nice spot to stop for refreshments and reflection. There are also a tram, a gift shop, and a café. ✉ *1418 Descanso Dr., La Cañada/Flintridge* ☎ *818/949–4200* ⊕ *www.descanso.com* 💰 *$7* ⊙ *Daily 9–4:30.*

❷ Fenyes Mansion. With its elegant dark wood paneling and floors, curved staircases, and a theatrical stage in the parlor, it's easy to envision how this 1905 mansion along Pasadena's Millionaire's Row once served as gathering place for the city's elite. Most rooms on the ground and second floors are still fitted with original furniture; you can peek into these roped-off spaces, now home to mannequins dressed in period clothing, to get a sense of what life was like a century ago. Docent-led tours are available, which give an extensive history of the home and its owners, many of whom can be seen in the mansion's many impression-

A GOOD TOUR

Numbers in the text correspond to numbers in the margin and on the Pasadena Area, Highland Park & San Marino map.

A good place to start a short driving tour of Pasadena is on Orange Grove Boulevard, aka Millionaire's Row, where wealthy Easterners built grand mansions. One example is the **Wrigley Mansion** ❶, an Italian Renaissance wedding cake of a house with grounds and gardens reminiscent of the neighborhood in the old days. To get there, take the Orange Grove exit off the Ventura Freeway (Highway 134); turn right at Orange Grove and travel five blocks. From the Pasadena Freeway (Highway 110), stay on the freeway until it ends at Arroyo Parkway. From Arroyo Parkway turn left at California Boulevard and then right at Orange Grove.

From the Wrigley Mansion, travel north on Orange Grove to Walnut Street and the **Fenyes Mansion** ❷, now headquarters of the Pasadena Historical Society. Continue on Orange Grove to Arroyo Terrace, where a left turn will take you into an architectural wonderland. Greene and Greene, the renowned Pasadena architects, designed all of the houses on Arroyo Terrace, as well as others in the area. To view their Craftsman masterpiece, the three-story, shingled **Gamble House** ❸, turn right on Westmoreland Place. Also in this section is the Frank Lloyd Wright–designed Millard House ("La Miniatura"), on Prospect Crescent (from Westmoreland, turn left onto Rosemont Avenue, right on Prospect Terrace, and right onto Prospect Crescent to No. 645). The

famous **Rose Bowl** ❹ is nestled in a gully just to the west off Arroyo Boulevard. Leave this area via Rosemont Avenue, driving away from the hills to the south. From Rosemont, turn right onto Orange Grove Boulevard. Then, at Colorado Boulevard, turn left. Immediately on the left is the contemporary, austere **Norton Simon Museum** ❺, a familiar backdrop to so many viewers of the annual New Year's Day Tournament of Roses Parade. Inside are outstanding collections of Impressionist and Asian art—if you're a fan of Degas's work, don't miss this musuem. West of the museum, paralleling the modern freeway bridge, Colorado crosses the historic concrete-arched Colorado Street Bridge, built in 1913.

East of the Norton Simon Museum, you'll enter **Old Town Pasadena** ❻. You'll want to walk around this section of Pasadena, heading east on Colorado. Parking's easy to find; look for signposted lots, often behind the main line of shops. Take a right on South Raymond Avenue and walk a block and a half down to the **Castle Green,** a former grand hotel and architectural gem. For a look at domed Pasadena City Hall, turn left from Colorado Boulevard onto Fair Oaks Avenue, then right on Holly Street. Garfield Avenue will bring you back to Colorado. The next intersection is Los Robles Avenue. One-half block north on Los Robles, the **Pacific Asia Museum** ❼ literally sticks out by virtue of its pagoda-style roofline. Back on Los Robles, head north and make a quick right onto East Union Street to find the stark

Pasadena Museum of California Art ❽. This is a small but interesting spot, well worth a quick dip into the native art scene.

From this point hop back in your car for a short drive south on El Molino to California Boulevard, where a left turn will take you into San Marino and the **Huntington Library, Art Collections, and Botanical Gardens** ❾ (follow the signs). In this sprawling estate, it's easy to forget you're in a city, as the sweeping grounds surround you with specially themed gardens. Though there's some renovation happening this year, you can still see the British paintings for which the museum's best known. Also in this area is the historic **Old Mill** ❿. This is a lot of sightseeing to cram into one day, so you may need to save the sights in the Highland Park neighborhood—**Heritage Square** and the **Southwest Museum**—for another afternoon. These three sights are within a short drive of each other, though, just south of Pasadena down the Arroyo Seco Parkway.

🕐 TIMING TIPS➜ If you want to see the Descanso Gardens, start early and see them first. Otherwise, get a late-morning or early-afternoon start to see the important architectural sights on this tour, saving Old Pasadena for last since it offers an outstanding evening street scene. Shops and restaurants stay open late in this relatively safe neighborhood, and it's easy to find parking in nearby garages.

A stop at the Gamble House shouldn't take more than an hour, leaving plenty of time for an afternoon visit to the Norton Simon Museum. Unless you're planning on seeing a game or hitting the flea market, you will probably want to skip the Rose Bowl. Set aside most of a day for the Huntington—in summer, visit the gardens in the morning to avoid the midday heat. Keep in mind that many museums are closed Monday, though the Norton Simon's closed Tuesday.

1

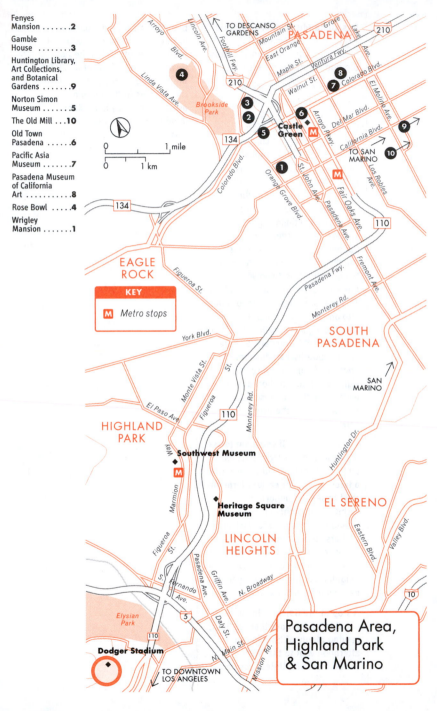

Pasadena Area,
Highland Park
& San Marino

ist paintings. Also be sure to take a moment to visit the adjacent Historical Center Gallery dedicated to the art and culture of Pasadena. ✉ *470 W. Walnut St., Pasadena* ☎ *626/577–1660* ⊕ *www.pasadenahistory.org* ✑ *Tour $4; museum $5* ☉ *Wed.–Sun. noon–5.*

★ ❸ **Gamble House.** Built by Charles and Henry Greene in 1908, this is a spectacular example of American Arts and Crafts bungalow architecture. The term *bungalow* can be misleading, since the Gamble House is a huge three-story home. To wealthy Easterners such as the Gambles (as in Procter & Gamble), this type of vacation home seemed informal compared with their mansions back home. What makes admirers swoon is the incredible amount of handcraftsmanship, including a teak staircase and cabinetry, Greene and Greene–designed furniture, and an Emil Lange glass door. The dark exterior has broad eaves, with sleeping porches on the second floor. An hour-long, docent-led tour of the Gamble's interior will draw your eye to the exquisite details. If you want to see more Greene and Greene homes, buy a self-guided tour map of the neighborhood in the bookstore. ✉ *4 Westmoreland Pl., Pasadena* ☎ *626/793–3334* ⊕ *www.gamblehouse.org* ✑ *$10* ☉ *Thurs.–Sun. noon–3; tickets go on sale at 10, 1-hr tour every 20 min.*

OFF THE BEATEN PATH

HERITAGE SQUARE MUSEUM – Looking like a prop street set up by a film studio, Heritage Square sticks out like a row of bright dollhouses in the modest Highland Park neighborhood. Five 19th-century residences, a train station, a church, and a carriage barn, built between the Civil War and World War I, were moved to this small park from various locations in southern California to save them from the wrecking ball. Docents dressed in period costume lead visitors through the lavish homes, giving an informative picture of what life in Los Angeles was like a century ago. The latest addition is a 1907 boxcar, now parked next to the Palms Depot, originally part of the Southern Pacific Railroad. The grounds are free, open Friday 10:30–3:30, but the buildings are closed. They are open, however, on holiday Mondays. ✉ *3800 Homer St., off Ave. 43 exit, Highland Park* ☎ *626/449–0193* ✑ *$10* ☉ *Fri.–Sun. noon–5.*

❾ **Huntington Library, Art Collections, and Botanical Gardens.** If you have time

Fodor'sChoice
★

for only one stop in the Pasadena area, it should be the Huntington, built in the early 1900s as the home of railroad tycoon Henry E. Huntington. Henry and his wife, Arabella (who was his aunt by marriage), voraciously collected rare books and manuscripts, botanical specimens, and 18th-century British art. The institution they established became one of the most extraordinary cultural complexes in the world.

■ **TIP➡** **If you're seeking the fine art here, take note: there will be some switcheroos in 2007. The Huntington Gallery, housed in the original 1911 Georgian mansion, is closed for renovations until 2008. Its world-famous collection of British paintings will instead be shown in the Erburu Gallery.** Among the highlights are John Constable's intimate *View on the Stour near Dedham* and the monumental *Sarah Siddons as the Tragic Muse,* by Joshua Reynolds. In a too-cute pairing, Gainsborough's *Blue Boy* faces *Pinkie,* by Thomas Lawrence. Once the British paintings return to the mansion, the Erburu will be filled with American artworks. Meanwhile, in the

Virginia Steele Scott Gallery of American Art you can see paintings by Mary Cassatt, Frederic Remington, and more.

The library contains more than 600,000 books and some 300 manuscripts, including such treasures as a Gutenberg Bible, the Ellesmere manuscript of Chaucer's *Canterbury Tales,* George Washington's genealogy in his own handwriting, scores of works by William Blake, and an unrivaled collection of early editions of Shakespeare. In the library's hallway are five tall hexagonal towers displaying important books and manuscripts.

Although the art collections are increasingly impressive here, don't resist being lured outside into the stunning Botanical Gardens. From the main buildings, lawns and towering trees stretch out toward specialty areas. The 12-acre Desert Garden, for instance, has the world's largest group of mature cacti and other succulents, arranged by continent. (Visit this garden on a cool morning or in the late afternoon, since a hot midday walk may be too much verisimilitude.) In the Japanese Garden, an arched bridge curves over a pond; the area also has stone ornaments, a Japanese house, a bonsai court, and a Zen rock garden. There are collections of azaleas and 1,500 varieties of camellias, the world's largest public collection. The 3-acre rose garden is displayed chronologically, so the development leading to today's strains of roses can be observed; on the grounds is the charming **Rose Garden Tea Room,** where traditional high tea is served. There are also herb, palm, and jungle gardens, plus the Shakespeare Garden, which blooms with plants mentioned in Shakespeare's works.

The latest addition, opened in 2005, is the Rose Hills Foundation Conservatory for Botanical Science, a child-oriented center with dozens of hands-on exhibits to illustrate plant diversity in various environments. (These rooms are quite warm and humid, especially the central rotunda, which displays rain forest plants.) The Huntington also plans to begin work on an ambitious classical Chinese Garden, set to be the largest of its kind outside China. Work on this will be underway for the next several years. A 1¼-hour guided tour of the gardens is led by docents at posted times, and a free brochure with map and highlights is available in the entrance pavilion. ⊠ *1151 Oxford Rd., San Marino* ☎ *626/ 405–2100* ⊕ *www.huntington.org* ✉ *$15, free 1st Thurs. of month* ☉ *Tues.–Fri. noon–4:30, weekends 10:30–4:30.*

Kidspace Children's Museum. Built in 2004, this hands-on museum is a great activity-focused, kid-centric alternative to Pasadena's art collections. Imaginative exhibits invite kids to interact, while parents can gain tidbits of knowledge on earthquakes, animals, and insects. In the towering leaf climb inside a sunny atrium, kids assume the role of ant on their daring ascent. ⊠ *480 N. Arroyo Blvd., Pasadena* ☎ *626/449–9144* ⊕ *www.kidspacemuseum.org* ✉ *$8* ☉ *Daily 9:30–5.*

OFF THE BEATEN PATH

10

THE OLD MILL (EL MOLINO VIEJO) – Built in 1816 as a gristmill for the San Gabriel Mission, the mill is one of the last remaining examples in southern California of Spanish Mission architecture. The thick adobe walls and textured ceiling rafters give the interior a sense of quiet strength. Be sure to step into the back room, now a gallery with rotating quarterly exhibits in alliance with the California Art Club. Outside, a chipped section of the mill's exterior reveals the layers of brick, ground seashell paste, and oxblood used to hold the structure together. The surrounding gardens are reason enough to visit, with a flower-decked arbor and old sycamores and oaks. In summer the California Philharmonic ensemble performs in the garden. ✉ *1120 Old Mill Rd., San Marino* ☎ *626/ 449–5458* 🎫 *Free* ☺ *Tues.–Sun. 1–4.*

SOUTHWEST MUSEUM – Readily spotted from the Pasadena Freeway (Highway 110), this huge Mission Revival building, now added to the National Register of Historic Places, stands halfway up Mt. Washington. Inside is an extensive collection of Native American art and artifacts, with special emphasis on the people of the Plains, the Northwest and Southwest coasts, and California. Highlights include a replica of a Santa Susana Mountains Chumash Indian rock art site and an 18-foot Southern Cheyenne tepee. The outstanding basketry collection is one of the largest in the country. ✉ *234 Museum Dr., Highland Park* ☎ *323/ 221–2163* ⊕ *www.southwestmuseum.org* 🎫 *$7.50* ☺ *Tues.–Sun. 10–5.*

5

Fodor'sChoice
★

Norton Simon Museum. Long familiar to television viewers of the New Year's Day Rose Parade, this low-profile brown building is more than just a background for the passing floats. It's one of the finest small museums anywhere, with an excellent collection that spans more than 2,000 years of Western and Asian art. It all began in the 1950s when Norton Simon (Hunt-Wesson Foods, McCalls Corporation, and Canada Dry) started collecting the works of Degas, Renoir, Gauguin, and Cézanne. His collection grew to include old masters, impressionists, and modern works from Europe and Indian and Southeast Asian art. After he retired, Simon reorganized the failing Pasadena Art Institute and continued to assemble one of the world's finest collections.

Today the Norton Simon Museum is richest in works by Rembrandt, Goya, Picasso, and, most of all, Degas: this is one of the only two U.S. institutions to hold the complete set of the artist's model bronzes (the other is New York's Metropolitan Museum of Art). Renaissance, baroque, and rococo masterpieces include Raphael's profoundly spiritual *Madonna with Child with Book* (1503), Rembrandt's *Portrait of a Bearded Man in a Wide-Brimmed Hat* (1633), and a magical Tiepolo ceiling, *The Triumph of Virtue and Nobility Over Ignorance* (1740–50). The museum's collections of impressionist (van Gogh, Matisse, Cézanne, Monet, Renoir) and cubist (Braque, Gris) works are extensive. Several Rodin sculptures are placed throughout the museum. Head down to the bottom floor to see the phenomenal Southeast Asian and Indian sculptures and artifacts, where graceful pieces like a Ban Chiang blackware vessel date to well before 1000 BC. Don't miss a living artwork outdoors: the garden, conceived by noted southern California landscape designer Nancy Goslee Power. The tranquil pond was inspired by Monet's gardens at Giverny. ✉*411 W. Col-*

orado Blvd., Pasadena ☎ *626/449–6840* ⊕ *www.nortonsimon.org* ✉ *$8* ⊙ *Wed., Thurs., and Sat.–Mon. noon–6, Fri. noon–9.*

★ ❻ **Old Town Pasadena.** Once the victim of decay, the area was revitalized in the 1990s as a blend of restored 19th-century brick buildings with a contemporary overlay. A phalanx of chain stores has muscled in, but there are still some less familiar shops and plenty of tempting cafés and restaurants. In the evening and on weekends, streets are packed with people, and Old Town crackles with energy. The 12-block historic district is anchored along Colorado Boulevard between Pasadena Avenue and Arroyo Parkway.

NEED A BREAK?

Stop in **Leonidas Chocolate Cafe** (✉ 49 W. Colorado Blvd. ☎ 626/577–7121) for a cup of joe enriched with delectable Belgian chocolate. The "white hot cocoa," made with white chocolate, is heavenly creamy. Or, to cool off, follow the intoxicating aroma of freshly pressed waffle cones to **Tutti Gelati** (✉ 62 W. Union St., No. 1 ☎ 626/440–9800), an Italian gelateria behind Crate & Barrel on Colorado Boulevard. Flavors include zabaglione, *stracciatella* (chocolate chip), and hazelnut; many ingredients come directly from Milan, and everything is made on the premises.

❼ **Pacific Asia Museum.** Devoted to the arts and culture of Asia and the Pacific Islands, this manageably sized museum displays changing exhibits drawn from its permanent collection of 17,000 works and artifacts. It's not the place for blockbuster shows—instead, you'll find modest displays of ceramics, calligraphy, and the like. The building itself is worth a look: it's inspired by Han Dynasty structures and surrounds a koi fishpond. ✉ *46 N. Los Robles Ave., Pasadena* ☎ *626/449–2742* ⊕ *www.pacificasiamuseum.org* ✉ *$7, free 4th Fri. of month* ⊙ *Wed., Thurs., and weekends 10–5, Fri. 10–8.*

❽ **Pasadena Museum of California Art.** The first thing you see when you approach this museum is the graffiti-covered parking structure. Was it vandalized by local taggers? Nope—it's the handiwork of artist George Kenny Scharf as part of this museum's dedication to all forms of Californian art, architecture, and design from 1850 to the present. The regularly changing exhibits are focused and thoughtfully presented; you might find anything from early California landscapes to contemporary works on car culture. ✉ *490 E. Union St., Pasadena* ☎ *626/568–3665* ⊕ *www.pmcaonline.org* ✉ *$6, free 1st Fri. of month 5–8* ⊙ *Wed.–Sun. noon–5; 1st Fri. of month noon–8.*

❹ **Rose Bowl.** With an enormous rose, the city of Pasadena's logo, adorned on its exterior, it's hard to miss this 100,000-seat stadium, host of many Super Bowls and home to the UCLA Bruins. Set in Brookside Park at the wide bottom of an arroyo, the facility is closed except during games and special events such as the monthly Rose Bowl Swap Meet, which is considered the granddaddy of West Coast flea markets. ✉ *Rose Bowl Dr. at Rosemont Ave., Pasadena* ☎ *626/577–3100* ⊕ *www.rosebowlstadium.com* ✉ *$7–$20* ⊙ *Flea market 2nd Sun. of month 9–3.*

OFF THE BEATEN PATH

MISSION SAN GABRIEL ARCHANGEL – In 1771 Father Junípero Serra dedicated this mission to the divine messenger St. Gabriel. Within the next 50 years, the San Gabriel Archangel became the wealthiest of all California missions. In 1833 the Mexican government confiscated the mission, and it began to decline. The U.S. government returned the mission to the church in 1855, but by this time the Franciscans had departed. In 1908 the Claretian Missionaries took charge. Much care has since been poured into the mission; its unusual mosquelike appearance is thought to be modeled after the Cathedral in Córdoba, Spain. Public mass is held at the mission Sunday morning at 7 and 9:30. ⊠ *428 S. Mission Dr., San Gabriel* ☎ *626/457–3048* ⊕ *www.sangabrielmission.org* ☜ *$5* ⊙ *Daily 9–4:30.*

❶ Wrigley Mansion. Chewing-gum magnate William Wrigley purchased this white Italian Renaissance–style house in 1914. The mansion, with its green-tile roof and manicured rose garden with 1,500 floral varieties, is now the headquarters of the Tournament of Roses Association. The interior still provides a glimpse of the over-the-top style of the area in the early 20th century, though in its new role it may remind you more of a Marriott than a home. Tours of the house last about an hour. ⊠ *391 S. Orange Grove Blvd., Pasadena* ☎ *626/449–4100* ⊕ *www.tournamentofroses.com* ☜ *Free* ⊙ *Tours: Feb.–Aug., Thurs. 2–4; gardens: Feb.–Oct., daily sunrise–sunset.*

LONG BEACH, SAN PEDRO & PALOS VERDES

The coastline south of Venice mellows into a string of low-key beach communities. Those around the bulge of the Palos Verdes Peninsula—including Redondo Beach, Palos Verdes Estates, and Rancho Palos Verdes—are collectively called the South Bay. The Pacific Coast Highway dips inland, skimming above San Pedro and continuing to Long Beach at the tail end of Los Angeles County.

The hilly Palos Verdes Peninsula, an expensive, gentrified residential area, is edged with rocky cliffs and tide pools. Point Vicente, in Rancho Palos Verdes, is a good place for whale-watching during the gray whale migrations from January through March. The communities are zoned for horses, so you'll often see riders along the streets (they have the right of way). San Pedro (pronounced *Pee*–dro), L.A.'s working harbor, is an old seaport community full of small 1920s-era white clapboards. Greek and Yugoslav markets and restaurants abound here, underlining the town's strong Mediterranean flavor. San Pedro and neighboring Wilmington are connected to downtown Los Angeles by a narrow, 16-mi-long stretch of land, less than a ½ mi wide in most places, annexed in the late 19th century to preserve Los Angeles's transportation and shipping interests. ⚠ Unfortunately, gang activity sometimes flares up in San Pedro, especially around Cabrillo Beach, so avoid walking around here at night.

Long Beach, long stuck in limbo between Los Angeles and Orange County in the minds of visitors, is steadily rebuilding its place in the southern California scheme. Founded as a seaside resort in the 19th century, the city boomed in the early 20th century as oil discoveries drew in Midwesterners and Dust Bowlers. Bust followed boom and the city took on a somewhat raw, industrial, neglected feel. But a long-term redevelopment plan begun in the 1970s has finally come to fruition, turning the city back to its resort roots.

What to See

★ ❷ **Aquarium of the Pacific.** Sea lions, nurse sharks, octopuses, and . . . parrots—this aquarium focuses primarily on ocean life from the Pacific Ocean, with a detour into Australian birds. The main exhibits include lively sea lions, a crowded tank of various sharks, and ethereal sea dragons, which the aquarium has successfully bred in captivity. Most impressive is recently added multimedia attraction, *Whales: A Journey with Giants.* This panoramic film shows in the darkened core of the aquarium's Great Hall and nearly makes you feel you're swimming with the giants. Ask for showtimes at the information desk. For a nonaquatic experience, head over to Lorikeet Forest, a walk-in aviary full of the friendliest parrots from down under. Buy a cup of nectar and smile as you become a human bird perch. Since these birds spend most of their day feeding, you're guaranteed a noisy—and possibly messy—encounter. (A sink, soap, and towels are strategically placed at the exhibit exit.) If you've ever wondered how an aquarium functions, book the extensive hour-long Behind the Scenes Tour ($15) at the information desk. ✉ *100 Aquarium Way, Long Beach* ☎ *562/590–3100* ⊕ *www.aquariumofpacific. org* ✆ *$18.95* ☯ *Daily 9–6.*

❾ **Cabrillo Marine Aquarium.** Dedicated to the marine life that flourishes off the southern California coast, this Frank Gehry–designed center gives an intimate and instructive look at local sea creatures. Head to the Exploration Center and S. Mark Taper Foundation Courtyard for kid-friendly interactive exhibits and activity stations. Especially fun is the "Crawl In" aquarium, where you can be surrounded by fish without getting wet. ■ **TIP→ From March through July the aquarium organizes a legendary grunion program, when you can see the small, silvery fish as they come ashore at night to spawn on the beach.** After visiting the museum, you can stop for a picnic or beach stroll along Cabrillo Beach. ✉ *3720 Stephen M. White Dr., San Pedro* ☎ *310/548–7562* ⊕ *www.cabrilloaq. org* ✆ *$5 suggested donation, parking $7* ☯ *Tues.–Fri. noon–5, weekends 10–5.*

OFF THE BEATEN PATH

GENERAL PHINEAS BANNING RESIDENCE MUSEUM AND BANNING PARK – General Phineas Banning, an early entrepreneur in Los Angeles, is credited with developing the Los Angeles Harbor into a viable economic entity and naming the area Wilmington (he was from Delaware). Part of his estate has been preserved in a 20-acre park. (The picnicking possibilities here are excellent.) A 100-year-old wisteria, near the arbor, blooms in spring. You can see the interior of the house on docent-led tours. ✉ *401 E. M St., Wilmington* ☎ *310/548–7777* ⊕ *www.banningmuseum.org* ✆ *Suggested donation for tours $5* ☯ *Guided tours Tues.–Thurs. 12:30, 1:30, and 2:30, weekends 12:30, 1:30, 2:30, and 3:30.*

❺ **Long Beach Museum of Art.** This museum fills a charming 1912 shingle-clad Arts and Crafts estate and an adjacent gallery with a small but

A GOOD TOUR

Numbers in the text correspond to numbers in the margin and on the Long Beach, San Pedro & Palos Verdes map.

Because a single drive around these three areas would encompass more than 100 mi, it's best to approach the area on two separate trips; both include a visit to an aquarium. If you're new here, Long Beach will likely be the more appealing pick.

Begin a tour of Long Beach at what is still the city's most famous attraction, the art deco ship the **Queen Mary** ❶. Then take the Queens Way Bridge back across the bay to the **Aquarium of the Pacific** ❷. From here, stops along Shoreline Drive at **Rainbow Harbor** ❸ or the colorfully painted waterfront shopping center, Shoreline Village, give the best views of the harbor and the Long Beach skyline. At Ocean Boulevard, Shoreline Drive turns into Alamitos Avenue. Continue on Alamitos to the corner of 7th Street and the **Museum of Latin American Art (MoLAA)** ❹. Return to Ocean Boulevard and turn east. Just past the commercial district lie the **Long Beach Museum of Art** ❺ and grand old homes dating from the early 1900s. From Ocean Boulevard, turn onto Livingston Drive and then 2nd Street to drive through Belmont Shores before arriving at Alamitos Bay and **Naples** ❻, a picturesque enclave of canals and marinas, and the place to take a gondola ride.

For an overview of Palos Verdes and San Pedro, begin at the Point Vicente Lighthouse, at Palos Verdes Drive and Hawthorne Boulevard. The lighthouse has stood here since 1926 and it's also a great spot for whale-watching between January and March. Nearby is Point Vicente Park, where you'll have a postcard view of the ocean. From there, take a leisurely coastline drive south on Palos Verdes Drive. Two miles down, on your left, you'll see the all-glass **Wayfarers Chapel** ❼. Continue south and you'll hit San Pedro and Los Angeles Harbor. Follow the signs to Cabrillo Beach, where you'll find the **Cabrillo Marine Aquarium** ❾. From here it's a quick hop over to **Ports O' Call** ❽ for a quick bite.

⏱ **TIMING TIPS→** In Long Beach, guided tours of the *Queen Mary* last about an hour. If you've planned in advance, you could end the day with a sunset gondola cruise on the canals in Naples. If you have kids in tow, expect to stay at least an hour at either the Long Beach or San Pedro aquariums. Don't forget to factor in 15 to 20 minutes' driving time between attractions, and remember that the museums and the Cabrillo Marine Aquarium are closed on Monday. If you're here anytime from January through March, you might be able to squeeze in some whale-watching during the gray whale migration.

captivating collection of Californian modernist works and landscapes. You might find it hard to tear yourself away from the stunning ocean view from the terrace, though. But don't overlook the Children's Art Gallery; it has some especially lively pieces. ✉ *2300 E. Ocean Blvd., Long Beach* ☎ *562/439–2119* 🌐 *www.lbma.org* 💲 *$7, free Fri.* ⏱ *Tues.–Sun. 11–5.*

Long Beach, San Pedro & Palos Verdes

NEED A BREAK? Stroll seaside to the Long Beach Museum of Art and grab a waterview table under a yellow umbrella at **Claire's at the Museum** (✉ 2300 E. Ocean Blvd. ☎ 562/439–2119). Grab a bite to eat or indulge in one of the signature desserts with the sun setting across the bay.

4 **Museum of Latin American Art (MoLAA).** At this writing, MoLAA was undergoing a massive renovation and expansion—when finished, in early 2007, it should be an even more impressive destination. It's the only museum on the West Coast devoted exclusively to contemporary art from Mexico and Central and South America; the permanent collection rotates and temporary shows cycle through, so there's always something new to see. The expansion will add an educational art studio, a research library, a film screening room, and an outdoor sculpture garden with creations by Latin American artists. The museum gift store is an especially good one, with carved masks, textiles, and other work by local and Latin American artists. Admission includes an informative audio tour. ✉ *628 Alamitos Ave., Long Beach* ☎ *562/437–1689* ⊕ *www.molaa. com* ✎ *$5, free Fri.* ☉ *Tues.–Fri. 11:30–7:00, Sat. 11–7, Sun. 11–6.*

6 **Naples.** Consisting of three small islands in man-made Alamitos Bay, Naples is best experienced on foot. Park near Bay Shore Avenue and 2nd Street and walk across the bridge to meander around the quaint streets with Italian names. This well-restored neighborhood has eclectic architecture: vintage Victorians, Craftsman bungalows, and Mission Revivals. You may spy a real gondola or two on the canals. (You can hire one for a ride, but generally not on the spur of the moment.) Reserve at least one week in advance for rides with **Gondola Getaway** (✉ 5437 E. Ocean Blvd., Naples, Long Beach ☎ 562/433–9595 ⊕ www. gondo.net). The one-hour rides are usually touted for romantic couples, although groups of up to 16 people can be accommodated. Bread, salami, and cheese are served—you bring the wine. Rides cost $65 per couple, $10–$17 each additional person, and run from 11 AM to 11 PM.

8 **Ports O' Call.** The cluster of buildings aims its restaurants and gift shops squarely at tourists, but locals can be lured here, too, especially for the harbor cruises. It's a great place to catch a boat for a whale-watching cruise or a trip out to Catalina. A stroll down this lively strip, along the Port of Los Angeles's Main Channel, leads you to the **Maritime Museum** (✉ Berth 84, at the end of 6th St., San Pedro ☎ 310/548–7618), which displays more 700 ship and boat models and a large collection of navigational gear. ✉ *1100 Nagoya Way, San Pedro* ☎ *310/652–4517.*

1 ***Queen Mary.*** There's a saying among staff members that the more you get to know the *Queen Mary,* the more you realize that she has a uniquely endearing personality as well as a wealth of history. The beautifully preserved ocean liner was launched in 1934 and made 1,001 transatlantic crossings before finally berthing in Long Beach in 1967. It has gone through many periods of renovations since, but in 1993, the RMS Foundation took over ownership and restored its original art deco style. On board, you can take one of five tours, such as the informative Behind the Scenes walk or the downright spooky Ghost and Legends tour. (Spirits have been spotted in the pool and engine room.) You could stay for dinner at one of the ship's restaurants or even spend the night in one of the wood-panel rooms. The ship's neighbor, a geodesic dome originally built to house Howard Hughes's *Spruce Goose* aircraft, now serves as a terminal for Carnival Cruise Lines, making the *Queen Mary* the perfect pit stop before or after a cruise. And an-

chored next to the *Queen* is the *Scorpion,* a Russian submarine you can tour for a look at Cold War history. ⊠ *1126 Queens Hwy., Long Beach* ☏ *562/435–3511* ⊕ *www.queenmary.com* ☒ *Tours $22.95–$31.95* ☉ *Call for times and frequency of guided tours.*

❸ Rainbow Harbor. In the quest to generate some commercial gold, this segment of the waterfront has been developed to complement Long Beach's other harbor attractions. The brightly painted clusters of restaurants, boutiques, and souvenir stores that make up **Shoreline Village** (⊠ Shoreline Dr. and Shoreline Village Rd., Long Beach ☏ 562/435–2668 ⊕ www.shorelinevillage.com) cap the area to the east. You can rent surreys, bikes, sailboats, or Jet Skis here; the Pelican Pier Pavilion has a small carousel and arcade games. The **Pike at Rainbow Harbor** is a stucco-clad collection of uninspired shops and restaurants found in malls across America. Depending on the season and day of the week, Rainbow Harbor is also the place to catch the city's AquaBus water shuttle to the *Queen Mary.* ⊠ *Shoreline Dr. between the Aquarium of Pacific and Shoreline Village, Long Beach* ⊕ *www.shopthepike.com.*

OFF THE BEATEN PATH **RANCHO LOS ALAMITOS HISTORIC RANCH AND GARDENS –** One of the country's oldest adobe one-story domestic buildings still standing, this landmark was built circa 1800, when the Spanish flag still flew over California. Docents lead guided tours of the house and barnyard; there are a working blacksmith shop in the barn and a stable of farm animals that include draft horses, sheep, and goats. ⊠ *6400 E. Bixby Hill Rd., enter at guard gate at Palo Verde and Anaheim Sts., Long Beach* ☏ *562/431–3541* ⊕ *www.rancholosalamitos.com* ☒ *Donation suggested* ☉ *Wed.–Sun. 1–5; free 90-min tour every ½ hr 1–4.*

★ **❼ Wayfarers Chapel.** A look at this stunning, all-glass Swedenborgian church is practically guaranteed to fill you with awe. Built in 1949 by architect Lloyd Wright (son of Frank Lloyd Wright), it intentionally blends in with the trees and lush garden setting on the Palos Verdes Peninsula. The flower-filled garden includes a number of plants that are mentioned in the Bible. On a clear day you can see straight across the ocean to Catalina Island. Little wonder the church is a very popular wedding destination; you'll see tributes to this in the dedication bricks along the Walk of Honor. ⊠ *5755 Palos Verdes Dr. S, Rancho Palos Verdes* ☏ *310/377–1650* ⊕ *www.wayfarerschapel.org* ☉ *Daily 7–5.*

Where to Eat

WORD OF MOUTH

"The food [at Patina] is consistently sophisticated, creative and excellent. . . . The chef's tasting menu is guaranteed to impress."

—Woody

"[A.O.C.] has amazing food, and friendly, non-snobby service. Make a reservation: it gets packed. Great for a special dinner, or just to stop in and taste some wine at the bar."

—J S

By Roger J. Grody

CELEBRITY IS BIG BUSINESS in Los Angeles, so it's no accident the concept of the celebrity chef—emerging from an exhibition kitchen to schmooze with an equally illustrious clientele—is a key part of the city's dining scene. Wolfgang Puck, whose culinary empire of restaurants, food products, and cooking shows has made him a household name across the nation, epitomizes this phenomenon. And L.A. keeps coming up with fresh stars to fill its ever-expanding universe of kitchens. For instance, Gino Angelini is adding a new dimension to Italian cooking at Angelini Osteria and La Terza, while David Myers spins one of the city's most ambitious contemporary menus at Sona. Innovative Suzanne Goin manages to deliver exciting results at both Cal-French Lucques and A.O.C., her Mediterranean-inspired wine bar.

Although Los Angeles doesn't pretend to rival New York in terms of high-end dining rooms, its strategic location contributes to a varied and imaginative local cuisine. Local produce is a linchpin; area restaurants benefit from the state's incredible agricultural yields. This is the bedrock of California cuisine: fresh, seasonal local ingredients. Increasingly, intriguing produce from specialty farms shows up at L.A.'s farmers' markets, where home cooks browse shoulder to shoulder with acclaimed chefs. (*See* Chapter 6 for a rundown on local markets.)

As one of the true capitals of the Pacific Rim, L.A. also absorbs the culinary influences of its various Asian communities. Asian flavors set off creative sparks in fusion kitchens and traditional establishments alike. You can dine at dim sum temples comparable to those in Hong Kong, for instance, or try a French-trained chef's spin on sashimi. In recent years, L.A. has emerged as quite possibly the best place to eat sushi outside of Japan, with a remarkable selection of high-end sushi bars serving both traditional and cutting-edge fare. The city's proximity to Latin America and its diverse Latino neighborhoods add further depth. Local chefs frequently incorporate ingredients indigenous to El Salvador, Colombia, and every culinary region of Mexico.

Beverly Hills, Century City & Hollywood

Beverly Hills

AMERICAN
$$$–$$$$

✗ **The Grill on the Alley.** Beverly Hills restaurants can take you many places, from Provence to Polynesia, but in this case it's just up the Golden State Freeway to a traditional San Francisco–style grill with dark-wood paneling and brass trim. The clubby chophouse, where movie industry execs power-lunch at the most coveted booths in town, creates tasty, simple American fare, including steaks, chicken potpies, crab cakes, Cobb salad, and homemade rice pudding. ⊠ *9560 Dayton Way, Beverly Hills* ☎ *310/276–0615* ⌳ *Reservations essential* ▤ *AE, DC, MC, V* ⊗ *No lunch Sun.*

AMERICAN-
CASUAL
$$–$$$$

✗ **Kate Mantilini.** Casual but hip—and with Beverly Hills prices for comfort food—this is a good place to remember when you're up early (breakfast served daily) or out and about after midnight (open until 2 AM on weekends). The lengthy menu lines up American evergreens like New England clam chowder, macaroni and cheese, meat loaf, and a white chili made with white beans and chicken. ⊠ *9101 Wilshire Blvd., Beverly Hills* ☎ *310/278–3699* ▤ *AE, DC, MC, V.*

KNOW-HOW

Dining out in Los Angeles tends to be a casual affair, and even at some of the most expensive restaurants you're likely to see customers in jeans (although this is not necessarily considered in good taste). It's very rare for L.A. restaurants to actually require a jacket and tie, but all of the city's more formal establishments appreciate a gentleman who dons a jacket—let your good judgment be your guide.

Despite its veneer of decadence, L.A. is not a particularly late-night city. The peak dinner times are from 7 to 9, and most restaurants won't take reservations after 10 PM. Unless otherwise noted, the restaurants listed in this guide are open daily for lunch and dinner. Generally speaking, restaurants are closed either Sunday or Monday; a few are shuttered both days. Most places—even the upscale spots—are open for lunch on weekdays, since plenty of Hollywood megadeals are conceived at that time.

L.A. is an extremely wine-friendly city. Although some profit-conscious restaurateurs are beginning to rebel, most are happy to assess a relatively modest corkage fee (typically $10 to $25 per bottle, sometimes less) for diners who bring their own wine. However, you should avoid bringing anything you would expect to find on the restaurant's wine list or anything too ordinary. Courtesy also demands that you offer the sommelier or your server a taste of what you've brought.

Smokers should keep in mind that California law forbids smoking in all enclosed areas, including bars. Smoking is not necessarily permitted even on patios, so call ahead to find out a restaurant's policy.

All restaurants in Los Angeles County—everything from hole-in-the-wall takeout joints to opulent dining rooms—are required to post the letter grade (A, B, or C) on the premises that reflects the score received from Los Angeles County health officials, who regularly inspect kitchen and storage facilities. Establishments that fail are closed until the deficiencies are corrected.

As for reservations, keep in mind that they're nearly always advisable and are absolutely essential at many of the city's trendier venues. While making your reservation, inquire about parking. You'll find most places, except small mom-and-pop establishments, provide valet parking at dinner for reasonable rates (often under $5 plus tip).

Restaurants here are organized by location, cuisine, and price.

WHAT IT COSTS				
$$$$	$$$	$$	$	¢
AT DINNER over $32	$22–$32	$12–$22	$7–$12	under $7

Prices are per person for a main course, excluding 8.25% sales tax.

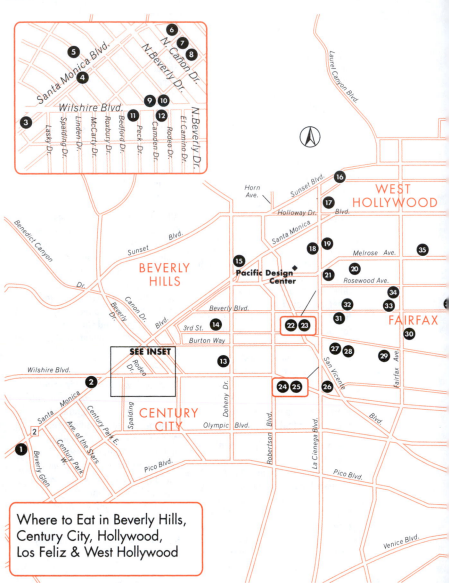

Where to Eat in Beverly Hills, Century City, Hollywood, Los Feliz & West Hollywood

KEY

Ⓜ Metro Stops

BRAZILIAN
$$$

✕ **Fogo de Chão.** *Churrascarias* (Brazilian steak houses) are suddenly commonplace in L.A. and Fogo de Chão is one of the best examples of the trend, with an elegant spin on the traditional meat fest. Start at the buffet, helping yourself to salads and sides. Back at your table, use the marker to signal for service; turn it to green and servers dressed as gauchos arrive with beautifully barbecued meats, carving them onto your plate from sword-like spits. There are about 15 different kinds of beef, chicken, lamb, and pork to try—when you can take no more, turn the marker to red. The dining room itself recalls a fine steak house with a hint of Vegas: white linen–topped tables, wooden wine racks, massive murals, and fountains. ⊠ *133 N. La Cienega Blvd., Beverly Hills* ☎ *310/289–7755* ⌂ *Reservations essential* ▤ *AE, D, MC, V* ☽ *No lunch weekends.*

> ## ROGER'S TOP 5
>
> - **Ocean Star** for fantastic dim sum.
> - **Patina,** inside Walt Disney Concert Hall.
> - **Philippe The Original** for a French Dip sandwich.
> - **Spago Beverly Hills,** stellar food *and* clientele.
> - **Urasawa** for a once-in-a-lifetime Japanese feast.

CONTEMPORARY
$$$–$$$$

✕ **The Belvedere.** In the entertainment industry's A-list hotel, the Peninsula, you're sure to be hobnobbing with power brokers, even if you don't recognize them. The refined cooking here elevates the opulent Belvedere far beyond the usual hotel dining room. You may want to start with the signature house-smoked salmon with scallion pancakes and chive crème fraîche, then indulge in Moroccan-spiced duck or Kansas City strip steak with peppercorn sauce. At lunch, deal makers convene over whimsical small bites (like shots of gazpacho and "tuna lollipops"), salads, and glamburgers like sautéed salmon with pinot noir–cured onions. Of course, the execs who favor this place are prone to special ordering; the staff graciously obliges. ⊠ *9882 S. Santa Monica Blvd., Beverly Hills* ☎ *310/788–2306* ▤ *AE, D, DC, MC, V.*

$$$–$$$$

✕ **Maple Drive.** The privacy of the high-backed booths here isn't the only lure for entertainment industry players—it's the sophisticated contemporary-American cuisine that keeps bringing them back. Look for duck breast with grilled foie gras and lavender-plum sauce, grilled rare bluefin tuna with niçoise olive *jus,* and a stellar rib eye with béarnaise. And for longtime regulars, Maple Drive classics like meat loaf and "kick-ass" chili are always available. ⊠ *345 N. Maple Dr., Beverly Hills* ☎ *310/274–9800* ⌂ *Reservations essential* ▤ *AE, DC, MC, V* ☽ *Closed Sun. No lunch weekends.*

$$$–$$$$
Fodor'sChoice
★

✕ **Spago Beverly Hills.** The flagship restaurant of Wolfgang Puck, the chef who helped define California cuisine, is justifiably a modern L.A. classic. The casually elegant restaurant centers on an outdoor courtyard. There, shaded by 100-year-old olive trees, you can glimpse the exhibition kitchen and, on occasion, the affable chef-owner greeting his famous friends. (The people-watching here is worth the price of admission.) The daily-changing menu could offer a tasting of five foie gras preparations, *côte de boeuf* with Armagnac-peppercorn sauce, Cantonese-style duck, and some traditional Austrian specialties. Acclaimed pastry chef Sherry Yard works magic with everything from a sophisticated tart inspired by the Twix candy bar to an Austrian *kaiserschmarren* (crème fraîche pancakes with fruit). ⊠ *176 N. Cañon Dr., Beverly Hills* ☎ *310/385–0880* ⚐ *Reservations essential* ▭ *AE, D, DC, MC, V* ⊘ *No lunch Sun.*

> ### WORD OF MOUTH
>
> "[Spago was] really one of the best meals we've ever had and they treated us like royalty (and we're 'no one')."   —Tess

$$–$$$$ ✕ **The Blvd.** Just off the lobby of the eternally fashionable Regent Beverly Wilshire hotel is this chic but laid-back venue. It's the kind of place where you could order either a pizza or a $185 martini (the Baccarat glass is a souvenir). Salads and truffled risotto are offered for grazing, while a more serious meal might begin with ahi tuna tartare, followed by seared scallops and sweetbreads, rotisserie chicken, or steak with Point Reyes blue-cheese sauce. A small terrace faces a Rodeo Drive lineup of Tiffany, Prada, and Cartier. ⊠ *Regent Beverly Wilshire, 9500 Wilshire Blvd., Beverly Hills* ☎ *310/275–5200* ⚐ *Reservations essential* ▭ *AE, D, DC, MC, V.*

DELICATESSENS ✕ **Barney Greengrass.** This *haute* deli on the fifth floor of Barneys de-
$–$$ partment store has an appropriately high-class aesthetic: limestone floors, mahogany furniture, and a wall of windows. On the outdoor terrace, at tables shaded by large umbrellas, you can savor flawless smoked salmon, sturgeon, and whitefish flown in fresh from New York. The deli closes at 6 PM. ⊠ *Barneys, 9570 Wilshire Blvd., Beverly Hills* ☎ *310/777–5877* ▭ *AE, DC, MC, V.*

ITALIAN ✕ **Enoteca Drago.** High-flying Sicilian chef Celestino Drago scores with this
★ **$$–$$$** sleek but unpretentious version of an *enoteca* (a wine bar serving small snacks). It's an ideal spot for sampling interesting Italian wines—more than 50 available by the glass—and enjoying a menu made up of small plates such as deep-fried olives, chicken liver pâté served in a rustic jar, and grilled baby octopus. Although the mushroom-filled ravioli bathed in foie gras-truffle sauce is a bit luxurious for an enoteca, it's one of the city's best pasta dishes. Larger portions and pizzas are also available here, but the essence of an enoteca is preserved. ⊠ *410 N. Cañon Dr., Beverly Hills* ☎ *310/786–8236* ⚐ *Reservations essential* ▭ *AE, DC, MC, V.*

$–$$ ✕ **Da Pasquale.** An affordable meal is hard to find here in the land of Gucci, which is one reason to visit Da Pasquale. An even better reason is the wonderful thin-crust pizza topped with ingredients like fresh tomato, garlic, and basil or three cheeses and prosciutto. The kitchen also excels at familiar pastas and roasted chicken. Despite the talent-agency regulars, the homey Old Napoli interior and friendly staff make everybody feel welcome. ⊠ *9749 S. Santa Monica Blvd., Beverly Hills* ☎ *310/859–3884* ▭ *AE, MC, V* ⊘ *Closed Sun. No lunch Sat.*

JAPANESE ✕ **Urasawa.** Shortly after celebrated sushi chef Masa Takayama packed
$$$$ his knives for the Big Apple, his protégé Hiroyuki Urasawa settled into
Fodor's Choice the master's former digs. The understated sushi bar has preciously few
★ seats, resulting in incredibly personalized service. At a minimum of $250 per person for a strictly *omakase* (chef's choice) meal, Urasawa is the priciest restaurant in town, but the endless parade of masterfully

crafted, exquisitely presented dishes renders few regrets. The maple sushi bar, sanded daily to a satinlike finish, is the scene of a mostly traditional cuisine with magnificent ingredients. You might be served velvety bluefin toro paired with beluga caviar or egg custard, *uni* (sea urchin) glittering with gold leaf. This is also the place to come during *fugu* season, when the legendary, potentially deadly blowfish is artfully served to adventurous diners. ⊠ *2 Rodeo, 218 N. Rodeo Dr., Beverly Hills* ☎ *310/247–8939* ⚐ *Reservations essential* ☐ *AE, DC, MC, V* ☻ *Closed Sun. No lunch.*

★ **$$$–$$$$** ✗ **Matsuhisa.** Freshness and innovation are the hallmarks of this flagship restaurant of superchef Nobu Matsuhisa's empire. The surprisingly modest-looking place draws celebrities and serious sushi buffs alike. Here you'll encounter such dishes as caviar-capped tuna stuffed with black truffles, squid "pasta" with garlic sauce, sea urchin wrapped in a *shiso* leaf, and monkfish liver pâté wrapped in gold leaf. Reflecting his past stint in Peru, Matsuhisa incorporates intriguing Latin ingredients into traditional Japanese cuisine. Regulars ask for the omakase, assured of an amazing culinary experience, and then steel themselves for a big tab. ⊠ *129 N. La Cienega Blvd., Beverly Hills* ☎ *310/659–9639* ⚐ *Reservations essential* ☐ *AE, DC, MC, V* ☻ *No lunch weekends.*

PAN-ASIAN ✗ **Trader Vic's.** Believe it or not, this kitschy restaurant-bar is the most **$$–$$$$** restrained of the late Victor Bergeron's South Seas extravaganzas. Opened in 1955, it has outlasted nearly all of its competitors, thanks to new generations of admirers. Longtime favorites like crab Rangoon (wrapped in wonton noodles and deep-fried), skewered shrimp, grilled pork ribs, and peanut butter–barbecued lamb have been joined by lighter options such as sushi rolls, sesame seed–crusted ahi tuna, and Thai curries. ⊠ *Beverly Hilton, 9876 Wilshire Blvd., Beverly Hills* ☎ *310/276–6345* ⚐ *Reservations essential* ☐ *AE, D, DC, MC, V* ☻ *No lunch.*

STEAK ✗ **The Lodge Steakhouse.** Despite its prevalence of salad-picking starlets, **$$$–$$$$** L.A. is experiencing a stampede of contemporary steak houses, a trend well represented by the Lodge. With a neorustic motif devoid of the customary red leather and white linen, this hip establishment's only connections to the traditional American steak house—besides high prices—are its deftly seared prime beef, classic potato side dishes, and extensive selection of full-bodied red wines. ⊠ *14 N. La Cienega Blvd., Beverly Hills* ☎ *310/854–0024* ⚐ *Reservations essential* ☐ *AE, DC, MC, V* ☻ *No lunch.*

$$$–$$$$ ✗ **Mastro's Steakhouse.** With a prime Beverly Hills location and classic steak house menu, this Arizona import is proving to be a popular alternative to the old standbys. Starters include a shrimp cocktail dramatically presented in a cloud of dry ice. Massive steaks, swimming in butter, are served on the bone for maximum flavor. The downstairs dining room is appropriately sleek and studied, but Rat Pack–era gentlemen and their conspicuously younger companions sometimes let loose at a piano bar upstairs. ⊠ *246 N. Cañon Dr., Beverly Hills* ☎ *310/888–8782* ⚐ *Reservations essential* ☐ *AE, D, DC, MC, V* ☻ *No lunch.*

VIETNAMESE ✗ **Crustacean.** This head-turning venue is a surrealistic reproduction of **$$–$$$$** colonial Vietnam. Exotic fish swim in a floor-to-ceiling aquarium and through a glass-topped "river," sunk into the marble floor, that mean-

The Hotel Dining Room Revival

2

Some of L.A.'s best restaurants hold forth in hotels, and locals vie for tables along with the guests.

From the Cambodian silks to the French porcelain, **Jaan** (☎ 310/278–3344), at the Raffles L'Ermitage Hotel in Beverly Hills, swaddles you in luxe surroundings. Its inventive contemporary cuisine incorporates luxury ingredients—Kobe beef, black truffles, caviar—from around the world.

There's no false advertising at **Oceanfront** (☎ 310/581–7714), in Santa Monica's Casa del Mar. It serves crisply prepared meals in a sumptuous room right on the beach. At the nearby Viceroy Santa Monica, **Whist** (☎ 310/451–8711) serves market-driven contemporary fare in a dramatic dining room with rows of vintage English china, or at poolside cabanas.

The Tower Bar (☎ 323/848–6677), at Sunset Towers, is a seductive hideaway evoking its glamorous Hollywood history. The Ritz-Carlton Marina del Rey's **Jer-ne** (☎ 310/823–1700) excels with its colorful design and whimsical, globe-trotting menu. Celebrated Italian chef Gino Angelini didn't hesitate locating his sophisticated West Hollywood restaurant, **La Terza** (☎ 323/782–8384), at the Orlando Hotel.

Cut (☎ 310/276–8500), Wolfgang Puck's latest venture, brings a steakhouse to the Regent Beverly Wilshire.

The Ritz-Carlton Huntington Hotel & Spa is packed with amenities, but the cuisine at **The Dining Room** (☎ 626/577–2867) is reason enough to go.

–Roger J. Grody

ders toward the bar. The French-influenced Southeast Asian menu might include lemongrass-scented bouillabaisse or salmon in a ginger emulsion. From the restaurateur's "secret kitchen," in which only family members are allowed, comes colossal tiger prawns and whole Dungeness crab simmered in sake, chardonnay, and cognac. ⊠ *9646 Santa Monica Blvd., Beverly Hills* ☎ *310/205–8990* ♧ *Reservations essential* ▭ *AE, DC, MC, V* ☺ *Closed Sun. No lunch Sat.*

Century City

FRENCH

★ **$$$–$$$$**

✕ **La Cachette.** Owner-chef Jean-François Meteigner developed a following while cooking at L'Orangerie and Cicada. At his own restaurant, he combines traditional French fare—foie gras, Provençal bouillabaisse, rack of lamb—with a lighter, more modern cuisine reflected in dishes like roasted Maine cod with a passion fruit–ginger–plum sauce. A dressy (by L.A. standards) crowd makes sure that this elegant, flower-filled *cachette* (little hiding place) doesn't stay hidden. ⊠ *10506 Santa Monica Blvd., Century City* ☎ *310/470–4992* ♧ *Reservations essential* ▭ *AE, D, DC, MC, V* ☺ *No lunch weekends.*

Hollywood

AMERICAN

$$–$$$$

✕ **Musso & Frank Grill.** Liver and onions, lamb chops, goulash, shrimp Louis salad, gruff waiters—you'll find all the old favorites here in Hollywood's oldest restaurant. A film-industry hangout since it opened in 1919, Musso & Frank still welcomes the working studio set to its maroon faux-leather booths. Great breakfasts are served all day, but the kitchen's famous "flannel cakes" (pancakes) are served only until 3 PM. ✉ *6667 Hollywood Blvd., Hollywood* ☎ *323/467–7788* 🖃 *AE, DC, MC, V* ✆ *Closed Sun. and Mon.*

AMERICAN–CASUAL
¢

✕ **Pink's Hot Dogs.** Orson Welles ate 18 of these hot dogs in one sitting, and you, too, will be tempted to order more than one. The chili dogs are the main draw, but the menu has expanded to include an Ozzy Osbourne Dog (a spicy Polish sausage with cheese, grilled onions, guacamole, and tomatoes). Since 1939 Angelenos and tourists alike have been lining up to plunk down some modest change for one of the greatest guilty pleasures in L.A. Pink's is open until 3 AM on weekends. ✉ *709 N. La Brea Ave., Beverly–La Brea* ☎ *323/931–4223* ⌂ *Reservations not accepted* 🖃 *No credit cards.*

CONTEMPORARY
$$–$$$$

✕ **Ammo.** This hip canteen proves that the designers and photographers who are regulars here know good taste in food as well as fashion. Lunch might be French lentil salad; a prosciutto, mozzarella, and arugula sandwich; or a really great burger. Start dinner with one of the kitchen's market-fresh salads or yellowfin tuna carpaccio with avocado, then follow up with a grilled pork chop with caramelized apples. The crisp, minimal setting is cool but not chilly. ✉ *1155 N. Highland Ave., Hollywood* ☎ *323/871–2666* 🖃 *AE, MC, V* ✆ *No dinner Sun.*

$$–$$$$

✕ **Vert.** Here Wolfgang Puck turns his hand to a mix of traditional brasserie and contemporary California dishes. You'll find French classics like a *tarte flambé* (a rustic onion tart from Alsace) and *moules marinières* (mussels cooked with shallots and white wine) alongside grilled tuna and a hefty Gorgonzola-topped burger. Though it's hidden in the Hollywood & Highland center, the restaurant is always busy; the bar is backlighted in the namesake color (green), and the walls sprout abstract sculptures. ✉ *6801 Hollywood Blvd., Hollywood* ☎ *323/491–1300* ⌂ *Reservations essential* 🖃 *AE, D, DC, MC, V* ✆ *No lunch weekends.*

ITALIAN
$–$$$

✕ **Cheebo.** Everyone from kid-toting yuppies to tattooed and pierced rockers adores this Hollywood pizza joint splashed with orange paint, which offers much more than its signature rectangular pies (called "slabs"). The sandwiches (think pressed pork and Manchego cheese or the half-pound mesquite-grilled beef burger with cheddar) are crowd-pleasers, and the pastas are top-drawer. The more ambitious dinner menu includes cedar plank–grilled salmon and steak frites. ✉ *7533 Sunset Blvd., Hollywood* ☎ *323/850–7070* 🖃 *AE, MC, V.*

MEXICAN
$–$$

✕ **El Cholo.** The first of what's now a chain, this landmark south of Hollywood has been packing them in since the '20s. A hand-painted adobe ceiling and an outdoor patio with a fountain create a partylike atmosphere, which the bar's legendary margaritas can only enhance. The fare includes all kinds of Cal–Mex standards, including tacos, chicken enchiladas, *carnitas* (shredded fried pork), and, from July through October, their famous green-corn tamales. ✉ *1121 S. Western Ave., Hollywood* ☎ *323/734–2773* 🖃 *AE, DC, MC, V.*

$–$$

✕ **Guelaguetza.** This seek-it-out spot with lively musical accompaniment serves the complex but not overpoweringly spicy cooking of Oaxaca,

Local Chains Worth Stopping For

IT'S SAID THAT THE DRIVE-IN BURGER JOINT was invented in L.A., probably to meet the demands of an ever-mobile car culture. What's certain is that the fast food in L.A. tastes better than fast food elsewhere. For burgers—the original signature food of the metropolis—there are a couple chains worth noting. Cars line up at all hours at **In-N-Out Burger** (many locations), still a family-owned operation (and very possibly America's original drive-thru) whose terrific made-to-order burgers are revered by locals. There's even a "secret" menu with variations (for instance, "Animal style," "4x4") designed primarily for outrageous appetites. The company's Web site lists explanations for the most popular.

Tommy's sells a delightfully sloppy chili burger; the original location (2575 Beverly Blvd., Los Angeles, 213/ 389–9060) is a no-frills culinary landmark. For rotisserie chicken that will make you forget the Colonel forever, head to **Zankou Chicken** (5065 Sunset Blvd., Hollywood, 323/ 665–7845), a small chain noted for its golden crispy-skinned birds, potent garlic sauce, and Armenian specialties. Homesick New Yorkers will appreciate **Jerry's Famous Deli** (10925 Weyburn Ave., Westwood, 310/208– 3354), where the massive menu includes all the classic deli favorites. With a lively bar scene, good barbecued ribs, and contemporary takes on old favorites, the more upscale **Houston's** (202 Wilshire Blvd., Santa Monica, 310/576–7558) is a popular local hangout. And **Señor Fish** (422 E. 1st St., Downtown, 213/ 625–0566; other locations) is known for its healthy Mexican seafood specialties, such as scallop burritos and ceviche tostadas.

---

one of Mexico's most renowned culinary capitals. The standouts are the moles, whose intense flavors come from intricate combinations of nuts, seeds, spices, chilies, and bitter chocolate. But be sure to check out barbecued-goat tacos or pizzalike *clayudas* topped with white cheese and *tasajo* (dried beef) or *cecino* (chili-marinated pork) and chorizo. ⊠ *3337½ W. 8th St., Mid-City* ☎ *213/427–0601* ▭ *MC, V.*

MIDDLE EASTERN
¢–$

✗ **Zankou Chicken.** Forget the Colonel. Zankou's aromatic, Armenian-style rotisserie chicken with perfectly crisp, golden skin is one of L.A.'s truly great budget meals. It's served with pita bread, veggies, hummus, and unforgettable garlic sauce. If this doesn't do it for you, try the kebabs, falafel, or sensational *shawarma* (spit-roasted lamb or chicken) plates. ⊠ *5065 W. Sunset Blvd., Hollywood* ☎ *323/665–7845* ⌲ *Reservations not accepted* ▭ *No credit cards.*

RUSSIAN
$$

✗ **Uzbekistan.** Brightly colored murals lend a fittingly folksy air to this restaurant, which serves a mix of Russian and Central Asian cuisine. Start with any of the meat dumplings—*samsa* (baked), *manti* (steamed), or *pelmeni* (boiled)—and go on to eggplant *Samarkand* (sautéed with tomatoes and garlic), *lulya-kebab* (skewered ground lamb), or *akurma lagman* (a stir-fry of beef, noodles, and vegetables seasoned with cumin).

The atmosphere is upbeat—on those evenings when a combo plays, customers have been known to burst into their favorite songs. ⊠ *7077 Sunset Blvd., Hollywood* ☎ *323/464–3663* ▤ *MC, V.*

SEAFOOD
★ **$$$–$$$$**

✗ **Providence.** Since its highly anticipated opening in 2005, Providence has drawn considerable praise for the work of chef-owner Michael Cimarusti, formerly of downtown's Water Grill. Obsessed with quality and freshness, the meticulous chef maintains a network of specialty purveyors, some of whom tip him off to their catch before it even hits the dock. This exquisite seafood then gets the Cimarusti treatment of French technique, traditional American themes, and Asian accents. For instance, you might find foie gras paired with lobster, arctic char with a black tea infusion, or crayfish with sweetbreads, asparagus, and chive *espuma* (foam). ⊠ *5955 Melrose Ave., Hollywood* ☎ *323/460–4170* ▤ *AE, DC, MC, V* ☉ *No lunch Mon.,Tues., and weekends.*

SOUTHERN
$–$$

✗ **Roscoe's House of Chicken 'n Waffles.** The name of this casual eatery may strike you as odd, but don't be put off. Roscoe's is *the* place for real down-home Southern cooking. Just ask the patrons, who drive from all over L.A. for Roscoe's bargain-price fried chicken, wonderful waffles (which, by the way, turn out to be a great partner for fried chicken), tender chicken livers, and grits. Although Roscoe's has the intimate feel of a smoky jazz club, those musicians hanging out here are just taking five. ⊠ *1514 N. Gower St., Hollywood* ☎ *323/466–7453* ⌲ *Reservations not accepted* ▤ *AE, D, DC, MC, V.*

STEAK
$$$–$$$$

✗ **Dakota.** After years of neglect, the Hollywood Roosevelt Hotel got a face-lift and suddenly turned into party central for young Hollywood celebs. The opening of its contemporary steak house, though, is far from a superficial change, as it balances hipness with the spirit of an American classic. Snack on truffled Parmesan fries, tuck into a rib eye with *chimichurri* sauce, or try Scottish salmon in a sweet chili barbecue sauce. The decor follows a dress code of lots of leather and suede. ⊠ *Hollywood Roosevelt Hotel, 7000 Hollywood Blvd., Hollywood* ☎ *323/769–8888* ⌲ *Reservations essential* ▤ *AE, D, DC, MC, V.*

THAI
$–$$

✗ **Chan Dara.** Known for its head-turning waitresses and its rock-and-roll/showbiz crowd, this casual eatery is on the edge of charming Larchmont Village, the commercial district serving ritzy Hancock Park. Try any of the noodle dishes, especially those with crab and shrimp. Also on the extensive menu are *satay* (skewered meats with a tangy peanut sauce); Thai barbecued chicken, pork, or beef; and deep-fried whole catfish. In summer stop by for the seasonal mango tart. ⊠ *310 N. Larchmont Blvd., Hollywood* ☎ *323/467–1052* ▤ *AE, D, DC, MC, V.*

Los Feliz & Silver Lake

CARIBBEAN
$–$$

✗ **Cha Cha Cha.** Off-the-beaten-path Cha Cha Cha attracts an eclectic crowd. It's hip but neither pretentious nor overly trendy. A giant map on the wall suggests the restaurant's Caribbean influences. You can sit in the small dining room or on the enclosed tropical-à-la-Carmen-Miranda patio. Standard options include empanadas, Jamaican jerk chicken or pork, curried shrimp, fried plantain chips, and paella. Sangría is the drink of choice. ⊠ *656 N. Virgil Ave., Los Feliz* ☎ *323/664–7723* 🖃 *AE, D, DC, MC, V.*

CONTEMPORARY
$$–$$$

✗ **Vermont.** This stylish eatery kicked off a renaissance on its colorful namesake street. Vaulted ceilings, Persian rugs, and fresh flowers make the interior graceful and inviting. The modern menu starts with

the likes of crab cakes with mustard aïoli or beet salad with Roquefort, then moves on to crispy whitefish, braised lamb shank, and vegetarian risotto. Vermont is excellent for quiet business lunches, but the livelier dinner hour—an alluring lounge adjoins the restaurant—attracts everyone from Armani-clad studio suits to bohemian artists. ⊠ *1714 N. Vermont Ave., Los Feliz* ☎ *323/661–6163* 🖃 *AE, D, DC, MC, V* ☻ *No lunch weekends.*

ECLECTIC
¢–$$

✗ **Fred 62.** Funky L.A. chef-restaurateur Fred Eric has created a tongue-in-cheek take on the American diner. The usual burgers and shakes are joined by choices like grilled salmon, Southern-style brisket and a "Poorest Boy" sandwich (crispy fried chicken, onions, and rémoulade on a French roll). Toasters sit on every table and breakfasts consist of tofu scrambles, "Bearded Mr. Frenchy," and "punk tarts." Like the neighborhood itself, nobody is out of place here, with everybody from button-down businesspeople to tattooed musicians showing up at some point during its 24/7 cycle. ⊠ *1850 N. Vermont Ave., Los Feliz* ☎ *323/667–0062* ⌲ *Reservations not accepted* 🖃 *AE, DC, MC, V.*

INDIAN
$$

✗ **Tantra.** As the name suggests, this is a very sexy place, accented with bold colors, dramatic silk lighting fixtures, and a hanging curtain of oxidized metal. But it's not just about attitude: the regional Indian cuisine is first-rate, including mango-and-cheese samosas, *khoormani gosht* (lamb in apricot-curry sauce), tandoori monkfish, and a drink called *nimboo-paani* (sweetened lime juice with saffron). For dessert, snap up the chocolate-filled samosas. The adjoining bar-lounge has become a popular local haunt. ⊠ *3705 Sunset Blvd., Silver Lake* ☎ *323/663–8268* ⌲ *Reservations essential* 🖃 *AE, MC, V* ☻ *Closed Mon. No lunch.*

ITALIAN
$–$$

✗ **Trattoria Farfalla.** This reliable, brick-walled trattoria brought Los Feliz out of the spaghetti-and-meatballs mode in the '80s and has remained a favorite ever since, thanks in part to its fair prices. Regulars tend to order the Caesar salad on a pizza-crust bed, roasted herbed free-range chicken, and penne *alla Norma* (studded with rich, smoky eggplant). ⊠ *1978 N. Hillhurst Ave., Los Feliz* ☎ *323/661–7365* 🖃 *AE, DC, MC, V* ☻ *No lunch Sun.*

MEXICAN
¢

✗ **Yuca's Hut.** Blink and you'll miss this place, whose reputation far exceeds its size. It's known for carne asada, carnitas, and *cochinita pibil* (Yucatán-style roasted pork) tacos and burritos. This is a fast-food restaurant in the finest tradition—independent, family-owned, and sticking to what it does best. The liquor store next door sells lots of Coronas to Hut customers soaking up the sun on the makeshift parking-lot patio. There's no chance of satisfying a late-night craving, though; it closes at 6 PM. ⊠ *2056 N. Hillhurst Ave., Los Feliz* ☎ *323/662–1214* ⌖ *Reservations not accepted* ▭ *No credit cards* ☽ *Closed Sun.*

VIETNAMESE
$–$$

✕ **Gingergrass.** In the heart of increasingly trendy Silver Lake, traditional Vietnamese favorites emerge from this café's open kitchen, sometimes with a California twist. Consider classic crispy-skinned imperial rolls (filled with chicken, veggies, or crab and shrimp, served with lettuce and mint for wrapping), variations on *pho* (Vietnam's ubiquitous noodle soup), and Cal-light versions of *bánh mì* (baguette sandwiches that fuse French and Southeast Asian traditions), along with a refreshing basil-lime elixir. ⊠ *2396 Glendale Blvd., Silver Lake* ☎ *323/644–1600* ⌖ *Reservations not accepted* ▭ *AE, D, MC, V.*

West Hollywood

AMERICAN
$$–$$$$

✕ **Jar.** A contemporary sense of style layered with a retro, woodsy warmth frames the classic American cooking of chef Suzanne Tracht. The menu at this bastion of comfort cuisine represents a hit parade of all-American favorites. After crab deviled eggs, consider steak, rack of lamb, or a massive slab of tender pot roast that's a world apart from the one Mom used to make. You can finish with rich chocolate pudding or banana cream pie. ⊠ *8225 Beverly Blvd., south of West Hollywood* ☎ *323/655–6566* ▭ *AE, DC, MC, V* ☽ *No lunch Mon.–Sat.*

CAJUN–CREOLE
¢–$

✕ **Gumbo Pot.** Although not exactly "down by the bayou," this order-at-the-counter café does serve a mean gumbo rich in shrimp, chicken, and andouille sausage. It's also the place for New Orleans–style po'boy and *muffaletta* sandwiches, jambalaya, and *beignets* (the Big Easy's take on doughnuts). ⊠ *Farmers Market, 6333 W. 3rd St., Fairfax District* ☎ *323/933–0358* ⌖ *Reservations not accepted* ▭ *MC, V.*

CHINESE
¢–$$

✕ **Mandarette.** This inviting café, filled with intricate cherrywood accents and antique Chinese drums, began as a casual spin-off of the Mandarin in Beverly Hills, but the concept has outlasted its originator. Start with cucumber salad with spicy peanut dressing, scallion pancakes, or curried chicken dumplings before indulging in *kung pao* scallops or crispy sesame beef. ⊠ *8386 Beverly Blvd., Los Angeles* ☎ *323/655–6115* ▭ *AE, DC, MC, V.*

CONTEMPORARY
$$$$
Fodor'sChoice
★

✕ **Sona.** Young, intense David Myers—one of the city's most exciting and unpredictable chefs—shoots the works. A slab of polished granite topped with an exquisite orchid arrangement anchors the sleek dining room. The prix-fixe tasting menus are a good choice here, since they allow you to try several of Myers's unique dishes. An occasional item is too precious, but the successful dishes win out. Highlights might include Tahitian squash soup with amaretto duck confit agnolotti and chai foam, Australian sea bass with brandade-stuffed piquillo peppers, fennel confit, and lemon butter, and an elaborate three-course dessert tasting. ⊠ *401 N. La Cienega Blvd., West Hollywood* ☎ *310/659–7708* ⌖ *Reservations essential* ▭ *AE, D, DC, MC, V* ☽ *Closed Sun. No lunch.*

2

$$$–$$$$ ✕ **Asia de Cuba.** This hot spot, whose staying power on the fickle Sunset Strip is impressive, shares the Mondrian hotel's city views with Sky Bar, once the most exclusive nightspot in town. Prices are high but portions are often large enough to share. Signature dishes include a picadillo-style tuna tartare dubbed "Tunapica," "Lobster Mai Tai" flavored with rum and coconut, mojito-glaze steak, and Alaskan butterfish with Cuban black beans and edamame (soybean) salad. The cross-cultural experiments in the kitchen may yield mixed results, but the scene is always entertaining. ✉ *8440 Sunset Blvd., West Hollywood* ☎ *323/848–6000* ⚜ *Reservations essential* ▭ *AE, DC, MC, V.*

$$$–$$$$ ✕ **Grace.** After years of moving through the city's top kitchens, chef Neal Fraser is doing his best cooking yet in a place of his own. He mixes textures and contrasting flavors in dishes like risotto with pumpkin, sea urchin, and sweet shrimp; barbecued wild salmon in enoki mushroom sauce; and wild boar tenderloin in violet mustard sauce. Imaginative doughnuts, like a maple-glazed doughnut with candied walnuts and apple cider ice cream, highlight the compelling dessert menu. ✉ *7360 Beverly Blvd., south of West Hollywood* ☎ *323/934–4400* ⚜ *Reservations essential* ▭ *AE, MC, V* ⊘ *Closed Mon. No lunch.*

★ **$$$–$$$$** ✕ **Lucques.** Once silent-film star Harold Lloyd's carriage house, this brick building has morphed into a chic restaurant that's a big hit with the younger, well-heeled set. And the veggie-intense cooking by Suzanne Goin is smart, too: consider Italian heirloom pumpkin soup with sage and chestnut cream, pancetta-wrapped Alaskan cod with red potatoes, crushed grapes and crème fraîche, and short ribs with horseradish cream. ✉ *8474 Melrose Ave., West Hollywood* ☎ *323/655–6277* ⚜ *Reservations essential* ▭ *AE, D, DC, MC, V* ⊘ *No lunch Sun.*

★ **$$$** ✕ **Table 8.** It's worth seeking out this charmer, hidden behind a nondescript facade shared by a tattoo parlor upstairs. The subtly lighted dining room is cozy and sophisticated, and the sexy lounge makes a good place to sip a watermelon martini while snacking on truffled Gruyère fondue. Native Angeleno chef Govind Armstrong keeps it relatively straightforward but never boring, with a market-driven California cuisine free of excessive ethnic influences. Items such as wild Alaskan salmon with red onion *soubise* (a classic cream sauce) and salt-crusted porterhouse are simply delicious. ✉ *7661 Melrose Ave., south of West Hollywood* ☎ *323/782–8258* ⚜ *Reservations essential* ▭ *AE, D, MC, V* ⊘ *Closed Sun. No lunch.*

DELI ✕ **Canter's.** This granddaddy of L.A. delicatessens (it opened in 1928)
¢–$$ cures its own corned beef and pastrami and has an in-house bakery. It's not the best deli in town, but it's a true classic and open 24/7. Next door is the Kibitz Room, where there's live music every night. ✉ *419 N. Fairfax Ave., Fairfax District* ☎ *323/651–2030* ⚜ *Reservations not accepted* ▭ *MC, V.*

FRENCH ✕ **L'Orangerie.** Usually reserved for the most special of occasions, this
★ **$$$$** is the closest L.A. gets to a fine Parisian dining room. The regal setting channels the spirit of Versailles with soaring French doors, exquisite Louis XIV appointments, and dramatic floral arrangements. Chefs come and go, but standards are maintained at the highest levels. Current special-

ties include a "crème brûlée" of foie gras with green apple mousse, walnut-crusted squab with a date beignet, and tea-marinated sea bass. Service is attentive but not overbearing. ⊠ *903 N. La Cienega Blvd., West Hollywood* ☎ *310/652–9770* ⌂ *Reservations essential* ▣ *AE, D, DC, MC, V* ☉ *Closed Mon. No lunch.*

★ **$$$–$$$$** ✕ **Ortolan.** Despite a galaxy of crystal chandeliers, Ortolan attempts to take the pretentiousness out of haute cuisine. Here designer jeans outnumber designer suits. But ex-L'Orangerie chef Christophe Emé keeps up an impeccable standard in the kitchen with dishes such as Napa Valley escargots with lettuce emulsion and Parmesan crust, roasted squab with date puree, and what may be the silkiest foie gras in the city. Many creations are dramatically presented on stone slabs or in unique vessels. The one thing even Emé can't get you is the namesake game bird; it's endangered. ⊠ *8338 W. 3rd St., south of West Hollywood* ☎ *323/653–3300* ⌂ *Reservations essential* ▣ *AE, MC, V* ☉ *Closed Sun. No lunch.*

$$–$$$ ✕ **Mimosa.** If you're craving a perfect Provençal meal, turn to chef Jean-
FodorśChoice Pierre Bosc's menu. There's *salade Lyonnaise,* served with a poached
★ egg, bouillabaisse, and fillet of sole *au pistou* (with basil-garlic paste). The atmosphere is that of a classic bistro, with mustard walls, cozy banquettes, and jars of cornichons and olives delivered to every table on arrival. ⊠ *8009 Beverly Blvd., West Hollywood* ☎ *323/655–8895* ▣ *AE, DC, MC, V* ☉ *Closed Sun. and Mon. No lunch.*

GREEK ✕ **Sofi.** Hidden down a narrow passageway is this friendly little taverna
$$–$$$ where you can sample such Greek favorites as dolmades, *taramasalata* (a creamy, salty dip made from fish roe), spanakopita, and souvlaki. The casually smart dining room is more than comfortable, but try to sit outside on the lovely bougainvillea-shaded patio. All that's missing is a view of the Aegean Sea. ⊠ *8030¾ W. 3rd St., south of West Hollywood* ☎ *323/651–0346* ▣ *AE, D, DC, MC, V* ☉ *No lunch Sun.*

ITALIAN ✕ **Dolce Enoteca e Ristorante.** With a look-at-me decor, complete with fire
$$–$$$$ boxes and dramatic wine displays, this celebrity-owned restaurant is well known for its star-gazing opportunities. However, it also appeals to serious diners and, with a 40-plus page wine list, to oenophiles. The contemporary Italian cuisine includes dishes such as saffron risotto with veal, gold sea bass with fennel, and osso buco. To keep costs down, consider the enoteca menu, which lists interesting small plates. ⊠ *8284 Melrose Ave., south of West Hollywood* ☎ *323/852–7174* ⌂ *Reservations essential* ▣ *AE, D, DC, MC, V* ☉ *No lunch.*

$–$$$$ ✕ **Angelini Osteria.** You might not guess it from the modest, rather con-
FodorśChoice gested dining room, but this is one of L.A.'s most celebrated Italian restau-
★ rants. The key is chef-owner Gino Angelini's thoughtful use of superb ingredients, evident in dishes such as mussels and clams in garlic, parsley, and white wine and pumpkin tortelli with butter, sage, and asparagus. An awesome lasagna verde, inspired by Angelini's grandmother, is not to be missed. Whole branzino, crusted in sea salt, and unusual specials (e.g., tender veal kidneys) consistently impress. An intelligent selection of mostly Italian wines complements the menu, and desserts like the open-face marmalade tart are baked fresh daily. ⊠ *7313 Beverly Blvd., Beverly–La Brea* ☎ *323/297–0070* ▣ *AE, MC, V* ☉ *Closed Mon. No lunch weekends.*

$$–$$$ ✕ **Ca' Brea.** Starters make the meal at this reliable spot—try baked goat cheese wrapped in pancetta and served atop a Popeye-size mound of spinach. Among the entrées, look for the osso buco or the lamb chops with black-truffle and mustard sauce. The cozy loft is ideal for those seeking privacy. ✉ *346 S. La Brea Ave., Beverly-La Brea* ☎ *323/938–2863* ▭ *AE, D, DC, MC, V* ☾ *Closed Sun. No lunch Sat.*

JAPANESE
$$$–$$$$ ✕ **Koi.** Celebs and trendoids vastly outnumber sushi purists here. The sexy, understatedly exotic design includes several intimate spaces, both indoors and out—surely this is positive feng shui. The buzzing crowd indulges in well-executed dishes such as crispy rice topped with spicy tuna, Kobe beef carpaccio with crispy shiitake mushrooms and yuzu vinaigrette, and sesame-crusted lobster tail. ✉ *730 N. La Cienega Blvd., West Hollywood* ☎ *310/659–9449* 🥢 *Reservations essential* ▭ *AE, MC, V* ☾ *No lunch weekends.*

★ $$$–$$$$ ✕ **Wa Sushi & Bistro.** Founded by three alums from trendsetting Matsuhisa, Wa offers a more personalized experience with comparable high-quality sushi and intriguing Japanese cooking. Particularly rewarding are dishes enhanced with French-inspired sauces. For instance, Chilean sea bass could be napped with a port reduction, while uni-topped Santa Barbara prawns are dosed with beurre blanc. Although casual, Wa's second-story hillside location allows for seductive city views from a small handful of tables dressed up with linen and candles. ✉ *1106 N. La Cienega Blvd., West Hollywood* ☎ *310/854–7285* 🥢 *Reservations essential* ▭ *AE, MC, V* ☾ *No lunch.*

$$–$$$ ✕ **Yabu.** Soba's the name of the game here—you can choose from more than three dozen varieties of hot or cold soba preparations—but the menu extends far beyond these freshly made buckwheat noodles. The inner courtyard's grove of timber bamboo is a nice backdrop for grilled yellowtail collar, soup scented with *matsutake* mushrooms (prized for their mysteriously musty essence) and *toro* (tuna belly) sushi or sashimi. Yabu's proximity to the Beverly Center makes it a welcome alternative to the mall's chain restaurants. ✉ *521 N. La Cienega Blvd., West Hollywood* ☎ *310/854–0400* ▭ *AE, D, DC, MC, V* ☾ *No lunch Sun.*

MEDITERRANEAN
★ $$$–$$$$ ✕ **Campanile.** Chef-owner Mark Peel has mastered the mix of robust Mediterranean flavors with homey Americana. Occupying a 1926 building that once housed the offices of Charlie Chaplin, Campanile is one of L.A.'s most acclaimed and beloved restaurants. Appetizers may include sweetbread ravioli with pancetta and lobster, while grilled snapper with Meyer lemon aïoli and prime rib with tapenade appear as entrées. For dessert, consider a pecan-caramel tart or chocolate beignets. Thursday night, grilled cheese sandwiches are a huge draw, as the beloved five-and-dime classic morphs into creations like goat cheese and marinated fennel on walnut toast. For an ultimate L.A. experience, come for weekend brunch on the enclosed patio. ✉ *624 S. La Brea Ave., Miracle Mile* ☎ *323/938–1447* 🥢 *Reservations essential* ▭ *AE, D, DC, MC, V* ☾ *No dinner Sun.*

$$–$$$
Fodor's Choice
★ ✕ **A.O.C.** Since it opened in 2002, this restaurant and wine bar has revolutionized dining in L.A., pioneering the small-plate format that has now swept the city. The space is dominated by a long, candle-laden bar

serving more than 50 wines by the glass. There's also an L.A. rarity, a charcuterie bar. The tapaslike menu is perfectly calibrated for the wine list; you could pick duck confit, smoked trout, an indulgent slab of pork *rillettes* (a sort of pâté), or just plunge into one of the city's best cheese selections. Named for the acronym for Appellation d'Origine Contrôlée, the regulatory system that ensures the quality of local wines and cheeses in France, A.O.C. upholds the standard of excellence. ⊠ *8022 W. 3rd St., south of West Hollywood* ☎ *323/653–6359* ⌖ *Reservations essential* ▭ *AE, MC, V* ⊗ *No lunch.*

SPANISH
$$

✕ **Cobras & Matadors.** A bustling storefront spot, Cobras & Matadors hits the mark with numerous appetizers and tapas, among them traditional gazpacho, Galician-style grilled octopus with salsa verde, and sautéed green lentils with Serrano ham. Larger plates may include roast game hen with Catalan sweet-and-sour sauce or chorizo in red wine with white beans. There's no wine list here, but you can buy a bottle from the owner's wine shop next door, where the intriguing inventory is almost exclusively Spanish, or bring your own for a modest corkage fee. ⊠ *7615 Beverly Blvd., south of West Hollywood, Beverly-La Brea* ☎ *323/932–6178* ▭ *MC, V* ⊗ *No lunch.*

STEAK
$$–$$$$

✕ **The Palm.** All the New York elements are present at this West Coast replay of the famous Manhattan steak house—mahogany booths, tin ceilings, a boisterous atmosphere, and New York–style, no-nonsense waiters rushing you through your cheesecake (flown in from the Bronx). This is where you'll find the biggest and best lobster, good steaks, prime rib, chops, great French-fried onion rings, and paper-thin potato slices. When writers sell a screenplay, they celebrate with a Palm lobster. ⊠ *9001 Santa Monica Blvd., West Hollywood* ☎ *310/550–8811* ▭ *AE, DC, MC, V* ⌖ *Reservations essential* ⊗ *No lunch weekends.*

Downtown

AMERICAN
$$–$$$

✕ **Engine Co. No. 28.** A restored 1912 fire station, where everything down to the original brass sliding pole has been preserved, now rushes out solid, old-fashioned comfort food. The long bar is a popular hangout for downtown workers not eager to hit the rush-hour freeways. The kitchen does a fine job with crab cakes, chili, macaroni and cheese, and thick slabs of terrific meat loaf. Specials showcase recipes inspired by firehouse cooking across the country. ⊠ *644 S. Figueroa St., Downtown* ☎ *213/624–6996* ▭ *AE, DC, MC, V* ⊗ *No lunch weekends.*

AMERICAN–
CASUAL
¢–$
Fodor'sChoice
★

✕ **Philippe the Original.** Not only is this L.A.'s oldest restaurant (1908), but it may also be where the French dip sandwich originated. Here you can get one made with beef, pork, ham, lamb, or turkey on a freshly baked roll; the house hot mustard is as famous as the sandwiches. Philippe earns its reputation by maintaining its traditions, from sawdust on the floor to long, wooden tables where customers can sit and socialize. The home cooking includes hearty breakfasts, chili, pickled eggs, and an enormous pie selection. The best bargain: a cup of java for only 9¢! ⊠ *1001 N. Alameda St., Downtown* ☎ *213/628–3781* ⌖ *Reservations not accepted* ▭ *No credit cards.*

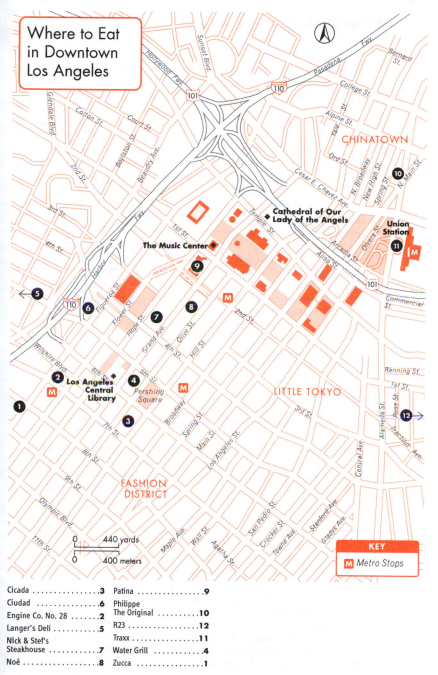

Where to Eat in Downtown Los Angeles

CHINATOWN

Cathedral of Our Lady of the Angels

The Music Center

Union Station

LITTLE TOKYO

Los Angeles Central Library

Pershing Square

FASHION DISTRICT

0 — 440 yards
0 — 400 meters

KEY

Ⓜ *Metro Stops*

Good Morning, L.A.

IN L.A., many a big-screen megahit has been conceived over a breakfast of yogurt and granola or huevos rancheros. At **Hugo's** (✉ 8401 Santa Monica Blvd., West Hollywood ☎ 323/654-3993), one of the city's top morning destinations, breakfast specialties include pumpkin pancakes and "Pasta Mama" (pasta scrambled with eggs, garlic, and Parmesan cheese). A favorite of Hollywood heavy-hitters is **Gardens** (✉ Four Seasons Hotel, 300 S. Doheny Dr., Beverly Hills ☎ 310/273-2222), where an occasional dollop of caviar turns up on the breakfast menu. But for a thoroughly unpretentious L.A. AM experience, head over to the Westside's **John O'Groats** (✉ 10516 W. Pico Blvd., West L.A. ☎ 310/204-0692), where the good old-fashioned American breakfasts are accompanied by signature homemade biscuits.

In Pasadena, folks line up outside **Marston's** (✉ 151 E. Walnut St. ☎ 626/796-2459), a cozy bungalow.

Over in Century City a modest café called **Clementine** (✉ 1751 Ensley Ave. ☎ 310/552-1080) reels in fans with fresh scones and buttermilk biscuit egg-and-ham sandwiches. City Hall power brokers convene over eggs Benedict or USDA Prime roast beef hash at **Pacific Dining Car** (✉ 1310 W. 6th St. ☎ 213/483-6000), a venerable downtown steak house, or at **The Original Pantry Café** (✉ 877 S. Figueroa St., Downtown ☎ 213/972-9279), both open all night. In Beverly Hills, New York expats huddle at **Nate 'n' Al's** (✉ 414 N. Beverly Dr. ☎ 310/274-0101) over matzo brei or corned beef hash. And for a truly authentic Japanese breakfast—complete with *natto* (a gooey fermented soybean product difficult for Westerners to appreciate), head to **A Thousand Cranes** (✉ 120 S. Los Angles St. ☎ 213/253-9255), a serene garden restaurant at Little Tokyo's New Otani Hotel.

CONTEMPORARY
$$$

✗ **Noé.** This surprising hotel restaurant, a short walk from Disney Hall, has a patio with striking downtown views. You might start with a ginger–butternut squash "cappuccino" or king crab and asparagus rolls with sesame-honey dressing, then move on to duck with a roasted pear and parsnip puree or Scottish salmon with Madras curry oil, all presented with artistic flourishes that may include a flute of mango frappé. ✉ *Omni Los Angeles Hotel, 251 S. Olive St., Downtown* ☎ *213/356–4100* ⟐ *Reservations essential* ▭ *AE, D, DC, MC, V* ☉ *Closed for lunch.*

★ **$$–$$$**

✗ **Traxx.** Hidden inside historic Union Station, this intimate restaurant is an art deco delight. Its linen-topped tables spill out onto the main concourse. Chef-owner Tara Thomas's menu gussies up popular favorites; for example, crab cakes come with chipotle rémoulade, while striped bass gets a hit of caramelized fennel and coriander vinaigrette. The jacaranda-shaded courtyard is a local secret. The well-stocked bar, occupying what was originally the station's telephone room, is just across the concourse. ✉ *Union Station, 800 N. Alameda St., Downtown* ☎ *213/625–1999* ▭ *AE, D, MC, V* ☉ *Closed Sun. No lunch Sat.*

2

DELICATESSEN
$

✗ **Langer's Deli.** With fluorescent lighting and Formica tables, Langer's has the look of a no-frills Jewish deli back in New York. The draw here is the hand-cut pastrami, which is relatively lean, peppery, and robustly flavorful—those who swear it's the best in town have a strong case. Some regulars opt for the legendary #19 (pastrami with Swiss and coleslaw piled high on twice-baked rye), but purists prefer it straight up with Russian dressing. The neighborhood is rough around the edges, but the nearby metro station brings plenty of businesspeople here from the heart of downtown. ⊠ *704 S. Alvarado St., Downtown* ☎ *213/483–8050* ⚇ *Reservations not accepted* 🖃 *MC, V* ⊘ *Closed Sun. No dinner.*

FRENCH
$$$$
Fodor'sChoice
★

✗ **Patina.** In a bold move, chef-owner Joachim Splichal moved his flagship restaurant from Hollywood to downtown's striking Frank Gehry–designed Walt Disney Concert Hall. The contemporary space, surrounded by a rippled "curtain" of rich walnut, is an elegant, dramatic stage for the acclaimed restaurant's contemporary French cuisine. Specialties include seared foie gras with Pear William ice cream, wild pheasant breast with juniper berry sauce, and a formidable *côte de boeuf* for two, carved tableside. Finish with a hard-to-match cheese tray and sensual desserts. ⊠ *Walt Disney Concert Hall, 141 S. Grand Ave., Downtown* ☎ *213/972–3331* ⚇ *Reservations essential* 🖃 *AE, D, DC, MC, V* ⊘ *No lunch weekends.*

ITALIAN
★ **$$–$$$$**

✗ **Cicada.** Cicada, certainly one of the most romantic and architecturally dramatic dining venues in L.A., occupies the ground floor of the 1928 art deco Oviatt Building. The glass doors are Lalique, carved maple columns soar two stories to a gold leaf ceiling, and from the balcony, a glamorous bar overlooks the spacious dining room. "Modern Italian" best describes the menu: shrimp ravioli in curry sauce, Maine lobster crepes, and braised veal shank with dried-fruit risotto. ⊠ *617 S. Olive St., Downtown* ☎ *213/488–9488* ⚇ *Reservations essential* 🖃 *AE, DC, MC, V* ⊘ *Closed Sun. No lunch.*

$$–$$$

✗ **Zucca.** Here superchef-restaurateur Joachim Splichal turns his attention to Italian cuisine, leavening sophistication with earthy flavors. The Murano glass chandeliers and mural of a Venetian carnival scene energize the seductive but noisy dining room. You can opt for dishes like pumpkin tortelloni—*zucca*, after all, is squash in Italian—with butter-sage sauce, osso buco, and a whole Mediterranean-style *branzino* (sea bass). This spot's a good option for pretheater dining. ⊠ *801 S. Figueroa St., Downtown* ☎ *213/614–7800* ⚇ *Reservations essential* 🖃 *AE, D, DC, MC, V* ⊘ *No lunch weekends.*

JAPANESE
$$–$$$$

✗ **R23.** A few blocks east of Little Tokyo in the artsy loft district, this redbrick, beamed dining room was carved out of a former railroad loading dock. This surprisingly peaceful and visually stunning place is at its best with sashimi, sushi, and *chirashi sushi* ("scattered sushi," with toppings layered on vinegar rice rather than formed into rolls). Deceptively simple preparations such as flash-fried blue crabs and grilled yellowtail tuna are also well done, but the complicated, sauced dishes fall behind. ⊠ *923 E. 2nd St., Downtown* ☎ *213/687–7178* 🖃 *AE, DC, MC, V* ⊘ *Closed Sun. No lunch Sat.*

LATIN
$$–$$$

✗ **Ciudad.** The colorful interior perfectly complements the new-wave culinary tour of the Americas offered by celebrity chefs Mary Sue Milliken and Susan Feniger. Ordering a selection of appetizers is the way to go here. Start off with a Brazilian *caipirinha* or Cuban *mojito* cocktail; then tuck into starters like Bolivian sweet corn tamales, Colombian *arepas* (corn cakes stuffed with sausage) or Peruvian ceviche. Entrées include tamarind-glazed salmon and an Argentine steak with garlicky *chimichurri* sauce. ⊠ *445 S. Figueroa St., Downtown* 🕾 *213/486–5171* 🖃 *AE, MC, V* ⊗ *No lunch weekends.*

SEAFOOD
★ **$$$–$$$$**

✗ **Water Grill.** There's a bustling, enticing rhythm here as platters of glistening shellfish get whisked from the oyster bar to the cozy booths. Chef David LeFevre's menu shows off his slow-cooking skills. Entrées such as olive oil–poached salmon with a mushroom vinaigrette and slow-steamed Alaskan halibut with kalamata olive puree exemplify his light, expert touch. Excellent desserts and a fine wine list round out this top-notch experience. ⊠ *544 S. Grand Ave., Downtown* 🕾 *213/891–0900* 🖰 *Reservations essential* 🖃 *AE, DC, MC, V* ⊗ *No lunch weekends.*

STEAK
$$$–$$$$

✗ **Nick & Stef's Steakhouse.** The beef palace of restaurateurs Joachim and Christine Splichal, named after their twin boys, has been so successful they've replicated the concept in other cities. The restaurant is modern, but elements of the traditional steak house—cozy booths, crisp white linen, wood accents—remain. The choice steaks come from a glassed-in, on-site aging chamber; build up your order by deciding among a dozen sauces and an equal number of potato side dishes. The wine list, deep in California reds, is predictably strong. ⊠ *330 S. Hope St., Downtown* 🕾 *213/680–0330* 🖰 *Reservations essential* 🖃 *AE, MC, V* ⊗ *No lunch weekends.*

Coastal & Western Los Angeles

Bel Air

AMERICAN
$$$–$$$$

✗ **Vibrato Grill, Jazz, etc.** Co-owned by trumpeter Herb Albert, Vibrato takes a high-road approach to a jazz club: this is a stylish, acoustically perfect venue where every table has a line of sight to the stage. The kitchen is as notable as the music; it turns out contemporary American fare such as surf-and-turf tartare (ahi and prime beef) and coffee-rubbed Kurobuta pork chop (Kurobuta is a dark, richly marbled pork). The art on the walls was painted by the Grammy winner himself. ⊠ *2930 Beverly Glen Cir., Bel Air* 🕾 *310/474–9400* 🖰 *Reservations essential* 🖃 *AE, DC, MC, V* ⊗ *No lunch.*

CONTEMPORARY
★ **$$$–$$$$**

✗ **Hotel Bel-Air.** This secluded hotel's restaurant spills into a lush garden, with a terrace overlooking a pond patrolled by swans. A meal at this special-occasion spot will make you feel like a Hollywood insider—keep an eye out for celebs. But the restaurant's not just a pretty face; look for seasonal appetizers such as seared scallops and crispy sweetbreads with cauliflower cream or the signature tortilla soup. Entrées could include poached Maine lobster, Kobe beef paired with foie gras, or grilled rack of lamb. The hotel also hosts a superlative high tea, and Sunday brunch on the terrace can be magical. ⊠ *701 Stone Canyon Rd., Bel Air* 🕾 *310/ 472–5234* 🖰 *Reservations essential* 🖃 *AE, DC, MC, V.*

Culver City

CONTEMPORARY
★ $$

✕ **Beacon.** Trendsetting chef Kazuto Matsusaka—his resume includes Spago, Chinois on Main, and Buddha Bar in Paris—has opened this unpretentious restaurant in Culver City. Here he specializes in a Pacific Rim cuisine that's refreshingly grounded and restrained. His alluring menu offers crispy fried oysters wrapped in lettuce with a tartar sauce, a pastrylike "pizza" layered with wasabi mayo and ahi tuna, grilled hanger steak, delicate miso-glazed black cod, and green-tea cheesecake. The expansive space is casual and fun (and a bit noisy), fueling the revitalization of this sleepy Westside community. ⊠ *3280 Helms Ave., adjacent to Culver City* ☎ *310/838–7500* ⌨ *Reservations essential* ▭ *AE, MC, V* ☾ *No dinner Mon. No lunch Sun.*

FRENCH
$$–$$$

✕ **Bistro de l'Hermitage.** The charming looks of this bistro near the Kirk Douglas Theatre would lend it credibility on a Parisian side street. Its menu (including a chalkboard of nightly specials) maintains its reputation, with French classics prepared quite well for this side of the Atlantic. Start with traditional escargots or foie gras terrine, then move on to duck confit or filet mignon. You might end with a cheese plate or a tarte Tatin (apple tart). ⊠ *9727 Culver Blvd., Culver City* ☎ *310/815–8222* ⌨ *Reservations essential* ▭ *AE, D, DC, MC, V* ☾ *Closed Sun. No dinner Mon.*

Los Angeles International Airport

CONTEMPORARY
$$–$$$$

✕ **Encounter.** If you're flying to L.A., you can begin or end your trip with a stop by the dramatic Theme Building for a meal with a runway view. Designers from Walt Disney Imagineering whipped up the intergalactic atmosphere. Choices such as tuna tartare, Peking-style duck, and roasted chicken with a mustard cream sauce certainly beat airplane fare. The place, with its colorful, futuristic design and close encounters with rumbling 747s, is a delight for kids of all ages. ⊠ *209 World Way, LAX* ☎ *310/215–5151* ▭ *AE, MC, V.*

Malibu

ITALIAN
$–$$$

✕ **Tra di Noi.** The name means "among us," and Malibu natives are trying to keep this simple *ristorante* just that—a local secret. Regular customers and film celebrities turn up here, but it's also a great place to bring kids. Nothing fancy or *nuovo* on the menu, just hearty lasagna, freshly made pasta, chicken and veal dishes, and fresh salads. An Italian buffet is laid out for Sunday brunch. ⊠ *3835 Cross Creek Rd., Malibu* ☎ *310/456–0169* ▭ *AE, MC, V.*

JAPANESE
$$$–$$$$

✕ **Nobu Malibu.** At famous chef-restaurateur Nobu Matsuhisa's coastal outpost, a casually chic clientele swarms over morsels of the world's finest fish. In addition to stellar sushi, Nobu serves many of the same ingenious specialties offered at his flagship, Matsuhisa. You'll find exotic species of fish artfully accented with equally exotic South American peppers, ultratender Kobe beef, and a broth perfumed with rare matsutake mushrooms. ⊠ *3835 Cross Creek Rd., Malibu* ☎ *310/317–9140* ⌨ *Reservations essential* ▭ *AE, DC, MC, V* ☾ *No lunch.*

MEDITERRANEAN
$$–$$$$

✕ **Beau Rivage.** One of the few Malibu restaurants with a view of the beach and ocean, this romantic Mediterranean villa–style dining room

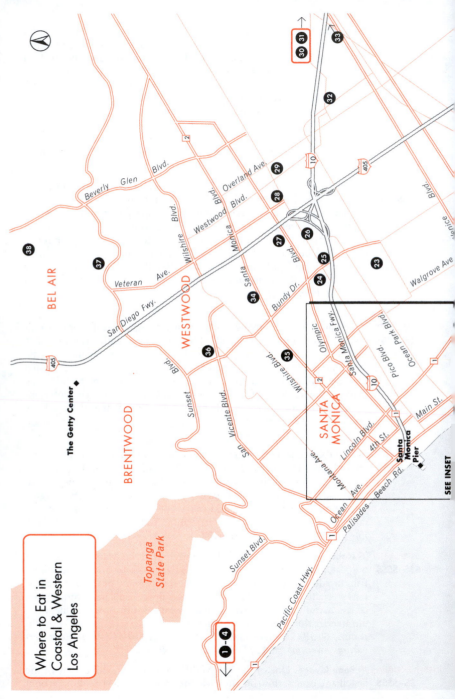

Where to Eat in
Coastal & Western
Los Angeles

BEL AIR

BRENTWOOD

WESTWOOD

SANTA
MONICA

The Getty Center

Topanga
State Park

SEE INSET

Santa
Monica
Pier

Streets and roads

Beverly Glen Blvd.
Wilshire Blvd.
Westwood Blvd.
Overland Ave.
Santa Monica Blvd.
Veteran Ave.
San Diego Fwy.
Sunset Blvd.
San Vicente Blvd.
Bundy Dr.
Wilshire Blvd.
Olympic
Santa Monica Fwy.
Pico Blvd.
Ocean Park Blvd.
Main St.
Lincoln Blvd.
4th St.
Montana Ave.
Ocean Ave.
Palisades Beach Rd.
Pacific Coast Hwy.
Walgrove Ave.
Venice Blvd.

405

2

10

PACIFIC OCEAN

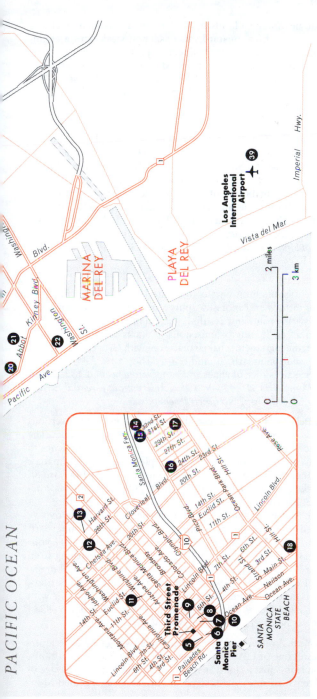

has copper domes and lush landscaping. The expansive menu includes filet mignon with a three-mustard sauce, salmon steak with a champagne-raspberry sauce, and a strong lineup of pastas, risotto, and gnocchi. In contrast to that of some trendier Malibu haunts, the staff here is warm and welcoming. ✉ *26025 Pacific Coast Hwy., Malibu* ☎ *310/456–5733* ⚲ *Reservations essential* 🖃 *AE, D, DC, MC, V* ⊙ *No lunch Mon.–Sat.*

Pacific Palisades

AMERICAN-CASUAL

$$$–$$$$

✕ **Gladstone's Malibu.** Gladstone's is one of the most popular restaurants along the southern California coast; its demand has even spawned a sister restaurant in Universal Studios' CityWalk, whose lack of beachfront makes it far less attractive. The food is notable mostly for its Brobdingnagian portions: giant bowls of crab chowder, mounds of steamed clams, and the famous mile-high chocolate cake, which can easily feed a small regiment. The real reason to visit Gladstone's is the glorious vista of sea, sky, and beach. It's also a good breakfast spot. ✉ *17300 Pacific Coast Hwy., at Sunset Blvd., Pacific Palisades* ☎ *310/454–3474* 🖃 *AE, D, DC, MC, V.*

Santa Monica

AMERICAN

$$

✕ **Violet.** Twentysomething chef-owner Jared Simons, with his anti-establishment tattoos and mohawk, puts a new spin on the neighborhood bistro with promising results. The small-plates menu, which Simons describes as "eating promiscuously," kicks comfort food up a notch with terrific ingredients: baked macaroni with Gruyère cheese and Serrano ham, venison meatballs, and braised short ribs. All this is bolstered by an eclectic choice of wines and handcrafted beers. ✉ *3221 Pico Blvd., Santa Monica* ☎ *310/453–9113* ⚲ *Reservations essential* 🖃 *AE, D, MC, V* ⊙ *Closed Mon. No lunch weekends.*

AMERICAN-CASUAL

$–$$

✕ **Broadway Deli.** The name tells just half the story. This lively, cavernous place is a cross between a European brasserie and an upscale diner. The huge menu goes way beyond corned-beef and pastrami sandwiches to include pizzas, an ostrich burger, shepherd's pie, even duck enchiladas. Breads are baked on-site, and there's also a kids' menu. ✉ *1457 3rd St. Promenade, Santa Monica* ☎ *310/451–0616* ⚲ *Reservations not accepted* 🖃 *AE, MC, V.*

¢–$

✕ **The Counter.** Angelenos still adore the venerable Apple Pan, but they've also embraced this upscale, contemporary burger-joint counterpart. Here, you can select beef, turkey, or veggie patties, then specify your preferred cheeses, toppings, one of 17 different sauces (anything from honey-mustard to peanut), and bun (or, for carb counters, a "burger-in-a-bowl"). Even with the slick surroundings and wild combinations, the Counter is a nostalgic reminder of L.A.'s ongoing love affair with the burger. ✉ *2901 Ocean Park Blvd., Santa Monica* ☎ *310/399–8383* ⚲ *Reservations not accepted* 🖃 *AE, MC, V.*

CONTEMPORARY

★ $$$–$$$$

✕ **Chinois on Main.** A once-revolutionary outpost in Wolfgang Puck's repertoire, this is still one of L.A.'s most crowded—and noisy—restaurants. The jazzy interior is just as loud as the clientele. The happy marriage of Asian and French cuisines yields signature dishes such as grilled Mon-

CLOSE UP

A Table Outdoors

IT'S NOVEMBER OR MARCH, but the request is still possible: "We'd like a table outdoors." Thanks to L.A.'s weather, you can eat outside nearly year-round, and there are dozens of alfresco options from Malibu to Pasadena. Some restaurants give you an ocean view, some evoke Provençal herb gardens, and others line up sidewalk tables for great people-watching. If an outdoor table is your goal, be sure to specify one when making reservations.

Begonias, burbling fountains, and candlelighted tables fill the patio at **Il Cielo** (⌧ 9018 Burton Way, Beverly Hills ☎ 310/276–9990). On a moonlight night, it's romantic enough to elicit the unthinkable from a confirmed bachelor.

For stunning coastal views, head to **Geoffrey's** (⌧ 27400 Pacific Coast Hwy., Malibu ☎ 310/457–1519), where you'll be sandwiched between surf and stars. The olive tree–shaded patio

at **Dominick's** (⌧ 8715 Beverly Blvd., West Hollywood ☎ 310/652–2335) draws a new generation of wannabe Rat Packers.

The best tables at **Michael's** (⌧ 1147 3rd St., Santa Monica ☎ 310/451–0843), the early landmark of California cuisine, are in its enchanting garden. At **Chez Mimi** (⌧ 246 26th St., Santa Monica ☎ 310/393–0558), simple French fare is served on a brick patio with vine-covered trellises and trees entwined with lights.

For a true star-gazing experience, consider **The Ivy** (⌧ 113 N. Robertson Blvd., Beverly Hills ☎ 310/274–8303), whose picket fence–enclosed patio is often filled with famous faces. To watch bustling Old Pasadena pass before you, head to **Mi Piace** (⌧ 25 E. Colorado Blvd. ☎ 626/795–3131), a popular Italian spot.

–Roger J. Grody

2

golian lamb chops with wok-fried vegetables, Shanghai lobster with spicy ginger-curry sauce, and Cantonese duck with fresh plum sauce. ⌧ *2709 Main St., Santa Monica* ☎ *310/392–9025* ⌚ *Reservations essential* ▭ *AE, D, DC, MC, V* ⊗ *No lunch Sat.–Tues.*

★ **$$$–$$$$** ✕ **JiRaffe.** The wood-clad, two-story dining room with ceiling-high windows is as handsome as the menu is tasteful. Chef-owner Raphael Lunetta turns out seasonal appetizers such as a delicate roasted-tomato tart or a roasted-beet salad with caramelized walnuts and dried bing cherries. They're worthy preludes to main dishes such as a truly memorable crispy-skinned salmon with parsnip puree, braised fennel, and sweet balsamic reduction. ⌧ *502 Santa Monica Blvd., Santa Monica* ☎ *310/917–6671* ⌚ *Reservations essential* ▭ *AE, DC, MC, V* ⊗ *No lunch.*

$$$–$$$$ ✕ **Wilshire.** The woodsy patio at Wilshire is one of the most coveted spaces on the L.A. dining circuit—its candlelight, firelight, and gurgling fountain lure in a hip crowd beneath a cloud of canvas. The cuisine emphasizes organic market-fresh ingredients. You might try red kuri squash–Asian pear soup with cinnamon cream, a rack of lamb with farro, or roasted chicken with Swiss chard and chanterelles.

There's a lively bar scene here, too. ✉ *2454 Wilshire Blvd., Santa Monica* ☎ *310/586–1707* ⌕ *Reservations essential* 🖃 *AE, D, DC, MC, V* ⊘ *No lunch weekends.*

$$–$$$$ ✕ **Josie.** Done in understated taupe hues with generously spaced tables, this rather sophisticated establishment feels like it belongs in San Francisco instead of more laid-back L.A. You'll find outstanding game dishes here, such as wild boar tenderloin and venison in burgundy-pear sauce or a foie gras–topped buffalo burger. ✉ *2424 Pico Blvd., Santa Monica* ☎ *310/581–9888* ⌕ *Reservations essential* 🖃 *AE, D, MC, V* ⊘ *No lunch.*

FRENCH ✕ **Mélisse.** In a city where informality reigns, this is one of L.A.'s more
$$$$ dressy—but not stuffy—restaurants. A crystal chandelier hangs in the
Fodor's Choice dining room, above well-spaced tables topped with flowers and Limo-
★ ges china. The garden room loosens up with a stone fountain and a retractable roof. Chef-owner Josiah Citrin enriches his modern French cooking with seasonal California produce. Consider seared foie gras with figs poached in sweet wine and huckleberry sorbet, lobster Thermidor, or seared venison in chocolate sauce. The cheese cart is loaded with domestic and European selections. ✉ *1104 Wilshire Blvd., Santa Monica* ☎ *310/395–0881* ⌕ *Reservations essential* 🖃 *AE, D, DC, MC, V* ⊘ *Closed Sun. and Mon. No lunch.*

ITALIAN ✕ **Valentino.** Renowned as one of the country's top Italian restaurants,
$$$$ Valentino has a truly awe-inspiring wine list. The list itself goes on for
Fodor's Choice more than 120 pages and the cellar overflows with 100,000 bottles. In
★ the 1970s, suave owner Piero Selvaggio introduced L.A. to his exquisite modern Italian cuisine, and he continues to impress guests with dishes like spaghetti with garlic and *bottarga* (tuna roe), sautéed sweetbreads in a *vin santo* (sweet wine) sauce, and quails in a chardonnay–black truffle sauce. The menu recently changed to a prix-fixe format, starting at a reasonable $45. ✉ *3115 Pico Blvd., Santa Monica* ☎ *310/829–4313* ⌕ *Reservations essential* 🖃 *AE, DC, MC, V* ⊘ *Closed Sun. No lunch Sat. and Mon.–Thurs.*

★ **$$–$$$$** ✕ **Drago.** Native Sicilian Celestino Drago's home-style fare is carefully prepared and attentively served in stark designer surroundings. White walls and white linen–covered tables line both sides of a floating service station dressed up with a towering arrangement of fresh flowers. The menu adds sophisticated finishes to rustic foundations in dishes such as pappardelle tossed in a pheasant and morel mushroom sauce, squid-ink risotto, or pan-roasted rabbit in sweet-and-sour sauce. ✉ *2628 Wilshire Blvd., Santa Monica* ☎ *310/828–1585* 🖃 *AE, DC, MC, V* ⊘ *No lunch weekends.*

MEXICAN ✕ **Border Grill.** This busy restaurant's massive, colorful murals—a bit
★ **$$–$$$** primeval—are a perfect complement to modern interpretations of ancient Mayan dishes such as *cochinita pibil* (achiote-marinated pork). Other favorites include a wild-mushroom quesadilla, vinegar-and-pepper-grilled turkey, and daily ceviche specials. Celebrity chef-owners Mary Sue Milliken and Susan Feniger display a passion for Mexican cuisine here, but they do mellow the dishes to suit a broad audience. ✉ *1445 4th St., Santa Monica* ☎ *310/451–1655* 🖃 *AE, D, DC, MC, V.*

PAN-ASIAN
$$

✕ **Typhoon.** Owner Brian Vidor, who traveled the world as a rock musician and naturalist, brings home some of his favorite gastronomic experiences to this restaurant. If you can tear your attention away from the windows overlooking the Santa Monica Airport flight paths, the exhibition kitchen, and the mirrored weather map above a crowded bar, you can embark on a culinary grand tour of Asia. You'll find sashimi from Japan, samosas from India, and curries from Thailand. For even more adventure—or bragging rights—you can order stir-fried crickets, Manchurian mountain ants, or scorpions, all beautifully seasoned. ✉ *3221 Donald Douglas Loop S, Santa Monica* ☎ *310/390–6565* ⌾ *Reservations essential* ▭ *AE, DC, MC, V* ⊘ *No lunch Sat.*

SEAFOOD
$$–$$$$

✕ **The Lobster.** Anchoring the beach end of the festive Santa Monica Pier, the Lobster usually teems with locals and tourists alike, who come here for the hip scene, the great view, and the comfort seafood of chef Allyson Thurber. Start with lobster cocktail with tarragon-lemon aïoli, lobster salad with sweet corn pancakes, spicy snow crab soup, or fried calamari. For entrées, the restaurant's namesake is the main attraction—you'll find both Maine and Pacific spiny varieties—but dishes like king salmon in herb sauce are equally satisfying. Weather permitting, request a table on the terrace, both for the views and for an escape from the high-decibel interior. ✉ *1602 Ocean Ave., Santa Monica* ☎ *310/458–9294* ⌾ *Reservations essential* ▭ *AE, D, MC, V.*

$$–$$$$

✕ **Ocean Avenue Seafood.** Operating since 1946, this cavernous restaurant isn't right on the water, but the Pacific is just across the street—ask for a table by the window for an ocean view. Low ceilings, dim lighting, well-spaced tables, and attentive service create a close-knit mood. There are plenty of lobster dishes, but other popular choices include paella, Kona Coast big-eye tuna, and prime steaks. The oyster bar offers a dizzying selection. ✉ *1401 Ocean Ave., Santa Monica* ☎ *310/394–5669* ▭ *AE, D, DC, MC, V.*

STEAK
$$$–$$$$

✕ **BOA Steakhouse.** This is not your father's steak house; businessmen and somber mahogany have been traded in for a fun-loving crowd in an avant-garde room with multicolor lighting fixtures. But you can still start with a prawn cocktail or a traditional Caesar salad prepared tableside before slicing your Languiole knife into a dry-aged prime New York strip or rib eye. Although the beef may not need any frills, you could opt for an embellishment such as a blue cheese or a cabernet reduction sauce. ✉ *101 Santa Monica Blvd., Santa Monica* ☎ *310/899–4466* ⌾ *Reservations essential* ▭ *AE, D, DC, MC, V.*

Venice

AMERICAN
$$–$$$

✕ **James' Beach.** With a menu that's more old-school American than those at most of its peers in now-trendy Venice, this coastal hot spot seems just right for a seaside lunch or supper, inside or out on the patio. The menu focuses on classics like meat loaf, chicken potpie, and fried chicken, but you can also find tuna tartare, ceviche, and scallops with truffle sauce. If you're so inclined, sip your dessert wine between shots at the billiard table in a bungalow behind the patio. It's open until 1 AM Thursday–Saturday. ✉ *60 N. Venice Blvd., Venice* ☎ *310/823–5396* ▭ *AE, D, DC, MC, V* ⊘ *No lunch Mon. and Tues.*

CONTEMPORARY
$$$

✕ **Joe's Restaurant.** In what was originally a turn-of-the-20th-century beach house, Joe Miller has created the definitive neighborhood restaurant with a citywide reputation. His French-influenced California cooking puts fresh ingredients to imaginative uses. Start with tuna tartare or five kinds of heirloom tomatoes, each paired with a different sauce, and continue with Kurobuta pork cassoulet or potato-crusted red snapper in port wine sauce. For dessert, try the kirsch-flavored Boston cream pie. Lunch is a terrific value—all entrées are $15 or less and come with soup or salad. ✉ *1023 Abbott Kinney Blvd., Venice* ☎ *310/399–5811* ▭ *AE, D, DC, MC, V* ☉ *Closed Mon.*

> **WORD OF MOUTH**
>
> "I've been going [to the Apple Pan] since I was a kid, and now bring my kid here. . . .Sometimes it's nice when nothing changes, especially in L.A., where everything does."
>
> —Shannon

FRENCH
$$

✕ **Lilly's French Café & Bar.** Forget *haute* cuisine—Lilly's celebrates the robust flavors of French regional and bistro cooking. Start with *flamiche* (a northern French goat cheese and leek tart) or that bistro warhorse, escargots with garlic-herb butter. Then go on to duck breast with wild cherry sauce or entrecôte with béarnaise sauce and finish with profiteroles or a lemon tart. The daily prix-fixe lunch is a great value: soup or salad plus a glamorous sandwich or omelet for about $10. ✉ *1031 Abbot Kinney Blvd., Venice* ☎ *310/314–0004* ▭ *AE, MC, V.*

ITALIAN
★ **$–$$$**

✕ **Piccolo.** A block from Venice Beach, but closer in spirit to the real Venezia, this charmer's sophisticated fare is a refreshing departure from the interchangeable menus at most L.A. trattorias. Here you might start with duck prosciutto drizzled with mild Gorgonzola cream, followed by porcini risotto studded with blueberries or *cassunziei* (beet-stuffed ravioli with poppy seeds in a brown butter and cheese sauce), a specialty of the owner's hometown in northern Veneto. Main courses include pistachio-crusted lamb loin with garlic-herb puree. ✉ *5 Dudley Ave., Venice* ☎ *310/314–3222* ▭ *AE, D, MC, V* ☉ *No lunch.*

West Los Angeles

AMERICAN–
CASUAL
★ **¢**

✕ **The Apple Pan.** A burger-insider haunt since 1947, this unassuming joint with a horseshoe-shape counter—no tables here—turns out one heck of a good burger topped with Tillamook cheddar, plus a hickory burger with barbecue sauce. You'll also find great fries and, of course, an apple pie good enough to name a restaurant after (although many regulars argue that the banana cream deserves the honor). Be prepared to wait. ✉ *10801 W. Pico Blvd., West L.A.* ☎ *310/475–3585* ⊜ *Reservations not accepted* ▭ *No credit cards* ☉ *Closed Mon.*

BARBECUE
$–$$$

✕ **Mr. Cecil's California Ribs.** A rib-loving movie-studio exec opened this eatery in a tiny, circular hatbox of a building. The meaty, tender St. Louis–style ribs are particularly outstanding, with a spirited but not overpowering sauce. Aficionados of pecan pie should also keep this place in mind. Plus, it's the only rib joint in town where you can order a bottle of Château Lafite Rothschild! ✉ *12244 W. Pico Blvd., West L.A.* ☎ *310/442–1550* ▭ *AE, MC, V.*

CHINESE
$–$$$

✕ **JR Seafood.** Westsiders once had to drive to Monterey Park to get shrimp in spicy salt; now they can get this and other favorites right in their own neck of the woods. The Hong Kong–style restaurant serves all the Chinese seafood house standards—seafood soup, rock cod in garlic sauce, kung pao scallops—that are so plentiful in the San Gabriel Valley but so scarce in these parts. The service can be slow, but as long as the shrimp keeps coming, no one seems to mind. ⊠ *11901 Santa Monica Blvd., West L.A.* ☎ *310/268–2463* ▤ *MC, V.*

CUBAN
$–$$

✕ **Versailles.** Despite its decidedly no-frills dining room, Versailles's respectable, bargain-price Cuban food has people lining up outside the door. Most are crazy about the citrusy *mojo*-marinated chicken seasoned with loads of garlic. Others prefer oxtail, *ropa vieja* (shredded beef), or paella. ⊠ *10319 Venice Blvd., West L.A.* ☎ *310/558–3168* ⌲ *Reservations not accepted* ▤ *AE, D, MC, V.*

INDIAN
★ **$–$$**

✕ **Bombay Cafe.** Some of the dishes at Bombay Cafe are strictly authentic, others have been lightened up a bit to suit southern California sensibilities, and a few are truly innovative. Regulars (and there are many) swear by the chili-laden lamb *frankies* (burritolike snacks sold by vendors on the beaches of Bombay) and *sev puri* (wafers topped with onions, potatoes, and chutneys). ⊠ *12021 Pico Blvd., West L.A.* ☎ *310/473–3388* ▤ *MC, V* ⊗ *No lunch weekends.*

ITALIAN
$$–$$$$

✕ **Vincenti.** A big open kitchen with a mammoth, revolving rotisserie is the heart of this handsome, white-tile restaurant. Off the spit come roasted pork, veal, venison, or whole spit-roasted fish such as arctic char. A rustic sausage plate or prosciutto paired with creamy *burrata* cheese are fine ways to begin, and pasta courses (like gnocchi with rabbit ragù) are always skillfully prepared. ⊠ *11930 San Vicente Blvd., Brentwood* ☎ *310/207–0127* ⌲ *Reservations essential* ▤ *AE, MC, V* ⊗ *Closed Sun. No lunch Sat. and Mon.–Thurs.*

$$–$$$

✕ **Cucina Paradiso.** With its linen-draped tables, attentive service, and marble-topped wine bar, this eager-to-please trattoria feels homey and approachable. The menu bears out that impression with choices like garlicky scampi, porcini risotto, osso buco, and a terrific filet mignon in Gorgonzola cream. During autumn's truffle season, a luxurious perfume wafts through the dining room as dishes are generously topped with shavings of the prized fungus. ⊠ *3387 Motor Ave., West L.A.* ☎ *310/839–2500* ⌲ *Reservations essential* ▤ *AE, D, DC, MC, V* ⊗ *No lunch weekends.*

JAPANESE
$$$–$$$$
Fodor's Choice
★

✕ **Mori Sushi.** Only a small fish logo identifies the facade of this restaurant, but many consider it the best sushi bar in L.A. and Morihiro Onodera one of the great sushi masters in America. The austere whitewashed space stands in contrast to the chef's artful presentations of pristine morsels of seafood, all served on ceramic plates he makes himself. Allow him to compose an entire meal for you—this can be an expensive proposition—and he'll send out eye-popping presentations of sushi or sashimi accented with touches of rare sea salts, yuzu, and freshly ground wasabi, as well as intricately conceived salads, housemade tofu, and soups. ⊠ *11500 Pico Blvd., West L.A.* ☎ *310/479–3939* ▤ *AE, MC, V* ⊗ *Closed Sun. No lunch Sat.*

★ **$$-$$$$** ✕ **Kiriko.** Here in "Little Tokyo West," this understated restaurant with contemporary art and rough-timbered sushi bar distinguishes itself from the competition. Friendly chef-owner Ken Namba might send out beautifully marbled salmon, smoked in-house and crowned with caviar, or lightly seared toro topped with a tiny dollop of minced chili. Sea urchin risotto and rice turtle soup provide soul-warming breaks from a parade of beautifully presented, but never overwrought, sushi. Regulars finish with housemade sesame ice cream while contemplating their next visit. ✉ *Olympic Collection, 11301 Olympic Blvd., #102, West L.A.* ☎ *310/ 478–7769* ⌕ *Reservations essential* ▭ *AE, MC, V* ⊗ *Closed Mon. No lunch weekends.*

MEXICAN
★ **$-$$** ✕ **La Serenata Gourmet.** Even now that it has expanded, crowding into this Westside branch of the East L.A. original can be uncomfortable, but the restaurant scores points for its flavorful Mexican cuisine. Pork dishes and moles are delicious, but seafood is the real star—there are chubby *gorditas* (cornmeal pockets stuffed with shrimp), juicy shrimp enchiladas in *tomatillo* sauce, and simply grilled fish that sings with flavor. If your experience with Mexican food has been on the Tex-Mex end of the spectrum, come here to broaden your taste bud horizons. ✉ *10924 W. Pico Blvd., West L.A.* ☎ *310/441–9667* ⌕ *Reservations not accepted* ▭ *AE, D, MC, V.*

$ ✕ **Monte Alban.** This family-owned café serves the subtle cooking of one of Mexico's most respected culinary regions, Oaxaca. Flavors here are intense without being fiery. Try their version of chiles rellenos (bright green chili peppers stuffed with chicken, raisins, and groundnuts); any of the complex moles with chicken, pork, or salmon; or extra-tender stewed goat with toasted avocado leaves. For dessert, there's fried, sliced sweet plantain topped with crème fraîche. ✉ *11927 Santa Monica Blvd., West L.A.* ☎ *310/444–7736* ▭ *AE, DC, MC, V.*

San Fernando Valley

Burbank

CONTEMPORARY
$$ ✕ **Bistro Provence.** The contemporary, French-inspired cooking of chef-owner Miki Zivkovic is waking up the Burbank dining scene. While the restaurant's shopping center location may be less than glamorous, the candlelighted interior is warm and inviting. The daily menu could include sweet tomato and olive risotto, *pissaladière* (a pizzalike tart hailing from Nice), bouillabaisse, or paella. Zivkovic pulls all this off so deftly that the already reasonable prices seem like a steal. ✉ *345 N. Pass Ave., Burbank* ☎ *818/840–9050* ⌕ *Reservations essential* ▭ *AE, MC, V* ⊗ *Closed Sun. No lunch Sat.*

Calabasas

CONTEMPORARY
$$$-$$$$
Fodor'sChoice
★ ✕ **Saddle Peak Lodge.** When you've had enough big-city attitude, head for this romantic retreat in the Santa Monica Mountains—it feels a thousand miles from L.A. What was once a bordello is now a restaurant oozing with rustic elegance. Mounted stag and moose heads watch over roaring fireplaces and mountain views. They also hint at the lodge's specialty: game. Bring out the knives for wood-fired rack of venison, roasted elk

KEY

Ⓜ *Metro Stops*

Where to Eat in the
San Fernando Valley

2

tenderloin with creamy wild-mushroom sauce, and buffalo with béarnaise sauce. The sprawling terrace is an idyllic spot for Sunday brunch. ✉ *419 Cold Canyon Rd., Calabasas* ☎ *818/222–3888* ⌁ *Reservations essential* ▭ *AE, MC, V* ⊗ *Closed Mon. and Tues. No lunch Wed.–Sat.*

North Hollywood

ITALIAN
$$–$$$

✕ **Ca' del Sole.** With antique wood hutches, copper moldings, and a fireplace, this studio-area establishment draws showbiz and nonshowbiz types in search of such classics as pancetta-wrapped quail and pumpkin-filled *mezzelune* in a sauce of butter, sage, and Parmesan. Finish up with a giant hunk of Italian-style cheesecake covered with marinated strawberries. The wine list is solid and moderately priced. Weather permitting, you can sit on the walled patio that, despite its proximity to L.A. traffic, feels wonderfully escapist. ✉ *4100 Cahuenga Blvd., North Hollywood* ☎ *818/985–4669* ▭ *AE, DC, MC, V* ⊗ *No lunch Sat.*

Sherman Oaks

CONTEMPORARY
$$–$$$

✕ **Max.** Chef Andre Guerrero hits his stride with contemporary, Asian-influenced cooking. The dining room butters you up with earth tones, textured wall coverings, and a couple of cozy alcoves. The friendly, professional staff serves shrimp and pork *lumpia* (Filipino spring rolls), delicious little towers of tuna tartare, and tandoori salmon with coriander-mint chutney. ✉ *13355 Ventura Blvd., Sherman Oaks* ☎ *818/784–2915* ⌕ *Reservations essential* ▭ *AE, D, MC, V* ☾ *No lunch.*

★ **$$** ✗ **Café Bizou.** Housed in an old bungalow that complements its casual brand of elegance, Café Bizou is *the* place for fine California-French bistro fare at bargain prices. Sauces are classic, soups are rich (try the luscious lobster bisque), and combinations are creative. If it's on the menu, order the homemade ravioli appetizer, stuffed with lobster and salmon puree. A winning entrée is the sesame seed–coated salmon on potato-pancake triangles. Those who bring their own bottle pay a mere $2 corkage fee. ✉ *14016 Ventura Blvd., Sherman Oaks* ☎ *818/788–3536* ⌕ *Reservations essential* ▭ *AE, D, DC, MC, V.*

Studio City

DELICATESSEN ✗ **Art's Delicatessen.** One of the best kosher-style delis in the city, Art's
★ **$–$$** serves mammoth corned beef and pastrami sandwiches to hungry hordes from the nearby studios. Matzo-ball and sweet-and-sour cabbage soups, chopped liver, and knishes reel in regulars. This is one of the few delis with valet parking. ✉ *12224 Ventura Blvd., Studio City* ☎ *818/762–1221* ⌕ *Reservations not accepted* ▭ *AE, D, DC, MC, V.*

FRENCH ✗ **Pinot Bistro.** This was the first—and probably still the best—of Joachim
★ **$$–$$$** Splichal's chain of Pinot restaurants. The main dining room is standard SoCal, but the bar area is a lovely re-creation of a Parisian bistro, with mustard walls, polished wood, and black-and-white-tile floors. The varied menu pairs French mainstays such as cassoulet and braised lamb shank with modern dishes such as trout tartare with yuzu and cold-poached Atlantic salmon with green apple and curry. For dessert, don't miss the chocolate croissant bread pudding with a bourbon sauce. ✉ *12969 Ventura Blvd., Studio City* ☎ *818/990–0500* ▭ *AE, D, DC, MC, V* ☾ *No lunch weekends.*

JAPANESE ✗ **Asanebo.** Don't let its nondescript minimal location deter you: rela-
$$–$$$$ tively undiscovered Asanebo is one of L.A.'s finest Japanese restaurants.
Fodor'sChoice Once strictly a sashimi bar, Asanebo introduced top-quality sushi to sat-
★ isfy increasing local demand and also offers a wealth of innovative dishes. The affable chefs will introduce you to memorable specialties such as a caviar-topped lobster cocktail and succulent seared toro drizzled with a light garlic cream. ✉ *11941 Ventura Blvd., Studio City* ☎ *818/760–3348* ⌕ *Reservations essential* ▭ *AE, D, DC, MC, V* ☾ *Closed Mon. No lunch weekends.*

Universal City

ECLECTIC ✗ **minibar.** In a cultural limbo land between trendy Hollywood and the
$$–$$$ staid San Fernando Valley, this restaurant appeals to both sides of the divide. The look smacks of a Vegas lounge, with oversize art and bold colors. On the menu you'll find eclectic small plates meant for sharing: duck confit egg rolls, Creole crawfish empanadas, and Marrakesh chicken wings, glazed with an orange-pomegranate reduction sauce. It's virtually impossible to be bored with the extensive cross-cultural menu. ✉ *3413 Cahuenga Blvd. W., near Universal City* ☎ *323/882–6965* ⌕ *Reservations essential* ▭ *AE, MC, V* ☾ *No lunch.*

Pasadena, Glendale & San Gabriel Valley

Glendale

CONTEMPORARY
★ $$

✗ **Bistro Verdu.** The soul of a true neighborhood bistro beams from this low-profile spot, thanks largely to the increasingly inspired cooking of chef-owner Michael Ruiz. A welcoming staff oversees an intimate dining room and adjoining tapas bar. The sophisticated, multidimensional menu spans everything from macaroni and goat cheese to short ribs braised in chocolate stout to venison tenderloin with a nifty bone marrow–Rioja reduction. ✉ *3459 N. Verdugo Rd., Glendale* ☎ *818/541–1532* ⌂ *Reservations essential* ▭ *AE, D, MC, V* ◷ *Closed Mon. No lunch Sat.*

MEXICAN
★ $

✗ **La Cabañita.** Although only minutes from downtown Glendale and Pasadena, this is one of the few "secret" restaurants in the L.A. area. Pretend you've never had Mexican cooking before and savor fresh, thick handmade tortillas either wrapped around *picadillo* (ground beef with raisins, almonds, and cinnamon) or with roasted mild poblano chiles with sour cream and black beans. Then go on to *chuletas* (fall-off-the-bone-tender pork) in a delicate pasilla chili sauce. This is as far from the rice-and-beans routine as you can get. ✉ *3447 N. Verdugo Rd., Glendale* ☎ *818/957–2711* ▭ *AE, MC, V.*

Monterey Park

CHINESE
★ $–$$$$

✗ **Ocean Star.** Reminiscent of Hong Kong's dim sum palaces, this stronghold of Chinese seafood is so vast—it seats 800—that the staff resorts to walkie-talkies. It's known for the quality and freshness of its fish and shellfish, and you're free to select your meal from one of the many aquariums lining the marble walls. Try the boiled-live shrimp with soy-chili dipping sauce, huge scallops served in their shell, king crabs with black-bean sauce, any of the whole steamed fish, or the delicately sautéed snow-pea sprouts. The best way to experience Ocean Star is to bring a whole gang for a dim sum lunch. ✉ *145 N. Atlantic Blvd., Monterey Park* ☎ *626/308–2128* ▭ *MC, V.*

$–$$$

✗ **Lake Spring Shanghai Restaurant.** There are countless good Chinese restaurants in the San Gabriel Valley, but Lake Spring stands out; in fact, it's one of the most renowned Shanghai-style eateries in America. Unlike many of its frenetic, no-frills neighbors, Lake Spring's dining room exudes a refreshing calm. Devotees come for the tender, slow-cooked pork rump; spinach-tinted jade shrimp; cured pork with bamboo-shoot casserole; and plump scallops in garlic sauce. ✉ *219 E. Garvey Ave., Monterey Park* ☎ *626/280–3571* ▭ *MC, V.*

Pasadena

AMERICAN
$–$$$

✗ **Smitty's Grill.** Straightforward American fare is what Smitty's is all about. Black-and-white photos of Joltin' Joe, Ike, and a young Liz Taylor crowd the walls. You can depend on the steaks (half the price of a high-end steak house yet nearly as satisfying), but you'll also find respectable mac and cheese, barbecued ribs, creamed spinach, and corn bread baked in an iron skillet. If you're not in the mood for a fancy meal but don't feel like slumming it, Smitty's is the ideal place. ✉ *110 S. Lake Ave., Pasadena* ☎ *626/792–9999* ⌂ *Reservations essential* ▭ *AE, D, MC, V* ◷ *No lunch Sun.*

AMERICAN–CASUAL
¢–$

✕ **Pie 'N Burger.** A legendary Cal-tech hangout, this place serves up a burger the locals justifiably worship, plus potpies, a bargain lover's steak, traditional fountain drinks, and good pies (especially peach, pecan, or peanut butter). There are only a few tables, but you'll be treated right at a long counter filled with astrophysicists. ⊠ *913 E. California Blvd., Pasadena* ☎ *626/795–1123* ⚐ *Reservations not accepted* ▭ *No credit cards.*

CHINESE
$$–$$$
Fodor'sChoice
★

✕ **Yujean Kang's Gourmet Chinese Cuisine.** Forget any and all preconceived notions of what Chinese food should look and taste like—Kang's cuisine is nouvelle Chinese. Start with tender slices of veal on a bed of enoki mushrooms, topped with a tangle of quick-fried shoestring yams; or sea bass with kumquats and passion-fruit sauce. Even familiar dishes, such as the crispy sesame beef, result in nearly revelatory culinary experiences. Finish off with sweet bean-curd crepes or delicate mandarin orange cheesecake. ⊠ *67 N. Raymond Ave., Pasadena* ☎ *626/585–0855* ▭ *AE, D, DC, MC, V.*

CONTEMPORARY
$$$–$$$$

✕ **Derek's Bistro.** This casually elegant restaurant pioneered contemporary cuisine in what was once strictly meat-and-potatoes territory. Dinner might start with seared foie gras with caramelized mangos or ethereal deep-fried oysters, followed by wild salmon in a mustard beurre blanc or a rosy rack of lamb. Sate your sweet tooth with warm brioche bread pudding with crème anglaise or a refreshing cassis granita. ⊠ *181 E. Glenarm St., Pasadena* ☎ *626/799–5252* ▭ *AE, D, MC, V* ✆ *Closed Mon. No lunch Fri.*

$$$–$$$$
Fodor'sChoice
★

✕ **The Dining Room.** Until the arrival of charismatic chef Craig Strong, there wasn't much to say about this high-price hotel dining room. But Strong brought with him global inspirations and a culinary finesse beyond his years. A perfectionist (he insists, for instance, on importing butter from Normandy), Strong continually surprises with dishes such as ginger-crusted Alaskan halibut in coconut sauce, seared ahi tuna and foie gras in a red wine–raspberry reduction, and cabbage-wrapped pheasant in *salmis* (a classic game ragoût). The chef relishes the opportunity to personalize his cuisine, so consider springing for a customized tasting menu. ⊠ *Ritz-Carlton Huntington Hotel & Spa, 1401 S. Oak Knoll Ave., Pasadena* ☎ *626/577–2867* ▭ *AE, D, DC, MC, V* ✆ *Closed Sun. and Mon. No lunch.*

$$–$$$

✕ **Shiro.** Chef Hideo Yamashiro made quite a splash when he first began serving sizzling whole catfish with a tangy soy-citrus ponzu sauce, and his contemporary, Asian-influenced cooking remains exciting and fresh. Beyond the signature catfish you'll find yellowtail carpaccio with ginger dressing, shrimp with a curry and champagne sauce, and duck with juniper-berry sauce. For a sweet conclusion, try the passion-fruit mousse or the warm chocolate soufflé torte. ⊠ *1505 Mission St., South Pasadena* ☎ *626/799–4774* ⚐ *Reservations essential* ▭ *AE, DC, MC, V* ✆ *Closed Mon. and Tues. No lunch.*

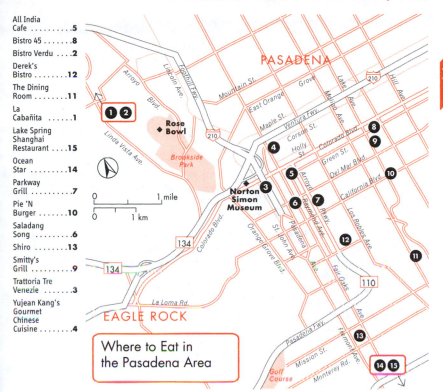

Where to Eat in
the Pasadena Area

2

ECLECTIC
$$–$$$
✗**Parkway Grill.** This ever-popular, influential restaurant (sometimes called the Spago of Pasadena) looks all-American with its brick walls, a carved-wood bar, and a prominent fireplace. The food wanders farther afield, incorporating influences from Italian to Southwestern to Thai. In one sitting you might have black bean soup or a pizza topped with blue cheese–stuffed dates, then Chinese-style roasted crispy duck, and s'mores for dessert. ⊠ *510 S. Arroyo Pkwy., Pasadena* ☎ *626/795–1001* ☏ *Reservations essential* ▭ *AE, DC, MC, V* ⊗ *No lunch weekends.*

FRENCH
$$–$$$$
✗**Bistro 45.** As stylish and sophisticated as anything on the Westside, Bistro 45 blends rustic French cooking—cassoulet, bouillabaisse, tarte tatin—with more modern and fanciful California hybrids, such as seared ahi tuna with a black-and-white-sesame crust. The art deco bungalow has been tailored into a sleek environment. The wine list is among the best in town, and owner Robert Simon regularly hosts lavish winemaker dinners. ⊠ *45 S. Mentor Ave., Pasadena* ☎ *626/795–2478* ☏ *Reservations essential* ▭ *AE, DC, MC, V* ⊗ *Closed Mon. No lunch weekends.*

INDIAN
$–$$
✗**All India Cafe.** Old Pasadena may be the last place you'd expect to find an authentic Indian restaurant, but authentic this is. Ingredients are fresh, and flavors are bold without depending on overpowering spici-

ness. Start with the *bhel puri,* a savory puffed rice-and-potatoes dish. In addition to meat curries and tikkas, there are many vegetarian selections and some hard-to-find items such as the burritolike frankies, a favorite Bombay street food. The prices are as palatable as the meals: a full lunch costs less than $9. ⊠ *39 Fair Oaks Ave., Pasadena* ☎ *626/440–0309* ⊟ *AE, MC, V.*

ITALIAN
★ **$$–$$$$**
✗ **Trattoria Tre Venezie.** An Italian restaurant has to be special to get noticed. This one does it by excelling in specialties from a trio of Italy's northernmost regions along the Austrian border, collectively referred to as Tre Venezie. Sparked with unusual ingredients and sauces, the menu can challenge your preconceptions about Italian food. Start with *jota* (a traditional sweet-and-sour soup) before enjoying the signature smoked pork chop with sauerkraut and a light Gorgonzola sauce. ⊠ *119 W. Green St., Pasadena* ☎ *626/795–4455* ⊟ *AE, DC, MC, V* ☺ *Closed Mon. No lunch Tues. or weekends.*

THAI
$–$$
✗ **Saladang Song.** The owners of Saladang, a standard Thai restaurant next door, concoct a more interesting menu here, going well beyond the usual satays and pad thai. It's a striking Thai-tech pavilion surrounded by outdoor tables and towering, ornamental pierced-steel panels that put this eatery in its own graciously hermetic world. For lunch or dinner, consider the spicy fish cakes or salmon with curry sauce. Or for a rarer treat, come for a Thai breakfast, with *kao-tom-gui* (rice soup with or without various meats and seafood) and *joak* (the Thai-style rice porridge), with sweet potato, taro, and pumpkin. ⊠ *383 S. Fair Oaks Ave., Pasadena* ☎ *626/793–5200* ⊟ *AE, DC, MC, V.*

Where to Stay

WORD OF MOUTH

"L.A. is so vast that [it's] best to decide exactly what you want to see and do and then choose a well-located hotel."

—tracys2cents

"The Beverly Hills geographic area is fairly large, and the general name encompasses some parts of West L.A. and West Hollywood. . . . There are many reasonably priced restaurants in the area, so you can eat well without spending a lot of green. And you are definitely centrally located to most tourist stuff. . . ."

—rjw_lgb_ca

Revised by
Kathy A.
McDonald

LOS ANGELES BEING THE TOWN OF EXCESS, there's no shortage of decadent palaces in which to rest your head. But whether you're going high style or budget, make sure to consider location when selecting your hotel. Planning to hit the beach? Give some thought to Santa Monica. Want to stay out late and enjoy L.A.'s legendary nightlife? Stay in West Hollywood or the Hollywood Boulevard area. For upscale and posh, you can't do better than Beverly Hills. In Pasadena you can enjoy the charm of Old Town and some of the best public gardens in the area. The downtown area, though gaining ground in the tourist department, is still frequented mostly by conventioneers and business travelers. The one thing that's hard to find: a small bed-and-breakfast. The rare standout B&Bs tend to be in Santa Monica, Hollywood, and Pasadena.

With so many lodging selections, Los Angeles hoteliers need to keep up with the Hiltons (so to speak). Virtually all in the $$$ and $$$$ categories have high-speed Internet access in guest rooms and business centers. Some, such as Shutters in Santa Monica and the Regent Beverly Wilshire, have wireless Internet access throughout the property and even poolside. Trendy hotels are also plumping up their outdoor offerings, with tricked-out cabanas and al fresco massages.

Several established properties got extreme makeovers in the past year. The Sunset Tower Hotel is hotelier Jeff Klein's remake of the art deco Argyle. New York's Thompson Hotels made their mark in L.A. with the reinvention of the Hollywood Roosevelt; now a Thompson Beverly Hills is on the drawing boards. The most stylish revamps in 2006 include the Sofitel and Chamberlain, both in West Hollywood; Santa Monica's Huntley and the Sheraton Delfina; and the Luxe Hotel Sunset Boulevard. One of the most dramatic transformations was the Hotel Angeleno, once a Holiday Inn below the Getty Center and now a supermod spot. At this writing, Hyatt planned to undertake a penthouse-to-ballroom renovation in the former Westin Century Plaza in Century City. As for the iconic but closed Ambassador Hotel: it was demolished in 2006 to make way for a school.

Beverly Hills, Century City, Hollywood & West Hollywood

Beverly Hills & Vicinity

$$$$ 🏨 **Beverly Hills Hotel.** Ever since its opening in 1912, the "Pink Palace" has attracted Hollywood's elite. Celebrity guests favor the private bungalows, which come with *all* of life's little necessities (the Presidential bungalow, for example, has its own lap pool and Jacuzzi). Standard rooms are also nothing to sniff at, with original artwork, butler service, Frette linens and duvets, walk-in closets, and huge marble bathrooms. Swiss skincare company La Prairie runs the hotel's swanky day spa, which specializes in de-aging treatments. The Polo Lounge remains an

> ### WORD OF MOUTH
>
> "If you want to do [an] Ironic Hip L.A. stay, might I also recommend the Beverly Hills Hotel? This pink palace still stands out as old Hollywood glamour, and it's still architecturally notable. . . ."
>
> –rjw_lgb_ca

KNOW-HOW

Most hotels have air-conditioning, cable TV, and in-room irons and ironing boards. Those in the moderate and expensive price ranges often have voice mail, coffeemakers, bathrobes, and hair dryers as well. Most also have at least dial-up Internet service in guest rooms, with a 24-hour use fee (though at a few hotels it's free). High-speed wireless access (Wi-Fi) is now common even at budget properties. Southern California's emphasis on being in shape means most hotels have fitness facilities; if the one on-site is not to your liking, ask for a reference to a nearby sports club or gym.

If a particular amenity is important to you, ask for it; many hotels will provide extras upon request. Also double-check your bill at checkout. These days, hotels are fond of tacked-on charges such as a "minibar restocking fee" or cleaning charges for smokers. If a charge seems unreasonable, ask to remedy it at checkout. If you're traveling with pets, note that pet policies do change and some hotels require substantial cleaning fees. A cautionary note to smokers: some hotels are entirely smoke-free, meaning even smoking outdoors is frowned upon or prohibited.

PRICES

Tax rates for the area will add 9% to 15.5% to your bill depending on where in Los Angeles County you stay; some hoteliers tack on energy or occupancy surcharges. Because you'll need a car no matter where you stay in Los Angeles, parking is another expense to consider. Though a few hotels have free parking, most charge for the privilege—and some resorts only have valet parking, with fees as high as $31 per night.

When looking for a hotel, don't write off the pricier establishments immediately. Price categories are determined by "rack rates"—the list price of a hotel room, which is usually discounted. Specials abound, particularly downtown on the weekends. Many hotels have packages that include breakfast, theater tickets, spa services, or exotic rental cars. Pricing is very competitive, so always check out the hotel Web site in advance for current special offers.

Finally, when making reservations, particularly last-minute ones, check the hotel's Web site for exclusive Internet specials or call the hotel directly.

WHAT IT COSTS					
	$$$$	**$$$**	**$$**	**$**	**¢**
FOR 2 PEOPLE	over $325	$200–$325	$125–$200	$75–$125	under $75

The lodgings we list are the top selections of their type in each price category. Price categories are assigned based on the range between the least and most expensive standard double rooms in nonholiday high season, on the European Plan (no meals) unless otherwise noted. Taxes (9%–15.5%) are extra. In listings, we always name the facilities available, but we don't specify whether they cost extra. When pricing accommodations, always ask what's included.

Where to Stay in Beverly Hills, Century City, Hollywood & West Hollywood

KEY

M *Metro Stops*

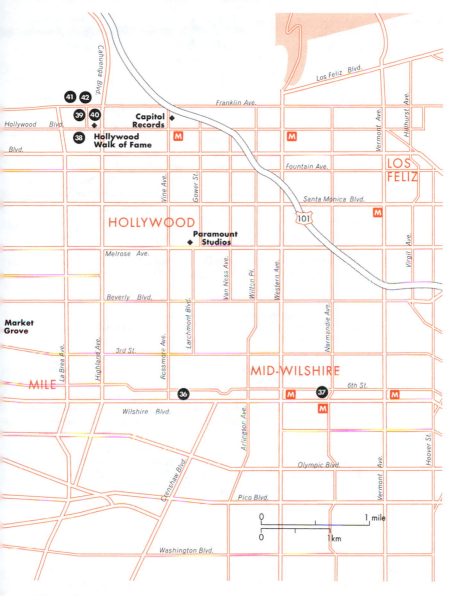

iconic Hollywood meeting place. Canine guests are also pampered here; 24-hour dog-walking service is available. ⊠ *9641 Sunset Blvd., Beverly Hills 90210* ☎ *310/276–2251 or 800/283–8885* 🖷 *310/887–2887* ⊕ *www.beverlyhillshotel.com* ➟ *204 rooms, 21 bungalows* ♨ *4 restaurants, coffee shop, room service, BBQs, in-room fax, in-room safes, some kitchenettes, minibars, cable TV with movies and video games, in-room DVDs, in-room VCRs, in-room broadband, golf privileges, 2 tennis courts, pool, gym, hair salon, hot tub, spa, 2 bars, lobby lounge, piano bar, shops, babysitting, dry cleaning, laundry service, concierge, Internet room, business services, meeeting rooms, parking (fee), some pets allowed (fee), no-smoking rooms* ▭ *AE, DC, MC, V.*

$$$$ 🎫 **Four Seasons Hotel Los Angeles at Beverly Hills.** High hedges and patio
Fodor'sChoice gardens make this hotel a secluded retreat that even the hum of traffic
★ can't permeate. It's a favorite of Hollywood's elite, so don't be surprised by a well-known face poolside or in the Windows bar. The staff here will make you feel pampered, as will the lavish guest rooms, which have beds with Frette linens, soft robes and slippers, and French doors leading to balconies. Extras include 24-hour business services, overnight shoe shine, and a morning newspaper. For a relaxing meal, you can dine poolside on the tropically landscaped terrace. Massages are available in a cabana near the pool. ⊠ *300 S. Doheny Dr., Beverly Hills 90048* ☎ *310/273–2222 or 800/332–3442* 🖷 *310/859–3824* ⊕ *www.fourseasons.com/losangeles* ➟ *187 rooms, 98 suites* ♨ *2 restaurants, café, room service, minibars, cable TV with movies and video games, in-room DVD/VCR, in-room broadband, pool, gym, hot tub, sauna, spa, steam room, bar, babysitting, dry cleaning, laundry service, concierge, business services, meeting rooms, car rental, parking (fee), some pets allowed (fee), no-smoking rooms.* ▭ *AE, DC, MC, V.*

$$$$ 🎫 **Le Meridien at Beverly Hills.** On the edge of Beverly Hills, near the restaurant hub of La Cienega Boulevard, you'll find this contemporary choice. Rooms are spacious and quiet with lots of gadgets: bedside controls can adjust the lights, TV, VCR, and CD player, too. Off the atrium lobby, a business lounge has Internet access and rooms for video- and teleconferencing. ⊠ *465 S. La Cienega Blvd., Beverly Hills 90048* ☎ *310/247–0400 or 800/645–5624* 🖷 *310/247–0315* ⊕ *www.beverlyhills.lemeridien.com* ➟ *245 rooms, 55 suites* ♨ *Restaurant, room service, in-room fax, minibars, cable TV with movies and video games, in-room VCRs, in-room broadband, pool, gym, massage, sauna, shop, babysitting, laundry service, concierge, Internet room, business services, meeting rooms, parking (fee), some pets allowed (fee), no-smoking rooms* ▭ *AE, D, DC, MC, V.*

$$$$ 🎫 **Luxe Hotel Rodeo Drive.** Refined design rules at this boutique hotel discreetly tucked away on Rodeo Drive between Valentino and Michael Kors boutiques. Streetside rooms look out over Gucci and the extravagant Prada Epicenter store. Dark mahogany and brushed metals fill the lobby, and the compact rooms go glam with black-and-white photography, 8-foot-high mirrors, Egyptian linens, and Frette robes and slippers. Café Rodeo, Luxe's intimate skylight restaurant, draws a well-heeled local lunch crowd with upscale comfort food and potent martinis. ⊠ *360 N. Rodeo Dr., Beverly Hills 90210* ☎ *310/273–0300 or 866/589–3411* 🖷 *310/859–8730* ⊕ *www.luxehotels.com* ➟ *84 rooms, 4* *suites ☐ Restaurant, room service, in-room safes, refrigerators, cable TV with movies, in-room broadband, Wi-Fi, gym, bar, babysitting, laundry service, concierge, business services, meeting room, car rental, parking (fee), no-smoking rooms ☐ AE, D, DC, MC, V.*

$$$$
Fodor'sChoice
★

Peninsula Beverly Hills. They seem to think of everything at this French Riveria–style palace. It's a favorite of Hollywood bold-face names, but all kinds of visitors consistently describe their stay as near perfect, though very expensive. Rooms overflow with antiques, artwork, and marble; high-tech room amenities

KATHY'S TOP 5

■ **Four Seasons Hotel Los Angeles at Beverly Hills** for chic seclusion.

■ **Peninsula Beverly Hills,** very French Riviera.

■ **Renaissance Hollywood Hotel,** stylish and sceney.

■ **Shutters on the Beach** to be right on the sand.

■ **Hotel Bel-Air** for bungalows that feel like a (princely) home.

are controlled by a bedside panel. Service is exemplary and always discreet. Soak up the sun by the fifth-floor pool with its fully outfitted cabanas or sip afternoon tea in the living room under ornate chandeliers. Belvedere, the hotel's flower-filled restaurant, is a lunchtime favorite for film business types. A complimentary Rolls Royce is available for short jaunts in Beverly Hills. ⊠ *9882 S. Santa Monica Blvd., Beverly Hills 90212 ☎ 310/551–2888 or 800/462–7899 ☐ 310/788–2319 ⊕ www. peninsula.com ☞ 166 rooms, 36 suites, 16 villas ☐ Restaurant, room service, in-room fax, in-room safes, minibars, cable TV with movies and video games, in-room DVDs, in-room VCRs, in-room broadband, pool, gym, hair salon, outdoor hot tub, sauna, spa, steam room, bar, lobby lounge, piano, shops, babysitting, dry cleaning, laundry service, concierge, business services, meeting rooms, travel services, parking (fee), some pets allowed (fee); no smoking ☐ AE, D, DC, MC, V.*

$$$$ **Raffles L'Ermitage Beverly Hills.** Enormous, uncluttered rooms discreetly decorated with rich fabrics and maple wood, make this very private hotel distinctly sophisticated. French doors open to remarkable views of the city or the mountains. Business-minded guests appreciate the direct-dial phones with private numbers, four multiline phones, and combination fax-copier-printers. The rooftop pool area has drop-dead views, teak furniture, and classy poolside cabanas with fax, phone, and TV. Exclusively for guests, the Amrita Spa has Asian-style beauty treatments. You could rub elbows with industry types in the Writer's bar, which is hung with framed film scripts. ⊠ *9291 Burton Way, Beverly Hills 90210 ☎ 310/ 278–3344 or 800/800–2113 ☐ 310/278–8247 ⊕ www.raffles-lermitagehotel.com ☞ 111 rooms, 13 suites ☐ Restaurant, room service, in-room fax, in-room safes, minibars, cable TV with movies, in-room DVD/VCR, in-room broadband, Web TV, Wi-Fi, pool, gym, sauna, spa, steam room, bar, lobby lounge, dry cleaning, laundry service, concierge, Internet room, business services, meeting room, parking (fee), some pets allowed, no-smoking rooms ☐ AE, D, DC, MC, V.*

$$$$ **Regent Beverly Wilshire.** Built in 1928, the Italian Renaissance–style Wilshire wing of this fabled hotel is replete with elegant details: crystal chandeliers, oak paneling, walnut doors, crown moldings, and pink marble. The contemporary Beverly wing, added in 1971, lacks the Wilshire wing's panache, as the rooms are smaller and plainer. Rodeo Drive beckons outside; a complimentary Rolls Royce can drive you anywhere within 3 mi of the hotel. Paneled in leather and wood, with soaring ceilings, The Blvd is the hotel's posh dining room. ⊠ *9500 Wilshire Blvd., Beverly Hills 90212* ☎ *310/275–5200 or 800/427–4354* 🖷 *310/274–2851* ⊕ *www.fourseasons.com* 🛏 *262 rooms, 137 suites* ⌂ *2 restaurants, room service, in-room safes, minibars, cable TV with movies and video games, in-room DVDs, in-room broadband, Wi-Fi, pool, gym, health club, hair salon, outdoor hot tub, sauna, spa, 2 bars, piano, shops, babysitting, dry cleaning, laundry service, concierge, business services, convention center, parking (fee), some pets allowed, no-smoking floors* ▭ *AE, DC, MC, V.*

$$$$ 🏨 **Sofitel Los Angeles.** From this perch bordering busy La Cienega Boulevard, you'll be a short drive from some of the city's best restaurants and nightlife. A renovation in 2006 gave the hotel a cool lounge from nightclub impresario Rande Gerber, a spa specializing in thalassotherapy (seawater-based treatments), and a 24-hour fitness center. Guest rooms went from Provençal flourishes to a cool urban look, all grays and blacks, with Hollywood Regency-style furniture, flat-screen TVs, and frosted-glass sliding doors leading to the bathrooms. Blond wood paneling sets off the feather duvet–topped beds. ■ **TIP→ For the best view, ask for a room facing the hills—otherwise you'll be facing the monolithic Beverly Center mall.** ⊠ *8555 Beverly Blvd., West Hollywood 90048* ☎ *310/278–5444 or 800/521–7772* 🖷 *310/657–2816* ⊕ *www.sofitel.com* 🛏 *267 rooms, 28 suites* ⌂ *Restaurant, room service, in-room safes, minibars, cable TV with movies and video games, in-room broadband, Wi-Fi, pool, health club, spa, bar, shop, dry cleaning, laundry service, concierge, business services, meeting rooms, parking (fee), some pets allowed, no-smoking floors* ▭ *AE, DC, MC, V.*

$$$–$$$$ 🏨 **Mosaic Hotel.** Stylish, comfortable, and outfitted with the latest electronics, the Mosaic is on a quiet side street that's central to Beverly Hills's business district. Iridescent mosaic tiles shimmer on the surfaces, while the teak-furnished, poolside lounging area gets an atmosphere boost with grand palms and simulated moonlight at night. Room amenities are posh: Frette linens and robes, gold brocades, and both a toiletries and a martini bar. The lobby restaurant and bar feels like a private club; at night, a candle wall adds a warm glow. An extra perk: guests have access to the nearby, huge Sports Club/LA for a nominal fee. ⊠ *125 S. Spalding Dr., Beverly Hills 90212* ☎ *310/498–3833 or 800/463–4466* 🖷 *310/278–1728* ⊕ *www.mosaichotel.com* 🛏 *44 rooms, 5 suites* ⌂ *Restaurant, room service, in-room safes, minibars, cable TV with movies and video games, in-room broadband, pool, gym, massage, bar, dry cleaning, laundry service, concierge, business services, car rental, parking (fee), some pets allowed, no-smoking floors* ▭ *AE, DC, MC, V.*

$$$ 🏨 **Avalon.** This relaxed but cosmopolitan boutique hotel combines space-age architectural details like large lobby plate-glass windows and terazzo floors with tech-savvy substance. Rooms at the three-building property incorporate '50s retro design, with classic pieces from George Nelson and Charles Eames; there are also Frette linens, chenille throws, and a menu of spa treatments that can be ordered in-room. For extended stays, the Avalon also has stylish apartments that come with all hotel services, including twice-daily housekeeping. Weather permitting, things get busy poolside and in the fun private cabanas. ⊠ *9400 W. Olympic Blvd., Beverly Hills 90212* ☎ *310/277–5221 or 800/535–4715* 🖷 *310/ 277–4928* ⊕ *www.avalonbeverlyhills.com* 🛏 *76 rooms, 10 suites* ♨ *Restaurant, room service, in-room fax, in-room safes, minibars, cable TV with movies and video games, in-room DVDs, in-room broadband, pool, gym, massage, bar, dry cleaning, laundry facilities, laundry service, concierge, business services, meeting room, parking (fee), some pets allowed (fee), no-smoking rooms* 🚬 *AE, DC, MC, V.*

$$$ 📺 **Beverly Hilton.** Home of the Golden Globe Awards, the Beverly Hilton is as polished as its glitzy address. Tower rooms have spectacular views of Beverly Hills. Room bathrooms, though compact, feel expansive with glass-walled showers, an opaque glass wall, and pocket door. Walls are creamy white; furnishings include versatile, leather-top, oval-shape work desks that swivel to the side. Flat-screen TVs and CD players are standard in every room. You can find action without ever leaving the grounds: Trader Vic's restaurant-bar is a kitschy classic that's popular at happy hour. The pool is almost Olympic size. A complimentary town car can ferry you within a 3-mi radius. ⊠ *9876 Wilshire Blvd., Beverly Hills 90210* ☎ *310/274–7777 or 877/414–8018* 🖷 *310/285–1313* ⊕ *www.beverlyhilton.com* 🛏 *469 rooms, 101 suites* ♨ *2 restaurants, room service, in-room safes, refrigerators, cable TV with movies and video games, in-room broadband, Wi-Fi, golf privileges, pool, gym, hair salon, massage, 2 bars, lobby lounge, piano, shops, babysitting, dry cleaning, laundry service, concierge, business services, convention center, travel services, parking (fee), some pets allowed (fee), no-smoking rooms* 🚬 *AE, D, DC, MC, V.*

★ **$$$** 📺 **The Crescent.** Built in 1926 as a dorm for silent film actors, the Crescent is now a sleek boutique hotel within walking distance of the Beverly Hills shopping triangle. Low couches and tables, an indoor-outdoor fireplace, French doors that open to the streetside patio restaurant, and shimmering candlelight at night give the hotel's public areas a welcoming and sophisticated look. Guest rooms are small, but platform beds and built-in furniture maximize the space. Bathrooms are finished in concrete—utilitarian but also coolly cozy. High-tech amenities include flat-screen TVs, in-room iPods, and a library of the latest CDs and DVDs. ⊠ *403 N. Crescent Dr., Beverly Hills 90210* ☎ *310/247–0505* 🖷 *310/ 247–9053* ⊕ *www.crescentbh.com* 🛏 *35 rooms* ♨ *Restaurant, room service, minibars, cable TV, Wi-Fi, massage, lobby lounge, dry cleaning, laundry service, parking (fee); no smoking* 🚬 *AE, D, MC, V.*

$$$ 📺 **Maison 140.** Colonial chic reigns in this three-story, 1930s spot, Beverly Hills's most grandly designed boutique hotel. The look mixes French and Far East with gleaming antiques, textured wallpaper, and colorfully painted rooms. (And these dramatic visuals compensate for compact rooms and bathrooms.) Refinements include down comforters and Frette linens and bathrobes. Take advantage of the pool and restaurant at the sister property, the Avalon hotel, 1 mi away. Beverly Hills's golden triangle of shopping is within close walking distance. The hotel's ebony and blood-red *Bar Noir* inspires intrigue. ⊠ *140 S. Lasky Dr., Beverly Hills 90212* ☎ *310/281–4000 or 800/670–6182* 🖷 *310/281–4001* ⊕ *www.*

Spa Specialists

SELF-INDULGENCE IS AN ART FORM in L.A. hotel day spas: urban sanctuaries that promise relaxation and revitalization, if you're willing to pay the price. A one-hour massage can set you back as much as $200. However, high prices don't seem to daunt many beauty-crazy Los Angelenos. Some spas are booked to capacity each weekend. Pampering is first and foremost for hotel guests, so it's a good idea to book Thursday-night through Sunday-afternoon treatments well in advance.

Each spa has its own personality, with masseurs, facialists, and aestheticians often operating according to a certain theme. The **Spa at the Four Seasons, Beverly Hills** (⊠ 300 S. Doheny Dr., Beverly Hills ☎ 310/273-2222 or 310/786-2229) concentrates on traditional body treatments in small, private quarters. Choose your own music or sounds in the deluxe treatment rooms; the spa even offers a calming facial for teenagers. The **Peninsula Spa at the Peninsula Beverly Hills** (⊠ 9882 S. Santa Monica Blvd., Beverly Hills ☎ 310/975-2854 or 800/462-7899) is an exclusive rooftop retreat; rarefied treatments here include massages with oils laced with pulverized precious stones.

The formal and quiet **Ritz-Carlton Huntington Hotel & Spa** (⊠ 1401 S. Oak Knoll Ave., Pasadena ☎ 626/568-3900) has a signature five-color clay massage treatment, during which you're rubbed with essential oils and clays. The rose aromatherapy massage is a nice touch in this City of Roses.

At the **Spa Mystique** (⊠ Century Plaza Hotel, 10220 Constellation Ave., Century City ☎ 310/551-3251 or 877/544-2256 ⊕ www.spamystique.com),

Asian therapies are a specialty: they include the Twin Tigers massage, conducted by two masseurs, and the Bamboo Awakening massage, during which a gentle bamboo whisking encourages circulation. Within the spa is the **Yamaguchi Salon** (☎ 310/551-7577), whose hair and makeup artists adhere to feng shui principles. At the nearby **Kara** (⊠ Park Hyatt, 2151 Ave. of the Stars, Century City ☎ 310/552-0425), treatments are offered in expansive "spa villas"—hotel-size rooms with chromatherapeutic, deep soaking tubs, a private outdoor patio, and massage tables.

In Santa Monica, Hollywood skin-care guru Ole Henriksen is behind the treatments at **One** (⊠ Shutters on the Beach, 1 Pico Blvd., Santa Monica ☎ 310/587-1712). Signature facials restore skin tone and shine using botanical emollients crafted by Henriksen. Meanwhile, at the **Mondrian** (⊠ 8440 Sunset Blvd., West Hollywood ☎ 323/848-6070) the Agua Bathouse spa is an all-white, Zen-like sanctuary.

When booking a massage, specify your preference for a male or female therapist. Expect to pay a minimum of $100 for a one-hour massage, with extras such as hot stones or an application of essential oils additional. One-hour facials start at $95; express facials go for about $65. You should tip at least 15% to 20%. Most reservations must be guaranteed by a credit card. The Blackberry-addicted take note: cell phones and PDAs are now banned in most spas.

maison140beverlyhills.com ⇨43 rooms ⌂ Room service, in-room safes, minibars, cable TV with movies, in-room DVDs, in-room broadband, gym, massage, lobby lounge, dry cleaning, laundry service, concierge, parking (fee), no-smoking rooms ▤ AE, DC, MC, V.

$$ 🏨 **Beverly Hills Plaza Hotel.** Looking for lots of space in which to spread out without heading into four-star territory? Try this all-suite hotel midway between Beverly Hills and Westwood. Warm tones of beige, gold, and cream and outdoor gardens with a waterfall and koi pond make for a relaxed atmosphere. You'll find bathrobes, hair dryers, movies, and Nintendo in the suites; VCRs can be rented at the front desk. The lowest-priced suites are accessible via stairs only. ⊠ *10300 Wilshire Blvd., Beverly Hills 90024* ☎ *310/275–5575 or 800/800–1234* 🖷 *310/278–3325* ⊕ *www.beverlyhillsplazahotel.com* ⇨ *116 suites* ⌂ *Restaurant, room service, in-room safes, some kitchens, some kitchenettes, minibars, cable TV with movies and video games, in-room broadband, pool, gym, hot tub, massage, bar, laundry service, concierge, business services, car rental, travel services, parking (fee), some pets allowed (fee), no-smoking rooms* ▤ *AE, D, DC, MC, V.*

$$ 🏨 **Loews Beverly Hills Hotel.** Expect lots of space and an explosion of color from the plush rooms here: they've got candy-stripe walls, peach oversize furniture, and creamy white duvets. All guest rooms have writing desks, private balconies, and sleep-inducing Tempur-Pedic mattresses. The lobby has a wood-burning fireplace and adjoining terrace. Lot 1224, the hotel's indoor–outdoor restaurant, is a popular lunchtime meeting place for studio types; expect a lively cocktail hour. ■ **TIP➔ Rooms facing busy Olympic Boulevard can be noisy; ask for one facing north if quiet is a priority.** ⊠ *1224 S. Beverwil Dr., Beverly Hills 90035* ☎ *310/277–2800 or 800/235–6397* 🖷 *310/203–9537* ⊕ *www.loewshotels.com* ⇨ *129 rooms, 8 suites* ⌂ *Restaurant, room service, in-room fax, in-room safes, some in-room hot tubs, minibars, cable TV with movies, in-room VCRs, in-room broadband, pool, gym, outdoor hot tub, bar, lounge, dry cleaning, laundry service, concierge, concierge floor, business services, meeting rooms, parking (fee), some pets allowed, no-smoking floors* ▤ *AE, D, DC, MC, V.*

$ 🏨 **Best Western Carlyle Inn.** Niceties like a full-breakfast buffet, a sundeck, and bathrobes make this small, four-story inn a good choice. Despite somewhat nondescript furniture and decor, the rooms are comfy; some include a sitting area and sofa bed. The hotel is in a quiet residential neighborhood close to restaurants, Century City, and Beverly Hills. ⊠ *1119 S. Robertson Blvd., West L.A., 90035* ☎ *310/275–4445 or 800/322–7595* 🖷 *310/859–0496* ⊕ *www.carlyle-inn.com* ⇨ *32 rooms* ⌂ *In-room safes, minibars, cable TV, in-room VCRs, Wi-Fi, gym, hot tub, laundry service, business services, parking (fee), no-smoking rooms* ▤ *AE, D, DC, MC, V* ❙◎❙ *BP.*

$ 🏨 **Hotel Beverly Terrace.** If you're looking to be close to the Sunset Strip and don't need many frills, you might give this a whirl. The rooms are basic but cheerful, with comfortable beds and bathrooms with shower stalls instead of tubs. Still, the rates are reasonable considering the upscale location on the West Hollywood–Beverly Hills border. Complimentary continental breakfast, which visitors give high marks, is served outside by the pool. ⊠ *469 N. Doheny Dr., Beverly Hills 90210* ☎ *310/274–*

8141 or 800/842–6401 🖷 *310/385–1998* ⊕ *www.hotelbeverlyterrace. com* 🖙 *39 rooms* ⚘ *Restaurant, some refrigerators, cable TV, Wi-Fi, pool, free parking, some pets allowed (fee); no smoking* ▭ *AE, D, DC, MC, V* ⅠⓄⅠ *CP.*

Century City

$$–$$$$ 🏨 **Hyatt Regency Century Plaza.** New management means the Century Plaza (formerly the Westin) will be revamped in 2006. For now, the two-story lobby lounge remains as well as the inviting pool and cabanas. You can count on the guest rooms having large bathrooms, balconies, and stunning city views. Seafood is the specialty at the hotel's well-reviewed restaurant, Breeze. Lighter, healthful choices are found at the spa café next to the Spa Mystique, known for its Asian-inspired treatments. The Westfield Shoppingtown and its state-of-the-art movie theaters are across the street. ⊠ *2025 Ave. of the Stars, Century City, 90067* ☎ *310/ 228–1234 or 800/633–7313* 🖷 *310/551–3355* ⊕ *www.hyatt.com* 🖙 *728 rooms, 14 suites* ⚘ *Restaurant, café, room service, in-room safes, minibars, cable TV with movies, in-room broadband, pool, health club, hair salon, outdoor hot tub, sauna, spa, steam room, bar, lobby lounge, dry cleaning, laundry service, concierge, business services, meeting rooms, convention center, car rental, parking (fee), some pets allowed; no smoking* ▭ *AE, D, DC, MC, V.*

$$$ 🏨 **Park Hyatt.** This hotel's proximity to 20th Century Fox Studios appeals especially to those in the industry, but the central Westside location is handy for all kinds of visits. There's a decent-size balcony off every room; most have excellent views. Ask for a room facing west for brilliant sunsets (smog permitting). Desks are computer ready with convenient cordless phones. Bathrooms have marble vanities and separate shower and tub. Nightly turndown, complimentary shoeshine, and complimentary town car service within Century City and Beverly Hills are nice touches. Spa treatments, offered in four spa villas with deep soaking tubs and a private outdoor patio, are a soothing indulgence. ⊠ *2151 Ave. of the Stars, Century City, 90067* ☎ *310/277–1234 or 866/333– 8881* 🖷 *310/785–9240* ⊕ *www.hyatt.com* 🖙 *185 rooms, 180 suites* ⚘ *Restaurant, room service, in-room fax, in-room safes, minibars, cable TV with movies, in-room broadband, pool, health club, outdoor hot tub, spa, steam room, bar, lobby lounge, shops, babysitting, dry cleaning, laundry service, concierge, business services, meeting rooms, parking (fee), no-smoking floors* ▭ *AE, D, DC, MC, V.*

$$ 🏨 **Courtyard by Marriott Century City/Beverly Hills.** Near Beverly Hills, this Marriott has a good location near the Century City business complex and nearby medical center. Wedged as it is into a compact lot overlooking busy Olympic Boulevard, rooms at the back of the hotel are quietest. The decor is basic, but desks have space to spread out. The hotel staff is friendly and helpful. ⊠ *10320 W. Olympic Blvd., Century City, 90064* ☎ *310/556–2777 or 800/321–2211* 🖷 *310/203–0563* ⊕ *www. courtyard.com* 🖙 *135 rooms* ⚘ *Restaurant, coffee shop, microwaves, refrigerators, cable TV with movies and video games, in-room broadband, gym, outdoor hot tub, babysitting, laundry facilities, laundry service, concierge, business services, meeting room, airport shuttle, car rental, parking (fee); no smoking* ▭ *AE, D, DC, MC, V.*

Hollywood & Vicinity

$$$–$$$$ **Hollywood Roosevelt Hotel.** A renovation and a pair of hot nightspots breathed new life into the Roosevelt. The Spanish tiles, painted ceilings, arches, and other details in this hotel's Spanish Colonial Revival main building are still here to evoke early Hollywood glamour. Rooms in the main building have contemporary platform beds, while those surrounding the pool have dark-wood furnishings and mirrored walls—think hip bachelor pad. The David Hockney–painted pool adds to the playful vibe. A Metro stop is one block away. ⊠ *7000 Hollywood Blvd., Hollywood, 90028* ☎ *323/466–7000 or 800/950–7667* 🖨 *323/462–8056* ⊕ *www. hollywoodroosevelt.com* 🛏 *305 rooms, 48 suites* ♿ *Restaurant, room service, in-room safes, minibars, cable TV with movies and video games, Wi-Fi, pool, gym, massage, 3 bars, lobby lounge, nightclub, shops, dry cleaning, laundry service, concierge, business services, meeting rooms, parking (fee), no-smoking rooms* 🖃 *AE, D, DC, MC, V.*

★ **$$$** **Renaissance Hollywood Hotel.** Part of the massive Hollywood & Highland shopping and entertainment complex, this 20-story Renaissance is at the center of Hollywood's action. Contemporary art (notably by L.A. favorites Charles and Ray Eames), retro '60s furniture, terrazzo floors, a Zen rock garden, and wood and aluminum accents greet you in the lobby. Rooms are vibrant: chairs are red, table lamps are molded blue plastic. Blackout shades keep the fierce sun at bay. For the ultimate party pad, book the Panorama Suite, with angled floor-to-ceiling windows, vintage Eames furniture, a grand piano, and a sunken Jacuzzi tub with a view. ⊠ *1755 N. Highland Ave., Hollywood, 90028* ☎ *323/856–1200 or 800/468–3571* 🖨 *323/856–1205* ⊕ *www.renaissancehollywood.com* 🛏 *604 rooms, 33 suites* ♿ *Restaurant, room service, in-room safes, minibars, cable TV with movies and video games, in-room broadband, pool, gym, 2 bars, lobby lounge, shop, babysitting, dry cleaning, laundry service, concierge, concierge floor, business services, meeting rooms, convention center, parking (fee), no-smoking rooms* 🖃 *AE, D, DC, MC, V.*

$$–$$$ **Magic Castle Hotel.** Close to the action and traffic of Hollywood, this former apartment building faces busy Franklin Avenue and is a quick walk to a nearby Red Line stop at Hollywood & Highland. There's nothing theme-y about the guest room decor, but larger rooms have kitchens with eating areas. There's a decent-size pool and patio with lots of greenery. ■ **TIP→** Guests at the hotel can secure dinner reservations and attend nightly magic shows at the Magic Castle, a private club for magicians and their admirers that's housed in a 1908 mansion next door. (Jacket and tie are required for men; kids are allowed only during Sunday brunch.) ⊠ *7025 Franklin Ave., Hollywood, 90028* ☎ *323/851–0800 or 800/741–4915* 🖨 *323/851–4926* ⊕ *www.magiccastlehotel.com* 🛏 *10 rooms, 30 suites* ♿ *In-room safes, some kitchenettes, refrigerators, cable TV, Wi-Fi, pool, laundry facilities, parking (fee); no smoking* 🖃 *AE, D, DC, MC, V.*

$$ **Radisson Wilshire Plaza Hotel.** A handy midcity location ensures a steady stream of bookings here; the bustling lobby and café give a good first impression. Guest rooms are nothing to write home about, but they have all the necessary amenities, plus oak desks and floor-to-ceiling windows with good views. Rooms on the business floor are virtual offices with fax/copier/printers and two-line phones. Across the street from a Red

3

Line station, the hotel gives you easy access to downtown and Hollywood. A limo rental service is available on-site. Authentic Japanese food and sushi can be found in Sake-E, off the lobby; Korean and Japanese breakfasts are available there, too. ✉ *3515 Wilshire Blvd., Mid-Wilshire, 90010* ☎ *213/381–7411 or 800/333–3333* 🖨 *213/386–7379* ⊕ *www.radwilshire.com* 🛏 *380 rooms, 13 suites* ♨ *3 restaurants, café, room service, some in-room faxes, in-room safes, minibars, cable TV with movies, in-room data ports, pool, gym, massage, lobby lounge, shop, laundry service, concierge, business services, meeting room, car rental, parking (fee), no-smoking rooms* ⊟ *AE, D, DC, MC, V.*

★ **$–$$** 📺 **Farmer's Daughter Hotel.** Tongue-in-cheek country style is the name of the game at this motel: rooms are upholstered in blue gingham with denim bedspreads, and staff members all wear overalls. A curving blue wall secludes the interior courtyard, where there's comfy patio furniture and an open-air lobby. Rooms are snug but outfitted with whimsical original art and amenities such as CD and DVD players. It's a favorite of *The Price Is Right* hopefuls; the TV show tapes at the CBS studios nearby. ■ **TIP➔ The cheap eats at the Farmers Market, as well as The Grove, L.A.'s popular outdoor shopping and entertainment mall, are directly across Fairfax Avenue.** ✉ *115 S. Fairfax Ave., Fairfax District, 90036* ☎ *323/937–3930 or 800/334–1658* 🖨 *323/932–1608* ⊕ *www.farmersdaughterhotel.com* 🛏 *64 rooms, 2 suites* ♨ *Restaurant, room service, In-room safes, refrigerators, cable TV, in-room DVDs, in-room broadband, pool, babysitting, dry cleaning, laundry service, concierge, meeting room, car rental, parking (fee), some pets allowed (fee), no-smoking rooms.* ⊟ *AE, D, DC, MC, V.*

$ 📺 **Dunes Inn–Wilshire.** Centered between downtown Los Angeles and Beverly Hills, the Dunes is a classic roadside motel with a 1960s vibe, complete with an oval pool and basic decor. Its midcity location and low price are an increasingly rare combination in metro L.A. ✉ *4300 Wilshire Blvd., Hancock Park, 90010* ☎ *323/938–3616 or 800/452–3863* 🖨 *323/938–8661* ⊕ *www.dunesla.com* ♨ *Some kitchenettes, refrigerators, cable TV, pool, laundry facilities, laundry service, car rental, free parking, no-smoking rooms* ⊟ *AE, D, DC, MC, V.*

$ 📺 **Highland Gardens Hotel.** A large, sparkling pool and a lush, if somewhat overgrown, tropical garden sets this hotel apart from other budget lodgings. Spacious but basic units have either two queen-size beds, or a king bed with a queen-size sleeper sofa, plus a desk and sitting area with Formica tables. Rooms facing busy Franklin Avenue are noisy; ask for one facing the courtyard. The hotel is just blocks from the Walk of Fame and a Metro Rail station and a few minutes' drive off the Sunset Strip. ✉ *7047 Franklin Ave., Hollywood, 90028* ☎ *323/850–0536 or 800/404–5472* 🖨 *323/850–1712* ⊕ *www.highlandgardenshotel.com* 🛏 *70 rooms, 48 suites* ♨ *Some kitchenettes, refrigerators, cable TV, Wi-Fi, pool, laundry facilities, free parking, some pets allowed; no smoking* ⊟ *AE, MC, V* ⏐♨⏐ *CP.*

¢ 🏨 **Orange Drive Manor Hostel.** Once an elegant Hollywood mansion, the Orange Drive Manor now hosts budget-conscious travelers who also like its central Hollywood location. Accommodations are sometimes rented as dorms and other times as private rooms, depending on occupancy. The rooms are spare but clean and light-filled. The hostel is near the Hollywood & Highland complex and a Metro Rail stop. A common kitchen is available for those who like DIY meals. Only cash and traveler's checks are accepted. ✉ *1764 N. Orange Dr., Hollywood, 90028* ☎ *323/850–0350* 📠 *323/969–8164* ⊕ *www.orangedrivehostel.com* ➪ *25 rooms* ♨ *Fans, Wi-Fi, airport shuttle, parking (fee); no a/c, no room phones, no room TVs, no smoking* ▭ No credit cards.

West Hollywood

$$$$ 🏨 **Bel Age Hotel.** Studio apartment–style suites at this nine-story, art-filled hotel near the Strip are very spacious. Each has a private terrace and work desk with spiffy Aeron chair. South-facing suites have the best views overlooking the L.A. skyline, and on a clear day you can see as far as the Pacific. Views are also spectacular from the rooftop pool and hot tub. Sink into a chair at the low-rise reception desk to check in. Weekend nights, there's live jazz in the hotel's view-rich restaurant—Ten20. A complete remodel of the hotel is expected to be completed in 2007; the hotel will then reopen as the London LA. ✉ *1020 N. San Vicente Blvd., West Hollywood 90069* ☎ *310/854–1111 or 800/996–3426* 📠 *310/854–0926* ⊕ *www.wyndham.com* ➪ *200 suites* ♨ *2 restaurants, room service, some kitchenettes, minibars, cable TV with movies, in-room broadband, Wi-Fi, pool, gym, hair salon, hot tub, massage, bar, piano bar, shops, babysitting, dry cleaning, laundry service, concierge, business services, meeting rooms, parking (fee), some pets allowed (fee), no-smoking floors* ▭ *AE, D, MC, V.*

$$$$ 🏨 **Chateau Marmont Hotel.** The Chateau's swank exterior disguises its lurid place in Hollywood history—many remember it as the scene of John Belushi's fatal overdose in 1982, and in 2004 controversial photographer Helmut Newton died in a car crash on his way out of the hotel. Actors like Johnny Depp and Keanu Reeves appreciate the hotel for its secluded cottages, bungalows, and understated suites and penthouses. The interior is 1920s style, although some of the decor looks dated rather than vintage. The Wi-Fi throughout the hotel means that you can surf the 'Net while seated on the hotel's scenic, landscaped terrace with drop-dead sunset views. ✉ *8221 Sunset Blvd., West Hollywood 90046* ☎ *323/656–1010 or 800/242–8328* 📠 *323/655–5311* ⊕ *www.chateaumarmont.com* ➪ *11 rooms, 63 suites* ♨ *Restaurant, room service, in-room fax, in-room safes, minibars, cable TV with movies, in-room DVDs, in-room data ports, Wi-Fi, pool, gym, massage, bar, babysitting, dry cleaning, laundry service, concierge, business services, parking (fee), some pets allowed (fee), no-smoking rooms* ▭ *AE, DC, MC, V.*

★ $$$$ 🏨 **Mondrian.** Ian Schrager, famed for his stylish hotels, created this all-white, high-rise, urban resort. Mod, apartment-size accommodations have floor-to-ceiling windows, slipcovered sofas, and marble coffee tables; all have kitchens. Desks and multiline phones could help you be productive, but the happening social scene in the lobby will certainly distract. The Asia de Cuba restaurant is known for its amazing views, sparkling cocktails, and scads of beautiful people. The one downside: rooms on the lower floors facing Sunset are unbearably noisy, so you should insist on a room that faces west. ⊠ *8440 Sunset Blvd., West Hollywood 90069* ☎ *323/650–8999 or 800/697–1791* 🖷 *323/650–5215* ⊕ *www.mondrianhotel.com* 🛏 *53 rooms, 185 suites* ⚒ *Restaurant, café, room service, in-room safes, kitchens, refrigerators, cable TV with movies, in-room VCRs, Web TV, Wi-Fi, pool, gym, sauna, spa, steam room, 2 bars, shop, laundry service, concierge, business services, meeting room, parking (fee), no-smoking rooms* 🗀 *AE, D, DC, MC, V.*

$$$$ 🏨 **Sunset Marquis Hotel and Villas.** If you're in town to cut your new hit single, you'll appreciate the two on-site recording studios here. But even the musically challenged will appreciate this property on a quiet cul-de-sac just off the Sunset Strip. Suites and ultraprivate villas, which are set amid lush gardens, are roomy and plush, with soundproof windows and blackout curtains for total serenity. (New villas are set to open at the start of 2007.) All have stereo systems; some have grand pianos. ⊠ *1200 N. Alta Loma Rd., West Hollywood 90069* ☎ *310/657–1333 or 800/858–9758* 🖷 *310/652–5300* ⊕ *www.sunsetmarquishotel.com* 🛏 *102 suites, 12 villas* ⚒ *2 restaurants, room service, in-room safes, minibars, refrigerators, cable TV with movies, in-room broadband, 2 pools, gym, outdoor hot tub, massage, sauna, babysitting, dry cleaning, laundry service, concierge, business services, meeting room, travel services, parking (fee); no smoking* 🗀 *AE, D, DC, MC, V.*

$$$ 🏨 **Chamberlain.** On a leafy residential side street, the Chamberlain is steps from Santa Monica Boulevard and close to the Sunset Strip. Rooms are handsomely tailored in gray and teal, with snappy gray and white Regency-style furniture. The work desks are oversize, but the bathrooms are compact (those in grand rooms have separate shower and tub). Tech extras include flat-screen TVs, cordless phones, and CD players. Beds have pillow-top mattresses. You can soak up the sunshine next to the rooftop pool with dramatic city and Hollywood Hills views. The guests-only dining room and bar serves potent cocktails and a tasty but limited menu. ⊠ *1000 Westmount Dr., West Hollywood 90069* ☎ *310/657–7400 or 888/622–4567* 🖷 *310/854–6744* ⊕ *www. chamberlainwesthollywood.com* 🛏 *96 rooms, 16 suites* ⚒ *Dining room, room service, in-room safes, some kitchenettes, minibars, cable TV with movies, in-room DVD/VCR, in-room broadband, Wi-Fi, pool, gym, massage, bar, babysitting, dry cleaning, laundry service, business services, meeting room, parking (fee), some pets allowed (fee), no-smoking rooms* 🗀 *AE, D, DC, MC, V.*

$$$ 🏨 **The Grafton on Sunset.** It's easy to tap into the Sunset Strip energy here, especially since the hotel's hip steak house, BOA, is usually packed. Rooms are small, but large windows with plantation shutters and full-length mirrors help open the space up. Ask for a room facing the interior courtyard, both to avoid noise from the Strip and to overlook the heated pool area with its mosaic-tiled waterfall and striped lounge chairs. Extra touches include portable room phones that work poolside, bathrobes, nightly turndown service, CD players, and free transportation within 3 mi. Expect to pay higher rates weekends due to the Sunset Strip's fun factor. ⊠ *8462 W. Sunset Blvd., West Hollywood 90069* ☎ *323/654–4600 or 800/821–3660* 🖷 *323/654–5918* ⊕ *www.graftononsunset. com* 🛏 *103 rooms, 5 suites* ⚒ *Restaurant, room service, minibars, re-*

frigerators, cable TV with movies, in-room VCRs, in-room data ports, Wi-Fi, pool, gym, massage, sauna, lounge, dry cleaning, laundry service, concierge, business services, meeting room, parking (fee), some pets allowed (fee), no-smoking rooms ☐ AE, D, MC, V.

$$$ ☒ **Le Montrose Suite Hotel.** Once an apartment building, this hotel plays host to those in the entertainment business and is a notably good deal for the rate (it's at the bottom of this price category). Close to Beverly Hills and Hollywood and a short drive from the Valley, it's just off the busy Sunset Strip on a quiet residential block. Loftlike suites, with sunken living room, fireplace, and private balcony, have chocolate brown walls, lightened by a geometric patterned duvet. Couches are covered in plush corduroy, and the TV and DVD player are hidden inside a dark wood sideboard. Bathrooms are small, with combination showers and tubs. You can relax on the rooftop pool next to the tennis court. ⊠ *900 Hammond St., West Hollywood 90069* ☎ *310/855–1115 or 800/776–0666* 🖷 *310/ 657–9192* ⊕ *www.lemontrose.com* ⇨ *132 suites* ₺ *Dining room, room service, in-room faxes, some kitchenettes, microwaves, refrigerators, cable TV with movies and video games, in-room DVDs, in-room broadband, tennis court, pool, gym, outdoor hot tub, massage, bicycles, lobby lounge, babysitting, dry cleaning, laundry service, concierge, Internet room, business services, meeting rooms, car rental, travel services, parking (fee), some pets allowed (fee), no-smoking floors ☐ AE, D, DC, MC, V.*

$$$ ☒ **Le Parc Suite Hotel.** On a tree-lined residential street close to CBS Television City and the Pacific Design Center, this congenial low-rise hotel aims to make guests feel coddled, with extremely personalized service and a strong commitment to privacy. Even the most basic suites here are spacious (650 square feet); they also have sunken living rooms with fireplaces and private balconies. Other extras include CD players, bathrobes, and slippers. A complimentary town car will chauffeur guests within a 3-mi radius. There's a grand view from the rooftop pool deck. ⊠ *733 W. Knoll Dr., West Hollywood 90069* ☎ *310/855–8888 or 800/578–4837* 🖷 *310/ 659–7812* ⊕ *www.leparcsuites.com* ⇨ *154 suites* ₺ *Restaurant, room service, kitchenettes, minibars, microwaves, cable TV with movies and video games, in-room DVD/VCR, in-room broadband, tennis court, pool, gym, hot tub, massage, sauna, dry cleaning, laundry facilities, laundry service, concierge, business services, meeting room, parking (fee), some pets allowed (fee); no smoking ☐ AE, D, DC, MC, V.*

$$$ ☒ **The Sunset Tower Hotel.** A clubby style infuses the 1929 art deco landmark formerly known as the Argyle. The lobby sets the tone with dark wood, mauve accents, and marble floors; vintage Hollywood star photos add retro glamour. Sink into couches and cozy upholstered corners while taking in the dramatic city views: the poolside city views are equally impressive. Guest rooms soft-pedal the look with art deco–inspired fixtures and walnut armoires. The spa and elaborate beauty salon add to the resort-in-the-city feel. Most of the Sunset Strip's clubs, bars, and hot spots are within walking distance. ⊠ *8358 Sunset Blvd., West Hollywood 90069* ☎ *323/654–7100 or 800/225–2637* 🖷 *323/654– 9287* ⊕ *www.sunsettowerhotel.com* ⇨ *20 rooms, 44 suites* ₺ *Restaurant, room service, in-room data ports, Wi-Fi, in-room safes, some in-room hot tubs, minibars, cable TV with movies, pool, gym, hair salon, spa, steam room, bar, piano bar, shop, babysitting, dry cleaning, laun-*

dry service, concierge, Internet room, business services, parking (fee), some pets allowed (fee), no smoking rooms ⊟ *AE, D, DC, MC, V.*

$$–$$$ 🔲 **Élan Hotel Modern.** Small but spirited, this hotel has an enviable location within walking distance of some of the city's best restaurants and the Beverly Center. The guest room decor focuses on texture with softly colored, inviting fabrics and coverings: mohair, chenille, and down bedding. In the streetside lounge you can have coffee while you navigate the 'Net. ⊠ *8435 Beverly Blvd., West Hollywood 90048* ☎ *323/658–6663 or 888/611–0398* 🖷 *323/658–6640* ⊕ *www.elanhotel.com* ↪ *46 rooms, 4 suites* ♿ *Room service, in-room safes, minibars, cable TV, in-room VCRs, in-room broadband, Wi-Fi, gym, massage, bar, laundry service, concierge, airport shuttle, car rental, parking (fee); no smoking* ⊟ *AE, D, DC, MC, V* ⦿ *CP.*

$$ 🔲 **Hyatt West Hollywood.** This hotel's busy Sunset Strip location guarantees lots of activity—and a bit of a test to pull into the curved drive and parking lot. Once known as the "riot house" for its boisterous musician guests, the hotel is now staid and even a bit tired, definitely in need of its planned renovation. (A revamp is slated for 2006.) Rooms that face the Sunset Strip have balconies; those facing the hills do not. Some rooms have aquariums, too. The view from the rooftop pool is extraordinary and favored for location shoots. Chi, the hotel's eye-catching Chinese restaurant, basks in the glow of its own outdoor fire pit. ⊠ *8401 Sunset Blvd., West Hollywood 90069* ☎ *323/656–1234 or 800/233–1234* 🖷 *323/650–7024* ⊕ *www.hyatt.com* ↪ *241 rooms, 21 suites* ♿ *Restaurant, room service, in-room safes, cable TV with movies, in-room data ports, pool, gym, bar, shop, dry cleaning, laundry service, business services, meeting rooms, parking (fee), no-smoking rooms* ⊟ *AE, D, DC, MC, V.*

$$ 🔲 **Ramada Plaza West Hollywood.** Popular with Aussie and Kiwi tour groups, this Ramada outlet has a prime West Hollywood/Sunset Strip position. Although the exterior is vibrantly colorful, inside the decor shows wear and tear and the guest room air-conditioners can be noisy. However, its location and its party vibe guarantees sold-out holiday weekends. (Halloween is particularly raucous.) Parking is an extra $25 per night—unusually steep for such a modest establishment. ⊠ *8585 Santa Monica Blvd., West Hollywood 90069* ☎ *310/652–6400 or 800/845–8585* 🖷 *310/652–4207* ⊕ *www.ramadaweho.com* ↪ *130 rooms, 45 suites* ♿ *Restaurant, room service, in-room safes, some kitchenettes, refrigerators, cable TV with movies and video games, in-room broadband, Web TV, Wi-Fi, pool, gym, bar, dry cleaning, laundry facilities, laundry service, concierge, business services, meeting room, car rental, travel services, parking (fee), some pets allowed (fee), no-smoking floors* ⊟ *AE, D, DC, MC, V.*

$$ 🔲 **The Standard, Hollywood.** Hotelier André Balazs created this cheap-and-chic Sunset Strip hotel out of a former retirement home. The aes-

---

WORD OF MOUTH

"This seems to be a pattern, closing the chain hotels in and around L.A., renovating, and opening as a boutique (and usually much more expensive) hotel. . . . A good thing for those looking for a nicer and more upscale hotel, but a bad thing for the wallet."   —emd

thetic is '70s kitsch: pop art, shag carpets and ultrasuede sectionals fill the lobby, while the rooms have inflatable sofas, beanbag chairs, surfboard tables, and Warhol poppy-print curtains. DJs spin nightly and lobby socializing begins at the front desk and extends to the blue AstroTurfed pool deck outside. ■ TIP→ **Especially on weekends and holidays, expect a young party scene that can drift noisily into the halls.** The 24-hour coffee shop is quite good, more modern classic than greasy spoon. ✉ *8300 Sunset Blvd., West Hollywood 90069* ☎ *323/650–9090* 🖨 *323/650–2820* 🌐 *www.standardhotel.com* 🛏 *137 rooms, 2 suites* ♦ *Coffee shop, room service, minibars, cable TV with movies, in-room broadband, pool, hair salon, bar, lobby lounge, shop, laundry service, concierge, meeting room, parking (fee), some pets allowed (fee)* ▤ *AE, D, DC, MC, V.*

$ 🏨 **Beverly Laurel Motor Hotel.** A family-run operation for more than 40 years, the Beverly Laurel stands out for its low rates and central city location. Touring bands and up-and-coming actors stay here on their way to the big time. An indifferent staff and small shaded pool are downsides. The ground floor is home to Swingers coffee shop, which is popular with the actors, models, and musicians who also frequent the motel. ✉ *8018 Beverly Blvd., West Hollywood 90048* ☎ *323/651–2441, 800/ 962–3824 outside CA* 🖨 *323/651–5225* 🛏 *52 rooms* ♦ *Coffee shop, some kitchenettes, microwaves, refrigerators, cable TV, in-room data ports, pool, free parking, some pets allowed (fee), no-smoking rooms* ▤ *AE, D, MC, V.*

Downtown

★ **$$$** 🏨 **Hilton Checkers Los Angeles.** Opened as the Mayflower Hotel in 1927, Checkers retains much of its original character; its various-size rooms all have charming period details, although they also have modern luxuries like pillow-top mattresses, coffeemakers, 24-hour room service, and cordless phones. The rooftop pool deck overlooks the L.A. library and nearby office towers. The plush lobby bar and lounge look like they belong in a private club, with comfortable leather chairs and a large plasma-screen TV. In the mornings, the complimentary car service can drive you anywhere within a 2-mi radius. ✉ *535 S. Grand Ave., Downtown, 90071* ☎ *213/624–0000 or 800/445–8667* 🖨 *213/626–9906* 🌐 *www. hiltoncheckers.com* 🛏 *188 rooms, 9 suites* ♦ *Restaurant, room service, cable TV with movies and video games, in-room broadband, pool, gym, outdoor hot tub, massage, sauna, spa, steam room, bar, library, dry cleaning, laundry service, concierge, business services, meeting room, parking (fee), some pets allowed (fee), no-smoking rooms* ▤ *AE, D, DC, MC, V.*

$$$ 🏨 **Los Angeles Marriott Downtown.** Near the U.S. 101 and I–110 freeways and five blocks north of the Staples Center and the L.A. Convention Center, the 14-story, glass-wall Marriott is an especially good choice if you're traveling on business. Guest rooms are oversize with marble baths and huge windows. Stay plugged in at the business center, which has computers, copiers, and fax machines. If you've grown weary of standard restaurant breakfast fare, choose the Japanese buffet (miso soup and salmon) for a new spin on the most important meal of the day. ✉ *333 S. Figueroa St., Downtown, 90071* ☎ *213/617–1133 or 800/228–9290*

213/613–0291 ⊕ www.marriott.com ⤶ 400 rooms, 69 suites △ 3 restaurants, room service, in-room safes, minibars, cable TV with movies, Wi-Fi, pool, gym, 2 bars, piano bar, 4 cinemas, dry cleaning, laundry service, concierge, concierge floor, business services, meeting rooms, convention center, car rental, parking (fee), no-smoking floors ▭ AE, D, DC, MC, V.

$$$

Fodor'sChoice

★

Millennium Biltmore Hotel. One of downtown L.A.'s true treasures, the gilded 1923 beaux arts masterpiece exudes ambiance and history. The lobby (formerly the Music Room) was the local headquarters of JFK's presidential campaign, and the ballroom hosted some of the earliest Academy Awards. These days, the Biltmore hosts business types drawn by its central downtown location, ample meeting spaces, and services such as a well-outfitted business center that stays open 24/7. Some of the guest rooms are small by today's standards, but all have classic, formal furnishings, shuttered windows, and marble bathrooms. Stay on the Club Level for excellent views and complimentary breakfast and evening cocktails. And bring your bathing suit for the vintage tiled indoor pool and adjacent steam room. *⊠ 506 S. Grand Ave., Downtown, 90071 ☎ 213/624–1011 or 800/245–8673 🖷 213/612–1545 ⊕ www. millenniumhotels.com ⤶ 627 rooms, 56 suites △ 3 restaurants, 2 cafés, room service, in-room safes, minibars, cable TV with movies and video games, in-room data ports, indoor pool, health club, hot tub, massage, sauna, steam room, 3 bars, lobby lounge, sports bar, shops, babysitting, laundry service, concierge, concierge floor, Internet room, business services, convention center, car rental, parking (fee), no-smoking floors ▭ AE, D, DC, MC, V.*

$$$

New Otani Hotel and Garden. Fittingly enough, this branch of a Japanese chain is on the edge of Little Tokyo. Its "Japanese Suites" have tatami mats, futon beds, extra-deep bathtubs, and paper screens on the windows. The American-style rooms are somewhat plain and compact. Two of the restaurants serve Japanese cuisine at authentically steep Tokyo prices. The third serves straightforward contemporary food, including a daily lunch buffet for downtown's office crowd. The hotel is close to the Civic Center and state and federal courthouses. For those who seek a contemplative moment (or a scenic wedding spot), there's a ½-acre Japanese garden on the roof. The on-site spa specializes in Shiatsu massage. *⊠ 120 S. Los Angeles St., Little Tokyo, 90012 ☎ 213/629–1200 or 800/639–6826 🖷 213/622–0980 ⊕ www.newotani.com ⤶ 414 rooms, 20 suites △ 3 restaurants, room service, in-room safes, minibars, cable TV with movies, in-room broadband, gym, hair salon, hot tub, massage, sauna, spa, 3 bars, shops, dry cleaning, laundry service, concierge, business services, meeting rooms, car rental, parking (fee), no-smoking rooms ▭ AE, D, DC, MC, V.*

$$$

Omni Los Angeles Hotel at California Plaza. The 17-story Omni is in downtown's cultural and business heart, just steps from the Museum of Contemporary Art and the Los Angeles Philharmonic's home, Disney Hall. The airy rooms have a cheery, California-casual look. ■ **TIP→ Ask for a western view to take advantage of the floor-to-ceiling windows.** Business rooms have all the necessities, including extra power strips, an oversize desk, and office supplies. Portable treadmills are available for in-room workouts. You can have breakfast or lunch on the Grand

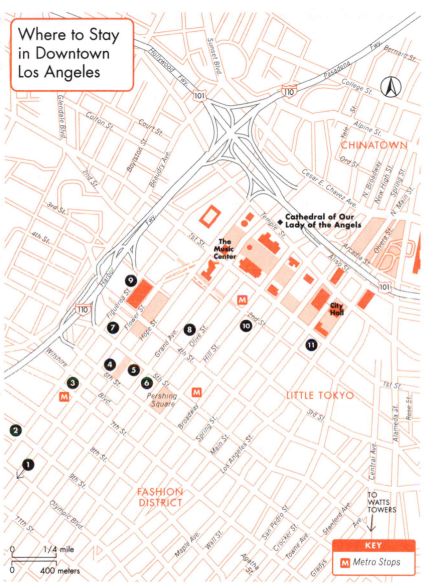

Where to Stay in Downtown Los Angeles

KEY

M Metro Stops

Café's pleasant outdoor terrace, which overlooks the Museum of Contemporary Art's entrance. Nightly, Noe serves Asian-influenced California cuisine. ⊠ *251 S. Olive St., Downtown, 90012* ☎ *213/617–3300 or 800/442–5251* 🖶 *213/617–3399* 🌐 *www.omnihotels.com* 🛌 *439 rooms, 14 suites* ♨ *2 restaurants, room service, minibars, cable TV with movies and video games, Wi-Fi, pool, gym, sauna, spa, steam room, bar, shop, babysitting, dry cleaning, laundry service, concierge, concierge floor, business services, meeting rooms, car rental, parking (fee), some pets allowed (fee), no-smoking floors* 🖃 *AE, D, DC, MC, V.*

$$$ 🏨 **Westin Bonaventure Hotel & Suites.** L.A.'s largest hotel has five towers, each mirrored, cylindrical, and 35 stories tall. Inside the futuristic lobby are fountains, an indoor lake, an indoor track, and 12 glass elevators. Color-coded hotel floors and numerous signs help newcomers navigate the hotel. Standard rooms are on the small side, but the suites are expansive and come with practical extras such as two-line speaker phones and ergonomic office chairs. All rooms have floor-to-ceiling windows, many with terrific views. Perk up with a shiatsu or chair massage at the Asian-theme spa. On clear days, check out the 34th-floor revolving lounge and its spectacular views. ⊠ *404 S. Figueroa St., Downtown, 90071* ☎ *213/624–1000 or 800/937–8461* 🖶 *213/612–4800* 🌐 *www.westin.com* 🛌 *1,354 rooms, 135 suites* ♨ *17 restaurants, room service, in-room safes, minibars, cable TV with movies, in-room broadband, in-room data ports, pool, gym, hair salon, sauna, spa, steam room, 5 bars, shops, laundry service, concierge, business services, meeting rooms, convention center, airport shuttle, car rental, travel services, parking (fee); no smoking* 🖃 *AE, D, DC, MC, V.*

$$–$$$ 🏨 **Wilshire Grand Hotel & Centre.** Wedged in among the other high-rises at the start of Wilshire Boulevard, this sprawling 16-story hotel is two blocks from the Staples Center and is the closest hotel to the convention center. The location and services are the strong suits; guest rooms are small for the price, and the decor begs for an update. Dining choices include Seoul Jung, serving savory Korean barbecue. Point Moorea, the lower lobby sports bar, makes good martinis and attracts a lively post-workday scene. A Metro stop one block away is a plus. ⊠ *930 Wilshire Blvd., Downtown, 90017* ☎ *213/688–7777 or 888/773–2888* 🖶 *213/612–3977* 🌐 *www.wilshiregrand.com* 🛌 *865 rooms, 35 suites* ♨ *4 restaurants, room service, minibars, cable TV with movies and video games, Wi-Fi, pool, gym, hair salon, outdoor hot tub, shops, dry cleaning, laundry service, concierge, concierge floor, business services, meeting rooms, convention center, car rental, travel services, parking (fee), no-smoking floors* 🖃 *AE, D, DC, MC, V.*

★ $$ 🏨 **Figueroa Hotel.** On the outside, it's Spanish Revival; on the inside, this 1926, 12-story hotel is a mix of Southwestern, Mexican, and Mediterranean styles, with earth tones, hand-painted furniture, and wrought-iron beds. You can lounge around the pool and bubbling hot tub surrounded by tropical greenery under the shadow of downtown skyscrapers. (Make it even better with a soothing drink from the back patio bar.) ▮ **TIP→** Watch the calendar when reserving: since it's next to the convention center and Staples Center, this well-priced hotel books up months in advance of major events. ⊠ *939 S. Figueroa St., Downtown, 90015* ☎ *213/627–8971 or 800/421–9092* 🖶 *213/689–0305* 🌐 *www.*

figueroahotel.com ⌗ *285 rooms, 2 suites* ⌂ *Restaurant, café, some fans, refrigerators, cable TV, in-room data ports, Wi-Fi, pool, outdoor hot tub, 2 bars, dry cleaning, laundry facilities, concierge, parking (fee); no smoking* ▭ *AE, DC, MC, V.*

★ **$$** 🏠 **Inn at 657.** Proprietor Patsy Carter runs a homey, welcoming bed-and-breakfast near the University of Southern California. Rooms in this 1904-built Craftsman have down comforters, Oriental silks on the walls, and needlepoint rugs. The vintage dining room table seats 12; conversation is encouraged. You're also welcome to hang out with the hummingbirds in the private garden. All rooms includes a hearty breakfast, homemade cookies, and free local phone calls. ⊠ *657 W. 23rd St., Downtown, 90007* ☎ *213/741–2200 or 800/347–7512* ⊕ *www. patsysinn657.com* ⌗ *11 rooms* ⌂ *Dining room, fans, some microwaves, refrigerators, cable TV, in-room VCRs, in-room broadband, Wi-Fi, massage, laundry service, business services, free parking; no smoking* ▭ *MC, V* ⦿ *BP.*

$–$$ 🏠 **The Standard, Downtown LA.** Built in 1955 as Standard Oil's company's
Fodor'sChoice   headquarters, the building was completely revamped under the sharp
★   eye of owner André Balazs. The large guest rooms are practical and funky: all have orange built-in couches; windows that actually open; and platform beds. (Some also have large plush toys in the shape of human feet—not practical, but definitely fun). Bathrooms have extra-large tubs. The indoor–outdoor rooftop lounge has a preening social scene and stunning setting, but be prepared for some attitude at the door. Daytime traffic and the nightly bar scene make some rooms noisy. ⊠ *550 S. Flower St., Downtown, 90071* ☎ *213/892–8080* 🖷 *213/892–8686* ⊕ *www. standardhotel.com* ⌗ *205 rooms, 2 suites* ⌂ *Restaurant, room service, in-room safes, minibars, cable TV with movies and video games, in-room broadband, in-room DVDs, pool, gym, hair salon, massage, billiards, 2 bars, lobby lounge, dry cleaning, laundry service, concierge, business services, meeting rooms, parking (fee), some pets allowed, no-smoking rooms* ▭ *AE, D, DC, MC, V.*

$ 🏠 **Kawada Hotel.** This modest, four-story redbrick hotel near the Disney Hall, Music Center, and local government buildings is at the foot of Bunker Hill. The immaculate guest rooms are on the small side but come with two phones and a wet bar. Studios are available for stays of one month or longer. Weekend rates can be as low as $79 per night. ⊠ *200 S. Hill St., Downtown, 90012* ☎ *213/621–4455 or 800/752–9232* 🖷 *213/687–4455* ⊕ *www.kawadahotel.com* ⌗ *115 rooms, 1 suite* ⌂ *Restaurant, room service, kitchenettes, refrigerators, cable TV, in-room VCRs, laundry facilities, laundry service, concierge, business services, meeting room, parking (fee); no smoking* ▭ *AE, D, DC, MC, V.*

Coastal & Western Los Angeles

Bel Air

$$$$ 🏠 **Hotel Bel-Air.** In a wooded canyon with lush gardens and a swan-filled
Fodor'sChoice   lake, the Hotel Bel-Air's distinctive luxury and seclusion have made it
★   a favorite of discreet celebs and royalty for decades. Bungalow-style rooms feel like fine homes, with country-French, expensively upholstered furniture in silk or chenille; many have hardwood floors. Several rooms

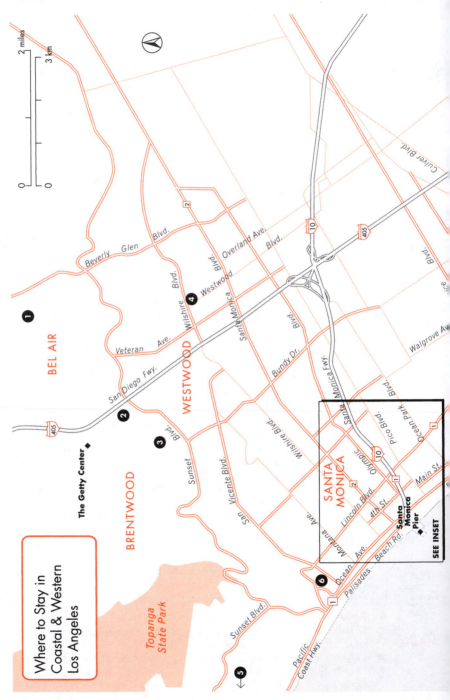

Where to Stay in Coastal & Western Los Angeles

2 miles
3 km

BEL AIR

1

BRENTWOOD

The Getty Center ◆

405

2

3

WESTWOOD

Beverly   Glen   Blvd.

2

Westwood Blvd.

Wilshire

4

Overland Ave.   Blvd.

Santa Monica   Blvd.

Veteran   Ave.

San Diego Fwy.

Sunset

Blvd.

San Vicente Blvd.

Montana Ave.

Wilshire Blvd.

Bundy Dr.

Santa Monica Fwy.

10

405

Culver Blvd.

Walgrove Av.

Blvd.

Pico Blvd.

Ocean park   Blvd.

1

SANTA MONICA

10

2

Olympic

Lincoln Blvd.

4th St.

Main St.

Santa

1

Santa Monica Pier ◆

SEE INSET

Topanga State Park

6

Ocean   Ave.

Palisades   Beach Rd.

1

Sunset Blvd.

Pacific   Coast Hwy.

5

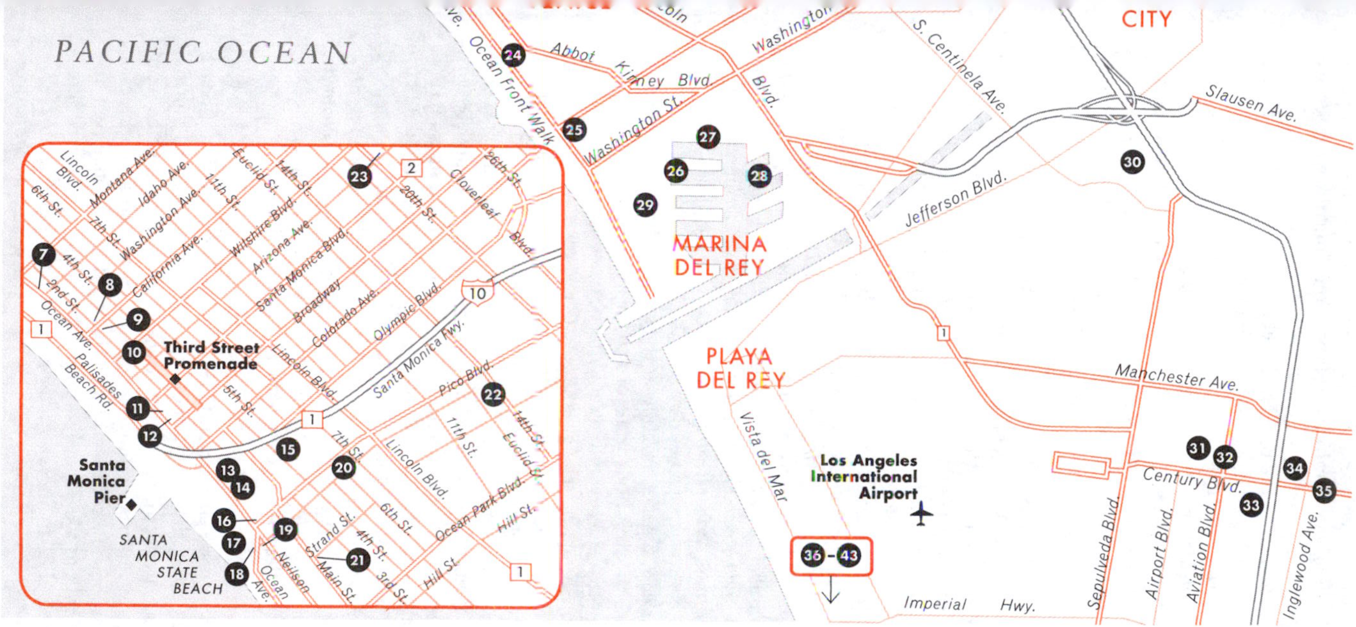

CITY

PACIFIC OCEAN

Los Angeles
International
Airport

MARINA
DEL REY

PLAYA
DEL REY

Vista del Mar

SANTA
MONICA
STATE
BEACH

Santa
Monica
Pier

Third Street
Promenade

have wood-burning fireplaces (the bell captain will build a fire for you). Eight suites have private outdoor hot tubs. Complimentary tea service greets you upon arrival; enjoy it on the terrace warmed by heated tiles. A pianist plays nightly in the bar. The hotel's excellent restaurant spills into the garden and a heated, vine-draped terrace. ⊠ *701 Stone Canyon Rd., Bel Air, 90077* ☎ *310/472–1211 or 800/648–4097* 🖷 *310/476– 5890* ⊕ *www.hotelbelair.com* 🛏 *52 rooms, 39 suites* ♨ *Restaurant, room service, in-room safes, minibars, cable TV with movies and video games, in-room VCRs, in-room broadband, pool, gym, massage, piano bar, shop, babysitting, dry cleaning, laundry service, concierge, business services, meeting rooms, free parking, some pets allowed (fee), no-smoking rooms* ▭ *AE, DC, MC, V.*

$$$ 🏨 **Luxe Hotel Sunset Boulevard.** On seven landscaped acres near the Getty Center, the Luxe feels like a secluded country club—but it's also next to the I–405, so you can quickly hit the road. After an overhaul in 2006, the guest rooms now have a comfortable residential look, with a taupe-and-brown color scheme, feather duvets, flat-screen TVs, iPod base stations on bedside tables. Book lessons with the hotel's tennis pro or head for the spa, which offers 16 kinds of massage. The Café Bel-Air is a neighborhood favorite for lunch on the sunny patio. ⊠ *11461 Sunset Blvd., Bel Air, 90049* ☎ *310/476–6571 or 866/589–3411* 🖷 *310/471–6310* ⊕ *www. luxehotels.com* 🛏 *110 rooms, 51 suites* ♨ *Restaurant, room service, in-room safes, minibars, cable TV with movies and video games, Wi-Fi, tennis court, pool, gym, spa, bar, shop, babysitting, dry cleaning, laundry service, concierge, business services, convention center, parking (fee), some pets allowed (fee), no-smoking rooms* ▭ *AE, D, DC, MC, V.*

$$ 🏨 **Hotel Angeleno.** Opened in 2006 at the crossroads of Sunset Boulevard and the I–405, this hotel transformed the local landmark of a mod, cylindrical tower. Inside, everything couldn't be more up-to-date and cleverly designed. Compact, triangle-shaped rooms, each with a tiny balcony, give views of Bel Air's hills or the freeway, a serpentine river of lights at night. Granite counters and stone-lined showers add a bit of luxury to the bathrooms. Instead of closets, you'll find armoires with conveniently placed hooks outside. On the 17th floor, complete with panoramic views, West is hotel's coppery, wood-accented restaurant serving robust Italian specialties. ⊠ *170 N. Church La., Bel Air, 90049* ☎ *310/ 476–6411 or 800/264–3536* 🖷 *310/476–1157* ⊕ *www.hotelangeleno. com* 🛏 *206 rooms, 3 suites* ♨ *Restaurant, room service, in-room safes, minibar, cable TV with movies, Wi-Fi, pool, gym, lounge, dry cleaning, laundry service, concierge, Internet room, business services, meeting rooms, parking (fee), no smoking* ▭ *AE, D, DC, MC, V.*

Long Beach

$$–$$$ 🏨 **Renaissance Long Beach Hotel.** Directly across from the Long Beach Convention Center, the Renaissance uses a sun, sea, and sand motif in the 16,000 square feet it uses for its own meeting space. The contemporary guest rooms have pillow-top mattresses and large work desks. Ask for a harbor-view room to take in those SoCal sunsets. From here it's an easy walk to the Aquarium of the Pacific or the touristy Shoreline Village. ⊠ *111 E. Ocean Blvd., Long Beach 90802* ☎ *562/437– 5900 or 800/468–3571* 🖷 *562/499–2509* ⊕ *www.renaissancehotels.com*

🛏 *360 rooms, 14 suites* ⌘ *2 restaurants, coffee shop, room service, mini-bars, cable TV with movies, in-room broadband, Web TV, pool, gym, hot tub, massage, sauna, bar, shop, laundry service, concierge, concierge floor, business services, convention center, car rental, parking (fee), some pets allowed (fee), no-smoking rooms* ▭ *AE, D, DC, MC, V.*

$–$$ 🏨 **Queen Mary.** Rich in history and tradition, the legendary (and allegedly haunted) *Queen Mary*, once the reigning maritime monarch of the Atlantic, transports its guests to a bygone era. The ship's first-class staterooms and suites are decorated in the classic art deco of the 1930s. There's plenty of nightime entertainment, from a comedy club to live theater to jazz. Holidays are big on the *Queen Mary;* New Year's Eve and July 4 are famously spectacular. Room stays include a self-guided tour of the venerable vessel. Wi-Fi is available in the lobby only. ✉ *1126 Queens Hwy., Long Beach 90802* ☎ *562/435–3511 or 800/437–2934* 🖷 *562/437–4531* ⊕ *www.queenmary.com* 🛏 *357 staterooms, 8 suites* ⌘ *3 restaurants, room service, cable TV, gym, spa, bar, cabaret, comedy club, nightclub, shops, laundry service, business services, meeting rooms, car rental, parking (fee), no-smoking rooms* ▭ *AE, DC, MC, V.*

Los Angeles International Airport

$$$ 🏨 **Los Angeles Airport Marriott.** Popular with single-overnight travelers and conventioneers, this 18-story Marriott hums year-round. A well-outfitted business center with FedEx and Kinko's services caters to business needs. Rooms are on the small side but soundproof (a good thing, since many face a busy runway). Champions, the hotel's TV-filled sports bar, attracts many local sports fans. ✉ *5855 W. Century Blvd., LAX, 90045* ☎ *310/641–5700 or 800/228–9290* 🖷 *310/337–5358* ⊕ *www.marriott.com* 🛏 *988 rooms, 22 suites* ⌘ *3 restaurants, café, room service, cable TV with movies and video games, in-room broadband, Web TV, pool, gym, hair salon, outdoor hot tub, massage, sauna, 2 bars, lobby lounge, sports bar, shop, babysitting, dry cleaning, laundry facilities, concierge, concierge floor, Internet room, business services, convention center, airport shuttle, car rental, parking (fee), some pets allowed, no-smoking floors* ▭ *AE, D, DC, MC, V.*

★ $$$ 🏨 **Sheraton Gateway Hotel.** LAX's coolest-looking hotel is so swank that guests have been known to ask to buy the black-and-white photos hanging behind the front desk. Extras for in-transit visitors include 24-hour room service, a 24-hour fitness center, currency exchange, a business center, and a 24-hour airport shuttle. Rooms are compact but soundproof and have helpful extras such as coffeemakers, hooks for hanging garment bags, and oversize work desks. Faux animal-skin headboards and ebonized furniture make the guest rooms feel more sophisticated than corporate. ✉ *6101 W. Century Blvd., LAX, 90045* ☎ *310/642–1111 or 800/325–3535* 🖷 *310/645–1414* ⊕ *www.sheraton.com* 🛏 *702 rooms, 102 suites* ⌘ *2 restaurants, café, room service, some in-room faxes, cable TV with movies and video games, in-room broadband, Wi-Fi, pool, gym, hot tub, bar, shop, babysitting, dry cleaning, concierge, concierge floor, Internet room, business services, convention center, airport shuttle, helipad, parking (fee), some pets allowed; no smoking* ▭ *AE, D, DC, MC, V.*

$$$ 🏨 **Westin Los Angeles Airport.** Close to the I–405 and on the airport's hotel corridor, the jumbo Westin offers reasonable park-and-ride packages. But there are strong suits here other than convenience and the long list of amenities. The guest rooms are spacious and many suites have private outdoor hot tubs. They also offer special pet amenities; ask ahead for the doggie bed. ✉ *5400 W. Century Blvd., LAX, 90045* ☎ *310/216–5858 or 800/937–8461* 🖷 *310/417–4545* ⊕ *www.westin. com* 🛏 *723 rooms, 42 suites* ♨ *Restaurant, room service, some in-room faxes, in-room safes, minibars, refrigerators, cable TV with movies, in-room broadband, Wi-Fi, pool, gym, hot tub, sauna, billiards, bar, children's programs (ages 6–13), laundry service, concierge, business services, meeting room, airport shuttle, car rental, some pets allowed (fee), parking (fee); no smoking* ▭ *AE, D, DC, MC, V.*

$$–$$$ 🏨 **Hilton Los Angeles Airport.** Coming and going at odd hours? This hotel could fill the bill as it ticks away 24/7 with arriving flight crews, businesspeople, and international visitors. The multilingual staff, currency exchange, 24-hour bistro, 24-hour business center, and an absurdly large 24-hour health club cover all sorts of needs no matter what the hour. Rooms are done in basic browns and beiges and come with a large work desk. ■ **TIP→** Hallways are immense; be prepared for a long walk to the guest rooms. ✉ *5711 W. Century Blvd., LAX, 90045* ☎ *310/410–4000 or 800/321–3232* 🖷 *310/410–6250* ⊕ *www.hilton.com* 🛏 *1,234 rooms, 152 suites* ♨ *3 restaurants, café, room service, cable TV with movies and video games, in-room broadband, Wi-Fi, pool, gym, 3 outdoor hot tubs, bar, lobby lounge, shop, babysitting, laundry service, concierge, concierge floor, business services, convention center, airport shuttle, car rental, parking (fee), some pets allowed (fee), no-smoking floors* ▭ *AE, D, DC, MC, V.*

$$ 🏨 **Radisson Los Angeles Westside.** Just 3 mi north of LAX, the Radisson Westside is close to freeways and a good value for those who want to fly in and find a hotel right away. Weekend rates can be as low as $109. The contemporary rooms may not have much personality but they are spacious. Executive-floor perks include late checkout, pillow-top mattresses, free high-speed Internet access, and a complimentary pass to the nearby Spectrum Club deluxe gym. ✉ *6161 Centinela Ave., Culver City 90231* ☎ *310/649–1776 or 800/333–3333* 🖷 *310/649–4411* ⊕ *www.radisson.com* 🛏 *365 rooms, 3 suites* ♨ *Restaurant, room service, refrigerators, cable TV with movies, in-room broadband, pool, gym, outdoor hot tub, bar, sports bar, shop, laundry service, business services, meeting room, airport shuttle, car rental, parking (fee), some pets allowed, no-smoking rooms* ▭ *AE, D, DC, MC, V.*

$$ 🏨 **Summerfield Suites.** There's room to spread out in these extra-large one- and two-bedroom suites; there are even living-room sleeper sofas. Cook in the fully outfitted kitchens or on the gas grills outside. The staff will stock your refrigerator with groceries (the service is free, but you'll have to pay for the groceries). Weeknights, the hotel welcomes you to a happy hour with complimentary drinks and snacks. ✉ *810 S. Douglas Ave., El Segundo 90245* ☎ *310/725–0100 or 800/996–3426* 🖷 *310/725–0900* ⊕ *www.summerfieldsuites.com* 🛏 *122 suites* ♨ *Dining room, kitchens, in-room fax, refrigerators, cable TV, in-room VCRs, in-room broadband, pool, gym, hot tub, basketball, laundry facilities,* *laundry service, business services, meeting rooms, free parking, some pets allowed (fee), no-smoking rooms* ⊟ *AE, D, DC, MC, V* ⫟ *BP.*

$–$$ ▦ **Holiday Inn LAX.** Close to the intersection of the I–405 and I–105 freeways, this 12-story hotel appeals to families as well as businesspeople. Twenty-four-hour services include a shuttle to the airport and a business center. Although lacking in charm, accommodations are functional: there's free Wi-Fi and coffeemakers. For those who need to park and fly, you can stay one night and receive up to 14 nights' free parking. ⊠ *9901 La Cienega Blvd., LAX, 90045* ☎ *310/649–5151 or 800/624–0025* ⊟ *310/670–3619* ⊕ *www.holiday-inn.com* ⫧ *405 rooms, 2 suites* ⟡ *Restaurant, room service cable TV with movies and video games, in-room broadband, Wi-Fi, pool, gym, bar, dry cleaning, laundry facilities, concierge, business services, airport shuttle, car rental, parking (fee), no-smoking rooms* ⊟ *AE, D, DC, MC, V.*

Hermosa Beach

★ $$$ ▦ **Beach House at Hermosa.** Sitting right on the sand, bordering SoCal's famous beach bike path, the Strand, the Beach House looks like a New England sea cottage from a century ago. Outside it's all gray shingles and overhanging white eaves, but inside you'll find contemporary amenities in split-level, loftlike rooms. Ocean-front rooms facing the Strand have terrific sunset views and small balconies. All rooms have two TVs, four multiline phones, CD player, fireplace, wet bar, and extra sound-proofing. Expect to pay more for ocean-view rooms and weekend stays. ⊠ *1300 The Strand, Hermosa Beach, 90254* ☎ *310/374–3001 or 888/895–4559* ⊟ *310/372–2115* ⊕ *www.beach-house.com* ⫧ *96 suites* ⟡ *Dining room, room service, kitchenettes, minibars, microwaves, cable TV, in-room data ports, gym, outdoor hot tub, massage, beach, dry cleaning, laundry service, concierge, business services, meeting rooms, parking (fee); no smoking* ⊟ *AE, D, DC, MC, V* ⫟ *CP.*

Malibu

$–$$$ ▦ **Casa Malibu.** A charming, family-run inn, the Casa Malibu sits directly on the beach. All that's between you and the ocean in the beach-front rooms are sliding-glass doors and a small deck. Ask for a room with a fireplace for the complete experience. Room decor is unremarkable, but with the ocean just outside, it's hardly a drawback. The Casa Malibu's private stretch of beach is raked each morning; guests get the use of beach chairs, towels, and umbrellas. Most of Malibu's best restaurants are close by. Book early for summer months or weekends. ⊠ *22752 Pacific Coast Hwy., Malibu 90265* ☎ *310/456–2219 or 800/831–0858* ⊟ *310/456–5418* ⊕ *www.casamalibu.com* ⫧ *19 rooms, 2 suites* ⟡ *Room service, some fans, some kitchens, cable TV, in-room DVD/VCR, in-room data ports, Wi-Fi, golf privileges, beach, babysitting, dry cleaning, laundry service, free parking; no a/c in some rooms, no smoking* ⊟ *AE, MC, V* ⫟ *CP.*

Manhattan Beach

$$$–$$$$ ▦ **shade.** Super-contemporary design makes this place feel like an adults-only playground. Rooms come with a sunken whirlpool tub surrounded by a movable shoji-like screen, a sculptural fireplace, a martini shaker, and overhead "chromatherapy" lighting that changes color via digital touch plates. Up on the roof is a sundeck and workout area; stand on tiptoe to see the ocean. The hotel's just a short walk to the beach, the local pier, and some of the area's best restaurants and shops. ✉ *1221 N. Valley Dr., Manhattan Beach 90266* ☎ *310/546–4995 or 866/987–4233* 🖨 *310/546–4985* ⊕ *www.shadehotel.com* 🛏 *33 rooms, 5 suites* ♨ *Restaurant, room service, in-room safes, in-room hot tubs, minibars, cable TV with movies, in-room DVDs, in-room broadband, Wi-Fi, outdoor hot tub, massage, bicycles, bar, lobby lounge, babysitting, dry cleaning, laundry service, concierge, Internet room, meeting rooms, parking (fee); no smoking* ▤ *AE, D, DC, MC, V.*

★ **$$** 🏨 **Ayres Hotel.** Though the rates are modest, the style here is grand. The building resembles a stone-clad chateau—but it's close to the I–405 rather than in the French countryside. Inside you'll find high ceilings, oil paintings, and formal furniture: in short, not the typical casual beachy look. The kitchen facilities in the guest rooms are a thoughtful plus. A free shuttle runs within a 3-mi area. ✉ *14400 Hindry Ave., Hawthorne 90250* ☎ *310/536–0400 or 800/675–3550* 🖨 *310/536–7665* ⊕ *www. ayresmanhattanbeach.com* 🛏 *173 rooms* ♨ *Restaurant, room service, microwaves, refrigerators, cable TV with movies, in-room broadband, pool, outdoor hot tub, laundry facilities, laundry service, concierge, meeting rooms, free parking, no-smoking rooms* ▤ *AE, D, DC, MC, V* ⦿ *BP.*

Marina del Rey

★ **$$$$** 🏨 **Ritz-Carlton Marina del Rey.** You might have a sense of déjà vu here since this resort, overlooking L.A.'s largest marina, is a favorite location of dozens of TV and film productions. Traditionally styled rooms in warm, gold tones have French doors, marble baths, and featherbeds, but the true luxury is in the spectacular, panoramic views. Book early for the popular Sunday champagne brunch at the waterside restaurant, Jer-ne. Check out the chlorine-free pool: it uses a balance of minerals to keep the water clean. If you sail into Los Angeles, docking fees at one of the hotel's 14 slips includes use of the fitness center and dockside room service. ✉ *4375 Admiralty Way, Marina del Rey, 90292* ☎ *310/823–1700 or 800/241–3333* 🖨 *310/823–2403* ⊕ *www.ritzcarlton.com* 🛏 *304 rooms, 12 suites* ♨ *Restaurant, snack bar (seasonal), room service, in-room safes, minibars, cable TV with movies and video games, in-room broadband, Wi-Fi, 2 tennis courts, pool, gym, outdoor, hot tub, sauna, spa, dock, bicycles, basketball, bar, lobby lounge, shop, babysitting, dry cleaning, laundry service, concierge, concierge floor, Internet room, business services, convention center, car rental, some pets allowed (fee), parking (fee), no-smoking rooms* ▤ *AE, D, DC, MC, V.*

$$$ 🏨 **Marina del Rey Marriott.** A total interior revamp in 2006 made this Marriott cooler than most. Guest rooms and public areas have a streamlined, contemporary look; happily, they don't go overboard with a nautical theme. Ask for upper-floor rooms facing the marina for the best views. Working in-room is made easier by two movable desks, ergonomic chairs, multiline phones, and high-speed Internet access. Wi-Fi is available in the lobby lounge. ✉ *4100 Admiralty Way, Marina del Rey, 90292* ☎ *310/301–3000 or 800/228–9290* 🖨 *310/448–4870* ⊕ *www.marriotthotels.com* 🛏 *332 rooms, 38 suites* ♨ *Restaurant, room service, in-room safes, refrigerators, cable TV with movies, in-room* *broadband, Web TV, Wi-Fi, pool, gym, bar, shop, babysitting, laundry service, concierge, concierge floor, business services, meeting rooms, car rental, parking (fee); no-smoking ⊟ AE, D, DC, MC, V.*

$–$$ 🏨 **Marina del Rey Hotel & Marina.** The balconies, patios, and harbor-view rooms take full advantage of the hotel's waterfront position. Cruises and charters are easily accessible from nearby slips; bike and in-line skate rentals are nearby, too. You can take advantage of complimentary access to a fitness club five blocks away or simply relax by the pool or gazebo. ⊠ *13534 Bali Way, Marina del Rey, 90292* ☎ *310/301–1000 or 800/882–4000* 🖷 *310/301–8167* ⊕ *www.marinadelreyhotel.com* 🛏*156 rooms, 2 suites* ⚭ *Restaurant, room service, cable TV with movies and video games, in-room data ports, pool, outdoor hot tub, bar, laundry service, concierge, meeting room, airport shuttle, free parking, no-smoking rooms* ⊟ *AE, DC, MC, V.*

$ 🏨 **Marina International Hotel & Bungalows.** A villagelike feel is evoked by white shutters on each window and private balconies overlooking the flower-filled courtyard. Large rooms have contemporary decor and French doors; some have partial views of the water. The split-level bungalows, each with its own private entrance, are huge. ■ **TIP→ Because it's across from a sandy beach within the marina, the hotel is a good choice for families with children.** ⊠ *4200 Admiralty Way, Marina del Rey, 90292* ☎ *310/301–2000 or 800/529–2525* 🖷 *310/301–6687* ⊕ *www. marinaintlhotel.com* 🛏 *110 rooms, 24 bungalows* ⚭ *Restaurant, room service, minibars, cable TV with movies, in-room data ports, pool, hot tub, bar, laundry service, concierge, business services, meeting room, airport shuttle, free parking, no-smoking rooms* ⊟ *AE, DC, MC, V.*

Redondo Beach

★ $$$ 🏨 **Crowne Plaza Redondo Beach & Marina Hotel.** This suburban five-story hotel feels like a resort—the beach is a short walk away, with a 22-mi bike path bordering the property. Across the street from King Harbor Marina, the hotel is a five-minute walk from the Redondo Beach Pier restaurants, shops, and arcade. Most rooms have balconies with a water view. A free shuttle is available to the two major shopping malls nearby. A favorite guest perk: stays include use of the on-site Gold's Gym. ⊠ *300 N. Harbor Dr., Redondo Beach 90277* ☎ *310/318–8888 or 877/227–6963* 🖷 *310/376–1930* ⊕ *www.redondobeach.crowneplaza.com* 🛏 *334 rooms, 5 suites* ⚭ *Restaurant, room service, in-room safes, minibars, cable TV with movies, in-room broadband, Web TV, Wi-Fi, tennis court, pool, health club, hair salon, outdoor hot tub, sauna, spa, bicycles, bar, laundry facilities, laundry service, concierge, concierge floor, business services, car rental, parking (fee), no-smoking rooms* ⊟ *AE, D, DC, MC, V.*

$$$ 🏨 **The Portofino Hotel & Yacht Club.** Reach out and touch the Pacific Ocean from this secluded South Bay hotel. There's water everywhere, and all rooms have views of either the ocean or King Harbor; you'll pay a premium for the ocean view. The resort atmosphere encourages guests to explore: borrow a bike, swim, rent a boat, or go fishing. In the nautically themed room, you can listen to the sounds of the marina and sink into the brightly colored overstuffed furniture. ⊠ *260 Portofino Way, Redondo Beach 90277* ☎ *310/379–8481 or 800/468–4292* 🖷 *310/372–7329* ⊕ *www. hotelportofino.com* 🛏 *161 rooms, 2 suites* ⚭ *Restaurant, room service,*

minibars, cable TV, in-room broadband, pool, outdoor hot tub gym, marina, bicycles, laundry service, concierge, business services, meeting rooms, parking (fee), no-smoking rooms ▤ AE, D, DC, MC, V.

Santa Monica

$$$$ ⊞ **Fairmont Miramar Hotel Santa Monica.** A mammoth Moreton Bay fig tree dwarfs the main entrance of this sprawling place. Residential-style bungalows, built between 1920 and 1946, are extremely private and a favorite of visiting VIPs. Standard rooms in the 10-story tower have no room to spare, but they do come with beautiful ocean views, alabaster light fixtures, carved wood armoires, Bose stereo systems, and down duvets. Although you're not right on the beach, the Third Street Promenade is close by. ⊠ *101 Wilshire Blvd., Santa Monica 90401* ☎ *310/576–7777 or 800/257–7544* 🖷 *310/458–7912* ⊕ *www.fairmont.com/santamonica* 🛏 *251 rooms, 51 suites, 32 bungalows* ⚷ *Restaurant, room service, in-room safes, minibars, cable TV with movies and video games, in-room data ports, in-room broadband, Wi-Fi (lobby only), pool, gym, hair salon, outdoor hot tub, sauna, spa, steam room, bicycles, bar, lobby lounge, shop, babysitting, dry cleaning, laundry service, concierge, business services, convention center, car rental, travel services, parking (fee), some pets allowed (fee), no-smoking rooms* ▤ *AE, D, DC, MC, V.*

★ **$$$$** ⊞ **Hotel Casa del Mar.** In the 1920s it was a posh beach club catering to the city's elite; now the Casa del Mar is one of SoCal's most luxurious beachfront hotels, with three extravagant two-story penthouses, a raised deck and pool, and an elegant ballroom facing the sand. Guest rooms, designed to evoke the old days with furnishings like overstuffed chaise lounges and vintage-style armoires are filled with contemporary amenities like flat-screen TVs, CD players, and supremely comfortable beds with sumptuous linens. Bathrooms are gorgeous, with sunken whirlpool tubs and glass-enclosed showers. Spa services use deliciously scented Murad products. ⊠ *1910 Ocean Front Way, Santa Monica 90405* ☎ *310/581–5533 or 800/898–6999* 🖷 *310/581–5503* ⊕ *www.hotelcasadelmar.com* 🛏 *129 rooms, 4 suites* ⚷ *2 restaurants, room service, in-room safes, minibars, cable TV with movies and video games, in-room VCRs, in-room broadband, pool, gym, spa, bar, lobby lounge, shop, dry cleaning, laundry service, concierge, business services, meeting room, parking (fee), some pets allowed; no smoking* ▤ *AE, D, DC, MC, V.*

$$$$ ⊞ **Hotel Oceana.** Generous-size suites, Matisse cutouts on the headboards, a leafy courtyard, and ocean proximity add up to a delightful boutique hotel. The Oceana is unpretentious and casual but has excellent service and luxe touches, including fine Egyptian linens, plush bathrobes, in-room spa services, and Aveda bath products. It's an easy walk to prime shopping on Montana Avenue and the Third Street Promenade, the Palisades park, or the beach. ⊠ *849 Ocean Ave., Santa Monica 90403* ☎ *310/393–0486 or 800/777–0758* 🖷 *310/458–1182* ⊕ *www.hoteloceanasantamonica.com* 🛏 *63 suites* ⚷ *Room service, fans, in-room safes, kitchenettes, microwaves, refrigerators, cable TV with movies and video games, in-room VCRs, in-room data ports, Wi-Fi, pool, gym, massage, lounge, babysitting, dry cleaning, laundry service, concierge, business services, meeting room, parking (fee), no-smoking rooms* ▤ *AE, D, DC, MC, V.*

With Children?

MOST HOTELS IN LOS ANGELES allow children under a certain age to stay in their parents' room at no extra charge, but others charge for them as extra adults; be sure to find out the cutoff age for children's discounts.

Hotel pools are dependable distractions for kids, but some are better than others. The **Beverly Hilton** has an almost Olympic-size pool that's perfect for splash time. Santa Monica's **Le Merigot Beach Hotel & Spa** has a small pool and even bigger beach out the back door. Kids get all the makings for sand castles: small shovel, bucket, and sand shapes. At the **Beverly Hills Hotel** there are a lifeguard and swimming lessons and pool toys for children. Turndown for kids includes cookies, milk, and a teddy bear.

The **Omni Los Angeles** greets young guests with a gift bag of games. Kids' suites at **Beverly Garland's Holiday Inn** come with bunk beds and PlayStations. Also in the Valley, the venerable **Sportsman's Lodge** is close to Universal Studios, but a world unto itself: there's plenty of room for kids to roam safely. Prior to arrival at the **Loews Santa Monica** a family concierge can suggest family-friendly vacation ideas. The hotel also offers childproofing kits and special children's menus. **Shutters on the Beach** has weekly juggling and magic lessons and provides portable DVD players and kids' menus in its restaurants. Teens will like the **Renaissance Hollywood Hotel,** which links directly to Hollywood & Highland's shopping and Mann Theaters. The **Magic Castle Hotel,** more reasonably priced, is also close to Hollywood's action; kids can attend the famed magic show here only at Sunday brunch.

In summer, Pasadena's **Ritz-Carlton Huntington Hotel & Spa** entertains kids 7 to 12 with swimming, scavenger hunts, and tennis during half- or full-day packages. Additionally, depending on demand, children 5 to 12 are supervised for dinner and a movie while parents dine in romantic privacy.

$$$$ ⬛ **Loews Santa Monica Beach Hotel.** Walk to the ocean side of the soaring atrium here and you'll feel like you're on a cruise ship. Huge petrified palm trees loom over the dramatic lobby. Rooms that face the ocean are definitely worth the extra cost. In all rooms you'll find sunken bathtubs, stone counters, wood armoires, and CD players. You can order lunch poolside while lounging on bright-yellow terry-cloth chaises. Ocean & Vine, the hotel's restaurant, aptly pairs small plates with select wines and has a fun outdoor patio complete with firepits. Pets go first-class at Loews: each receives a treat upon arrival. ✉ *1700 Ocean Ave., Santa Monica 90401* ☎ *310/458–6700 or 800/235–6397* 🖷 *310/458–6761* ⊕ *www.loewshotels.com* ⇨ *323 rooms, 19 suites* ⚷ *2 restaurants, snack bar, room service, minibars, cable TV with movies, in-room broadband, pool, health club, hair salon, hot tub, sauna, spa, steam room, beach, bicycles, shops, babysitting, dry cleaning, laundry service, concierge, business services, meeting rooms, car rental,* *travel services, parking (fee), some pets allowed, no-smoking rooms* ⊟ *AE, D, DC, MC, V.*

$$$$
Fodor'sChoice
★

Shutters on the Beach. Set right on the sand, this gray-shingle inn has become synonymous with in-town escapism. Guest rooms have those namesake shutter doors, pillow-top mattresses, and white built-in cabinets filled with art books and curios. Bathrooms are luxe, each with a whirlpool tub, a raft of bath goodies, and a three-nozzle, glass-walled shower. While the hotel's service gets mixed reviews from some readers, the beachfront location and showhouse decor make this one of SoCal's most popular luxury hotels. ⊠ *1 Pico Blvd., Santa Monica 90405* ☎ *310/458–0030 or 800/334–9000* 🖷 *310/458–4589* ⊕ *www. shuttersonthebeach.com* ⬐ *186 rooms, 12 suites* ⌓ *2 restaurants, room service, in-room safes, in-room hot tubs, minibars, cable TV with movies and video games, in-room DVDs, in-room broadband, Wi-Fi, pool, gym, outdoor hot tub, sauna, spa, steam room, beach, bicycles, bar, lobby lounge, piano, shop, babysitting, dry cleaning, laundry service, concierge, business services, meeting rooms, parking (fee), no-smoking rooms* ⊟ *AE, D, DC, MC, V.*

$$$–$$$$ **The Huntley.** A school of 300 ceramic fish crossing a lobby wall signals the Huntley's stylish but unstuffy approach. The location's terrific, close to the beach, the Third Street Promenade, and chic Montana Avenue. In the thoughtfully designed guest rooms, large framed mirrors help enlarge the space. Earth tones and tufted suede headboards keep things mellow. Work desks are ample and come with some very retro accessories: a quill pen and inkwell. Other gadgets are thoroughly of-the-moment: plasma-screen TV, Wi-Fi, and room numbers projected onto walls from mini spotlights. Corner rooms have the best views. ⊠ *1111 2nd St., Santa Monica 90403* ☎ *310/394–5454* 🖷 *310/458–9776* ⊕ *www. preferredhotels.com* ⬐ *188 rooms, 21 suites* ⌓ *Restaurant, room service, in-room safes, minibars, cable TV with movies and video games, in-room DVDs, in-room data ports, Wi-Fi, gym, bar, shop, babysitting, dry cleaning, laundry service, concierge, business services, meeting rooms, car rental, parking (fee), no-smoking floors* ⊟ *AE, D, DC, MC, V.*

$$$ **The Georgian.** You can't miss the Georgian: the art deco exterior is aqua, with ornate bronze grillwork and a charming oceanfront veranda. Built in 1933, the hotel retains its retro character with cream-color walls, vintage tiles, marble floors accented with sea-foam green and silver blue, and individually styled rooms with cherrywood furnishings and gold and silver accents. Popular with visiting Europeans, the hotel has a lobby that echoes with multiple languages and accents. Sit on the veranda to best appreciate the beach, ocean, and Santa Monica views. Though there's a dining room, it's used for breakfast only. ⊠ *1415 Ocean Ave., Santa Monica 90401* ☎ *310/395–9945 or 800/538–8147* 🖷 *310/656–0904* ⊕ *www. georgianhotel.com* ⬐ *56 rooms, 28 suites* ⌓ *Dining room, room service, fans, in-room safes, minibars, cable TV with movies and video*

games, in-room data ports, Wi-Fi, gym, lobby lounge, dry cleaning, laundry service, concierge, meeting rooms, car rental, parking (fee), some pets allowed (fee) ▭ *AE, D, DC, MC, V.*

★ **$$$** ▦ **Le Merigot Beach Hotel & Spa.** Steps from Santa Monica's expansive beach, Le Merigot caters to a corporate clientele (it's a JW Marriott property). Upper floors have panoramic views of the Santa Monica Pier and the Pacific; many rooms have terraces. The contemporary rooms have featherbeds and Frette linens, and bathrooms come with playful bath toys and votive candles. Expect a seashell (not chocolate) at turndown. A checkerboard slate courtyard, including a pool, cabanas, fountains, and outdoor living room, is the center of activity. You can book a massage at the spa for a true attitude adjustment, or dine in French country style at the comfortable Cézanne restaurant. ✉ *1740 Ocean Ave., Santa Monica 90405* ☏ *310/395–9700 or 888/539–7899* 🖷 *310/395–9200* ⊕ *www.lemerigothotel.com* ⇴ *175 rooms, 15 suites* ⌂ *Restaurant, room service, in-room safes, minibars, cable TV with movies and video games, in-room broadband, in-room data ports, pool, fitness classes, gym, hair salon, sauna, spa, steam room, beach, bicycles, bar, shop, babysitting, dry cleaning, laundry service, concierge, business services, meeting rooms, parking (fee), some pets allowed (fee), no-smoking rooms* ▭ *AE, D, DC, MC, V.*

$$$ ▦ **Sheraton Delfina.** A spiffy renovation transformed this Sheraton from tired to trendy. The homey lobby, with plump armchairs and divans, welcomes business types who fill the hotel on weekdays. Rooms are done in calming ocean colors and the textured headboards look like crocodile skin—if crocodiles were blue. Oversize work desks are practical and ergonomic. Most rooms have balconies, and those facing west on the upper floors have expansive views of the ocean and Santa Monica Mountains. On the ground floor, banquettes, cabanas, and a teak deck surround the pool, primed for socializing. The Tide Shuttle makes short local jaunts to the nearby Third Street Promenade and Santa Monica's lively Main Street. ✉ *530 W. Pico Blvd., Santa Monica 90405* ☏ *310/399–9344 or 888/627–8532* 🖷 *310/399–2504* ⊕ *www.sheratonsantamonica.com* ⇴ *297 rooms, 11 suites* ⌂ *Restaurant, in-room safes, minibars, cable TV with movies and video games, in-room broadband, pool, gym, outdoor hot tub, massage, bar, dry cleaning, laundry facilities, laundry service, concierge, concierge floor, business services, convention center, parking (fee), some pets allowed (fee), no-smoking floors* ▭ *AE, D, DC, MC, V.*

$$$ ▦ **Viceroy.** Whimsy abounds at this stylized seaside escape—there are porcelain dogs as lamp bases and Spode china plates mounted on the walls. The compact rooms all have French balconies, and the mostly marble bathrooms have seated vanities. The glamorous socialize in the pool and cabana area amid all-white armchairs and divans. Spa services, from energizing massage to detox facials, are available in-room and poolside from nearby Fred Segal Beauty. ✉ *1819 Ocean Ave., Santa Monica 90401* ☏ *310/260–7500 or 800/622–8711* 🖷 *310/260–7515* ⊕ *www.viceroysantamonica.com* ⇴ *158 rooms, 5 suites* ⌂ *Restaurant, room service, in-room safes, minibars, cable TV with movies and video games, in-room DVDs, in-room broadband, 2 pools, gym, massage, bar, lobby* *lounge, library, dry cleaning, laundry service, concierge, meeting rooms, parking (fee), some pets allowed, no-smoking rooms* ⊟ *AE, DC, MC, V.*

$$–$$$ ★ **The Ambrose.** An air of tranquillity pervades the four-story Ambrose, which blends right into its mostly residential Santa Monica neighborhood. The decor incorporates many Asian accents, following the principles of feng shui. There's a Zen garden and koi pond at the entrance and Japanese wood-block prints throughout. Rooms have deluxe extras like chenille throws, Italian linens, Frette towels and robes, and a minibar with health-oriented elixirs. Windows are double-paned for quiet; upper floors have partial ocean views. Room service and the breakfast buffet include healthy choices. A vintage London taxi is on call for free short jaunts in the area. ⊠ *1255 20th St., Santa Monica 90404* ☎ *310/315–1555 or 877/262–7673* 🖷 *310/315–1556* ⊕ *www.ambrosehotel. com* 🖙 *77 rooms* ⚲ *Room service, some fans, in-room safes, minibars, cable TV, in-room VCRs, in-room broadband, fitness classes, gym, massage, bicycles, library, babysitting, dry cleaning, laundry service, concierge, meeting room, car rental, free parking, some pets allowed, no-smoking rooms* ⊟ *AE, D, DC, MC, V* ⦿ *CP.*

★ **$$–$$$** ★ **Channel Road Inn.** A quaint surprise in southern California, the Channel Road Inn is every bit the country retreat B&B lovers adore, with canopy beds with fluffy duvets and a cozy living room with fireplace. Rooms are old-fashioned, but each has a private bath (one room has only a shower, and a few have hot tubs). A sumptuous home-cooked breakfast is included; enjoy it downstairs or in your room. Walk a block to the beach or borrow one of the bicycles. Unwind in the lovely rose garden or book an in-room massage. ⊠ *219 W. Channel Rd., Santa Monica 90402* ☎ *310/459–1920* 🖷 *310/454–9920* ⊕ *www.channelroadinn. com* 🖙 *14 rooms* ⚲ *Some refrigerators, cable TV, in-room VCRs, in-room data ports, hot tubs, bicycles, Internet room, free parking; no smoking* ⊟ *AE, MC, V* ⦿ *BP.*

$$–$$$ ★ **Doubletree Guest Suites.** Sunlight streams through the glass-enclosed atrium and spills over a patiolike sitting area in the lobby. One- and two-bedroom soundproofed suites include a separate living room with a large desk, wet bar, and sofa bed; microwaves and refrigerators are available upon request. Just off the busy Santa Monica Freeway (I–10), the hotel is within walking distance of the Third Street Promenade, beaches, and the pier. ⊠ *1707 4th St., Santa Monica 90401* ☎ *310/395–3332 or 800/222–8733* 🖷 *310/452–7399* ⊕ *doubletree.hilton.com* 🖙 *253 suites* ⚲ *Restaurant, room service, minibars, cable TV with movies and video games, in-room broadband, Wi-Fi, pool, gym, outdoor hot tub, sauna, billiards, bar, shop, laundry facilities, laundry service, concierge, business services, meeting rooms, car rental, parking (fee), no-smoking rooms* ⊟ *AE, D, DC, MC, V.*

$$ ★ **Cal Mar Hotel Suites.** On a residential street one block from the Third Street Promenade and within a short walk to the beach, this low-profile, two-story, all-suite hotel is a comparative bargain. In summer, though, a three-night minimum stay is required. Standard and master one-bedroom suites have king or twin beds and a full-size sofa bed. Furnishings are contemporary and comfortable without much thought given to decorating, but the atmosphere is friendly and informal. Rooms wrap around an interior courtyard with pool and windows open to the street or back alley, adding up to city sounds and noise both day and night. ✉ *220 California Ave., Santa Monica 90403* ☎ *310/395–5555 or 800/776–6007* 📠 *310/451–1111* 🌐 *www.calmarhotel.com* 🛏 *36 suites* 🛎 *Fans, kitchens, microwaves, refrigerators, cable TV, in-room data ports, Wi-Fi, pool, laundry facilities, free parking, no-smoking rooms; no a/c* ▭ *AE, MC, V.*

$$ 🏨 **Hotel Carmel.** Price and location are the calling cards of this older, unpretentious hotel, favored by international travelers. Basic rooms are small; some have ocean views. Continental breakfast is served next door at Interactive Café. You can stroll to the Third Street Promenade or to the beach a couple of blocks away. In summer, rooms often sell out early so make reservations months ahead. ✉ *201 Broadway, Santa Monica 90401* ☎ *310/451–2469 or 800/445–8695* 📠 *310/393–4180* 🌐 *www.hotelcarmel.com* 🛏 *96 rooms, 8 suites* 🛎 *Cable TV, in-room data ports, laundry service, parking (fee), no-smoking rooms* ▭ *AE, D, DC, MC, V* ▥ *CP.*

$ 🏨 **Bayside Hotel.** Room decor is modest, but you can't beat the location of this hotel, just across the street from the beach and blocks from the Third Street Promenade and Santa Monica Pier. If keeping cool is a must, request one of the seven rooms with air-conditioning or one of those with unobstructed ocean views and balconies. Book early for summer weekends; the hotel typically sells out then. ✉ *2001 Ocean Ave., Santa Monica 90405* ☎ *310/396–6000 or 800/525–4447* 📠 *310/396–1000* 🌐 *www.baysidehotel.com* 🛏 *45 rooms* 🛎 *Some fans, some kitchens, some microwaves, some refrigerators, cable TV, in-room data ports, airport shuttle, car rental, free parking; no a/c in some rooms* ▭ *AE, D, MC, V.*

$ 🏨 **Sea Shore Motel.** On Santa Monica's busy Main Street, the Sea Shore is a throwback to Route 66 and to '60's-style roadside motels. The neighborhood around it is now as trendy as they come, and just two blocks from the beach and bike path. Rooms have tile floors and basic amenities. The rooftop sundeck is a prime spot come sunset, and Amelia's, the motel's sidewalk café, is popular with locals. Santa Monica's Big Blue Bus line passes out front. The Sea Shore is popular in summer; book early. ✉ *2637 Main St., Santa Monica 90405* ☎ *310/392–2787* 📠 *310/392–5167* 🌐 *www.seashoremotel.com* 🛏 *21 rooms, 4 suites* 🛎 *Restaurant, café, some kitchens, refrigerators, cable TV, in-room data ports, Wi-Fi, dry cleaning, laundry facilities, business services, free parking, some pets allowed (fee); no smoking* ▭ *AE, D, MC, V.*

¢–$ 🏨 **Palm Motel.** Right along Santa Monica's Big Blue Bus line, this cheerful budget motel is popular with Europeans in the summer. The spartan bungalows were built in the 1920s. You can grab a snack of free coffee and cookies to enjoy outside in the bougainvillea-filled courtyard. ✉ *2020 14th St., Santa Monica 90405* ☎ *310/452–3861 or 877/822–7256* 📠 *310/450–8635* 🌐 *www.palmmotel.homestead.com* 🛏 *26 rooms* 🛎 *Fans, Wi-Fi, free parking, some pets allowed (fee); no a/c, no smoking* ▭ *AE, MC, V.*

Venice

$$ 🏨 **Venice Beach House.** A vestige of Venice's founding days, the Venice Beach House was one of the seaside enclave's first mansions. Many Craftsman-era details remain: dark woods, the glass-enclosed breakfast nook, a lattice-framed portico, and many stairs. Privacy is not why guests stay here—soundproofing is circa 1911 standards. However, historic charm radiates and the location, steps from the beach and boardwalk, is what southern California is all about. ✉ *15 30th Ave., Venice, 90291* ☎ *310/832–1966* 🖷 *310/823–1842* ⊕ *www.venicebeachhouse.com* 🛏 *4 rooms without baths, 5 suites* ♨ *Dining room, fans, cable TV, in-room broadband, beach, parking (fee); no a/c, no smoking* ▭ *AE, MC, V* ❏ *CP.*

$–$$ ▨ **Best Western Marina Pacific Hotel & Suites.** The price is right at this hotel, which is steps from the beach and one of the world's most vibrant boardwalks. Surrounded by art galleries, shops, and offbeat restaurants, there's never a lack of things to do. Stroll the scenic Venice canals, or rent bikes or skates nearby; racquetball and tennis courts are also close. Good-size rooms are contemporary; some have balconies and views of the beach. ✉ *1697 Pacific Ave., Venice, 90291* ☎ *310/452–1111 or 800/786–7789* 🖷 *310/452–5479* ⊕ *www.mphotel.com* 🛏 *57 rooms, 35 suites* ♨ *Dining room, refrigerators, cable TV, in-room broadband, laundry service, meeting room, parking (fee), no-smoking rooms* ▭ *AE, D, DC, MC, V* ❏ *CP.*

Westwood

$$ ▨ **Doubletree Hotel.** In the middle of the high-rise condos that predominate in the mostly upscale residential Wilshire Corridor, this tastefully appointed, 19-story hotel blends in quietly with its surroundings. It's an ideal choice for visitors to the UCLA campus—there's a free shuttle to take you there. Rooms have standard hotel furnishings, with two double beds or one king; you get fresh chocolate-chip cookies at check-in. ✉ *10740 Wilshire Blvd., Westwood, 90024* ☎ *310/475–8711* 🖷 *310/475–5220* ⊕ *www.doubletreelawestwood.com* 🛏 *281 rooms, 14 suites* ♨ *Restaurant, room service, cable TV with movies and video games, in-room data ports, Wi-Fi, pool, gym, outdoor hot tub, bar, shop, dry cleaning, laundry service, concierge, business services, meeting rooms, parking (fee), no-smoking rooms* ▭ *AE, D, DC, MC, V.*

San Fernando Valley

Burbank

★ $$$ ▨ **The Graciela Burbank.** Close to Burbank's TV and movie studios, the smartly designed Graciela feels like a Beverly Hills boutique hotel. Over the years, it has become a favorite of women business travelers, who like its understated look (muted beiges and greens) and residential vibe. The lobby is a welcoming living room with glass fireplace and corners for quiet conversation or cocktails. Featherbeds are covered in comfy duvets; thoughtful touches include monogrammed pillowcases and plush bathrobes. Generous work spaces have state-of-the-art lighting. Bathrooms have granite vanities, makeup mirrors, and shelves for storage. The rooftop sundeck has a brightly striped cabana and view of the nearby hills. ✉ *322 N. Pass Ave., Burbank 91505* ☎ *818/842–8887 or 888/956–1900* 🖷 *818/260–8999* ⊕ *www.thegraciela.com* 🛏 *91 rooms, 10 suites* ♨ *Dining room, room service, in-room safes, some kitchenettes, microwaves, refrigerators, cable TV with movies and video games, in-room DVDs, in-room broadband, Wi-Fi, gym, outdoor hot tub, massage, sauna, bar, lobby lounge, babysitting, dry cleaning, laundry service, concierge, business services, meet-*

Where to Stay in the
San Fernando Valley

KEY

Ⓜ Metro Stops

ing rooms, airport shuttle (Burbank), parking (fee), some pets allowed (fee), no-smoking rooms ⊟ *AE, D, DC, MC, V.*

$$ 🏨 **Coast Anabelle Hotel.** This small hotel's location on Burbank's main drag is handy, especially for those on studio business since it's a straight-shot mile from NBC and 3 mi from Warner Bros. However, this setting also translates into guest reports of traffic noise and poor soundproofing. Nightly turndown, in-room coffee, a morning paper, and free Internet access are part of the stay. Guest can use the pool next door at the hotel's sister property, the Safari Inn. ⊠ *2011 W. Olive Ave., Burbank 91506* ☏ *818/845–7800 or 800/716–6199* 🖷 *818/845–0054* 🌐 *www.coasthotels.com* 🛏 *40 rooms, 7 suites* ⚖ *Restaurant, room service, in-room safes, refrigerators, cable TV with movies and video games, in-room data ports, Wi-Fi, gym, lobby lounge, laundry facilities, laundry service, airport shuttle (Burbank), free parking, no-smoking floors* ⊟ *AE, DC, MC, V.*

$–$$ 🏨 **Hilton Burbank Airport & Convention Center.** Across the street from the Burbank Airport and staffed with multilingual personnel, this contemporary Hilton is geared to business travelers. Rooms have ergonomic office chairs and work desks; furniture is all warm cherrywood. The reliable Daily Grill provides 24-hour room service. A free shuttle and discounted tickets to Universal Studios are a big plus. Ask for rooms in the

East Tower, facing away from the airport, for the quietest stay. ✉ *2500 Hollywood Way, Burbank 91505* ☎ *818/843–6000 or 800/774–1500* 🖷 *818/842–9720* 🌐 *www.burbankairport.hilton.com* 🛏 *411 rooms, 77 suites ☖ Restaurant, room service, cable TV with movies, in-room broadband, 2 pools, gym, outdoor hot tub, bar, shop, dry cleaning, laundry service, concierge, business services, meeting rooms, convention center, airport shuttle (Burbank), car rental, parking (fee), some pets allowed (fee), no-smoking floors* ▤ *AE, D, DC, MC, V.*

North Hollywood

$–$$ 🏨 **Beverly Garland's Holiday Inn.** This lodgelike hotel is in two separate buildings near Universal Studios. Rooms have an early California look, with distressed furniture, muted color schemes, and private balconies or patios. The hotel is next to the Hollywood Freeway, which can be noisy, so ask for a room facing Vineland Avenue. Transportation to Universal Studios and a nearby Metro stop is free. Special kids' suites have bunk beds and PlayStation 2. ✉ *4222 Vineland Ave., North Hollywood, 91602* ☎ *818/980–8000 or 800/238–3759* 🖷 *818/766–0112* 🌐 *www. beverlygarland.com* 🛏 *245 rooms, 10 suites ☖ Restaurant, café, room service, some microwaves, cable TV with movies, 2 tennis courts, pool, sauna, bar, shop, dry cleaning, laundry facilities, laundry service, business services, meeting rooms, car rental, parking (fee), no-smoking rooms* ▤ *AE, D, DC, MC, V.*

Studio City

$$ 🏨 **Sportsmen's Lodge.** This five-story, English country–style structure shares grounds with waterfalls, a swan-filled lagoon, and a gazebo; the pool area and lush garden make you forget you're near a city. Rooms are simply furnished and decorated in a flowery style. The restaurant overlooks the gardens and is a Valley favorite for brunch; on weekends, live entertainment and happy hours bring in the crowds from nearby TV studios. ■ **TIP→** **The hotel offers discount tickets and a complimentary shuttle to Universal Studios.** ✉ *12825 Ventura Blvd., Studio City, 91604* ☎ *818/ 769–4700 or 800/821–8511* 🖷 *818/769–4798* 🌐 *www.slhotel.com* 🛏 *177 rooms, 13 suites ☖ 3 restaurants, room service, cable TV, in-room data ports, Wi-Fi, pool, gym, hair salon, outdoor hot tub, lounge, pub, shop, dry cleaning, laundry facilities, laundry service, meeting rooms, airport shuttle (Burbank), car rental, travel services, free parking, no-smoking rooms* ▤ *AE, D, DC, MC, V.*

Universal City

$$$ 🏨 **Hilton Universal City and Towers.** This modern tower has surprisingly cozy rooms with marble baths and good views from floor-to-ceiling windows. Complimentary trams can take you to Universal Studios and the adjacent CityWalk. ✉ *555 Universal Hollywood Dr., Universal City, 91608* ☎ *818/506–2500 or 800/445–8667* 🖷 *818/509–2058* 🌐 *www. hilton.com* 🛏 *483 rooms, 9 suites ☖ Restaurant, room service, in-room safes, minibars, cable TV with movies and video games, in-room data ports, Wi-Fi, pool, hot tub, spa, lobby lounge, piano, shop, babysitting, laundry service, concierge floor, business services, meeting rooms, car rental, parking (fee), no-smoking rooms* ▤ *AE, D, DC, MC, V.*

$$$ 🏨 **Sheraton Universal.** With a bit of glitz, lots of comforts, and a veteran staff, the Sheraton Universal has become a favorite among those visiting Universal Studios and the nearby CityWalk. On the back lot of the famed movie studio and theme park, rooms have floor-to-ceiling windows, some with remarkable Hollywood views. In season, you can dine poolside at the Baja Bar. ⊠ *333 Universal Hollywood Dr., Universal City, 91608* ☎ *818/980–1212 or 800/325–3535* 🖷 *818/985–4980* ⊕ *www.sheraton.com* 📞 *436 rooms, 25 suites* ⛉ *Restaurant, room service, in-room safes, minibars, cable TV with movies and video games, in-room broadband, pool, gym, hot tub, massage, sauna, bar, babysitting, dry cleaning, laundry service, concierge, concierge floor, business services, meeting rooms, convention center, car rental, parking (fee), no-smoking rooms.* ▭ *AE, D, DC, MC, V.*

Woodland Hills

$$–$$$ 🏨 **Hilton Woodland Hills.** If you're doing business in the west San Fernando Valley, this location can't be beat. The Hilton is within the Warner Center business hub, near shopping, restaurants, and movie theaters. A complimentary shuttle will drive you within a 3-mi radius. Comfortable guest rooms, with a touch of Mediterranean style, have armoires, marble-tile bathrooms, and large work desks. Across the driveway is a full-service health club available free to hotel guests. ⊠ *6360 Canoga Ave., Woodland Hills, 91367* ☎ *818/595–1000 or 800/922–2400* 🖷 *818/595–1090* ⊕ *www.hilton.com* 📞 *295 rooms, 23 suites* ⛉ *Restaurant, room service, minibars, cable TV with movies, in-room broadband, 12 tennis courts, pool, health club, bar, lounge, shop, babysitting, dry cleaning, laundry, concierge, concierge floor, business services, meeting rooms, car rental, parking (fee), some pets allowed (fee), no-smoking floors* ▭ *AE, D, DC, MC, V.*

Pasadena

$$$$ 🏨 **Ritz-Carlton Huntington Hotel & Spa.** An azalea-filled Japanese garden
Fodor'sChoice and the unusual Picture Bridge, with murals celebrating California's history, make this an especially scenic place to stay. The Mediterranean-style main building is surrounded by 23 acres of green lawns. The service is truly outstanding; everyone from the valet to the poolside attendant is warm, attentive, and observant. Traditional guest rooms are handsome if a bit small; all have been updated in shades of gold and blue. Brocade fabrics are found throughout, as are flat-screen TVs and CD players. The hotel's formal restaurant, the Dining Room, can be counted on for a rarefied contemporary dining experience. The children's programs are offered in summer only. ⊠ *1401 S. Oak Knoll Ave., Pasadena 91106* ☎ *626/568–3900 or 800/241–3333* 🖷 *626/568–3700* ⊕ *www.ritzcarlton.com* 📞 *361 rooms, 31 suites* ⛉ *2 restaurants, room service, in-room safes, minibars, cable TV with movies, in-room broadband, Wi-Fi, 3 tennis courts, pool, health club, hair salon, outdoor hot tub, sauna, spa, steam room, bicycles, bar, lobby lounge, shops, babysitting, children's programs (ages 7–12), dry cleaning, laundry service, concierge, concierge floor, business services, meeting rooms, convention center, car rental, travel services, parking (fee), some pets allowed (fee), no-smoking rooms* ▭ *AE, D, DC, MC, V.*

$$$ 🏨 **Hilton Pasadena Hotel.** The Hilton Pasadena is across from the Pasadena Convention Center, the Paseo Colorado outdoor mall, and within walking distance of trendy Old Town. A light and airy sandstone lobby says California casual, as do the bright and spacious rooms done in soft gold and tan colors. Business travelers appreciate the Smart Desk with ergonomically correct chair. A state-of-the-art fitness center includes the latest in cardiovascular equipment. ⊠ *168 S. Los Robles Ave., Pasadena 91101* ☎ *626/577–1000 or 800/445–8667* 🖷 *626/584–3148* ⊕ *www.hilton.com* 🛏 *285 rooms, 11 suites* ⌁ *Restaurant, room service, minibars, cable TV with movies and video games, in-room data ports, Wi-Fi, pool, gym, hair salon, outdoor hot tub, massage, sports bar, shops, dry cleaning, laundry facilities, laundry service, business services, meeting rooms, car rental, parking (fee), some pets allowed (fee), no-smoking rooms* ▭ *AE, D, DC, MC, V.*

$$ 🏨 **Artists' Inn & Cottage.** This charming 1895 B&B is in a quiet residential neighborhood of Craftsman bungalows, not far from the antiques shops of South Pasadena. Once a chicken farm, the Artists' Inn still retains a country air with more than 100 rosebushes in the garden, wicker furniture on the front porch, and home-cooked breakfasts and afternoon tea. Some rooms have fireplaces; all have themes relating to a particular period of art (like impressionism) or famous artist (Degas, van Gogh, O'-Keeffe). Close by is a Gold Line Metro stop for easy access to downtown L.A. Room rates include parking and Internet access. ⊠ *1038 Magnolia St., Pasadena 91030* ☎ *626/799–5668 or 888/799–5668* 🖷 *626/799–3678* ⊕ *www.artistsinns.com* 🛏 *10 rooms* ⌁ *In-room data ports, Wi-Fi, free parking; no TV in some rooms, no smoking* ▭ *AE, MC, V* ⍟ *BP.*

$$ 🏨 **Westin Pasadena.** Hand-painted tile work and bountiful floral displays greet you in the lobby. Rooms range from spacious to modest in size, and some come with plantation shutters, picture windows, and window seats. The concierge floor offers in-room fax machines, breakfast and snacks in the Executive Club, and private access. The hotel caters to businesspeople on weekdays; nonholiday weekend rates are less. ⊠ *191 N. Los Robles Ave., Pasadena 91101* ☎ *626/792–2727 or 800/937–8461* 🖷 *626/792–3755* ⊕ *www.westin.com* 🛏 *348 rooms, 2 suites* ⌁ *2 restaurants, room service, in-room fax, cable TV with movies, in-room data ports, in-room broadband, pool, gym, massage, sauna, steam room, 2 bars, shop, dry cleaning, laundry service, concierge, concierge floor, meeting rooms, car rental, parking (fee); no-smoking* ▭ *AE, D, DC, MC, V.*

Nightlife & the Arts

WORD OF MOUTH

"The screen, sound system, projection, and seats [at Grauman's Chinese] are amazing. [They] play their movies louder than most movie theaters do, so don't bring your grandmother to an action movie there if she doesn't like loud noises."

—Movie Fan

"The club hot spots are along the east–west axes of Sunset and Santa Monica boulevards between Santa Monica and downtown LA . . . and in Hollywood proper, although I've generally found the Hollywood clubs to be a bit younger and more punkish."

—Big_Money_D

Revised & updated by Lina Lecaro

THE TURNOVER AMONG L.A.'S NIGHTSPOTS can be enough to make your head spin—it's almost as dizzying as the diversity that's available virtually every night of the week. Hollywood and West Hollywood, where hip and happening nightspots liberally dot Sunset and Hollywood boulevards, are the epicenter of L.A. nightlife. The city is one of the best places in the world for seeing soon-to-be-famous rockers as well as top jazz, blues, and classical performers. Movie theaters are naturally well represented here, but the worlds of dance, theater, and opera have flourished in the past few years as well.

For a thorough listing of local events, www.la.com and *Los Angeles Magazine* are both good sources. The Calendar section of the *Los Angeles Times* (⊕ www.calendarlive.com) also lists a wide survey of Los Angeles arts events, especially on Thursday and Sunday, as do the more alternative publications, the *LA Weekly* and the *Citybeat Los Angeles* (both free, and issued every Thursday). Call ahead to confirm that what you want to see is ongoing.

THE ARTS

The outdated belief that Los Angeles is a plastic city devoid of real culture continues to wither with each new cutting-edge performance that happens here. Placido Domingo has put the Los Angeles Opera on the map, while the museums, galleries, and theaters in town continue to push the boundaries of expression, showcasing out-of-the-box performance, dance, and visual artists from all around the world.

Concerts

Major Concert Halls

Built in 2003 as a grand addition to L.A.'s Music Center, the 2,265-seat **Walt Disney Concert Hall** (⊠ 151 S. Grand Ave., Downtown ☎ 323/850–2000) is now the home of the Los Angeles Philharmonic and the Los Angeles Master Chorale. A sculptural monument of gleaming, curved steel, the theater is part of a complex that includes a public park, gardens, and shops as well as two outdoor amphitheaters for children's and preconcert events. ■ TIP→ **In the main hall, the audience completely surrounds the stage, so it's worth checking the seating chart when buying tickets to gauge your view of the performers.** The acoustics are just as excellent as they're cracked up to be.

Fodor's Choice ★

Also part of the Music Center, the 3,200-seat **Dorothy Chandler Pavilion** (⊠ 135 N. Grand Ave., Downtown ☎ 213/972–7211) presents an array of music programs and the L.A. Opera's classics from September through June. Music director Plácido Domingo encourages fresh work; in 2006, for instance, he ushered in *Grendel*, a new opera staged by the hypercreative director Julie Taymor. There's also a steady flow of touring ballet and modern ballet companies.

In Griffith Park, the open-air auditorium known as the **Greek Theater** (⊠ 2700 N. Vermont Ave., Los Feliz ☎ 323/665–1927), complete with Doric columns, presents big-name performers in its mainly pop-rock-jazz schedule from June through October.

★ Ever since it opened in 1920, in a park surrounded by mountains, trees, and gardens, the **Hollywood Bowl** (✉ 2301 Highland Ave., Hollywood ☎ 323/850–2000 ⊕ www.hollywoodbowl.com) has been one of the world's largest and most atmospheric outdoor amphitheaters. Its season runs from early July through mid-September; the L.A. Philharmonic spends its summers here. There are performances daily except Monday (and some Sundays); the program ranges from jazz to pop to classical. Concertgoers usually arrive early, bringing picnic suppers; there are plenty of picnic tables. Additionally, a moderately priced outdoor grill and a more upscale restaurant are among the dining options operated by the Patina Group. ■ TIP→ Be sure to bring a sweater—it gets chilly here in the evening. You might also bring or rent a cushion to apply to the wood seats. Avoid the hassle of parking by taking one of the Park-and-Ride buses, which leave from various locations around town; call the Bowl for information.

> **TICKET SOURCES**
>
> In addition to contacting venues directly, try these sources.
>
> ■ **Good Time Tickets** (☎ 323/464–7383 ⊕ www.goodtime-tickets.com). Sells harder-to-get tickets—and charges accordingly.
>
> ■ **Razor Gator** (☎ 800/542–4466 ⊕ www.razorgator.com). Covers events at museums and small theaters, plus some stadium fare.
>
> ■ **Theatre League Alliance L.A** (⊕ www.theatrela.org). Score discounted theater tickets.
>
> ■ **Ticketmaster** (☎ 213/480–3232, 213/365–3500 fine arts ⊕ www.ticketmaster.com). Still the all-around top dog.

Fodor'sChoice ★ The jewel in the crown of Hollywood & Highland is the **Kodak Theatre** (✉ 6801 Hollywood Blvd., Hollywood ☎ 323/308–6363 ⊕ www.kodaktheatre.com). Created as the permanent host of the Academy Awards, the lavish 3,500-seat theater is also used for music concerts and ballets. Seeing a show here is worthwhile just to witness the gorgeous, crimson-and-gold interior, with its box seating and glittering chandeliers.

The one-of-a-kind, 6,300-seat ersatz-Arabic **Shrine Auditorium** (✉ 665 W. Jefferson Blvd., Downtown ☎ 213/748–5116), built in 1926 as Al Malaikah Temple, hosts touring companies from all over the world, assorted gospel and choral groups, and other musical acts as well as high-profile televised awards shows, including the Latin Grammys.

★ It's used mainly for sporting events, but the **Staples Center** (✉ 1111 S. Figueroa St., Downtown ☎ 213/742–7300 ⊕ www.staplescenter.com) also offers blockbuster concerts. Megaband U2 took their big-budget show to this huge arena last year.

> **WORD OF MOUTH**
>
> "The perfect evening in L.A. during the summer is to go to the Hollywood Bowl with a picnic for a jazz or classical concert. . . . Also look into concerts at the Greek Theatre in Griffith Park—an incredible setting for a concert—tends toward more hip/rock/contemporary music."　　　　　–Renee

Adjacent to Universal Studios, the 6,250-seat **Gibson Amphitheater** (✉ 100 Universal City Plaza, Universal City ☎ 818/622–4440) holds more than 100 performances a year, including the Radio City Christmas Spectacular, star-studded benefit concerts, and all-star shindigs for local radio station KROQ 106.7.

The **Wiltern LG Theater** (✉ 3790 Wilshire Blvd., Mid-Wilshire ☎ 213/388–1400), a green terracotta, art deco masterpiece constructed in 1930, is a fine place to see pop, rock, jazz, and dance performances. The main space is standing room only, but there are a few seats on the balcony.

Dance

The dance scene in Los Angeles has faced its challenges, with lackluster ticket sales at the top of the list. Though there may not be much of an audience here for ballet, forms of more modern dance are quite popular—after all, most music videos are filmed here. You can see many of the industry's choreographers and backup grinders at many of the theaters listed above and at various clubs around town (try the Key Club and its bimonthly "Choreographer's Ball"). The venues listed below offer the most dance-related fare, including ballet and boogie-woogie.

At its state-of-the-art Luckman Theater, **Cal State L.A.'s Dance Department** (✉ 5151 State University Dr., East Los Angeles ☎ 323/343–5124) presents several prominent dance events each year—including the Dance Fair in March and Dance Kaleidoscope in July. The **Kodak Theatre** (✉ 6801 Hollywood Blvd., Hollywood ☎ 323/308–6363) hosts various ballet performances each year, including *The Nutcracker,*. **Shrine Auditorium** (✉ 665 W. Jefferson Blvd., Downtown ☎ 213/748–5115) hosts touring dance companies, such as the Kirov, the Bolshoi, and the American Ballet Theater (ABT). **UCLA Center for the Performing Arts** (✉ 405 N. Hilgard Ave., Westwood ☎ 310/825–4401 or 310/825–2101) welcomes visiting companies, such as the Hubbard Street Dance Company and Paul Taylor. The **REDCAT** (Roy and Edna Disney Cal Arts Theater; ✉ 631 W. 2nd St., Downtown ☎ 213/237–2800) is a 260-seat space that hosts performance of all kinds, including international dance groups that tend toward the avant-garde.

Film

Spending two hours at a movie while visiting Los Angeles doesn't have to mean taking time out from sightseeing. Some of the country's most historic and beautiful theaters are found here, and they host both first-run and revival films. Movie listings are advertised daily in the *Los An-*

geles Times Calendar section. Admission to first-run movies is usually about $9.

Art & Revival Houses

The **American Cinemathèque Independent Film Series** (✉ 6712 Hollywood Blvd., Hollywood ☎ 323/466–3456 ⊕ americancinematheque.com) screens classics plus recent independent films, sometimes with question-and-answer sessions with the filmmakers. The main venue is the Lloyd E. Rigler Theater, within the 1922 Egyptian Theater, which combines an exterior of pharaoh sculptures and columns with a modern, high-tech design inside. The Cinemathèque also screens movies at the 1940 **Aero Theater** (✉ 1328 Montana Ave., Santa Monica ☎ 323/466–3456).

Fodor's Choice ★ Taking the concept of dinner and a movie to a whole new level, **Cine-space** (✉ 6356 Hollywood Blvd., Hollywood ☎ 323/817–3456 ⊕ www.cine-space.com) screens classics and alternative flicks in its digital the-ater-restaurant. Comfort food is served during the films, which could be documentaries as easily as they could be old-school faves like *Grease*. The movies are often followed by popular club nights. DJ–provided music and a smoking patio that hovers over bustling Hollywood Boulevard attract indie rockers on Tuesday and hip-hop hellraising on weekends.

★ **UCLA** has two fine film series. The programs of the **Film and Television Archives at the James Bridges Theater** (✉ Hilgard Ave. near Sunset Blvd., Westwood ☎ 310/206–3456 or 310/206–8013 ⊕ www.cinema.ucla.edu) might cover the works of major directors, documentaries, children's films, horror movies—just about anything. The **School of Film & Television** (⊕ www.tft.ucla.edu) also uses the Bridges Theater, but it has its own program of newer, avant-garde films. Enter the campus at the north-easternmost entrance. Street parking is available on Loring Avenue (a block east of the campus) after 6 PM, or park for a small fee in Lot 3 (go one entrance south to Wyton Drive to pay at the kiosk before 7, after 7 at the lot itself).

The best of Hollywood classics and kitsch, foreign films, and, occasion-ally, documentaries are on tap at the **New Beverly Cinema** (✉ 7165 Bev-erly Blvd., Hollywood ☎ 323/938–4038), where there's always a double bill. **Nuart** (✉ 11272 Santa Monica Blvd., West L.A. ☎ 310/281–8223) is the best-kept of L.A.'s revival houses, with good seats, an excellent screen, and special midnight shows.

Fodor's Choice ★ The **Silent Movie Theater** (✉ 611 N. Fairfax Ave., Fairfax District ☎ 323/655–2520 ⊕ www.silentmovietheater.com) is a treasure. Thursday through Sunday it screens exclusively the cream of the pretalkies era with live musical accompaniment. Shorts precede the films. Each show is made to seem like an event in itself, and it's just about the only such theater of its kind.

Movie Palaces

The **Arclight** (✉ 6360 Sunset Blvd., Hollywood ☎ 323/464–4226) in-cludes as its centerpiece the geodesic Cinerama Dome, the first theater in the United States designed specifically for the large screen and sound system that went with Cinerama. The complex now includes 14 addi-tional screens, a mall, and a restaurant and bar. The only theater in L.A.

CLOSE UP

Cheap Thrills

YOU DON'T HAVE TO BE LOADED to load up on after-dark entertainment in L.A. From live music to TV show tapings to karaoke, there's plenty of low-cost and free fun to be had.

Audiences Unlimited (✉ 100 Universal City Plaza, Bldg. 153, Universal City 91608 ☎ 818/506–0043 ⊕ www.tvtickets.com) helps fill seats for television programs (and sometimes for televised award shows). The free tickets are distributed on a first-come, first-served basis. Shows that may be taping or filming include *King of Queens*. Note: you must be 16 or older to attend a television taping.

Santa Monica's **Mor Bar** has top-notch DJs every night of the week, but on Tuesday you get all the body rockin' rhythms you can handle for just two bucks.

The popular dive the **Smog Cutter** and its low-cost libations make for a rip-roaring karaoke party. You may have to wait a while for your turn, but at least you don't have to pay.

Order a snack and enjoy **Cinespace's** movies free. Then, stay and soak up the scene before the crowds come (drinks are often free or cheap before 11).

Monday at **Spaceland** spotlights promising and extremely varied (punk, country, alternative) artists with monthlong (and free) residencies, so you have up to four chances to catch them.

Ruby Tuesday at the Key Club gives rock fans of all ages a chance to see up-and-coming bands (many of them still in their teens) without depleting your allowance money.

to begin movies with greetings and background commentary by theater staff, the Arclight also designates some screenings as "premium," which lets you reserve the best seats for an extra fee. "Over 21" shows let you bring cocktails into designated screening rooms.

Bridge Cinema De Lux (✉ 6081 Center Dr., in the Promenade at Howard Hughes Center, West L.A. ☎ 310/568–3375) comes by its name honestly, with superwide screens, leather recliners, and top-notch food and drink. Sip a cocktail at the bar or order a meal to take into the theater. Regular ticket prices start at $9.75, with prices higher for Directors' Hall seating (reserved seats and even bigger screens).

Fodor's Choice ★ **Grauman's Chinese Theatre** (✉ 6925 Hollywood Blvd., Hollywood ☎ 323/464–6266), open since 1927, is perhaps the world's best-known theater, the home of the famous concrete walkway marked by movie stars' hand- and footprints and traditional gala premieres. There are additional, smaller screens at the Mann Chinese Six, in the adjoining Hollywood & Highland Complex.

Across the street from Grauman's is the **Pacific's El Capitan** (✉ 6838 Hollywood Blvd., Hollywood ☎ 323/467–7674), an art deco masterpiece meticulously renovated by Disney. First-run movies alternate with Disney revivals, and the theater often presents live stage shows in conjunction with Disney's animated pictures.

At the intersection of Hollywood and Sunset boulevards, the 1923 **Vista Theater** (⌧ 4473 Sunset Dr., Los Feliz ☎ 323/660–6639), now showing first-run films, was once Bard's Hollywood Theater, used for vaudeville shows in the '20s. A Spanish-style facade leads to an ornate, Egyptian-style interior.

Theater

Los Angeles isn't quite the "Broadway of the West," as some have claimed—the scope of theater here doesn't compare to that in New York. Still, the theater scene's growth has been impressive. Small theaters are blossoming all over town, and the larger houses, despite price hikes to as much as $70 for a single ticket, are usually full. Even small productions might boast big names from the entertainment industry.

Now Playing (⊕ www.reviewplays.com) lists what's currently in L.A. theaters and what's coming up in the next few months. **LA Stage Alliance** (⊕ www.lastagealliance.com) also gives information on what's playing in Los Angeles, albeit with capsules that are either noncommittal or overly enthusiastic. Its LAStageTIX service allows you to buy tickets online the day of the performance at roughly half price.

Major Theaters

Jason Robards and Nick Nolte got their starts at **Geffen Playhouse** (⌧ 10886 Le Conte Ave., Westwood ☎ 310/208–5454 ⊕ www.geffenplayhouse.com), an acoustically superior, 498-seat theater that showcases new plays in summer—primarily musicals and comedies. Many of the productions here are on their way to or from Broadway.

In addition to theater performances, lectures, and children's programs, free summer jazz, dance, cabaret, and occasionally Latin and rock concerts take place at the **John Anson Ford Amphitheater** (⌧ 2580 Cahuenga Blvd. E, Hollywood ☎ 323/461–3673 ⊕ www.fordamphitheater.org), a 1,300-seat outdoor venue in the Hollywood Hills. Winter shows are typically staged at the smaller indoor theater, **Inside the Ford.**

There are three theaters in the big downtown complex known as **The Music Center** (⌧ 135 N. Grand Ave., Downtown ☎ 213/972–7211 ⊕ www.musiccenter.org). The 2,140-seat **Ahmanson Theatre** (☎ 213/628–2772 ⊕ www.taperahmanson.com) presents both classics and new plays; the 3,200-seat **Dorothy Chandler Pavilion** shows a smattering of plays between the more prevalent musical performances; and the 760-seat **Mark Taper Forum** (☎ 213/628–2772 ⊕ www.taperahmanson.com) presents new works that often go on to Broadway, such as Tony Kushner's *Caroline, or Change.*

The home of the Academy Awards telecast from 1949 to 1959, the **Pantages Theatre** (⌧ 6233 Hollywood Blvd., Hollywood ☎ 323/468–1770 ⊕ www.nederlander.com) is a massive (2,600-seat) and splendid example of high-style Hollywood art deco, presenting large-scale Broadway musicals such as *The Lion King.*

The **Ricardo Montalbán Theatre** (⌧ 1615 N. Vine St., Hollywood ☎ 323/462–6666 ⊕ www.nosotros.org) has an intimate feeling despite its

1,038-seat capacity. It presents plays, concerts, seminars, and workshops with an emphasis on Latin culture.

The 1,900-seat, art deco **Wilshire Theatre** (⊠ 8440 Wilshire Blvd., Beverly Hills ☎ 323/468–1716 ⊕ www.nederlander.com) presents Broadway musicals and occasional concerts.

Smaller Theaters

★ The founders of **Actors' Gang Theater** (⊠ 9070 Venice Blvd., Hollywood ☎ 310/838–4264 ⊕ www.theactorsgang.com) include actor Tim Robbins; the fare has included Molière, Eric Bogosian, and international works by traveling companies.

☾ The **Bob Baker Marionette Theater** (⊠ 1345 W. 1st St., at Glendale Blvd., Downtown ☎ 213/250–9995 ⊕ www.bobbakermarionettes.com) has been a staple for L.A. youth since 1963. Kids sit on a carpeted floor and get a close-up view of the intricate puppets; ice cream and juice are served after the shows.

City Garage (⊠ 1340½ 4th St. Alley, between the 3rd St. Promenade and 4th St., Santa Monica ☎ 310/319–9939 ⊕ www.citygarage.org) really *was* a garage for the city and the police department in the 1930s. Since 1987 it has hosted the **Aresis Ensemble,** whose French artistic director, Frédérique Michel, has maintained a largely European orientation in selecting plays and a casually continental attitude in their execution—don't be surprised by incidental nudity.

Excellent original musicals and new dramas are the specialties at the 99-seat **Coast Playhouse** (⊠ 8325 Santa Monica Blvd., West Hollywood ☎ 323/650–8507).

The **Coronet Theatre** (⊠ 366 N. La Cienega Blvd., between Beverly Blvd. and Melrose Ave., West Hollywood ☎ 310/657–7377 ⊕ www.coronettheatre.com) proves good things come in small packages. It's actually three small theaters in one, with consistently funny comedy or one-person performance pieces (sometimes audience-interactive) running on all stages simultaneously.

Deaf West Theater (⊠ 5112 Lankershim Blvd., North Hollywood ☎ 818/762–2998 ⊕ www.deafwest.org) presents productions that are simultaneously spoken and signed, and therefore accessible to both hearing and deaf audience members, in its own home space. Its ingenious (and award-winning) revivals include *A Streetcar Named Desire,* the musical *Oliver!* and *Big River.*

East West Players (⊠ 120 Judge John Aiso St., Little Tokyo ☎ 213/625–7000) is a well-respected, small theater company dedicated to the Asian-American voice, with performances that include original works and musical revivals.

Architect Frank Gehry designed the **Edgemar Center for the Arts** (⊠ 2437 Main St., Santa Monica ☎ 310/399–3666 ⊕ www.edgemarcenter.org), an industrial-styled complex of two theaters, offices, and classrooms where the nonprofit performance group holds dramatic performances, dance, music, and film events, as well as outreach programs and workshops.

It has such supporters as Neil Simon, Jason Alexander, and Kate Capshaw in its corner.

The **Evidence Room** (⊠ 2220 Beverly Blvd., Downtown ☎ 213/381–7118 ⊕ www.evidenceroom.com) is a group of actors, directors, and designers who've earned themselves a raftful of honors. It draws some of the city's best performance artists.

The **Falcon Theatre** (⊠ 4252 Riverside Dr., Burbank ☎ 818/955–8101 ⊕ www.falcontheatre.com) is the brainchild of TV and movie producer-director-writer Garry Marshall (*Laverne & Shirley, Pretty Woman*). The well-appointed theater is a stone's throw from the Warner Bros. lot; you'll often find one of Marshall's cronies looking to have fun on stage again in works like *Arsenic and Old Lace*.

Though not in the most fashionable neck of the woods, the **Fremont Center Theatre** (⊠ 1000 Fremont Ave., Pasadena ☎ 626/441–5977 ⊕ www.fremontcentretheatre.com) has nonetheless turned out its share of critically appreciated revivals and more obscure dramas. It's also the home of the **Pasadena Shakespeare Company** (☎ 626/799–1860 ⊕ www.pasadenashakespeare.com).

Three performance venues and a coffee bar in one, the **Hudson Theatres** (⊠ 6539 Santa Monica Blvd., Hollywood ☎ 323/856–4249) are popular with TV actors longing to tread the boards during their summer vacations. What's more, the resident company, the Hudson Guild, has a reputation for some of the finest traditional theater in town—with raves for its reinterpretations of the likes of *Twelfth Night* and *Hedda Gabler*—as well as more experimental fare.

Whether putting on classic Chekhov or more obscure current fare, the **Interact Theatre Company** (⊠ 5215 Bakman Ave., North Hollywood ☎ 818/765–8732) earns nominations and awards from the L.A. Drama Critics Circle, Theatre L.A., *Back Stage West,* and others.

Though relatively new on the scene, the **Kirk Douglas Theatre** (⊠ 9820 Washington Blvd., Culver City ☎ 213/628–2772) has built a strong reputation for well-staged contemporary drama and comedy. It's got solid backing, too, as it's in the same family as the Ahmanson and the Mark Taper Forum.

The **Knightsbridge Theatre** (⊠ 1944 Riverside Dr., Silver Lake ☎ 323/667–0955 ⊕ www.knightsbridgetheatre.com) has a reputation as one of the city's chief performers of classic theater, both famous (*All's Well That Ends Well*) and less so (Gilbert & Sullivan's *Ruddygore*). The results range from the solid to the sensational.

The **Odyssey Theater** (⊠ 2055 S. Sepulveda Blvd., West L.A. ☎ 310/477–2055) presents largely traditional dramas (plays you may not know but should) in an intimate space, typically with astute direction and taut, powerful acting.

Pacific Resident Theatre (⊠ 703 Venice Blvd., Venice ☎ 310/822–8392 ⊕ www.pacificresidenttheatre.com) has earned 30 L.A. Drama Critics Awards since its first season as an actors' co-op in '85. It hones in on topical dramas and comedies.

The **Pasadena Playhouse** (✉ 39 S. El Molino Ave., Pasadena ☎ 626/356–7529 ⊕ www.pasadenaplayhouse.org) largely offers well-done middle-of-the-road fare that occasionally stars name TV and film actors.

The 99-seat **Santa Monica Playhouse** (✉ 1211 4th St., Santa Monica ☎ 310/394–9779 ⊕ www.santamonicaplayhouse.com) is worth visiting for its cozy, librarylike atmosphere, as well as its high-quality comedies, dramas, and musicals like *Funny You Don't Look Like a Grandmother* and children's programs such as *Hansel and Gretel*.

The **Theatre of NOTE** (✉ 1517 Cahuenga Blvd., north of Sunset Blvd., Hollywood ☎ 323/856–8611 ⊕ www.theatreofnote.com) has made a critical impact with both full-length plays (classic and new) and evenings of one-act works.

Ⓒ Founded in 1962, the nonprofit theater co-op **Theatre West** (✉ 3333 Cahuenga Blvd. W, North Hollywood ☎ 323/851–7977 or 818/761–2203 ⊕ www.theatrewest.org) has produced a lauded body of work. Its plays have gone on to Broadway (*Spoon River Anthology*) and been made into films (*A Bronx Tale*), and stars like the late Carroll O'Connor and Richard Dreyfuss have acted with the company. Its interactive **Storybook Theatre** (for three- to nine-year-olds) is a long-running favorite.

Theater Ensembles

The **Cornerstone Theater Company** (☎ 213/613–1700 ⊕ www.cornerstonetheater.org) doesn't need a home of its own: it integrates drama into locations like city buses and shopping malls. Having hopped through rural communities in 10 states since its founding, the company is now based in L.A., where it covers everything from Shakespeare adaptations to exploratory faith-themed productions.

★ **Circle X** (☎ 213/804–5491 ⊕ www.circlextheatre.org) is one of the most lauded and loved acting groups in the city. The traveling troupe continues to win local theater awards thanks to its continuing quest to find and mount exciting new works on a shoestring budget.

NIGHTLIFE

Despite the high energy level of the L.A. nightlife crowd, don't expect to be partying until dawn—this is still an early-to-bed city. Liquor laws require that bars stop serving alcohol at 2 AM, and it's safe to say that by this time, with the exception of a few after-hours venues and coffeehouses, most jazz, rock, and disco clubs have closed for the night. Due to the smoking ban, most bars and clubs with a cover charge allow "in and outs"—patrons may leave the premises and return (usually with a hand stamp or paper bracelet). Some newer clubs offer outdoor smoking patios—a great way to enjoy the city's consistently warm evenings.

While the ultimate in velvet-roped vampiness and glamour used to be the Sunset Strip, in the past couple of years the glitz has definitely shifted to Hollywood Boulevard and its surrounding streets. The lines are as long as the skirts are short outside the Hollywood club du jour (which changes so fast, its often hard to keep track). But the Strip still has plenty going for it, with comedy clubs, hard-rock spots, and restaurants. West Hollywood's Santa Monica Boulevard bustles with gay and lesbian bars and clubs. For less conspicuous—and congested—alternatives, check out the events in downtown L.A.'s performance spaces and galleries. Silver Lake and Echo Park are best for boho bars and live music clubs.

Foxy females, fat-walleted businessmen, and tabloid-familar faces have no problem getting in anywhere. But there's hope for the rest of us, too. ■ TIP→ Try popping in early or going on a weeknight . . . or just be very patient. If you wait in line and pay the cover, you'll get in eventually.

Note that parking, especially after 7 PM, is at a premium in Hollywood. In fact, it's restricted on virtually every side street along the "hot zone" of West Hollywood (Sunset Boulevard from Fairfax to Doheny). Posted signs indicate the restrictions, but these are naturally harder to notice at night. Paying $5 to $10, and at some venues even $15, for valet or lot parking is often the easiest way to go.

> ## A RIDE HOME
>
> If you're not in shape to drive after a night out, call on a chauffeur agency to drive you home in your car; rates start at $30. Drivers for **Autopilots** (☎ 213/201–4141 ⊕ www.autopilotsla.com) arrive on foldable scooters that they stash in your car trunk before taking you home.

Bars

Despite its well-publicized penchant for hedonism, Los Angeles, unlike New York, Chicago, and San Francisco, has never been much of a saloon town. But Hollywood's renaissance is changing that part of the equation. Thanks to vibrant new drinking and dining spaces along Cahuenga, Las Palmas, and Ivar, Tinseltown finally feels like a lively—somewhat safe—area to stroll at night, a real bar-hopper zone. In fact, with all the traffic generated by the new additions, it's smart to park in one place and walk or even (gasp!) use the subway to explore the area's hipster joints. There's even a trolley that trundles between various bars along the boulevard (see the Holly Trolley box, *below*). But Hollywood Boulevard aside, to quench your thirst in other parts of La-La Land, you'd still better be prepared to do some driving.

Hollywood

★ The **Beauty Bar** (✉ 1638 Cahuenga Blvd., Hollywood ☎ 323/464–7676) offers manicures and makeovers along with perfect martinis, but the hotties who flock to this retro salon-bar (the little sister of the Beauty Bars in NYC and San Fran) don't really need the cosmetic care—this is where the edgier beautiful people hang.

The dark and groovy **Burgundy Room** (✉ 1621½ N. Cahuenga Blvd., Hollywood ☎ 323/465–7530) has been a Hollywood favorite for some time, attracting an unpretentious rock-and-roll crowd most nights.

The namesakes of the **Cabana Club** (✉ 1439 N. Ivar Ave., Hollywood ☎ 323/463–0005) are built for, as the tabs say, canoodling, whether you want to be seen or not (curtains can be drawn for privacy). DJs spin everything from lounge to techno to rock.

The **Cat & Fiddle Pub** (✉ 6530 Sunset Blvd., Hollywood ☎ 323/468–3800) is a SoCal hacienda-style venue with a touch of England. Happy hours are weekdays 4–7, with a pint of that day's special beer for $3. You can play darts or check the memorabilia displays or loll on the patio, where jazz is played Sunday night 7–11 (free).

You get the feeling Sinatra would have hung out at the dimly lighted **Daddy's** (✉ 1610 N. Vine St., Hollywood ☎ 323/463–7777) as much for the swingin' vibe as for the good-looking crowd. Sounds range from soul to jazz; the drinks are nice and strong.

In a two-tier strip mall, **Lava Lounge** (✉ 1533 N. La Brea Ave., Hollywood ☎ 323/876–6612) is one of L.A.'s favorite dimly lighted dens of Polynesian pleasure. Look for the faux lava-rock fountain and weird lounge acts (was that a xylophonist?) mixed in with disco, blues, and DJ mixes. The cover is $1–$5, except Sunday's karaoke night, which is free.

Film-studio moguls, movie extras, and those longing for a look at a Hollywood watering hole of yesteryear flock to **Musso & Frank Grill** (✉ 6667 Hollywood Blvd., Hollywood ☎ 323/467–5123). This former haunt of F. Scott Fitzgerald is the city's oldest restaurant, established in 1919 and still at the same location. The bar serves up the Rob Roys smooth. Stick with them, or if you *must* eat (and "enjoy" the famous attitude of the waiters), go for the steaks.

Another one of those trendy spots way too cool to put a sign out front, the very exclusive **Nacional** (✉ 1645 Wilcox Ave., Hollywood ☎ 323/962–7712) always has a line out front, especially on weekends. Owned by the team behind the Ivar, this space has a woody yet highly modern feel with an open-air rooftop patio, fireplaces, and DJs spinning obscure funk and soul.

Rockers Tommy Lee and Dave Navarro, along with DJ Paul Oakenfold, invested in **Rokbar** (✉ 1710 N. Las Palmas Ave., Hollywood ☎ 323/461–5600), a slick (what else?) rock-and-roll-theme drinking spot. The DJs play AC/DC, the Stones, anything good and loud to keep regulars like George Clooney dancing. With rock-theme art on the walls and fancy bar snacks, it's an upscale alternative to the city's grungier rock pubs.

Dark and sequestered, the **Room** (✉ 1626 N. Cahuenga Blvd., Hollywood ☎ 323/462–7196) promises some of the town's hottest DJs every night. The accent is on hip-hop, but Thursday–Saturday, *anything* is fair game. Enter on the alley.

Want women to come to your new hangout? Give 'em what they love. That's the premise behind **Star Shoes** (✉ 6364 Hollywood Blvd., Hollywood ☎ 323/462–7827), the vintage-shoe store and bar from the people behind the equally kitschy

HOLLY TROLLEY

Looking for a way to bar-hop without driving in Hollywood? Try the "Holly Trolley" (www.ladottransit.com/other/trolley/), which shuttles between designated lots along Hollywood Boulevard. Tokens, available at most local watering holes, are $1 each and the trolley runs from 8 PM to 4 AM, Thursday through Saturday.

and conceptual Beauty Bar. Of course, the place attracts both sexes with its stiff drinks and DJ music ranging from funky to rocking. But it's the cool shoe displays that make it a step above the rest.

★ The casually hip **Three Clubs** (✉ 1123 N. Vine St., Hollywood ☎ 323/462–6441) is furtively located in a strip mall, beneath the Bargain Clown Mart discount store. The DJs segue through the many faces and phases of rock-and-roll and dance music. With dark-wood paneling, lamp-lighted tables, and even some sofas, you could be in a giant basement rec room from decades past—no fancy dress required, but fashionable looks suggested.

The **Tropicana Bar** (✉ 7000 Hollywood Blvd., Hollywood ☎ 323/466–7000), an outdoor, poolside lounge in the Roosevelt Hotel, had so much buzz the management had to tone it down. After the hotel's revamp in 2005 and the arrival of lightning-rod promoter Amanda Scheer Demme (now gone), the place became ridiculously fabulous, a hot spot for celebs and their tantalizing misbehavior. Inside the hotel, the even more exclusive **Teddy's** packs in celebutants trying to avoid the paparazzi.

★ **Vine** (✉ 1235 N. Vine St., Hollywood ☎ 323/960–0800) beckons from the cluster of bars north of Hollywood Boulevard. It's now a black-and-red-lacquered rock-and-roll bar with indie-music DJs and their haphazardly hip followers. The popular Friday night Pash parties have an invite list, so if you're not on it, come good and early.

★ A lovely L.A. tradition is to meet at **Yamashiro** (✉ 1999 N. Sycamore Ave., Hollywood ☎ 323/466–5125) for cocktails at sunset. In the elegant restaurant, waitresses glide by in kimonos, and entrées can zoom up to $39; on the terrace, a spectacular hilltop view spreads out before you. ■ TIP➔ **Mandatory valet parking is $3.50, but happy hour drinks are just a bit more than that.**

West Hollywood

As at so many other nightspots in this neck of the woods, the popular-
★ ity and clientele of **Bar Marmont** (✉ 8171 Sunset Blvd., West Hollywood ☎ 323/650–0575) bulged—and changed—after word got out it was a favorite of celebrities. Lately, it's gotten a second wind thanks to a strong DJ selection and luscious cocktails. The bar is next to the inimitable hotel Chateau Marmont, which bold-face names continue to haunt.

Half bar, half restaurant, and home to what the owners call "L.A.'s second-best chili" and the equally touted chili burger, **Barney's Beanery** (✉ 8447 Santa Monica Blvd., West Hollywood ☎ 323/654–2287) serves more than 200 different beers. Established in 1920, it's second only to Musso & Frank in restaurant longevity in L.A. The funky decor, long bar, two pool tables, and assortment of air hockey, video, and even pinball games keep the relatively hip but unaffected crowd amused and coming back for more.

At a busy intersection also featuring gaudy Miyagi's Restaurant and long-time strip club the Body Shop, **Dublin's Irish Whiskey Pub** (✉ 8240 Sunset Blvd., West Hollywood ☎ 323/656–0100) is among the top attractions on the Strip almost any night, with two pool tables, four bars, an upstairs dance floor (open after 7 PM), and a menu with clever variations on pub grub. Satellite multifeeds with 100 TV screens show virtually any ball game nationwide, and weekend mornings—especially football-season Sundays—are suitably boisterous.

Decent Chinese food and pretty good drinking are on offer at the **Formosa Cafe** (✉ 7156 Santa Monica Blvd., West Hollywood ☎ 323/850–9050), but it was featured in 1997's noir *L.A. Confidential* because it's a rare, still-intact remnant of that bygone Hollywood era. Its railroad-car design allows lots of booths, and the walls are a pictorial shrine to the film community, many of whom have frequented the place (it's across from the former Warner Hollywood lot).

Get up close and personal with Hollywood hipsters at **Jones** (✉ 7205 Santa Monica Blvd., West Hollywood ☎ 323/850–1727). It's too dark and crowded for you to be able to tell, but this is an authentically preserved old showbiz haunt, with secluded booths, scrumptious food, and very loud music.

A hetero hangout in a very gay neighborhood, **J. Sloan's** (✉ 8623 Melrose Ave., at Huntley Dr., West Hollywood ☎ 310/659–0250) has been around since 1919, first as a speakeasy and since the '30s as a legit bar. These days, its 10 TVs cover nearly all the sports on the satellite dish, plus there are karaoke and live blues bands.

★ The **Rainbow Bar & Grill** (✉ 9015 Sunset Blvd., West Hollywood ☎ 310/278–4232), in the heart of the Strip and next door to the legendary Roxy, is a landmark in its own right as *the* drinking spot of the '80s hair-metal scene—and it still attracts a music-industry crowd.

To enter **Skybar** (✉ 8440 Sunset Blvd., West Hollywood ☎ 323/650–8999), the poolside bar at the Hotel Mondrian, you must have a Mondrian room key, a screen credit, or a spot on the guest list. The view is phenomenal, as is the staying power of its cachet.

★ Wouldn't you know, a nursing home in the happening part of Sunset Strip gets converted into a smart, brash-looking hotel, the **Standard** (✉ 8300 Sunset Blvd., West Hollywood ☎ 323/650–9090), for the young, hip, and connected. Its impressive bar is popular with those in the biz.

Los Feliz, Silver Lake & Atwater Village

A space that's as popular with nonlocals as it is with the neighborhood's bohemian barflys, **4100** (✉ 4100 Sunset Blvd., Silver Lake ☎ 323/666–4460) is a great place to meet and be merry. A lively jukebox mixing rock and roll and soul, plus seating around the bar, makes it a hip, no-hassle hookup spot.

Akbar (✉ 4356 Sunset Blvd., Silver Lake ☎ 323/665–6810) has retained its friendly neighborhood feel, even after an expansion brought a bigger dance floor and sound system. The largely gay crowd tends be artier than the WeHo pretty boy set, and it's also less of a meat market.

Big Foot Lodge (✉ 3172 Los Feliz Blvd., Los Feliz ☎ 323/662–9227) has a cheeky outdoors theme, with a life-size, animated Smokey the Bear,

CLOSE UP

Glam vs. Grit

MEDIA SPIN may make L.A.'s nightlife seem like a blur of glossy bars, hip clubs, power brokers, and poseurs, but the after-dark scene has as much diversity and creativity as frivolity. The city has a special knack for mixing extremes, though; you may run into celebs in a dingy pub or see a rocker in one of the poshest venues.

The heavily promoted swanky scene (where anyone willing to pay for bottle service, usually starting at about $200, is guaranteed a well-placed table and "somebody" status for a night) is thoroughly prowled by the tanned devotees of personal trainers. Places like these are in especially sharp contrast to the unpretentious dive bars, where smoky voices and well-worn glasses evoke Tom Waits rather than the latest starlet. Expect to pay a $15–$20 cover to get into high-end hot spots (add another $20–$50 if you want to bypass the line by tipping the doorman). The more casual hangouts, on the other hand, rarely charge more than $5. Drink prices are similarly varied, with posh clubs asking $10 and above for specialty drinks, and dive bars selling $2 beers and well drinks. But which places are the best in their respective fields? Let this tally of the top gritty dives and glitzy dens be your guide.

For glitz: the Standard (Downtown L.A. and Sunset Strip); Forty Deuce; Ivar; Spider Club; Privilege; Mood; LAX.

For grit: Burgundy Room; Short Stop; Echo; Room; Smog Cutter; Mr. T's Bowl; the Smell; Silver Lake Lounge.

---

but the twentysomething crowd tends toward the rock and rockabilly set. Different DJs each night offer sounds from '80s metal to '60s French pop. If you're feeling campfire nostalgia, try the Toasted Marshmallow, a creamy drink topped with a flaming marshmallow.

★ **Cha Cha Lounge** (✉ 2375 Glendale Blvd., Silver Lake ☎ 323/660–7595), Seattle's coolest rock bar, now aims to repeat its success with this colorful, red-lighted space. Think part tiki hut, part tacky Tijuana party palace. The tabletops pay homage to the lounge's former performers; they've got portraits of Latin drag queens.

A '40s-style bar that was rediscovered during the mid-'90s lounge craze and immortalized in the film *Swingers,* **Dresden Room** (✉ 1760 N. Vermont Ave., Los Feliz ☎ 323/665–4294) is still a popular hangout with old-timers and Gen X lounge lizards alike. Marty and Elayne (also seen in the film) are still burning up the joint with inimitable covers of "Staying Alive" and "Livin' La Vida Loca" (nightly, except Sunday, 9 PM–1:30 AM). No cover, but there's a two-drink minimum.

★ The **Echo** (✉ 1822 Sunset Blvd., Echo Park ☎ 213/413–8200) sprang from the people behind the Silver Lake rock joint Spaceland. Most evenings it's a chill spot for artsy locals, but things rev up when DJs spin reggae, rock, and funk. Indie bands play a few nights a week.

The red-lighted, Chinese-motif **Good Luck Bar** (⊠ 1514 Hillhurst Ave., Los Feliz ☎ 323/666–3524) teems with young singles looking to meet someone, and the sexy vibe (helped along with soul tunes and strong spirits) means this place often lives up to its name.

★ It got its name thanks to its proximity to Dodger Stadium, but for decades the **Short Stop** (⊠ 1455 Sunset Blvd., Echo Park ☎ 213/482–4942) was even better known for its regulars—the LAPD. Under new ownership for the past couple of years, the dark dive still has cop memorabilia on the walls, but now it attracts artsy, fashionable locals. There's a great dance room with DJs spinning all sorts of sounds Thursday through Saturday.

It may be in an iffy part of town, but the **Smog Cutter** (⊠ 864 N. Virgil Ave., Silver Lake ☎ 323/667–9832) still attracts a fun cross-section of local barflies and Hollywood hipsters. Come for its raucous karaoke nights and cheap drinks.

★ **Tiki Ti** (⊠ 4427 W. Sunset Blvd., Silver Lake ☎ 323/669–9381) is one of the most charming drinking huts in the city. You can spend hours just looking at the Polynesian artifacts strewn all about the place, but be careful—time flies in this tiny tropical bar, and the colorful drinks can be so potent that you may have to stay marooned for a while.

Coastal & Western Los Angeles

SANTA MONICA & VENICE The retro charm of **The Brig** (⊠ 1515 Abbot Kinney Blvd., Venice ☎ 310/399–7537) suits the beachy locals just fine, but with DJs spinning cool sounds and stylish drinks (including a tasty blood-orange martini), it has become a destination for commuting clubbers, too.

The **Chez Jay** (⊠ 1657 Ocean Ave., Santa Monica ☎ 310/395–1741) saloon, near the Santa Monica Pier, has endured since 1959. With only 10 tables, checkered tablecloths, and sawdust on the floor, it's a shabby but charming setting for inventive seafood fare and regular celebrity sightings.

Circle Bar (⊠ 2926 Main St., Venice ☎ 310/450–0508) gets its name from the bar's circular-shape interior, a setup that helps make it a see-and-be-seen beachside "it" spot. On weekends DJs spin electronic dance beats, hip-hop, and rock for casually dressed twentysomethings.

Thick with nautical mementos, the **Galley** (⊠ 2442 Main St., Santa Monica ☎ 310/452–1934) is tiny but recommended for nostalgics who want to recapture Santa Monica circa 1940.

Carved wooden tribal masks and other Indian and Southeast Asian items make **Monsoon** (⊠ 1212 Third St. Promenade, Santa Monica ☎ 310/576–9996) one of the most elegant spots on the always-jumping Promenade. The restaurant serves South Asian cuisine, and there's live music (from so-so to pretty good) in the upstairs bar most nights.

A couple of popular L.A. DJs run **Mor Bar** (⊠ 2941 Main St., Santa Monica ☎ 310/455–6720). The music ranges from salsa to '80s, but the owner's own nights behind the turntables (Friday and Sunday) are always the liveliest, with raucously remixed house, hip-hop, and Top 40 packing the dance floor.

Spacious **The Otheroom** (✉ 12012 Abbot Kinney Blvd., Venice ☎ 310/396–6230) may be a recent harbinger of Abbot Kinney's gentrification, but it's still got that laid-back Venice vibe. In fact, it fits into this neighborhood well enough that you'd never guess the original's from Manhattan. There's an impressive selection of microbrews and wines.

MALIBU If it's surfer boys or girls you're after, **Duke's Barefoot Bar** (✉ 21150 Pacific Coast Hwy., Malibu ☎ 310/317–0777) will be your new favorite hangout. The tiki-decorated oceanside drinking spot—named after famed surf god Duke Kahanamoku—is a casual place, with a patio right near the waves and an adjoining restaurant offering tasty finger foods.

WEST LOS ANGELES The Westside's contribution to cocktail culture, **Liquid Kitty** (✉ 11780 W. Pico Blvd., West L.A. ☎ 310/473–3707) is a swanky hangout with DJs (or live lounge jazz Sunday night) and no cover. You can't miss this place: just look for the neon martini glass on the outside.

HERMOSA BEACH The **Lighthouse Cafe** (✉ 30 Pier Ave., Hermosa Beach ☎ 310/376–9833) has a full bar and free live music weeknights. Music starts at 9 (4 on Friday). A $5–$10 cover is charged on Friday and Saturday; weekend mornings jazz is on offer at 11.

ALoha Sharkeez (✉ 52 Pier Ave., Hermosa Beach ☎ 310/374–7823) is a lively Polynesian-theme bar where beach babes sip sweet bowl-size drinks and dance and romance amid DJ–supplied dance music.

The **Underground** (✉ 1332 Hermosa Ave., Hermosa Beach ☎ 310/318–3818) is a British pub and sports bar offering imported beers and alcohol-absorbing greasy food, plus darts, pool, and DJs spinning dance hits on the weekends.

Downtown

The 1940s-style **Broadway Bar** (✉ 830 S. Broadway, Downtown ☎ 213/614–9909) feels swanky but avoids velvet-rope syndrome. The two-level, chandeliered room is more Rat Pack than brat pack; it's got stiff drinks, a jukebox filled with rock and lounge, and a smoking balcony overlooking the boulevard.

FodorsChoice ★ The **Downtown L.A. Standard** (✉ 550 S. Flower St., Downtown ☎ 213/892–8080) has a groovy lounge with pink sofas and DJs, as well as an all-white restaurant that looks like something out of *2001: A Space Odyssey*. But it's the rooftop bar, with an amazing view of the city's illuminated skyscrapers, a heated swimming pool, and private, podlike water-bed tents, that's worth waiting in line to get into. And wait you probably will, especially on weekends and in summer.

The old-school vibe of the **Golden Gopher** (✉ 417 W. 8th St., Downtown ☎ 213/623–9044) is as much about where it's at as about what it is. Don't be surprised if you're panhandled on your way inside this downtown spot, which manages simultaneously to be swanky (art deco columns, Victorian wallpaper), kitschy (golden gopher-shape lamps, video games), and divey (there's a small liquor store inside the place for stocking up for later).

Atop the 32-story Transamerica Building, **Windows** (⊠ 1150 S. Olive St., Downtown ☎ 213/746–1554) is an elegant cocktail bar and restaurant with an unbeatable view and live music on the weekends.

Mid-Wilshire Area

Another dark drinkin' hole where seasoned neighborhood swiggers and Sex on the Beach–sipping barhoppers peacefully coexist is **The Dime** (⊠ 442 N. Fairfax Ave., Fairfax District ☎ 323/651–4421). This low-key option gets energetic on weekends—and when DJs take over the sound system with a mix of rock and chilled electro beats.

After-work business types frequent **HMS Bounty** (⊠ 3357 Wilshire Blvd., Mid-Wilshire ☎ 213/385–7275), an elegant old watering hole in the historic Gaylord apartment building. Be sure to check out the brass plates above each booth—they bear the names of Hollywood heavies who once held court here. The reasonably priced drinks are impressive; so is the jukebox.

Molly Malone's (⊠ 575 S. Fairfax Ave., Fairfax District ☎ 323/935–1577) is a small, casual pub where the only posturing is in the pro-Irish posters on the wall. The nightly live music tends to the Irish flavored, but snappy blues and alternative-rock bands shake up the mix; the cover varies from $3 to $7.

Eastern Los Angeles

The people from the Short Stop bar in Echo Park set up **Footsies** (⊠ 2640 N. Figueroa St., Cypress Park ☎ 323/221–6900) way off the beaten path. At this cozy joint, hipsters who opted for more affordable housing on L.A.'s outskirts can get liquored up with likeminded artists and professionals. It has a great jukebox, but on weekends, the soundtrack is even more dynamic, as DJs man the decks.

Another bar in an up-and-coming neighborhood, **Chalet** (⊠ 1630 Colorado Blvd., Eagle Rock ☎ 323/258–8800) has a woodsy, calm feel. Regulars get toasty by the '70s-style fireplace while sipping brandies. It's a great place for a date, although weekends are a tad too lively for romancing.

Pasadena

Domenico's (⊠ 82 N. Fair Oaks Ave., Pasadena ☎ 626/449–1948) is a multiroom sports bar–restaurant–live performance space, with billiards, TVs tuned to sports, and live music and DJs spinning nightly. There's always something going on here in addition to the great Italian food, which helps it maintain its reign as the liveliest place in the area.

It's all about the beer at **Lucky Baldwin's** (⊠ 17 S. Raymond Ave., Pasadena ☎ 626/795–0652), an Old Town hangout known for its robust brews and warm British pub atmosphere. Occasional live music, tasty food, and brew-related events add to the sudsy fun.

A frat-style crowd frequents **Moose McGillycuddy's** (⊠ 119 E. Colorado Blvd., Pasadena ☎ 626/304–9955) for tasty fried fare and beers galore. An adjoining room offers weekly heavy metal shows, karaoke, and disco DJs.

The San Fernando Valley

Aura (✉ 12215 Ventura Blvd., Studio City ☎ 818/487–1488) might be in the back of minimall, but the club is actually one of the more chic Valley nightlife options, with a throbbing sound system and separate rooms for VIPs. DJs spin a mix of hip-hop and high-energy dance hits.

Polynesian kitsch enthusiasts from all around town hit **Lucky Tiki** (✉ 15420 Chatsworth Ave., Mission Hills ☎ 818/892–2688), a tropical hangout from the minds behind the Bigfoot Lodge. It throws itself into the theme with totem poles, hula dancer figurines, and thatch-hut touches.

The Valley may not be as bustling as Hollywood, but it has slowly been building its own after-dark scene, especially on the weekends. **Sapphire** (✉ 11938 Ventura Blvd., Studio City ☎ 818/506–0777) is one of the glossiest spots in the area, with slick decor, plush seating, and a jukebox full of sexy grooves and rousing rock.

Melding Hollywood hip and neighborhood nonchalance, **Nobar** (✉ 10622 Magnolia Blvd., North Hollywood ☎ 818/753–0545) is a welcoming watering hole attracting regulars from nearby galleries and theaters.

Blues

A half-dozen bars and eateries have live blues on weekend nights, in addition to the clubs below.

Babe & Ricky's Inn (✉ 4339 Leimert Blvd., Leimert Park ☎ 323/295–9112) is an old blues favorite. The great jukebox and photo-poster gallery and the barbecue and brew (or wine) will get you in the mood. It's closed Tuesday; covers vary from $4 to $10, and for Monday night's jam, admission will also get you a fried-chicken dinner, served at 10 PM.

B. B. King's Blues Bar (✉ 1000 Universal Center Dr., Universal City ☎ 818/622–5464) is a spacious, three-story venue at Universal CityWalk, with music nightly (at 8), Southern cooking, and gospel brunch every Sunday. Cover runs from $5 to $15.

Café Boogaloo (✉ 1238 Hermosa Ave., near Pier Ave., Hermosa Beach ☎ 310/318–2324 ⊕ www.boogaloo.com) is a small, down-to-earth, Louisiana-style-flavored restaurant and bar; more than two dozen microbrews are on tap. Live blues is also on tap nearly every night. The cover ranges from free to $10.

A young crowd, many of them regulars, packs **Harvelle's** (✉ 1432 4th St., Santa Monica ☎ 310/395–1676) on the weekends; come early or be prepared to stand in line. Watch from the back if you want, but down front, you'll be dancing. The cover's $3 weekdays, $5–$7 on weekends; a two-drink minimum is sometimes enforced.

Cabaret, Performance & Variety

L.A. may be a film-, television-, and music-industry mecca, but under the surface, other, more experimental forms of entertainment continue to burgeon and gain attention, most notably a local burlesque revival. Troupes such as the Pussycat Dolls (now a bona fide pop music group) and the edgier Lucha Va Voom (featuring tattooed rock chicks and gals of all shapes and sizes performing alongside Mexican wrestling matches) regularly take over local theaters and nightclubs. Cabaret crooners aren't limited to loungey locales; many can be found at rock venues and bars on designated evenings.

Beyond Baroque (✉ 681 Venice Blvd., Venice ☎ 310/822–3006 ⊕ www. beyondbaroque.org), in the old Venice Town Hall, is a performance space and bookstore dedicated to the literary arts, with popular poetry and literature readings that have included the likes of Viggo Mortensen and offbeat offerings like a night of "Crap Poetry."

★ Stoke the old-fashioned burlesque revival at **Forty Deuce** (✉ 5574 Melrose Ave., Hollywood ☎ 323/465–4242 ⊕ www.fortydeuce.com), where sultry yet relatively demure strip shows recall another era. The eye candy here is nonstop, but not just on stage—the lounge-bar is one of the most celeb-studded hangouts in town. This is the brainchild of club impresario Ivan Kane.

★ With seating for 120, **Highways Performance Space** (✉ 1651 18th St., Santa Monica ☎ 310/453–1755 or 310/315–1459) is one of the primary venues for avant-garde, offbeat, and alternative performance art as well as theater, dance, and comedy programs. It also has two art galleries.

Coffeehouses

★ **Highland Grounds** (✉ 742 N. Highland Ave., Hollywood ☎ 323/466–1507) is one of L.A.'s oldest coffeehouses. It serves meals, plus it has a balcony, a patio, and a selection of beer as good as that of coffee. Nightly entertainment is mostly acoustic.

Newsroom Espresso Café (✉ 530 Wilshire Blvd., near 5th St., Santa Monica ☎ 310/319–9100) is a habitat for tightly wired media junkies: you can catch CNN updates while sipping on highly caffeinated Jolt soda. Normal, well-adjusted types will enjoy the large magazine rack and tasty entrées, including tandoori chicken and pesto pizza.

With a trippy, sci-fi, Tolkienesque motif, **Nova Express Cafe** (✉ 426 N. Fairfax Ave., Fairfax District ☎ 323/658–7533) serves coffee, tea, and other snacks until 4 AM. Try the Galaxy 69, a banana smoothie with a shot of espresso. Suitably atmospheric DJs spin tunes some evenings.

One of the best reasons to venture off the beaten path is **Sacred Grounds** (✉ 399 W. 6th St., San Pedro ☎ 310/514–0800), one of the area's classic beatnik coffeehouses. There's coffee, tea, bagels, pastries, art on the walls, comfortable couches, and music almost every night (poetry on Monday). It opens at 6 AM daily and stays open until the shows are over (midnight weekdays, a little later on weekends). Covers range from free to $5.

A good place to take a break from the nonstop fun you've been having in L.A. and write about it in your journal is the **Un-urban Coffee House** (✉ 3301 Pico Blvd., at Urban Ave., Santa Monica ☎ 310/315–0056). Enjoy a stiff cup of coffee or some luscious chai tea, scarf down the good but inexpensive breakfast or a sandwich, and hear the music or spoken-word performances on Sunday during the day or on weekend evenings.

Comedy & Magic

Note that in addition to the clubs below, a number of nightspots not specializing in comedy have a hot comedy night every week, and there are some comedy events at a passel of places best rounded up in the listings at ⊕ www.LA.com.

The **Acme Comedy Theater** (⊠ 135 N. La Brea, Hollywood ☎ 323/525–0202) is really what its name suggests, the height of zaniness—mainly improv, sketch comedy, or both in the same production. The fare is consistently nutty, including an improvised game show and an improvised '40s-style radio drama.

★ A nightly premier comedy showcase, **Comedy Store** (⊠ 8433 Sunset Blvd., West Hollywood ☎ 323/656–6225) has been going strong for more than two decades, with three stages (with covers ranging from free to $20) to supply the yuks. Famous comedians occasionally make unannounced appearances.

★ More than a quarter century old, **Groundling Theatre** (⊠ 7307 Melrose Ave., Hollywood ☎ 323/934–9700) has been a breeding ground for *Saturday Night Live* performers; alumni include Lisa Kudrow and *Curb Your Enthusiasm*'s Cheryl Hines. The primarily sketch and improv comedy shows run Thursday–Sunday, costing $12–$18.50.

Since 1960, **Ice House Comedy Club and Restaurant** (⊠ 24 N. Mentor Ave., Pasadena ☎ 626/577–1894) has featured comedians, celebrity impressionists, ventriloquists, and magicians from Las Vegas as well as from TV. Shows take place nightly; reservations are strongly advised on weekends. Covers vary; there's a two-drink minimum.

Richard Pryor got his start at the **Improv** (⊠ 8162 Melrose Ave., West Hollywood ☎ 323/651–2583), a renowned establishment showcasing stand-up comedy. Drew Carey's *Totally Improv* is Thursday night on a semiregular basis. Reservations are recommended. Cover is $10–$15, and there's a two-drink minimum.

Improv Olympic West (⊠ 6366 Hollywood Blvd., Hollywood ☎ 323/962–7560 ⊕ www.iowest.com) showcases thematic improv and revues among its nightly shows, with covers from free to $10. It's known for Second City comedy troupe's long-form improv called "the Harold."

Fodor's Choice
★ Look for top stand-ups—and frequent celeb residents, like Bob Saget, or unannounced drop-ins, like Chris Rock—at **Laugh Factory** (⊠ 8001 Sunset Blvd., West Hollywood ☎ 323/656–1336). The club has shows nightly at 8 PM, plus added shows at 10 and midnight on Friday and Saturday; the cover is $10–$12.

It may be in a low-rent strip mall, but **M-Bar** (⊠ 1253 N. Vine St., Hollywood ☎ 323/856–0036) attracts some big names from the comedy world on a regular basis. *Arrested Development*'s David Cross and his sitcom pals make appearances here often.

New York's **Upright Citizens Brigade** (⊠ 5919 Franklin Ave., Hollywood ☎ 323/908–8702) marched in with a mix of sketch comedy and wild improvisations skewering pop culture. Members of the L.A. Brigade include VH1 commentator Paul Scheer and Mad TV's Andrew Daly.

Country Music

Boulevard Music (✉ 4316 Sepulveda Blvd., Culver City ☎ 310/398–2583) is, like McCabe's, primarily a musical instruments store, but most weekend nights it hosts live music. Although the music may be of any genre, it's more countrified than anything else. The cover varies from $12 to $20. No booze is served; all ages are okay.

Rustling up fun since the '70s, **Cowboy Palace Saloon** (✉ 21635 Devonshire Blvd., Chatsworth ☎ 818/341–0166) might just be L.A.'s last honky-tonk; if you want to tie up your horse, you can use the hitching post out back. Dance lessons nightly and music (around 9) are free of charge. There's a weakly enforced two-drink minimum; on Sunday there's a complimentary barbecue.

Viva Cantina (✉ 900 Riverside Dr., Burbank ☎ 818/845–2425) is mainly a family-oriented Mexican restaurant, but the large, ranch-style bar area is more for grown-ups. That's where the country music happens every night, from the best of the locals to the occasional legendary old-timer like Red Simpson. Music starts at 7:30, and there's no cover.

Dance Clubs

Though the establishments listed below are predominantly dance clubs as opposed to live music venues, there's often some overlap. A given club can vary wildly in genre from night to night, or even on the same night. ■ **TIP→** Gay and promoter-driven theme nights tend to "float" from venue to venue. Call ahead to make sure you don't end up looking for retro '60s music at an industrial bondage celebration (or vice versa). Covers vary according to the night and the DJs.

In the Corner Club space at Hollywood and Vine formerly known as Deep, is **Basque** (✉ 1707 N. Vine St., Hollywood ☎ 323/464–1654), a venue that's just as sexy as its predecessor. Corset-wearing bartenders and an elevated dance floor make for nonstop ogling. DJs spin mostly hip-hop.

★ As a bar, **Boardner's** (✉ 1652 N. Cherokee Ave., Hollywood ☎ 323/769–5001) has a multidecade history (in the '20s it was a speakeasy), but with the adjoining ballroom, which was added a couple of years ago, it's now a state-of-the-art dance club. DJs may be spinning electronica, funk, or something else depending on the night—at the popular Saturday Goth event "Bar Sinister," patrons must wear black or risk not getting in. The cover here is anywhere from free to $10.

Club Lingerie (✉ 6507 Sunset Blvd., Hollywood ☎ 323/466–3416) has endured several name changes, but one thing hasn't changed: the turnover rate for outside promoters is still—unfortunately for the club—unusually high. Weekends, which lean toward hip-hop or electronic sounds, still manage to pack 'em in. The cover range is $10–$20.

The surprisingly unswank **Concorde** (✉ 1835 N. Cahuenga Blvd., Hollywood ☎ 323/464–5662) started out hot but has now throttled back a bit. With a large outdoor area and minimalist decor, it still offers plenty of opportunities for people-watching, but no longer of the tabloid kind. DJs spin a mix of hip-hop, '80s, and Top 40 music.

Like Concorde, **El Centro** (✉ 1069 N. El Centro Ave. ☎ 323/957–1066) packs in pretty young things on weekends, but the celeb scene has moved elsewhere. It may be because all those limos stuck out like sore thumbs in its rundown Hollywood locale. The outdoor patio and comfy booths are still a draw, though.

Fais Do-Do (✉ 5257 W. Adams Blvd., West L.A. ☎ 323/954–8080) is all about rotating theme nights—roots-rock, reggae, hip-hop, and blues have all had their times. The sounds primarily come from DJs; there's a liberal sprinkling of bands, but they're not the main draw. The Cajun-California cuisine (paired with beer or wine; no hard drinks) doesn't hurt either. The cover is $3–$15.

The 18-and-over set crowds into **Florentine Gardens** (✉ 5951 Hollywood Blvd., Hollywood ☎ 323/464–0706) on weekends. DJs from local radio stations often take over the turntables, and the crowd is usually made up of kids who drive in from Hollywood's outskirts.

Gabah (✉ 4658 Melrose Ave., Hollywood ☎ 323/664–8913) is Arabic for "jungle," and it's a fitting moniker for a place offering such exotic and diverse music. DJs spin everything from hip-hop to dub to reggae to obscure rarities during the long-running Saturday Chocolate Bar.

Garden of Eden (✉ 7080 Hollywood Blvd., Hollywood ☎ 323/465–3336) is an exotically decorated space hosting four nights of dancing (Wednesday–Saturday) for a dapper, youngish crowd: yes, there's a dress code. Music leans toward house and funk or Euro-house and trip-hop. There are three bars, a smoking patio, and valet parking; the cover is generally $15.

Ivar (✉ 6356 Hollywood Blvd., Hollywood ☎ 310/829–1933) has been attracting the model-actor "discover me" set with weekly hip-hop, electronic, and old-school music promotions. VIPs get to hang in a two-level, neon-lighted cylindrical area that looks like something out of *Star Trek,* but for the most part, that A-list set has moved on. Still, expect lines around the block on weekends.

The wait outside **LAX** (✉ 1714 Las Palmas Ave., Hollywood ☎ 323/464–0171) can often be as bad as the baggage check-in lines at its namesake. DJ AM (Nicole Richie's squeeze once upon a time) mans the decks most nights with a mash-up mix style that pumps out everything from Journey to Kanye West.

Mood (✉ 6623 Hollywood Blvd., Hollywood ☎ 323/464–6663) creates its namesake with candles, sculptures, and a shrinelike bar, but it's the beautiful people who get worshipped here. Wednesday and Saturday are the hot ticket nights, with DJs spinning hip hop and rock.

Prey (✉ 643 N. La Cienaga Blvd., West Hollywood ☎ 310/652–2012) changes its look more often than it changes its lightbulbs, but no matter what the decor, the place continues to attract models and actors. (The club was featured as a hangout in the HBO series *Entourage*.) Music leans toward hip-hop and house.

★ Owned by nightlife impresario Sam Nazarian, **Privilege** (✉ 8117 Sunset Blvd., Hollywood ☎ 323/654–0030) gets a makeover as often as its clientele, like Nazarian's other club, Prey. The prominent location at the start of the Sunset Strip ensures that the club remains consistently packed, though. As of this writing, the Saturday party, thrown by über-promoter Brent Bolthouse, was luring in the party girls (Hiltons, Simpsons, you get the picture).

The **Ruby** (✉ 7070 Hollywood Blvd., Hollywood ☎ 323/467–7070) is a popular three-room dance venue for young indie-rock and retro-loving twentysomethings. You might find anything from doomy Goth and industrial ("Perversion") to '80s retro ("Beat It") to '60s–'70s Brit pop and soul ("Bang") to trance and techno. Cover charges are $8–$12.

Sugar (✉ 814 Broadway, Santa Monica ☎ 310/889–1989) is a hot spot for cool electronica, with noted DJs and lively, young regulars.

Tempest (✉ 7323 Santa Monica Blvd., West Hollywood ☎ 323/960–7920), a restaurant-nightclub in the heart of gay West Hollywood, attracts mostly the young and straight hipsters to its dance nights, the most popular of which is the Friday Brit pop-rock club called Underground.

White Lotus (✉ 1743 N. Cahuenga Blvd., Hollywood ☎ 323/463–0060) is a restaurant and nightclub attracting scantily clad, sake-sipping cuties and the fellas who chase them. Its simple design (a clean, very white color palate, Asian antiques, statues at the entrance, and breezy outdoor patio) make it a fun place to eat (sushi's the specialty) and party. Various promoters come in during the week, bringing with them DJs spinning hit mixes.

With stripper poles and a red-and-black bordello look, **XES** (✉ 1716 N. Cahuenga Blvd., Hollywood ☎ 323/461–8190) has a not-so-subtle risqué appeal. Look no farther than its name: "sex" spelled backwards and pronounced "excess." The vampy venue pumps out rock and hip-hop.

Hip-hop and funk rule at the DJ-driven **Zanzibar** (✉ 1301 5th St., Santa Monica ☎ 310/451–2221), a warm and inviting spot from the people behind Temple Bar. Sounds ranging from Latin jazz to soul to deep house attract a mix of locals and commuting Hollywood clubsters.

Gay & Lesbian Clubs

Some of the most popular gay and lesbian "clubs" are weekly theme nights at various venues, so read the preceding list of clubs, *LA Weekly* listings, and gay publications such as *Odyssey* in addition to the following recommendations.

An ethnically mixed gay and straight crowd flocks to **Circus Disco and Arena** (✉ 6655 Santa Monica Blvd., Hollywood ☎ 323/462–1291 or 323/462–0714), two huge, side-by-side discos with techno and rock music, as well as a full bar and patio, open Tuesday, Thursday, and Friday 9–2. Only certain nights are gay themed. Saturday "Spundae" is for everyone: top local and international DJs spin funk, house, trance, disco, and more until 4 AM. The cover can range from $3 to $20.

The **Factory** (✉ 652 La Peer Dr., West Hollywood ☎ 310/659–4551) churns out dance music for those who like to grind. In the adjoining **Ultra Suede** (✉ 661 N. Robertson Blvd., West Hollywood), there's '80s–'90s pop on Wednesday and Friday. Saturday, the two houses combine for an event called "The Factory." Covers range from $5 to $15.

★ Nowhere is more gregarious than **Here** (✉ 696 N. Robertson Blvd., West Hollywood ☎ 310/360–8455), where there are hot DJs and an even hotter clientele. Though it's usually a boys' hangout, you'll find WeHo's wildest ladies' night at Tuesday's Fuse gathering.

Jewel's Catch One (✉ 4067 W. Pico Blvd., Mid-City ☎ 323/734–8849) is a lively hangout for just about anyone, with male and female dancers and lip-synching shows, karaoke, and DJs spinning hip-hop and disco.

The gay bar **MJ's** (✉ 28120 Hyperion Ave., Silver Lake ☎ 323/660–1503) is laid-back enough to attract locals of every persuasion. DJs spin an array of diva disco, electro, and mash-ups (DJ Paul V's Megamonday).

A long-running gay-gal fave, the **Palms** (✉ 8572 Santa Monica Blvd., West Hollywood ☎ 310/652–6188) continues to thrive thanks to great DJs spinning dance tunes Wednesday–Sunday. There are also an outdoor patio, pool tables, and an occasional live performance.

Peanuts (✉ 7969 Santa Monica Blvd., West Hollywood ☎ 323/654–0280) has groovy bordello-esque decor and mixed–gay theme nights, including the stripper rock-and-roll night called "Club Vodka" and the campy dance shindig "Velvet."

Rage (✉ 8911 Santa Monica Blvd., West Hollywood ☎ 310/652–7055) is a longtime favorite of the "gym boy" set, with DJs following a different musical theme every night of the week (alternative rock, house, dance remixes, etc.). The cover is free to $10.

Jazz

Powerhouse jazz and blues please crowds at the tiny **Baked Potato** (✉ 3787 Cahuenga Blvd. W, North Hollywood ☎ 818/980–1615). The star of the menu is, of course, the baked potato, jumbo and stuffed with everything from steak to vegetables. The music's on every night, with a $10 cover.

After moving to a bigger space in 2005, **Catalina** (✉ 6725 W. Sunset Blvd., Hollywood ☎ 323/466–2210) is hotter than ever, with top-notch jazz bookings ranging from classic Chicago style to Latin-flavored.

Charlie O's Bar & Grill (✉ 13725 Victory Blvd., Van Nuys ☎ 818/994–3058) has some pretty nifty local jazzers playing nightly, plus steak, chops, and ribs on the bill of fare; and there's no cover or minimum.

A tasty array of comfort food complements the nightly happy hour and later evening jazz shows at **Jaxx** (✉ 339 N. Brand Blvd., Glendale ☎ 818/500–1604) as does the cozy, Tiffany-lamped interior. Bookings range from piano-bar ticklers to slightly more boisterous horn blowers. There's no cover or minimum.

Come to **Jazz Bakery** (✉ 3233 Helms Ave., Culver City ☎ 310/271–9039) for world-class jazz nightly at 8 and 9:30, in a quiet, respectful concert-like setting. The cover is $10–$25; parking is free.

You can't eat or drink—but you can see great jazz—at the no-frills **World Stage** (✉ 4344 Degnan Blvd., Leimert Park ☎ 323/293–2451). It's the brainchild of storied drummer Billy Higgins, and some of his big-name friends are known to stop by. The schedule of workshops, jam sessions, and concerts—many featuring young aspiring musicians—changes frequently; so call ahead.

Latin

There's no ideal label for it, but this section includes venues for samba as well as salsa, rumba, rock *en español,* and even flamenco. A number of other venues offer such music one or more nights a week and information on them can be found in papers like the *LA Weekly,* but it's always wise to call and check.

Fodor'sChoice ★ The **Conga Room** (✉ 5364 Wilshire Blvd., Mid-Wilshire ☎ 323/938–1696), which is co-owned by local celebs, including Jimmy Smits, presents Latin music (primarily salsa) and the odd rock or soul show. The tropical interiors and hot music may not soften the blow to your wallet; regular admission is $10–$20, but VIP treatment, which is the only way to get the good seats, costs $30–$40.

The Cuban food at **El Floridita** (✉ 1253 N. Vine St., Hollywood ☎ 323/871–0936) is anywhere from good to great—and the music (Monday, Friday, and Saturday) is anywhere from very good to through the roof. A frequent guest is the salsa bandleader Johnny Polanco, backed by the sizzling Conjunto Amistad. Watching some of the paying customers who get up to dance alone is worth the price of admission (usually $10, or free with dinner).

L.A.'s top Latin bands all make their way to **Mama Juanas** (✉ 3707 Cahuenga Blvd., Studio City ☎ 818/505–8636), a colorful restaurant and live music venue with salsa, Afro-Cuban grooves, and an all-female group (the Mariachi Divas) on various nights. You can enjoy a spicy meal and follow it up with some spicier moves on its large dance floor.

Rock & Other Live Music

In addition to the venues listed below, many smaller bars book live music, if less frequently or with less publicity.

Soundcheck

WITH SO MANY PEOPLE vying for a mike in this town, it can often be difficult to weed out the worthwhile music nights. Here are a few (many of them jam nights that showcase more local talent for your buck) definitely worth checking out:

Monday. **The Joint:** This jam with guitarist Waddy Wachtel not only has occasional big-name guests but frequent drop-ins by accomplished session players and back-up band musicians from groups such as Tom Petty and the Rolling Stones. The **Key Club:** House band Metal Skool, a campy cover band that does hilarious but surprisingly good renditions of '80s hair-rock hits, plays at midnight, and up-and-coming rock acts perform here, too. Big names like Steven Tyler, Slash, and even Tommy Lee (with ex Pamela Anderson dancing on stage) have been known to join the band.

Wednesday. **Star Shoes:** Hot new-wave-flavored rockers take a break from the stage and hit the decks at "Radio." Björk and Peaches as well as members of Interpol and the Faint have been known to give the turntables a whirl. If a big alternative band is in town, this is the place where band members often to choose to hang.

Thursday and Sunday. **Cat Club:** This little hangout attracts a lot of the '80s musicians for whom metal just won't die—it did, after all, blow up right here on the Strip. Sunday's "Happenin' Harry Jam" reels in plenty of them, and Thursday, owner Slim Jim rocks out with a stellar array of pals.

The landmark formerly known as the Palace is now the **Avalon** (✉ 1735 N. Vine St., Hollywood ☎ 323/462–3000). The multilevel art deco building opposite Capitol Records has a fabulous sound system, four bars, and a balcony. Big-name rock and pop concerts hit the stage during the week, but on weekends the place becomes a dance club, with the most popular night the DJ-dominated Avaland. Upstairs, but with a separate entrance, you'll find celeb hub the **Spider Club**, a Moroccan-style room where celebs and their entourages are frequent visitors.

For the sake of pithiness, the **California Institute for Abnormal Arts** (✉ 11334 Burbank Ave., North Hollywood ☎ 818/506–6353 ⊕ www. ciabnormalarts.com) abbreviates its name to CIA. Its nuttiness (bands and multimedia events) is let loose Thursday–Saturday. It's been said that on "weekends it's a giant magnet for every loose screw in town." No alcohol is served.

Slim Jim Phantom, former drummer of the Stray Cats, is the man behind the **Cat Club** (✉ 8911 Sunset Blvd., West Hollywood ☎ 310/657–0888). Bands play nightly, and Mr. Phantom sometimes comes out to play with buds like ex–Guns N' Roses axman Gilby Clarke. There are an upstairs and a back patio, but it's still, to euphemize, "intimate." Covers range from free to $7.

Dark and grungy, **Dragonfly** (✉ 6510 Santa Monica Blvd., Hollywood ☎ 323/466–6111) showcases a mix of live rock and rock hybrids seven nights a week. After the bands on Friday and Saturday, it morphs into a dance club. On Thursday, it's reggae all night. When you need to cool off, there's an outdoor patio with bar. Cover is $5–$15.

About 8 or 10 times a month, the gloriously restored art deco **El Rey Theater** (⊠ 5515 Wilshire Blvd., Mid-Wilshire ☎ 323/936–4790) showcases concerts, often by top-name bands on national tours, as well as an assortment of theme nights. Covers are $10–$30.

14 Below (⊠ 1348 14th St., Santa Monica ☎ 310/451–5040) is a comfy hangout, but the booking policy (as many as five bands in a night) is a bit erratic, scheduling some of L.A.'s finest, some turkeys, and lots of bands doing re-creations of the Dead, the Stones, and more. Mingle with the postcollegiates in the bar, shoot some pool, or go around to the adjacent restaurant. Cover varies from free to $12.

At the longtime music-industry hangout known as **Genghis Cohen Cantina** (⊠ 740 N. Fairfax Ave., Hollywood ☎ 323/653–0640), you can hear hopefuls and veteran performers of the singer-songwriter sort and sample the kosher Chinese cuisine at the same time.

The comfortable **Gig** (⊠ 7302 Melrose Ave., Hollywood ☎ 323/936–4440) combines a bar, some cushy sofas, and a low-lighted environment, where mostly no-name bands (some great, some ghastly) can get a shot at Hollywood crowds. Covers range from $5–$15.

The **House of Blues** (⊠ 8430 Sunset Blvd., West Hollywood ☎ 323/848–5100) is a club that functions like a concert venue, hosting popular jazz, rock, and blues performers such as Etta James, Lou Rawls, Joe Cocker, Cheap Trick, Pete Townshend, and the Commodores. ■ **TIP→ Avoid industry idiots who prefer talking to listening by skipping the tables and bar areas for the central open floor.** Occasional shows are presented cabaret style and include dinner in the restaurant area upstairs; you can *sort of* see from some of it. Every Sunday there's a gospel brunch.

Every night the petite **Joint** (⊠ 8771 W. Pico Blvd., West L.A. ☎ 310/275–2619) puts on live music from mostly local, mostly so-so rockers. The real reason to come is its "Big Monday" jam with guitar hero Waddy Wachtel and stellar—and we do mean stellar—guest drop-ins. Recent surprise jammers have included Roger Daltrey, George Clinton, and Keith Richards.

The **Key Club** (⊠ 9039 Sunset Blvd., West Hollywood ☎ 310/274–5800) is a flashy, multitier rock club with four bars presenting current artists of all genres (some on national tours, others local aspirants). After the concerts, there's dancing with DJs spinning techno and house.

Everything from Latin rhythms to electronic music to raging punk sounds can found at the roomy **King King** (⊠ 6555 Hollywood Blvd., Hollywood ☎ 323/960–9234). Good acoustics, even better crowd. The entrance from the parking-lot side of the building helps you avoid slack-jawed tourists on the Walk of Fame.

 The **Knitting Factory** (⊠ 7021 Hollywood Blvd., Hollywood ☎ 323/463–0204) is the L.A. offshoot of the downtown New York club of the same name. The modern, medium-size room seems all the more spacious for its balcony-level seating and sizable stage. Despite its dubious location on Hollywood Boulevard's tourist strip, it's a great set-up for the arty, big-name performers it presents. There's live music almost every night in the main room and in the smaller Alter-Knit Lounge. Covers are free to $40.

Musician-producer Jon Brion (Fiona Apple, Aimee Mann, and others) shows off his ability to play virtually any instrument and any song in the rock lexicon—and beyond—as host of a popular evening of music every Friday at **Largo** (✉ 432 N. Fairfax Ave., Hollywood ☎ 323/852–1073). Other nights, low-key rock and singer-songwriter fare is offered at this cozy supper club–bar. And when comedy comes in, about one night a week, it's usually one of the best comedy nights in town, with folks like Margaret Cho. Reservations are required for tables, but bar stools are open.

The funky people behind Santa Monica's Temple Bar and Zanzibar moved east for their warm, more intimate spot, **Little Temple** (✉ 4159 Santa Monica Blvd., Santa Monica ☎ 323/660–4550). The DJs and live acts focus on soul, Latin, and reggae music.

McCabe's Guitar Shop (✉ 3101 Pico Blvd., Santa Monica ☎ 310/828–4497, 310/828–4403 for concert information) is rootsy-retro-central, where all things earnest and (preferably) acoustic are welcome—chiefly folk, blues, bluegrass, and rock. It *is* a guitar shop (so no liquor license), with a room full of folding chairs for concert-style presentations. Make reservations well in advance.

Enter **Mr. T's Bowl** (✉ 5261½ N. Figueroa Ave., Highland Park ☎ 323/256–7561) through the rear parking lot. It used to be a bowling alley; now, five or six nights a week (but not Monday), it offers some of L.A.'s weirdest—and most fun—rockers. (Beck played here during his folky phase.) There's a full bar, the cover is usually $3–$5, and food is available.

The **Roxy** (✉ 9009 Sunset Blvd., West Hollywood ☎ 310/276–2222), a Sunset Strip fixture for decades, hosts local and touring rock, alternative, blues, and rockabilly bands. Not the comfiest club around, but it's the site of many memorable shows.

When you're not gawking at the many vintage surf boards on the walls and ceiling of **Rusty's Surf Ranch** (✉ 256 Santa Monica Pier, Santa Monica ☎ 310/393–7386), you can watch rock-and-roll bands, singer-songwriters, or blues boppers.

Neighborhoody and relaxed, **Silver Lake Lounge** (✉ 2906 Sunset Blvd., Silver Lake ☎ 323/666–2407) draws a mixed collegiate and boho crowd. The club is very unmainstream "cool," the booking policy an adventurous mix of local and touring alt-rockers. Bands play three to five nights a week; covers vary but are low.

The **Smell** (✉ 247 S. Main St., Downtown ☎ No phone) may have bands only two or three nights a week (Wednesday, Friday, or Saturday), but they're often choice—in the alternative fringe world, anyway. If they're not playing at the Knitting Factory, Spaceland, or the Silver Lake Lounge, they just might be at the Smell. There's no liquor, the cover's usually $5, and there's also an art gallery. Enter via the back alley.

★ The hottest bands of tomorrow, surprises from yesteryear, and unclassifiable bands of today perform at **Spaceland** (✉ 1717 Silver Lake Blvd., Silver Lake ☎ 323/661–4380 ⊕ www.clubspaceland.com), which has a bar, jukebox, and pool table. Monday is always free, with monthlong gigs by the indie fave du jour. Spaceland has a nice selection of beers, some food if you're hungry, and a hip but relaxed interior.

There's a real community feeling at **Temple Bar** (✉ 1026 Wilshire Blvd., Santa Monica ☎ 310/393–6611), which books some of the most rhythmic acts in town. Live hip-hop and funk bands dominate here, but DJs often set the mood.

The **Troubadour** (✉ 9081 Santa Monica Blvd., West Hollywood ☎ 310/276–6168), one of the best and most comfortable clubs in town, has weathered the test of time since its '60s debut as a folk club. After surviving the '80s heavy-metal scene, this all-ages, wood-panel venue has caught a second (third? fourth?) wind by booking hot alternative rock acts. There's valet parking, but if you don't mind walking up Doheny a block or three, there's usually ample street parking (check the signs carefully).

Actor Johnny Depp sold his share of the infamous **Viper Room** (✉ 8852 Sunset Blvd., West Hollywood ☎ 310/358–1880) in 2004, but the place continues to rock with a motley live music lineup (Monday, local radio station Indie 103.1 presents new rock), if a less stellar crowd.

Whisky-A-Go-Go (✉ 8901 Sunset Blvd., West Hollywood ☎ 310/652–4202) is the most famous rock-and-roll club on the Strip, where back in the '60s, Johnny Rivers cut hit singles and the Doors, Love, and the Byrds cut their musical eyeteeth. It's still going strong, with up-and-coming alternative, hard rock, and punk bands. Mondays launch L.A.'s cutting-edge acts.

The nightly music at **Zen** (✉ 2609 Hyperion Ave., Silver Lake ☎ 323/665–2929) is as raw as the sushi on the menu: punk, indie, and art rock. Its three rooms, each with a different sound, are an upstairs loft-style space, a red-hue rock room, and the restaurant itself, where sounds lean toward the acoustic.

Sports & the Outdoors

WORD OF MOUTH

"The thing we enjoyed most was taking an early-morning drive down Canaan Road to Malibu, then going up to Zuma Beach. It was beautiful and peaceful."

—BTilke

"Ready to enjoy some nature? The Santa Monica Mountains, between Thousand Oaks and the Pacific Ocean, are a great escape. . . . The trails are pretty easy to navigate, and once in a while you might encounter some people, but overall it is not exactly overcrowded out there."

—hsv

Updated by
Laura Randall

SURFERS AND BODYBUILDERS AT THE BEACH, Jack Nicholson courtside at the Staples Center cheering on the Lakers, blissed-out yoga practitioners, sweat-suited power-walkers pacing through Beverly Hills—all have ingrained L.A. as a sports-focused city in the public imagination. These scenarios are just the tip of the iceberg, though; from rock climbing to whale-watching, L.A. has an enviable scope of activities. Given the right weather conditions, it's possible to choose between skiing and a trip to the beach. Some days begin overcast but become, after the clouds' late-morning "burn-off," simply glorious.

■ **TIP→** A word to the wise: the air is dry, so bottled water and lip balm can prove invaluable. Also, don't forget sunscreen; even on overcast days the sunburn index can be high. (Check the *Los Angeles Times*'s weather page or local AM radio news stations like KFWB 980 and KNX 1070.)

BEACHES

L.A.'s beaches are an integral part of the southern California lifestyle; getting some sand on the floor of your car is practically a requirement. From downtown, the easiest way to hit the coast is by taking the Santa Monica Freeway (I–10) due west. Once you reach the end of the freeway, I–10 runs into the famous Highway 1. Better known as the Pacific Coast Highway, or PCH, Highway 1 continues north to Sonoma County and south to San Diego. MTA buses run from downtown along Pico, Olympic, Santa Monica, Sunset, and Wilshire boulevards westward to the coast.

Los Angeles County beaches (and state beaches operated by the county) have lifeguards on duty year-round, with expanded forces during the summer. Public parking is usually available, though fees can be as much as $8; in some areas, it's possible to find free street and highway parking. Both restrooms and beach access have been brought up to the standards of the Americans with Disabilities Act. Generally, the northernmost beaches are best for surfing, hiking, and fishing, and the wider and sandier southern beaches are better for tanning and relaxing. ⚠ Almost all are great for swimming, but beware: pollution in Santa Monica Bay sometimes approaches dangerous levels, particularly after storms. Call ahead for **beach conditions** (☎ 310/457–9701) or go to www.watchthewater.com for specific beach updates. The following beaches are listed in north–south order:

Leo Carrillo State Beach. On the very edge of Ventura County, this narrow beach is better for exploring than for swimming or sunning. On your own or with a ranger, venture down at low tide to examine the tide pools among the rocks. Sequit Point, a promontory dividing the northwest and southeast halves of the beach, creates secret coves, sea tunnels, and boulders on which you can perch and fish. Generally, anglers stick to the northwest end of the beach; experienced surfers brave the rocks to the southeast. Campgrounds are set back from the beach; call ahead to reserve campsites. ⊠ *35000 PCH, Malibu* ☎ *818/880–0350, 800/444–7275 for camping reservations* ☞ *Parking, lifeguard (year-round, except only as needed in winter), restrooms, showers, fire pits.*

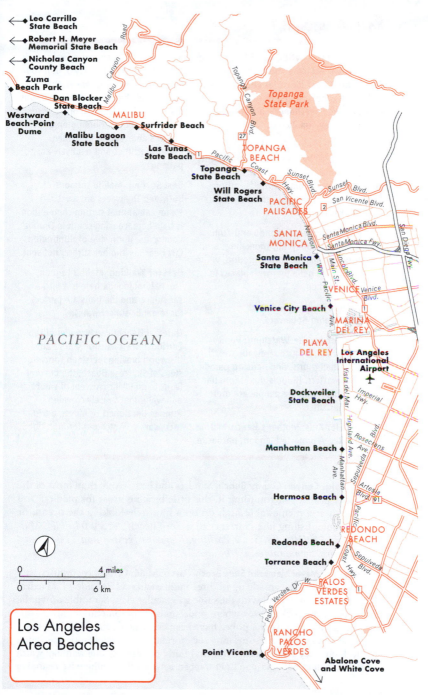

Leo Carrillo
State Beach

Robert H. Meyer
Memorial State Beach

Nicholas Canyon
County Beach

Zuma
Beach Park

Dan Blocker
State Beach

MALIBU

Surfrider Beach

Westward
Beach-Point
Dume

Malibu Lagoon
State Beach

Las Tunas
State Beach

Topanga
State Park

TOPANGA
BEACH

Topanga
State Beach

Will Rogers
State Beach

PACIFIC
PALISADES

SANTA
MONICA

Santa Monica
State Beach

VENICE

Venice City Beach

MARINA
DEL REY

PLAYA
DEL REY

Los Angeles
International
Airport

PACIFIC OCEAN

Dockweiler
State Beach

Manhattan Beach

Hermosa Beach

REDONDO
BEACH

Redondo Beach

Torrance Beach

PALOS
VERDES
ESTATES

4 miles

6 km

RANCHO
PALOS
VERDES

Point Vicente

Abalone Cove
and White Cove

Los Angeles
Area Beaches

L.A.'s Best Beaches

MOST LOS ANGELES BEACHES are pretty spectacular, but some are better suited for certain activities and people than others. Here's a longtime beachgoer's breakdown, quality by quality.

Best All-Around Beach: Santa Monica. A wide swath of sand, plenty of people-watching, good swimming, great views from the bluffs—other than its surfing (nil), this beach hits the key marks.

Best Activities: Redondo and Zuma. Both have volleyball, snorkeling, and fishing. Zuma has a playground, while Redondo's got a pier with places to eat and shop.

Easiest Parking: Venice at Washington Boulevard.

Best for People-Watching: Venice City Beach, for its boardwalk, volleyball courts, and nonstop parade of characters. Runner-up: Manhattan Beach, though the people are more cookie-cutter.

Best for Kids: Mother's Beach/Marina del Rey. A protected lagoon, barbecue pits, and a cool playground mean you can easily make a full day of it. If your kids want to go in the water, though, you should check the water conditions first, as pollution's been on the rise. In Orange County, Huntington State Beach stands out for its family-friendly facilities and relatively easy parking.

Best Surfing: Malibu Lagoon/ Surfrider. The waves are awesomely steady; an annual surfing competition is held here. Looking south to Orange County, the north side of Huntington City Beach is another surfing hot spot.

Best for Walking: Malibu Lagoon. The natural lagoon here is a bird sanctuary, and the trails are perfect for romantic sunset walks.

Quietest Beach: Western end of Leo Carrillo. If it's seclusion you're after, it's worth braving the steep concrete steps of Staircase Beach; the descent leads to an idyllic crescent of sand and water that's rarely crowded. Runner-up: Robert H. Meyer, a trio of rocky coves. (Watch out for high tide.)

Nicholas Canyon County Beach. Sandier and less private than most of the rocky beaches surrounding it, this little beach is great for picnics. You can sit at a picnic table high up on a bluff overlooking the ocean, or cast out a fishing line. Surfers call it Zero Beach. ⊠ *33904 PCH, Malibu* ☎ *310/305–9503* ☞ *Parking, lifeguard (year-round), restrooms, showers, picnic tables, barbecues.*

Fodor'sChoice ★ **Robert H. Meyer Memorial State Beach.** Part of Malibu's most beautiful coastal area, this beach is made up of three minibeaches: El Pescador, La Piedra, and El Matador—all with the same spectacular view. Scramble down the steps to the rocky coves where nude sunbathers sometimes gather—although in recent years, police have been cracking down. "El Mat" has a series of caves, Piedra some nifty rock formations, and Pescador a secluded feel, but they're all picturesque and fairly private. ⚠ **One warning: watch the incoming tide and don't get trapped between those otherwise charming**

boulders. ✉ *32350, 32700, and 32900 PCH, Malibu* ☎ *818/880–0350* ☞ *Parking, 1 roving lifeguard unit, restrooms.*

Zuma Beach Park. Zuma, 2 mi of white sand usually littered with tanning teenagers, has it all: from fishing and diving to swings for the kids to volleyball courts. Beachgoers looking for quiet or privacy should head elsewhere. The surf is rough and inconsistent. ✉ *30050 PCH, Malibu* ☎ *818/880–0350* ☞ *Parking, lifeguard (year-round, except only as needed in winter), restrooms, food concessions, playground.*

Westward Beach–Point Dume. Go tide-pooling, fishing, snorkeling, or bird-watching (prime time is late winter–early spring). Hike to the top of the sandstone cliffs to whale-watch—their migrations can be seen between December and April. Westward is a favorite surfing beach, but the steep surf isn't for novices. ■ TIP➔ Bring your own food, since the nearest concession is a longish hike away. ✉ *South end of Westward Beach Rd., Malibu* ☎ *310/305–9503* ☞ *Parking, lifeguard (year-round, except only as needed in winter), restrooms, showers.*

Dan Blocker State Beach. Originally owned jointly by the stars of the *Bonanza* TV series, this little stretch of beach was donated to the state after Blocker (who played Hoss) died in 1972. It's great for scuba diving, bird-watching, surfing, swimming, and fishing. ✉ *25560 PCH, at Corral Canyon Rd., Malibu* ☎ *310/305–9503* ☞ *Parking, lifeguard (year-round, except only as needed in winter), restrooms.*

Malibu Lagoon State Beach/Surfrider Beach. Steady 3- to 5-foot waves make this beach, just west of Malibu Pier, a popular surfing location. The International Surfing Contest is held here in September—the surf is best around that time. Water runoff from Malibu Canyon forms a natural lagoon that's a sanctuary for 250 species of birds. Unfortunately, the lagoon is often polluted and algae filled. If you're leery of going into the water, you can bird-watch, play volleyball, or take a walk on one of the nature trails, which are perfect for romantic sunset strolls. ✉ *23200 PCH, Malibu* ☎ *310/305–9503* ☞ *Parking, lifeguard (year-round), restrooms, picnic tables.*

Las Tunas State Beach. This small beach known for its groins (metal gates constructed in 1929 to protect against erosion) has good swimming, diving, and fishing conditions and a rocky coastline. ✉ *19444 PCH, Malibu* ☎ *310/305–9503* ☞ *Parking on highway only, lifeguard (year-round, except only as needed in winter).*

LAURA'S TOP 5

- **Angeles National Forest's Gabrielino Trail,** where you can hike in a bird-filled oak forest.
- **Dodger Stadium** for a baseball game.
- **Huntington Library, Art Collections, and Botanical Gardens,** especially the cactus garden with its giant aloes.
- **South Bay Bicycle Trail,** biking and people-watching nonstop from Santa Monica to Venice Beach.
- **Zuma Beach, Malibu,** perfect for riding the waves followed by an open-air seafood dinner.

5

Topanga State Beach. The beginning of miles of public beach, Topanga has good surfing at the western end (at the mouth of the canyon). Close to a busy section of the PCH and rather narrow, Topanga is not serene; hordes of teenagers zip over Topanga Canyon Boulevard from the Valley. Fishing and swings for children are available. ⊠ *18700 block of PCH, Malibu* ☎ *818/880–0350* ☞ *Parking, lifeguard (year-round, except only as needed in winter), restrooms, food concessions.*

Will Rogers State Beach. This clean, sandy, 3-mi beach, with a dozen volleyball nets, gymnastics equipment, and playground equipment for kids, is an all-around favorite. The surf is gentle, perfect for swimmers and beginning surfers. However, beware after a storm, when untreated water flows from storm drains into the sea. ⊠ *15100 PCH, 2 mi north of Santa Monica Pier, Pacific Palisades* ☎ *818/880–0350* ☞ *Parking, lifeguard (year-round, except only as needed in winter), restrooms.*

★ **Santa Monica State Beach.** It's the first beach you'll hit after the Santa Monica Freeway (I–10) runs into the PCH, and it's one of L.A.'s best known. Wide and sandy, Santa Monica is *the* place for sunning and socializing: be prepared for a mob scene on summer weekends, when parking becomes an expensive ordeal. Swimming is fine (with the usual poststorm pollution caveat); for surfing, go elsewhere. For a memorable view, climb up the stairway over the PCH to Palisades Park, at the top of the bluffs. Summer-evening concerts are often held here. ⊠ *1642 Promenade, PCH at California Incline, Santa Monica* ☎ *310/305–9503* ☞ *Parking, lifeguard (year-round), restrooms, showers.*

Venice City Beach. The surf and sand of Venice are fine, but the main attraction here is the boardwalk scene. There are also swimming, fishing, surfing, basketball (it's the site of some of L.A.'s most hotly contested pickup games), racquetball, handball, and shuffleboard. You can rent a bike or some in-line skates and hit the Strand bike path. ⊠ *West of Pacific Ave., Venice* ☎ *310/577–5700* ☞ *Parking, restrooms, food concessions, showers, playground.*

Dockweiler State Beach. The longest (4-mi) strip of beach in the county, Dockweiler has almost all the makings of a perfect beach: a campground, RV park, playground, separate bike trail, barbecue pits, mild surf, nice sand. If only the planes from LAX weren't taking off directly overhead and factories weren't puffing out fumes right behind you. If you don't mind that, you'll find plenty of room to spread out. An additional bonus is the hang-gliding facility (right in front of the water-treatment plant). Contact **Windsports International** (☎ 818/367–2430 ⊕ www.windsports.com); $120 will get you a full lesson with equipment. ⊠ *8255 Vista del Mar, west end of Imperial Hwy., Playa del Rey*

☎ *310/372–2166* ☞ *Parking, lifeguard (year-round), restrooms, showers, volleyball.*

Manhattan Beach. A wide, sandy strip with good swimming and rows of volleyball courts, Manhattan Beach is the preferred destination of muscled, tanned young professionals and dedicated bikini-watchers. There are also a separate bike path, a playground, fishing equipment for rent, a bait shop, and a sizable fishing pier. ⊠ *Manhattan Beach Blvd. and N. Ocean Dr., Manhattan Beach* ☎ *310/372–2166* ☞ *Parking, lifeguard (year-round), restrooms, food concessions, showers.*

Hermosa Beach. South of Manhattan Beach, Hermosa Beach has all the amenities of its neighbor—down to the fishing tackle and bait shop— but it attracts more of a teenage party crowd. Swimming takes a backseat to the volleyball games and party on the pier and boardwalk. ⊠ *Hermosa Ave. and 33rd St., Hermosa Beach* ☎ *310/372–2166* ☞ *Parking, lifeguard (year-round), restrooms, food concessions, showers, wheelchair access to pier.*

★ **Redondo Beach.** The Redondo Beach Pier marks the starting point of this wide, sandy, busy beach along a heavily developed shoreline community. Restaurants and shops flourish along the pier, excursion boats and privately owned craft depart from launching ramps, and a reef formed by a sunken ship creates prime fishing and snorkeling conditions. If you're adventurous, you might try to kayak out to the buoys and hobnob with pelicans and sea lions. A series of free rock and jazz concerts takes place at the pier every summer. ⊠ *Torrance Blvd. at Catalina Ave., Redondo Beach* ☎ *310/372–2166* ☞ *Parking, lifeguard (year-round), restrooms, food concessions, showers.*

Torrance Beach. This little-known beach where the Strand walkway–bicycle path finally comes to an end has no pier or other such attractions, just a small snack shop. But it's a great place to swim and bodysurf and has a park with great vistas, volleyball, a swingset, and a Fido fountain just for dogs. ⊠ *3897 Taseo de la Playa, Torrance* ☎ *310/372–2166* ☞ *Parking, restrooms, food concessions, showers.*

GARDENS

★ **Descanso Gardens** (⊠ 1418 Descanso Dr., La Cañada/Flintridge ☎ 818/ 949–4200 ⊕ www.descanso.com) is a perfect place to come in search of wonderful scents—between the lilacs, the acres of roses, and the forest of California redwoods, pines, and junipers, you can sniff all sorts of fragrances. Also be sure to check out the 600 varieties of camellias and the Japanese teahouse and garden. On hot days, the lush fern garden is a cool retreat. Classes (yoga and watercolor painting, for example), night walks, and activities for families are scheduled throughout the year. The oak-framed main lawn is a lovely setting for summer concerts. The garden's open daily 9–5; admission is $7.

★ While wandering the 150-acre grounds of the **Huntington Library, Art Collections, and Botanical Gardens** (⊠ 1151 Oxford Rd., San Marino ☎ 626/405–2100 or 626/405–2141 ⊕ www.huntington.org), you can truly forget you're in a city. Just over the Pasadena line in San Marino, the former estate of railroad baron Henry Huntington sprawls out in an incredible display of manicured gardening. Among the specialized gardens are a rose garden with 1,200 species from all over the world; a walled Japanese garden with reflecting ponds, a moon bridge, and a bonsai court; and a children's garden of topiary animals, pint-size fountains, and mazes. The stunning desert garden bristles with yellow-spined desert cacti, giant South African aloes, and beds of fiery red and orange succulents. Coming up next: an elaborate Chinese garden and cultural center, due to open in 2008. The Huntington grounds are open Tuesday–Friday noon–4:30 and weekends 10:30–4:30; entry is $15 but is free the first Thursday of every month.

At the **Los Angeles County Arboretum** (✉ 301 N. Baldwin Ave., Arcadia ☎ 626/821–3222 ⊕ www.arboretum.org), you can wander from a piece of South Africa to the Australian outback and even through a bit of tropical forest. One highlight is the tropical greenhouse, with carnivorous-looking orchids and a pond full of brilliant Chinese goldfish. The house and stables of the eccentric real-estate pioneer Lucky Baldwin are well preserved and worth a visit. The Santa Anita Racetrack is across the street, but you'll very seldom see it as you wander these 40 acres. Don't miss the grove of Engleman oaks above the waterfall. To get there, go east on I–210 just past Pasadena, exit in Arcadia on Baldwin Avenue and go south, and you will soon see the entrance. It's open daily 9–5 and costs $7.

SPORTS

L.A.'s near-perfect climate allows sports enthusiasts the privilege of being outside year-round. The **City of Los Angeles Department of Recreation and Parks** (✉ 200 N. Main St., Suite 1350, 90012 ☎ 888/527–2757 ⊕ www.cityofla.org/rap) has information on city parks. For information on county parks contact the **Los Angeles County Department of Parks and Recreation** (✉ 433 S. Vermont Ave., 90020 ☎ 213/738–2961 ⊕ parks.co.la.ca.us).

Los Angeles is home to some of the greatest franchises in pro basketball and baseball, and the greater L.A. area has two pro teams in each of those sports, as well as hockey. Who knows if L.A.'s quest for a pro football team to replace the Rams and Raiders will succeed—at this writing, negotiations with the NFL were underway to bring a team to the Los Angeles Coliseum. In the meantime, there's always the rough-and-tumble arena football of the Avengers, as well as the ferocious college rivalry of USC and UCLA. **Ticketmaster** (☎ 213/480–3232 ⊕ www.ticketmaster.com) sells tickets to most sporting events in town.

Baseball

You can watch the **Dodgers** take on their National League rivals while you munch on pizza, tacos, or a foot-long "Dodger dog" at one of the game's most comfortable ball parks, **Dodger Stadium** (⊠ 1000 Elysian Park Ave., exit off I–110, Pasadena Fwy. ☎ 323/224–1448 ticket information ⊕ www.dodgers.com). The **Los Angeles Angels of Anaheim** won the World Series in 2002, the first time since the team formed in 1961. For Angels ticket information, contact **Edison International Field** (⊠ 2000 Gene Autry Way, Anaheim ☎ 714/663–9000 ⊕ www.angelsbaseball.com). Several colleges in the area also have baseball teams worth watching, especially USC, which has been a perennial source of major-league talent.

Basketball

College

Most of these schools put consistently competitive women's fives, as well as men's, on their respective courts. The Trojans of the **University of Southern California** (☎ 213/740–4672 ⊕ usctrojans.collegesports.com) play at the **L.A. Sports Arena** (⊠ 3911 S. Figueroa St., Downtown ☎ 213/748–6136). The Bruins of the **University of California at Los Angeles** (☎ 310/825–2101 ⊕ uclabruins.collegesports.com) play at Pauley Pavilion on the UCLA campus. These schools go head to head in Pac 10 competition each year. A lesser-known team that has lately stirred the waters is Malibu's own Waves of **Pepperdine University** (☎ 310/506–4935 ⊕ www.pepperdinesports.collegesports.com). The 49ers of **California State University at Long Beach** (CSULB or Long Beach State; ⊠ State University Dr. near Bellflower Blvd., Long Beach ☎ 562/985–4949 ⊕ www.longbeachstate.com) are known to mix it up pretty well on the court in their arena, the Pyramid. Another local team worth watching is the Lions at **Loyola Marymount University** (⊠ 2700 LMU Dr., Westchester ☎ 310/338–6095 ⊕ www.lmulions.com).

Professional

L.A.'s pro basketball teams play at the Staples Center. The **Los Angeles Lakers** (☎ 310/426–5000 ⊕ www.nba.com/lakers) still attract a loyal following that includes celebrity fans like Jack Nicholson, Dyan Cannon, and Leonardo DiCaprio. The 2005 return of head coach Phil Jackson, who led the team to three NBA championships, recharged fans after the 2004 departure of superstar Shaquille O'Neal. L.A.'s "other" team, the much-maligned but newly revitalized **Clippers** (☎ 888/895–8662 ⊕ www.nba.com/clippers), sells tickets that are generally cheaper and easier to get than those for Lakers games. The **Los Angeles Sparks** (☎ 310/426–6031 ⊕ www.wnba.com/sparks) have built a WNBA dynasty around former USC star Lisa Leslie.

Bicycling

When you plan to bicycle in the L.A. area, consider the logistics of transportation, rentals, and your chosen terrain. If you plan to get to your bike route via bus, you can do so only if the bus has a rack on its front (if not, you're out of luck). Taking a bike on the subway requires a permit; to apply for one, call the **MTA** (☎ 213/922–7023 or 800/266–6883). The permit's free but is sent to you by mail, so do this well in advance. You can get maps of L.A.'s bike trails and information leaflets on bus bike racks from the MTA or the **Department of Transportation** (☎ 213/580–1177) or through the Web site www.bicyclela.org. A word to the wise: don't cruise deep into the national parks and forests by yourself.

For an L.A.-area overview, including maps and useful links, check out **Los Angeles Bike Paths** (⊕ www.labikepaths.com). For bike-route suggestions or a little company, you can get in touch with the **San Fernando Valley Bicycle Club** (☎ 818/347–6148 ⊕ www.sfvbc.org). Mountain-biking enthusiasts should visit the **South Bay Mountain Biking Club** (⊕ www.sbmbc.com); find a date–route rated for your skill level on this Web site, contact the leader for that group, show up with your bike and gear, and you're good to go. Gay and lesbian folks can check in with **Different Spokes Bicycle Club** (⊕ www.differentspokes.com) for info on recreational rides and events (it has a newsletter, too).

Any L.A.–area yellow pages will yield a bunch of retail bicycle shops where you can rent wheels, pick the brain of a savvy salesperson or customer, or at least pick up the twice-yearly *Bicycling Event Guide*. **MyBikeSite.com** (⊕ www.mybikesite.com) posts extensive national information, including good coverage of southern California. Also worth a look is the **Los Angeles County Bicycle Coalition** (⊕ www.labikecoalition.org); though primarily an advocacy group, it also sponsors events.

The Pacific Coast

The most famous bike path in the city runs along the Pacific Ocean. The 22-mi concrete route from Will Rogers State Beach down to Torrance Beach, known as the **Strand,** attracts cyclists of all levels. They share the path with joggers, skateboarders, in-line skaters, walkers, and other non-vehicular traffic (although for some stretches, bikes have their own parallel path). Except for a couple of short city-street detours around the Marina del Rey Harbor and the Redondo Beach Pier, the sunny beach scenery is uninterrupted. The ride can be done in a long leisurely afternoon, with plenty of time for stops along the way: rest assured that there's more than enough to see to make the round-trip worthwhile. You can rent a bike at one of many shops along the Strand's middle section between Santa Monica and Venice. (*See* Bike Rentals, *below.*) Cyclists often refer to the 18.4-mi section south of the Santa Monica Pier as the South Bay Bicycle Trail.

South of the Strand, following the brief and pathless "RAT" (Right After Torrance) beach, is a 23-mi loop with good views of the winding hills and clear ocean views on the relatively untrammeled **Palos Verdes Peninsula.** The trip, which takes at least three hours, is best attempted on a temperate morning when fog isn't obscuring the ocean. The marked bike lanes come and go, so be careful.

Other Excursions

Nod to the brown pelicans in the wetlands as you cruise westward along the **Ballona Creek** path from National and Jefferson boulevards in Culver City; you can hook up with the Strand at the other end. Santa Monica's **San Vicente Boulevard** has a wide, 3-mi cycling lane that parallels the sidewalk. **Balboa Park,** in the San Fernando Valley, is another haven for two-wheelers, although beware after a heavy rain; it'll be flooded. The flat, 3-mi paved path around **Lake Hollywood** is a great place to take in views of the HOLLYWOOD sign. Griffith Park, Malibu Creek State Park, and Topanga State Park are all part of the **Santa Monica Mountains,** which have good mountain-biking paths. Griffith Park also has a flat family-friendly 4.7-mi path that runs along Crystal Springs Drive and Zoo Drive, then turns back along the Los Angeles River and ends on Fletcher Drive near the main entrance.

For some solitude and rural terrain, visit **Angeles National Forest** (☎ 626/574–5200 forest service), in the northern reaches of L.A. County. The mostly flat and shaded **Gabrielino Trail** along the upper Arroyo Seco is a favorite of mountain bikers, runners, birders, and horseback riders. To get there, exit the 210 Freeway at Arroyo Boulevard–Windsor Avenue in Altadena. Drive three-quarters of a mile north and look for the small parking lot just before you reach Ventura Avenue.

Bike Rentals

Bike rentals usually cost $6–$10 an hour or $15–$40 a day. You'll likely also need to hand over a photo ID and credit card before cycling off. Double-check the helmet situation with your chosen rental outfitter; some places rent helmets, some only sell, and a couple charge a nominal fee if you're renting a bike for several days.

Perry's has three locations along the Strand: **Perry's Bike & Skate** (⊠ 2600 Ocean Front Walk, Venice ☎ 310/452–1507), **Perry's Beach Rentals** (⊠ 2400 Ocean Front Walk, Venice ☎ 310/452–7609), and **Perry's Cafe & Sports Rentals** (⊠ 1200 The Promenade, Santa Monica ☎ 310/485–3975). **Spokes 'N Stuff** (⊠ Griffith Park, 4400 Crystal Springs Dr., Los Feliz ☎ 323/653–4099 ⊠ Strand, 1700 Ocean Ave., Santa Monica ☎ 310/395–4748 ⊠ Strand, 4175 Admiralty Way, Marina del Rey ☎ 310/306–3332) has a rental shop behind the ranger station in Griffith Park and two rental places on the Strand. **Venice Pier Bike Shop** (⊠ 24 Washington Blvd., just east of Strand, Venice ☎ 310/301–4011) rents bikes and other beach-sport stuff.

Bowling

A year after the 2002 demise of the storied Hollywood Star Lanes, **Lucky Strike** (⊠ 6801 Hollywood Blvd. ☎ 323/467–7776) opened nearby with 12 lanes, sit-down dining, and Star Lanes' trademark retro decor. After 7 PM the place turns into a 21-and-over nightclub. Another colorful alley is **Allstar Lanes** (⊠ 4459 Eagle Rock Blvd., Eagle Rock ☎ 323/254–2579), where there are a Chinese restaurant and specialty nights that might include karaoke or rock bands.

Boxing & Wrestling

Championship competitions take place in both of these sports year-round at the **Forum** (⊠ 3900 W. Manchester Blvd., off I–405 at Century Blvd., Inglewood ☎ 310/330–7300).

Fishing

There's plenty of freshwater fishing in the lakes dotting the city and in the Angeles National Forest. A license is required: they're available at many sporting-goods stores. (Out-of-state visitors can get two-day licenses for $18, or one-day licenses for $12.) The **Fish and Game Department** (☎ 562/342–7100, 562/590–5020 lake-stocking information) can answer questions about licenses and give advice.

Shore fishing and surf casting are excellent on many of the beaches, and pier fishing is popular because no license is necessary to fish off public piers. The **Santa Monica, Redondo Beach** and **Malibu** piers have bait-and-tackle shops with everything you'll need.

If you want to break away from the piers, sign up for a boat excursion with one of the local charters, most of which will sell you a fishing license and rent tackle. Most also offer whale-watching excursions. **Del Rey Sport Fishing** (✉ 13759 Fiji Way, Marina del Rey ☎ 310/822–3625) runs excursions for $30 per half day and $45 for three-quarters of a day, with tackle rental another $8–$11. **Redondo Sport Fishing Company** (✉ 233 N. Harbor Dr., Redondo Beach ☎ 310/372–2111) has half-day charters starting at $32. Sea bass, halibut, bonita, yellowtail, and barracuda are the usual catch.

Twenty Second Street Landing (✉ 141 W. 22nd St., San Pedro ☎ 310/832–8304) leads an overnight charter ($110) that lets you stargaze while waiting for a bite. Day charters are $35–$50. **L.A. Harbor Sportfishing** (✉ 1150 Nagoya Way, Berth 79 at harbor, San Pedro ☎ 310/547–9916), which sails some of the area's best charter boats, offers excursions ranging from half a day ($28) to two-day runs in summer.

FISHING FINGERS

The most popular and most unusual form of fishing in the L.A. area involves no hooks, bait, or poles. The great **grunion runs,** which take place from March through July, occur when hundreds of thousands of small silver fish called grunion wash up on southern California beaches to lay their eggs in the sand. The fish can be picked up by hand while they are briefly stranded on the sand. All that's required is a fishing license and a willingness to get your toes wet. San Pedro's **Cabrillo Marine Aquarium** (☎ 310/548–7562 ⊕ www.cabrilloaq.org) hosts programs about grunion throughout most of their spawning season. During certain months you're not allowed to touch the grunion; call the Fish and Game Department for details.

Golf

The City Parks and Recreation Department lists seven public 18-hole courses in Los Angeles, and L.A. County runs some good ones, too. **Rancho Park Golf Course** (✉ 10460 W. Pico Blvd., West L.A. ☎ 310/838–7373) is one of the most heavily played links in the country. It's a beautifully designed course, but the towering pines present an obstacle for those who slice or hook. There's a two-level driving range, a 9-hole pitch 'n' putt, a snack bar, and a pro shop where you can rent clubs.

Several good public courses are in the San Fernando Valley. The **Sepulveda Golf Complex** (✉ 16821 Burbank Blvd., Encino ☎ 818/995–1170) has the Balboa course (par 70) and the longer Encino course (par 72), plus a driving range. Five lakes and occasional wildlife spottings make the **Woodley Lakes Golf Course** (✉ 6331 Woodley Ave., Van Nuys ☎ 818/780–6886) fairly scenic. It's flat and thus somewhat forgiving, but the back 9 is more challenging, with only one par 4 under 400 yards.

★ If you want a scenic course, you've got it in spades at the county-run, par-71 **Los Verdes Golf Course** (✉ 7000 W. Los Verdes Dr., Rancho Palos Verdes ☎ 310/377–7370). You get a cliff-top view of the ocean—time it right and you can watch the sun set behind Catalina Island.

Griffith Park has two splendid 18-hole courses along with a challenging 9-hole course. **Harding Municipal Golf Course** and **Wilson Municipal Golf Course** (✉ 4730 Crystal Springs Dr., Los Feliz ☎ 323/663–2555) are about 1½ mi inside the park entrance, at Riverside Drive and Los Feliz Boulevard. Bridle paths surround the outer fairways, and the San Gabriel Mountains make a scenic background. The 9-hole **Roosevelt Municipal Golf Course** (✉ 2650 N. Vermont Ave., Los Feliz ☎ 323/665–2011) can be reached through the park's Vermont Avenue entrance.

Sitting on landfill, the **Scholl Canyon Golf Club** (✉ 3800 E. Glenoaks Blvd., Glendale ☎ 818/243–4100) may only be a par 60, but it's fun and challenging, attractive for its top condition as well as its ups and downs and elevated views. You may recall the 9-hole pitch 'n' putt **Los Feliz Municipal Golf Course** (✉ 3207 Los Feliz Blvd., Los Feliz ☎ 323/663–7758) from the movie *Swingers*. The **Holmby Park Pitch 'n' Putt** (✉ 601 Club View Dr., near Beverly Glen ☎ 310/276–1604) is truly cozy: the longest hole is 68 yards.

For those who love to watch the pros in action, the hot golf ticket in town each February is the PGA **Nissan Open** (☎ 800/752–6736). The $4.8 million purse attracts the best golfers in the world to its week of competition at the Riviera Country Club in Pacific Palisades.

Football

For a city that lost not one but two NFL teams, there's a lot of football to be seen in the area. The **L.A. Avengers** (☎ 213/480–3232 Ticketmaster ⊕ www.laavengers.com) are the city's entry into arena football, playing at the **Staples Center** (✉ 1111 S. Figueroa St., Downtown ☎ 213/742–7340 box office ⊕ www.staplescenter.com). Football fever in L.A., however, still revolves primarily around the college teams.

College

The **USC Trojans** (☎ 213/740–4672 ⊕ usctrojans.collegesports.com) play at the **L.A. Memorial Coliseum** (✉ 3939 S. Figueroa St., Downtown ☎ 213/748–6136), both a state and federal historic landmark. The **UCLA Bruins** (☎ 310/825–2101 ⊕ uclabruins.collegesports.com) pack 'em in at the **Rose Bowl** (✉ 1010 Rose Bowl Dr., Pasadena ☎ 626/449–7673).

Every year, the two teams face off in one of college football's oldest and most exciting rivalries.

Health Clubs

If you belong to national chains, like **24-Hour Fitness** or **Bally's**, you'll find plenty of branches here. If not, they and the many local clubs and chains in the city usually sell daily or weekly memberships. **Meridian** (✉ 1950 Century Park E, Century City ☎ 310/789–1111) has a full range of aerobics classes including aerobic boxing and kickboxing for $20 per day; there are also branches in the Miracle Mile and Beverly-La Brea areas. The state-of-the-art **Crunch Fitness** (✉ 8000 Sunset Blvd., in Virgin Megastore complex, West Hollywood ☎ 323/654–4550) is popular with celebrities for its expansive facilities. It costs $24 per day; for Chateau Marmont or Standard guests bearing room keys, it's $12.

Probably the most famous body-pumping facility in the city is **Gold's Gym** (✉ 360 Hampton Dr., Venice ☎ 310/392–6004 ✉ 1016 N. Cole Ave., Hollywood ☎ 323/462–7012). In addition to using the two flagship locations mentioned here, local hulks turn themselves into veritable muscle sculptures at two additional locations in the San Fernando Valley and another in Redondo Beach. For $20 a day or $59 a week, several tons of weights and body-building machines can be yours.

Hiking

"Nobody Walks in L.A." sang the Missing Persons back in the '80s, and it's as true as ever—but people do like to hike. With so many different land- and seascapes to explore, hiking is a major pastime for many Angelenos who crave an escape from city life, heading for the hills en masse on weekends, often with dogs in tow. From almost anywhere in L.A., you should find a fine trail a surprisingly short hop away. ■ TIP➔ **Remember, the region can be dry and hot at most times of the year, so take plenty of water and liberally apply (and reapply) sunblock.** Hats and sunglasses help with hydration and UV protection.

The coast, the Hollywood Hills, and the parent range of the latter, the Santa Monica Mountains, are convenient getaways. If you're in the Pasadena area, you'll have easy access to the surprisingly wild San Gabriel Mountains of the Angeles Crest National Forest and the gentler San Gabriel Valley. Farther afield, look into some more extensive hikes in the Verdugo or Santa Susana Mountains. ⚠ **Don't venture deep into the national parks and forests alone. Griffith Park is one thing; the Angeles National Forest is quite another.** Despite an active park ranger presence there, the Angeles Forest is rugged, parts of it are quite dense, and a person alone and injured could face serious difficulties.

For information on hiking locations and scheduled outings in Los Angeles, contact the **Sierra Club** (✉ 3435 Wilshire Blvd., Suite 320, Los Angeles 90010 ☎ 213/387–4287 ⊕ www.sierraclub.org). Or, check out *Outdoors,* the quarterly calendar of events put out by the **Santa Monica Mountains National Recreation Area** (✉ 401 W. Hillcrest Dr., Thousand Oaks 93160 ☎ 805/370–2301 ⊕ www.nps.gov/samo).

Hollywood Hills

One of the best places to begin is **Griffith Park** (⊠ Ranger station, 4730 Crystal Springs Dr., Los Feliz); pick up a map from the ranger station. Many of the paths in the park are not shaded and can be quite steep. A nice, short hike from Canyon Drive, at the southwest end of the park, takes you to **Bronson Caves**, where the *Batman* television show was filmed. Begin at the Observatory for a 3-mi round-trip hike to the top of **Mt. Hollywood**.

★ For a walk, run, or bike ride, the **Hollywood Reservoir (aka Lake Hollywood) Trail** is probably one of the best spots in all L.A. The 4-mi flat walk around the reservoir provides great views of hillside mansions (including the spread once owned by Madonna, with its controversial striped retaining wall), the HOLLYWOOD sign, and the reservoir itself. The park is open dawn to dusk. To get there, exit U.S. 101 at Barham Boulevard (near Universal City). Look for Lake Hollywood Drive soon on your right and take it, making sure you stay the course through its tricky turns. Park when you see the gate. The reservoir was built by the god of Los Angeles water, William Mulholland; its dam has a memorable movie cameo in Roman Polanski's *Chinatown*.

The 3-mi **Mt. Lee Trail,** which begins in Hollywood near the junction of Beachwood and Hollyridge drives, climbs 500 feet to L.A.'s most famous landmark, the HOLLYWOOD sign. You can't walk around the sign, but you can get about 100 yards from it, which is pretty good for snapshots.

The stroll in **Franklin Canyon** is just above the northern reaches of Beverly Hills. Less than 2½ mi, it's often used by film crews. Pick up a map from the visitor center (follow Franklin Canyon Drive to Lake Drive, then turn right to find the Franklin Canyon Ranch House). Docent-led walks are also available.

Santa Monica Mountains

The Santa Monica Mountains are an unlikely swath of natural beauty that extend into the city. Although the climate is Mediterranean, the plants suggest more of a prairie, with golden grasses and gnarled live oak. Some of Los Angeles's best-known natural beauty spots, such as Topanga Canyon and Leo Carrillo State Park (with its tide pools and coves), are within the bounds of the Santa Monicas, or you can head farther out of the city to the wilder terrain of Point Mugu State Park.

★ Who knows how many of Will Rogers's famed witticisms came to him while he and his wife hiked or rode horses along the **Inspiration Point Trail** from their ranch, now **Will Rogers State Historic Park** (⊠ 1501 Will Rogers State Park Rd., Pacific Palisades ☎ 310/454–8212). The point is on a detour off the lovely 2-mi loop, which you pick up right by the riding stables beyond the parking lot ($7 per car). On a clear (or even just semiclear) day, the panorama is one of L.A.'s widest and most "wow" inducing, from the peaks of the San Gabriel Mountains in the distant east to the Oz-like cluster of downtown L.A. skyscrapers to Catalina Island looming off the coast to the southwest. If you're looking for a longer trip, the top of the loop meets up with the 65-mi Backbone Trail, which connects to Topanga State Park. And don't forget

Will Rogers's home, slated to reopen for tours in spring 2006 after extended renovations.

Malibu Creek State Park (✉ 1925 Las Virgenes Rd., Calabasas ☎ 818/880–0367) has some of the best hiking in the area, and if you bring a swimsuit, you can take a dip in the rock pool. See the wild country that has doubled as Korea in the *M*A*S*H* TV show and as assorted alien worlds in the original *Star Trek* series.

★ Another way into the Santa Monicas is via the Trippet Ranch entrance to **Topanga State Park** (✉ Entrada Rd., Malibu ☎ 310/455–2465), which gives you several options: a ½-mi nature loop, a 7-mi round-trip excursion to the Parker Mesa Overlook (breathtaking on a clear day), or a 10-mi trek to the Will Rogers park. Parking is $4. (Exit U.S. 101 onto Topanga Canyon Boulevard in Woodland Hills and head south until you can turn left onto Entrada; if going north on PCH, turn onto Topanga Canyon Boulevard—a bit past Sunset Boulevard—and go north until you can turn right onto Entrada.)

Hockey

The National Hockey League's **L.A. Kings** (☎ 213/480–3232 Ticketmaster ⊕ www.lakings.com) are playoff contenders at the **Staples Center** (✉ 1111 S. Figueroa St., Downtown ☎ 213/742–7340 box office ⊕ www.staplescenter.com). The **Anaheim Ducks** (☎ 714/704–2701 ⊕ www.mightyducks.com) push the puck at **Arrowhead Pond** (✉ 2695 E. Katella Ave., Anaheim ☎ 714/704–2500). Long an underdog team, they made it to the Stanley Cup finals in 2003. Hockey season runs from October through April. If the major-league clubs are out of town, in the doldrums, or just too darned pricey, try the rough-and-tumble minor leaguers, the **Long Beach Ice Dogs** (✉ Long Beach Arena, 300 E. Ocean Blvd., Long Beach ☎ 562/423–3647 ⊕ www.icedogshockey.com).

Horse Racing & Shows

Santa Anita Race Track (✉ 285 W. Huntington Dr., at Colorado Pl., Arcadia ☎ 626/574–7223 ⊕ www.santaanita.com ⊡ $5–$20) is a beautiful facility that has the San Gabriel Mountains for a backdrop. It's still the dominant site for thoroughbred racing from late September to November 1 and from December 16 to late April; the centerpiece of the season is the Breeders' Cup in late October. Seabiscuit tram tours, covering the history of the legendary racehorse, are offered free on weekends from January to April. **Hollywood Park** (✉ 1050 S. Prairie Ave., at Century Blvd., Inglewood ☎ 310/419–1500 ⊡ $7–$15), next to the Forum, is another favorite venue to see thoroughbreds race. It's open from early November to Christmas Eve and from late April to mid-July. Several grand-prix jumping competitions and Western riding championships are held throughout the year at the **Los Angeles Equestrian Center** (✉ 480 Riverside Dr., Burbank ☎ 818/563–3252, 818/840–9066 box office ⊕ www.la-equestriancenter.com).

Horseback Riding

For adults and kids 7 and over, **Bar S Stables** (⊠ 1850 Riverside Dr., just northeast of Griffith Park, Glendale ☎ 818/242–8443) is a no-frills outfit charging $20 per hour and $12 for each additional hour; lessons are also available. Starting at $60 for 70 minutes, the **Escape on Horseback Dude Ranch** (⊠ 2623 Old Topanga Rd., Topanga ☎ 818/591–2032 ⊕ www.losangeleshorsebackriding.com) has guided rides past the giant rock formations of the Santa Monica/Malibu Mountains Conservancy and through countless wildflowers nestled in the area's unique red soil, plus panoramic vistas of Catalina Island and the Pacific Ocean. There's also a romantic sunset ride for $85 per person.

Every day, 8 AM to 5 PM, more than 50 mi of Griffith Park's beautiful bridle trails are open to the public via **Griffith Park Horse Rentals** (⊠ 480 Riverside Dr., Burbank ☎ 818/840–8401) inside the L.A. Equestrian Center. Rates are $25 for one hour, $30 for 1½ hours, and $35 for two hours (the max). In summer, the Sunset Dinner Ride is a 1½-hour ride plus a Mexican dinner for $40. At **J.P. Stables** (⊠ 1914 Mariposa St., Burbank ☎ 818/843–9890), the only limit to your riding time is the endurance of your wallet and your behind; the cost is $25 for the first hour and $15 each additional hour. Hours are 7:30–4:30. Rates at **Sunset Ranch** (⊠ 3400 Beachwood Dr., at Griffith Park's southwestern end ☎ 323/469–5450 🖷 323/461–3061) are $20 for one hour, $35 for two hours (the maximum). Among the package rides are a sunset ride to Mt. Hollywood ($40–$65) and a Friday-evening trail ride over the hill into Burbank, where riders dine at a Mexican restaurant (starting at $60, dinner not included).

A caveat or two: as docile as the horses may seem, they are not golf carts! Total newbies should stick with the easiest rides. Additionally, novice or not, you are wise to check (or ask the stable folks) that the saddle cinch is tight enough. Many stables have an upper weight limit of around 200–250 pounds. Some of the rental stables offer lessons, or you can go for the package (evaluation, five lessons, and a horsemanship class) offered at the L.A. Equestrian Center by the **Traditional Equitation School** (⊠ 480 Riverside Dr., Burbank ☎ 818/569–3666 ⊕ www.teslaec.com), for $195 and up.

In-Line & Roller-Skating

All of the paths mentioned in Bicycling are also excellent for in-line and roller-skating, though cyclists have the right of way. The **Strand**, specifically the part of it that passes through Venice Beach, is the skating mecca of the area. Distance skaters can hook up with the **Friday Night Skate** (☎ 310/577–5283 ⊕ www.fridaynightskate.org). Every Friday night at 8 (weather permitting), skaters gather at the entrance to the Santa Monica Pier. From here, everyone zips off on a 10-mi route through city streets—you just follow the pack, behind the guy with the boom box strapped to his body.

Jack Skate Park (⊠ 23415 Civic Center Way, Malibu ☎ 310/317–1364) is good for both in-line and roller-skating. It's closed to the public on Tuesday and Thursday.

To rent in-line skates, try **Boardwalk Skates** (✉ 201½ Ocean Front Walk, Venice ☎ 310/450–6634). You can rent both in-line and roller skates by the day or hour from **Sea Mist Rentals** (✉ 1619 Ocean Front Walk, at Santa Monica Pier, Santa Monica ☎ 310/395–7076).

Polo

Will Rogers State Historic Park (✉ 1501 Will Rogers State Park Rd., Pacific Palisades ☎ 310/573–5000) was donated by Rogers's estate on the condition that the outdoor regulation-size field (now the only one in the nation) be maintained for polo. From April through September, games are played Saturday at 2 PM and Sunday at 10 AM (weather permitting). Parking costs $7 per car.

Rock Climbing

Los Angeles has several excellent indoor facilities, but you came here for the great outdoors, and there's lots of that to be had. In the San Fernando Valley, **Stoney Point** (✛ Off Topanga Canyon Blvd. south of Hwy. 18 in northern Chatsworth) is the top choice, both historically—it's where Patagonia founder Yvon Chouinard made his name as a rock climber—and practically, since the 300-foot-high boulders can accommodate all skill levels. If a bit of a journey, **Vasquez Rocks** is pretty surreal and offers good climbing for beginners and the more experienced. The area, named for the 19th-century bandit who hid out among the rocks, is in northeastern L.A. County. For more information, check with the **County Department of Parks and Recreation** (☎ 213/738–2961 ⊕ parks.co.la. ca.us). Near the **Malibu Creek State Park visitor center** (✛ 4 mi south of U.S. 101 on Las Virgenes–Malibu Canyon Rd.), the Planet of the Apes Wall and the Ghetto Wall make for good climbing, but not for beginners. It's busy on weekends. The cliffs behind beautiful **Point Dume Beach** (✛ South end of Westward Beach Rd.) in Malibu are likewise pretty challenging and hopping on weekends. Check out **www.socalclimbingclub. com** for some opinionated advice on climbing in the L.A. area.

If you're a total beginner, for your own safety you're best off starting out at an indoor facility; and the best of L.A.'s have engaging routes for advanced climbers, too. One centrally located indoor rock gym is **Rockreation** (✉ 11866 La Grange Ave., West L.A. ☎ 310/207–7199 ⊕ www. rockreation.com/lahome.html). It has 9,000 square feet of climbing space, with 24 routes on approximately 20- to 25-foot walls. Belayers (spotters) keep an eye on you and give lessons.

Running

Exposition Park has a scenic course popular with students and downtown workers. The jogging trail circles the Coliseum and Sports Arena, with pull-up bars and other simple workout equipment placed every several hundred yards. **San Vicente Boulevard** in Santa Monica has a wide, grassy median that splits the street for several picturesque miles. The Hollywood Hills' **Runyon Canyon** has a 3-mi loop with a steep section for those seeking a rugged run. The reservoir at **Lake Hollywood,** just east of Cahuenga Boulevard in the Hollywood Hills, is encircled by a 3.3-mi asphalt path with a view of the HOLLYWOOD sign. Within Hollywood's hilly **Griffith Park** are thousands of acres' worth of hilly paths and challenging terrain; **Crystal Springs Drive,** from the main entrance at Los Feliz to the zoo, is a relatively flat 5 mi, and near its midpoint is a ranger station where you can get a park map. **Circle Drive,** around the perimeter of UCLA in Westwood, provides a 2½-mi run through academia. Running along the outer edge of the campus can enlarge the jaunt to just under 4 mi. Near several major hotels, lovely **Beverly Gardens** extends along the north side of Santa Monica Boulevard through Beverly Hills; bracketed by ornate fountains, its leafy paths pass by the Beverly Hills Library and City Hall and through a delightful, block-long cactus garden. Continuing around on Wilshire to Whittier and right onto Elevado, or at the other end up Doheny and left onto Elevado, yields a 3½-mi route. The 22 mi of bike path known as the **Strand,** along the coast from Will Rogers Beach to Torrance Beach, is a great place for a run—especially in the Venice Beach and Santa Monica sections. Beware of cyclists and skaters zipping by at high speeds. If you like races, you'll want to check out *Raceplace* (⊕ www.raceplace.com) in advance of your trip. For you long-range trail runners, see the Topanga State Park listing above in Hiking. The truly ambitious can check out *50 Trail Runs in Southern California,* by Stan Swartz et al. (Mountaineer Books, 2000).

Skiing & Snowboarding

Cross-Country

Ski season in southern California generally runs from Thanksgiving until Memorial Day. **Idyllwild** (☎ 951/659–3259 ⊕ www.idyllwildchamber. com), near Palm Springs, has excellent cross-country trails.

Downhill

East of town, at the San Bernardino County line, is **Mt. Baldy** (☎ 909/ 981–3344 ⊕ www.mtbaldy.com), the largest and steepest ski area in southern California with 26 runs over 400 acres. Despite rustic facilities and limited snowmaking facilities, it's beloved for its varied and challenging terrain. Take the I–10 or the I–210 over the San Bernardino County line to Mountain Avenue, which you'll take north for 16 mi to Mt. Baldy Road; then continue north. Count on a two- to three-hour drive from downtown L.A.

Big Bear (☎ 909/866–4607 ⊕ www.bigbear.com), about 100 mi northeast of Los Angeles, is one of the most popular ski retreats on the West Coast, with a full range of accommodations, several ski lifts, night skiing, and one of the largest snowmaking operations in California. To get here, take the I–10 San Bernardino Freeway east past the city of San Bernardino to Highway 30 headed for Highway 330; that goes northeast and becomes Highway 18, which eventually goes around Big Bear Lake. The drive takes at least two hours.

> **WORD OF MOUTH**
>
> "There are times when you can lay out on a sunny beach in the morning, then drive to Big Bear at night and go snow skiing. Welcome to L.A."   −Thyra

Another ski and snowboard area in the vicinity of Big Bear is **Bear Mountain** (☎ 888/786–6481), where freestyle terrain tends to attract young thrill-seekers. To get to the lake, take the I–10 San Bernardino Freeway east past the city of San Bernardino to Highway 30. Then connect to Highway 330 going northeast; Highway 330 becomes Highway 18, which circumvents Big Bear Lake. **Snow Valley** (✉ 35100 Hwy. 18, Running Springs ⊕ www.snow-valley.com ☎ 909/867–5151) has snowmaking capabilities, a kids' snowmobile park, and a designated sledding area. **Mountain High** (✉ Hwy. 138 west to Hwy. 2, 3 mi past Wrightwood ☎ 888/754–7878 ⊕ www.mthigh.com), as do most of these areas, has lights for night skiing. It's also got a kid-friendly tubing park. The easy-to-navigate facilities and calm vibe at **Snow Summit** (✉ 3 mi past Wrightwood ☎ 909/866–5766) make it a good spot for beginners, families with small children, and skiers seeking traditional downhill runs without fuss.

Soccer

The 2002 MLS champions, the **Los Angeles Galaxy** (☎ 626/432–1540 or 877/342–5299 ⊕ www.lagalaxy.com), play March through September at the new stadium at the **Home Depot Center** (✉ 18400 Avalon Blvd., Carson ☎ 877/342–5299 ⊕ www.homedepotcenter.com).

Tennis

L.A. Department of Recreation and Parks (✉ 200 N. Main St., Downtown ☎ 213/473–7070 ⊕ www.laparks.org/dos/sports/tennis.htm) has a complete list of the city's more than 75 public tennis courts. Some are always free, others only weekdays; others charge $5–$10 an hour per court, depending on time of day. Reservations are a must during peak hours at the most popular pay courts; to make them, apply for a reservation card (click on "Permits") at the Web site or call 323/644–3536.

The **Poinsettia Tennis Center** (✉ 7341 Willoughby Ave., Hollywood ☎ 323/512–8234) is a pay-to-play facility with eight lighted courts.

West L.A. has a number of locations with well-maintained, lighted courts: the courts at **Westwood Park** (✉ 1375 Veteran Ave., Westwood ☎ 310/575–8299) are $8 an hour. The four courts at the **Barrington Recreational Center** (✉ Barrington Ave. south of Sunset Blvd., Brentwood) are always free. And the 14 courts at **Cheviot Hills** (✉ 2551 Motor Ave., just south of 20th Century Fox lot ☎ 310/836–8879) are always pay-to-play.

Griffith Park has a dozen lighted courts at the **Griffith-Riverside Pay Tennis Complex** (✉ 3401 Riverside Dr., at Los Feliz Blvd., Los Feliz ☎ 323/661–5318). There are a dozen unlighted courts at Griffith Park's **Griffith-Vermont Pay Tennis Complex** (✉ 2715 N. Vermont Ave., Los Feliz ☎ 323/664–3521).

La Cienega Tennis Center (✉ 325 S. La Cienega Blvd., Beverly Hills ☎ 310/550–4767) has 16 lighted courts available for $7–$9 per hour; you can reserve up to four days in advance if you have a Leisure Services Card ($14.25 for non–Beverly Hills residents), which can be purchased at the center. Those who don't have the card can call ahead to see how busy it is.

If you're interested in watching the pros, the **Mercedes Benz Cup** (Formerly the Infiniti Open; ☎ 310/825–2101 tickets, 310/824–1010 info ⊕ www.mercedes-benzcup.com), held in summer at UCLA, usually attracts some of the top-seeded players on the pro tennis circuit.

Volleyball

The casual beach volleyballer can find pickup games at beaches the length of the coast; more serious players might want to concentrate on the **Santa Monica State Beach** nets or those at **Manhattan Beach** (which has about 200 nets). If you are truly obsessed, contact the **California Beach Volleyball Association** (☎ 800/350–2282) to see about amateur tournaments (grass-court play as well as sand); its California Cup State Championship tourney is held in late July and early August.

As for **pro volleyball,** the beach volleyball played by two-person teams, check out the men's and women's tournaments held at city beaches in June, July, and August. The Web site of the **Association of Volleyball Professionals** (⊕ www.avp.com) is the best place for information.

Water Sports

Boating, Kayaking & Jet Skiing

Long Beach Windsurf & Kayak Center (✉ 3850 E. Ocean Blvd., near Belmont Pier, Long Beach ☎ 562/433–1014) gives kayaking lessons starting at $90 an hour and in-line skating lessons ($45 an hour). For boat and Jet Ski rentals in spring and summer, call **Offshore Water Sports** (✉ 128 E. Shoreline Dr., Rainbow Harbor, Long Beach ☎ 562/436–1996). **Marina Boat Rentals** (✉ 13719 Fiji Way, Marina del Rey ☎ 310/574–2822), behind the El Torito eatery in Fisherman's Village, rents single and double kayaks as well as speedboats, cruisers, and sailboats by the hour or half day. **Malibu Ocean Sports** (✉ 22935 PCH, across from pier at Malibu Point, Malibu ☎ 310/456–6302) has kayak rentals and lessons, as well as moonlight kayak cruises in Marina Del Rey and kayak tours along the Malibu coast. Jack Galper's **Pacific Paddlers** (☎ 877/776–5292 ⊕ www.pacificpaddlers.com) is a great choice for introductory kayaking lessons. Each person is paired with an instructor in a two-person boat before advancing to a single boat. Galper also organizes a weekly paddling club. **Rocky Point Marine Fuels** (✉ 310 Portofino Way, Redondo Beach ☎ 310/374–9858) rents single and double kayaks.

Scuba Diving & Snorkeling

Anyone who can swim can snorkel, but you'll have to show proof of certification to strap on a scuba tank. L.A. is probably not the best place to start learning scuba—the water's rough—but you can get certified at one of the dive centers listed below. Snorkeling and scuba diving require calm waters, and despite its name, the Pacific Ocean does not quite fit the bill. However, there's good diving to be had if you know where to look. Try **Leo Carrillo State Beach** in Malibu; **Abalone Cove, Malaga Cove,** and **Christmas Tree Cove** at Palos Verdes; or, a few minutes farther east, the **Underwater Dive Trail** at White Point, just east of Royal Palms State Beach, which winds by rope through kelp beds, sulfurous hot springs, and underwater coves. Farther afield, there are **Catalina Is-**

land, and the **Channel Islands,** or go down the coast to **Laguna Beach.** Web sites such as ⊕ www.ladiver.com can give you guidance.

If you or your diving partner is injured in a diving-related accident, the 24-hour staff at the **U.S. National Diving Accident Network** (☎ 919/684–8111) can help you find a doctor trained to treat divers.

All the scuba equipment (and diving lessons) you'll need can be obtained from the following shops. Most rent standard scuba gear packages for $50 and up (some do discounts for multiple days or weekends). That does *not* include basic snorkeling gear (mask, snorkel, booties, fins, and, optional, but recommended, gloves), which runs about $20 per day (or which you may be required to buy, for $200–$300). Some shops arrange diving charters to Catalina Island and the Channel Islands. ■ TIP→ **Most certification packages include an open-water training trip to Catalina Island, but ask about ancillary costs such as whether the boat trip and equipment are included, for example.**

You might use **Pacific Wilderness and Ocean Sports** (⊠ 1719 S. Pacific Ave., near Cabrillo Marina, San Pedro ☎ 310/833–2422) if you're diving at White Point or Palos Verdes. **Divers Discount** (⊠ 3575 Cahuenga Blvd., Universal City ☎ 323/850–5050) guarantees the lowest gear-rental rates in the area. **Malibu Divers** (⊠ 21231 PCH, Malibu ☎ 310/456–2396 ⊕ www.malibudivers.com) may well be on your way to the diving area at Leo Carrillo State Beach, but be warned: its certification classes are so popular that rental gear may be scarce on weekends. It's just a short stroll from many popular hotels to the **Reef Seekers Dive Company** (⊠ 8612 Wilshire Blvd., Beverly Hills ☎ 310/652–4990 ⊕ www. reefseekers.com).

Swimming

The first-rate **Santa Monica Swim Center** (⊠ 1700 Pico Blvd., Santa Monica ☎ 310/458–8700) is open for lap swims every day (nonresidents pay $5). There's a separate pool for children and families.

Inland swimmers head to the **Rose Bowl Aquatic Center** (⊠ 36 N. Arroyo Blvd., Pasadena ☎ 626/564–0330 ⊕ www.rosebowlaquatics.com ✆ $10 day pass) for its Olympic-length lap pool. It's open daily.

Surfing

Surfing is the sport that truly symbolizes L.A. and southern California in general; it has a long cultural history here. If you're not a strong swimmer, though, think twice before jumping in; fighting the surf to where the waves break is a strenuous proposition.

A lesson from **Malibu Ocean Sports** (⊠ 22935 PCH, across from pier at Malibu Point ☎ 310/456–6302) will keep you on the sand for at least 45 minutes explaining the basics. **Surf Academy** (⊠ 302 19th St., Hermosa Beach ☎ 310/372–2790 ⊕ www.surfacademy.org) teaches at El Segundo (Dockweiler) and Manhattan Beach, with lessons starting at $45. When you hit the surfing hot spots, surf shops with rentals will be in long supply. Competition keeps prices comparable; most rent long and short boards and miniboards (kid-size surfboards) from $18 per day and wet suits from $8 per day (some give discounts for additional days).

Call the **L.A. County Lifeguards** (☎ 310/457–9701) for a prerecorded surf-conditions hotline or go to www.watchthewater.com for specific beach reports up and down the coast.

Whale-Watching

From December to March or April, California gray whales migrate from northern waters to warmer breeding and birthing waters off the coast of Mexico. To get an up-close look at these magnificent animals as they pass close to shore, hop aboard one of the **whale-watching tours** that depart from Long Beach and San Pedro; prices are $9–$18 per person, and reservations are recommended. ■ **TIP→ Bring binoculars, dress warmly, and be warned that winter seas can be rough.** Contact any of the expedition companies listed under Fishing, *above;* they all have whale-watching outings, too. Or call one of the following tour operators: **Spirit Cruises** (☎ 310/548–8080 ⊕ www.spiritdinnercruises.com) or **Long Beach Sportfishing** (☎ 562/432–8993 ⊕ www.longbeachsportfishing.com).

START-UP SURFING

Your welcome in the water likely won't be a shining example of gender equality. Beginning female surfers often get encouragement from local hotshots. A hapless guy, however, should expect a few sneers. Be as polite and mellow as possible. Give other surfers plenty of space—do *not* cut them off—and avoid swimmers. Beginners should avoid Palos Verdes; surfers there are notoriously territorial. Once in the water, beware of rocks and undertows. Surfing calls for caution: that huge piece of flying fiberglass beneath you could kill someone. The best and safest way to learn is by taking a lesson.

Windsurfing

Good windsurfing can be found all along the coast. Reserve in advance for lessons. **Long Beach Windsurf & Kayak Center** (✉ 3850 E. Ocean Blvd., near Belmont Pier, Long Beach ☎ 562/433–1014) provides lessons for $180, including gear and wet suit. At **Captain Kirk's** (✉ 525 N. Harbor Blvd., near Slip 93 of L.A. Harbor, San Pedro ☎ 310/833–3397), you can get a basic beginner's setup for $45 a day. More advanced gear will run you up to $60 a day, and beginner lessons start at $99, which includes equipment and three hours of instruction.

Yoga

Los Angeles has nearly as many yoga studios as coffee shops, and most of them are quite good. You'll find schools teaching a variety of styles, including the athletic ashtanga (aka "power yoga"), flowing vinyasa, meditative breathing and stretching classes for senior citizens, pre- and postnatal workouts, and yoga for children; but most schools emphasize one particular style. Some do have more spiritual orientations than others, but this is kept generally low-key. *Yoga Journal* (⊕ www.yogajournal. com) is an excellent source of information for finding studios as well as yoga retreats and more information.

 Ganga (Frank) White founded **Center for Yoga** (✉ 230½ N. Larchmont Blvd., Hancock Park ☎ 323/464–1276) in 1967. To this day it stays true to his vision of integrating various strands of hatha yoga, such as

Iyengar, anusara, ashtanga, and vinyasa. **Golden Bridge** (✉ 6322 De Longpre Ave., Hollywood ☎ 323/936–4172 ⊕ www.goldenbridgeyoga. com) is centered on the teachings of Gurmukh Khalsa, whose approach to kundalini yoga stresses the mind–body connection (yoga for expectant moms is a specialty). **Sacred Movement** (✉ 245 S. Main St., Venice ☎ 310/450–7676) has a meditative feel without being prescriptively spiritual. Kundalini master Yogi Bhajan has made the focus of **Yoga West** (✉ 1535 S. Robertson Blvd., Los Angeles ☎ 310/552–4647) meditation, breathing, and asanas (poses). A large faculty and schedule help make **Yoga Works** (✉ 1426 Montana Ave., Santa Monica ☎ 310/393–5150) live up to its name; friendly staffers will help you choose from among classes in ashtanga, Iyengar, and "Yoga Works Style" (combining elements of these with vinyasa).

Shopping

WORD OF MOUTH

"Melrose Avenue shopping is always fun on a Saturday. . . . If you're in a Ladies Who Lunch mode, hit Montana Avenue in Santa Monica. . . . Venice Beach has some cool shops scattered all over."
—rjw_lgb_ca

"L.A. is the only place on the planet that has a gift shop at the coroner's department. The gift shop is on the second floor, you have to be buzzed and signed in, but sure enough there's a shop where you can buy all sorts of oddly fun things like toe-tag key chains, and beach blankets with chalk outlines. T-shirts, tote bags, books. I spent $80."
—thelmaandlouise

By Kristina
Brooks

THINK OF SHOPPING IN L.A. AS A SPORT, and you won't be far off the mark. To "win," plan ahead to maximize your shopping versus driving time; keep your eyes peeled for dressed-down celebs; and aim to have fun. One of the greatest pleasures is shopping alfresco, since even most malls here are outdoors, with courtyards for people-watching or a chai break. Although the city is notoriously vast, concentrated shopping areas in many neighborhoods will provide hours of browsing bang for your parking buck. ■ **TIP→** One rule of thumb about business hours: the funkier the neighborhood, the later the shops open.

But where to start? Rodeo Drive is the name visitors tend to be most familiar with, and its stores uphold its longtime reputation for expensive, international fashion. Eager for some celebrity sightings? The showy boutiques on Robertson Boulevard may be your best bet. For boho-chic style, try the vintage shops and new cluster of boutiques (Marc Jacobs, Paul Smith, Marni) on Melrose Avenue and Melrose Place in West Hollywood or the offbeat stores along Abbot Kinney Boulevard in Venice. If clean and conservative is more your speed, browse along Santa Monica's Montana Avenue. The Avenues of Art and Design (Beverly and Robertson boulevards and upper Melrose Avenue) offer design showrooms galore, antiques vendors, and art galleries. For the best selection of edgy clothes and artsy accessories, Silver Lake, Los Feliz, and Echo Park are the neighborhoods to hit. The influence of Hollywood is most apparent in the city's impressive selection of music stores (many with regular live performances) and bookstores that specialize in film, theater, and other arts.

Around Beverly Hills

The "Golden Triangle" formed by Santa Monica and Wilshire boulevards and Beverly Drive contains, like a pearl, famed **Rodeo Drive.** Consider a tour of Beverly Hills a field trip, since most of the boutiques display their wares like works of art, and many of the toned, polished shoppers look air-brushed. Although you may feel cowed by some of the astronomical prices or cooler-than-thou attitudes among salespeople, most shops present a friendly sales front to the public. Also, a recent influx of midrange stores has supposedly "democratized" the street. Around this tourist hot spot, many celebrities sneak into their favorite shops before or after hours or through back entrances. Keep in mind that some stores are by appointment only. ■ **TIP→** There are several well-marked, free (for two hours) parking lots around the core shopping area.

SALES SPIEL

Seasonal sales in August, September, December, and January are supplemented by other sale periods throughout the year. "Benefit shopping" at sales that support various causes is popular. Although most are private events, keep your eyes peeled for announcements of public sales. The *Los Angeles Times* and *LA Weekly* are both good sources for sale info. If you're curious about who's shopping where (after all, this is L.A.), take a peek at monthly glossies *In Style* or *Los Angeles.*

Shopping Centers & Malls

★ **Beverly Center.** Given the neighborhood, this mall is a reliable celebrity magnet. Macy's and Bloomingdale's anchor the shopping zone (the sixth through the eighth floors in the eight-story building), with outlets such as Apple, A/X Armani Exchange, Diesel, and DKNY alongside the usual Banana Republics and Pottery Barns. There's a terrific view of the city from the top-floor terrace and rooftop food court. ⊠ *8500 Beverly Blvd., bounded by Beverly, La Cienega, and San Vicente Blvds. and 3rd St., between Beverly Hills and West Hollywood* ☎ *310/854–0071.*

> **KRISTINA'S TOP 5**
>
> ■ **3rd Street,** between La Cienega and Fairfax, a cluster of small but very chic boutiques.
>
> ■ **Abbot Kinney Boulevard,** with its local, quirky shops and mellow Venice vibe.
>
> ■ **Farmers Market and The Grove,** great Siamese twins for shopping and snacking.
>
> ■ **Melrose Avenue,** especially where it meets Melrose Place, for tempting boutiques.
>
> ■ **Rodeo Drive** for unabashed, over-the-top luxury.

Department Stores

Barneys New York. Luring in young Hollywood types with sophisticated, edgy designs, this L.A. outpost of the New York department store also has highly regarded makeup salesfolk. Shop for couture on the second floor, young avant-garde designers on the third, and guys' offerings on the fourth. ⊠ *9570 Wilshire Blvd., Beverly Hills* ☎ *310/276–4400.*

Neiman Marcus. The store sometimes referred to as "Needless Markups" nevertheless attracts a loyal, local following of the rich and sometimes famous for classic to avant-garde clothing and accessories. The couture salon frequently trots out designer trunk shows. ⊠ *9700 Wilshire Blvd., Beverly Hills* ☎ *310/550–5900.*

Saks Fifth Avenue. Saks is still a terrific resource for designer clothing, accessories, shoes, and fragrances, as the moneyed, old-Hollywood patrons will attest. ⊠ *9600 and 9634 Wilshire Blvd., Beverly Hills* ☎ *310/ 275–4211.*

Specialty Stores

ART GALLERIES **Gagosian Gallery.** Designed by Richard Meier (who also designed the Getty Center), this light-filled space shows blue-chip modern and contemporary artists such as Francesco Clemente, Cy Twombly, Andy Warhol, and Richard Serra. ⊠ *456 N. Camden Dr., Beverly Hills* ☎ *310/271–9400.*

FOR CHILDREN **Oilily.** This Dutch company is known for brightly colored, whimsically patterned clothing and gear for babies, kids, and their moms. ⊠ *9520 Brighton Way, Beverly Hills* ☎ *310/859–9145.*

HOME FURNISHINGS & GIFTS **Del Mano Gallery.** One of the best sources for wood turnings, this store also specializes in fine fiber arts, ceramics, jewelry, and art teapots by contemporary American and international artisans. ⊠ *11981 San Vicente Blvd., Brentwood* ☎ *310/476–8508.*

6

CLOSE UP

Rodeo Drive Deluxe

THE BEAUTIFUL THINGS FOR BEAUTIFUL PEOPLE tour begins at **Via Rodeo,** a cobblestoned one-block section of Rodeo closest to Wilshire Boulevard (at Dayton Way). With its temple dome ceiling and recherché design **Gianni Versace** (✉ 248 N. Rodeo Dr., Beverly Hills ☎ 310/205–3921), pays tribute to the late designer famed for red-carpet gowns. His sister Donatella keeps the flame alive with must-have bags and sunglasses and *Miami Vice*-flavored menswear. For more drop-dead gowns, but in a softer vein, hit *Vogue* favorite **Badgley Mischka** (✉ 202 N. Rodeo Dr., Beverly Hills ☎ 310/248–3750). **Porsche Design** (✉ 236 N. Rodeo Dr., Beverly Hills ☎ 310/205–0131) has been called the "only guy store on the block." Car-obsessed celebs visit for the Porsche dashboard dial watches, but you can peek in for the who-would-have-thought? factor. But in fact there's another guy-friendly spot in the zone: **Vilebrequin** (✉ 9519 Wilshire Blvd., Beverly Hills ☎ 310/205–9087), purveyor of St. Tropez–style swim trunks.

Leaving the V of Via Rodeo, you'll spot the adjoining men's and women's boutiques of the trendsetting Italian design house, **Dolce & Gabbana** (✉ 312 and 314 N. Rodeo Dr., Beverly Hills ☎ 310/888–8701). A wet bar for celeb clients gives away its target audience, but anyone can browse the logoed velvet eye masks and slippers, bags, and power pumps. Known for pioneering the tux for women, **Yves Saint Laurent** (✉ 326 N. Rodeo Dr., Beverly Hills ☎ 310/271–4110) is freshly popular for accessories like the "muse" satchel and square-toe satin pumps. For the casual-chic clothing favored by Gwyneth Paltrow and

Charlize Theron, stop in to **Michael Kors** (✉ 360 N. Rodeo Dr., Beverly Hills ☎ 310/777–8862) for the carefully tailored, earthen-tone sportswear (not to mention fur-draped furniture).

At the corner of Brighton Way, **Chanel** (✉ 400 N. Rodeo Dr., Beverly Hills ☎ 310/278–5500) proves that even those in the land of flip-flops have an appetite for these ultra-elegant suits, bags, and two-tone shoes. Another classic label, **Giorgio Armani** (✉ 436 N. Rodeo Dr., Beverly Hills ☎ 310/271–5555), shows off perfectly draped suits, gowns, and couture, with the requisite video of runway shows providing running commentary. For a respite from this European-designer vibe, stop at **Ralph Lauren** (✉ 444 N. Rodeo Dr., Beverly Hills ☎ 310/281–7200), where a greenery-lined corridor with lazily spinning fans and burbling fountains ushers you into high-WASP rooms stocked with preppy clothes galore.

Cross the street and enter the fashion candy shop that is **Etro** (✉ 461 N. Rodeo Dr., Beverly Hills ☎ 310/248–2855). You'll find stacks of shirts and ties in yummy colors (magenta, key lime, tangerine) and scads of gorgeous scarves. This Milanese label's hallmark vibrant stripes, paisleys, and plaids should clash but somehow go together. In the next block, two very different Italian showcases are well worth a visit: Gucci and the Prada "epicenter." **Gucci** (✉ 347 N. Rodeo Dr., Beverly Hills ☎ 310/278–3451) goes for the stridently modernist aesthetic, with lean, sexy, and mainly black clothing upstairs and cube displays for signature bags downstairs. The Rem

Koolhaas–designed **Prada** (✉ 343 N. Rodeo Dr., Beverly Hills ☎ 310/278–8661), on the other hand, is way more fun than most art galleries, as it nearly obscures its classy clothes, shoes, and bags with huge mannequins, 20-foot-wide staircases, Swiss-cheese plastic walls, and funhouse curves. Derek Lam is now designing for **Tod's** (✉ 333 N. Rodeo Dr., Beverly Hills ☎ 310/285–0591), home of comfortable but hip loafers, boots, slides, moccasins, and beautiful leather goods from wallets to man purses.

Ba-da-bling! Time for some diamonds? **Cartier** (✉ 370 N. Rodeo Dr., Beverly Hills ☎ 310/275–4272) has a bridal collection to sigh for in its chandeliered and respectfully hushed showroom, along with more playful colored stones and an Asian-inspired line. Blueblood **Tiffany & Co.** (✉ 210 N. Rodeo Dr., Beverly Hills ☎ 310/273–8880) is the most inviting of Rodeo Drive's jewelry boutiques. The first floor (enter on Wilshire) is for classic and contemporary jewelry and watches. Head up to the second level (enter on Rodeo) for crystal, silver, china, and gifts like an Elsa Peretti sterling silver teething ring. Bold, contemporary Italian jewelry, watches, and other luxurious necessities are the order of the day at **Bulgari** (✉ 201 N. Rodeo Dr., Beverly Hills ☎ 310/858–9216). In business for over a century, **Van Cleef & Arpels** (✉ 300 N. Rodeo Dr., Beverly Hills ☎ 310/276–1161) still designs elegant and distinctive pieces, with lots of pavé floral designs. And perhaps the most locally famous jeweler is **Harry Winston** (✉ 310 N. Rodeo Dr., Beverly Hills ☎ 310/271–8554), *the* source for Oscar-night jewelry loans. The three-level space, with a bronze sculptural facade, velvet-panel walls, private salons, and a rooftop patio, is as glamorous as the gems.

Looking for something more down-to-earth? A few midrange stores have shouldered their way in among the couture designers. **BCBG Max Azria** (✉ 443 N. Rodeo Dr., Beverly Hills ☎ 310/275–3024) led the "democratization" of Rodeo Drive with relatively affordable designs that attract young celebs: romantic dresses, teeny toppers, halters, and fun accessories. One of the last of the indie clothing stores on Rodeo, **Theodore** (✉ 453 N. Rodeo Dr., Beverly Hills ☎ 310/276–0663) is a haven for the young and perhaps rebellious to find James Perse skinny tees, jeans of many labels, and hoodies aplenty. Upstairs, browse the avant-garde designer wear (Ann Demeulemeester, Jean Paul Gaultier). Next door, Theodore Man has faux-scruffy tees, jeans, and leather jackets for the guys. Though sizes 0 and 2 are the neighborhood norm, **Marina Rinaldi** (✉ 319 N. Rodeo Dr., Beverly Hills ☎ 310/860–9793) bucks the trend by carrying stylish, understated (and still pricey) Italian-made clothes in sizes 10 through 22 from the Max Mara line.

6

Gearys of Beverly Hills. Since 1930, this has been the ultimate destination for those seeking the most exquisite fine china, crystal, silver, and jewelry, mostly from classic sources like Steuben to Orrefors. ✉ *351 N. Beverly Dr., Beverly Hills* ☏ *310/273–4741.*

Le Palais des Thés. Some like it hot, some like it iced. Choose from 250 varieties of tea in tins lining the walls, color-coded by the tea's region of origin. Gifts like tea baskets, box sets, and teapots make original souvenirs. ✉ *401 N. Canon Dr., at Brighton Way, Beverly Hills* ☏ *310/271–7922.*

Taschen. Philippe Starck designed the space to evoke a cool 1920s Parisian salon. Framed plasma TVs line dark-wood walls, which are filled with coffee-table books about architecture, travel, and (often racy) photography. A suspended glass-cube gallery space in back shows rotating art and photo exhibits. ✉ *354 N. Beverly Dr., Beverly Hills* ☏ *310/274–4300.*

MENSWEAR **Anto Distinctive Shirt Maker.** With an archive of movie industry clients' measurements and shirt styles dating back to 1955, Anto can reproduce a Frank Sinatra or Sammy Davis shirt for current customers who want some borrowed class. ✉ *268 N. Beverly Dr., Beverly Hills* ☏ *310/278–4500.*

Carroll & Co. In business since 1949, this is one of a dying breed: a full-service, traditional men's clothing store. Icons of menswear such as Cary Grant and Clark Gable were Richard Carroll's friends and customers. You'll still find quality goods, excellent service, and styles that endure. (Another branch is in Pasadena.) ✉ *425 N. Canon Dr., Beverly Hills* ☏ *310/273–9060.*

SHOES **Jimmy Choo.** Dedicated fashionistas shop here for the latest and greatest shoes. Despite the sometimes dizzying heel heights, women claim their Choos bring them nothing but comfort. Popular Ramona bags are also in stock. ✉ *469 N. Canon Dr., Beverly Hills* ☏ *310/860–9045.*

VINTAGE CLOTHING **Fodor'sChoice ★** **Lily et Cie.** Some consider this the premier vintage shop in the country and cite founder Rita Watnick as the inspiration for Hollywood's ongoing love affair with vintage wear. Chanel cocktail dresses and Galanos evening gowns are some of the gems here that date from 1900 to the present. This is no thrift shop; a vintage gown from the owner's private collection can run $100,000. ✉ *9044 Burton Way, Beverly Hills* ☏ *310/724–5757.*

WOMEN'S & MEN'S CLOTHING **Burberry.** Here's proof that everything old can be new again, as British designer Christopher Bailey made the distinctive plaid—on everything from tot-size kilts to sexy swimwear—a must-have for stylish Angelenos. ✉ *9560 Wilshire Blvd., Beverly Hills* ☏ *310/550–4500.*

Emporio Armani. A steady stream of young customers heads here for Armani cachet and the trendiness of this line. Jeans, men's jackets, and women's suitings are ever popular. ✉ *9533 Brighton Way, Beverly Hills* ☏ *310/271–7790.*

Niketown. Ironically, this two-story mecca for athletic gear is one of the few Beverly Hills stores with an elevator. The industrial design of the store doesn't upstage the famous Nike swoosh on clothes, shoes, and gear. ⊠ *9560 Wilshire Blvd., Beverly Hills* ☎ *310/275–9998.*

Ron Herman. You may know the name from the city's Fred Segal stores. This stand-alone shop is more relaxed but just as plugged-in, with an eclectic mix of local and European designs. ⊠ *325 N. Beverly Dr., Beverly Hills* ☎ *310/550–0910.*

Traffic Men. Those with a taste for luxe but not stuffy styles come here for Paul Smith, Costume National, or Vivienne Westwood. The adjoining **Traffic Women** (☎ 310/659–3438) has everything from Juicy Jeans to Alexander McQueen. ⊠ *Beverly Center, 6th fl., 8500 Beverly Blvd., between Beverly Hills and West Hollywood* ☎ *310/659–4313.*

Century City Area

Century City is L.A.'s errand central, where entertainment executives and industry types do their serious shopping. In general, it's more affordable than Beverly Hills. A nascent art scene is blossoming in Culver City, along the intersection of La Cienega and Washington boulevards and the Santa Monica Freeway, and down side streets like Comey Avenue. To the west, Westwood is dominated by its largest resident, UCLA.

> Pull yourself away from the eye candy in Rodeo Drive's boutique windows to glance down at the "Walk of Style," which honors fashion industry stars such as Giorgio Armani, Tom Ford, Edith Head, and Salvatore Ferragamo with sidewalk plaques.

Shopping Malls

★ **H.D. Buttercup.** Built to celebrate the 1932 Olympics, the art deco Helms Bakery has been reborn as a "manutailer" furniture mart, where middlemen are banished. Airy showrooms for some 50 manufacturers offer antiques, artwork, handmade bedding, discounted designer clothing, fine textiles, designer lighting, furniture, and more. Park once and shop all day. ⊠ *3225 Helms Ave., between Venice and Washington Blvds., Culver City* ☎ *310/277–3898.*

Westfield Century City. Known locally as the Century City Shopping Center, this open-air mall is set among office buildings on what used to be the Twentieth Century Fox studios' back lot. A decent selection of upscale shops (Brooks Brothers, Sigrid Olson) are anchored by Macy's and Bloomingdale's. ⊠ *10250 Santa Monica Blvd., Century City* ☎ *310/277–3898.*

Specialty Stores

ART GALLERY **Blum & Poe.** Tim Blum and Jeff Poe's big orange box anchors the up-and-coming part of Culver City, where art spaces are elbowing their way in among auto repair shops. Takashi Murakami and Sam Durant are among the high-profile artists on the gallery's roster. ⊠ *2754 S. La Cienega Blvd., near Washington Blvd., Culver City* ☎ *310/836–2062.*

BOOKS **Mystery Bookstore.** If L.A. brings out your darker instincts, this is the place to indulge in the latest murder mystery or English cozy. Employees are helpful aficionados of every subgenre and the store hosts several signings every week by the likes of Robert B. Parker and Linda Fairstein. ⊠ *1036-C Broxton Ave., between Weyburn and Kinross Aves., Westwood* ☎ *310/209–0415.*

FOR CHILDREN **Allied Model Trains.** A replica of L.A.'s Union Station, Allied claims to be the "largest train store ever built." It feels like a clacking, whistling train museum, with several operating choo-choos. Besides the huge selection of model trains, Allied also sells Department 56 villages and Playmobil toys. ⊠ *4411 S. Sepulveda Blvd., Culver City* ☎ *310/313–9353.*

Children's Book World. More than 80,000 titles for children cram a trio of storefronts. Saturday-morning story time and a play area absorb the kids while parents browse through acres of books, music, videos, games, and kits. It's just southwest of Century City. ⊠ *10580½ W. Pico Blvd., West L.A.* ☎ *310/559–2665.*

WINE & SPIRITS **Wally's.** It may be known as the wine store to the stars, but regular folks
★ also delve into the vast selection of wines and liquor, fine chocolates, imported cheeses, and the impressive assortment of cigars. Saturday-afternoon wine tastings make a visit all the sweeter. ⊠ *2107 Westwood Blvd., West L.A.* ☎ *310/475–0606.*

The Wine House. This beverage warehouse in the shadow of I–405 carries everything from $10 table wines to $500 first-growth Bordeaux and the right cigars to go with them. The scope of the selection can be daunting, but friendly staffers help neophytes find the perfect bottle at the perfect price. ⊠ *2311 Cotner Ave., between Pico and Olympic Blvds., West L.A.* ☎ *310/479–3731.*

WOMEN'S **Last Chance.** Grab a bargain from the end of the fashion cycle—items
CLOTHING from Gucci, Marc Jacobs, and hot local designers are at 60%–80% off retail prices. Although the store is off the beaten path, bargain hunters will find the trip worthwhile. ⊠ *8712 Washington Blvd., between La Cienega and National Blvds., Culver City* ☎ *310/287–1919.*

Downtown

Dotted with ethnic neighborhoods (Olvera Street, Chinatown, Koreatown, Little Tokyo) and several large, open-air shopping venues (the Fashion District, the Flower Market, Grand Central Market, the Toy District, and the Jewelry District), downtown L.A. offers an urban bargain hunter's shopping experience to counterbalance the precious atmosphere and mile-high prices of the Westside's boutiques.

Shopping Centers & Streets

Citadel Factory Stores. Wonder what's behind the Babylonian-motif wall you see from the I–5? The former Uniroyal Tire factory (and *Ben Hur* backdrop) morphed into L.A.'s first factory outlet, with brands like Calvin Klein, Tommy Hilfiger, and Puma, plus a decent outdoor food court. ⊠ *5675 E. Telegraph Rd., off I–5, exit Atlantic Blvd., City of Commerce* ☎ *323/888–1724.*

★ **The Fashion District.** Although this 90-block hub of the West Coast fashion industry is mainly a wholesale market, more than 1,000 independent stores sell to the general public (and some wholesalers do so on

Out-of-the-Ordinary Souvenirs

IN A CITY with so many exceptional shops, it would be a shame to go home with a ho-hum "Hollywood" T-shirt. Some quirky museum gift-shop finds could surprise the folks back home: celebrity-worn clothes at the Hollywood Entertainment Museum; vintage-car models at the Petersen; or a kid-friendly bottle of (fake) tar and bones from the Page Museum.

For rare and cool kitsch, go to L.A.'s most off-the-wall gift shops, like Los Feliz's Soap Plant Wacko (for tiki candle holders or a new fez), or Downtown's Indio Products (for love potions 9 to 99). At the L.A. County Coroner's gift shop, **Skeletons in the Closet** (⊠ 1104 N. Mission Rd., at Morengo St. ☎ 323/343−0760), you can snag coroner toe-tag key chains, a "body bag" garment bag, or a body-outline beach towel. Browsing for a budding screenwriter? Head to **Hollywood Book City** (⊠ 6627−6631 Hollywood Blvd. ☎ 323/466−2525) to choose from thousands of film books, scripts, and autographed celebrity photos. Shopping for a music buff? Pick up a pair of Hollywood Bowl bowls at the **Bowl Store** (⊠ 2301 N. Highland Ave., Hollywood ☎ 323/850−2085), next to the outdoor music venue.

6

Saturday, too, when elbow room is scarce). Bargaining is expected, most sales are cash only, and dressing rooms are rare. Explore **Santee Alley** (between Santee Street and Maple Avenue, from Olympic Boulevard to 11th Street) for back-alley deals on the same sunglasses, jewelry, handbags, shoes, and clothing you'll see in Beverly Hills. Be prepared to haggle, and don't lose sight of your wallet. Visit the fashion district's Web site for maps and tips. ⊠ *Roughly between I−10 and 7th St., San Pedro and Main Sts., Downtown* ⊕ *www.fashiondistrict.org.*

Grand Central Market. Since 1917, this open-air market has tempted Angelenos with all kinds of produce, fresh meats and seafood, spices, and fresh tortillas. Burritos, Cuban sandwiches, and kebabs satisfy shoppers on the go. ⊠ *317 S. Broadway, between 3rd and 4th Sts., Downtown* ☎ *213/624−2378.*

The Jewelry District. It's like a slice of Manhattan, with the crowded sidewalks, diverse aromas, and haggling bargain hunters to prove it. Expect to pay 50% to 70% off retail for everything from wedding bands to sparkling belt buckles. The more upscale stores are along Hill Street between 6th and 7th streets. There's a parking structure next door on Broadway. ⊠ *Between Olive St. and Broadway, from 5th to 8th St., Downtown* ⊕ *www.lajd.net.*

Fodor's Choice ★ **Olvera Street.** Historic buildings line this redbrick walkway overhung with grape vines. At dozens of clapboard stalls you can browse south-of-the-border goods—leather sandals, woven blankets, devotional candles, and the like—as well as cheap toys and tchotchkes. With the musicians and cafés providing background noise, the area is constantly lively. ⊠ *Between Cesar Chavez Ave. and Arcadia St., Downtown.*

Southern California Flower Mart. Shop with the pros at the largest flower market in the country, in this very location since 1923. Cut, potted, dried, and silk—they're all here amid a riot of colors and scents. Pay wholesale prices during public shopping hours: Tuesday, Thursday, and Saturday 6 AM–noon, and Monday, Wednesday, and Friday 8 AM–noon. There's a $1–$2 fee per person. Park in the lot on Maple Avenue between 7th and 8th streets. ✉ *766 Wall St., between 7th and 8th Sts., Downtown.*

The Toy District. This 12-block area of wholesale toy dealers is for the adventurous bargain hunter looking for knock-off versions of popular toys. From 25-cent stuffed animals to $150 gas-powered pocket bikes, toys arrive here directly from factories in China. Most vendors sell wholesale only, but plenty will also sell to individuals bearing cash. ✉ *Between 3rd and 5th Sts., and Los Angeles and San Pedro Sts., Downtown.*

Specialty Stores

ART GALLERIES **China Art Objects.** Of the recent wave of cutting-edge galleries that are replacing the knickknack shops and restaurants along dilapidated Chung King Road, this is the first and still the best. The gallery mounts shows of emerging local and international artists. ✉ *933 Chung King Rd., between Hill and Yale Sts., Chinatown* ☎ *213/613–0384.*

HOME FURNISHINGS & GIFTS **Indio Products.** Get your kitsch fix at this mammoth factory store for spiritual and New Age products. "Tie Up Your Man" oil, tarot cards in several languages, and "Luck in a Hurry" spray are great for a superstition or a laugh. ✉ *236 W. Manchester Ave., south of downtown, off I–110* ☎ *323/778–2233.*

Museum of Contemporary Art Store. It figures that the MOCA gift shop would be a terrific source for exhibit-related designer goods (Alessi bottle openers, Jonathan Adler vases, Jeff Koons balloon dogs), art posters, books, and children's toys. Three other branch stores in L.A. have similar contemporary art and design items: **MOCA Store Geffen Contemporary** (☎ 213/633–5323), **MOCA Santa Monica** (☎ 310/396–9833), and **MOCA at the Pacific Design Center** (☎ 310/289–5223), which has a selection of art catalogues and rare art books. ✉ *250 S. Grand Ave., Downtown* ☎ *213/621–1710.*

Hollywood

Local shops may be a mixed bag, but at least you can read the stars below your feet as you browse along Hollywood Boulevard. Lingerie and movie memorabilia stores predominate here, but the retail-hotel-dining-entertainment complex Hollywood & Highland has helped revitalize the Hollywood scene. Clowns, break dancers, and other street entertainers now draw sizable crowds of tourists that jam Hollywood Boulevard's sidewalks. Along La Brea Avenue, you'll find plenty of trendy, quirky, and hip merchandise, from records to furniture and clothing.

Shopping Center

Hollywood & Highland. Dozens of stores, the Kodak Theatre, and a slew of eateries fill this outdoor complex, which mimics cinematic glamour. Sweeping "Miss America" steps take you between floors of designer shops (Polo, Ralph Lauren, Louis Vuitton) and chain stores (Banana Republic, Planet Funk, Virgin Megastore). From the upper levels, there's a camera-perfect view of the famous HOLLYWOOD sign. On the second level, next to the Kodak Theatre, is a **Visitor Information Center** (☎ 323/467–6412) with a multilingual staff, maps, attraction brochures, and information about services. ✉ *Hollywood Blvd. and Highland Ave., Hollywood* ☎ *323/817–0220.*

Specialty Stores

BOOKS & MUSIC

Fodor's Choice
★

Amoeba Records. Although megasize, Amoeba acts like an independent record store, reflecting its Berkeley roots. The "Homegrown" display highlights local artists, and bands play here several times a week. With a rich stock of used CDs, an impressive cache of rarities and collectibles (like the Beatles' "Butcher" cover), and an encyclopedic range of indie releases, Amoeba pulls in Hollywood freethinkers. ✉ *6400 Sunset Blvd., at Cahuenga Blvd., Hollywood* ☎ *323/245–6400.*

★ **Larry Edmunds Bookshop.** After more than 60 years on the boulevard, this cinema and theater bookstore maintains old-school courtesy and charm. With more than 6,000 movie posters (including the $4,000 poster for *Gentleman Jim* that greets customers), a million photographs, and, of course, books, this store can mesmerize both casual and obsessive fans. ✉ *6644 Hollywood Blvd., Hollywood* ☎ *323/463–3273.*

FOR CHILDREN **Lost & Found.** The owner, a former stylist, describes this place as "Alice in Wonderland meets Jimi Hendrix." Visit for trippy boys' and girls' clothing (up to size 12) from Asia, Europe, and beyond. ✉ *6314 Yucca Ave., Hollywood* ☎ *323/856–0921.*

HOME FURNISHINGS **Lost & Found, etc.** For adults who just want to have fun, this colorful auxiliary to the nearby children's store has one-of-a-kind gifts, art, textiles, clothes, and tchotchkes. Choices include brass jewelry from France, African silk batiks, Stella Forest clothing, and other goodies handpicked from around the world. ✉ *6320 Yucca St., Hollywood* ☎ *323/856–5872.*

LINGERIE **Frederick's of Hollywood.** Why not visit Frederick's *in* Hollywood for bra enhancers, corsets, and velvet and marabou numbers? Climb upstairs on a leopard-print carpet to view celeb bras behind glass. ✉ *6751 Hollywood Blvd., Hollywood* ☎ *323/957–5953.*

TOYS & GAMES
★
Hollywood Magic Shop. A Tinseltown institution since the 1970s, and possibly the friendliest store in town, this place draws novices and special effects experts alike. Prices range from a buck for a gag to $6,000 for a stage illusion. You're virtually guaranteed to leave laughing. ✉ *6614 Hollywood Blvd., Hollywood* ☎ *323/464–5610.*

VINTAGE CLOTHING **Jet Rag.** Dig for just the right polyester or denim vintage gear. Known for its reasonable prices, Jet Rag takes it one step further on Sunday from 11:30 to dusk with a big parking-lot sale: all items go for $1. ✉ *825 N. La Brea Ave., near Hollywood* ☎ *323/939–0528.*

Los Feliz, Silver Lake & Echo Park

Although these edgy neighborhoods are in the process of gentrifying, they still give off jolts of innovation. Come for homegrown, funky galleries, vintage shops, and local designers' boutiques. Shopping areas are concentrated along Vermont Avenue and Hollywood Boulevard in Los Feliz; Sunset Boulevard in both Silver Lake (known as Sunset Junction) and Echo Park; and Echo Park Avenue in Echo Park. ■ TIP→ **Keep in mind that things are spread out enough to necessitate a couple of short car trips, and many shops in these neighborhoods don't open until noon.**

Specialty Stores

ANTIQUES   **Peter Vanstone, Inc.** Decorators and dealers visit this courteous merchant for his eclectic selection of art, antiques, and furnishings priced anywhere from $5 to $4,000. ✉ *2211 Sunset Blvd., Silver Lake* ☎ *213/413–5964.*

BOOKS   **Skylight Books.** A neighborhood bookshop through and through, complete with Lucy, the resident cat, Skylight has excellent coverage of L.A. travel, current affairs, children's books, fiction, and film, plus 'zines and journals. Frequent author events draw L.A.'s groovers and thinkers. ✉ *1818 N. Vermont Ave., Los Feliz* ☎ *323/660–1175.*

CANDY   **Zanzabelle.** An ice-cream and novelty candy store across the street from the local elementary school: how cool is that? Tracy James sells old-fashioned candies (Necco wafers, Violet Crumble bars, fresh caramels), handmade Pez dispensers, and penny candies stuffed in vintage boxes decorated with images of Flash Gordon and Bing Crosby. The locally made ice cream goes down smooth. ✉ *2912 Rowena Ave., Silver Lake* ☎ *323/663–9900.*

CLOTHING & ACCESSORIES   **Dean.** Danny Dean Davis made a splash with his '70s-style wide leather watchbands and oversize watch faces. His shop is stuffed with bags and watches, all made locally and many handmade, in a rainbow of colors. ✉ *3918 W. Sunset Blvd., Silver Lake* ☎ *323/665–2766.*

La La Ling. A must for moms who are dressing junior to stand out in a crowd, La La Ling carries the hippest baby clothes and gear around (like teensy Pumas and Paulina Quintana distressed leather diaper bags). Their star item is a line of vintage concert T-shirts that are cut and re-sewn to fit tykes smaller than size 6. ✉ *1810 N. Vermont Ave., Los Feliz* ☎ *323/664–4400.*

Panty Raid. For a lot of guys, being in a lingerie store can be worse than a visit to the dentist, but this one features a "boyfriend corner" with a PlayStation and men's magazines. Gals can browse the piles of Cosabella, Huit, and Hanky Pankys in peace. ✉ *2378½ Glendale Blvd., Silver Lake* ☎ *323/668–1888.*

Patty Faye. A child-size table with paper and markers keeps kids distracted while moms explore this friendly boutique. Erin Anderson and Carla Helmholz named the shop for their moms (Patty and Faye), and they have great eyes for clothing, shoes, and accessories that are cool without trying too hard. A store within the store, **Truth & Beauty** (☎ 323/664–6522) stocks aromatherapy goodies, skincare lines, home furnishings, and specialty chocolates. ✉ *2910 Rowena Ave., Silver Lake* ☎ *323/667–1954.*

Show Pony. This art-meets-fashion installation space is a true community resource and haven for local designers and artists. Limited hours (Wednesday–Sunday afternoons) are supplemented by viewing by appointment. ⊠ *1543 Echo Park Ave., Echo Park* ☎ *213/482–7676, 213/250–3381 for appointments.*

Steinberg & Sons. This petite shop offers indie and hard-to-find designers, with an emphasis on structural and asymmetrical shapes. Striving to be a center for the neighborhood's creative types, the **Little Knittery** (inside the store) offers knitting, crocheting, yarn painting, and other artsy classes, plus rare and exotic yarns. ⊠ *4712 Franklin Ave., just off N. Vermont Ave., Los Feliz* ☎ *323/660–0294.*

White Trash Charms. Begun as a jewelry brand, White Trash Charms has expanded into a boutique for those with a badass attitude and a loaded wallet. "Born to Lose" bags, Gwen Stefani's LAMB clothing line, and lots of retro-ironic charms like "trophy chick" or loaded dice are highlights. ⊠ *1951 N. Hillhurst Ave., Los Feliz* ☎ *323/666–9585.*

X-Large. Co-owned by members of the Beastie Boys, X-Large carries baggy, sturdy, urban-edge clothes and accessories. Check out the cooler full of tees. ⊠ *1768 N. Vermont Ave., Los Feliz* ☎ *323/666–3483.*

COSMETICS **Le Pink.** LOVE STINKS, BUT EVERYTHING IN HERE SMELLS GOOD, reads Laura Walden's welcome sign. Going for an old-time apothecary feeling, Laura stocks skin and bath products and cosmetics like Dr. Hauschka, Mustela, and Kneipp. Vintage girls' bedroom decor includes sock monkey dolls made by Laura's mom back in Arkansas. ⊠ *3820 Sunset Blvd., Silver Lake* ☎ *323/661–7465.*

HOME **Now/Again L.A.** An inviting mess of post-1950s furnishings, art, and light-
FURNISHINGS ing has all been handpicked by owner Dan Jordan for its eclectic appeal. ⊠ *3815 W. Sunset Blvd., Silver Lake* ☎ *323/662–4338.*

POP CULTURE **Glory.** A fleet of vintage British motorcycles from the 1940s to 1960s, with vintage equipment to go with it, attracts collectors from both sides of the pond. American-made denim and motorcycle-themed clothing is here for the more casual fan. ⊠ *4659 Hollywood Blvd., Los Feliz* ☎ *323/644–5679.*

Fodor'sChoice **Soap Plant Wacko/La Luz de Jesus Gallery.** This pop-culture supermar-
★ ket packs in art books (from erotica to "deviant literature"), action figures, goofy toys, and back-of-comic-book novelties such as X-ray specs and hula dancer lamps. The in-store gallery focuses on underground and "lowbrow" art; openings are flooded with hundreds of fans. ⊠ *4633 Hollywood Blvd., Los Feliz* ☎ *323/663–0122 or 323/666–7667.*

Y-Que Trading Post. Pronounced "ee-kay," this place churns out T-shirts with topical, tongue-in-cheek slogans (like "Run Katie Run," referring to the younger half of TomKat), as well as naughty novelties, gag gifts, and retro lunch boxes. On weekends, crowds of revelers shop here until midnight. ⊠ *1770 Vermont Ave., Los Feliz* ☎ *323/664–0021.*

SHOES **Camille Hudson.** Psst! Want an exclusive source for unique women's shoes straight out of France, Italy, Belgium, Spain, and Japan? This boutique has gorgeous footwear (just one pair in each size) you won't find elsewhere, including the in-house line. ⊠ *4685 Hollywood Blvd., near Vermont Ave., Los Feliz* ☎ *323/953–0377.*

VINTAGE CLOTHING

Flounce Vintage. Owner Lisa Gerstein has her faves—like '50s cardigans and '30s dresses—but she stocks everything from gloves to shoes to frocks from the Victorian era to the 1960s. More about the look than the label, her collection offers great values for vintage fans. ⊠ *1555 Echo Park Ave., Echo Park* ☎ *213/481–19757.*

Ozzie Dots. Come for ties, scarves, glasses, wigs, boas, fake weaponry, Hawaiian shirts, hats, boots, rubber snakes—did we mention the color-coded racks of old clothes? This costume shop caters to the entertainment industry and designers looking for vintage inspiration. ⊠ *4637 Hollywood Blvd., Los Feliz* ☎ *323/663–2867.*

SquaresVille. With Juan Miró-ish walls, and a "what we need" white-board, SquaresVille is one of a dwindling number of buy–sell–trade vintage shops in L.A. They cater to folks with little cash but lots of imagination. ⊠ *1800 N. Vermont Ave., Los Feliz* ☎ *323/669–8464.*

WINE & SPIRITS

Silver Lake Wine. Boutique, small-production wineries from 'round the world provide this shop with bottles that fill vertical racks from floor to ceiling. The knowledgeable staff will steer you to the right wine or spirits for any occasion. You can wet your whistle at tastings on Sunday, Monday, and Thursday. ⊠ *2395 Glendale Blvd., Silver Lake* ☎ *323/662–9024.*

West Hollywood & Melrose Avenue

West Hollywood is prime shopping real estate. And you know what they say about location, location, location? Depending on the street address, West Hollywood has everything from upscale art, design, and antiques store to ladies-who-lunch clothing boutiques to megamusic stores and specialty book vendors. Melrose Avenue, for instance, is part bohemian-punk shopping district (from North Highland to Sweetzer) and part up-scale art and design mecca (upper Melrose Avenue and Melrose Place). Discerning locals and celebs haunt the posh boutiques around Sunset Plaza (Sunset Boulevard at Sunset Plaza Drive), on Robertson Boulevard (between Beverly Boulevard and 3rd Street), and along upper Melrose Avenue.

The huge, blue Pacific Design Center, on Melrose at San Vicente Boulevard, is the focal point for the neighborhood's art- and interior design–related stores, including many on nearby Beverly Boulevard. The Beverly–La Brea neighborhood also claims a number of trendy clothing stores. Perched between Beverly Hills and West Hollywood, 3rd Street (between La Cienega and Fairfax) is a magnet for small, friendly designer boutiques. Finally, the Fairfax District, along Fairfax below Melrose, encompasses the flamboyant, historic Farmers Market, at Fairfax Avenue and 3rd Street; the adjacent shopping extravaganza, The Grove; and some excellent galleries around Museum Row at Fairfax Avenue and Wilshire Boulevard.

Shopping Centers

Fodor'sChoice
★

Farmers Market and The Grove. The granddaddy of L.A. markets dates to 1935, and the amazing array of clapboard stalls (selling everything from candy to hot sauce, fresh fruit to fresh lamb), wacky regulars, and

CLOSE UP

Melrose Place

Melrose Place is once again hot. With the opening of **Marc Jacobs**'s three new boutiques—one for his women's collection (at 8400 Melrose Place), one for his men's line (at 8409 Melrose Place), and the third (at 8410 Melrose Avenue) for his more affordable Marc by Marc bridge line—the area on and around this one-block street is back on the fashion radar. Nearby, **Diane von Furstenberg**'s shop (at 8407 Melrose Avenue) flaunts her classic wrap dresses and distinctive geometric prints. At 8428 Melrose Place, **Tracy Feith Men** pairs candy-color velvet blazers and handmade surfboards, while a few doors down, at 8446, his St. Barths-meets-Marrakesh dresses continue to dazzle the ladies. Next door, at 8440, hair maven Sally Hershberger snips shags (her signature cut) for a mere $600—if you can even score an appointment. Meanwhile, jeweler **Joann Smyth,** at 8444 Melrose Place, sells lariats and pearls at relatively affordable prices. At the end of the block, at 8460, the Italian label **Marni** exhibits bohemian luxury wear (like cropped furs and chunky bead accents) in a fabulously modernist space.

6

a United Nations of food choices must be experienced to be appreciated. Employees from the nearby CBS studios mingle with hungover clubbers and elderly locals at dozens of eateries and shops under one huge roof. The "Red Car" trolley shuttles visitors between the Farmers Market and the nearby **Grove**, a wildly popular outdoor mall with an ersatz European feel and a fabulous people-watching scene. Although many of the stores are familiar mall faces (Nordstrom, Abercrombie & Fitch, the Apple Store, American Girl Place), the elaborate setting, with winding tile walkways, a stream, and a fountain, put this shopping center over the top. ⊠ *6333 W. 3rd St., at Fairfax Ave., Fairfax District* ☎ *323/933–9211 Farmers Market, 323/900–8080 The Grove.*

Specialty Stores

ANTIQUES **Blackman Cruz.** Browse among David Cruz and Adam Blackman's offbeat pieces (like 1940s New York subway signs) as well as fine Continental and Asian furniture from the 18th to the mid-20th century. ⊠ *800 La Cienega Blvd., West Hollywood* ☎ *310/657–9228.*

Licorne Antiques. Among the fine 16th- to 19th-century European furnishings and decorative arts here, there's an emphasis on 17th-century Spanish and Italian pieces. ⊠ *8432 Melrose Pl., near West Hollywood* ☎ *323/852–4765.*

ART GALLERIES **Jan Kesner Gallery.** For more than 20 years, this excellent photography gallery has been devoted to international and California-based 20th-century photographers. It represents Nancy Burson, Richard Misrach, and Rubén Ortiz Torres, among others, and is open by appointment. ⊠ *164 N. La Brea Ave., Beverly–La Brea* ☎ *323/938–6834.*

Margo Leavin Gallery. This has been a preeminent L.A. gallery for more than 30 years, exhibiting contemporary American and European painters,

Farmers' Markets

CHEFS BY THE BUSHEL, parents, kids in strollers, artists, and fixed-income senior citizens mingle and sample their way through the best of southern California's fresh produce at Los Angeles's farmers' markets. Got a craving for sun-ripened, just-in-season strawberries? Want to try a cherimoya or pomelo? Hit a market.

Markets are held every day of the week, but weekends are the most popular. Many have special events like cooking classes, pet adoptions, or live music to accompany the fresh bounty. Check with the **Southland Farmers' Market Association** (☎ 310/481–0167 ⊕ www.cafarmersmarkets.org) for locations, days, and times of the more than 70 local markets. Here are a few of the best. The **Beverly Hills Farmers' Market** (✉ Civic Center Dr. between Alpine Dr. and Foothill Rd. ☎ 310/550–4796), held Sunday 9–1, is the only California market to carry wine (no sampling allowed). The

Chinatown Farmers' Market (✉ 727 N. Hill St., between Alpine and Ord Sts. ☎ 213/680–0243), held Thursday 2–6, specializes in Asian produce. The **West Hollywood Farmers' Market** (✉ 1200 N. Vista St., at Fountain Ave. ☎ 323/848–6502), on Monday 9–2, is as busy and cheerful as a street fair. The greatest of all is the **Santa Monica Wednesday market** (✉ Arizona Ave. at 2nd St. ☎ 310/458–8712). Running from 8:30 to 1:30, it draws all the area's top chefs and those who just love produce. Depending on the time of year, you might be tempted by heirloom tomatoes, Chinese long beans, Persian cucumbers, or blood oranges. On Saturday 8:30–1, there's an organic produce market at this same location. Other Santa Monica markets are held Saturday at Pico and Cloverfield boulevards (8–1) and Sunday at Main Street and Ocean Park Boulevard (9:30–1).

sculptors, photographers, and artists working on paper. ✉ 812 N. Robertson Blvd., West Hollywood ☎ 310/273–0603.

★ **Regen Projects.** Regen has expanded its gallery space as its reputation continues to grow. Local and international contemporary artists such as Wolfgang Tillmans, John Bock, and Liz Larner are representative. ✉ 633 N. Almont Dr., between Melrose Ave. and Santa Monica Blvd., West Hollywood ☎ 310/276–5424.

★ **6150 Wilshire Boulevard.** Seven contemporary galleries (including Acme, Kopeikin, and Roberts & Tilton) fill two floors around a central outdoor courtyard. Outside Chinatown, this may be the best spot for edgy, mainly local artists. ✉ Crescent Heights Blvd. and Fairfax Ave., Miracle Mile.

BOOKS & MUSIC **A Different Light.** Frequent book signings and readings pull in the locals for books by and about gays, lesbians, bisexuals, and the transgendered. ✉ 8853 Santa Monica Blvd., West Hollywood ☎ 310/854–6601.

Bodhi Tree Bookstore. Incense wafts around a huge selection of spiritual (more Buddhist than Christian) books, gifts, music, and videos. Psychic readings, signings, lectures, and workshops are held regularly. Behind the store, Bodhi's used-book shop also sells herbs and teas. ✉ *8585 Melrose Ave., West Hollywood* ☎ *310/659–1733.*

Fodor's Choice ★ **Book Soup.** One of the best independent bookstores in the country, Book Soup has been serving Angelenos for more than 30 years. Given its Hollywood pedigree, it's especially deep in books about film, music, art, and photography. Fringe benefits include an international newsstand, a bargain-book section, and author readings several times weekly. ✉ *8818 Sunset Blvd., West Hollywood* ☎ *310/659–3110.*

★ **Cook's Library.** Foodies unite! This shop stocks roughly 7,000 books about food and cooking. Sink into a comfy chair, and browse a cookbook in peace. ✉ *8373 W. 3rd St., near West Hollywood* ☎ *323/655–3141.*

Meltdown. The largest comic-book store on the West Coast (and a female-friendly one to boot!) is a monument to the artistry, wit, and downright weirdness of comics. Toys, art books, graphic novels, tees (from Tintin to Teen Titans), posters, and a gallery with comic-related art and photography supplement the scores of comic books. **Drunken Master** (☎ 323/850–5758), inside Meltdown, stocks a few thousand Asian and world cinema DVDs, has all-region DVD players, and certifies its products as 100% bootleg free. ✉ *7522 Sunset Blvd., near West Hollywood* ☎ *323/851–7223.*

Tower Records. When it opened in 1970, this was the world's largest record store. Tower is rock, rap, and pop central and also has a deep Latin music section. If you don't find what you want here, try across the street at **Tower Records Sunset Video** (☎ 310/657–3344) or **Tower Records Sunset Classical** (☎ 310/657–3910). ✉ *8801 Sunset Blvd., West Hollywood* ☎ *310/657–7300.*

Traveler's Bookcase. Nearly 24,000 titles will tempt you to take another trip. Along with vacation guides, this store has travel literature, a round-the-world photography section, and books to give kids the travel bug. ✉ *8375 W. 3rd St., near West Hollywood* ☎ *323/655–0575.*

Virgin Megastore. The racks here reveal an international, Brit-inflected pop perspective. Listening and DVD preview stations enable instant sampling, with more than 2 million song clips available. Ample underground parking is a huge plus. ✉ *8000 Sunset Blvd., West Hollywood* ☎ *323/650–8666.*

CAMERAS & ELECTRONICS **Samy's Camera.** This is a we'll-meet-or-beat-any-price kind of place, with cameras, video equipment, lighting, and studio equipment, used wares, collectibles, rentals and repairs, and digital imaging services. Other branches are in Pasadena and Venice. ✉ *431 S. Fairfax Ave., south of W. 3rd St., Fairfax District* ☎ *323/938–2420.*

FOR CHILDREN **Sugar Baby.** "Rocker moms, not soccer moms" is the slogan and the vibe of this friendly but edgy shop. The "Rock & Roll Saves Lives" tees for tots are best-sellers, but you'll also find retro kids' books, and even goodies for moms, like jewelry and lotion. ✉ *7523 W. Sunset Blvd., near West Hollywood* ☎ *323/969–9143.*

Sunset Kids. Designer duds for the junior set (newborn to size 16) include Flowers by Zoe, Queen Bee, and Cakewalk, luring in celeb moms like Faith Hill. ✉ *8669 Sunset Blvd., West Hollywood* ☎ *310/659–4411.*

Armani Casa. Enter the world of Armani world, where the clean and classic lines of black, white, and mocha furniture and home accessories cast their spell. ✉ *157 N. Robertson Blvd., at Beverly Blvd., West Hollywood* ☎ *310/248–2440.*

Futurama. Amoeba-shape couches and matching Boomarama chairs in lots of colors draw hipsters into this retro-furnishings emporium. ✉ *446 N. La Brea Ave., Beverly–La Brea* ☎ *323/937–4522.*

Hollyhock. Outstanding 18th- and 19th-century antiques casually nestle among more modern pieces here. Acclaimed for its quality and eclecticism, Hollyhock is a prime place to pick up treasures and design ideas. ✉ *817 Hilldale Ave., off Santa Monica Blvd., West Hollywood* ☎ *310/777–0100.*

Jonathan Adler. Gabe, a pug, greets visitors at this mecca for fans of the New York–based kitsch-tastic designer. Mid-century and country club styles get retooled in pottery, fun pillows, graphic textiles, and a furniture line. ✉ *8125 Melrose Ave., near West Hollywood* ☎ *323/658–8390.*

O.K. An über–gift shop, O.K. stocks the classy (Scandinavian stemware, vintage candelabras) to the goofy (macramé dog collars, bejeweled Pez holders) and specializes in architecture and design books. ✉ *8303 W. 3rd St., near West Hollywood* ☎ *323/653–3501.*

Soolip. As though the desk accoutrements, custom letterpress stationery, and handmade papers from nearly 50 countries weren't enough, this *paperie* also does a brisk business in couture wrapping. The space includes a bungalow with clothing, accessories, furnishings, and gifts, as well as a florist service. ✉ *8646 Melrose Ave., West Hollywood* ☎ *310/360–0545.*

Table Art. If you're hooked on shelter mags, the porcelain (Meissen, KPM, Royal Copenhagen), mouthblown glass, Belgian linens, and Thomas Goode (dealer to Queen Elizabeth) tableware here will set your pulses racing. Prices range from $13 to $23,000. ✉ *7977 Melrose Ave., near West Hollywood* ☎ *323/653–8278.*

Zipper. In what the owner calls a "modernist general store," gift seekers can find Mathmos lamps, locally designed pottery and jewelry, kids' novelties, photography, and a sizable design-book section. ✉ *8316 W. 3rd St., near West Hollywood* ☎ *323/951–0620.*

arp. This is L.A.'s only outlet for Ted Muehling's exquisite, museum-quality jewelry and houseware designs. His own organic and restrained jewelry (think coral and seashell shapes) shares the spotlight with that of his protégés: Gabriella Kiss, Annette Ferdinandsen, and Maria Beaulieu. ✉ *8311½ W. 3rd St., near West Hollywood* ☎ *323/653–7764.*

C by Karina. When J.Lo ignites a new trend in eyewear, it's most likely that she bought her shades here. Let the always-cool Karina help you find a flattering vintage style or a pair of cat-eye frames of your very own. ✉ *116 S. Robertson, between Beverly Hills and West Hollywood* ☎ *310/777–0231.*

Kaviar and Kind. By appointment only, this trendsetting boutique may be worth the effort. Owners Katherine Azarmi and Sunrise Ruffalo (yes, she's the wife of actor Mark Ruffalo) frequently rotate jewelry, art, handmade clothing, and bags by artists the world over, so you're guaranteed originality and up-to-the-minute cachet. ⊠ *8533 Sunset Blvd., West Hollywood* ☎ *310/659–8857.*

MENSWEAR **Alpha.** This guy-everything boutique is for the man who wants his barbecue to be as stylish as his cufflinks. Quirky additions like the "third date corner" help those in a new relationship find the perfect gift. ⊠ *8625 Melrose Ave., West Hollywood* ☎ *310/855–0775.*

J Ransom. TVs tuned to sports and news, leather couches, and cabinets stocked with rock-and-roll-friendly clothes—this store wears its testosterone on its sleeve. Morphine Generation (an L.A. brand developed by local musicians) and Kings of Glory shirts are accessorized with wide leather belts and crucifix jewelry. Mick Jagger has been known to visit. ⊠ *151 S. La Brea, Beverly–La Brea* ☎ *323/936–1675.*

John Varvatos. The celebrated menswear designer's showroom has vaulted, beamed ceilings and a separate VIP room for celebrities. The "L.A. look" of sport coat, jeans, and Converse sneakers is a staple here. ⊠ *8800 Melrose Ave., at Robertson Blvd., West Hollywood* ☎ *310/859–2791.*

Lo-Fi. Vintage concert tees, Levis, and old-school hooded sweatshirts are an L.A. uniform for guys. With more than 1,000 collectible shirts and an occasional jaw-dropping price tag (a "Ziggy Stardust" original is $1,000), Lo-Fi is a must for a hit of nostalgia. ⊠ *1038 N. Fairfax Ave., West Hollywood* ☎ *323/654–5634.*

SHOES **Boot Star.** A huge selection of boots here spells heaven to urban cowboys and -girls. You'll find everything from calfskin to alligator, turquoise cobra skin to hand-tooled skulls and crossbones, with most boots handmade in Mexico and Texas. Custom sizing is available. ⊠ *8493 Sunset Blvd., West Hollywood* ☎ *323/650–0475.*

Sigerson Morrison. The strappy sandals, polished flats, and mod boots from this British designer have inspired many a pedicure. ⊠ *8307 W. 3rd St., near West Hollywood* ☎ *323/655–6133.*

Undefeated. Glide through the pneumatic door to find retro and old-school Adidas, Nike, and Reebok sneakers for those with better cash flow than dunk shots. There's another branch on Main Street in Santa Monica. ⊠ *112½ S. La Brea Ave., Beverly–La Brea* ☎ *323/937–6077.*

VINTAGE CLOTHING ★ **Decades.** Cameron Silver has made this a primo vintage source, with a stellar selection of 1960s–'70s designers (Hermès, Pucci, Gucci). On the street level, **Decades Two** (☎ *323/655–1960*) resells contemporary designer and couture clothing (often worn once by celeb clientele) at up to 80% off. ⊠ *8214 Melrose Ave., near West Hollywood* ☎ *323/655–0223.*

Resurrection. Stylists head here for high-quality 1960s–'80s vintage wear from the likes of Ossie Clark, Halston, YSL, and Pucci, as well as vintage Levis, Gucci accessories, and such. ⊠ *8006 Melrose Ave., near West Hollywood* ☎ *323/651–5516.*

The Way We Wore. A gold-lamé-draped ceiling and leopard-print stairs set the scene for a range of women's 20th-century clothes. Upstairs, couture from Halston, Dior, and Chanel can cost up to $20,000. ⊠ *334 S. La Brea, Beverly–La Brea* ☎ *323/937–0878.*

WOMEN'S & MEN'S CLOTHING

American Rag Cie. Locals and Japanese tourists compete for the high-end, mainly European new and vintage clothing, shoes, and accessories. Browse the mainly French home furnishings and European CDs in the store's annex, **Maison Midi** (☎ 323/935–3157), or take an espresso break in the bistro–café. ⊠ *150 S. La Brea Ave., Beverly–La Brea* ☎ *323/935–3154.*

Built by Wendy. Wendy Mullin, now designing for Wrangler, built her rep with her Brooklyn-meets-Cheyenne aesthetic. Think overalls, tie-dye jeans, and *Bad News Bears* tees. ⊠ *7938 W. 3rd St., near West Hollywood* ☎ *323/651–1902.*

Chrome Hearts. If Cher and P. Diddy are your fashion idols, this is your place for handmade, chunky silver jewelry, studded leather pants, sunglasses, gadgets, and furniture. ⊠ *600 N. Robertson Blvd., at Melrose Ave., West Hollywood* ☎ *310/854–9800.*

Fodor'sChoice ★ Fred Segal. A longtime L.A. fashion landmark, this is a store like no other. Intense and condensed, it is one space subdivided into miniboutiques that range from couture clothing to skateboard fashions. The entertainment industry's fashion fiends are addicted to the exclusive goods here, like European Levi lines and cult L.A. designers. There's free parking off Crescent Heights Boulevard. ⊠ *8100 Melrose Ave., at Crescent Heights Blvd., near West Hollywood* ☎ *323/651–4129.*

H. Lorenzo. Funky, high-end designer clothes (D-Squared, Junya Watanabe, Jaded by Knight) attract stylists and a young Hollywood crowd, people who don't blink at paying $250 for jeans. Next door, **H. Men** (☎ 310/652–7039) provides the same hot styles for the guys. ⊠ *8660 Sunset Blvd., West Hollywood* ☎ *310/659–1432.*

Henry Duarte. The denim king of L.A., at home on the Sunset Strip, uses rock-and-roll art to set off his cast-bronze buckles and custom-tooled leather bags, belts, and jackets. ⊠ *8747 Sunset Blvd., West Hollywood* ☎ *310/652–3500.*

★ **Kitson.** In L.A., this store has gotten more press than Paris Hilton. Known as celebrity central, it's packed with shoppers pawing through the cashmere sweaters, hoodies, jeans, Pucci scarves, Nicky Hilton hats, and unusual pampering products. Across the street, **Kitson Kids** (☎ 310/246–3829) helps Britney clothe her spawn in style. ⊠ *115 S. Robertson Blvd., between Beverly Hills and West Hollywood* ☎ *310/859–2652.*

Kristin Londgren. Opened as a showcase for her scrumptious clothes (bias-cut dresses, hand-knit and hand-dyed wraps), Kristin has branched out to include jewelry, fetchingly displayed in acrylic light boxes, Scandinavian vintage glass, recycled traffic-cone bags, and anything else that catches her fancy. ⊠ *8303 W. 3rd St., near West Hollywood* ☎ *323/653–9200.*

Fodor'sChoice ★ Maxfield. L.A.'s temple of high fashion carries labels like Thomas Wylde, Comme des Garçons, Christian Dior, and Yohji Yamamoto for those with deep cash reservoirs. The atmosphere is quite serious, as those with virtual PhDs in fashion study the vintage Hermès and latest Balenciaga. ⊠ *8825 Melrose Ave., at Robertson Blvd., West Hollywood* ☎ *310/274–8800.*

Maxfield Bleu. Score 50%–65% discounts on last season's Gucci, Prada, Armani, Christian Dior, and other labels from the high-fashion mothership, Maxfield. ⊠ *151 N. Robertson Blvd., between Beverly Hills and West Hollywood* ☎ *310/275–7007.*

Miu Miu. In the youthful extension of the Prada line, body-conscious fashions for men and women are

> "At 9 AM [in the top farmers' markets], you'll find sous-chefs from the top-end restaurants shopping for that evening's specials. By lunchtime, everyone's there—executives from surrounding office buildings, bodybuilders looking for organic salad fixings, leaflet distributers. . . . You get to walk around in the sun, taking in the produce and the people. It's just really cool."   –rjw_lgb_ca

complemented by famously well-constructed bags and often exaggerated footwear. ⊠ *8025 Melrose Ave., near West Hollywood* ☎ *323/651–0073.*

Fodor's Choice
★

Paul Smith. You can't miss the shocking pink "shoebox" that houses Paul Smith's fantastical collection of clothing, vintage books, luggage, boots, hats, and objets d'art. The interior has multiple "stage sets," some taken whole from European chateaux and others with props that wink and nod to old Hollywood glamour. The clothing, in signature colors like hot pink and mustard yellow, likewise mixes old and new. ⊠ *8221 Melrose Ave., near West Hollywood* ☎ *323/951–4800.*

Suss Design. When stars like Julia Roberts flashed their needles, knitting became Hollywood chic. Suss caters to fashionistas with fine Italian yarn, tempting knitwear (cashmere scarves, sweater dresses, baby sweaters), knitting classes, and couches for—what else?—knitting. ⊠ *7350 Beverly Blvd., Beverly–La Brea* ☎ *323/954–9637.*

Ted Baker. A "best in show" theme permeates this British designer's color-crazy boutique, where prize ribbons adorn the fuschia sport coats, and mechanical puppies wag tails at the wildly striped shirts. ⊠ *131 N. Robertson Blvd., between Beverly Hills and West Hollywood* ☎ *310/550–7855.*

WOMEN'S CLOTHING

Agent Provocateur. British naughtiness tickles L.A. with fishnets, corsets, and silk and handmade lace-adorned negligees and undergarments that leave modesty in the dust. ⊠ *7961 Melrose Ave., near West Hollywood* ☎ *323/653–0229.*

Beige. Despite the name, Beige carries edgy and local designers (Michelle Mason, James Coviello, and Louis Verdad) for those who like to stand out in a crowd. ⊠ *7274 Beverly Blvd., Beverly–La Brea* ☎ *323/549–0064.*

Bleu. Ever dream of getting a fresh look without lifting a finger? The friendly, style-savvy staff will size you up in minutes and deliver just the right party frocks, jeans, or teeny sweaters (with the jewelry, shoes, and undies to match) to your dressing room. Body-conscious designer labels include DVF and No.l.ita. ⊠ *454 S. La Brea Ave., Beverly–La Brea* ☎ *323/939–2228.*

Brunette. Who says blondes have more fun? From lingerie to shoes to beautiful dresses, this shop gets girly without the frou-frou. Look for Desanka flowy dresses, lingerie-inspired Geren Ford, and Ya Ya. Guys can chill on the couch and play video games while waiting. ⊠ *8025 Sunset Blvd., near West Hollywood* ☎ *323/650–9018.*

Curve. Layers of chiffon, lace, silk, mesh, and leather separates will take you beyond jeans and a tank. Curve's own line rubs shoulders with up-and-comers like Inhabit and Michelle Mason. ⊠ *154 N. Robertson Blvd., between Beverly Hills and West Hollywood* ☎ *310/360–8008.*

Hillary Rush. A third-generation shopkeeper, Hillary showcases eclectic new clothing designers (like herself) in this East-Village-on-the-West-Coast shop. Her "anti-Robertson" vibe encourages shoppers to schmooze and pet her pooch, Calzone, while sifting through the racks. ⊠ *8222 W. 3rd St., near West Hollywood* ☎ *323/852–0088.*

Leona Edmiston. The "queen of frocks" in her native Australia, Leona Edmiston has brought her 1930s- and 1940s-inspired designs to L.A. Her dresses—bonus!—are wrinkle-free for traveling. A smaller shop is on Montana Avenue in Santa Monica. ⊠ *8591 Sunset Blvd., West Hollywood* ☎ *310/855–9121.*

Lisa Kline. For that very L.A. look, visit this dependable, celebrity-friendly shop for Juicy Couture, Kooba purses, Anna Sui, and those all-important underpinnings for revealing outfits. ⊠ *136 S. Robertson Blvd., between Beverly Hills and West Hollywood* ☎ *310/246–0907.*

Naissance on Melrose. Tired of hiding that bump under a frumpy smock? This is the place for hip and trendy maternity clothes, plus diaper bags, bedding, and baby books for those bundles of joy. ⊠ *8254 Melrose Ave., near West Hollywood* ☎ *323/653–8850.*

Nanette Lepore. The floor-to-ceiling pink glow is not your imagination. Sweetly girlish and whimsical women's wear fairly floats off the hangers. You can count on details like eyelet, big chintzy florals, and ruffles. ⊠ *114 S. Robertson Blvd., between Beverly Hills and West Hollywood* ☎ *310/281–0004.*

Satine. The opaque window is a clue that paparazzi-shy celebs love this retro-theme place for its well-edited collection of emerging indie brands (Wayf) and popular designer labels (Stella McCartney). ⊠ *8117 W. 3rd St., near West Hollywood* ☎ *323/655–2142.*

South Willard. For hard-to-find European and Brazilian lines, hit this store–design lab. The unusual, sober-hue collections include Raf Simons and Bernhard Willhelm. ⊠ *8038 W. 3rd St., near West Hollywood* ☎ *323/653–6153.*

Stella McCartney. Edgy chicks and girly-girls flock to this ivy-covered shop to score the season's hottest items, such as white flowy dresses and cropped jackets. The parking in the back makes it hard to pass by. ⊠ *8823 Beverly Blvd., West Hollywood* ☎ *310/323–7051.*

Tracey Ross. Chandeliers, black-and-beige decor, and French pop music set the mood. Designer labels include Roland Mouret, Stella McCartney, Jimmy Choo, and everything Chloé. ⊠ *8595 Sunset Blvd., West Hollywood* ☎ *310/854–1996.*

Trina Turk. Bubblelike lamps light this pale pink paradise. Shop for bold mod prints and colors on dresses and separates that are cut to fit like a dream. ⊠ *8008 W. 3rd St., near West Hollywood* ☎ *323/651–1382.*

Santa Monica & Venice

The breezy beachside communities of Santa Monica and Venice are ideal for leisurely shopping. Scads of tourists (and some locals) gravitate to the Third Street Promenade, a popular pedestrians-only strolling–shopping area. A number of modern furnishings stores are nearby on 4th and 5th streets. Main Street between Pico Boulevard and Rose Avenue offers upscale chain stores, cafés, and some original shops, while Montana Avenue is a great source for unique boutiques and child-friendly shopping, especially between 7th and 17th streets. ■ **TIP→ Parking in Santa Monica is next to impossible on Wednesday, when some streets are blocked off for the farmers' market, but there are several parking structures with free parking for an hour or two.** In Venice, Abbot Kinney Boulevard (or simply, the Street) is abuzz with midcentury furniture stores, offbeat galleries and boutiques, yoga studios, and cafés, particularly between Venice Boulevard and Main Street.

Shopping Centers

Brentwood Country Mart. Back in the day, Liz Taylor and Joan Crawford used to stop here for burgers. A preservationist has restored this faux country market with its red-barn backdrop and cobblestone courtyards. The dozen or so fun stores specialize in textiles, clothing, toys, and stationery. And you can still grab a burger here. ⊠ *225 26th St., at San Vicente Blvd., Santa Monica.*

★ **Third Street Promenade.** Whimsical dinosaur-shaped, ivy-covered fountains and buskers of every stripe set the scene along this pedestrians-only shopping stretch. Stores are mainly the chain variety (Restoration Hardware, Von Dutch, Apple), but movie theaters, bookstores, pubs, and restaurants ensure that virtually every need is covered. ⊠ *3rd St. between Broadway and Wilshire Blvd.*

Specialty Shops

ART GALLERIES **Angles.** With one room graced by 16-foot skylighted ceilings, this is undoubtedly one of L.A.'s most beautiful gallery spaces. Come for contemporary international artists working in all mediums, like Tom LaDuke, David Bunn, Linda Besemer, and Kevin Appel. ⊠ *2230 and 2222 Main St., Santa Monica* ☎ *310/396–5019.*

★ **Bergamot Station.** A former trolley stop on the old L.A.–Santa Monica Red Line has become a contemporary art complex with more than 30 galleries, 10 shops, and a café, plus the Santa Monica Museum of Art. Even kids are entertained by the funky setting and diversity of art here. It's closed Sunday. ⊠ *2525 Michigan Ave., at 26th St., Santa Monica* ☎ *310/453–7535.*

L.A. Louver. Since it opened in 1976—a lifetime ago by L.A. standards—this gallery has shown contemporary local artists in an international context (David Hockney alongside Leon Kossoff, for instance). ✉ *45 N. Venice Blvd., Venice* ☎ *310/822–4955.*

Ten Women Venice. Twenty-one diverse, local women artists, not just 10, participate in this co-op. Glass art, jewelry, ceramics, paintings, photography, sculptures, and knitwear are all lovingly displayed. ✉ *1237 Abbot Kinney Blvd., Venice* ☎ *310/452–2256.*

BOOKS & MUSIC **Arcana.** A treasure trove for filmmakers, this store boasts a serious collection of new and out-of-print books on art, architecture, design, and fashion. ✉ *1229 Third Street Promenade, Santa Monica* ☎ *310/458–1499.*

Barnes & Noble. Don't be surprised if your cashier is a moonlighting actor at this triple-decker book and music stalwart. You can sample and search CDs, and signings and workshops by entertainment industry folks happen frequently. ✉ *1201 Third Street Promenade, at Wilshire Blvd., Santa Monica* ☎ *310/260–9110.*

Borders. DVDs, self-help books, and a British line of paper goods are big sellers at this three-story bookstore, where rows of browsing tables invite lingering, and an in-store café provides fuel. ✉ *1415 Third Street Promenade, Santa Monica* ☎ *310/393–9290.*

★ **Dutton's Brentwood Bookstore.** Remember the noncorporate bookstore, with its distinctive musty odor? Wander through the rooms of crowded, floor-to-ceiling bookshelves, or ask the helpful staff for a suggestion. Children's and music books are special strengths. A second store is in Beverly Hills for the Eastside crowd. ✉ *11975 San Vicente Blvd., Brentwood* ☎ *310/476–6263.*

Equator. The bright, slightly garagelike space can feel more like a gallery than a bookstore—and in fact, exhibits (like photographs of Mexican wrestlers) rotate through along with the books. It's a great source for out-of-print and collectable volumes, especially art, photo, design, architecture, poetry, and fiction. Offbeat subgenres include surf and skate, circus freaks, and bullfighting. ✉ *1103 Abbot Kinney Blvd., Venice* ☎ *310/399–5544.*

★ **Hear Music.** Pick up a latte in the entryway and take it to a burn-and-print station, where you can burn your own compilation, choose your own cover art, and walk away minutes later with a new CD. With its excellent selection of jazz, folk, world, electronica, and alternative music, the store will take you out of your comfort zone. On weekend nights, the burn stations are jammed. ✉ *1429 Third Street Promenade, Santa Monica* ☎ *310/319–9527.*

Hennessey + Ingalls Bookstore. A stop here would make a perfect end to a day at the Getty. In L.A., this is the largest collection of books on graphic design, art, architecture, and photography. ✉ *214 Wilshire Blvd., between 2nd and 3rd Sts., Santa Monica* ☎ *310/458–9074.*

COSMETICS **Kiehl's.** Bringing its 150-plus years of experience in skin and hair care to the extremely tanned locals, Kiehl's soothes with its trademark plain packaging and pure ingredients. Another branch is on Robertson Boulevard, in West Hollywood. ✉ *1516 Montana Ave., Santa Monica* ☎ *310/255–0055.*

FOR CHILDREN **Acorn.** Remember when toys didn't require computer programming? Ellen
★ West's old-fashioned shop sparks kids' imaginations with dress-up
clothes, books, and hand-painted wooden toys: no batteries or plastic
allowed! Closed Sunday and Monday. ⊠ *1220 5th St., near Wilshire
Blvd., Santa Monica* ☎ *310/451–5845.*

Every Picture Tells a Story. This one-of-a-kind gallery deals in original art
(Maurice Sendak, Hilary Knight, Dr. Seuss) from children's books. Although adults are the target customers, there are also books for non-art-
loving kids. ⊠ *1311-C Montana Ave., Santa Monica* ☎ *310/451–2700.*

Puzzle Zoo. Anyone with a taste for play will find something among the
puzzles galore, unusual chess sets, Disney toys, action figures, Madame
Alexander dolls, collectors' toy soldiers and movie-inspired figures.
⊠ *1413 Third Street Promenade, Santa Monica* ☎ *310/393–9201.*

FOR DOGS **The Wagging Tail.** No ordinary pet shop, this is practically a dog department store, where you can find anything from faux-fur-trimmed rain-
coats to Parisian shampoo to fresh "cannoli." You can even commission
your pooch's likeness on a mug, a Pop Art portrait, belt buckle, or tile.
Dogs are as welcome as their owners. ⊠ *1123 Montana Ave., Santa Monica* ☎ *310/656–9663.*

HOME
FURNISHINGS **Design Within Reach.** Form follows function in this high-end, modernist
showroom, whether in the curvy children's furniture, Eames chairs, or
$6,000 Noguchi sofa. ⊠ *332-A Santa Monica Blvd., at 4th St., Santa
Monica* ☎ *310/899–6000.*

Raw Style. "Be happy" is Pearl Maremont's emphatic message with her
riotously colorful gallery–store, chock-full of shell-encrusted chairs,
teapots, and all manner of offbeat handmade arts, crafts, and furniture
designed by some 300 American artists. ⊠ *1511 Montana Ave., Santa
Monica* ☎ *310/458–7662.*

Tortoise. On buying trips to Japan, Keiko and Taku Shinomoto gather up
all sorts of intriguing items, often with a traditional craftsmanship behind
them, such as *tenugi* (printed Japanese tea towels), tea ceremony objects,
and cedar bentwood dishes. This is a rare source for gifts. Closed Monday and Tuesday. ⊠ *1208 Abbot Kinney Blvd., Venice* ☎ *310/314–8448.*

MENSWEAR **Sean.** Emile Lafaurie's "not too now or too wow" clean and classic
clothes have just enough polish: button-downs with a narrow cut, boxy
painter's jackets, sedate suits. **Station 25,** an in-store shoe boutique,
provides the finishing touches.
⊠ *1609 Montana Ave., Santa
Monica* ☎ *310/260–5616.*

POP CULTURE **Kidrobot.** Underground art is the
draw at this toy boutique for grown-
ups. Ugly dolls, Dunnys, Ice-Bots,
and other limited-edition figures
draw collectors and the curious.
⊠ *1407 Third Street Promenade,
Santa Monica* ☎ *310/576–7766.*

> **WORD OF MOUTH**
>
> "As for the Rose Bowl [Flea Mar-
> ket], my advice is to arrive really
> early (even pay the extra to get in
> early) because parking and crowds
> can be a problem."   –P. Olson.

6

WOMEN'S &   **Fred Segal.** Larger and less frenetic than its sister store on Melrose, this
MEN'S CLOTHING branch offers the latest in trendy clothing and accessories in two build-
★   ings full of pricey miniboutiques. The Comfort Café and a hair salon
provide reprieves from shopping. ⊠ *500 and 420 Broadway, Santa
Monica* ☎ *310/458–8100 or 310/394–9814.*

The Levi's Store. Tired of trying on dozens of jeans to find the right pair?
Step into the Fit Locator booth here for a full body scan and printout
of your best fit and size. This is the largest Levi outlet in southern California, with thousands of jeans in various colors and configurations (including a $1,000 pair of collectors' Levi's). Vests, jackets, shirts, and
boots break up the sea of denim. ⊠ *1409 Third Street Promenade, Santa
Monica* ☎ *310/393–4899.*

WOMEN'S   **Cabaña.** Ceiling fans and dressing-room cabañas are the perfect back-
CLOTHING drop for Lily Pulitzer's trademark pink-and-green shifts and beachy bags
(by Eliza Gray) and sandals (from Miss Trish of Capri). ⊠ *1511-A Montana Ave., Santa Monica* ☎ *310/394–5123.*

Heist. Former investment banker Nilou Ghodsi considers this a giant version of her closet, and a fabulous closet it is. In a warm yet minimalist
setting, the Denim Table, baskets of sandals and handmade jewelry, and
hand-chosen designer separates virtually beg to move to your closet.
⊠ *1104 Abbot Kinney Blvd., Venice* ☎ *310/450–6531.*

Jill Roberts. New York, Hamptons style, gets a West Coast twist here.
Trina Turk, Phillip Lim, and Bernardo flip-flops draw in neighborhood
moms with 10 minutes to spare. The Beverly Hills branch also carries
menswear. ⊠ *920 Montana Ave., Santa Monica* ☎ *310/260–1966.*

Moondance Jewelry Gallery. Each case here highlights an individual designer, from modish to antique: Me + Ro, Jeanine Payer, and Gabrielle
Sanchez are among them. Trunk shows and special events are given several times a year. ⊠ *1530 Montana Ave., Santa Monica* ☎ *310/395–5516.*

Pamela Barish. Former designer to the (rock) stars, Pamela Barish slowed
down and opened this white boutique to showcase her seductive designs—
filmy tunics, satin frocks, and cut-to-there wear. ⊠ *1327½ Abbot Kinney Blvd., Venice* ☎ *310/314–4490.*

San Fernando & San Gabriel Valleys

Over "the Hill" and into the San Fernando Valley, Studio City's Ventura Boulevard is the vital artery of Valley shopping. Mimicking Hollywood, stars line this shopping drag, but here they honor past TV shows.
Only 20 freeway minutes over another hill east of Hollywood are the
San Gabriel Valley communities of Burbank and Pasadena. In Pasadena,
the stretch of Colorado Boulevard between Pasadena Avenue and Arroyo Parkway, known as Old Town, is a popular pedestrian shopping
mecca, with stores like Crate & Barrel, Abercrombie & Fitch, Pottery
Barn, and J. Crew. A few blocks west on Colorado, the open-air "urban
village" known as Paseo Colorado mixes residential, retail, dining, and
entertainment spaces along Colorado Boulevard between Los Robles and
Marengo avenues. Enter on Colorado or Marengo for free parking.

CLOSE UP

Flea Markets

FLEA MARKETS are a fantastic resource for those who love all things vintage. Flea market culture has a few rules: arrive early (the "great finds" tend to go fast), polite haggling is allowed, and remember that what you see is what you get (no, those Pumas from the '70s don't come in other colors).

Held every Sunday 9–5 in Fairfax High School's parking lot, the **Melrose Trading Post** (✉ Fairfax Blvd. and Melrose Ave. ☎ 323/655–7679 🌐 www.melrosetradingpost.org) is hip, fairly junk-free, and popular with Hollywood denizens. Live music and fresh munchies entertain vintage hunters and collectors, but bargains are rare. Take heart, though, because the market benefits Fairfax High's clubs and organizations. Parking is free, but admission is $2.

Huge and hyped, the **Rose Bowl Flea Market** (✉ 1001 Rose Bowl Dr., Pasadena ☎ 323/560–7469 🌐 www.

rgcshows.com), happens on the second Sunday of every month, rain or shine. If you expect bargains, you're in for a shock unless you're an expert haggler. This extremely popular market attracts more than 2,200 vendors looking for top dollar for their antiques, crafts, and new furniture. It's an especially good source for pop culture odds and ends (like a $100 Partridge Family lunchbox). Admission is $7 from 9 to 3; more expensive special passes will get you in one to three hours ahead of time.

For better bargain hunting and less stress, try the **Pasadena City College Flea Market** (✉ 1570 E. Colorado Blvd., at Hill Ave., Pasadena ☎ 626/585–7906), on the first Sunday of each month. With 500 vendors (70 of them selling records), this is a great source for collectibles, furniture, and clothing at prices that won't break the bank. Admission and parking are free 8–3.

6

Specialty Stores

ART GALLERY **Mendenhall Sobieski Gallery.** In a historic brick building (a former site of printing-press classes), this gallery is now home to works by contemporary artists like Squeak Carnwath, Robert Williams, and Mark Ryden. Openings are lively at this hip, attitude-free space. ✉ *40 Mills Pl., just west of Colorado Blvd., Pasadena* ☎ *626/535–9757.*

BOOKS **Distant Lands.** An amazing selection of maps, gear, guides, and literature will put you in travel mode. Knowledgeable staff and an in-store travel agency make another trip a snap. ✉ *56 S. Raymond Ave., just south of Green St., Pasadena* ☎ *626/449–3220 or 800/310–3220.*

Storyopolis. If Oprah shops here for baby shower gifts, why shouldn't you? Lots of readings, music, dancing, arts and crafts activities for kids leave parents free to shop for books and other goodies. ✉ *12348 Ventura Blvd., Studio City* ☎ *818/509–5600.*

★ **Vroman's Bookstore.** Southern California's oldest and largest (27,000 square feet) independent bookseller is justly famous for great service. An attached newsstand, café, and adjacent gift and stationery store boost the total shopping experience. Some 400 author events annually, plus a fab kids' zone complete with play area, make this a truly outstanding spot. ⊠ *695 E. Colorado Blvd., Pasadena* ☎ *626/449–5320.*

COSMETICS **Lather.** Take a deep breath. Is that geranium or yuzu you smell? Giant soap blocks, aromatherapy candles, a blending bar, and private spa room cover all the bases. Products use all-natural ingredients, too. ⊠ *106 W. Colorado Blvd., Pasadena* ☎ *626/396–9636.*

HOME FURNISHINGS & GIFTS **Rm. 107.** A light-filled, barrel-vaulted former warehouse now sets off a lovely mix of restored vintage and newly designed furniture and objects with mid-20th-century style. Closed Monday and Tuesday. ⊠ *174 S. De Lacey Ave., south of Colorado Ave., Pasadena* ☎ *626/432–4867.*

WOMEN'S & MEN'S CLOTHING **Tryst.** A young Frenchman and his wife stock this West Hollywood–esque space with European designers (Mange Tout) and rock star tees (Buddhist Punk) and fill the "Denim Bar" with young celeb favorites (Energie). Weekend events might include bubbly and Krispy Kremes to the beat of Euro-pop music. ⊠ *13023 Ventura Blvd., Studio City* ☎ *818/906–7761.*

It's a Wrap. Looking for castoffs from *Six Feet Under, General Hospital,* or the latest Disney Studios production? The wardrobe departments of movie and TV studios and production companies ship clothes here daily. A "letter of authenticity" accompanies each bargain (that's 35%–95% off retail). Another store is open near Beverly Hills, on S. Robertson Boulevard. ⊠ *3315 W. Magnolia Blvd., at California St., Burbank* ☎ *818/567–7366.*

WOMEN'S CLOTHING ★ **Camille Frances Depedrini.** One space is home to four unique shopping gems, the diamond of which is wedding dress designer Camille Frances Depedrini. Inspired by 1920s–'50s gowns, she turns out gorgeous and unusual dresses, cloaks, sweet suede shoes, and handpainted scarves. The other shops are **Koi,** a source for exotic, folk-ethnic clothing, jewelry, and bags; **Marz,** an alternative paper and gift shop; and **Rue de Mimo,** an incredible collection of architectural clothing from sources in both L.A. and countries like Poland, Israel, and Portugal. ⊠ *1007 Fair Oaks Ave., just south of I–110, South Pasadena* ☎ *626/441–7868.*

Dari. William Shatner's daughter Melanie's boutique appeals to stylish schoolgirls and their moms with designer lines like Rebecca Taylor, C by Chloé, and 12th Street by Cynthia Vincent. ⊠ *12184 Ventura Blvd., Studio City* ☎ *818/762–3274.*

debout. At this exclusive shoe salon, Luc Berjen, Leopoldo Giordano, and other European lines will tempt some try-ons. Venetian coin purses, Chie Mihara bags, and other accessories are also highly browsable. ⊠ *13023 Ventura Blvd., Studio City* ☎ *818/906–7761.*

Elisa B. Elisa's small but well-edited collection of up and coming L.A. designers (Wasabi, Adina) and established favorites (Trina Turk, Rebecca Taylor) draw women of all ages to this friendly Old Town boutique. ⊠ *12 Douglas Alley, Pasadena* ☎ *818/906–7761.*

Faire Frou Frou. Slink in here for underwear that could pass as outerwear: lace-trimmed chemises, silk camisoles, bustiers. A Rosamosario silk gown goes for a grand, but you can also find cheap, fun cotton knickers. ✉ *18017-A Ventura Blvd., near Coldwater Canyon Ave., Studio City* ☎ *818/783–4974.*

Playclothes Vintage Fashions. Costumers and designers rely on this mega-vintage store, with 3,500 square feet of clothing, accessories, collectibles (including a special Western section), and furniture from the 1920s to the '70s. ✉ *11422 Moorpark St., Studio City* ☎ *818/755–9559.*

6

Orange County & Catalina Island

WORD OF MOUTH

"After going to it for 38 years, I still rate the original Disneyland as the best and happiest vacation destination on earth—and I'm not that easy to please."

—Kiki

"Laguna is more interesting and picturesque than Newport, but [Newport is] easier to access and has more lodging options (although the Montage in Laguna is breathtaking—have a sunset drink upstairs there!)."

—wherenext

By Kathy
Bryant

FEW OF THE CITRUS GROVES that gave Orange County its name remain. This region south and east of Los Angeles is now ruled by tourism and high-tech business instead of farmers. Angelenos may make cracks about theme parks being the extent of culture here, but there's much more to the area than mouse ears and laid-back beach towns. You can get an evocative dose of history by visiting the 18th-century Mission San Juan Capistrano or find a thriving performing arts center (albeit near the massive shopping center South Coast Plaza). Several major bands got started here, including ska-infected No Doubt, thrash metal Korn, and the punk band Social Distortion. And while local style was long focused on hometown surf-gear companies like Quiksilver and Billabong, its edgier elements mean that Orange County gets profiled in *Vogue*.

With its tropical flowers and palm trees, the stretch of coast between Seal Beach and San Clemente is often called the California Riviera. Exclusive Newport Beach, artsy Laguna, and the up-and-coming surf town of Huntington Beach are the stars, but lesser-known gems on the glistening coast—such as Corona del Mar—are also worth visiting. Offshore, meanwhile, lies gorgeous Catalina Island, a terrific spot for diving, snorkeling, and hiking. And despite a building boom that began in the 1990s, the area is still a place to find wilderness trails, canyons, greenbelts, and national parks.

Some of Orange County's towns are now high-profile, thanks to Fox's spoiled-teen drama *The O.C.* and *Laguna Beach*, MTV's "reality soap." But life here is much more diverse than the McMansion world shown on TV. A strong Mexican influence contributes to the cuisine and architecture; the largest Vietnamese community outside Asia is that of Westminster's Little Saigon. And please don't tell the 3 million locals that they live in a suburb of Los Angeles. Orange County is different, with its own concerns. It's more relaxed, more family oriented, and friendlier. (Not every waiter here is trying to break into the movies.)

About the Hotels & Restaurants

Restaurants in Orange County are often more casual than in L.A. You'll rarely see men in jackets and ties. Of course, there's also a swath of supercasual places along the beachfronts—fish-taco takeout, taquerias, burger joints—that won't mind if you wear flip-flops. Reservations are recommended for the nicest restaurants. Many places don't serve past 11 PM, and locals tend to eat early. Remember that according to California law, smoking is prohibited in all enclosed areas.

Along the coast there's been a small flurry of luxury resort openings in the past few years; Laguna's Montage resort made a big splash in 2003, followed by Newport Beach's Balboa Bay Club and Huntington Beach's Hyatt Regency Resort and Spa. (In most cases, you can take advantage of some of the facilities of such resorts, such as restaurants or spas, without being an overnight guest.) There are also plenty of low-key hotels in the area, and those around the theme parks are very family friendly.
■ TIP→ Prices are often lower in winter, especially near Disneyland, unless there's a convention in Anaheim, and weekend rates are often rock bottom at business hotels. It's worth calling around to search for bargains.

	WHAT IT COSTS				
	$$$$	**$$$**	**$$**	**$**	**¢**
RESTAURANTS	over $32	$22–$32	$12–$22	$7–$12	under $7
HOTELS	over $325	$200–$325	$125–$200	$75–$125	under $75

Restaurant prices are per person for a main course, excluding 8.25% sales tax. Hotel prices are for two people in a standard double room in nonholiday high season on the European Plan (no meals) unless otherwise noted. Taxes (9%–14%) are extra. In listings we always name the facilities available, but we don't specify whether they cost extra. When pricing accommodations, always ask about what's included.

Exploring Orange County

Like Los Angeles, Orange County stretches over a large area, lacks a singular focal point, and has limited public transportation. You'll need a car and a sensible game plan to make the most of your visit. If you're headed to Disneyland, you'll probably want to stay in or near Anaheim and take excursions to the coast. If the Mouse's kingdom is not part of your itinerary, try staying at a midpoint location such as Irvine or Costa Mesa, both equidistant from inland tourist attractions and the coast. These towns are less crowded than Anaheim and less expensive than the beach cities. Of course, if you can afford it, staying at the beach is always recommended.

Numbers in the text correspond to numbers in the margin and on the Orange County map.

Timing

The sun shines year-round in Orange County, though in early summer there are the occasional "June gloom" days, when skies are overcast. Beat the crowds and the heat by visiting in winter, spring, or fall. Smart parents give kids their Disney fix on weekdays or during the winter months whenever possible.

INLAND ORANGE COUNTY

About a 35-minute drive from downtown Los Angeles on I–5 (also known as the Santa Ana Freeway) is Anaheim, Orange County's tourist hub, which centers on the big D. The inland part of the county is often seen as an ever-spreading morass of middle- and upper-middle-class housing developments and strip malls. True, you'll see plenty of indistinguishable tract housing and may wonder how anyone finds the way home. If you get off the freeways, though, you can find diverse and distinctive areas. In the Old Towne section of Orange, for instance, hundreds of antiques and collectibles dealers fill early-20th-century buildings. Little Saigon, a large Vietnamese community with around 3,500 businesses, is between Westminster and Garden Grove. Farther south and inland, the Santiago, Silverado, and Modjeska canyons meander toward the marvelous Cleveland National Forest, which stretches from Orange County to San Diego.

GREAT ITINERARIES

Although you could visit Orange County as a day trip from L.A., it would mean roughly three hours, if not more, in the car. If possible, make a trip here an overnight—at least. With all the beach communities along with the theme parks, you'll have more than enough to keep you busy for a few days.

IF YOU HAVE 1 DAY

Who are we kidding? You're going to **Disneyland** ❶.

IF YOU HAVE 3 DAYS

You're still going to **Disneyland** ❶ (stay overnight in 🏨 **Anaheim**), and if it's up to the kids, you could add **Disney's California Adventure** to the mix and easily devote all three days (and a considerable amount of money) to the Disneyland Resort. If you'd prefer to escape the Magic Kingdom or avoid it altogether, get an early start and head to 🏨 **Laguna Beach** ⓰ before the crowds arrive. Breakfast alfresco and then take a walk on the sand. Afterward, stroll around the local streets lined with boutiques and art galleries or go for a hike in the coastal canyons. If you'd like to splurge on a fancy dinner, this would be the town to do it in. On Day 3, visit **Newport Beach** or **Huntington Beach**; then head inland to **Costa Mesa**, where you can browse through **South Coast Plaza** ❾, one of the world's largest retail, entertainment, and dining complexes, or visit the smaller nearby shopping centers. Alternatively, catch an early boat out to **Catalina Island** for the day.

7

Disneyland Resort

26 mi southeast of Los Angeles, via I–5.

The snowcapped Matterhorn, the centerpiece of the Magic Kingdom, punctuates the skyline of **Anaheim.** Since 1955, when Walt Disney chose this once-quiet farming community for the site of his first amusement park, Disneyland has attracted more than 450 million visitors and thousands of workers, and Anaheim has been their host. To understand the symbiotic relationship between Disneyland and Anaheim, you need only look at the $4.2 billion spent in a combined effort by the Walt Disney Company and Anaheim, the latter to revitalize the city's tourist center and run-down areas, the former to expand and renovate the Disney properties into

KATHY'S TOP 5

- **Catalina Island,** a short ferry ride and you'll feel 1,000 miles away.

- **Disneyland,** the first is still the best.

- **Huntington Beach** for surfing, even if you're just watching.

- **Laguna Beach,** for its beautiful cove and canyon, art galleries, and spectacular resort hotels.

- **Mission San Juan Capistrano** for an evocative look into southern California's colonial history.

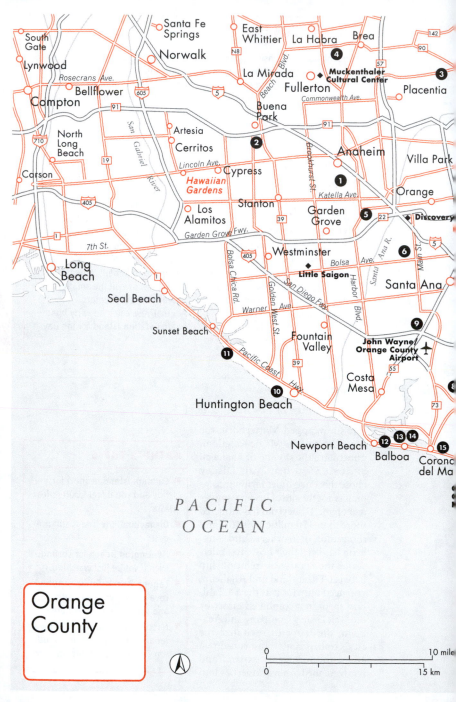

Orange
County

PACIFIC
OCEAN

0 _____ 10 mile
0 _____ 15 km

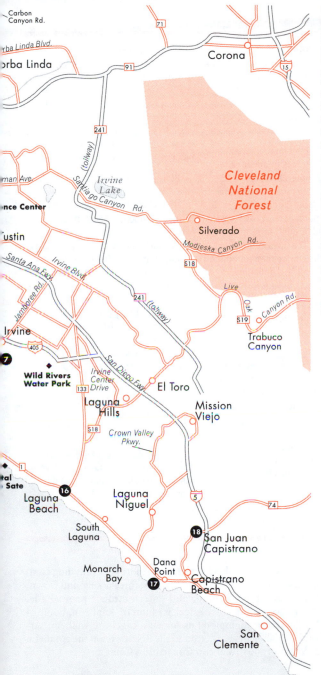

Disney Strategies

ON YOUR MARK, get set . . . a trip to Disneyland Resort gets the adrenaline pumping, but to most enjoy your visit, study these helpful tips. If you're traveling with children, check out the book *Fodor's Disneyland & Southern California with Kids* for more practical advice.

■ **Buy entry tickets in advance.** Many nearby hotels sell park admission tickets; you can also buy them through the Disney Web site. If you book a package deal, such as those offered through AAA, tickets are included, too. The lines at the ticket booths can take more than an hour on busy days, so you'll definitely save time by buying in advance.

■ **Come midweek.** Weekends, especially in summer, are a mob scene. A winter weekday is often the least crowded time to visit.

■ **Plan your times to hit the most popular rides.** If you're at the park when the gates open, make a beeline for the top rides before the crowds reach critical mass. Another good time to avoid lines is in the evening, when the hordes thin out somewhat, and during a parade or other show. Save the quieter attractions for midafternoon.

■ **Look into Fastpasses.** These passes allow you to reserve your place in line at some of the most crowded attractions (only one at a time). Distribution machines are posted near the entrances of each attraction. Feed in your park admission ticket, and you'll receive a pass with a printed time frame (generally up to 1–1½ hours later) during which you can return to wait in a much shorter line.

■ **Plan your meals to avoid peak mealtime crowds.** Start the day with a big breakfast so you won't be too hungry at noon, when restaurants and vendors get swarmed. Wait to have lunch until after 1. If you want to eat at the **Blue Bayou** in New Orleans Square, it's best to make reservations in person as soon as you get to the park. Another (cheaper) option is to bring your own food. There are areas with picnic tables set up for this. And it's always a good idea to bring water and a few nonmeltable snacks with you.

■ **Check the daily events schedule.** During parades, fireworks, and other special events, sections of the parks clog with crowds. This can work for you or against you. An event could make it difficult to get around a park–but if you plan ahead, you can take advantage of the distraction to hit popular rides.

what is known now as **Disneyland Resort.** The resort is a sprawling complex that includes Disney's two amusement parks; three hotels; and Downtown Disney, a shopping, dining, and entertainment promenade. Anaheim's tourist center includes Angel Stadium of Anaheim, home of baseball's World Series Champion Los Angeles Angels of Anaheim; Arrowhead Pond, which hosts concerts and the hockey team the Anaheim Ducks; and the enormous Anaheim Convention Center.

Fodor'sChoice
★

① One of the biggest misconceptions people have about **Disneyland** is that they've "been there, done that" if they've visited either Florida's mammoth Walt Disney World or one of the Disney parks overseas. But Disneyland, opened in 1955 and the only one of the kingdoms to be overseen by Walt himself, has a genuine historic feel and occupies a unique place in the Disney legend. There's plenty here that you won't find anywhere else: for example, Storybook Land, with its miniature replicas of animated Disney scenes from classics such as *Pinocchio; Alice in Wonderland*; and the Indiana Jones Adventure ride.

The eight themed lands here comprise more than 60 major rides, 50 shops, and 30 restaurants. You enter the park through a re-created 19th-century railroad station, which opens onto **Main Street, U.S.A.** Walt's hometown of Marceline, Missouri, was the inspiration behind this romanticized image of small-town America, circa 1900. Trolleys, double-decker buses, and horse-drawn wagons travel up and down the scaled-down thoroughfare, and the sidewalks are lined with rows of shops selling everything from crystal ware to sports memorabilia to photo supplies. ■ **TIP→** Main Street opens half an hour before the rest of the park, so it's a good place to explore if you're getting an early start to beat the crowds. If you want to save some of the walking for later, board the Disneyland Railroad at the park entrance; it tours all the lands.

Directly across from Main Street, Sleeping Beauty's Castle marks the entrance to **Fantasyland,** where you can fly on Peter Pan's Flight, take an aerial spin with Dumbo the Flying Elephant, bobsled through the **Matterhorn,** and float through It's a Small World. Fantasyland Theater has *Snow White,* a free musical that's geared to younger children. The steamboat *Mark Twain* and the sailing ship *Columbia* both set sail from **Frontierland,** where you can also raft to **Tom Sawyer Island** for an hour or so of climbing and exploring.

Inspired by some of the more exotic corners of the world, **Adventureland** is home to the popular **Jungle Cruise** and the **Indiana Jones Adventure,** which has special effects and decipherable hieroglyphics to distract you while you're standing in line. **Critter Country,** populated by animated bears, is where to find **Splash Mountain,** Disney's steepest, wettest adventure. In **Tomorrowland,** you can ride on the futuristic Astro Orbitor rockets, race through **Space Mountain,** tinker with the toys of tomorrow at Innoventions, and zap your neighbors with laser beams in the interactive **Buzz Lightyear Astro Blasters.** ■ **TIP→** Kids love getting soaked on rides like Splash Mountain and the Cosmic Wave. Either save these for the end of the day, bring a change of clothes, or expect to shell out for dry (and pricey) T-shirts.

Dixieland musicians play in the twisting streets of **New Orleans Square,** where you'll find theme shops selling everything from hats to gourmet foods. This is also where to catch the always-popular **Pirates of the Caribbean** and **Haunted Mansion** rides. (Pirates now has a Jack Sparrow character.) **Mickey's Toontown** is a land where kids feel like they're

7

actually in a cartoon. They can climb up a rope ladder on the *Miss Daisy* (Donald Duck's boat), walk through Mickey's House to meet the famous mouse, and take a spin on the **Roger Rabbit Car Toon Spin.**

Besides the eight lands, the daily live-action shows and parades are always crowd pleasers. **Fantasmic!** is a musical, fireworks, and laser show in which Mickey and friends wage a spellbinding battle against Disneyland's darker characters; and the daytime and nighttime Parade of Dreams features just about every animated Disney character ever drawn. ■ **TIP→** Arrive early to secure a good view; if there are two shows scheduled for the day, the second one tends to be less crowded. A fireworks display sparks up Friday and Saturday evenings. Brochures with maps, available at the entrance, list show- and parade times.

Characters appear for autographs and photos throughout the day; guidebooks at the entrances give times and places. You can also meet some of the animated icons at one of the character meals served at the three Disney hotels (open to the public).

You can store belongings in lockers just off Main Street; purchases can also be sent to the package pickup desk, at the front of the park. Main Street stays open an hour after the attractions close, so you may want to save your shopping for the end of your visit. ■ **TIP→** If you plan to visit for more than a day, you can save money by buying three- and four-day Park Hopper tickets that grant same-day "hopping" privileges between Disneyland and Disney's California Adventure. ✉ *1313 Harbor Blvd., Anaheim* ☎ *714/781–4565* ⊕ *www.disneyland.com* ✉ *$59* ◷ *Daily year-round; longer hrs weekends, holidays, and summer. Call for specific times.*

> Walt Disney himself would sometimes stay in an apartment over Main Street's fire station. Now a light always stays on in the apartment's window in his honor.

★ ☾ The sprawling 55-acre **Disney's California Adventure,** right next to Disneyland (their entrances face each other), pays tribute to the Golden State with four theme areas. **Paradise Pier** re-creates the glory days of California's seaside piers. If you're looking for thrills, the **California Screamin'** roller coaster takes its riders from 0 to 55 mph in about four seconds and proceeds through scream tunnels, steeply angled drops, and a 360-degree loop. The Sun Wheel, a giant Ferris wheel, provides a good view of the grounds at a more leisurely pace.

At the **Hollywood Pictures Backlot,** Disney Animation gives you an insider's look at the work of animators and how they create characters. **Turtle Talk with Crush** lets kids have an unrehearsed talk with computer-animated Crush, a sea turtle from *Finding Nemo.* The Hyperion theater hosts **Aladdin—A Musical Spectacular,** a 45-minute live performance with terrific visual effects. ■ **TIP→** Plan on getting in line about an hour in advance: the show is well worth the wait. On the latest film-inspired ride, **Monsters, Inc. Mike & Sulley to the Rescue,** you climb into taxis and travel the streets of Monstropolis on a mission of safely returning Boo to her bedroom. A major draw for older kids is the looming *Twilight Zone Tower of Terror,* which drops riders 13 floors.

A bug's land, inspired by the 1998 film *A Bug's Life,* skews its attractions to an insect's point of view. Kids can cool off (or get soaked) in the water jets and giant garden hose of Princess Dot Puddle Park, or hit the pill bug–shaped bumper cars. The short show *It's Tough to Be a Bug!* gives you a 3-D look at insect life.

Golden State celebrates California's history and natural beauty with six regions, including the Bay Area, Pacific Wharf, and Condor Flats, where you can enjoy Soarin' Over California, a spectacular simulated hang-glider ride over California terrain. The film *Golden Dreams* is a senti-mental dash through California history with Whoopi Goldberg. There's also a working 1-acre farm and winery, a 40,000-square-foot anima-tion exhibit, Broadway-style theater, nature trail, and tortilla factory. Like its sister park, California Adventure has a parade every day. ✉ *1313 Harbor Blvd., Anaheim* ☎ *714/781–4565* ⊕ *www.disneyland.com* 🖃 *$59* ⊙ *Daily year-round; longer hrs weekends, holidays, and sum-mer. Call for specific times.*

Downtown Disney is a 20-acre promenade of dining, shopping, and en-tertainment that connects the Disneyland Resort hotels and theme parks. Restaurant-nightclubs here include the **House of Blues,** which spices up its Delta-inspired ribs and seafood with various live music acts on an in-timate two-story stage. At **Ralph Brennan's Jazz Kitchen** you can dig into New Orleans–style food and music. Sports fans gravitate to **ESPN Zone,** a sports bar–restaurant–entertainment center with American grill food, interactive video games, and 175 video screens telecasting worldwide sports events. There's also an **AMC** multiplex movie theater with stadium-style seating that plays the latest blockbusters and, naturally, a couple of kids' flicks. Promenade shops sell everything from Disney goods to fine art. ✉ *Disneyland Dr. between Ball Rd. and Katella Ave., Anaheim* ☎ *714/300–7800* ⊕ *www.disneyland.com* 🖃 *Free* ⊙ *Daily 7 AM–2 AM; hrs at shops and restaurants vary.*

Where to Stay & Eat

The Anaheim area has more than 50,000 rooms in hotels, family-style inns, and RV parks. ■ **TIP→ One handy perk of staying in a Disney hotel: you can charge anything you buy in either park, such as food and souvenirs, to your room, so you don't have to carry around a lot of cash. (This doesn't hold true for Downtown Disney, though.)**

An Anaheim Resort Transit (ART) bus can take you around town for $3. The buses run every 10 minutes during peak times, 20 minutes oth-erwise. They go between major hotels, Disney attractions, the Anaheim Convention Center, and restaurants and shops. See the ART Web site (www.rideart.org) for more information. In addition, many hotels are within walking distance of the Disneyland Resort.

Unlike Disneyland, which is dry, Disney's California Adventure has restaurants that serve beer and wine. In addition, a small winery there has grapevines growing on the hillside and illustrations showing the trans-formation from grapes to wine.

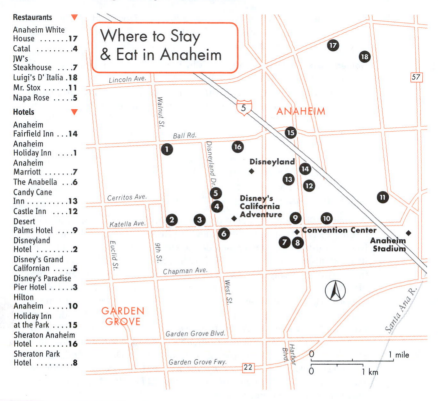

Where to Stay & Eat in Anaheim

$$$–$$$$ ✕ **Anaheim White House.** Several small dining rooms are set with crisp linens and candles in this flower-filled 1909 mansion. The northern Italian menu includes pasta, rack of lamb, and a large selection of fresh seafood. A three-course prix-fixe lunch, served weekdays, costs $16. ✉ *887 S. Anaheim Blvd., Anaheim* ☎ *714/772–1381* ▭ *AE, MC, V* ☉ *No lunch weekends.*

★ **$$$–$$$$** ✕ **Napa Rose.** In sync with its host hotel, this restaurant is done in a lovely Arts and Crafts style. The contemporary cuisine here is matched with an extensive wine list (600 bottles on display). For a look into the open kitchen, sit at the counter and watch the chefs as they whip up signature dishes such as Gulf of California rock scallops in a sauce of lemon, lobster, and vanilla and spit-roasted prime rib of pork with ranch-style black beans. A four-course prix-fixe menu ($75 without wine, $120 with wine) changes weekly. ✉ *Grand Californian Hotel, 1600 S. Disneyland Dr.* ☎ *714/300–7170* ▭ *AE, D, DC, MC, V.*

$$–$$$$ ✕ **JW's Steakhouse.** This subdued steak house inside the Anaheim Marriott specializes in aged beef but also serves seafood. The clubby, gentleman's library–style room has sectioned-off dining booths. The extensive wine list includes some double bottles. ✉ *700 W. Convention Way, Anaheim* ☎ *714/750–8000* ▭ *AE, D, DC, MC, V* ☉ *No lunch.*

$$–$$$$ ✗ **Mr. Stox.** Intimate booths and linen tablecloths create an elegant setting at this family-owned restaurant. Prime rib, mesquite-grilled rack of lamb, and fresh fish specials are excellent; the pasta, bread, and pastries are made in-house; and the wine list is wide-ranging. ✉ *1105 E. Katella Ave., Anaheim* ☎ *714/634–2994* ▭ *AE, D, DC, MC, V* ◷ *No lunch weekends.*

$$–$$$ ✗ **Catal Restaurant & Uva Bar.** Famed chef Joachim Splichal takes a more casual approach at this bilevel Mediterranean spot—with tapas breaking into the finger-food territory. At the Uva (Spanish for "grape") bar on the ground level you can graze on olives and Spanish ham, choosing from 40 wines by the glass. Upstairs, Catal's menu spans paella, rotisserie chicken, and salads. ✉ *1580 Disneyland Dr., Suite 103, Downtown Disney* ☎ *714/774–4442* ▭ *AE, D, DC, MC, V.*

$–$$ ✗ **Luigi's D'Italia.** Despite the simple surroundings—red vinyl booths and plastic checkered tablecloths—Luigi's serves outstanding Italian cuisine: spaghetti marinara, cioppino, and all the classics. Kids will feel right at home here; there's even a children's menu. ✉ *801 S. State College Blvd., Anaheim* ☎ *714/490–0990* ▭ *AE, D, DC, MC, V.*

$$$–$$$$
Fodor'sChoice
★ 🏨 **Disney's Grand Californian.** The newest of Disney's Anaheim hotels, this Craftsman-style luxury property has guest rooms with views of the California Adventure park and Downtown Disney. They don't push the Disney brand too heavily; rooms are done in dark woods with amber-shaded lamps and just a small Bambi image on the shower curtain. Restaurants include the Napa Rose dining room, Hearthstone Lounge, and Storytellers Cafe, where Disney characters entertain children at breakfast. Of the three pools, the one shaped like Mickey Mouse is just for kids, and there's an evening child activity center. Room-and-ticket packages are available; the hotel has its own entry gate to California Adventure. The new Mandara spa has a couple's suite with Balinese-inspired art and textiles. ✉ *1600 S. Disneyland Dr., Disneyland Resort, 92803* ☎ *714/956–6425* 🖷 *714/300–7701* ⊕ *www.disneyland.com* 📨 *701 rooms, 44 suites* ⌕ *2 restaurants, room service, in-room safes, minibars, cable TV, in-room broadband, pool, health club, hot tub, 2 lounges, video game room, shop, children's programs (ages 5–12), dry cleaning, laundry service, concierge, business services, parking (fee); no smoking* ▭ *AE, D, DC, MC, V.*

$$$–$$$$ 🏨 **Hilton Anaheim.** Next to the Anaheim Convention Center, this busy Hilton is the largest hotel in southern California: it even has its own post office, as well as shops, restaurants, and cocktail lounges. Rooms are pleasingly bright, and a shuttle runs to Disneyland, or you can walk the few blocks. Special summer children's programs include the "Vacation Station Lending Desk," with games, toys, and books, as well as children's menus. There's a $12 fee to use the health club. ✉ *777 Convention Way, Downtown Anaheim, 92802* ☎ *714/750–4321 or 800/445–8667* 🖷 *714/740–4460* ⊕ *www.anaheim.hilton.com* 📨 *1,492 rooms, 95 suites* ⌕ *4 restaurants, room service, cable TV with movies, Wi-Fi, pool, health club, hot tub, massage, sauna, 2 lounges, piano, children's programs (ages 3–12), laundry service, concierge, business services, meeting rooms, car rental, travel services, parking (fee), no-smoking floor* ▭ *AE, D, DC, MC, V.*

7

$$$ 🏨 **Disneyland Hotel.** Not surprisingly, the first of Disney's three hotels is the one most full of Magic Kingdom magic, with Disney-theme memorabilia and Disney music. Check out the Peter Pan–theme pool, with its wooden bridge, 110-foot waterslide, and relaxing whirlpool. The cove pools' sandy shores are great for sunning and playing volleyball. East-facing

rooms in the Sierra Tower have the best views of the park, while west-facing rooms look over gardens. At Goofy's Kitchen, kids can dine with Disney characters. Room-and-ticket packages are available. ⊠ *1150 Magic Way, Disneyland Resort, 92802* ☎ *714/778–6600* 🖷 *714/956–6582* ⊕ *www.disneyland.com* ⇨ *990 rooms, 62 suites* ⌂ *5 restaurants, café, room service, in-room safes, minibars, cable TV, in-room broadband, 3 pools, health club, hot tub, massage, sauna, spa, beach, 2 bars, video game room, children's programs (ages 5–12), laundry service, concierge, business services, airport shuttle, car rental, parking (fee); no smoking* 🖃 *AE, D, DC, MC, V.*

$$$ 🏨 **Disney's Paradise Pier Hotel.** The Paradise Pier has many of the same Disney touches as the Disneyland Hotel, but it's a bit quieter and tamer. From here you can walk to Disneyland or pick up a shuttle or monorail. SoCal style manifests itself in seafoam-green guest rooms with lamps shaped like lifeguard stands, and surfboard motifs. A new wooden roller-coaster-inspired waterslide takes adventurers to a high-speed splashdown. Room-and-ticket packages are available. ⊠ *1717 S. Disneyland Dr., Disneyland Resort, 92802* ☎ *714/999–0990* 🖷 *714/776–5763* ⊕ *www.disneyland.com* ⇨ *502 rooms, 38 suites* ⌂ *3 restaurants, room service, in-room safes, minibars, cable TV, in-room broadband pool, wading pool, health club, 2 lounges, video game room, children's programs (ages 5–12), dry cleaning, laundry service, concierge, business services, parking (fee); no smoking* 🖃 *AE, D, DC, MC, V.*

$$–$$$ 🏨 **Anaheim Marriott.** Rooms at this busy convention hotel are well equipped for business travelers, with desks, two phones, and data ports. Some rooms have balconies. Discounted weekend and Disneyland packages are available. ⊠ *700 W. Convention Way, Anaheim 92802* ☎ *714/750–8000 or 800/228–9290* 🖷 *714/750–9100* ⊕ *www.marriott.com* ⇨ *1,031 rooms, 52 suites* ⌂ *2 restaurants, room service, in-room safes, cable TV with movies, in-room data ports, 2 pools, health club, 2 hot tubs, lounge, piano, video game room, laundry facilities, laundry service, concierge, meeting rooms, car rental, parking (fee), some pets allowed (fee), no-smoking floors, Internet* 🖃 *AE, D, DC, MC, V.*

★ $$–$$$ 🏨 **Sheraton Anaheim Hotel.** If you're hoping to escape from the commercial atmosphere of the hotels near Disneyland, consider this sprawling replica of a Tudor castle. In the flower- and plant-filled lobby you're welcome to sit by the grand fireplace, watching fish swim around in a pond. Rooms are sizable; some first-floor rooms open onto interior gardens and a pool area. A shuttle to Disneyland is available. ⊠ *900 S. Disneyland Dr., Anaheim 92802* ☎ *714/778–1700 or 800/325–3535* 🖷 *714/*

535–3889 ⊕ www.starwoodhotels.com ⌦ 447 rooms, 26 suites
⌂ Restaurant, café, room service, cable TV with movies and video
games, in-room data ports, pool, health club, outdoor hot tub, bar, video
game room, laundry facilities, laundry service, meeting rooms, parking
(fee), no-smoking rooms ▭ AE, D, DC, MC, V.

$–$$ ▥ **The Anabella.** This Spanish Mission–style hotel is across from Dis-
neyland Resort on the convention center campus. The hotel's Oasis, with
a hot tub and pool, plus an adults-only pool, is a perfect place for relaxing. The Tangerine Grill and Patio serves a fantastic tangerine cheesecake. ⊠ 1030 W. Katella Ave., Anaheim 92802 ☎ 714/905–1050 or
800/863–4888 🖷 714/905–1054 ⊕ www.anabellahotel.com ⌦ 359
rooms ⌂ Restaurant, room service, in-room safes, refrigerators, TV with
movies and video games, in-room data ports, 2 pools, health club, outdoor hot tub, lounge, laundry facilities, laundry service, concierge floor,
business services, free parking ▭ AE, D, DC, MC, V.

★ $–$$ ▥ **Candy Cane Inn.** One of the Disneyland area's first hotels (deeds were
executed Christmas Eve, hence the name), the Candy Cane is one of Anaheim's most relaxing properties. Rooms are spacious and understated,
while the palm-fringed pool is especially inviting. The hotel is just steps
from the Disneyland parking lot. A free Disneyland shuttle runs every
half hour. ⊠ 1747 S. Harbor Blvd., Anaheim 92802 ☎ 714/774–5284
or 800/345–7057 🖷 714/772–5462 ⊕ www.candycaneinn.net ⌦ 170
rooms ⌂ Refrigerators, cable TV, pool, wading pool, outdoor hot tub,
laundry facilities, laundry service, free parking, no-smoking rooms
▭ AE, D, DC, MC, V ⏐⊙⏐ CP.

$–$$ ▥ **Holiday Inn Anaheim at the Park.** Families frequent this Mediter-
ranean-style hotel. Some rooms have separate sitting areas. ⊠ 1221 S.
Harbor Blvd., Anaheim 92805 ☎ 714/758–0900 or 800/545–7275
🖷 714/533–1804 ⊕ www.holiday-inn.com ⌦ 252 rooms, 2 suites
⌂ Restaurant, room service, cable TV with movies and video games,
in-room data ports, pool, outdoor hot tub, bar, video game room, meeting rooms, free parking, no-smoking floor ▭ AE, D, DC, MC, V.

$–$$ ▥ **Sheraton Park Hotel at the Anaheim Resort.** Sheraton took over this hotel
in 2006 and freshened up the decor in guest rooms and public spaces.
Rooms have balconies, and those in the tower have good views of Disneyland's summer fireworks shows. You can also relax in the nicely landscaped outdoor area or take a dip in the oversize pool. ⊠ 1855 S.
Harbor Blvd., Anaheim 92802 ☎ 714/750–1811 or 800/716–6199
🖷 714/971–3626 ⊕ www.sheraton.com ⌦ 490 rooms ⌂ Restaurant,
coffee shop, room service, refrigerators, cable TV with movies and
video games, in-room broadband, pool, outdoor hot tub, lounge, laundry service, meeting room, car rental, parking (fee), no-smoking floor
▭ AE, D, DC, MC, V.

$ ▥ **Anaheim Fairfield Inn by Marriott.** A chain hotel with character, the
Anaheim Fairfield provides friendly, detail-oriented service and spacious rooms, most with sleeper sofas as well as beds. A five-minute walk
gets you to Disneyland. In summer keep an eye out for the magician who
roams the premises, entertaining adults and kids alike. ⊠ 1460 S. Harbor Blvd., Anaheim 92802 ☎ 714/772–6777 or 800/228–2800 🖷 714/
999–1727 ⊕ www.marriott.com ⌦ 467 rooms ⌂ Restaurant, room service, some microwaves, refrigerators, cable TV with movies, pool, out-

7

door hot tub, recreation room, travel services, free parking, no-smoking floor ▭ *AE, D, DC, MC, V.*

$ 🏨 **Castle Inn and Suites.** Faux-stone trim and towers, shield decor, and replica gas lamps dress up the Castle Inn, which is across the street from Disneyland. Suites have microwaves. ✉ *1734 S. Harbor Blvd., Anaheim 92802* ☎ *714/774–8111* 🖶 *714/956–4736* ⊕ *www.castleinn.com* 📮 *150 rooms, 50 suites* ♿ *Some in-room hot tubs, some microwaves, refrigerators, cable TV, pool, wading pool, outdoor hot tub, laundry facilities, laundry service, free parking, no-smoking rooms* ▭ *AE, D, DC, MC, V.*

$ 🏨 **Desert Palms Hotel and Suites.** This hotel midway between Disneyland and the convention center is a great value, with some $79 one-bedroom suites that can accommodate a group of four or more. Book well in advance, especially when large conventions are in town. ✉ *631 W. Katella Ave., Anaheim 92802* ☎ *714/535–1133 or 888/788–0596* 🖶 *714/491–7409* ⊕ *www.desertpalmshotel.com* 📮 *50 rooms, 50 suites* ♿ *Refrigerators, cable TV with movies, in-room broadband, pool, outdoor hot tub, video game room, laundry facilities, laundry service, free parking; no smoking* ▭ *AE, D, DC, MC, V* 🍴 *CP.*

¢–$ 🏨 **Anaheim Holiday Inn.** The warmth of Old California is found in this Holiday Inn, where the walls are furnished with historic photos and water paths snake through the grounds. The residential location makes for quiet evenings. ✉ *1240 S. Walnut Ave., Anaheim 92802* ☎ *714/535–0300 or 800/824–5459* 🖶 *714/491–8953* ⊕ *www.holidayinn-anaheim.com* 📮 *255 rooms, 28 suites* ♿ *Restaurant, room service, some microwaves, cable TV, pool, exercise equipment, outdoor hot tub, bar, video game room, laundry service, business services, meeting rooms, free parking, no-smoking rooms* ▭ *AE, D, DC, MC, V.*

Nightlife

★ The little red roadhouse known as the **Doll Hut** (✉ 107 S. Adams, Anaheim ☎ 714/533–1286) was once a truck stop between L.A. and San Diego. Southern California music booster Linda Jemison then turned it into a great place to hear about-to-break bands. In 2001 she turned it over to new owners, who are maintaining its rep for supporting up-and-comers and those below industry radar. Rockabilly, big-band, punk—no matter what kind of show is appearing, it will have a low cover.

Grove of Anaheim (✉ 2200 E. Katella Ave. ☎ 714/712–2700 ⊕ www. thegroveofanaheim.com) is a midsize concert venue, which means nearly every seat is a good one. It books all kinds of bands and the occasional comedy act; the Gipsy Kings, Modest Mouse, Willie Nelson, and Blondie have all hit the stage here.

At the **House of Blues** (☎ 714/778–2583 ⊕ www.hob.com), in the Downtown Disney promenade, you can catch some of the best bands from the 1980s and '90s for a relatively low cover. The Southern-style restaurant has the fun Sunday Gospel Brunch. Shows often sell out, so call ahead.

Sports

Pro baseball's **Los Angeles Angels of Anaheim** play at **Angel Stadium Anaheim** (✉ 2000 State College Blvd., East Anaheim ☎ 714/634–2000 ⊕ www.angelsbaseball.com). An "Outfield Extravaganza" celebrates great plays on the field, with fireworks and a geyser exploding over a model evoking the California coast. The National Hockey League's **Anaheim Ducks** play at **Arrowhead Pond** (✉ 2695 E. Katella Ave., East Anaheim ☎ 714/704–2400 ⊕ www.mightyducks.com).

Knott's Berry Farm

25 mi south of Los Angeles, via I–5, in Buena Park

The land where the boysenberry was invented (by crossing red raspberry, blackberry, and loganberry bushes) is now occupied by Knott's Berry Farm. You can see the park in a day, but plan to start early and finish fairly late. Traffic can be heavy, so factor in time for delays. ■ TIP→ It's a good idea to confirm the park's opening hours, which change relatively often.

★ ☻ ❷ **Knott's Berry Farm** got its start in 1934, when Cordelia Knott began serving chicken dinners on her wedding china to supplement her family's income. Or so the story goes. The dinners and her boysenberry pies proved more profitable than husband Walter's berry farm, so the two moved first into the restaurant business and then into the entertainment business. The park is now a 150-acre complex with 100-plus rides and dozens of restaurants and shops. While it has some good attractions for small children, the park is best known for its roster of awesome thrill rides. And, yes, you can still get that boysenberry pie (and jam, juice—you name it.)

Old West Ghost Town is made up of authentic old buildings relocated from their original mining-town sites. You can stroll down the street, stop and chat with the blacksmith, pan for gold, crack open a geode, ride in an authentic 1880s passenger train, or take the **Gold Mine** ride and descend into a replica of a working gold mine. A real treasure here is the antique Dentzel carousel. **GhostRider** towers over it all; it's Orange County's first wooden roller coaster. Traveling up to 56 mph and reaching 118 feet at its highest point, the coaster is riddled with sudden dips and curves, subjecting riders to forces up to three times that of gravity. The **Timber Mountain Log Ride** is a worthwhile flume ride, especially if you're with kids who don't make the height requirements for the flumes at Disneyland.

Smaller fry will want to head straight for **Camp Snoopy,** a miniature High Sierra wonderland where the *Peanuts* gang hangs out. At nearby **Big Foot Rapids** you can ride white water in an inner tube. At the **Boardwalk,** you'll find the *Boomerang* roller coaster and the **Perilous Plunge,** billed as the world's tallest, steepest, and—thanks to its big splash—wettest thrill ride. The 1950s hot rod–theme **Xcelerator** launches you hydraulically into a superslow U-turn, topping out at 205 feet. On the Western-theme **Silver Bullet,** riders are sent to a height of 146 feet and then back down 109 feet. Riders spiral, corkscrew, fly into a cobra roll, and experience overbanked curves. It's not for the squeamish. Over in **Fiesta Village** are two more musts for adrenaline junkies: **Montezooma's Revenge,** a roller coaster that goes from 0 to 55 mph in less than five seconds, and **Jaguar!** which simulates the motions of a cat stalking its prey, twisting, spiraling, and speeding up and slowing down as it takes you on its stomach-dropping course.

Knott's Soak City Water Park is directly across from the main park and is on 13 acres in front of Independence Hall. It has 21 major water

7

rides; the latest is **Pacific Spin,** an oversize water slide that drops riders 75 feet into a catch pool. Soak City is only open late May through late September.

■ **TIP➜** **If you think you'll only need a few hours at the main park, you can save significant money by coming after 4 PM, when admission fees drop to $22.50. This deal is offered year-round.** ✉ *8039 Beach Blvd., Buena Park, between La Palma Ave. and Crescent St., 2 blocks south of Hwy. 91* ☎ *714/220–5200* ⊕ *www.knotts. com* ✑ *$45* ⌚ *June–mid-Sept., daily 9 AM–midnight; mid-Sept.–May, weekdays 10–6, Sat. 10–10, Sun. 10–7; closed during inclement weather.*

> ### SCARY FARM
>
> In October, Knott's shifts into Scary Farm gear at night. To celebrate Halloween, the attractions take on scary new guises, with prowling costumed cast members out to spook you. They go all out to creep you out, so the Scary Farm is not recommended for kids under 13.

Where to Stay & Eat

$$$$ ✕ **Pirate's Dinner Adventure.** During this interactive pirate-theme dinner show, 150 actors/singers/acrobats (some quite talented) perform on a galleon while you eat a three-course meal. Food is mediocre and seating is tight, but kids love making a lot of noise to cheer on their favorite pirate. ✉ *7600 Beach Blvd., Buena Park* ☎ *866/439–2469* ▭ *AE, D, MC, V.*

$$ ✕ **Mrs. Knott's Chicken Dinner Restaurant.** Cornelia Knott's fried chicken and boysenberry pies drew crowds so big that Knott's Berry Farm was built to keep the hungry customers occupied while they waited. The restaurant's current incarnation (outside the park's entrance) still serves crispy fried chicken, along with tangy coleslaw, and Mrs. Knott's signature chilled cherry-rhubarb compote. Long lines on weekends may make eating here not worth your time. ✉ *Knott's Berry Farm, 8039 Beach Blvd., Buena Park* ☎ *714/220–5080* ▭ *AE, D, DC, MC, V.*

$-$$ ▥ **Knott's Berry Farm Resort Hotel.** The only hotel on the Knott's Berry Farm grounds has family-oriented "camp rooms" that are decorated in a Camp Snoopy motif. Shuttle service to Disneyland and nearby golf courses is available. Ask about packages that include entry to Knott's Berry Farm. ✉ *7675 Crescent Ave., Buena Park 90620* ☎ *714/995–1111* 🖷 *714/828–8590* ⊕ *www.radisson.com* ⇜ *320 rooms, 16 suites* ♨ *Restaurant, room service, cable TV with movies and video games, Wi-Fi, tennis court, pool, health club, hot tub, basketball, bar, video game room, laundry facilities, concierge* ▭ *AE, D, DC, MC, V.*

Yorba Linda, La Habra & Brea

7–12 mi north of Anaheim, via Hwy. 57.

Clustered together just north of Anaheim, these quiet suburban towns are characterized by lush parks and family-oriented shopping centers with huge movie theaters. The redevelopment of downtown Brea has brought shopping, dining, and entertainment to the Birch Street Promenade. After 20 years of redevelopment projects, Old Towne Fullerton now has more than 70 restored historic houses, restaurants, and shops; tree-lined walkways; and lots of free parking. Away from the town center, house styles become more varied, incorporating Victorian up through Moderne touches.

3 Yorba Linda's main claim to fame is the **Richard Nixon Presidential Library and Birthplace,** final resting place of the 37th president and his wife, Pat. Exhibits illustrate the checkered career of Nixon, from heralded leader of the free world to beleaguered resignee. You can listen to the so-called smoking-gun tape from the Watergate days, among other recorded material. Life-size sculptures of foreign world leaders, gifts Nixon received from international heads of state, and a large graffiti-covered section of the Berlin Wall are on display. You can also visit Pat Nixon's tranquil rose garden and the small farmhouse where Richard Nixon was born in 1913. Don't miss the bookstore, selling everything from birdhouses to photos of Nixon with Elvis. ⊠ *18001 Yorba Linda Blvd., at Imperial Hwy., Yorba Linda* ☎ *714/993–3393* ⊕ *www.nixonlibrary.org* ⊡ *$8* ☾ *Mon.–Sat. 10–5, Sun. 11–5.*

4 The **Children's Museum at La Habra** is in a 1923-vintage Union Pacific railroad depot, with old railroad cars resting nearby. The hands-on exhibits here are for children from preschool to fourth grade. They can ride a kid-size carousel, watch five railroad trains, or drive a bus. The park next door has tables for bring-your-own picnics. ⊠ *301 S. Euclid St., La Habra* ☎ *562/905–9793* ⊕ *www.lhcm.org* ⊡ *$5* ☾ *Mon.–Sat. 10–5, Sun. 1–5.*

The 18-room Italian Renaissance–style mansion that's now the **Muckenthaler Cultural Center** offers year-round art exhibits from the California Watercolorist Finalists to paintings of autos. A new repertory theater presents plays in summer and cabaret the rest of the year. ⊠ *1201 W. Malvern Ave., Fullerton* ☎ *714/738–6595* ⊕ *www.muckenthaler.org* ⊡ *Free* ☾ *Wed.–Sun. noon–4.*

Where to Eat

$$$$ ✕ **La Vie en Rose.** It's worth the detour to Brea to sample the traditional French cuisine served in this faux Norman farmhouse. The menu hits many familiar favorites like onion soup and steak au poivre, but you can also find Normandy's characteristic ingredients: shellfish, apples, and rich, creamy sauces. For dessert, try the apple tart or Grand Marnier soufflé. ⊠ *240 S. State College Blvd., across from Brea mall, Brea* ☎ *714/529–8333* ▭ *AE, MC, V* ☾ *Closed Sun.*

$$–$$$ ✕ **The Cellar.** Choosing a vintage to pair with your classic panfried Dover sole with lemon-caper butter sauce or your veal Oscar with crabmeat and asparagus might prove a formidable task here. True to its name, the stone-walled underground French restaurant has one of the finest wine collections in the West, with more than 1,400 vintages from 15 countries. ⊠ *305 N. Harbor Blvd., Fullerton* ☎ *714/525–5682* ▭ *AE, D, DC, MC, V* ☾ *Closed Sun. and Mon. No lunch.*

Garden Grove & Orange

South of Anaheim, via I–5 to Hwy. 22.

The city of Orange started as a legal fee; the parcel of land that became the town center was given to a pair of lawyers as payment for services back in 1871. The town square they staked out is now Orange Plaza (or Orange Circle, as locals call it), the heart of **Old Towne Orange,** around the intersection of Glassell Street and Chapman Avenue. ■ TIP➔ **The area is a must-stop for antiques browsers and architecture aficionados. You can scout out everything from antique armoires to flapper-era accessories to 1950s toys.** So vintage is this area that movies like *That Thing You Do!* (early roles for Liv Tyler and Charlize Theron) and *First Daughter* were filmed here. Locals take great pride in their many California Craftsman cottages; Christmas is a particularly lovely time to visit, when many of the area's homes are festooned with elaborate decorations.

Orange isn't all history, though. **Block at Orange** (⊠ 20 City Blvd., W. Orange ☎ 714/769–3800 ⊕ www.theblockatorange.com), a major mall complex near the I–5 and I–22 freeways, has a strong calling card in its **Vans Skatepark** (⊠ 1 City Blvd. ☎ 714/769–3800 ⊕ www.vans. com), where skaters swoop through specially designed bowls and courses. You can rent boards, pads, and helmets to hit the ramps; there's a special area for kids and beginners.

⑤ In Garden Grove the main attraction is the **Crystal Cathedral,** the domain of television evangelist Robert "*Hour of Power*" Schuller. Designed by the late architect Philip Johnson, the sparkling glass structure resembles a four-pointed star, with more than 10,000 panes of glass covering a weblike steel truss to form transparent walls. Two annual pageants, "The Glory of Christmas" and "The Glory of Easter," feature live animals, flying angels, and other special effects. ⊠ *12141 Lewis St. (take I–5 to Chapman Ave. W), Garden Grove* ☎ *714/971–4000* ⊕ *www. crystalcathedral.org* 🎟 *Pageants $18–$40* ⊙ *Guided tours weekdays 9–3:30; call for schedule. Sun. services at 9:25 and 11:05.*

OFF THE BEATEN PATH

LITTLE SAIGON – Little Saigon encompasses much of the city of Westminster. But the heart of the action is around Magnolia and Bolsa streets, where the colorful Asian Garden Mall tempts shoppers with jewelry and gift shops (bargaining on the prices is expected), Asian herbalists, and informal family restaurants. For a snack, try the *pho* (beef and noodle soup) at Pho 79. Note that the mall gets extremely crowded on weekends and is total madness around the Chinese New Year. ⊠ *Bolsa St. between Bushard and Magnolia Sts., Westminster.*

Where to Stay & Eat

★ **$$–$$$$** ✕ **La Brasserie.** You'll find the perennial elements of a fine French restaurant here: a warm welcome, a softly lighted dining room with oil paintings, and classic fare. You could start with vichyssoise or terrine of foie gras before sampling the chef's veal special. ⊠ *202 S. Main St., Orange* ☎ *714/978–6161* ▭ *AE, DC, MC, V* ⊙ *Closed Sun.*

$$–$$$ ✕ **Citrus City Grille.** The surroundings may be Old Towne, but the menu certainly isn't. Choices range from vegetable spring rolls to pot roast, but the roast duck and Chilean sea bass are particular standouts. The inviting half-moon bar is a surefire lively gathering place. ⊠ *122 N. Glassell St., Orange* ☎ *714/639–9600* ▭ *AE, D, DC, MC, V* ⊙ *Closed Sun.*

$$ ✕ **PJ's Abbey.** Locals come to this 1891 former Baptist church to enjoy American favorites such as pork chops with garlic-mashed potatoes, rack of lamb, and fresh-baked desserts. ✉ *182 S. Orange St., Old Towne Orange* ☎ *714/771–8556* ▭ *AE, D, DC, MC, V* ⊙ *Closed Mon.*

$ ✗ **Felix Continental Cafe.** Facing Orange Circle's park, Felix's serves Cuban and Spanish dishes. The casual spot fills up for lunch and early dinners; try for an outdoor table and order up a chicken special with garlicky *mojo* sauce. ✉ *36 Plaza Sq., Orange* ☎ *714/633–5842* ▭ *AE, DC, MC, V.*

¢–$ ✗ **Da Lat Bistro.** A rare Little Saigon restaurant with a distinct decor, this spot has a Southeast Asia feel with bamboo-covered walls and a thatched bar. Try the *goi thom* (pork salad), pineapple shrimp salad, or the skewers of pork, shrimp, and beef. A green pennywort drink, Rua Ma, is sweet, tasty, and supposed to be good for you, too. ✉ *16525 Brookhurst St., Fountain Valley* ☎ *714/839–8338* ▭ *AE, MC, V* ⊙ *Closed Tues.*

¢–$ ✗ **Thanh My Restaurant.** Though frill-free, one of Little Saigon's oldest restaurants offers a deliciously wide range of Vietnamese cuisine. Try the hot pot: it comes boiling to the table, and then you add fish, vegetables, spices or the fresh egg rolls. It's also a good idea to ask your server for suggestions (and for a gauge of how spicy the dishes will be). ✉ *9553 Bolsa Ave., Westminster* ☎ *714/531–9540* ▭ *AE, MC, V.*

$–$$ 🏨 **Doubletree Hotel Anaheim/Orange.** This contemporary 20-story hotel has a dramatic lobby of marble and granite, with waterfalls cascading down the walls. The hotel is near the Block, Anaheim Stadium, and the Anaheim Convention Center. ✉ *100 The City Dr., Orange 92868* ☎ *714/634–4500 or 800/222–8733* 📠 *714/978–3839* ⊕ *www.doubletreehotels. com* 🛏 *454 rooms, 11 suites* 🍴 *Restaurant, cable TV with movies, in-room broadband, pool, health club, bar, concierge floor, meeting rooms, parking (fee), no-smoking rooms* ▭ *AE, D, DC, MC, V.*

Santa Ana

12 mi south of Anaheim, via I–5 to Hwy. 55.

⟳ ❻ The main attraction in the county seat is the **Bowers Museum of Cultural Art.** Permanent exhibits include Pacific Northwest wood carvings; beadwork of the Plains cultures; clothing, cooking utensils, and silver-adorned saddles used on early California ranches; and California impressionist paintings. Special exhibits such as a show of Egyptian mummies rotate through on a regular basis. As of this writing, a new wing was due to open in fall 2006, with a 300-seat auditorium and an Asian art gallery. The **Bowers Kidseum** (✉ 1802 N. Main St.) has interactive exhibits geared toward kids ages 6–12, in addition to classes, storytelling, and arts-and-crafts workshops. Admission is included in the general museum ticket. ✉ *2002 N. Main St., off I–5, Santa Ana* ☎ *714/567–3600* ⊕ *www. bowers.org* 🖼 *$17; free on 2nd and 4th Tues.* ⊙ *Tues.–Sun. 11–6.*

⟳ With a 108-foot tilting architectural cube beckoning from the I–5 freeway, the **Discovery Science Center** is easy to spot. The hands-on exhibits are for kids from preschool through teens (they especially like the Virtual Volleyball). Kids with an interest in dinosaurs will hit the jackpot: there are life-size dinosaur models, a giant walk-through Argentinosaurus, a fossil dig, and online game of Dinosaur Quest. Other fun activities include lying on a bed of nails, climbing a rock wall, and making tidal waves. ✉ *2500 N. Main St.* ☎ *714/542–2823* ⊕ *www.discoverycube.org* 🎟 *$12* ⊙ *Daily 10–5, except major holidays.*

Where to Eat

★ **$–$$** ✗ **Zov's Bistro.** There's a well-worn path to both sides of Zov's. The restaurant out front prepares bistro favorites with a deft Middle Eastern spin, such as rack of lamb with pomegranate sauce or chicken *geras* (stuffed with wild rice and almonds, with sour cherry sauce). Go around back and you'll find a separate café and bakery filled with locals picking up fresh-baked pastries or deciding between the sirloin burger or mezes (appetizers) for lunch. Both sides have patio tables. The restaurant is just on the other side of the Highway 55 freeway from Santa Ana; take the 17th Street exit. ✉ *Enderle Center, 17440 E. 17th St., Tustin* ☎ *714/838–8855* ▭ *AE, D, DC, MC, V.*

$ ✗ **Tangata.** Inside the Bowers Museum, this eatery has a menu overseen by owner-executive chef Joachim Splichal. Choose among salads, pastas, soups, French-style roasted chicken, lamb shank over polenta, and tasty desserts. Dine on the patio or, in the main dining room, watch the "chef theater." ✉ *2002 N. Main St., Santa Ana* ☎ *714/550–0906* ▭ *AE, D, DC, MC, V* ⊙ *Closed Mon. No dinner.*

Nightlife & the Arts

The 500-seat **OC Pavilion** theater opened in 2005; its performance slate ranges from comedians to Kenny G to Kool & The Gang. State-of-the-art acoustics and comfortable, wide seats are pluses. There are also a jazz lounge and a posh contemporary restaurant. ✉ *801 N. Main St., Santa Ana* ☎ *714/550–0880* ⊕ *www.ocpavilion.com.*

Toward Cleveland National Forest

4 mi east of Santa Ana.

Need a breath of nonurban air? Back in the eastern part of the county, the housing sprawl peters out into beautiful, still largely open country, a mix of parkland and privately held areas. A few two-lane, gently winding roads reach into these toast-color hills, heading toward the Cleveland National Forest. The main roads are named for the canyons they follow: Santiago, Modjeska, and Silverado. It's chaparral country, with dry grasses, hawks overhead, stands of live oak, and the smell of coastal sage. While development is creeping in, especially along Santiago Canyon Road, the canyons are known for their small, fiercely independent communities of longtime residents. ⚠ **Santiago is also a favorite for cyclists, so watch for them on the shoulder of the road.**

Driving along Santiago Canyon Road from the border of Orange, you'll pass Irvine Lake, a reservoir, on your left. The road dips and curves for a few miles before you'll reach an intersection with Silverado Canyon Road branching off to the left. Silverado Canyon Road is the usual entry point to **Cleveland National Forest** (☎ 909/736–1811 ⊕ www.fs.fed.us/r5/cleveland). However, the road is sometimes closed due to fire risk or for environmental reasons; always call ahead. Also, check with the ranger station about any activities you may have in mind: You may need to get a day pass.

The next offshoot, another few miles ahead, is Modjeska Canyon Road, to the left. The canyon is named for Helena Modjeska, a famed Polish actress who emigrated to what was an extremely remote area in the late 1800s. After a failed attempt at communal farm living with a group of fellow Polish emigrés—none of whom had any agricultural experience—she went back to the stage and became one of the most acclaimed actresses in America in the 1880s and '90s. (Modjeska's exceptional life was the basis for Susan Sontag's 2001 novel *In America*.) **Arden** (☎ 949/923–2230), the Stanford White–designed home she occupied at the end of her life, still stands; you can see it on tours given by the Heritage Hill Historical Park four times a month January–November; make reservations in advance.

Continue on Santiago and you may see a gleam of chrome where Live Oak Canyon Road forks to the left—the shine from rows of motorcycles parked in front of **Cook's Corner** (✉ 19122 Live Oak Canyon Rd. ☎ 949/858–0266), a gritty, decades-old roadhouse. Kick back with a beer or a burger in the dark bar or out on the patio—it's a friendly, no-fuss place, a favorite with "weekend warrior" bikers. Soak it up while you can; encroaching development is threatening this classic canyon spot.

Why the anteater mascot for UCI? It was chosen during the 1960s; it's a character from the syndicated comic "B.C." Hence the call of "zot!" in the fight song.

7

Irvine

6 mi south of Santa Ana, via Hwy. 55 to I–405, 12 mi south of Anaheim, via I–5.

Irvine—characterized by its rows of large, cream-color tract homes, tree-lined streets, uniformly manicured lawns, and pristine parks—may feel strange to people not used to such uniformity. The master-planned community has top-notch schools, a university and a community college, dozens of shopping centers, and a network of well-lighted walking and biking paths.

7 Some of the Californian impressionist paintings on display at the small yet intriguing **Irvine Museum** depict the state's rural landscape in the years before massive freeways and sprawling housing developments. The paintings, which are displayed on the 12th floor of the cylindrical marble-and-glass Tower 17 building, were assembled by Joan Irvine Smith, granddaughter of James Irvine, who once owned a quarter of what is now Orange County. ✉ 18881 Von Karman Ave., at Martin St. north of UC Irvine campus, Irvine ☎ 949/476–2565 ⊕ www.irvinemuseum. org ⊠ Free ☉ Tues.–Sat. 11–5.

8 The **University of California at Irvine** (UCI) was established on 1,000 acres of rolling ranch land donated by the Irvine family in the mid-1950s. The campus contains more than 11,000 trees from around the world and features a stellar biological science department and creative writing program. The **Irvine Barclay Theater** (☎ 949/854–4646 ⊕ www.thebarclay.org) presents an impressive roster of music, dance, and dramatic events, and there's not a bad seat in the house. The **Art Gallery at UC Irvine** (☎ 949/824–3508 ⊕ beallcenter.uci.edu) sponsors exhibitions of student and professional art. The **Beall Center for Art & Technology** (☎ 949/824–4339 ⊕ beallcenter.uci.edu) shows the works of emerging international artists. The center and the gallery are both open from mid-September to mid-June, Tuesday and Wednesday noon–5 and Thursday to Saturday noon–8. ⊠ *I–405 to Jamboree Rd., west to Campus Dr. S, Irvine* ☎ *949/824–5011* ⊕ *www.uci.edu.*

🌀 **Wild Rivers Water Park** has more than 40 rides and attractions, including a wave pool, daring slides, and a river inner-tube ride. ⊠ *8770 Irvine Center Dr., off I–405, Irvine* ☎ *949/768–9453* ⊕ *www.wildrivers.com* 🖭 *$29* ⊙ *Late May–Sept.; call for hrs.*

Where to Stay & Eat

$$–$$$ ✕ **Bistango.** A sleek, art-filled bistro serves first-rate American cuisine with a European flair: salads, steak, seafood, pasta, and pizzas. Try the tuna grilled rare. An attractive group comes to savor the food, listen to live jazz, and mingle with well-dressed peers (book ahead). There's live entertainment seven nights a week and a happy hour on weekdays 5–7. ⊠ *19100 Von Karman Ave., Irvine, near John Wayne/Orange County Airport* ☎ *949/752–5222* ⊟ *AE, D, DC, MC, V* ⊙ *No lunch weekends.*

$$–$$$ ✕ **Il Fornaio.** Two weeks a month, regional dishes from Tuscany or Puglia supplement the regular fare—house-made pastas, pizza, veal scallopine, succulent grilled eggplant with goat cheese—at this airy Italian chain eatery. ■ **TIP→** This branch stands out by virtue of its pair of boccie courts; borrow a boccie set and play a game before your meal. ⊠ *18051 Von Karman Ave., Irvine* ☎ *949/261–1444* ⊟ *AE, D, DC, MC, V* ⊙ *No lunch Sun.*

★ $$–$$$ ✕ **Prego.** Reminiscent of a Tuscan villa, this is a much larger version of the Beverly Hills Prego, with soft lighting, golden walls, and an outdoor patio. Try the spit-roasted meats and chicken, charcoal-grilled fresh fish, or pizzas from the oak-burning oven. California and Italian wines are reasonably priced. ⊠ *18420 Von Karman Ave., Irvine* ☎ *949/553–1333* ⊟ *AE, D, DC, MC, V* ⊙ *No lunch weekends.*

$–$$ ✕ **Kitima Thai Cuisine.** Tucked away on the ground floor of an office building, this small, reliable Thai restaurant is a favorite with the business-lunch crowd. Try Bangkok duck and cashew chicken; the kitchen will regulate the spiciness depending on your heat tolerance. ⊠ *2010 Main St., Suite 170, Irvine* ☎ *949/261–2929* ⊟ *AE, DC, MC, V* ⊙ *Closed Sun.*

$$$–$$$$ 🏨 **Irvine Marriott John Wayne Airport.** Towering over Koll Business Center, the Marriott offers a convenient location and amenities designed to appeal to business travelers. Despite its size, the hotel has an intimate feel, due in part to the convivial lobby and evening entertainment. There's a courtesy van to South Coast Plaza and the airport. ⊠ *18000 Von Karman Ave., Irvine 92612* ☎ *949/553–0100 or 800/228–9290* 📠 *949/261–7059* ⊕ *www.marriott.com* 🛏 *485 rooms, 10 suites* ♨ *3 restaurants, cable TV with movies, Wi-Fi, 2 tennis courts, pool, health club, hot tub, business services, meeting rooms, airport shuttle* ⊟ *AE, D, DC, MC, V.*

$$$ 🏨 **Fairmont Newport Beach.** An eye-catching ziggurat design is the trademark of this modern hotel in Koll Center. Bought by Fairmont in 2005, the hotel's undergone some long-needed refurbishment. Guest rooms and public spaces are now done in rich chocolate, gold, and carnation red; the heated pool is now surrounded by cabanas. Although technically in Newport Beach, the hotel is near John Wayne Airport. ⊠ *4500 MacArthur Blvd., Newport Beach 92660* ☎ *949/476–2001 or 800/243–4141* 🖷 *949/476–0153* ⊕ *www.fairmont.com* 🛏 *444 rooms, 50 suites* 🛆 *2 restaurants, cable TV with movies, in-room broadband, 2 tennis courts, pool, health club, bar, concierge, business services, airport shuttle* ☰ *AE, D, DC, MC, V.*

$–$$$ 🏨 **Hyatt Regency Irvine.** The sleek, ultramodern rooms here offer practical amenities such as coffeemakers, irons, and hair dryers. Special golf packages at nearby Oak Creek and Pelican Hills are available. In 2006 a restaurant opened, 6ix Park Grill, run by Yves Fournier, as did bar8. ⊠ *17900 Jamboree Rd., near John Wayne/Orange County Airport, Irvine 92614* ☎ *949/975–1234 or 800/233–1234* 🖷 *949/852–1574* ⊕ *www.hyatt.com* 🛏 *536 rooms, 21 suites* 🛆 *2 restaurants, cable TV with movies, Wi-Fi, 4 tennis courts, pool, health club, bicycles, babysitting, 2 bars, concierge, business services* ☰ *AE, D, DC, MC, V.*

Nightlife

It's worth checking the performance schedules at the UCI venues (above), as they consistently bring in interesting acts.

🕐 The 32-acre **Entertainment Center at Irvine Spectrum** contains a huge, 21-theater cinema complex (with a six-story IMAX 3-D theater), several lively restaurants (including Crazy Horse Nightclub, a local bastion of country music) and cafés, and 150 shops, as well as a Giant Wheel and carousel. Other highlights are Dave and Buster's, with games for kids, and the Improv, for adult comedy. ⊠ *Exit Irvine Center Dr. at intersection of I–405, I–5, and Hwy. 133, Irvine* ☎ *949/450–4900 film listings* ⊕ *www.irvinespectrum.com.*

The **Verizon Wireless Amphitheater** (⊠ 8808 Irvine Center Dr., Irvine ☎ 949/855–8095 or 949/855–6111), a 16,300-seat open-air venue, presents musical events from April through October.

Costa Mesa

6 mi northeast of Irvine, via I–405 to Bristol St.

Though it's probably best known for its shopping malls, Costa Mesa is also the performing-arts hub of Orange County, and a formidable local business center. Patrons of the domestic and international theater, opera, and dance productions fill area restaurants and nightspots. Movie buffs have several theaters to choose from, too.

If you look at the where-to-buy listings in the bottom of couture ads in glossy magazines, you'll often see, sandwiched between listings of shops in Paris and Tokyo, the name of Costa Mesa's most famous landmark, ★ ❾ **South Coast Plaza,.** This immense complex gets ritzier by the year as international designer boutiques jostle for platinum-card space. The original section has the densest concentration of shops: Gucci, Armani, Burberry, La Perla, Hermès, Versace, Chloe, and Prada. All the familiar mall names are here, too, from Sunglass Hut to Banana Republic. One standout is the excellent bookstore Book Soup. Major department stores, including

Saks and Nordstrom, flank the exterior. A pedestrian bridge crosses Bear Street to the second wing, a smaller offshoot with a huge Crate & Barrel. ✉ *3333 S. Bristol St., off I–405, Costa Mesa* ☎ *714/435–2000* ⊕*www.southcoastplaza.com* ⊗ *Weekdays 10–9, Sat. 10–7, Sun. 11–6:30.*

South Coast Plaza has gradually become surrounded by other shopping complexes with different twists. Across Sunflower Avenue is an outdoor shopping area called South Coast Plaza Village (technically in Santa Ana), while on the other side of Bear Street is Metro Pointe, a conglomerate mass of supersize, often bargain-oriented stores. Farther down Bristol on the other side of the I–405 you'll find SoBeCa (short for South on Bristol Entertainment, Culture & Arts), which is a more subculture- and youth-oriented area, anchored by the **Lab** (✉ 2930 Bristol St., Costa Mesa ⊕ www.sobeca.net or www.thelab.com), also known as the antimall. After a weakish start, the Lab now has funky shops, trendy restaurants, and places to hang out. Mull it over with a coffee in the kitschy Gypsy Den or while browsing for hats Arth (combines art and hat), for hard-to-find sneakers at Blends, and for cool clothes at Carve.

The **Camp** (✉ 2937 Bristol St. ⊕ www.thecampsite.net), another outdoor "retail community," takes a mellower, ecofriendly approach, devoting itself to sports-related stores like Adventure 16 and Cycle Werks. There's Native Foods, a vegan restaurant, plus Co-Op, an art gallery. Liburdi's Scuba Center even has a small pool for instruction. Grab a snack from the Village Bakery and hang out in the grassy bowl.

Costa Mesa's role in consumer consumption is matched by its arts venues. The **Orange County Performing Arts Center** (✉ 600 Town Center Dr., east of Bristol St. ☎ 714/556–2787) houses Segerstrom Hall for opera, ballet, symphony, and musicals and the more intimate Founders Hall for chamber music. Richard Lippold's enormous *Firebird,* an angular sculpture of polished metal that resembles a bird taking flight, extends outward from the glass-enclosed lobby. A new, 2,000-square-foot concert hall and 500-seat theater is set to open in fall 2006. Across a courtyard from the original center, the new glass-fronted concert hall will host the Orange County Philharmonic, while the theater will focus on jazz and cabaret concerts. Across the way is the highly regarded South Coast Repertory Theater (⇨ Nightlife & the Arts, *below*).

★ Tucked between mirror-glass office towers near the Performing Arts Center is the **California Scenario** (✉ 611 Anton Blvd.), a 1½-acre sculpture garden designed by Isamu Noguchi, who carved this compact space into distinct areas with his abstract designs. Each represents an aspect of the state's terrain. Smooth granite boulders punctuate the sweep of flat stone paving. A pine tree–trimmed grassy slope faces a circular area planted with cacti, while a sunken stream curls toward a low stone pyramid. ■ TIP→ The garden can be hard to find—it's a block from the South Coast Repertory Theater, by the Chat Noir restaurant—but it's well worth the effort.

Where to Stay & Eat

$$–$$$$ ✕ **Morton's of Chicago.** Hearty eaters flock to this wood-panel eatery, the quintessential steak house, for huge portions of prime aged beef and fresh seafood. During the week check out happy hour to soften the blow of

the check. The soft lighting contrasts with all the noise. ⊠ *South Coast Plaza Village, 1661 W. Sunflower Ave., Santa Ana* ☏ *714/444–4834* ▭ *AE, DC, MC, V* ⊘ *No lunch weekends.*

$–$$$$ ✕**Chat Noir.** With a decor that evokes Belle Epoque Paris, Chat Noir vamps it up with dark wood and red velvet. As it's near the theaters, it's especially handy for a preperformance meal. Live jazz, proximity to South Coast Plaza and businesses, and updated takes on French bistro classics such as omelets, escargots, and mussels and fries make for an eclectic crowd. ⊠ *655 Anton Blvd.* ☏ *714/557–6647* ▭ *AE, D, DC, MC, V.*

★ **$$–$$$** ✕ **Troquet.** The Chanel and Hermès boutiques of South Coast Plaza's main pavilion are in good company with this burnished French bistro. Soft lighting, a low-key atmosphere, and a perch one story above the shopping fray should encourage you to take your time with the menu. Classics like steak tartare and roast duck breast get a fresh slant with accompaniments like baby bok choy with a ginger-orange reduction sauce. ■ TIP➜ The prix-fixe menus at lunch and dinner are comparative bargains here. ⊠ *South Coast Plaza, 3333 Bristol St., Costa Mesa* ☏ *714/708–6865* ▭ *AE, MC, V.*

$$ ✕**Memphis Soul Café and Bar.** Southern food gets the SoCal treatment here—goat cheese and pesto bump up against gumbo and catfish. The retro setting and DJ nights give things an authentically lively vibe. ⊠ *2920 Bristol St., Costa Mesa* ☏ *714/432–7685* ▭ *AE, D, DC, MC, V.*

★ **$–$$** ✕ **Bangkok IV.** This restaurant's elegant interior, with striking flower arrangements on every table, defies conventional mall dining. The deep-fried catfish with a chili-garlic-lemongrass sauce is exceptional. You may also want to give the Thai noodle dishes a try. ⊠ *South Coast Plaza, 3333 Bear St., Costa Mesa* ☏ *714/540–7661* ▭ *AE, D, DC, MC, V.*

$–$$ ✕ **Habana Restaurant and Bar.** With rustic candelabras and murals in a candlelighted former industrial space, Habana serves up Cuban flavor with a hip modern flair. Chocolate lovers can't miss the Café Cubano—chocolate mousse topped with chocolate whipped cream and rum sauce. With entertainment two nights a week, this restaurant is a popular nightspot. ⊠ *The Lab, 2930 Bristol St., Costa Mesa* ☏ *714/556–0176* ▭ *AE, D, MC, V.*

★ **$–$$** ✕ **Karl Strauss Brewery Restaurant.** The menu here is a cut above the usual suds-house fare, with choices such as "firecracker" sirloin strips (with a spicy soy-sesame-ginger glaze) and blackened salmon. Belly up to the circular bar for a seasonal brew or the classic amber lager. ⊠ *901 South Coast Dr., Costa Mesa* ☏ *714/546–2739* ▭ *AE, D, DC, MC, V.*

$$$ 🏨 **Hilton Costa Mesa.** At this spacious hotel you can stay near John Wayne Airport without the air traffic sounding too close. In-room desks and business services make it a good stop if you're bound for the nearby office parks. ⊠ *3050 Bristol St., Costa Mesa 92626* ☏ *714/540–7000 or 800/445–8667* 🖷 *714/540–9176* ⊕ *www.hilton.com* ⇥ *486 rooms, 12 suites* ⌖ *Restaurant, cable TV with movies, Wi-Fi, pool, health club, hot tub, lobby lounge, laundry facilities, business services, meeting rooms* ▭ *AE, D, DC, MC, V.*

$–$$$ 🏨 **Country Inn and Suites.** The warm colors, art and antiques, and mahogany furniture help this hotel feel less corporate than some hotel chains. Refreshments are served in the evening Monday through Thursday.

⊠ *325 Bristol St., Costa Mesa 92626* ☎ *714/549–0300 or 800/322–9992* 🖷 *714/662–0828* ⊕ *www.ayreshotels.com* ⇨ *282 rooms* ⚬ *Restaurant, some microwaves, refrigerators, cable TV with movies and video games, 2 pools, gym, 2 hot tubs, bar, laundry facilities, meeting rooms, airport shuttle* ☰ *AE, D, DC, MC, V.*

$–$$$ 🏨 **Westin South Coast Plaza.** This high-rise adjoins the South Coast Plaza complex—you can roll out of bed and hit the stores. The beds in these comfortably sized rooms come with feather duvets. The atmospheric restaurant, Pinot Provence, is a longtime local favorite, although sometimes the decor outshines the food. Tennis courts are nearby. ⊠ *686 Anton Blvd., Costa Mesa 92626* ☎ *714/540–2500 or 888/627–7213* 🖷 *714/662–6695* ⊕ *www.westin.com* ⇨ *391 rooms, 5 suites* ⚬ *Restaurant, cable TV with movies, in-room broadband, pool, health club, business services, meeting rooms, some pets allowed* ☰ *AE, D, DC, MC, V.*

Nightlife & the Arts

★ The **Orange County Performing Arts Center** (⊠ 600 Town Center Dr., Costa Mesa ☎ 714/556–2787 ⊕ www.ocpac.org) consistently presents impressively far-reaching arts performances. Companies such as the American Ballet Theater make annual appearances, as do the touring groups of major Broadway hits. Other highlights range from the Kirov Ballet to the Count Basie Orchestra to Tony Bennett. Within the Center, a jazz club in the 250-seat Founders Hall hosts performances with club-style seating on Friday and Saturday. *See above* for more details on the new performance spaces, due to open in fall 2006.

The **South Coast Repertory Theater** (⊠ 655 Town Center Dr., Costa Mesa ☎ 714/708–5555 ⊕ www.scr.org) is a Tony Award–winning theater presenting new and traditional works on two stages.

THE COAST

Running along the Orange County coastline is scenic Pacific Coast Highway (Highway 1, known locally as PCH). Older beachfront settlements, with their modest bungalow-style homes, are joined by posh new gated communities. The pricey land between Newport Beach and Laguna Beach is where Laker Kobe Bryant, novelist Dean Koontz, and a slew of Internet and finance moguls live. Though the coastline is rapidly being filled in, there are still a few stretches of beautiful, protected open land. And at many places along the way you can catch an idealized glimpse of surfers hitting the beach, boards under their arms.

Huntington Beach

25 mi west of Anaheim, Hwy. 57 south to Hwy. 22 west to I–405; 40 mi southeast of Los Angeles, I–5 south to I–605 south to I–405 south to Beach Blvd.

Once a sleepy residential town with little more than a string of rugged surf shops, Huntington Beach has transformed itself into a resort destination. The town's appeal is its broad white-sand beaches with often-towering waves, complemented by a lively pier, shops, and restaurants on Main Street and the luxurious Hilton Waterfront Beach Resort and

CLOSE UP

The Great Outdoors

WATER SPORTS RULE the coast of Orange County. Those inexperienced at riding the waves along the coastline can get a feel for the waves by riding a boogie board at Seal Beach or at the Newport River jetties. Surfing is permitted at most beaches year-round (check local newspapers or talk to lifeguards for conditions), and surfboard-rental stands line the coast. The best waves are usually at San Clemente, Newport Beach, and Huntington Beach. From June through September the ocean temperature tops 70°F and lifeguards patrol almost every beach. Local newspapers print beach reports with wave information and notice of any closures. You can also check local news on surf and water quality through the **Surfrider Foundation** (⊕ www.surfrider.org).

Keep a lookout for signs warning of dangerous conditions: undertow, strong currents, and big waves can all be hazardous. Avoid swimming near surfers. When a yellow flag with a black circle is flying (known to locals as "black balling"), it means no hard boards are allowed, but swimming and bodyboarding are permitted.

If you'd like to explore the coastline by bike or on foot, the **Santa Ana Riverbed Trail** hugs the Santa Ana River for 20½ mi between the Pacific Coast Highway (PCH) at Huntington State Beach and Imperial Highway in Yorba Linda. Joggers have an uninterrupted path the whole way. There are entrances, restrooms, and drinking fountains at all crossings. A bike path winds south from Marina del Rey all the way to San Diego with only minor breaks. Most beaches have bike-rental stands.

You'll usually hear the name Irvine linked to soulless suburban sprawl, but balancing that is the **Irvine Ranch Land Reserve** (☎ 714/832-7478 ⊕ www.irvineranchlandreserve.org). These 50,000 protected acres stretch 22 mi from Weir Canyon to the coast, where the reserve meets the Laguna Coast Wilderness Park and Crystal Cove State Park. The Nature Conservancy manages the park and sponsors many activities, from tough mountain bike rides to leisurely family picnics in regional parks. You'll need advance reservations for any of their docent-led activities.

7

---

the Hyatt Regency. A draw for sports fans: the U.S. Open professional surf competition takes place here every July. Other top sporting events are the AVP Pro Beach Volleyball Tournament in August and the Core Tour Extreme BMX Skate Competition in September. There's even a Surfing Walk of Fame, with plaques set in the sidewalk around the intersection of the PCH and Main Street.

🔟 **Huntington Pier** stretches 1,800 feet out to sea, well past the powerful waves that made Huntington Beach America's "Surf City." A farmers' market is held on Friday; an informal arts fair sets up most weekends. At the end of the pier sits **Ruby's** (☎ 714/969–7829), part of a California chain of 1940s-style burger joints. The **Pierside Pavilion** (⊠ PCH across from Huntington Pier) has shops, restaurants, bars with live music, and a theater complex. The best surf-gear source is **Huntington Surf and Sport Pierside** (☎ 714/841–4000), staffed by true surf enthusiasts.

Just up Main Street from the pier, the **International Surfing Museum** pays tribute to the sport's greats with the Surfing Hall of Fame, which has an impressive collection of surfboards and related memorabilia. They've even got the Bolex camera used to shoot the 1966 surfing documentary *The Endless Summer.* ⊠ *411 Olive Ave., Huntington Beach* ☎ *714/960–3483* ⊕ *www.surfingmuseum.org* ✆ *$2* ☉ *June–Sept., daily noon–5; Oct.–May, Thurs.–Mon. noon–5.*

★ ⓫ **Bolsa Chica Ecological Reserve** beckons wildlife lovers and bird-watchers with an 1,180-acre salt marsh that is home to 200 species of birds, including great blue herons, snowy and great egrets, and brown pelicans. Throughout the reserve are trails for bird-watching, including a comfortable 1½-mi loop. Free guided tours depart from the walking bridge the first Saturday of each month at 9 AM. ⊠ *Entrance on PCH 1 mi south of Warner Ave., opposite Bolsa Chica State Beach at traffic light* ☎ *714/840–1575* ✆ *Free* ☉ *Daily dawn–sunset.*

Where to Stay & Eat

$–$$$$ ✕ **Tuna Town.** Korn drummer David Silvera, a Huntington Beach resident, owns this Japanese-Hawaiian restaurant. Korn memorabilia is on the walls, which reverberate with music and chatter. Try the sushi dinner or sautéed chicken in wasabi cream sauce. The food takes center stage when the chefs chop and grill the food right before your eyes. ⊠ *221 Main St.* ☎ *714/536–3194* ▭ *AE, D, MC, V* ☉ *No dinner May–Aug.*

$–$$$ ✕ **Duke's.** A perfect people-watching spot overlooking the beach, this seafood restaurant has fish, chicken, and salads with a Hawaiian accent. Try crispy coconut shrimp or a salad of hearts of palm and papaya. The view's the thing here, although the food comes in a close second. ⊠ *317 Pacific Coast Hwy.* ☎ *714/374–6446* ▭ *AE, D, MC, V.*

★ $–$$$ ✕ **Red Pearl Kitchen.** This slim, hip, lacquer-red space near Main Street may put its bar front and center, but the pan-Asian food is no wallflower. The menu, divided into small or large servings, could include hot chili-crusted calamari, green papaya salad, or Szechuan pepper steak with sweet-and-sour eggplant. Desserts are equally strong. ■ **TIP→ DJs spin several nights a week, upping the energy but making it difficult to talk.** If you come on a weekend, you'll likely need to wait awhile; reservations are a good idea. ⊠ *412 Walnut Ave., Huntington Beach* ☎ *714/969–0224* ▭ *AE, MC, V.*

¢–$$$ ✕ **Chimayo at the Beach.** At Chimayo, which is beneath Duke's and right on the beach, fish takes on a Mexican flavor: dishes include lobster tacos, shrimp with Mexican spices, and grilled seafood. You can almost reach out and touch the passing joggers, volleyball players, and skateboarders if you sit on the patio outside. ⊠ *315 PCH* ☎ *714/374–7273* ▭ *AE, D, MC, V.*

¢–$ ✕ **Sugar Shack.** The long lines in front testify to this local favorite, which has been owned by the same family since 1967. Breakfasts, served all day, are standouts, as are the hamburgers, salads, and sandwiches. Streetside sitting is so popular you have to sign a clipboard by the door and wait your turn. ⊠ *213½ Main St.* ☎ *714/536–0355* ▭ *AE, D, DC, MC, V* ☉ *No dinner Thurs.–Tues., Wed. dinner served until 8.*

¢ ✕ **Wahoo's Fish Taco.** Proximity to the ocean makes these mahimahi-filled tacos taste even better. This healthy fast-food chain brought Baja's fish tacos north of the border to quick success. Here, surf stickers cover the walls. ✉ *120 Main St., Huntington Beach* ☎ *714/536–2050* ▤ *MC, V.*

$$$–$$$$ ▥ **Hilton Waterfront Beach Resort.** Rising 12 stories above the surf, this Hilton caters to many kinds of travelers: couples, families, business types. All guest rooms have private balconies, many with panoramic ocean views. The grounds are extensive, including a sand volleyball court and a free-form pool; the staff can even arrange the fixings for a cookout on the beach. ✉ *21100 PCH, Huntington Beach 92648* ☎ *714/845–8000 or 866/387–5760* ▤ *714/845–8425* ⊕ *www.waterfrontresort.com* ⇨ *266 rooms, 24 suites* ⟁ *Restaurant, some microwaves, cable TV with movies, Wi-Fi, tennis court, pool, gym, hot tub, 2 bars, children's programs; ages 5–12), concierge floor, business services, meeting rooms, airport shuttle, some pets allowed (fee)* ▤ *AE, D, DC, MC, V.*

★ **$$$** ▥ **Hyatt Regency Huntington Beach Resort and Spa.** Sprawling along the PCH, almost every room in this Spanish-style hotel has an ocean view as well as a private balcony or terrace. With a nod to California's Mission period, the hotel includes courtyards, outdoor fireplaces, and fountains. Artwork with a beach theme is by local artists, and guest rooms and public spaces are decorated with artisan glass from Italy. This Hyatt aims to create a village atmosphere, and to a large extent it has succeeded. Beach access is via a bridge over the PCH. ✉ *21500 PCH, 92648* ☎ *714/698–1234 or 800/554–9288* ▤ *714/845–4620* ⊕ *www. huntingtonbeach.hyatt.com* ⇨ *517 rooms, 57 suites* ⟁ *3 restaurants, grocery, in-room safes, refrigerators, in-room broadband, 2 tennis courts, health club, hair salon, spa, shop, children's programs (ages 3–12), concierge floor* ▤ *AE, D, DC, MC, V.*

$–$$ ▥ **Hotel Huntington Beach.** This hotel offers a location midway between Anaheim and the beach areas. A free shuttle is available to take you to John Wayne Airport, South Coast Plaza, or the Huntington Beach pier. ✉ *7667 Center Ave., 92647* ☎ *714/891–0123 or 877/891–0123* ▤ *714/ 895–5491* ⊕ *www.hotelhb.com* ⇨ *224 rooms* ⟁ *Restaurant, Wi-Fi, in-room hot tubs, indoor pool, health club, bar, airport shuttle* ▤ *AE, D, DC, MC, V.*

$ ▥ **Best Western Regency Inn.** Forgo an ocean view here, and you can save a lot of money. This moderately priced, tidy hotel is near the PCH and close to the main drag and its restaurants and shops. Rooms are cookie-cutter, but some have private whirlpools. ✉ *19360 Beach Blvd., Huntington Beach 92648* ☎ *714/962–4244* ▤ *714/963–4724* ⊕ *www. bestwestern.com* ⇨ *64 rooms* ⟁ *Refrigerators, cable TV, in-room broadband, pool, hot tub, laundry facilities, meeting room* ▤ *AE, D, DC, MC, V.*

Sports & the Outdoors

BEACHES **Huntington City Beach** (☎ 714/536–5281) stretches for 3 mi from the pier area. The beach is most crowded around the pier; amateur and professional surfers brave the waves daily on its north side. As you continue north, **Huntington State Beach** (☎ 714/536–1454) parallels Pacific Coast Highway. On the state and city beaches there are changing rooms, concessions, lifeguards, and ample parking; the state beach also has barbecue pits. At the northern section of the city, **Bolsa Chica State Beach** (☎ 714/846–3460) has barbecue pits and RV campsites and is usually less crowded than its southern neighbors.

Dog Beach (✉ 19000 PCH ☎ 714/535–5281), just north of the pier, is the rare place that encourages dogs to run and splash sans leash. You might even see a dog surfing with his owner. The beach is open daily 5 AM–10 PM.

SURFING   **Corky Carroll's Surf School** (☎ 714/969–3959 ⊕ www.surfschool.net) organizes lessons, weeklong workshops, and surfing trips. You can rent surf- or boogie boards at **Dwight's** (☎ 714/536–8083), one block south of the pier. **HB Wahine** (✉ 301 Main St. ☎ 714/969–9399 ⊕ www.hbwahine.com) gives girls-only surf lessons, sells boards designed specially for them (narrower) and has cool surfing clothes, too. **Huntington Beach Surfing Instruction** (☎ 714/962–3515 ⊕ www.hbsurfing.com), a group of off-duty lifeguards, offers lessons by appointment only in summer and yearlong in Costa Rica.

Newport Beach

6 mi south of Huntington Beach, PCH.

Newport Beach has two distinct personalities. There's the island-dotted yacht harbor, where the wealthy play. (Newport is said to have the highest per-capita number of Mercedes-Benzes in the world.) And then there's inland Newport Beach, just southwest of John Wayne Airport, a business and commercial hub that's lined with high-rise office buildings, shopping centers, and hotels.

★ ⑫   **Newport Harbor,** which shelters nearly 10,000 small boats, may seduce even those who don't own a yacht. Exploring the charming avenues and surrounding alleys can be great fun.

Within Newport Harbor are eight small islands, including Balboa and Lido. The houses lining the shore may seem modest, but this is some of the most expensive real estate in the world. Marine Avenue, Balboa Island's main street, has shops, restaurants, and places to try the chocolate-covered Balboa Bar, a chocolate-dipped ice cream bar that was invented on the Balboa Peninsula. As you stroll the perimeters of the island, you can see houses that range in style from Moderne, designed by John Lautner, to the more traditional Cape Cod. Several grassy areas on primarily residential Lido Isle have views of Newport Harbor. In evidence of the upper-crust Orange County mind-set, each is marked PRIVATE COMMUNITY PARK.

Newport Pier, which juts out into the ocean near 20th Street, is the heart of Newport's beach community and a popular fishing spot. Street parking is difficult at the pier, so grab the first space you find and be prepared to walk. A stroll along West Ocean Front reveals much of the town's character. On weekday mornings, head for the beach near the pier, where you're likely to encounter dory fishermen hawking their predawn catches, as they've done for generations. On weekends the walk is alive with kids of all ages on in-line skates, skateboards, and bikes dodging pedestrians and whizzing past fast-food joints, shops, and bars.

Newport's best beaches are on **Balboa Peninsula,** whose many jetties pave the way to ideal swimming areas. The most intense body-surfing place in Orange County and arguably on the West Coast, known as the **Wedge,** is at the south end of the peninsula. Created by accident in the 1930s when the Federal Works Progress Administration built a jetty to protect Newport Harbor, the break is pure euphoria for highly skilled body surfers. ■ TIP➔ **Since the waves generally break very close to shore and rip currents are strong, lifeguards strongly discourage visitors from attempting it—but it sure is fun to watch an experienced local ride it.**

⓭ The **Balboa Pavilion,** on the bay side of the peninsula, was built in 1905 as a bath- and boathouse. Today it houses a restaurant and shops and is a departure point for harbor and whale-watching cruises. Look for it on Main Street, off Balboa Boulevard. Adjacent to the pavilion is the three-car ferry that connects the peninsula to Balboa Island. In the blocks around the pavilion you'll find restaurants, beachside shops, and the small **Fun Zone**—a local kiddie hangout with a Ferris wheel and a nautical museum. On the other side of the narrow peninsula is **Balboa Pier.** On its end is the original branch of Ruby's, a 1940s-esque burger-and-shake joint.

At its new location in the Balboa Fun Zone, the **Newport Harbor Nautical Museum** has exhibits on the history of the harbor as well as of the Pacific as a whole. For lovers of ship models, there are more than $3 million worth, some dating to 1798; one is made entirely of gold and silver. Another fun display is a virtual deep-sea fishing machine. ✉ 600 E. Bay Ave., Balboa ☎ 949/675–8915 ⊕ www.nhnm.org ✉ Free ☉ Tues.–Sun 10–5.

Try a one-hour cruise with the Gondola Company of Newport (949/675–1212, www.gondolas.com). It costs $85 for two.

7

Shake the sand out of your shoes to head inland to the ritzy **Fashion Island** outdoor mall, a cluster of arcades and courtyards, complete with koi pond, inside in a sea of parking spaces. Although it doesn't have quite the international-designer clout of South Coast Plaza, it has the luxe department store Neiman Marcus and expensive spots like L'Occitane, Kate Spade, Ligne Roset, and Design Within Reach. Chains, restaurants, and the requisite movie theater fill out the rest. ✉ 410 Newport Center Dr., between Jamboree and MacArthur Blvds., off PCH, Newport Beach ☎ 949/721–2000 ⊕ www.shopfashionisland.com.

Roger's Gardens. On 7 acres across from Fashion Island, this garden center has so many unusual specimens that even Martha Stewart didn't want to leave when she visited. Special exhibits during holidays like Christmas and Easter make it a good place to get creative ideas. ✉ 2301 San Joaquin Hills Rd. ☎ 800/647–2356 ⊕ www.rogersgardens.com.

★ ⓮ The **Orange County Museum of Art** gathers a collection of modernist paintings and sculpture by California artists and cutting-edge, international contemporary works. The collection includes works by such key California artists as Richard Diebenkorn, Ed Ruscha, Robert Irwin, and Chris Burden. The museum also displays some of its collection at a gallery at South Coast Plaza free of charge; it's open the same hours as the mall. Soups, salads, and daily specials are served at the Patina's Citrus Cafe.

✉ *850 San Clemente Dr., Newport Beach* ☎ *949/759–1122* ⊕ *www. ocma.net* ✉ *$10* ☉ *Tues., Wed., and Fri.–Sun. 11–5, Thurs. 11–8.*

Where to Stay & Eat

$–$$$ ✕ **Bluewater Grill.** On the site of an old sportfishing dock, this local spot has 15 types of fish, a bay view, and early-1900s fishing photos on the walls. Favorites include blue-nose seabass, local swordfish, and calamari steak, for those who miss the abalone that used to be common in the area. Wines are reasonably priced. ✉ *630 Lido Park Dr.* ☎ *949/675–3474* ▭ *AE, D, DC, MC, V.*

★ $–$$$ ✕ **The Cannery.** This 1920s cannery building still teems with fish, but now they go into dishes on the Pacific Rim menu rather than being packed into crates. Settle in at the sushi bar, dining room, or patio before choosing between sashimi or oven-roasted Chilean sea bass. On Tuesday night a selection of 50 wines is sold at 50% off. ✉ *3010 Lafayette Rd., Newport Beach* ☎ *949/566–0060* ▭ *AE, D, DC, MC, V.*

$$ ✕ **Pescadou Bistro.** Owned by a French family, this casual and fun bistro serves reasonably priced Provençal fare like rabbit in mustard sauce. Try the three-course prix-fixe menu at $20, a bargain in Newport. Across the street is the Lido Marina Village, a cluster of restaurants, shops, and boating businesses at the west end of Newport Harbor. ✉ *3325 Newport Blvd.* ☎ *949/675–6990* ▭ *AE, D, MC, V* ☉ *Closed Mon.*

★ ¢–$ ✕ **Taco Mesa.** This extremely popular taqueria is the reason that the Mc-Donald's parking lot next door is always empty. Other than a plastering of surf stickers and the friendliness of the staff, Taco Mesa is frill free; of the four branches in OC, this one has that intangible quality that makes it the best. Order at the counter; then grab a metal folding chair on the patio before gorging on fantastic carne asada (steak) tacos, giant burritos, and fresh salsa. Close to the end of the Highway 55 freeway, this stand is technically in Costa Mesa. ✉ *647 W. 19th St., Costa Mesa* ☎ *949/642–0629* ▭ *MC, V.*

★ $$$$ ⊞ **The Island Hotel.** A suitably stylish hotel in a very chic neighborhood (it's across the street from the Fashion Island mall), the 20-story tower caters to luxury seekers by offering weekend golf packages in conjunction with the nearby Pelican Hill golf course. Guest rooms have outstanding views, private bars, and original art. The spa does its bit for luxury with a pearl powder facial. For gustatory richness, try the Pavilion restaurant's contemporary menu, with choices such as macadamia-crusted Chilean sea bass. ✉ *690 Newport Center Dr., Newport Beach 92660* ☎ *949/759–0808 or 800/332–3442* 🖷 *949/759–0568* ⊕ *www. theislandhotel.com* ⇌ *295 rooms, 92 suites* ♨ *2 restaurants, room service, cable TV with movies and video games, WiFi, 2 tennis courts, pool, health club, sauna, spa, steam rooms, bar, concierge, business services, some pets allowed (fee),* ▭ *AE, D, DC, MC, V.*

$$$–$$$$ ⊞ **Balboa Bay Club and Resort.** Sharing the same frontage as the private Balboa Bay Club where Humphrey Bogart, Lauren Bacall, and the Reagans hung out, this hotel has one of the best bay views around. There's a yacht club vibe in the public spaces, especially in the nautical dining room. Rooms, which have either bay or courtyard views, have a beachy decor of rattan furniture, plantation shutters, and tropical-pattern drapes. Duke's Place, a bar named for John Wayne, a former member

and club governor, has photos of the star in his mariner-theme films. ✉ *1221 W. Coast Hwy., 92663* ☎ *949/645–5000 or 888/445–7153* 🖶 *949/630–4215* ⊕ *www.balboabayclub.com* ⤢ *150 rooms, 10 suites* ⚬ *3 restaurants, room service, health club, spa, bar, business services, airport shuttle (fee)* ▭ *AE, D, DC, MC, V.*

$$$ 🏨 **Newport Beach Marriott Hotel and Spa.** Here you'll be smack in the monied part of town: across from Fashion Island, next to a country club, and with a view toward Newport Harbor. Rooms have that no-fuss contemporary look: dark wood, granite bathroom counters. Depending on your 'druthers, ask for a room with a balcony or patio that provides a view of the property's lush gardens or toward the Pacific. Five penthouse suites overlooking the Pacific absorb the top floors. The latest addition is the full-service Pure Blu spa, opened in 2006. ✉ *900 Newport Center Dr., Newport Beach 92660* ☎ *949/640–4000 or 800/228–9290* 🖶 *949/640–5055* ⊕ *www.marriott.com* ⤢ *532 rooms, 20 suites* ⚬ *Restaurant, cable TV with movies, in-room broadband, Wi-Fi, 8 tennis courts, 2 pools, health club, spa, bar, concierge, business services, meeting rooms, airport shuttle* ▭ *AE, D, DC, MC, V.*

$$ 🏨 **Hyatt Regency Newport Beach.** The best aspect of this grand dame of Newport hotels is its green acres: 26 of them, overlooking the back bay. When booking your room, suite, or bungalow, let them know your preference of either bay, golf course, garden, or pool views. Each room has a balcony or veranda. ✉ *1107 Jamboree Rd., 92660* ☎ *949/792–1234* 🖶 *949/644–1552* ⊕ *www.hyattnewporter.com* ⤢ *388 rooms, 11 suites, 4 bungalows* ⚬ *Restaurant, refrigerators, in-room broadband, 9-hole golf course, 16 tennis courts, health club, hot tub, spa, bicycles, volleyball, 3 swimming pools, 9-hole golf course, meeting rooms, complimentary shuttle, bar, business services* ▭ *AE, D, DC, MC, V.*

¢–$$ 🏨 **Newport Dunes Waterfront Resort and Marina.** One of the world's richest RV parks, this destination has more than 100 acres of private beach along Newport's Back Bay. The Village Center has a pool, a spa, and a store, and the Back Bay Cafe serves breakfast and lunch. It's a good spot to launch a boat or watch others do it. Cottages ($65 and up for a small one; $150 and up for one with beachfront) have kitchens and screened porches; some have water views. ✉ *1131 Back Bay Dr., 92660* ☎ *949/729–3863 or 800/765–7661* 🖶 *949/729–1133* ⊕ *www.newportdunes.com* ⤢ *382 RV sites, 24 cottages* ⚬ *Restaurant, pool, beach, boating, bicycles, shop* ▭ *AE, D, MC, V.*

Sports & the Outdoors

BOAT RENTAL You can tour Lido and Balboa isles by renting kayaks ($15 an hour), sailboats ($35 an hour), small motorboats ($50 an hour), cocktail boats ($70 an hour), and ocean boats ($75–$85 an hour) at **Balboa Boat Rentals** (✉ 510 E. Edgewater Ave., Newport Beach ☎ 949/673–7200 ⊕ www.boats4rent.com). You must have a driver's license, and some knowledge of boating is helpful; rented boats must stay in the bay.

BOAT TOURS **Catalina Passenger Service** (✉ 400 Main St., Newport Beach ☎ 949/673–5245 ⊕ www.catalinainfo.com), at the Balboa Pavilion, operates 90-minute sightseeing tours for $10 and daily round-trip passage to Catalina Island for $44. Call first; winter service is often available only on weekends. **Hornblower Cruises & Events** (✉ 2431 West Coast Hwy., Newport Beach ☎ 949/646–0155 or 800/668–4322 ⊕ www.hornblower.com) books three-hour weekend dinner cruises with dancing for $65 Friday, $69 Saturday; the two-hour Sunday brunch cruise is $47.

GOLF **Newport Beach Golf Course** (✉ 3100 Irvine Ave., Newport Beach ☎ 949/852–8681), an 18-hole, par-59 course, is lighted for night play. Rates start at $10. Reservations are accepted up to one week in advance, but walk-ins are accommodated when possible.

RUNNING The **Beach Trail** runs along the coast from Huntington Beach to Newport. Paths throughout **Newport Back Bay** (☎ 949/640–6746 ⊕ www.newportbay.org) wrap around a marshy area inhabited by lizards, rabbits, and waterfowl. For information on free walking tours in this ecological reserve, call the **Newport Bay Naturalists.**

SPORTFISHING In addition to a complete tackle shop, **Davey's Locker** (✉ Balboa Pavilion, 400 Main St., Newport Beach ☎ 949/673–1434 ⊕ www.daveyslocker.com) operates sportfishing trips starting at $29, as well as private charters and, in winter, whale-watching trips for $21.

TENNIS Call the **recreation department** (☎ 949/644–3151 ⊕ recreation.city.newport-beach.ca.us) to find out about courts throughout Orange County where play is free and on a first-come, first-served basis. Reservations are required at the **Newport Beach Hotel and Spa** (✉ 900 Newport Center Dr., Newport Beach ☎ 949/640–4000). The cost is $10 per person per day for nonguests.

Corona del Mar

2 mi south of Newport Beach, via Hwy. 1.

A small jewel on the Pacific Coast, Corona del Mar (known by locals as "CDM") has exceptional beaches that some say resemble their majestic northern California counterparts. **Corona del Mar Beach** (☎ 949/644–3151) is actually made up of two beaches, Little Corona and Big Corona, separated by a cliff. Facilities include fire pits, volleyball courts, food stands, restrooms, and parking. ■ TIP➔ Two colorful reefs (and the fact that it's off-limits to boats) make Corona del Mar great for snorkelers and for beachcombers who prefer privacy.

FodorśChoice ★ Midway between Corona del Mar and Laguna, stretching along both sides of Pacific Coast Highway, **Crystal Cove State Park** is a favorite of local beachgoers and wilderness trekkers. It encompasses a 3½-mi stretch of unspoiled beach and has some of the best tide-pooling in southern California. Here you can see starfish, crabs, and other sea life on the rocks. The park's 2,400 acres of backcountry are ideal for hiking, horseback riding, and mountain biking, but stay on the trails to preserve the beauty. Environmental camping is allowed in one of the three campgrounds. Bring water, food, and other supplies; there's a pit toilet but no shower. Open fires and pets are forbidden. Parking costs $8. Rental cottages are scheduled to open in 2006. ☎ 949/494–3539 ⊕ *www.crystalcovestatepark.com* ⊗ *Daily 6–sunset.*

15 **Sherman Library and Gardens,** a 2½-acre botanical garden and library specializing in the history of the Pacific Southwest, makes a good break from the sun and sand. You can wander among cactus gardens, rose gardens, a wheelchair-height touch-and-smell garden, and a tropical conservatory. There's a good gift shop, too. Cafe Jardin serves lunch on weekdays plus Sunday brunch. ✉ *2647 PCH, Corona del Mar* ☎ *949/673–2261, 949/673–0033 lunch reservations* ⊕ *www.slgardens.org* 🎫 *$3* ⏰ *Daily 10:30–4.*

WORD OF MOUTH

"One beach in Orange County that is particularly good for families is Corona del Mar, just south of Newport Beach. It's quieter and a little more laid back than most other beaches. Also, it's close to the jetty for Newport Harbor and it can be fun for little ones to watch the sailboats coming in and out of the harbor (more sailboats on weekends) . . .."   –Chele60

Where to Eat

$–$$$$ ✗ **Gulfstream.** This trendy restaurant has an open kitchen, comfortable booths, and outdoor seating on warm evenings. Especially tasty are the short ribs with mustard barbecue sauce, served with fries and slaw; the most popular item is a tuna burger. Salads are healthy and good—particularly the grilled vegetables. Things get noisy near the bar area, so come early if you like quiet. ✉ *850 Avocado Ave.* ☎ *949/718–0187* 💳 *AE, D, MC, V.*

★ **$$–$$$** ✗ **Oysters.** This hip but convivial seafood restaurant, which has a bustling bar and frequent live music, caters to a late-night crowd. The eclectic menu might include fire-roasted artichokes and terrific ahi tuna dishes. There's also a substantial list of outstanding desserts, cognacs, and dessert wines. ✉ *2515 E. Coast Hwy., Corona del Mar* ☎ *949/675–7411* 💳 *AE, D, DC, MC, V* ⏰ *No lunch.*

★ **$$** ✗ **Sage on the Coast.** Between Newport and Laguna in the Crystal Cove Promenade, Sage serves contemporary American food, which may include sweet-potato fries, roasted-beet salad, and fish-of-the-day specials. A recommended small plate is the grilled beef fillet medallion and spinach with portobello mushrooms. ✉ *7862 E. Coast Hwy.* ☎ *949/715–7243* 💳 *AE, D, DC, MC, V.*

¢–$$ ✗ **Caffee Panini.** Serving good, reasonable food with an Italian accent, the café serves breads straight from the oven, salads, pizzas and other traditional Italian entrées, such as chicken pesto farfalle, panini di prosciutto, and a salad of tomatoes and mozzarella. Open 7 AM–10 PM, this is the place to see Newporters kick back. ✉ *2333 E. Coast Hwy.* ☎ *949/675–8101* 💳 *AE, D, MC, V.*

¢–$ ✗ **Pacific Whey Cafe & Baking Company.** The ovens rarely get a break here—everything is made from scratch daily. Pick up something to go here—perhaps a cinnamon-custard danish or a "B.L.T.A." (the A is for avocado)—and then venture across the street to Crystal Cove State Park for a picnic. If you stay for a hot meal, you could try lemon souffle pancakes or a steak sandwich oozing with melted brie. ✉ *7962 E. Coast Hwy., Crystal Cove Promenade* ☎ *949/715–2200* 💳 *AE, MC, V.*

7

Laguna Beach

16 *10 mi south of Newport Beach on Hwy. 1; 60 mi south of Los Ange-les, I–5 south to Hwy. 133, which turns into Laguna Canyon Rd.*

Fodor'sChoice
★ Even the approach tells you that Laguna Beach is exceptional. Driving in along Laguna Canyon Road from the I–405 freeway gives you the chance to cruise through a gorgeous coastal canyon, large stretches of which remain undeveloped (*see* the Laguna Coast Wilderness Park *in* Sports & the Outdoors, *below*). After winding through the canyon, you'll arrive at a glistening wedge of ocean, at the intersection with the PCH.

Laguna's welcome mat is legendary. For decades in the mid-20th century a local booster, Eiler Larsen, greeted everyone downtown. (There's now a statue of him on the main drag.) On the corner of Forest and Park avenues you can see a 1930s gate proclaiming, THIS GATE HANGS WELL AND HINDERS NONE, REFRESH AND REST, THEN TRAVEL ON. A gay community has long been established here; until relatively recently, this was quite the exception in conservative Orange County. The Hare Krishnas run a restaurant, environmentalists rally, artists continue to gravitate here—there seems to be room for everyone.

There's a definite arty slant to this tight-knit community. The California *plein air* art movement coalesced here in the early 1900s; by the middle of the century an annual arts festival was established. Art galleries now dot the village streets, and there's usually someone daubing up in Heisler Park, overlooking the beach. The town's main street, the Pacific Coast Highway, is referred to as either South Coast or North Coast Highway, depending on the address. From this waterfront, the streets slope up steeply to the residential areas. All along the highway and side streets, you'll find dozens of fine-art and crafts galleries, clothing boutiques, and jewelry shops.

Laguna's central beach gives you a perfect slice of local life. A stocky 1920s lifeguard tower marks **Main Beach Park**, at the end of Broadway at South Coast Highway. A wooden boardwalk separates the sand from a strip of lawn. Walk along this, or hang out on one of its benches, to watch people body-surfing, playing sand volleyball, or scrambling around one of two half-basketball courts. The beach also has children's play equipment, picnic areas, restrooms, and showers. Across the street is a lovely old movie theater.

The **Laguna Art Museum** displays American art, with an emphasis on California artists and works. Special exhibits change quarterly.

ODDBALL ART

An outdoor amphitheater near the mouth of the canyon hosts the annual **Pageant of the Masters** (☎ 949/494–1145 or 800/487–3378 ⊕ www.foapom.com), Laguna's most impressive event. Local participants arrange tableaux vivants, in which live models and carefully orchestrated backgrounds merge in striking mimicry of classical and contemporary paintings. The pageant is part of the **Festival of Arts**, held in July and August; tickets are much in demand, so plan ahead.

■ **TIP→** Galleries throughout the area stay open late in coordination with the museum on the first Thursday of each month (visit www.firstthursdaysartwalk. com for more information). A free shuttle service runs from the museum to galleries and studios. ⊠ *307 Cliff Dr., Laguna Beach* ☎ *949/494–6531* ⊕ *www.lagunaartmuseum.org* ☞ *$10* ☉ *Daily 11–5.*

Where to Stay & Eat

★ **$$$$** ✗ **Studio.** In a nod to Laguna's art history, Studio has food that entices the eye as well as the palate. You can't beat the location, on a 50-foot bluff overlooking the Pacific Ocean—every table has an ocean view. Executive chef James Boyce changes the menu daily to reflect the seafood and the fresh ingredients on hand (he even has a "personal forager"). Among the standouts you might find grilled rib-eye steak and a salad of seared Catalina yellowtail with Hawaiian green papaya and lemongrass. A prix-fixe tasting menu is $115; with wine it's $170. Nonalcoholic beverages can be paired with the food, too. ⊠*Montage Hotel, 30801 S. Coast Hwy.* ☎ *949/715–6420* ⌲ *Reservations essential* ▭ *AE, D, DC, MC, V* ☉ *Closed Mon. No lunch.*

★ **$$–$$$** ✗ **Five Feet.** Others have attempted to mimic this restaurant's innovative blend of Chinese and French cooking styles, but Five Feet remains the leader of the pack. Among the standout dishes is the house catfish. The setting is pure Laguna: exposed ceiling, open kitchen, high noise level, and brick walls hung with works by local artists. ⊠ *328 Glenneyre St., Laguna Beach* ☎ *949/497–4955* ▭ *AE, D, DC, MC, V* ☉ *No lunch.*

$$–$$$ ✗ **French 75.** Locals love this bistro and champagne bar for its intimate, opulent feel inspired by a 1940s-style Paris supper club. It's definitely a change from the usual bright, casual restaurant look; this space has low lighting, dark-wood paneling, and a mural of cherubs spritzing bubbly. The menu focuses on bistro classics with the occasional curveball, like duck in a caramelized honey and tangerine sauce. One constant: the Callebaut chocolate soufflé. ⊠ *1464 S. Coast Hwy., Laguna Beach* ☎ *949/494–8444* ▭ *AE, D, DC, MC, V* ☉ *No lunch.*

$–$$$ ✗ **Mosun.** Fans of this restaurant-nightclub favor the Pacific Rim cuisine, fresh sushi, and large selection of sake. Among the entrées are teriyaki steak and pan-seared, five-spice duck breast. ⊠ *680 S. Coast Hwy., Laguna Beach* ☎ *949/497–5646* ⌲ *Reservations essential* ▭ *AE, D, DC, MC, V* ☉ *No lunch.*

$$ ✗ **Ti Amo.** A romantic setting and creative Mediterranean cuisine have earned this place acclaim. Try the seared ahi with a sesame-seed crust. All the nooks and crannies are charming, candlelighted, and private, but to maximize romance, request a table in the enclosed garden in back. ⊠ *31727 S. Coast Hwy., Laguna Beach* ☎ *949/499–5350* ▭ *AE, D, DC, MC, V* ☉ *No lunch.*

¢–$$ ✗ **Taco Loco.** This may look like a fast-food taco stand, and the hemp brownies on the menu may make you think the kitchen's *really* laid-back, but the quality of the food here equals that in many higher-price restaurants. Some Mexican standards get a Louisiana twist, like Cajun-spiced seafood tacos. Other favorites include blackened lobster tacos and the mushroom-and-tofu burgers. It stays open late on Friday and Saturday, till 2 AM. ⊠ *640 S. Coast Hwy.* ☎ *949/497–1635* ▭ *AE, MC, V.*

$ ✕ **Café Zinc.** Laguna Beach cognoscenti gather at the tiny counter and plant-filled patio of this vegetarian café serving breakfast and lunch. Oatmeal is sprinkled with berries in season, poached eggs are dusted with herbs, and the orange juice is fresh squeezed. For lunch, try the spicy Thai pasta, asparagus salad with orange peel and capers, or one of the pizzettes. ⊠ *350 Ocean Ave., Laguna Beach* ☎ *949/494–6302* 🖃 *AE, MC, V* ⊗ *No dinner.*

¢–$ ✕ **The Stand.** If an eatery can be called typically Laguna, this is it. Only organic vegan ingredients are used in preparations. There are around 20 spaces to eat outside, read the supplied tracts and newspapers, and maybe argue a point or two. Smoothies, salads, and pita sandwiches are favorites. The Stand is open 7–7 daily. ⊠ *238 Thalia St., near PCH* ☎ *949/ 494–8101* 🖃 *AE, D, MC, V.*

$$$$
FodorsChoice
★
🏨 **Montage Resort & Spa.** Laguna's connection to the Californian *plein air* artists is mined for inspiration at this head-turningly fancy hotel. The Montage uses the local Craftsman style as a touchstone. Shingled buildings ease down a bluff to the cove beaches; inside, works by contemporary and early-20th-century California artists snare your attention. Guest rooms balance ease and refinement; all have ocean views and amenities such as CD/DVD players and extra-deep tubs. Of the restaurants, Studio is the fanciest, with more sweeping Pacific views and a refined contemporary menu. At the oceanfront spa and fitness center, you can indulge in a sea-salt scrub, take a yoga class, or hit the lap pool. ⊠ *30801 S. Coast Hwy., Laguna Beach 92651* ☎ *888/715–6700* 🖷 *949/715–6100* ⊕ *www.montagelagunabeach.com* 🛏 *211 rooms, 51 suites* ♨ *3 restaurants, room service, in-room safes, minibars, in-room data ports, 3 pools, health club, outdoor hot tub, spa, beach, 4 bars, children's programs (ages 5–12), dry cleaning, laundry service, concierge, business services, meeting rooms, parking (fee)* 🖃 *AE, MC, V.*

★ $$$$ 🏨 **Surf & Sand Resort.** Your parents may have stayed here decades ago, but there's nothing dated about it. Guest rooms seem to hover over the beach; most have private balconies. The decor uses soft, monochromatic colors and sand-color sisal rugs. Rooms in the Towers have whirlpool tubs in the bathrooms. If you've gotten a bit too much sun, sign up for the aloe vera wrap in the spa. ⊠ *1555 S. Coast Hwy., Laguna Beach 92651* ☎ *949/497–4477 or 888/869–7569* 🖷 *949/494–2897* ⊕ *www.surfandsandresort.com* 🛏 *155 rooms, 13 suites* ♨ *Restaurant, minibars, cable TV with movies, in-room broadband, pool, health club, spa, beach, bar, concierge, meeting rooms* 🖃 *AE, D, DC, MC, V.*

★ $$–$$$$ 🏨 **Hotel Casa del Camino.** This Spanish-style hotel was built in 1927. Its ace in the hole is its large rooftop terrace, with clear ocean views—an ideal spot at sunset. Rooms have

WORD OF MOUTH

"Laguna's charm is partly based on the fact that we have cove beaches as opposed to those long (dull) stretches of sand. Laguna's Main Beach is the 'safest' as it is the widest beach and the lifeguard headquarters is there . . . please do yourself a favor and acquaint yourself with the city's tram service. Laguna's traffic (especially getting in and out of town at 'tourist rush hour') can be really bad . . ."   –skateboardmom2

warm color schemes; beds have feather duvets to ward off the seaside chill. ✉ *1289 S. Coast Hwy., Laguna Beach 92651* ☎ *949/497–2446 or 888/367–5232* 📠 *949/494–5581* 🌐 *www.casacamino.com* 🛏 *42 rooms, 7 suites* 🍴 *Restaurant, cable TV, Wi-Fi, bar, free parking, some pets allowed* 🖃 *AE, D, DC, MC, V.*

$$–$$$$ 🏨 **Inn at Laguna Beach.** On a bluff overlooking the ocean, the inn is on Main Beach and steps from shops and art galleries. Location and price are the key to this good hotel. ✉ *211 N. Coast Hwy., Laguna Beach 92651* ☎ *949/497–9722 or 800/544–4479* 📠 *949/497–9972* 🌐 *www. innatlagunabeach.com* 🛏 *70 rooms* 🍴 *Minibars, some microwaves, refrigerators, cable TV, in-room VCRs, in-room data ports, pool, meeting rooms* 🖃 *AE, D, DC, MC, V.*

★ $$–$$$ 🏨 **Eiler's Inn.** Named for Laguna's late official greeter, this B&B is centered on a bright courtyard with a fountain. Every room is different, but all are full of antiques and travelers' journals for you to write in. Afternoon wine and cheese are served in the courtyard or in the cozy reading room, where you'll find the inn's only TV. A sundeck in back has an ocean view. ✉ *741 S. Coast Hwy., Laguna Beach 92651* ☎ *949/ 494–3004 or 866/617–2696* 📠 *949/497–2215* 🛏 *12 rooms* 🍴 *No room phones, no room TVs, no a/c* 🖃 *AE, D, DC, MC, V* 🍽 *BP.*

$–$$$ 🏨 **Hotel Laguna.** The oldest hotel in Laguna (opened in 1888) has manicured gardens, beach views, and an ideal location downtown. Among the perks is access to the hotel's private beach, where guests are provided with lounges, umbrellas, and towels and can order lunch or cocktails from the Beach Club menu. ✉ *425 S. Coast Hwy., Laguna Beach 92651* ☎ *949/494–1151 or 800/524–2927* 📠 *949/497–2163* 🌐 *www. hotellaguna.com* 🛏 *65 rooms* 🍴 *2 restaurants, in-room DVDs, Wi-Fi, beach, bar, meeting rooms, parking (fee); no a/c* 🖃 *AE, DC, MC, V* 🍽 *CP.*

Nightlife & the Arts

The **Laguna Playhouse** (✉ 606 Laguna Canyon Rd., Laguna Beach ☎ 949/497–2787 🌐 www.lagunaplayhouse.com), dating to the 1920s, mounts a variety of productions, from classics to youth-oriented plays. The **Sawdust Arts Festival** (☎ 949/494–3030 🌐 www.sawdustartfestival. org), held in July and August opposite the Festival of the Arts amphitheater, always hosts musicians and entertainers.

The **Boom Boom Room** (✉ Coast Inn, 1401 S. Coast Hwy., Laguna Beach ☎ 949/494–7588) is the town's most popular gay club. The **Sandpiper** (✉ 1183 S. Coast Hwy., Laguna Beach ☎ 949/494–4694), a hole-in-the-wall dancing joint, attracts an eclectic crowd. **White House** (✉ 340 S. Coast Hwy., Laguna Beach ☎ 949/494–8088), a chic club on the main strip, has nightly entertainment and dancing.

Sports & the Outdoors

BEACHES There are a handful of lovely beaches around town besides the Main Beach (*above*). **Aliso Creek County Beach** (☎ 714/834–2400), in south Laguna, has a playground, fire pits, parking, food stands, and restrooms. **1,000 Steps Beach,** off South Coast Highway at 9th Street, is a hard-to-find locals' spot with great waves. There aren't really 1,000 steps down to it, it just seems that way. **Woods Cove,** off South Coast Highway at Diamond Street, is especially quiet during the week. Big rock formations hide lurking crabs. As you climb the steps to leave, you can see a Tudor-style mansion that was once the home of Bette Davis.

BICYCLING Mountain bikes and helmets can be rented at **Rainbow Bicycles** (✉ 485 N. Coast Hwy., Laguna Beach ☎ 949/494–5806 ⊕ www.teamrain.com).

GOLF **Aliso Creek Golf Course** (✉ 31106 S. Coast Hwy., Laguna Beach ☎ 949/499–1919 ⊕ www.alisocreekinn.com) is a scenic 9-hole facility with a putting green. Greens fees are $20–$30; carts (optional) cost $3 for a pull cart or $10 for a motorized one. Reservations are accepted up to a week in advance.

HIKING The **Laguna Coast Wilderness Park** (☎ 949/923–2235 ⊕ www. lagunacanyon.org) is spread over 19 acres of fragile coastal territory, including the canyon. The trails are great for hiking and mountain biking and are open daily, weather permitting. Docent-led hikes are given regularly; call for information.

TENNIS Six metered courts can be found at **Laguna Beach High School.** Two courts are available at the **Irvine Bowl.** Six courts are available at **Alta Laguna Park** on a first-come, first-served basis. For more information, call the **City of Laguna Beach Recreation Department** (☎ 949/497–0716).

WATER SPORTS Because its entire beach area is a marine preserve, Laguna Beach is ideal for snorkelers. Scuba divers should head to the Marine Life Refuge area, which runs from Seal Rock to Diver's Cove. Rent bodyboards at **Hobie Sports** (✉ 294 Forest Ave., Laguna Beach ☎ 949/497–3304).

Shopping

Forest and Ocean avenues and Glenneyre Street are full of art galleries and fine jewelry and clothing boutiques.

Art for the Soul (✉ 272 Forest Ave., Laguna Beach ☎ 949/497–8700) has hand-painted furniture, crafts, and unusual gifts. **Artisance** (✉ 278 Beach St. ☎ 949/494–0687) pulls together posh tableware and decorative odds and ends, from shell-like porcelain by Ted Muehling to glossy coffee-table books. Get your sugar fix at the time-warped **Candy Baron** (✉ 231 Forest Ave. ☎ 949/497–7508), filled with old-fashioned goodies like gumdrops, bull's-eyes, and more than a dozen barrels of saltwater taffy. The **Crystal Image** (✉ 225 Forest Ave., Laguna Beach ☎ 949/497–3399) has an almost overwhelming trove of rare minerals, meteorites, fossils, jewelry, and art. Perfume bottles and boxes made from minerals are particularly eyecatching. Hit **Fetneh Blake** (✉ 427 N. Coast Hwy., Laguna Beach ☎ 949/494–3787) for pricey, Euro-chic clothes. The emerging designers found here lure Angelenos to make the trek south. Browse **Georgeo's Art Glass and Jewelry** (✉ 269 Forest Ave., Laguna Beach ☎ 949/497–0907) for a large selection of etched-glass bowls, vases, and fine jewelry. At **Trove** (✉ 1233 N. Coast Hwy., Laguna Beach ☎ 949/376–4640) you can rummage for estate jewelry, 18th- to 20th-century pieces, and odd, whimsical finds. The **Tung & Groov** (✉ 950 Glenneyre St., Laguna Beach ☎ 949/494–0768) carries an eclectic mix of hand-crafted and decorator items like traditional umbrellas from Bali, brass elephant bells from India, and papier-mâché boxes.

ART GALLERIES Most South Village art galleries line up along the South Coast Highway in the 900 to 2000 blocks. **DeRu's Fine Art** (✉ 1590 S. Coast Hwy., Laguna Beach ☎ 949/376–3785) specializes in California impressionist works by artists such as Guy Rose, William Wendt, and others. The **Redfern Gallery** (✉ 1540 S. Coast Hwy., Laguna Beach ☎ 949/497–3356) is another top source for California impressionists. You can see more of its collection at the Montage Resort. Since 1937, **Warren Imports** (✉ 1910 S. Coast Hwy., Laguna Beach ☎ 949/494–6505) has been the place to go for Asian art and antiques—everything from Chinese porcelain to Japanese iron teapots to carved Buddhas.

Dana Point

⑰ *10 mi south of Laguna Beach, via PCH.*

Dana Point's claim to fame is its small-boat marina tucked into a dramatic natural harbor and surrounded by high bluffs. **Dana Point Harbor** (☎ 949/923–2255 ⊕ www.danapointharbor.com) was first described more than 100 years ago by its namesake, Richard Henry Dana, in his book *Two Years Before the Mast.* At the marina are docks for small boats, marine-oriented shops, restaurants, and boat and bike rentals. In early March a **whale festival** (☎ 949/472–7888 or 888/440–4309 ⊕ www. festivalofwhales.org) celebrates the passing gray whale migration with concerts, films, sports competitions, and a weekend street fair.

At the south end of Dana Point, **Doheny State Beach** (☎ 949/496–6171, 714/433–6400 water quality information) is one of southern California's top surfing destinations, but there's a lot more to do within this 63-acre area. Divers and anglers hang out at the beach's western end, and during low tide, the tide pools beckon both young and old. You'll also find five indoor tanks and an interpretive center devoted to the wildlife of the Doheny Marine Refuge. There are food stands and shops, picnic facilities, volleyball courts, and a pier for fishing. Camping is permitted, though there are no RV hook-ups. ⚠ **Be aware that the waters here periodically do not meet health standards established by California (warning signs are posted if that's the case).**

Two indoor tanks at the **Ocean Institute** contain touchable sea creatures, as well as the complete skeleton of a gray whale. Anchored near the institute is *The Pilgrim,* a full-size replica of the square-rigged vessel on which Richard Henry Dana sailed. You can tour the boat Sunday 10–3. Weekend cruises are also available. In addition, marine-mammal exploration cruises are given January through March, and cruises to explore regional tide pools set out year-round. ✉ *24200 Dana Point Harbor Dr., Dana Point* ☎ *949/496–2274* ⊕ *www.ocean-institute.org* ✉ *$5* ☺ *Weekends 10–3:30.*

Where to Stay & Eat

$–$$$ ✕ **Luciana's Ristorante.** This intimate restaurant can be relied on for straightforward Italian meals. Dining rooms are small, warmed by two fireplaces; there's another fireplace on the patio. Try the freshly handmade pastas or the linguine with clams, prawns, calamari, and mussels in a light tomato sauce. ⊠ *24312 Del Prado Ave., Dana Point* ☎ *949/661–6500* ▭ *AE, DC, MC, V* ☺ *No lunch.*

$–$$$ ✗ **Wind & Sea.** An unblocked ocean view makes this a great place for lunch—and looking out on the Pacific might put you in the mood for a retro cocktail like a mai tai. Of the entrées, try the macadamia-crusted mahimahi. On warm days, patio tables beckon you outside. ⊠ *34699 Golden Lantern St., Dana Point* ☎ *949/496–6500* ▭ *AE, MC, V.*

¢–$$ ✗ **Turk's.** Once owned by Hollywood bit player/strongman Turk Varteresian, Turk's is now run by his daughter Candy. Aquariums give it a nautical feel, while the walls are filled with old pictures of Turk's movies and of various celebrities. Since the bar and grill is smack on the boardwalk and stays open until 2 AM, it's a big local favorite. ⊠ *34683 Golden Lantern St., Dana Point* ☎ *949/496–9028* ▭ *AE, MC, V.*

¢–$ ✗ **Proud Mary's.** On a terrace overlooking the harbor, this "Cheers" on the water serves burgers, steaks, and other American standards, and you can order breakfast all day. ⊠ *34689 Golden Lantern St., Dana Point* ☎ *949/493–5853* ▭ *AE, D, MC, V* ☺ *No dinner.*

$$$$
Fodor'sChoice
★ ✗🏨 **Ritz-Carlton, Laguna Niguel.** An unrivaled setting on the edge of the Pacific, combined with hallmark Ritz-Carlton service, has made this resort justly famous. The sleek, contemporary color scheme of cool blues, silver, and cream is punctuated with magenta accents. Rooms have 42-inch plasma TVs and DVD players, marble bathrooms, and private balconies with ocean or pool views. Restaurant 162', named for its site 162 feet above sea level, has sweeping views of the Pacific. The menu is divided into small, medium, and large plates. A small plate might be soup; a medium plate a pizza; and a large plate oven roasted cod or maple-chili-grilled rib-eye steak. The wood-panel former library was transformed into a bar and meeting place. This lobby lounge has musical performances Wednesday through Saturday evenings. ⊠ *1 Ritz-Carlton Dr., Dana Point 92629* ☎ *949/240–2000 or 800/241–3333* 🖷 *949/240–0829* ⊕ *www.ritzcarlton.com* ⊷ *363 rooms, 30 suites* ⌂ *3 restaurants, in-room safes, minibars, in-room data ports, Wi-Fi, 2 tennis courts, 2 pools, health club, hair salon, spa, lobby lounge, concierge, business services, meeting rooms* ▭ *AE, D, DC, MC, V.*

$$$$ ✗🏨 **St. Regis Monarch Beach Resort and Spa.** Exclusivity and indulgence carry the day here; you can even have someone unpack for you. The 172-acre grounds include a private beach club, an 18-hole Robert Trent Jones Jr.–designed golf course, and tennis courts across the street. Rooms have views of either the coast or the lush landscaping; such amenities as CD and DVD players and libraries are among the pluses. The best restaurant is Stonehill Tavern, which opened in 2006 under chef Michael Mina and serves modern American fare. Can't decide between appetizers? You can order a trio, three small plates, each focused on a key ingredient like lobster or duck. Entrées might include prime short rib with braised potatoes and truffles or shellfish stew with saffron broth. ⊠ *1 Monarch Beach Resort, off Niguel Rd., Dana Point 92629* ☎ *949/234–3200 or 800/722–1543* 🖷 *949/234–3201* ⊕ *www.stregismb.com* ⊷ *325 rooms, 75 suites* ⌂ *6 restaurants, in-room safes, minibars, cable TV with movies and video games, in-room data ports, Wi-Fi, 18-hole golf course, 3 pools, health club, hair salon, massage, spa, beach, bar, lobby lounge,* *dry cleaning, laundry facilities, concierge, business services, some pets allowed (free)* $\boxminus$ *AE, D, DC, MC, V.*

★ $$–$$$ 🏨 **Blue Lantern Inn.** Combining New England–style architecture with a southern California setting, this white-clapboard B&B rests on a bluff overlooking the harbor and ocean. A fire warms the intimate, inviting living area, where you may enjoy complimentary snacks and play backgammon every afternoon. The Nantucket–style guest rooms also have fireplaces and whirlpool tubs. The top-floor Tower Suite has a 180-degree ocean view. ⊠ *34343 St. of the Blue Lantern, Dana Point 92629* ☎ *949/661–1304 or 800/950–1236* 🖷 *949/496–1483* ⊕ *www. bluelanterninn.com* 🛏 *29 rooms* ♨ *In-room VCRs, in-room broadband, gym, concierge, meeting rooms; no smoking* $\boxminus$ *AE, DC, MC, V* ¶ *BP.*

Sports & the Outdoors

Inside Dana Point Harbor, **Swim Beach** has a fishing pier, barbecues, food stands, parking, restrooms, and showers. Rental stands for surfboards, Windsurfers, small powerboats, and sailboats can be found near most of the piers.

Dana Wharf Sportfishing & Whale Watching (⊠ 34675 Golden Lantern St., Dana Point ☎ 949/496–5794 ⊕ www.danawharfsportfishing.com) runs charters and whale-watching excursions from early December to late April. Tickets cost $25; reservations are required. **Embarcadero Marina** (⊠ 34512 Embarcadero Pl., Dana Point ☎ 949/496–6177 ⊕ www.danaharbor.com) has small powerboats and sailboats for rent near the launching ramp at Dana Point Harbor. **Hobie Sports** (⊠ 24825 Del Prado, Dana Point ☎ 949/496–2366) rents surfboards and boogie boards.

On **Capt. Dave's Dolphin Safari** (⊠ 34675 Golden Lantern, Dana Point ☎ 949/488–2828 ⊕ www.dolphinsafari.com), you have a good chance of seeing pods of dolphins, as many as 1,000, only a half mile from shore. Dave, a marine naturalist–filmmaker, and his wife run the safaris year-round. The endangered blue whale is sometimes seen in summer. Reservations are required for the safaris, which last 2½ hours and cost $45.

San Juan Capistrano

18 *5 mi north of Dana Point, Hwy. 74, 60 mi north of San Diego, I–5.*

San Juan Capistrano, one of the few noteworthy historical districts in southern California, is best known for its mission, to which the swallows traditionally return each year, migrating from their winter haven in Argentina, but these days they are more likely to choose other local sites for nesting. St. Joseph's Day, March 19, launches a week of festivities. After summering in the arches of the old stone church, the swallows head home on St. John's Day, October 23. Along Camino Capistrano are antiques stores ranging from pricey to cheap.

If you arrive by train, you'll be dropped off across from the mission at the San Juan Capistrano depot. With its appealing brick café and preserved Santa Fe cars, the depot retains much of the magic of early American railroads. If driving, park near Ortega and Camino Capistrano, the city's main streets.

7

Fodor$Choice
★

Mission San Juan Capistrano, founded in 1776 by Father Junípero Serra, was the major Roman Catholic outpost between Los Angeles and San Diego. The Great Stone Church, begun in 1797, is the largest structure created by the Spanish in California. Many of the mission's adobe buildings have been preserved to illustrate mission life, with exhibits of an olive millstone, tallow ovens, tanning vats, metalworking furnaces, and the padres' living quarters. The gardens, with their fountains, are a lovely spot in which to wander. The bougainvillea-covered Serra Chapel is believed to be the oldest building standing in California. Mass takes place daily at 7 AM in the chapel and 8:30 in the new church. ⊠ *Camino Capistrano and Ortega Hwy., San Juan Capistrano* ☎ *949/234–1300* ⊕ *www.missionsjc.com* ⊠ *$6* ⊗ *Daily 8:30–5.*

Near Mission San Juan Capistrano is the **San Juan Capistrano Library,** a postmodern structure built in 1983. Architect Michael Graves combined classical and Mission styles to striking effect. Its courtyard has secluded places for reading. ⊠ *31495 El Camino Real, San Juan Capistrano* ☎ *949/493–1752* ⊗ *Mon.–Wed. 10–8, Thurs. 10–6, Sat. 10–5, Sun. noon–5.*

Where to Eat

$$–$$$ ✕ **L'Hirondelle.** Roast duck, rabbit, and Belgian dishes are the hallmark of this French and Belgian restaurant, whose name is French for—surprise—the swallow. The extensive wine list is matched by an impressive selection of Belgian beers. You can dine inside or out on the patio. Sunday brunch is superb. ⊠ *31631 Camino Capistrano, San Juan Capistrano* ☎ *949/661–0425* ⊟ *AE, DC, MC, V* ⊗ *Closed Mon.*

$–$$$ ✕ **Cedar Creek Inn.** Equally suitable for family meals and romantic dinners, the inn has a children's menu as well as a secluded outdoor patio. The contemporary American menu features crowd pleasers like an ahi burger, rack of lamb, and herb-crusted halibut. ⊠ *26860 Ortega Hwy., San Juan Capistrano* ☎ *949/240–2229* ⊟ *AE, MC, V.*

$–$$ ✕ **The Ramos House Cafe.** Here's your chance to visit one of the historic district's simple, 19th-century homes. This café sits practically on the railroad tracks—nab a table on the patio and dig into a hearty breakfast, such as the mountainous wild-mushroom scramble. Patrons are occasionally saluted by the roar of a passing Amtrak. ⊠ *31752 Los Rios St., San Juan Capistrano* ☎ *949/443–1342* ⊟ *AE, D, DC, MC, V* ⊗ *Closed Mon.*

$$ ▦ **Mission Inn San Juan Capistrano.** Next door to the mission is this B&B on a 2-acre century-old family orchard where you can pick oranges right off the trees. Each of the guest rooms has a different theme and is named for one the California missions. ⊠ *26891 Ortega Hwy., 92675* ☎ *949/234–0249* ⊟ *949/234–0311* ⊕ *www.missioninnsjc.com* ⊐ *20 rooms* ⊘ *Refrigerators, cable TV, Wi-Fi, pool, free parking* ⊟ *AE, D, MC, V.*

Nightlife

Coach House (⊠ 33157 Camino Capistrano, San Juan Capistrano ☎ 949/496–8930 ⊕ www.thecoachhouse.com), a roomy, casual club with long tables and a dark-wood bar, draws crowds of varying ages for entertainment ranging from hip new bands to Dick Dale, the take-no-prisoners king of the surf guitar.

Prayer and misbehavior lie cheek by jowl; across the way from the mission you'll find a line of Harleys in front of the **Swallows Inn** (✉ 31786 Camino Capistrano, San Juan Capistrano ☎ 949/493–3188). Despite a somewhat tough look, it pulls in all kinds—bikers, college kids, Marines from San Diego, grandparents, all come for a drink, a casual bite, and some rowdy live music. There's no cover charge.

OFF THE BEATEN PATH

SAN CLEMENTE – Travelers who shun the throngs in favor of a low-key beach experience should drive 10 mi south of Dana Point on Pacific Coast Highway to San Clemente. There, 20 square mi of prime bicycling terrain await. Camp Pendleton, the country's largest Marine Corps base, welcomes cyclists to use some of its roads—just don't be surprised to see a troop helicopter taking off right beside you. Surfers favor **San Clemente State Beach** (☎ 949/492–3156), which has camping facilities, RV hookups, and fire rings. San Onofre State Beach, just south of San Clemente, is another surfing destination. Below the bluffs are 3½ mi of sandy beach, where you can swim, fish, and watch wildlife.

ORANGE COUNTY ESSENTIALS

To research prices, get advice from other travelers, and book travel arrangements, visit www.fodors.com.

AIR TRAVEL

It's easy to arrange for a flight into John Wayne Airport, conveniently near the intersection of the I–405 and Highway 55 freeways. From most destinations, you may have to book a connecting flight to get there. Long Beach Airport, near the south end of Los Angeles County by I–405, can also be handy. A hub for low-cost domestic airline JetBlue, it has many daily nonstop flights.

AIRPORTS

The county's main facility is John Wayne Airport Orange County (SNA), which is served by 11 major domestic airlines and 3 commuter lines. It's a glossy facility, complete with a statue of namesake Duke, and its relatively small size makes it easy to negotiate. Still, you should leave plenty of time for security checks and parking. Long Beach Airport (LGB) serves five airlines, including its major player, JetBlue. It's smaller and more low-key than John Wayne; it may not have many airport amenities, but parking is generally a snap. It's roughly 20–30 minutes by car from Anaheim. For details on other L.A. County airports, including Los Angeles International Airport (LAX), *see* the Smart Travel Tips chapter.
🚺 **Airport Information John Wayne Airport Orange County** ✉ MacArthur Blvd. at I–405, Santa Ana ☎ 949/252–5252 🌐 www.ocair.com. **Long Beach Airport** ✉ 4100 Donald Douglas Dr., Long Beach ☎ 562/570–6555 🌐 www.lgb.org.

AIRPORT TRANSFERS

Airport Bus, a shuttle service, carries passengers from John Wayne and LAX to Anaheim and Buena Park. The fare from John Wayne to Anaheim is $14, from LAX to Anaheim $19. Prime Time Airport Shuttle provides door-to-door service from Orange County hotels to LAX and the San Pedro cruise terminal. The fare is $13 per person and up, depending on where you're picked up and dropped off. SuperShuttle provides 24-hour door-to-door service from all the airports to all points in Orange County. The fare to the Disneyland area is $10 per person from John Wayne, $15 from LAX, and $30 from Long Beach Airport.

🛈 **Shuttles** Airport Bus ☎ 800/938–8933 ⊕ www.airportbus.com. **Prime Time Airport Shuttle** ☎ 800/262–7433 ⊕ www.primetimeshuttle.com. **SuperShuttle** ☎ 714/517–6600 ⊕ www.supershuttle.com.

BUS TRAVEL

The Los Angeles MTA has limited service to Orange County. From downtown L.A., Bus 460 goes to Knott's Berry Farm and Disneyland Resort. Greyhound serves Anaheim and Santa Ana. The Orange County Transportation Authority will take you virtually anywhere in the county, but it will take time; OCTA buses go from Knott's Berry Farm and Disneyland to Huntington Beach and Newport Beach. Bus 1 travels along the coast; Buses 701 and 721 provide express service to Los Angeles.

Fares for the OCTA local routes are $1.25 per boarding; you can also get a $3 local day pass (valid only on the date of purchase). Day passes can be purchased from bus drivers upon boarding. Express bus fare between Orange County and L.A. is $3.75 a pop, $2.50 if you have a day pass. The bus-fare boxes take coins and dollar bills, but you must use exact change.

🛈 **Bus Information** Greyhound ☎ 714/999–1256 or 800/231–2222 ⊕ www.greyhound.com. **Los Angeles MTA** ☎ 213/626–4455 ⊕ www.mta.net. **Orange County Transportation Authority (OCTA)** ☎ 714/636–7433 ⊕ www.octa.net.

CAR TRAVEL

The San Diego Freeway (I–405) and the Santa Ana Freeway (I–5) run north–south through Orange County. South of Laguna I–405 merges into I–5 (called the San Diego Freeway south from this point). A toll road, the 73 Highway, runs 15 mi from Newport Beach to San Juan Capistrano; it costs $3 and is usually less jammed than the regular freeways. Do your best to avoid freeways during rush hours (6–9 and 3:30–6:30).

Highways 55 and 91 head west to the ocean and east into the mountains. Highway 91, which goes to Garden Grove and inland points (Buena Park, Anaheim), has some express lanes for which drivers pay a toll, ostensibly to avoid the worst of rush-hour traffic. If you have three or more people in your car, though, you can use the Highway 91 express lanes most of the day for free (the exception being 4 PM–6 PM on weekdays, when you pay half-fare). Highway 55 leads to Newport Beach. The Pacific Coast Highway (Highway 1) allows easy access to beach communities and is the most scenic route.

Laguna Canyon Road, the beautiful route that winds through a coastal canyon, is undergoing a widening project begun in 2003. The work is expected to take four years, but the road will remain open throughout. ⚠ **The old road is quite narrow and used by cyclists as well as drivers, so especially cautious and turn on your headlights even in daytime.**

GOLF

Orange Country has some noteworthy golfing opportunities, thanks to the area's great weather and dozens of facilities. For more information contact the **Southern California Golf Association** (☏ 818/980–3630 ⊕ www.scga.org). Another resource is the **Southern California Public Links Golf Association** (☏ 714/994–4747 ⊕ www.plga.org).

MEDIA

Newspapers in Orange County include the *Orange County Register,* the *Los Angeles Times,* and the edgier, feature-heavy *OC Weekly.* All have up-to-date listings and events. There are also many ad-driven magazines and newsletters in the area: their recommendations should be taken with a big grain of salt.

Online, tap into the **OC Weekly** site (⊕ www.ocweekly.com) for events listings, reviews of inexpensive local restaurants (including a "hole-in-the-wall" column), and skewering takes on local politics. **Squeeze OK** (⊕ www. squeezeoc.com) gives descriptions and ratings of local restaurants, nightlife, shops, spas, and activities. The **Orange County Art Source** (⊕ www. ocartsource.org) posts events listings and links to local arts organizations.

TRAIN TRAVEL

When planning train travel, consider where the train stations are in relation to your ultimate destination. You may need to make extra transportation arrangements once you've arrived in town. From the station in San Juan Capistrano, for instance, you can walk through the historic part of town; the station in Anaheim, on the other hand, is not within walking distance of Disneyland.

Amtrak makes daily stops in Orange County at Fullerton, Anaheim, Santa Ana, Irvine, San Juan Capistrano, and San Clemente. Metrolink is a weekday commuter train that runs to and from Los Angeles and Orange County, starting as far south as Oceanside and stopping in Laguna Niguel, Tustin, San Juan Capistrano, San Clemente, Irvine, Santa Ana, Orange, Anaheim, and Fullerton. The Metrolink system is divided into a dozen zones; the fare you pay depends on how many zones you cover. Buy tickets from the vending machines at each station. Ticketing is on an honor system.

🚹 **Train Information Amtrak** ☏ 800/872–7245 ⊕ www.amtrak.com. **Metrolink** ☏ 800/ 371–5465 ⊕ www.metrolinktrains.com.

VISITOR INFORMATION

🚹 **Anaheim-Orange County Visitor and Convention Bureau** ✉ Anaheim Convention Center, 800 W. Katella Ave., Anaheim 92802 ☏ 714/765–8888 ⊕ www.anaheimoc. org. **Buena Park Convention and Visitors Office** ✉ 6601 Beach Blvd., Buena Park 90621 ☏ 800/541–3953 ⊕ www.buenapark.com. **Costa Mesa Conference and Visitors Bureau** ✆ Box 5071, Costa Mesa 92628 ☏ 714/384–0493 or 800/399–5499 ⊕ www. costamesa-ca.com. **Huntington Beach Conference and Visitors Bureau** ✉ 301 Main St., Suite 208, Huntington Beach 92648 ☏ 714/969–3492 ⊕ www.hbvisit.com. **Laguna Beach Visitors Bureau** ✉ 252 Broadway, Laguna Beach 92651 ☏ 949/376–0511 or 800/ 877–1115 ⊕ www.lagunabeachinfo.org. **Newport Beach Conference and Visitors Bureau** ✉ 3300 West Coast Hwy., Newport Beach 92663 ☏ 800/942–6278 ⊕ www. newportbeach-cvb.com. **San Juan Capistrano Chamber of Commerce and Visitors Center** ✉ 31781 Camino Capistrano, Suite 306, San Juan Capistrano 92693 ☏ 949/493–4700 ⊕ www.sanjuanchamber.com.

CATALINA ISLAND

Just 22 mi out from the L.A. coastline, across from Newport Beach and Long Beach, Catalina has virtually unspoiled mountains, canyons, coves, and beaches; best of all, it gives you a glimpse of what undeveloped southern California once looked like.

Summer, weekends, and holidays, Catalina crawls with thousands of L.A.-area boaters, who tie their vessels at protected moorings in Avalon and other coves. Although Catalina is not known for its beaches, sunbathing and water sports are big draws; divers and snorkelers come for the exceptionally clear water surrounding the island. The main town, Avalon, is a charming, old-fashioned beach community, where yachts bob in the crescent-shape bay. Wander beyond the main drag and you'll find brightly painted little bungalows fronting the sidewalks, with the occasional golf cart purring down the street.

Cruise ships sail into Avalon twice a week and smaller boats shuttle between Avalon and Two Harbors, a small isthmus cove on the island's western end. You can also take bus excursions beyond Avalon. Roads are limited and nonresident vehicles prohibited, so hiking (by permit only) and cycling are the only other means of exploring.

Perhaps it's no surprise that Catalina has long been a destination for filmmakers and movie stars. In its earlier past, however, the island also sheltered Russian fur trappers (seeking sea-otter skins), pirates, gold miners, and bootleggers (carrier pigeons were used to communicate with the mainland). In 1919 William Wrigley Jr., the chewing-gum magnate, purchased a controlling interest in the company developing Catalina Island, whose most famous landmark, the Casino, was built in 1929 under his orders. Because he owned the Chicago Cubs baseball team, Wrigley made Catalina the team's spring training site, an arrangement that lasted until 1951.

In 1975 the Santa Catalina Island Conservancy, a nonprofit foundation, acquired about 86% of the island to help preserve the area's natural resources. These days the conservancy is restoring the rugged interior country with plantings of native grasses and trees. Along the coast you might spot such oddities as electric perch, saltwater goldfish, and flying fish.

Although Catalina can be seen in a day, several inviting hotels make it worth extending your stay for one or more nights. A short itinerary might include breakfast along the boardwalk, a tour of the interior, a snorkeling excursion at Casino Point, and dinner in Avalon.

FUN FACT

Zane Grey, the writer who put the Western novel on the map, spent a lot of time on Catalina, and his influence is still evident in a peculiar way. When the movie version of Grey's book *The Vanishing American* was filmed here in 1924, American bison were ferried across from the mainland to give the land that Western plains look. When the moviemakers packed up and left, the buffalo stayed, and a small herd still remains, grazing the interior.

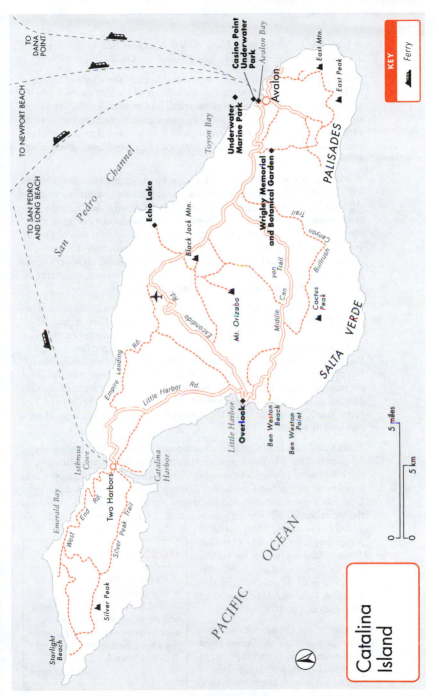

KEY

Ferry

TO DANA POINT

TO NEWPORT BEACH

TO SAN PEDRO AND LONG BEACH

San Pedro Channel

Casino Point Underwater Park

Avalon Bay

Avalon

Underwater Marine Park

Toyon Bay

Echo Lake

Black Jack Mtn.

Wrigley Memorial and Botanical Garden

PALISADES

East Mtn.

East Peak

Canyon Trail

Bullrush

Cactus Peak

Middle Can yon Trail

SALTA VERDE

Mt. Orizaba

Escondido Rd.

Rd.

Empire Landing Rd.

Little Harbor Rd.

Little Harbor Overlook

Ben Weston Beach

Ben Weston Point

Isthmus Cove

Two Harbors

Catalina Harbor

Emerald Bay

West End Rd.

Silver Peak Trail

Silver Peak

Starlight Beach

PACIFIC

OCEAN

0   5 miles

0   5 km

Catalina Island

Avalon

A 1- to 2-hr ferry ride from Long Beach, Newport Beach, or San Pedro; a 15-min helicopter ride from Long Beach or San Pedro.

Avalon, Catalina's only real town, extends from the shore of its natural harbor to the surrounding hillsides. Most of the city's activity, however, is centered along the pedestrian mall on Crescent Avenue, and most sights are easily reached on foot. Private cars are restricted and rental cars aren't allowed, but taxis, trams, and shuttles can take you anywhere you need to go. Bicycles and golf carts can be rented from shops along Crescent Avenue.

A walk along **Crescent Avenue** is a nice way to begin a tour of the town. Vivid art deco tiles adorn the avenue's fountains and planters—fired on the island by the now-defunct Catalina Tile Company, the tiles are a coveted commodity. Head to the **Green Pleasure Pier,** at the center of Crescent Avenue, for a good vantage point of Avalon. At the top of the hill you'll spot a big white building, the Inn at Mt. Ada, now a top-of-the-line B&B but originally built by William Wrigley Jr. for his wife. On the pier you'll find the Catalina Island Chamber of Commerce, snack stands, the Harbor Patrol, and scads of squawking seagulls.

★ On the northwest point of Avalon Bay (looking to your right from Green Pleasure Pier) is the majestic landmark **Casino.** This circular white structure is one of the finest examples of art deco architecture anywhere. Its Spanish-inspired floors and murals gleam with brilliant blue and green Catalina tiles. In this case, *casino,* the Italian word for "gathering place," has nothing to do with gambling. Rather, Casino life revolves around the magnificent ballroom. The same big-band dances that made the Casino famous in the 1930s and '40s still take place several times a year. The **New Year's Eve dance** (☎ 310/510–1520) is hugely popular and sells out well in advance.

Santa Catalina Island Company leads tours of the Casino, lasting about 55 minutes, for $9. You can also visit the **Catalina Island Museum,** in the lower level of the Casino, which investigates 7,000 years of island history; or stop at the **Casino Art Gallery** to see works by local artists. First-run movies are screened nightly at the **Avalon Theatre,** noteworthy for its classic 1929 theater pipe organ. ✉ *1 Casino Way, Avalon* ☎ *310/510–2414 museum, 310/510–0808 art gallery, 310/510–0179 Avalon Theatre* ☞ *Museum $4, art gallery free* ☉ *Museum: daily 10–4. Art gallery: mid-Mar.–Dec., daily 10:30–4; Jan.–mid-Mar, Tues. and Thurs.–Sun. 10:30–4.*

In front of the Casino are the crystal-clear waters of the **Casino Point Underwater Park,** a marine preserve protected from watercraft where moray eels, bat rays, spiny lobsters,

WORD OF MOUTH

"Catalina is a cool day trip. . . . We once rented golf carts to get around (there are no cars allowed) and we fell over laughing when we saw a town map on the steering wheel. Getting lost in Avalon? That'll be the day. . . ."

–WallyKringen

halibut, and other sea animals cruise around kelp forests and along the sandy bottom. It's a terrific site for scuba diving, with some shallow areas suitable for snorkeling. Scuba and snorkeling equipment can be rented on and near the pier. The shallow waters of **Lover's Cove**, east of the boat landing, are also good for snorkeling.

Two miles south of the bay via Avalon Canyon Road is **Wrigley Memorial and Botanical Garden.** Here you'll find plants native to southern California, including several that grow only on Catalina Island: Catalina ironwood, wild tomato, and rare Catalina mahogany. The Wrigley family commissioned the garden as well as the monument, which has a grand staircase and a Spanish mausoleum inlaid with colorful Catalina tile. (The mausoleum was never used by the Wrigleys, who are buried in Los Angeles.) Taxi service from Avalon is available, or you can take a tour bus from the downtown Tour Plaza or ferry landing. ⊠ *Avalon Canyon Rd., Avalon* ☎ *310/510–2897* ⊠ *$5* ⏲ *Daily 8–5.*

Where to Stay & Eat

$$–$$$ ✕ **Catalina Country Club.** The spring training clubhouse built for the Chicago Cubs now does duty as a restaurant for surf-and-turf standbys. The adjacent bar is great for an after-dinner drink; it connects to the old Cubs locker room. ⊠ *1 Country Club Dr., Avalon* ☎ *310/510–7404* ⌾ *Reservations essential* ▭ *AE, D, MC, V.*

$–$$$ ✕ **Steve's Steakhouse.** You won't lack for scenic distraction here; almost every table has a bay view. There are, of course, thick rib-eye and porterhouse steaks, but don't overlook the locally bought fish. Avalon-style shrimp from the Gulf of Mexico is also a favorite. ⊠ *417 Crescent Ave., Avalon* ☎ *310/510–0333* ▭ *AE, D, MC, V* ⏲ *No lunch Dec.–Apr.*

★ $$–$$$ ✕ **Channel House.** A longtime Avalon family owns this restaurant, serving dishes such as Catalina swordfish, coq au vin, and pepper steak. There's a patio facing the harbor, as well as an Irish bar. ⊠ *205 Crescent Ave., Avalon* ☎ *310/510–1617* ▭ *AE, D, MC, V* ⏲ *Closed Mon. mid-Oct.–Easter.*

¢–$ ✕ **Eric's on the Pier.** Stroll out on the pier to this laid-back counter spot for a buffalo burger to go or perhaps, should you snag a patio table, an order of fish-and-chips or nachos. ⊠ *Green Pier No. 2, Avalon* ☎ *310/510–0894* ▭ *AE, MC, V.*

¢–$ ✕ **Topless Taco.** This walk-up Mexican joint keeps it simple and satisfying: tacos, burritos, and homemade salsa and chips for hungry beachgoers and locals alike. ⊠ *313 Crescent Ave., Avalon* ☎ *310/510–0100* ▭ *No credit cards.*

$$$$ ⚏ **Inn on Mt. Ada.** Staying in the mansion where William Wrigley Jr. once lived gives you all the comforts of a millionaire's home—at a millionaire's prices, beginning at $360 a night in summer. Breakfast, lunch, beverages, snacks, and use of a golf cart are included. The guest rooms are traditional and elegant; some have fireplaces and all have water views. The hilltop view of the curve of the bay is spectacular, and service is discreet. ⊠ *398 Wrigley Rd., Avalon 90704* ☎ *310/510–2030 or 800/608–7669* ⊟ *310/510–2237* ⊕ *www.catalina.com/mtada* ⇆ *6 rooms* ⏶ *Dining room; no room phones, no kids under 14, no smoking, no a/c* ▭ *MC, V* ⎮◎⎮ *MAP.*

FodorsChoice ★

7

$$$ 🏨 **Hotel Metropole and Market Place.** This romantic hotel evokes the former look of New Orleans's French Quarter. Some guest rooms have balconies overlooking a flower-filled courtyard of restaurants and shops; others have ocean views. Many have fireplaces. For a stunning panorama, head for the rooftop deck. ⊠ *205 Crescent Ave., Avalon 90704* ☎ *310/510–1884 or 800/541–8528* 🖷 *310/510–2534* ⊕ *www.hotel-metropole. com* 🛏 *44 rooms, 4 suites* ♨ *Some in-room hot tubs, some minibars, cable TV, no-smoking rooms* ⊟ *AE, MC, V* ¶⊙¶ *CP.*

$$–$$$ 🏨 **Hotel Villa Portofino.** Steps from the Pleasure Pier, this hotel strikes a discreet note. Rooms are named after Italian cities, and most are decorated in deep jewel tones. Some ocean-facing rooms have open balconies, fireplaces, and marble baths. You can sunbathe on the private deck, or ask for beach towels and chairs to take to the cove. ⊠ *111 Crescent Ave., Avalon 90704* ☎ *310/510–0555 or 800/346–2326* 🖷 *310/510–0839* ⊕ *www.hotelvillaportofino.com* 🛏 *34 rooms* ♨ *Restaurant, minibars, cable TV* ⊟ *AE, D, DC, MC, V* ¶⊙¶ *CP.*

$–$$ 🏨 **Hotel Vista del Mar.** Contemporary rooms full of rattan furniture and greenery open onto a skylighted atrium. Some rooms have fireplaces, whirlpool tubs, and wet bars. Two larger rooms have ocean views. ⊠ *417 Crescent Ave., Avalon 90704* ☎ *310/510–1452 or 800/601–3836* 🖷 *310/510–2917* ⊕ *www.hotel-vistadelmar.com* 🛏 *15 rooms* ♨ *Some in-room hot tubs, minibars, refrigerators, cable TV, in-room VCRs, no-smoking rooms* ⊟ *AE, D, MC, V* ¶⊙¶ *CP.*

¢–$$ 🏨 **Hermosa Hotel and Catalina Cottages.** You'll find tiny, sparse rooms with shared baths in this 1890s hotel; the separate cottages have kitchens and private baths. The beach is a half block away. ⊠ *131 Metropole St., Avalon 90704* ☎ *310/510–1010 or 888/684–1313* 🖷 *310/510–2830* ⊕ *www.hermosahotel.com* 🛏 *35 rooms without bath, 14 cottages* ♨ *Some kitchens, cable TV; no room phones* ⊟ *AE, D, DC, MC, V.*

Nightlife

El Galleon (⊠411 Crescent Ave., Avalon ☎310/510–1188) has microbrews, bar nibbles, and karaoke. **Luau Larry's** (⊠ 509 Crescent Ave., Avalon ☎ 310/510–1919), famous for the potent blue Whicky Whacker cocktail, comes alive with boisterous tourists and locals on summer weekends.

Sports & the Outdoors

BICYCLING Bike rentals are widely available in Avalon for about $5 per hour and $12 per day. Look for rentals on Crescent Avenue and Pebbly Beach Road such as **Brown's Bikes** (⊠ 107 Pebbly Beach Rd., next to Island Rentals, Avalon ☎ 310/510–0986 🖷 310/510–0747 ⊕ www.catalinabiking. com). To bike beyond the paved roads of Avalon, you must buy a day-use permit from the Catalina Conservancy. There's a two-day minimum for the $10 passes, and you may not ride on hiking paths.

DIVING & SNORKELING The Casino Point Underwater Park, with its handful of wrecks, is best suited for diving. Lover's Cove is better for snorkeling (no scuba diving allowed, but you'll share the area with glass-bottom boats). Both are protected marine preserves. **Catalina Divers Supply** (⊠ Green Pleasure Pier ☎ 310/510–0330 ⊕ www.catalinadiverssupply.com) rents equipment, runs guided scuba and snorkel tours, gives certification classes, and more. It has an outpost at Casino Point.

HIKING   ■ **TIP→** **If you plan to backpack overnight, you'll need a camping reservation. The interior is dry and desertlike; bring plenty of water and sunblock.**

Permits from the **Santa Catalina Island Conservancy** (✉ 3rd and Claressa Sts., Avalon ☏ 310/510–2595) are required for hiking into Catalina Island's interior. The permits are free and can be picked up at the main house of the conservancy or at the airport. You don't need a permit for shorter hikes, such as the one from Avalon to the Botanical Garden. The conservancy has maps of the island's east-end hikes, such as Hermit's Gulch Trail. It's possible to hike between Avalon and Two Harbors, starting at the Hogsback Gate, above Avalon, though the 28-mi journey has an elevation gain of 3,000 feet and is not for the weak. ■ **TIP→** **For a pleasant 4-mi hike out of Avalon, take Avalon Canyon Road to Wrigley Gardens and follow the trail to Lone Pine. At the top, you'll have an amazing view of the Palisades cliffs and, beyond them, the sea.**

Another hike option is to take the **Airport Shuttle Bus** (☏ 310/510–0143) from Avalon to the airport for $17 round-trip. The 10-mi hike back to Avalon is mostly downhill, and the bus is an inexpensive way to see the interior of the island.

HORSEBACK RIDING   Horseback riders can wrangle four-legged transportation for scenic trail rides. Reservations must be made at the **Catalina Stables** (✉ 600 Avalon Canyon Rd., Avalon ☏ 310/510–0478), which has guided rides starting at $37 for a half hour.

Catalina Island Essentials

To research prices, get advice from other travelers, and book travel arrangements, visit www.fodors.com.

AIR TRAVEL

Island Express helicopters depart hourly from San Pedro and Long Beach (8 AM–sunset). The trip takes about 15 minutes and costs $87 one-way, $165.50 round-trip. Reservations a week in advance are recommended. 🛈 **Airlines & Contacts** Island Express ☏ 800/228–2566 ⊕ www.islandexpress.com.

BOAT & FERRY TRAVEL

Two companies offer ferry service to Catalina Island. The boats have both indoor and outdoor seating and snack bars. Excessive baggage is not allowed, and there are extra fees for bicycles and surfboards. The waters around Santa Catalina can get rough, so if you're prone to seasickness, come prepared.

Catalina Express makes an hourlong run from Long Beach or San Pedro to Avalon and a 90-minute run from Dana Point to Avalon. Round-trip fare for the various routes costs $54. Service from Newport Beach to Avalon is available through Catalina Passenger Service. Boats leave from Balboa Pavilion at 9 AM (in season), take 75 minutes to reach the island, and cost $44 round-trip. Return boats leave Catalina at 4:30 PM. Reservations are advised in summer and on weekends for all trips. ■ **TIP→** **Keep an eye out for dolphins, which sometimes swim alongside the ferries.**

7

FARES & SCHEDULES 🔢 **Boat & Ferry Information** Catalina Express ☎ 310/519–1212 or 800/481–3470 🖷 800/410–9159 ⊕ www.catalinaexpress.com. **Catalina Passenger Service** ☎ 949/673–5245 or 800/830–7744 🖷 949/673–8340 ⊕ www.catalinainfo.com.

GOLF CARTS

Golf carts constitute the island's main form of transportation. You can rent them along Avalon's Crescent Avenue and Pebbly Beach Road for about $35 per hour with a $30 deposit, payable via cash or travelers checks only.

🔢 **Local Agencies** Island Rentals ⊠ 125 Pebbly Beach Rd., Avalon ☎ 310/510–1456.

LODGING

■ **TIP→** Between Memorial Day and Labor Day be sure to make reservations *before* heading here. After late October, rooms are much easier to find on shorter notice, rates drop dramatically, and many hotels offer packages that include transportation from the mainland and/or sightseeing tours.

TOURS

Santa Catalina Island Company runs the following Discovery Tours: a summer-only coastal cruise to Seal Rocks; the *Flying Fish* boat trip (summer evenings only); a comprehensive inland motor tour (which includes an Arabian horse performance); a tour of Skyline Drive; a Casino tour; a scenic tour of Avalon; a glass-bottom-boat tour, an undersea tour on a semisubmersible vessel; and a tour of the Botanical Garden. Reservations are highly recommended for the inland tours. Tours cost $13.50 to $99. There are ticket booths on the Green Pleasure Pier, at the Casino, in the plaza, and at the boat landing. Catalina Adventure Tours, which has booths at the boat landing and on the pier, arranges similar excursions at comparable prices.

The Santa Catalina Island Conservancy organizes custom ecotours and hikes of the interior. Naturalist guides drive open Jeeps through some gorgeously untrammeled parts of island. Tours start at $98 per person for a three-hour trip (three-person minimum); you can also book half- and full-day tours. The tours run year-round.

🔢 **Catalina Adventure Tours** ☎ 310/510–2888 🖷 310/510–2797 ⊕ www.catalinaadventuretours.com. **Santa Catalina Island Company** ☎ 310/510–8687 or 800/626–1496 ⊕ www.scico.com. **Santa Catalina Island Conservancy** ⊠ 3rd and Claressa Sts., Avalon 90704 ☎ 310/510–2595 ⊕ www.catalinaconservancy.org.

VISITOR INFORMATION

🔢 **Tourist Information** Catalina Island Visitors' Bureau ⊠ Green Pleasure Pier, Box 217, Avalon 90704 ☎ 310/510–1520 or 714/449–3372 🖷 310/510–7606 or 714/870–0597 ⊕ www.catalina.com.

SMART TRAVEL TIPS

There are planners and there are those who, excuse the pun, fly by the seat of their pants. We happily place ourselves among the planners. Our writers and editors try to anticipate all the issues you may face before and during any journey, and then they do their research. This section is the product of their efforts. Use it to get excited about your trip to Los Angeles, to inform your travel planning, or to guide you on the road should the seat of your pants start to feel threadbare.

ADDRESSES

Expect sudden changes in street-address numbering as streets pass through neighborhoods, then incorporated cities, then back into neighborhoods. This can be most bewildering on Robertson Boulevard, an otherwise useful north–south artery that, by crossing through L.A., West Hollywood, and Beverly Hills, dips in and out of several such numbering shifts in a matter of miles.

In Santa Monica, odd numbers switch over from the north and west sides of streets to the south and east sides.

There are plenty of identical or extremely similar street names in L.A., so be as specific as you can when getting or checking directions.

AIR TRAVEL

Flights in and out of Los Angeles International Airport (LAX) are seldom delayed because of weather and generally run on time. Because of heavy traffic around the airport (not to mention the city's extended rush hours) and difficult parking, however, you should allow plenty of time to arrive at the airport prior to scheduled departure or arrival times. Some hotels near LAX offer air-travel perks, such as free shuttles to the airport. There are three other nearby airports that serve L.A. County; they're smaller and have more limited services but are worth investigating when booking flights (⇨ Airports). For instance, the Long Beach airport is a hub for the low-cost domestic airline JetBlue, while Southwest has a big presence at the Burbank (Bob Hope), Ontario, and Orange County airports.

CARRIERS

Delta and American have the most non-stop and direct flights to Los Angeles International Airport (LAX) from U.S. cities. JetBlue Airways, a low-fare domestic airline, has daily nonstop flights between Long Beach and Oakland; Salt Lake City; Las Vegas; New York City; Boston; Washington, D.C.; Atlanta; and Fort Lauderdale; it also recently added nonstop flights between Burbank and New York. Low-fare Southwest Airlines serves the LAX, Ontario, Burbank, and Orange County airports. AirTran Airways, another low-fare domestic airline, has two daily nonstop flights between L.A. and its hub in Atlanta.

🛪 **Major Airlines** Alaska Airlines ☎ 800/252-7522 or 206/433-3100 ⊕ www.alaskaair.com. **American Airlines** ☎ 800/433-7300 ⊕ www.aa.com. **America West** ☎ 800/235-9292 or 480/693-6701 ⊕ www.americawest.com. **ATA** ☎ 800/435-9282 or 317/282-8308 ⊕ www.ata.com. **Continental Airlines** ☎ 800/523-3273 for U.S. and Mexico reservations, 800/231-0856 for international reservations ⊕ www.continental.com. **Delta Airlines** ☎ 800/221-1212 for U.S. reservations, 800/241-4141 for international reservations ⊕ www.delta.com. **JetBlue** ☎ 800/538-2583 ⊕ www.jetblue.com. **Northwest Airlines** ☎ 800/225-2525 for U.S. reservations, 800/447-4747 for international destinations ⊕ www.nwa.com. **Southwest Airlines** ☎ 800/435-9792 ⊕ www.southwest.com. **United Airlines** ☎ 800/864-8331 for U.S. reservations, 800/538-2929 for international reservations ⊕ www.united.com. **US Airways** ☎ 800/428-4322 for U.S. and Canada reservations, 800/622-1015 for international reservations ⊕ www.usairways.com.

🛪 **Smaller Airlines** AirTran Airlines ☎ 800/247-8726 ⊕ www.airtran.com. **Hawaiian Airlines** ☎ 800/367-5320 ⊕ www.hawaiianair.com.

CHECK-IN & BOARDING

Plan to arrive at the airport about two hours before your scheduled departure time for domestic flights and 2½ to 3 hours before international flights. You may need to arrive earlier if you're flying from LAX or during peak air-traffic times.

Always **ask your carrier about its check-in policy.** Airport security is tight; all checked luggage is screened and some passengers and carry-on items may be chosen for a secondary screening either at the security checkpoints or at the departure gate. To avoid delays at airport-security checkpoints, try not to wear any metal. Jewelry, belt and other buckles, steel-toe shoes, barrettes, and underwire bras are among the items that can set off detectors. Also, do not bring beverages in metal containers, such as cans of soda.

Double-check your flight times, especially if you made your reservations far in advance. Airlines change their schedules, and alerts may not reach you. Always **bring a government-issued photo ID to the airport** (even when it's not required, a passport is best), and **arrive when you need to and not before.** Check in usually at least an hour before domestic flights and two to three hours for international flights. Many airlines have more stringent advance check-in requirements at some busy airports. The TSA estimates the waiting time for security at most major airports and publishes the information on its Web site. Note that if you aren't at the gate at least 10 minutes before your flight is scheduled to take off (sometimes earlier), you won't be allowed to board.

Don't stand in a line if you don't have to. Buy an e-ticket, check in at an electronic kiosk, or—even better—check in on your airline's Web site before you leave home. If you don't need to check luggage, you could bypass all but the security lines. These days, most domestic airline tickets are electronic; international tickets may be either electronic or paper.

You usually pay a surcharge (usually at least $25) to get a paper ticket, and its sole advantage is that it may be easier to endorse over to another airline if your flight is canceled and the airline with which you booked can't accommodate you on another flight. With an e-ticket, the only thing you receive is an e-mailed receipt citing your itinerary and reservation and ticket numbers. Be sure to carry this with you as you'll need it to get past security. If you lose you receipt, though, you can simply print out another copy or ask the airline to do it for you at check-in.

During busy travel seasons and around holiday periods, if a flight is oversold, the gate agent will usually ask for volunteers and will offer some sort of compensation if you're willing to take a different flight. **Know your rights.** If you're bumped from a flight *involuntarily,* the airline must give you some kind of compensation if an alternate flight can't be found within one hour. If your flight is delayed because of something within the airline's control (bad weather doesn't count), then the airline has a responsibility to get you to your destination on the same day, even if they have to book you on another airline and in an upgraded class if necessary. Read your airline's Contract of Carriage; it's usually buried somewhere on the airline's Web site.

Be prepared to quickly adjust your plans by programming a few numbers into your cell: your airline, an airport hotel or two, your destination hotel, your car service, and/or your travel agent. Bring snacks, water, and sufficient diversions, and you'll be covered if you get stuck in the airport, on the tarmac, or even in the air during turbulence.

CUTTING COSTS

Airfare wars come and go, but your best hope of obtaining the best price is to be flexible about the date and time you travel and to purchase three to six months in advance.

Depending on your route, **a flight to an alternative airport in metro L.A. may cost less than a flight to LAX.** Flying to a secondary airport may also save you time and ground-transportation costs.

The least expensive airfares to Los Angeles are priced for round-trip travel and must usually be purchased at least 7 days (and sometimes 14 to 21 days) in advance. Airlines generally allow you to change your return date for a fee; most low-fare tickets, however, are nonrefundable. It's always good to **comparison shop.** Web sites that consolidate listings and travel agents can have different arrangements with the airlines and offer different prices for exactly the same flight and day. Certain Web sites have tracking features that will e-mail you immediately when good deals are posted. Other people prefer to stick with one or two frequent-flier programs, racking up free trips and accumulating perks that can make trips easier. On some airlines, perks include a special reservations number, early boarding, access to upgrades, and more roomy economy-class seating.

Check early and often. Start looking for cheap fares up to a year in advance, and keep looking until you see something you can live with; you never know when a good deal may pop up. That said, **jump on the good deals.** Waiting even a few minutes might mean paying more. For most people, saving money is more important than flexibility, so the more affordable nonrefundable tickets work. Just remember that you'll pay dearly (often as much as $100) if you must change your travel plans. Check on prices for departures at different times of the day and to and from alternate airports, and **look for departures on Tuesday, Wednesday, and Thursday,** typically the cheapest days to travel. Remember to **weigh your options,** though. A cheaper flight might have a long layover rather than being nonstop, or landing at a secondary airport might substantially increase your ground transportation costs.

Note that many airline Web sites—and most ads—show prices *without* taxes and surcharges. Don't buy until you know the full price. Government taxes add up quickly. Also **watch those ticketing fees.** Surcharges are usually added when you buy your ticket anywhere but on an airline's own Web site. (By the way, that includes on the phone—even if you call the airline directly—and for paper tickets regardless of how you book.)

Also check the Web sites of individual airlines; some list special fares on their sites that are not available through consolidators. Southwest Airlines, for instance, posts weekly special discount fares exclusively on its Web site.

⚡ Online Consolidators AirlineConsolidator.com ⊕ www.airlineconsolidator.com, for international tickets. **Best Fares** ⊕ www.bestfares.com; $59.90 annual membership. **Cheap Tickets** ⊕ www.cheaptickets.com. **Expedia** ⊕ www.expedia.com. **Hotwire** ⊕ www.hotwire.com. **Kayak.com** ⊕ www.kayak.com does metasearches, pulling together deals from more than 100 different sites. **last-**

minute.com ⊕ www.lastminute.com specializes in last-minute travel; the main site is for the U.K., but it has a link to a U.S. site. **Luxury Link** ⊕ www.luxurylink.com has auctions (surprisingly good deals) as well as offers at the high-end side of travel. **Orbitz** ⊕ www.orbitz.com. **Onetravel.com** ⊕ www.onetravel.com. **Priceline.com** ⊕ www.priceline.com. **Travelocity** ⊕ www.travelocity.com.

ENJOYING THE FLIGHT

Get the seat you want. Avoid those on the aisle directly across from the lavatories. Most frequent fliers say those are even worse than the seats that don't recline (e. g., those in the back row and those in front of a bulkhead). For more legroom, you can request emergency-aisle seats, but only do so if you're capable of moving the 35- to 60-pound airplane exit door—a Federal Aviation Administration require-ment of passengers in these seats. Seats behind a bulkhead also offer more legroom, but they don't have under-seat storage. Often you can pick a seat when you buy your ticket on an airline's Web site. But it's not always a guarantee, par-ticularly if the airline changes the plane after you book your ticket; check back be-fore you leave. SeatGuru.com has more information about specific seat configura-tions, which vary by aircraft.

Fewer airlines are providing free food for passengers in economy class. **Don't go hun-gry.** If you're scheduled to fly during meal times, verify if your airline offers anything to eat; even when it does, be prepared to pay. If you have dietary concerns, request special meals. These can be vegetarian, low-cholesterol, or kosher, for example. It's a good idea to pack some healthful snacks and a small (plastic) bottle of water in your carry-on bag.

Ask the airline about its children's menus, activities, and fares. On some lines infants and toddlers fly for free if they sit on a parent's lap, and older children fly for half price in their own seats. Also ask about policies involving car seats; having one may limit where you can sit. While you're at it, ask about seatbelt extenders for car seats. And note that you can't count on a flight attendant to automatically produce an extender; you may have to inquire about it again when you board.

FLYING TIMES

Nonstop flights from New York to Los Angeles take about six hours; with the three-hour time change, you can leave JFK by 8 AM and be in L.A. by 11 AM. Some flights may require a midway stop, making the total excursion between 7½ and 8½ hours. Many of the flights out of Chicago are nonstop with a duration of four hours. Nonstop times are approximately three hours from Dallas, 10 hours from London, and 15 hours from Sydney.

HOW TO COMPLAIN

If your baggage goes astray or your flight goes awry, complain right away. Most car-riers require that you **file a claim immedi-ately.** The Aviation Consumer Protection Division of the Department of Transporta-tion publishes *Fly-Rights*, which discusses airlines and consumer issues and is avail-able online. You can also find articles and information on mytravelrights.com, the Web site of the nonprofit Consumer Travel Rights Center.

⚑ Airline Complaints Office of Aviation Enforce-ment and Proceedings (Aviation Consumer Protec-tion Division) ☎ 202/366-2220 ⊕ airconsumer.ost.dot.gov. **Federal Aviation Administration Con-sumer Hotline** ☎ 866/835-5322 ⊕ www.faa.gov.

AIRPORTS

The major gateway to L.A. is Los Angeles International Airport. Departures are from the upper level, and arrivals are on the lower level. LAX is serviced by more than 85 major airlines and is the third-largest airport in the world in terms of passenger traffic. Ontario International Airport, about 35 mi east of Los Angeles, serves the San Bernardino–Riverside area with a dozen airlines. Burbank's Bob Hope Air-port serves the San Fernando Valley with six airlines. Four airlines use Long Beach Airport. John Wayne/Orange County Air-port serves Orange County with 14 air-lines, including four commuter carriers.

It's generally easier to navigate the sec-ondary airports than to get through sprawling LAX. Bob Hope Airport in Bur-bank is closest to downtown L.A., and domestic flights to it can be cheaper than flights to LAX—it's definitely worth checking out. From Long Beach Airport it's equally convenient to go north to central Los Angeles or south to Orange County. Flights to Orange County's John Wayne Airport are often more expensive than those to the other secondary airports. Parking at the smaller airports is cheaper than at LAX.

Because all the airports are no-smoking facilities, you must leave the terminal buildings to smoke.

Long layovers don't have to be only about sitting around or shopping. These days they can be about burning off vacation calories. Check out www.airportgyms.com for lists of health clubs that are in or near many U.S. and Canadian airports.

⚡ Airlines & Airports Airline and Airport Links. com ⊕ www.airlineandairportlinks.com has links to many of the world's airlines and airports. **Bob Hope Airport** (BUR) ☎ 818/840–8830 ⊕ www. bobhopeairport.com. **John Wayne/Orange County Airport** (SNA) ☎ 949/252–5006 ⊕ www.ocair.com. **Long Beach Airport** (LGB) ☎ 562/570–2600 ⊕ www.lgb.org. **Los Angeles International Airport** (LAX) ☎ 310/646–5252 ⊕ www.lawa.org. **Ontario International Airport** (ONT) ☎ 909/937–2700 ⊕ www.lawa.org.

⚡ Airline Security Issues Transportation Security Agency ⊕ www.tsa.gov/public has answers for almost every question that might come up.

GROUND TRANSPORTATION

LAX provides free bus service from one terminal to another, and the car-rental companies also have gratis shuttles to their nearby branches. Some hotels, especially those near the airport, provide free airport shuttles for their guests. Driving times from LAX to different parts of the city vary considerably: it will take you at least 45 minutes to get downtown, 20 minutes to get to Santa Monica, 30 minutes to Beverly Hills, and 35–40 minutes to Van Nuys or Sherman Oaks (the central San Fernando Valley). With traffic, particularly on the 405 freeway, it can take much longer. From Burbank, it's 20 minutes to downtown, 40 minutes to Santa Monica, 35–40 minutes to Beverly Hills, and 15 minutes to the central San Fernando Valley. The

drive from downtown L.A. to the Ontario or Orange County airports takes at least an hour; plan on at least 45 minutes for the drive to Long Beach Airport.

By taxi: Taxis are the most convenient way to get between the city and the airports. It's a $38 flat rate between downtown L.A. and LAX in either direction, plus a $2.50 surcharge. Taxis to and from Ontario Airport run on a meter and can cost up to $50 or $60 depending on traffic; taxis between downtown and Bob Hope Airport are also metered and can cost $35 to $40. From Long Beach Airport to Long Beach hotels, some taxis offer a $17 flat rate; trips to downtown L.A. are metered and cost roughly $65.

By shuttle: For two or three travelers—particularly if you're going a longish distance, for example, to the San Fernando Valley from LAX—shuttle services are economical, $15–$21 per person. However, an individual traveler, depending on the destination, may end up paying more than by cab. Shuttle ride costs are determined by postal codes; fares increase depending on how many postal-code areas you pass. A shuttle ride generally takes longer than a cab ride. These big vans typically circle the airport repeatedly to fill up with passengers. Your travel time will be determined in part by how many other travelers are dropped off before you. At LAX, Prime Time and SuperShuttle allow walk-on shuttle passengers without prior reservations; otherwise, you'll need to make a reservation at least 24 hours in advance for a ride either to or from an airport.

By FlyAway bus: In 2006, the Los Angeles World Airports group started a nonstop bus service between Union Station in downtown L.A. and LAX. The ride takes about 45 minutes and costs $3 (cash only). Buses run 24 hours a day: every half hour between 5 AM and 1 AM, then every hour. They've got luggage bays on board.

By public transportation: If you don't have much to carry, are not in a hurry, and know your destination is near a bus or subway stop, consider taking public transit from LAX into L.A. Free shuttles take passengers from the arrivals levels of each terminal to public transit points; shuttle C will take you to parking lot C and MTA bus connections, while shuttle G goes to the Metro Rail Green Line Aviation station. The Green Line trains run every 15–20 minutes until 1 AM. Several bus lines include the airport, but they often don't stick to their schedule. It may take four times as long as it would by car, but the fare is usually $2 or less. From Burbank's airport, meanwhile, you can connect with Metrolink or Amtrak train service for a 20-minute trip to downtown Union Station. The fare is $5.50, but you may have to wait up to an hour between trains. There's no direct public transportation from the Ontario or Long Beach airports into Los Angeles proper.

🚺 **Shuttles** Xpress Shuttle ☎ 800/427–7483 🌐 www.expressshuttle.com. **Prime Time** ☎ 800/733–8267 🌐 www.primetimeshuttle.com. **Super-Shuttle** ☎ 323/775–6600, 310/782–6600, or 800/258–3826 🌐 www.supershuttle.com.

BUSINESS HOURS

Los Angeles is not a city that never sleeps, but through much of the area, business extends well into the evening, especially for the bigger stores and chains and malls. On Monday certain restaurants, nightclubs, and shops (such as outdoors sports-gear rental stores) are closed.

MUSEUMS

Many L.A. museums are closed on Monday and major holidays. However, a few of the preeminent art museums, including the Norton Simon and Los Angeles County Museum of Art, stay open on Monday. Instead, the Norton Simon is closed Tuesday, the Los Angeles County museum on Wednesday. Most museums close around 5 PM or 6 PM, and most stay open late at least one night a week, often Thursday. Many museums, large and small, have weekly or monthly free days or hours when no admission is charged.

SHOPS

Most stores in Los Angeles are open 10 to 6, although many stay open until 9 PM or later, particularly those in trendy areas such as Melrose Avenue and in Santa Monica. Tower Records on the Sunset Strip, for example, is open every day until midnight. Shops along Melrose, Abbot Kinney Boulevard in Venice, and in Los Feliz often don't get moving until 11 AM or noon. Most shops are open on Sunday at least in the afternoon.

BUS TRAVEL TO & FROM L.A.

The duration of a bus trip from other parts of California or nearby states can be comparable to the time it takes to take a plane, preflight waiting considered. The only Greyhound terminal is in an industrial area of downtown L.A., off Alameda Street. The waiting room and restrooms are clean, and there are individual pay TVs. The terminal is not close to other transit stations but by taking MTA Bus 58 you can get to Union Station. Taxis are also available at the terminal.

Greyhound has dozens of daily routes serving Los Angeles. It often has promotional fares from other West Coast cities to L.A. You can buy tickets by phone, on the Greyhound Web site, or in person at the terminal. The online purchasing service is called Will Call; you'll need to make the transaction at least two hours before departure.

🚺 **Bus Information** Greyhound ☎ 213/629–8405 or 800/231–2222 🌐 www.greyhound.com.

BUS TRAVEL WITHIN L.A.

Let's face it: in L.A., unless your car's in the shop, you're probably behind the wheel. Inadequate public-transportation systems have been an L.A. problem for decades. That said, many local trips can be made, with time and patience, by bus. In certain cases, it may be your best option; for example, visiting the Getty Center, going to Universal Studios and/or the adjacent CityWalk, or venturing into downtown. There's also a special Metropolitan Transit Authority (MTA) bus that goes between Union Station and Dodger Stadium for Friday night home games. It doesn't save money, but it can save you time and parking-related stress. For the fastest MTA service, look for the red-and-white Metro Rapid buses; these stop less frequently and are able to extend green lights. At this writing, there were six Rapid routes including routes on Wilshire and Vermont boulevards; over the next few years more Rapid routes will be added.

The Metropolitan Transit Authority DASH (Downtown Area Short Hop) minibuses cover six different circular routes in Hollywood, Mid-Wilshire, and the downtown area. The buses stop every two blocks or so. The Santa Monica Municipal Bus Line, also known as the Big Blue Bus, is a pleasant and inexpensive way to move around the Westside, where the MTA lines leave off. There's also an express bus to and from downtown L.A., and a shuttle bus, the Tide Shuttle, which runs between Main Street and the Third Street Promenade and stops at hotels along the way. Culver CityBus Lines run six routes through Culver City. Smoking is never allowed in the L.A. public transportation system.

FARES & SCHEDULES

MTA schedules are available through the information line below, but heavy local traffic can make them unreliable. Service is available at all hours. An MTA bus ride for both standard and Rapid service costs $1.25, plus 25¢ for each transfer between buses or from bus to subway. From 9 PM to 5 AM, the fare goes down to 75¢. You can also buy a one-day pass for $3, or a $15 weekly pass for unlimited travel on all Metro buses and trains (biweekly and monthly passes are also available). Passes are valid from Sunday through Saturday. EZ Transit passes are a long-term option; this $58 monthly pass covers transit on virtually all public transit options throughout the county.

DASH buses make pickups at five-minute intervals. You pay 25¢ every time you get on. Buses generally run weekdays 6 AM–7 PM and Saturday 10 AM–5 PM; a few downtown weekend routes run on Sunday as well. Note: the Downtown Discovery Route (DD) makes a continuous loop among downtown sites; Route E is a shopper's tour with stops in the Broadway, Jewelry, and Fashion districts, as well as at two downtown malls.

The Santa Monica Municipal Bus Line (the Big Blue Bus) costs 75¢, while Big Blue's Tide Shuttle is a quarter. Transfers

are free from one Big Blue Bus to another; to MTA or Culver CityBus it's 25¢. The Route 10 (downtown) express bus costs $1.75. Packs of 10 tokens are $7. You can also use a prepaid Metrocard, the Little Blue Card, and get the same discounted rate for multiple rides (70¢ per ride). The Big Blue buses generally run from 5 AM to midnight, while the Tide Shuttle runs Sunday to Thursday from noon until 8 PM and Friday and Saturday from noon to 10 PM.

Culver CityBus is 75¢ and runs 6 AM–midnight. The Santa Monica bus line's Metrocard can be used on this system but not Big Blue Bus tokens. Culver CityBuses also accept MTA tokens but not MTA passes. Children and people over 65 always pay less on all lines.

⚡ Bus Information California Smart Traveler ☎ 800/266-6883 ⊕ www.dot.ca.gov/caltrans511. **Culver CityBus Lines** ☎ 310/253-6500 ⊕ www.culvercity.org. **DASH** ☎ 213/626-4455 or 310/808-2273 ⊕ www.ladottransit.com/dash. **Metropolitan Transit Authority (MTA)** ☎ 213/626-4455 or 800/COMMUTE ⊕ www.mta.net. **Santa Monica Municipal Bus Line** ☎ 310/451-5444 ⊕ www.bigbluebus.com.

PAYING

You can pay your fare in cash on MTA, Santa Monica, and Culver City buses, but you must have exact change. You can buy MTA passes and tokens throughout the city at MTA customer centers and some convenience stores and grocery stores. Metrocards or tokens for the Santa Monica buses can be purchased at local libraries and retailers. Call or check the pertinent bus Web site for the retail location nearest you.

CAMERAS & PHOTOGRAPHY

Clicking photos of celebrities is a business in Hollywood—don't try it, unless you don't mind looking like a paparazzo wannabe and raising your subjects' ire (or that of their bodyguards). Otherwise L.A. is a great place to be a shutterbug. You can shoot both urban and natural spaces, not to mention iconic images such as the footprints in front of Grauman's Chinese Theatre. However, pictures of the great outdoors can be problematic in summer because of the smog. Try photographing in the early morning or late afternoon, when the light is mellower and shadows will give a sense of depth. If you're trying for a dramatic crashing-waves shot on a rocky stretch of coastline, snap an instant before the surf hits the rocks to maximize your chances of capturing the full crest of spray. At Disneyland, you'll have plenty of opportunities to take pictures with costumed characters. The *Kodak Guide to Shooting Great Travel Pictures* (available at bookstores everywhere) is loaded with tips.

EQUIPMENT PRECAUTIONS

Keep your camera protected at the beach, where tiny grains of sand can ruin lenses and jam mechanisms.

Don't pack film or equipment in checked luggage, where it's much more susceptible to damage. X-ray machines used to view checked luggage are extremely powerful and therefore are likely to ruin your film. Try to ask for hand inspection of film, which becomes clouded after repeated exposure to airport X-ray machines. Always keep film, tape, and computer disks out of the sun. Carry an extra supply of batteries, and be prepared to turn on your camera or laptop to prove to airport security personnel that the device is real.

CAR RENTAL

In Los Angeles, a car is a necessity. When renting one, keep in mind that you'll likely be spending a lot of time in it, and options like a CD player or power windows that might seem unnecessary may make a significant difference in your day-to-day comfort.

Major-chain rates in L.A. begin at $35 a day and $110 a week, plus 8.25% sales tax. Luxury and sport utility vehicles start at $49 a day. Note that the major agencies offer services for travelers with disabilities, such as hand-controls, for little or no extra cost.

Request car seats and extras such as GPS when you book, and make sure that a confirmed reservation guarantees you a car. Agencies sometimes overbook, particularly for busy weekends and holiday periods. Rates are sometimes—but not always—better if you book in advance or reserve

through a rental agency's Web site. There are other reasons to book ahead, though: for popular destinations, during busy times of the year, or to ensure that you get a certain type of car (van, SUV, exotic sports car).

Beverly Hills Budget Car Rental, with six locations, offers the widest range of vehicle rentals, including Hummers, convertibles, minivans, and economy cars. Daydreaming of a restored classic Chevy or the latest Porsche? Beverly Hills Rent-A-Car, a rental facility with branches in Santa Monica, Beverly Hills, and near LAX, rents exotics, classic cars, luxury models, economy cars (including Mini Coopers), vans, and SUVs. Midway Car Rental, with six offices on the Westside, in the Valley, and in Mid-Wilshire, has the usual, plus some extra-large vans and, in its "executive class," Lexus, BMW, Mercedes, and so on. Possibly the handiest in the lower-price range is Enterprise, with two dozen branches in the area (some have luxury vehicles as well). You can rent an ecofriendly electric or hybrid car through Budget; for more information contact EV Rental Cars.

CUTTING COSTS

Really weigh your options. Find out if a credit card you carry or organization or frequent-renter program to which you belong has a discount program. And check that such discounts really are the best deal. You can often do better with special weekend or weekly rates offered by a rental agency. (And even if you only want to rent for five or six days, ask if you can get the weekly rate; it may very well be cheaper than the daily rate for that period of time.)

Price local car-rental companies as well as the majors. Also investigate wholesalers, which don't own fleets but rent in bulk from those that do and often offer better rates (note you must usually pay for such rentals before leaving home). Consider adding a car rental onto your air–hotel vacation package; the cost will often be cheaper than if you had rented the car separately on your own.

Beware of hidden charges. Those great rental rates may not be so great when you add in taxes, surcharges, cancellation penalties, taxes, drop-off charges (if you're planning to pick up the car in one city and leave it in another), and surcharges (for being under or over a certain age, for additional drivers, or for driving over state or country borders or out of a specific radius from your point of rental).

Note that airport rental offices often add supplementary surcharges that you may avoid by renting from an agency whose office is just off airport property. Don't buy the tank of gas that's in the car when you rent it unless you plan to do a lot of driving. Avoid hefty refueling fees by filling the tank at a station well away from the rental agency (those nearby are often more expensive) just before you turn in the car.

Local Agencies Beverly Hills Budget Car Rental ☎ 310/274-9173 or 800/227-7117 ⊕ www. budgetbeverlyhills.com. **Beverly Hills Rent-A-Car** ☎ 310/337-1400 or 800/479-5996 ⊕ www. bhrentacar.com. **Enterprise** ☎ 800/736-8222 ⊕ www.enterprise.com. **EV Rental Cars** ☎ 877/ 387-3682 ⊕ www.evrental.com. **Midway Car Rental** ☎ 888/682-0166 ⊕ www.midwaycarrental. com. **Rent A Wreck** ☎ 800/944-7501 ⊕ www.rent-a-wreck.com. **Town Rent A Car** ☎ 310/973-6815 or 323/934-4780.

Major Agencies Alamo ☎ 800/462-5266 ⊕ www.alamo.com. **Avis** ☎ 800/230-4898 ⊕ www.avis.com. **Budget** ☎ 800/527-0700 ⊕ www.budget.com. **Hertz** ☎ 800/654-3131 ⊕ www.hertz.com. **National Car Rental** ☎ 800/ 227-7368 ⊕ www.nationalcar.com.

INSURANCE

Everyone who rents a car wonders about whether the insurance that the rental companies offer is worth the expense. No one—not even us—has a simple answer. It all depends on how much regular insurance you have, how comfortable you are with risk, and whether or not money is an issue.

If you own a car and carry comprehensive car insurance for both collision and liability, your personal auto insurance will probably cover a rental, but read your policy's fine print to be sure. If you don't have auto insurance, then you should probably buy the collision- or loss-damage waiver (CDW or LDW) from the rental company. This eliminates your liability for

damage to the car. Some credit cards offer CDW coverage, but it's usually supplemental to your own insurance and rarely covers SUVs, minivans, luxury models, and the like. If your coverage is secondary, you may still be liable for loss-of-use costs from the car-rental company (again, read the fine print). But no credit-card insurance is valid unless you use that card for *all* transactions, from reserving to paying the final bill.

You may also be offered supplemental liability coverage; the car-rental company is required to carry a minimal level of liability coverage that covers all renters, but it's rarely enough to cover claims in a really serious accident if you're at fault. Your own auto insurance policy will protect you if you own a car; if you don't, you have to decide if you are willing to take the risk.

U.S. rental companies sell CDWs and LDWs for about $15 to $25 a day; supplemental liability is usually more than $10 a day. The car-rental company may offer you all sorts of other policies, but they're rarely worth the cost. Personal accident insurance, which is basic hospitalization coverage, is an especially egregious rip-off if you already have health insurance.

Note that you can decline the insurance from the rental company and purchase it through a third-party provider such as Travel Guard (www.travelguard.com)—$9 per day for $35,000 of coverage. That's sometimes less than half the price of the CDW offered by some car-rental companies. Also, Diners Club offers primary CDW coverage on all rentals reserved and paid for with the card. This means that Diners Club's company—not your own car insurance—pays in case of an accident. It *doesn't* mean your car-insurance company won't raise your rates once it discovers you had an accident.

REQUIREMENTS & RESTRICTIONS

In California you must be 21 and have a valid credit card, often with $200–$300 available credit on it (regardless of how you'll ultimately pay), to rent a car; rates may be higher if you're under 25. There's no upper age limit.

CAR TRAVEL

Picture L.A. and you might see the mesh of multilane freeways with their hypnotic streams of cars. Once you've joined the multitudes you'll be caught up in the tempos of traffic: frustration, exhilaration, and crushing boredom. "Freeway culture" is one of the city's defining traits.

GETTING GAS

In L.A., as of this writing, gasoline costs around $3.15–$3.25 a gallon. There are plenty of stations in all areas; most stay open late, and some are open 24 hours. To find the stations with the lowest gas prices in town, visit www.losangelesgasprices. com. Prices are updated every 36 hours by a network of volunteer spotters.

EMERGENCY SERVICES

For lesser problems on L.A.'s freeways (being out of gas, having a blown tire, needing a tow to the nearest phone), Caltrans (California's Department of Transportation) has instituted the Freeway Service Patrol (FSP) 6:30 AM–7 PM. More than 145 tow trucks patrol the freeways offering free aid to stranded drivers. If your car breaks down on an interstate, try to pull over onto the shoulder and either wait for the state police to find you or, if you have other passengers who can wait in the car, walk to the nearest emergency roadside phone and call the state police. Another option is to dial 800/266–6883 and select the option for freeway patrol. When calling for help, note your location according to the small green mileage markers posted along the highway. Other highways are also patrolled but may not have emergency phones or mileage markers.

🚩 **Freeway Service Patrol** ☎ 213/922–2957 general information.

NAVIGATING LOS ANGELES

Finding your way by car in Los Angeles can be a piece of cake or a nightmare. If you're used to urban driving, you shouldn't have too much trouble, but if you're unused to driving in big cities, L.A. can be unnerving. The city may be sprawling and traffic clogged, but at least it has evolved with the automobile in mind. Streets are wide and parking garages abound, so it's more driver-friendly than many older big cities. Get a good map and remember a few of the pointers we list here, and you should be able to avoid confusion.

Be aware that a number of major streets have similar-sounding names (Beverly Drive and Beverly Boulevard, or numbered streets north to south downtown and east to west in Hollywood, West Hollywood, and Beverly Hills) or exactly the same name (San Vicente Boulevard in West L.A., Brentwood, Santa Monica, and West Hollywood). Also, some smaller streets seem to exist intermittently for miles, so unless you have good directions, you should use major streets rather than try for an alternative that is actually blocked by a dead end or detours, like the side streets off Sunset Boulevard. Try to **get clear directions and stick to them.** The *Thomas Guide,* a hefty, spiral-bound, super-thorough street guide and directory, is published annually and is available at bookstores, grocery stores, and the like. It's worth the money if you're planning to stay longer than a week and spend the majority of your time navigating the area in your car, but for most visitors the compact L.A. city maps available at auto clubs and retail shops are more manageable and work just fine.

If you get discombobulated while on the freeway, remember the rule of thumb: even-numbered freeways run east and west, odd-numbered freeways run north and south.

PARKING

For some shops and many restaurants and hotels in L.A., valet parking is virtually assumed. The cost is usually $3–$5 and/or an optional tip; **keep small bills on hand for the valets.**

But there are also some inexpensive and easy garage and lot parking options. For instance, the underground facility at the Hollywood & Highland entertainment and shopping complex, at 6801 Hollywood Boulevard, charges $2 for the first four hours and a maximum of $10 for the day; no validation is required.

In Beverly Hills, the first two hours are free at several lots on or around Rodeo

Drive (for a detailed map, visit www. beverlyhills.org). There's never a parking fee or a long wait to enter and exit at the Westside Pavilion's open-access garage at 10800 Pico Boulevard.

Parking in downtown L.A. can be tough, especially on weekdays, but the garage at the 7+Fig retail complex at Ernst and Young Plaza (725 South Figueroa Street) is spacious, reasonable, and visitor-friendly. Validation from a shop or restaurant gets you three hours free; otherwise, it's $7 after 4 PM and on weekends. Staples Center patrons should ask about the discounted rates.

Parking rules are strictly enforced in Los Angeles, so make sure you **check for parking signs and pay attention to their rules.** Illegally parked cars are ticketed or towed quickly (and the minimum ticket is $35). Parking is generally available in garages or parking lots; some public lots are free all or part of the day; otherwise prices vary from 25¢ (in the public lots) to $2 per half hour or from a few dollars to $25 per day. Downtown and Century City garage rates may be as high as $25 an hour, though prices tend to drop on weekends.

Speaking of posted limits, street parking in L.A. is confusing because of the many and varying restrictions (during the day, only at night, once a week during street-cleaning hours, etc.). When visiting residential areas, be sure to ask your hosts about parking restrictions since signs aren't always easy to find. If you have to park in a restricted space for even the briefest amount of time, put on your emergency blinkers.

Sometimes businesses will offer validated parking if you've parked in an affiliated lot; validation will give you free parking for a certain time period. At a restaurant, for instance, **ask for parking validation** from the host or hostess. Metered parking is also widely available; meter rates vary from 25¢ for 15 minutes in the most heavily trafficked areas to 25¢ for one hour; have a bunch of change available. In some areas, metered parking is free on weekends or on Sunday. Another bonus: if a meter is out of order (for example, if it is flashing the word *FAIL* where the time remaining would appear), parking is free for the posted time limit.

When parking in a large lot or parking garage, **note the section or level of your parking space.** Stadiums, malls, theme parks, and other venues with giant parking areas post signs, but some garages don't have much in the way of indicators.

ROAD CONDITIONS
Beware of weekday rush-hour traffic, which is heaviest from 7 AM to 10 AM and 3 PM to 7 PM. Both KFWB and KNX (⇨ Media) have frequent traffic reports; the Los Angeles city Web site has a real-time traffic information map, and the California Highway Patrol has a road-conditions line. To encourage carpooling, some crowded freeways reserve an express lane for cars carrying more than one passenger. Parallel streets can often provide viable alternatives to jam-packed freeways, notably Sepulveda Boulevard for I–405; Venice and Washington boulevards for I–10 from Mid-Wilshire west to the beach; and Ventura Boulevard, Moorpark Street, and/or Riverside Drive for U.S. 101 through the San Fernando Valley. Highway signage is on the whole good but can't substitute for maps and detailed directions.

Fog is generally equated with San Francisco, but the coastline of southern California does get some pea-soup conditions that are dangerous for drivers. In late 2002, for instance, nearly 200 cars piled up on the Long Beach Freeway due to heavy fog. If you encounter thick fog, slow down, switch on your low beams and fog lights, and watch carefully for the lights of other vehicles. If the fog is extremely heavy, pull over cautiously and wait for it to pass.

🚗 **California Highway Patrol** ☎ 323/906–3434 for road conditions, 800/427–7623 in California. **City of Los Angeles** ⊕ www.ci.la.ca.us.

RULES OF THE ROAD
The use of seat belts for all passengers is required in California, as is the use of car seats for children five years old or younger or 60 pounds or less. The speed limit is

25–35 mph on city streets and 65 mph on freeways unless otherwise posted. Turning right on a red light after a complete stop is legal unless otherwise posted. Many streets in downtown L.A. are one-way, and a left turn from one one-way street onto another is okay on a red light after a complete stop. On some major arteries, left turns are illegal during one or both rush hours (watch for signs). Certain car-pool lanes, designated by signage and a white diamond, are reserved for cars with more than one passenger. Freeway on-ramps often have stop-and-go signals to regulate the flow of traffic, but cars in high occupancy vehicle (HOV) lanes can pass the signal without stopping.

State law does not prohibit the use of a cellular telephone while driving, but the California Highway Patrol emphasizes the importance of using hands-free devices.

Some towns, including Beverly Hills and Culver City, use photo radar at stoplights to try to reduce speeding (these intersections are always identified with signs). LAX is notorious for handing out tickets to drivers circling its busy terminals; avoid the no-parking zones and keep loading or unloading to a minimum. Also keep in mind that pedestrians always have the right of way in California; not yielding to them, even if they're jaywalkers, may well result in a $100 ticket.

Speeding can earn you a fine of up to $500. It is illegal to drive in California with a blood alcohol content of .08% or above (.01% if you're under 21); the cost of driving while intoxicated can be a $390–$1,000 fine plus 48 hours to six months in jail for first offenders. The police are not easygoing about traffic offenses in general. They don't typically engage in selective enforcement when the flow of traffic exceeds the speed limit, but they'll then focus on the drivers making dicey moves. Parking infractions can result in penalties starting at $30 for a ticket on up to having your vehicle towed and impounded (at an ultimate cost of nearly $200 even if you pay up immediately, more if you don't). In California, radar detectors aren't illegal, but "scanners"

(which receive police radio signals) *are*; per the FCC, "jammers" (which interfere with signals) are illegal throughout the United States.

Relative to those in many of America's major urban areas, Los Angeles drivers generally have a higher standard of road courtesy (sometimes buttressed by law) regarding pedestrians, maintaining lanes, merging lanes, and so forth. This cuts both ways: they'll extend it to you and expect it from you.

CHILDREN IN LOS ANGELES

With its proximity to the beach and its handful of awesome nearby theme parks, Los Angeles was made for kids. Be sure to plan ahead and involve your youngsters as you outline your trip. When packing, **include things to keep them busy during extended stretches in the car.** On sightseeing days try to schedule activities of special interest to your children. Consult the lively by-parents, for-parents *Where Should We Take the Kids? California* or *Fodor's Around Los Angeles with Kids.* Both are available in bookstores everywhere and can help you plan your days with your children. *L.A. Parent* is a monthly magazine with events listings and resources, available free at supermarkets, libraries, and museums. The Children's Nature Institute, based in Franklin Canyon Park, is a good place to ask about hikes and other outdoor activities for toddlers and other young children.

If you're renting a car, don't forget to arrange for a car seat when you reserve.

🔲 **Local Information** Children's Nature Institute ☎ 310/860-9484 ⊕ www.childrensnature.org. *L.A. Parent* ☎ 818/846-0400 ⊕ losangeles. parenthood.com.

BABYSITTING

Hotel concierges often keep a roster of reliable sitters on hand and will provide names upon request. Agencies are also an option; the hourly rate is typically $15–$18, depending on the number and ages of the children, plus a flat driving fee of about $5. The bonded sitters of the Baby Sitters Guild are professionally trained in child care and range in age from 21 to 70. The Baby Sitters Agency of West L.A. serves hotels and homes on the Westside.

⨎ Agencies Baby Sitters Agency of West L.A. ☎ 310/306-5437. **Baby Sitters Guild** ☎ 310/837-1800.

FLYING
Experts agree that it's a good idea to use safety seats aloft for children weighing less than 40 pounds. Airlines set their own policies: if you use a safety seat, U.S. carriers usually require that the child be ticketed, even if he or she is young enough to ride free, because the seats must be strapped into regular seats. And even if you pay the full adult fare for the seat, it may be worth it, especially on longer trips. Do **check your airline's policy about using safety seats during takeoff and landing.** Safety seats are not allowed everywhere in the plane, so get your seat assignments as early as possible.

When reserving, request children's meals or a freestanding bassinet (not available at all airlines) if you need them. But note that bulkhead seats, where you must sit to use the bassinet, may lack an overhead bin or storage space on the floor.

SIGHTS & ATTRACTIONS
Places that are especially appealing to children are indicated by a rubber-duckie icon (🐤) in the margin.

CONCIERGES
Good hotel concierges are invaluable—for arranging transportation, getting reservations at the hottest restaurant, and scoring tickets for a sold-out show. They're in the know and well connected. That said, sometimes you have to take their advice with a grain of salt.

It's not uncommon for restaurants to ply concierges with free food and drink in exchange for steering diners their way. Indeed, European concierges often receive referral *fees*. Hotel chains usually have individual guidelines about what their concierges can accept. The best concierges, however, are above reproach. This is particularly true of those who belong to the prestigious international society of Les Clefs d'Or.

What can you expect of a concierge? At a typical tourist-class hotel, you can expect him or her to give you the basics: to show you something on a map, make a standard restaurant reservation, or help you book a tour or airport transportation. Savvy concierges at the finest hotels and resorts, though, can arrange for just about any good or service imaginable—and do so quickly. You should compensate them appropriately. A $10 tip is enough to show appreciation for a table at a hot restaurant. But the reward should really be much greater for tickets to that U2 concert that's been sold out for months.

DISABILITIES & ACCESSIBILITY
California is a national leader in making attractions and facilities accessible to travelers with disabilities. Since 1982 the state building code has required that all construction for public use include access for people with disabilities.

⨎ Local Resources Los Angeles Convention & Visitor Bureau ✉ 333 S. Hope St., 18th fl., Los Angeles 90071 ☎ 213/624-7300 ⊕ www.lacvb.com.

SIGHTS & ATTRACTIONS
Major attractions in the southern California area are wheelchair accessible, as are shopping malls, performance venues, and movie theaters. Guides for visitors with disabilities are available at Disneyland and Universal Studios. Griffith Park has a notable play area: Shane's Inspiration, a universally acceptable playground.

TRANSPORTATION
Most major car-rental agencies provide cars equipped for travelers with disabilities for little or no extra cost (⇨ Car Rental). State laws provide special privileges, such as license plates allowing special parking spaces, unlimited parking in time-limited spaces, and free parking in metered spaces. ID from states other than California is honored.

LAX offers a special assistance vehicle for passengers with disabilities or special needs. For a guide to the airport's facilities for travelers with disabilities, check LAX's Web site. SuperShuttle (⇨ Airport Transfers) can provide accessible airport shuttle service.

All public buses and rail transportation are accessible for people with disabilities; lifts or low floors accommodate wheelchairs and walkers. Braille signs are posted in rail stations.

The U.S. Department of Transportation Aviation Consumer Protection Division's online publication *New Horizons: Information for the Air Traveler with a Disability* offers advice for travelers with a disability and outlines basic rights. Visit DisabilityInfo.gov for general information.

🚩 **Information & Complaints Aviation Consumer Protection Division** (⇨ Air Travel for airline-related problems ⊕ airconsumer.ost.dot.gov/publications/ horizons.htm for airline travel advice and rights). **Departmental Office of Civil Rights** ☎ 202/366-4648, 202/366-8538 TTY ⊕ www.dotcr.ost.dot.gov. **Disability Rights Section** ☎ ADA information line 202/514-0301, 800/514-0301, 202/514-0383 TTY, 800/514-0383 TTY ⊕ www.ada.gov. **U.S. Department of Transportation Hotline** ☎ 800/778-4838 or 800/455-9880 TTY for disability-related air-travel problems.

🚩 **Local Resources Los Angeles International Airport Special Assistance Vehicle** ☎ 310/646-6402 or 310/646-8021 ⊕ www.lawa.org/lax.

TRAVEL AGENCIES

In the United States, the Americans with Disabilities Act requires that travel firms serve the needs of all travelers. Some agencies specialize in working with people with disabilities.

🚩 **Travelers with Mobility Problems Access Adventures/B. Roberts Travel** ☎ 800/444-6540 ⊕ www.brobertstravel.com, run by a former physical-rehabilitation counselor. **Accessible Vans of America** ☎ 877/282-8267 or 888/282-8267, 973/808-9709 reservations ⊕ www.accessiblevans.com. **CareVacations** ☎ 780/986-6404 or 877/478-7827 ⊕ www.carevacations.com, for group tours and cruise vacations. **Flying Wheels Travel** ☎ 507/451-5005 ⊕ www.flyingwheelstravel.com.

🚩 **Travelers with Developmental Disabilities New Directions** ☎ 805/967-2841 or 888/967-2841 ⊕ www.newdirectionstravel.com. **Sprout** ☎ 212/222-9575 or 888/222-9575 ⊕ www.gosprout.org.

DISCOUNTS & DEALS

A couple of CityPasses are worth looking into, but do the math in terms of what you plan to see and how much you'd save. For $49, the Hollywood CityPass lets you take the two-hour Starline Hollywood Tour and visit the Hollywood Entertainment Museum and the Kodak Theatre, home of the Oscars. The Hollywood pass is good for 30 days after the first use. The $199 Southern California CityPass lets you save on the area's main theme parks and attractions: Disneyland, Disney's California Adventure, Universal Studios, the San Diego Zoo, and SeaWorld. The Southern California pass is good for 14 days after its first use. You can buy passes online or at the participating locations. Added bonus: your CityPass booklet contains actual tickets, so you can avoid long lines.

For tips on getting a deal for your airplane ticket, rental car, and so on, check those appropriate sections.

🚩 **CityPass** ☎ 888/330-5008 ⊕ citypass.net.

GAY & LESBIAN TRAVEL

L.A. has a large and visible gay community, and West Hollywood, especially Santa Monica Boulevard, is at the heart of it, with Silver Lake another popular enclave. L.A. joins in Christopher Street West's Gay and Lesbian Pride Celebration each June, which culminates with a parade through the streets of West Hollywood. Santa Monica Boulevard sees extra action on Halloween with a massive costume carnival. Many of the bars and restaurants along Santa Monica Boulevard have flyers and free gay publications stacked near their entrances.

A variety of free monthly and weekly publications, including *Frontiers* and *Lesbian News*, provide up-to-date information on nightlife and entertainment. The West Hollywood Convention and Visitors Bureau gives details on local events and community services. The L.A. Gay and Lesbian Center is also a good resource.

🚩 **Gay- & Lesbian-Friendly Travel Agencies Different Roads Travel** ☎ 760/325-6964 or 800/429-8747 (Ext. 14) ✉ lgernert@tzell.com. **Skylink Travel and Tour/Flying Dutchmen Travel** ☎ 707/546-9888 or 800/225-5759; serving lesbian travelers.

🚩 **Local Resources L.A. Gay and Lesbian Center** ☎ 323/993-7400 ⊕ www.laglc.org. **West Hollywood Convention and Visitors Bureau** ☎ 800/368-6020 ⊕ www.gogaywesthollywood.com.

HEALTH

Air pollution in L.A. may affect sensitive people in different ways. During particularly bad days in summer (the media update pollution levels each day), it's a good idea to plan a day indoors or on a windy beach. The sun can burn even on overcast days, and the dry heat can dehydrate, **so wear hats, sunglasses, and sunblock and carry water** with you.

Do not fly within 24 hours of scuba diving, or you'll put your lungs at risk by going from a high-pressure environment to a low-pressure one.

INSURANCE

What kind of coverage do you honestly need? Do you even need trip insurance at all? Take a deep breath and read on.

We believe that comprehensive trip insurance is especially valuable if you're booking a very expensive or complicated trip (particularly to an isolated region) or if you're booking far in advance. Who knows what could happen six months down the road? But whether or not you get insurance has more to do with how comfortable you are assuming all that risk yourself.

Comprehensive travel policies typically cover trip cancellation and interruption, letting you cancel or cut your trip short because of a personal emergency, illness, or, in some cases, acts of terrorism in your destination. Such policies also cover evacuation and medical care. Some also cover you for trip delays because of bad weather or mechanical problems as well as for lost or delayed baggage. Another type of coverage to look for is financial default—that is, when your trip is disrupted because a tour operator, airline, or cruise line goes out of business. Generally you must buy this when you book your trip or shortly thereafter, and it's only available to you if your operator isn't on a list of excluded companies.

If you're going abroad, consider buying medical-only coverage at the very least. Neither Medicare nor some private insurers cover medical expenses anywhere outside of the United States besides Mexico and Canada (including time aboard a cruise ship, even if it leaves from a U.S. port).

Medical-only policies typically reimburse you for medical care (excluding that related to preexisting conditions) and hospitalization abroad and provide for evacuation. You still have to pay the bills and await reimbursement from the insurer, though.

Expect comprehensive travel insurance policies to cost about 4% to 7% of the total price of your trip (it's more like 12% if you're over age 70). A medical-only policy may or may not be cheaper than a comprehensive policy. Always read the fine print of your policy to make sure that you're covered for the risks that are of the most concern to you. Compare several policies to make sure you're getting the best price and range of coverage available.

Just as an aside: you know you can save a bundle on trips to warm-weather destinations by traveling in rainy season. But there's also a chance that a severe storm will disrupt your plans. The solution? Look for hotels and resorts that offer storm–hurricane guarantees. Although they rarely allow refunds, most guarantees do let you rebook later if a storm strikes.

Insurance Comparison Sites Insure My Trip. com ⊕ www.insuremytrip.com. **Square Mouth.com** ⊕ www.quotetravelinsurance.com.

Comprehensive Travel Insurers Access America ☎ 866/807-3982 ⊕ www.accessamerica.com. **CSA Travel Protection** ☎ 800/729-6021 ⊕ www. csatravelprotection.com. **HTH Worldwide** ☎ 610/254-8700 or 888/243-2358 ⊕ www.hthworldwide. com. **Travelex Insurance** ☎ 888/457-4602 ⊕ www.travelex-insurance.com. **Travel Guard International** ☎ 715/345-0505 or 800/826-4919 ⊕ www.travelguard.com. **Travel Insured International** ☎ 800/243-3174 ⊕ www.travelinsured.com.

Medical-Only Insurers Wallach & Company ☎ 800/237-6615 or 504/687-3166 ⊕ www.wallach. com. **International Medical Group** ☎ 800/628-4664 ⊕ www.imglobal.com. **International SOS** ☎ 215/942-8000 or 713/521-7611 ⊕ www. internationalsos.com.

FOR INTERNATIONAL TRAVELERS

CUSTOMS

U.S. Customs and Border Protection ⊕ www. cbp.gov.

CURRENCY

The dollar is the basic unit of U.S. currency. It has 100 cents. Coins are the penny (1¢), nickel (5¢), dime (10¢), quarter (25¢), and half-dollar (50¢); and the very rare golden $1 coin and even rarer silver $1. Bills are in denominations of $1, $5, $10, $20, $50, and $100, all mostly green and identical in size; designs and background tints vary. You may come across a $2 bill, but the chances are slim.

There are quite a few currency exchanges in the area, especially downtown and Beverly Hills. Below is a sampling of offices in a range of locations; between them, American Express and Thomas Cook have a total of nine in the L.A. area. Normal weekday business hours are generally 9 or 10 until 5 or 6 with some offices, including the Encino AmEx and Bank Notes Exchange, also open half a day on Saturday. Some Thomas Cook branches have regular or summer Saturday hours.

🚩 **Currency Exchanges American Express**
✉ 12050 Ventura Blvd., Studio City ☎ 818/506–3146. **Bretton Woods** ✉ 11659 San Vicente Blvd., Brentwood ☎ 800/439–2426. **Bank Notes Exchange** ✉ 520 S. Grand Ave., Suite L100, Downtown ☎ 213/627–5404 or 888/533–7283. **Travelex** ✉ 9595 Wilshire Blvd., Beverly Hills ☎ 310/247–0892.

DRIVING

Driving in the United States is on the right. Speed limits are posted in miles per hour along roads and highways (usually between 55 mph and 70 mph). Watch for lower limits in small towns and on back roads (usually 30 mph to 40 mph). Most states require front-seat passengers to wear seat belts; many states require children to sit in the back seat and to wear seat belts. In major cities, morning rush hour is between 7 and 10; afternoon rush hour is between between 4 and 7; expect heavy traffic. To encourage carpooling, some freeways have special lanes for so-called high-occupancy vehicles (HOV)—cars carrying more than one passenger, usually marked with a diamond.

Highways are well paved. Interstate highways—limited-access, multilane highways with numbers prefixed by "I–"—are the fastest routes. Interstates with three-digit numbers encircle urban areas, which may have other limited-access expressways, freeways, and parkways as well. Tolls may be levied on limited-access highways. So-called U.S. highways and state highways are not necessarily limited access but may have several lanes.

Gas stations are plentiful. Most stay open late (24 hours along large highways and in big cities), except in rural areas, where Sunday hours are limited and where you may drive long stretches without a refueling opportunity. Along larger highways, roadside stops with restrooms, fast-food restaurants, and sundries stores are well spaced. State police and tow trucks patrol major highways and lend assistance. If your car breaks down on an interstate, pull onto the shoulder and wait for help, or have your passengers wait while you walk to an emergency phone (available in most states). If you carry a cell phone, dial *55, noting your location on the small green roadside mileage markers.

ELECTRICITY

The U.S. standard is AC, 110 volts/60 cycles. Plugs have two flat pins set parallel to each other.

EMBASSIES

🚩 **Australia** ☎ 202/797–3000 ⊕ www.austemb.org. **United Kingdom** ☎ 202/588–7800 ⊕ www.britainusa.com. **Canada** ☎ 202/682–1740 ⊕ www.canadianembassy.org.

EMERGENCIES

For police, fire, or ambulance dial 911.

HOLIDAYS

Major national holidays are New Year's Day (Jan. 1); Martin Luther King Day (3rd Mon. in Jan.); Presidents' Day (3rd Mon. in Feb.); Memorial Day (last Mon. in May); Independence Day (July 4); Labor Day (1st Mon. in Sept.); Columbus Day (2nd Mon. in Oct.); Thanksgiving Day (4th Thurs. in Nov.); Christmas Eve and Christmas Day (Dec. 24 and 25); and New Year's Eve (Dec. 31).

MAIL

You can buy stamps and aerograms and send letters and parcels in post offices. Stamp-dispensing machines can occasionally be found in airports, bus and train stations, office buildings, drugstores, and the like. U.S. mailboxes are stout, dark blue, steel bins at strategic locations in major cities; pickup schedules are posted inside the bin (pull down the handle to see them). Parcels more than 1 pound must be mailed at a post office or at a private mailing center.

Within the United States, a first-class letter weighing 1 ounce or less costs 39¢, and each additional ounce costs 24¢; postcards cost 24¢. A 1-ounce airmail letter to most countries costs 84¢, an airmail postcard costs 75¢; to Canada and Mexico, a 1-ounce letter costs 63¢, a postcard 55¢. An aerogram—a single sheet of lightweight blue paper that folds into its own envelope, stamped for overseas airmail—costs 75¢ regardless of its destination.

To receive mail on the road, have it sent c/o General Delivery at your destination's main post office (use the correct five-digit ZIP code). You must pick up mail in person within 30 days and show a driver's license or passport.
🔹 **DHL** ☎ 800/225-5345 ⊕ www.dhl.com. **Federal Express** ☎ 800/463-3339 ⊕ www.fedex.com. **Mail Boxes, Etc.** (The UPS Store) ⊕ www.mbe.com. **United States Postal Service** ⊕ www.usps.com.

PASSPORTS & VISAS
Visitor visas aren't necessary for citizens of Australia, Canada, the United Kingdom, as well as for most citizens of European-Union countries if you're coming for tourism and staying for fewer than 90 days. If you require a visa, the cost is $100, and depending on where you live, the waiting time can be substantial. Apply for a visa at the U.S. consulate in your place of residence; look at the U.S. State Department's special visa Web site for further information.
🔹 **Visa Information** Destination USA ⊕ www.unitedstatesvisas.gov.

PHONES
All U.S. telephone numbers consist of a three-digit area code and a seven-digit local number. Within many local calling areas, you dial only the seven-digit number; in others, you must dial "1" first and

then the area code. To call between area-code regions, dial "1" then all 10 digits; the same goes for calls to numbers prefixed by "800," "888," "866," and "877"—all toll free. For calls to numbers preceded by "900" you must pay—usually dearly.

For international calls, dial "011" followed by the country code and the local number. For help, dial "0" and ask for an overseas operator. The country code is 61 for Australia, 64 for New Zealand, 44 for the United Kingdom. Calling Canada is the same as calling within the United States. Most phone books list country codes and U.S. area codes. The country code for the United States is 1.

For operator assistance, dial "0." To obtain someone's phone number, call directory assistance at 555–1212 or occasionally 411 (free at many public phones). You can reverse the charges on a long-distance call if you phone "collect"; dial "0" instead of "1" before the 10-digit number.

At pay phones, instructions often are posted. Usually you insert coins in a slot (usually 25¢–50¢ for local calls) and wait for a steady tone before dialing. When you call long-distance, the operator tells you how much to insert; prepaid phone cards, widely available in various denominations, can be used from any phone. Follow the directions to activate the card (there is usually an access number and then an activation code for the card), then dial your number.

The United States has several GSM (Global System for Mobile Communications) networks, so multiband mobile phones from most countries (except for Japan) work here. Unfortunately, it's almost impossible to buy a pay-as-you-go mobile SIM card in the United States—which allows you to avoid roaming charges—without a phone. That said, cell phones with pay-as-you-go plans are available for well under $100. The cheapest ones with decent national coverage are from Cingular, which offers the GoPhone, and Virgin Mobile, which only offers pay-as-you-go service.

📶 **Cell Phone Contacts Cingular** ☎ 888/333-6651 🌐 www.cingular.com. **Virgin Mobile** 🖀 No phone 🌐 www.virginmobileusa.com.

MEDIA

NEWSPAPERS & MAGAZINES

The *Los Angeles Times* is L.A.'s only major daily metropolitan newspaper. The *LA Weekly* is L.A.'s largest free weekly newspaper, containing extensive film, art, and music coverage in addition to social and political commentary, though its 2006 acquisition by former rival *New Times* left its editorial future uncertain at this writing. The conservative *Daily News* provides the full range of news coverage, with a particular emphasis on local San Fernando Valley news. The *L.A. Daily Journal* is L.A.'s legal newspaper. *La Opinion* is a daily Spanish-language newspaper providing coverage of news, sports, and entertainment. Its competitor, *Hoy Los Angeles,* hit the southern California market in 2004. *Los Angeles Magazine* is a glossy mix of celebrity, lifestyle, and food articles, plus extensive restaurant and activities listings.

RADIO & TELEVISION

Los Angeles radio stations include **KCBS** (93.1 FM aka Jack FM, classic rock), **KABC** (790 AM, talk radio), **KCRW** (89.9, public radio with an innovative weekday show called *Morning Becomes Eclectic*), **KROQ** (106.7 FM, rock and alternative), **INDIE** (103.1 FM, indie rock and some good local music), **K-EARTH** (101.1 FM, oldies), **KFWB** (980 AM, news), **KIIS-FM** (102.7 FM, Top 40), **KJAZ** (1240 AM, jazz), **KLON** (88.1 FM, jazz and blues), **KLOS** (95.5 FM, rock), **KMZT** (105.1 FM, classical), **KNX** (1070 AM, news, sports, and features), **KPFK** (90.7 FM, Pacifica, public radio), **KPCC** (89.3 FM, public radio), **KUSC** (91.5 FM, classical public radio), **KYSR** (98.7 FM, pop, rock, and alternative), and **KZLA** (93.9 FM, country).

Local Los Angeles television channels include **KCBS** (Channel 2, CBS affiliate), **KNBC** (Channel 4, NBC affiliate), **KTLA** (Channel 5, WB affiliate), **KABC** (Channel 7, ABC affiliate), **KCAL** (Channel 9, independent), **KTTV** (Channel 11, Fox affiliate), **KCOP** (Channel 13, UPN affiliate), and **KCET** (Channel 28, PBS), as well as **KMEX** (Channel 34, Univision) and **KVEA** (Channel 52, Telemundo), broadcasting in Spanish.

METRO RAIL TRAVEL

Metro Rail covers a limited area of L.A.'s vast expanse, but what there is, is helpful and frequent. The underground Red Line runs from Union Station downtown through Mid-Wilshire, Hollywood, and Universal City on its way to North Hollywood, stopping at the most popular tourist destinations along the way. The light commuter rail Green Line stretches from Redondo Beach to Norwalk, while the partially underground Blue Line goes from downtown to the South Bay (Long Beach/San Pedro). The Green and Blue lines are not often used by visitors. The monorail-like Gold Line, opened in summer 2003, begins at Union Station and heads northeast to Pasadena and Sierra Madre. The Orange Line, a 14-mi bus corridor connecting the North Hollywood subway station with the western San Fernando Valley, opened in fall 2005.

FARES & SCHEDULES

There's service from about 4:30 AM to 12:30 AM, every 5–15 minutes, depending on time of day and location. Buy a ticket from any station's vending machines (use bus tokens, coins, or $1 or $5 bills). It costs $1.25 plus 25¢ per transfer, or $3 for an all-day pass. The machines print your tickets and make change. (If you have a valid Metro Pass for buses, you don't need a ticket.) Metro Rail operates on the honor system; officers make periodic checks for valid tickets or passes onboard. Bicycles are not allowed during rush hours and then only with permits, but you can store them on a rack (free) or in a locker (fee). The Web site is the best way to get info on Metro Rail. See also "L.A. on the Fast Track" in Chapter 1.

📶 **Metro Rail Information Metropolitan Transit Authority (MTA)** ☎ 800/266-6883 or 213/626-4455 🌐 www.mta.net.

MONEY MATTERS

Prices throughout this guide are given for adults. Substantially reduced fees are almost always available for children, students, and senior citizens. For information on taxes, *see* Taxes.

Although not inexpensive, costs in Los Angeles tend to be a bit less than in other major cities such as New York and San Francisco. For instance, in a low-key local diner, a cup of coffee might cost a dollar. In high-profile or trendy establishments, though, costs escalate; a cup of coffee in an upscale restaurant can cost as much as $5.

CREDIT CARDS

Throughout this guide, the following abbreviations are used: **AE**, American Express; **D**, Discover; **DC**, Diners Club; **MC**, MasterCard; and **V**, Visa.

It's a good idea to inform your credit-card company before you travel, especially if you're going abroad and don't travel internationally very often. Otherwise, the credit-card company might put a hold on your card owing to unusual activity—not a good thing halfway through your trip. Record all your credit-card numbers—as well as the phone numbers to call if your cards are lost or stolen—in a safe place so you're prepared should something go wrong. Both MasterCard and Visa have general numbers you can call (collect if you're abroad) if your card is lost, but you're better off calling the number of your issuing bank because MasterCard and Visa usually just transfer you to your bank; your bank's number is usually printed on your card.

🚹 **Reporting Lost Cards** American Express ☎ 800/992-3404 in U.S., 336/393-1111 collect from abroad ⊕ www.americanexpress.com. Diners Club ☎ 800/234-6377 in U.S., 303/799-1504 collect from abroad ⊕ www.dinersclub.com. Discover ☎ 800/347-2683 in U.S., 801/902-3100 collect from abroad ⊕ www.discovercard.com. MasterCard ☎ 800/622-7747 in U.S., 636/722-7111 collect from abroad ⊕ www.mastercard.com. Visa ☎ 800/847-2911 in U.S., 410/581-9994 collect from abroad ⊕ www.visa.com.

TRAVELER'S CHECKS & CARDS

Some consider traveler's checks the currency of the cave man, and it's true that fewer establishments accept traveler's checks these days. Nevertheless, they're a cheap and secure way to carry extra money, particularly on trips to urban areas. Both Citibank (under the Visa brand) and American Express issue traveler's checks in the United States, but Amex is better known and more widely accepted; you can also avoid hefty surcharges by cashing Amex checks at Amex offices. Whatever you do, keep track of all the serial numbers in case the checks are lost or stolen.

American Express now offers a stored-value card called a Travelers Cheque Card, which you can use wherever American Express credit cards are accepted, including ATMs. The card can carry a minimum of $300 and a maximum of $2,700, and it's a safe way to carry your funds. Although you can get replacement funds in 24 hours if your card is lost or stolen, it doesn't really strike us as a very good deal. In addition to a high initial cost ($14.95 to set up the card, plus $5 each time you "reload"), you still have to pay a 2% fee for each purchase in a foreign currency (similar to that of any credit card). Further, each time you use the card in an ATM you pay a transaction fee of $2.50 on top of the 2% transaction fee for the conversion—add it all up and it can be considerably more than you would pay for using your own ATM card. Regular traveler's checks are just as secure and cost less.

🚹 **American Express** ☎ 888/412-6945 in U.S., 801/945-9450 collect outside of U.S. to add value or speak to customer service ⊕ www.americanexpress.com.

PACKING

Why do some people travel with a convoy of suitcases the size of large-screen TVs and yet never have a thing to wear? How do others pack a toaster-oven-size duffle with a week's worth of outfits *and* supplies for every possible contingency? We realize that packing is a matter of style—a very personal thing—but there's a lot to be said for traveling light. The tips in this section will help you win the battle of the bulging bag.

Make a list. In a recent Fodor's survey, 29% of respondents said they make lists (and often pack) at least a week before a trip. Lists can be used at least twice—once to pack and once to repack at the end of your trip. You'll also have a record of the contents of your suitcase, just in case it disappears in transit.

Think it through. What's the weather like? Is this a business trip or a cruise or resort vacation? Going abroad? In some places and/or sights, traditions of dress may be more or less conservative than you're used to. As your itinerary comes together, jot activities down and note possible outfits next to each (don't forget those shoes and accessories).

Edit your wardrobe. Focus on things you'd be likely to wear twice. Build around one or two neutrals and an accent (e.g., black, white, and olive green). For a week's trip, you can look smashing with three bottoms, four or five tops, a sweater, and a jacket you can wear alone or over the sweater. Since this is L.A., a stylish pair of jeans will take you almost everywhere.

Be practical. Put comfortable shoes at the top of your list. (Did we need to tell you this?) Pack items that are lightweight, wrinkle resistant, compact, and washable. (Or this?) Try a simple wrinkling test: intentionally fold a piece of fabric between your fingers for a couple minutes. If it refuses to crease, it will probably come out of your suitcase looking fresh. That said, if you stack and then roll your clothes when packing, they'll wrinkle less.

Check weight and size limitations. In the United States you may be charged extra for checked bags weighing more than 50 pounds. Abroad some airlines don't allow you to check bags weighing more than 60 to 70 pounds, or they charge outrageous fees for every pound your luggage is over. Carry-on size limitations can be stringent, too.

Be prepared to lug it yourself. If there's one thing that can turn a pack rat into a minimalist, it's a vacation spent lugging heavy bags over long distances. Unless you're on a guided tour or a cruise, select luggage that you can readily carry. Porters, like good butlers, are hard to find these days.

Lock it up. Several companies sell locks (about $10) approved by the Transporta-

tion Safety Administration that can be unlocked by all U.S. security personnel should they decide to search your bags. Alternatively, you can use simple plastic cable ties, which are sold at hardware stores in bundles.

Tag it. Always put tags on your luggage with some kind of contact information; use your business address if you don't want people to know your home address. Put the same information (and a copy of your itinerary) inside your luggage, too.

Don't check valuables. On U.S. flights, airlines are only liable for about $2,800 per person for bags. On international flights, the liability limit is around $635 per bag. But just try collecting from the airline for items like computers, cameras, and jewelry. It isn't going to happen; they aren't covered. And though comprehensive travel policies may cover luggage, the liability limit is often a pittance. Your home owner's policy may cover you sufficiently when you travel—or not. You're really better off stashing baubles and gizmos in your carry-on—right near those prescription meds.

Report problems immediately. If your bags—or things in them—are damaged or go astray, file a written claim with your airline *before you leave the airport*. If the airline is at fault, it may give you money for essentials until your luggage arrives. Most lost bags are found within 48 hours, so alert the airline to your whereabouts for two or three days. If your bag was opened for security reasons in the United States and something is missing, file a claim with the TSA.

WHAT YOU'LL NEED IN L.A.

Although casual dressing is a hallmark of the California lifestyle, the best restaurants and nightspots sometimes require a jacket and tie in the evening, and women usually wear something dressier than regulation sightseeing garb. If you're going to the trendier bars or clubs, you'll need a suitably trendy outfit.

The most important rule to bear in mind in packing for a southern California vacation is to **prepare for temperature**

changes. There can be significant temperature differences between inland areas and the shore, and temperatures can drop substantially at night. Clothes that can be layered are your best insurance.

Always **bring sunscreen.** Even if you're not planning on sunbathing per se, you can get burned quickly just being outdoors. If you'll be hitting the beach or a pool, pack a bathing suit, large towels, and flip-flops or slides.

Don't forget your bathing suit and a beach-friendly top layer like a zip-front sweatshirt, plus a plastic bag to stash them in should you need to pack them while they're still damp. If you're going anywhere near sand: **bring a casual pair of shoes you can easily slide on and off.**

Be sure you take comfortable walking shoes. People may say that nobody walks in L.A., but you will spend plenty of time on your feet.

RESTROOMS

Some restrooms in L.A. are clean as a whistle; others are pig-sty awful. You can assume that gas stations along the highways outside of town will have a bathroom available, but this isn't true of every station in L.A. itself. Restrooms in parks are often dirty. Restaurants and bars may have signs that read FOR PATRONS ONLY so that you're obliged to buy something to use the facilities. Better bets for relatively clean, obligation-free restrooms are those in department stores and large chain bookstores.

The Bathroom Diaries is a Web site that's flush with unsanitized info on restrooms the world over—each one located, reviewed, and rated.

Find a Loo The Bathroom Diaries ⊕ www.thebathroomdiaries.com

SAFETY

In L.A., as in any other major American city, street smarts and common sense are your best methods of staying safe. At night, **avoid areas that are deserted or unlighted.** When driving in unfamiliar areas, plan your route ahead of time rather than figuring it out on the way. Do not respond to people offering cab rides or help with your luggage.

Keep valuables out of sight on the street or, better yet, leave them at home. Men should carry wallets in front pants pockets rather than in back pockets. Do not hang purses or backpacks on the back of chairs or put them on empty neighboring seats. **Keep your belongings close**; for example, tuck your bag between your feet at a movie theater. Money belts and waist packs peg you as a tourist; if you carry a purse, consider one with a thick strap that can be worn across the body, bandolier-style. When leaving your car, put any valuables out of sight; put all the windows up and lock all doors and the trunk.

The most concentrated homeless population in the city is downtown, and on some blocks panhandling is common. Hollywood and Santa Monica are other areas where you're most likely to be approached for money or food.

After years in decline, gang-related violent crime has recently been on the rise, prompting aggressive new antigang initiatives. Gang-related street violence is concentrated in certain neighborhoods; South L.A., Compton, and Watts should be avoided, particularly at night.

Of the Metro lines, the Red and Green lines are the safest and are more heavily patrolled. The Blue Line can be sketchy after dark. Avoid riding in empty cars, and move with the crowd when going from the station to the street.

EARTHQUAKE SAFETY

Very minor earthquakes occur frequently in southern California; most of the time they're so slight that you won't notice them at all. If you do feel a stronger tremor, follow basic safety precautions. If you're indoors, take cover in a doorway or under a table or desk—whichever is closest to you. Protect your head with your arms. Stay clear of windows, mirrors, or anything that might fall from the walls. Do not use elevators. If you're in an open space, move away from buildings, trees, and power lines. If you're outdoors near buildings, duck into a doorway. If you're driving, slow down and pull over to the side of the road, avoiding overpasses, bridges, and power lines, and stay inside the car. Expect aftershocks; if you feel a smaller quake following a larger tremor, take cover again.

GOVERNMENT ADVISORIES

If you travel frequently also look into the Registered Traveler program of the Transportation Security Administration (TSA; www.tsa.gov). The program, which is still being tested in five U.S. airports, is designed to cut down on gridlock at security checkpoints by allowing prescreened travelers to pass quickly through kiosks that scan an iris and/or a fingerprint. How sci-fi is that?

SENIOR-CITIZEN TRAVEL

The minimum age to receive a senior-citizen discount to attractions, movies, and so on in Los Angeles varies from 55 to 65 years old.

To qualify for age-related discounts, mention your senior-citizen status up front when booking hotel reservations (not when checking out) and before you're seated in restaurants (not when paying the bill). Be sure to have identification on hand. When renting a car, ask about promotional car-rental discounts, which can be cheaper than senior-citizen rates.

Educational Programs Elderhostel ☎ 877/426-8056, 978/323-4141 international callers, 877/426-2167 TTY ⊕ www.elderhostel.org.

SMOKING

Smoking is prohibited in many parts of Los Angeles—inside and out. Violators face fines of $100–$500, so do your homework before lighting up. All enclosed public areas and workplaces, including restaurants, bars, and retail shops, are no-smoking zones. Recently passed ordinances have also banned cigarette smoking at Los Angeles County beaches and piers, as well as beaches in Santa Monica, Malibu, Newport Beach, and Huntington Beach. Owner-operated bars and restaurant patios are exempt from the smoking ban, but many follow a smoke-free policy anyway. Even outdoor malls may have designated smoking areas.

STUDENTS IN L.A.

Most museums and other major attractions have student discounts as do many movie theaters. Several theaters, including the Pasadena Playhouse and Geffen, offer discounted student rush tickets on the day of performance.

The city's two major universities, UCLA and USC, both have active campus scenes, and both have galleries, performances, and sports events open to the public. UCLA students hang out in adjacent Westwood Village and all over the upscale Westside. USC has a lovely campus, but the surrounding neighborhood can be dicey.

IDs & Services STA Travel ☎ 212/627-3111, 800/781-4040 24-hr service center ⊕ www.sta.com. **Travel Cuts** ☎ 800/592-2887 in U.S. ⊕ www.travelcuts.com.

TAXES

The sales tax in Los Angeles is 8.25%. There's none on most groceries, but there is on newspapers (unless bought from a coin-operated machine) and magazines. The tax on hotel rooms is 8.05%–12%.

TAXIS & LIMOUSINES

Don't even try to hail a cab on the street in Los Angeles. Instead, phone one of the many taxi companies. The metered rate is $2 per mile, plus a $2 per-fare charge. Taxi rides from LAX have an additional $2.50 surcharge. Be aware that distances between sights in L.A. are vast, so cab fares add up quickly. One relative bargain, though: for a $4 flat fare, up to four passengers may use a taxi to visit downtown attractions within the "One Fare Zone," which is bounded by the Harbor Freeway (I–110) to the west, Main Street to the east, Pico Boulevard to the south, and the Hollywood Freeway (U.S. 101) to the north. On the other end of the price spectrum, limousines come equipped with everything from a full bar and telephone to a hot tub. If you open any L.A.-area yellow pages, the number of limo companies will astound you. Most charge by the hour, with a three-hour minimum.

Limo Companies ABC Limousine & Sedan Service ☎ 818/980-6000 or 888/753-7500. **American Executive** ☎ 213/250-2121 or 800/927-2020. **Black**

& White Transportation Services ☎ 800/924-1624.
Chauffeur's Unlimited ☎ 310/645-8711 or 888/546-6019 ⊕ www.chaufusa.com. **Dav El Limousine Co.** ☎ 310/550-0070 or 800/922-0343 ⊕ www.davel.com. **First Class** ☎ 323/756-4894 or 310/676-9771 ⊕ www.first-classlimo.com. **ITS** ☎ 800/487-4255.
🛈 **Taxi Companies** **Bell Cab** ☎ 888/235-5222 ⊕ www.bellcab.com. **Beverly Hills Cab Co.** ☎ 800/273-6611. **Checker Cab** ☎ 800/300-5007. **Independent Cab Co.** ☎ 800/521-8294 ⊕ www.taxi4u.com. **United Independent Taxi** ☎ 800/411-0303 or 800/822-8294. **Yellow Cab/LA Taxi Co-Op** ☎ 800/200-1085 or 800/200-0011.

TIME

Los Angeles is in the Pacific time zone, two hours behind Chicago, three hours behind New York, eight hours behind London, and 18 hours behind Sydney.

TIPPING

The customary tip rate is 15%–20% for waiters and taxi drivers and 10%–15% for hairdressers and barbers. Bellhops and airport baggage handlers receive $1–$2 per bag; parking valets are usually tipped $1–$2. Bartenders are generally tipped $1 per drink. Hotel maids should generally receive $1–$3 per day of the stay. In upscale establishments, they should receive at least 4% of the room rate before taxes, unless the hotel charges a service fee that includes a gratuity. In restaurants, a handy trick for estimating the tip is to double the 8.25% tax.

TOURS & PACKAGES

You can explore L.A. from many vantage points and even more topical angles. Not surprisingly, lots of guides include dollops of celebrity history and gossip. Most tours run year-round, and most require advance reservations.

SCOOTER TOURS

For an unusual perspective on L.A.'s attractions, you can take a tour of the city via the Segway, the electric scooter and "human transporter" that debuted on city sidewalks in 2003. Tours range from $59 to $89 per person, and there are 15 different areas or themes from which to choose, including the UCLA campus, Santa Monica, and Rodeo Drive. All tours begin with

an instruction session, followed by a guided ride, totaling just over two hours.
🛈 **Fees & Schedules** **Segway Tours** ☎ 310/358-5900 ⊕ www.segwow.com.

BUS & VAN TOURS

Casablanca Tours, established in 1980, gives sightseeing tours all around L.A., but its specialty is an insider's look at Hollywood and Beverly Hills; it's available in two- and four-hour versions ($49–$76). Most tours are in minibuses with a maximum of 14 people; others are in 25-seaters. L.A. Tours and Sightseeing has several tours ($35–$109) by van and bus covering various parts of the city, including downtown, Hollywood, and Beverly Hills. The company also operates tours to Disneyland, Universal Studios, Six Flags Magic Mountain, beaches, and stars' homes. Starline Tours of Hollywood ($16–$100) picks up passengers from area hotels and from Grauman's Chinese Theatre. Universal Studios, Knott's Berry Farm, stars' homes, and Disneyland are some of the sights on this popular tour company's agenda.
🛈 **Fees & Schedules** **Casablanca Tours** ☎ 323/461-0156. **L.A. Tours and Sightseeing** ☎ 323/460-6490 ⊕ www.latours.net. **Starline Tours of Hollywood** ☎ 323/463-3333 or 800/959-3131 ⊕ www.starlinetours.com.

HELICOPTER TOURS

If you want an aerial tour, lift off with Orbic Helicopters. It offers two 30-minute tours (a general L.A. tour and a scenic shoreline/Westside tour) and a 45-minute tour combining those itineraries. Orbic's been flying its two- and four-passenger helicopters for more than a dozen years, and the pilots each have 16 or more years of flying experience. Flights cost $130–$180 per person; reserve via credit card and can-cel within 24 hours at no charge (no-shows pay full fare).
🛈 **Fees & Schedules** **Orbic Helicopters** ☎ 818/988-6532 ⊕ www.orbichelicopters.com.

PRIVATE GUIDES

L.A. Nighthawks will arrange your nightlife for you. For a rather hefty price (at least $99 a person), you'll get a limousine, a guide (who ensures you're in a safe environment at all times), and immediate entry into L.A.'s hottest nightspots.

📋 **Fees & Schedules L.A. Nighthawks** ☎ 310/392-1500.

SPECIAL-INTEREST TOURS

With Architecture Tours L.A., you can zip all over the city in a 1960s Cadillac on a private tour with an architectural historian. Rates start at $65. Architours customizes walking and driving tours for architecture buffs; these can include interior visits with architects, artists, and designers. Rates begin at $25 per hour.

The city of Beverly Hills operates two trolley tours, one focused on art and architecture, the other on local sights. From July through Labor Day and during the winter holidays the trolleys run Tuesday through Saturday; during the rest of the year they make the rounds on Saturday only. Tickets cost $5. Hollywood Fantasy Tours has daily van tours that take you through historic Hollywood, to the HOLLYWOOD sign, and past stars' homes in Beverly Hills. The tours cost $16–$31, but there are combo packages and group discounts. Soak up the shimmer and glow of classic neon signs from an open double-decker bus on a Neon Art Tour, given Saturday evening from May through October. Tickets cost $45 for nonmembers.

The Next Stage also has an innovative take on the city; it takes people by foot, bus, van, train, and helicopter on its tours. Favorites (mostly in the $30–$60 range) include the Insomniac's Tour, the Scentimental Journey, L.A. Has Its Ups and Downs (an escalator–elevator excursion), and a culinary tour. Take My Mother Please will arrange lively, thematic combination walking and driving tours; for instance, you could explore sights associated with Raymond Chandler's detective novels. Custom tours are also available. Rates start at $300 for a half day.

📋 **Fees & Schedules Architecture Tours L.A.** ☎ 323/464-7868 ⊕ www.architecturetoursla.com. **Architours** ☎ 323/294-5821 ⊕ www.architours.com. **City of Beverly Hills Trolley Tours** ☎ 310/285-2438 ⊕ www.beverlyhills.org. **Hollywood Fantasy Tours** ☎ 323/469-8184 or 800/782-7287 ⊕ www.hollywoodfantasytours.com. **Neon Art**

Tours ☎ 213/489-9918 Museum of Neon Art ⊕ www.neonmona.org. **The Next Stage** ☎ 626/577-7880 ⊕ www.nextstagetours.com. **Take My Mother Please** ☎ 323/737-2200 ⊕ www.takemymotherplease.com.

WALKING TOURS

Red Line Tours offers daily one- and two-hour walking tours of Hollywood behind the scenes and historic and contemporary downtown Los Angeles. Tours, which cost $10–$20, are led by a docent, and include live audio headsets to block out street noise.

The Los Angeles Conservancy's walking tours (each about 2½ hours long at a cost of $10 per person) chiefly cover the downtown area. The Historic Core tour showcases the city's art deco and Beaux-Arts past. A pleasant, self-guided walking tour of Santa Monica is detailed in a brochure available at the Santa Monica Visitors Information Center. You may also download street maps ahead of your trip at ⊕ www.santamonica.com.

📋 **Fees & Schedules Los Angeles Conservancy** ☎ 213/623-2489 ⊕ www.laconservancy.org. **Red Line Tours** ☎ 323/402-1074 ⊕ redlinetours.web.aplus.net. **Santa Monica Visitors Information Center** ☎ 310/393-7593 or 800/544-5319 ⊕ www.santamonica.com.

VACATION PACKAGES

Packages *are not* guided tours. Packages combine airfare, accommodations, and perhaps a rental car or other extras (theater tickets, guided excursions, boat trips, reserved entry to popular museums, transit passes), but they let you do your own thing. During busy periods, packages may be your only option because flights and rooms may be otherwise sold out. Packages will definitely save you time. They can also save you money, particularly in peak seasons, but—and this is a really big but—you should price each part of the package separately to be sure. And be aware that prices advertised on Web sites and in newspapers rarely include service charges or taxes, which can up your costs by hundreds of dollars.

Note that local tourism boards can provide information about lesser-known and small-niche operators that sell packages to just a few destinations. And don't always assume that you can get the best deal by booking everything yourself. Some packages and cruises are sold only through travel agents.

Each year consumers are stranded or lose their money when packagers—even large ones with excellent reputations—go out of business. How can you protect yourself? First, always pay with a credit card; if you have a problem, your credit-card company may help you resolve it. Second, buy trip insurance that covers default. Third, choose a company that belongs to the U.S. Tour Operators Association, whose members must set aside funds ($1 million) to cover defaults. Finally choose a company that also participates in the Tour Operator Program of the American Society of Travel Agents (ASTA), which will act as mediator in any disputes. You can also check on the tour operator's reputation among travelers by posting an inquiry on one of the Fodors.com forums.

Organizations American Society of Travel Agents (ASTA) ☎ 703/739−2782, 800/965−2782 24-hr hotline ⊕ www.astanet.com. **United States Tour Operators Association** (USTOA) ☎ 212/599−6599 ⊕ www.ustoa.com.

TRAIN TRAVEL

Union Station in downtown Los Angeles is one of the great American railroad stations. The interior is well kept and includes comfortable seating, a restaurant, and snack bars. As the city's rail hub, it's the place to catch an Amtrak train. Among Amtrak's southern California routes are 13 daily trips to San Diego and 7 to Santa Barbara. Amtrak's luxury *Coast Starlight* travels along the spectacular coastline from Seattle to Los Angeles in just a day and a half (though it's often a little late). The *Sunset Limited* goes to Los Angeles from Florida (via New Orleans and Texas), and the *Southwest Chief* from Chicago. You can make reservations in advance by phone or at the station. As with airlines, you usually get a better deal the farther in advance you book. You must show your ticket and a photo ID before boarding. Smoking is not allowed on Amtrak trains.

CUTTING COSTS

To save money, **look into rail passes.** But be aware that if you don't plan to cover many miles, you may come out ahead by buying individual tickets.

Train Information Amtrak ☎ 800/872-7245 ⊕ www.amtrak.com. **Union Station** ✉ 800 N. Alameda St. ☎ 213/683−6979.

TRAVEL AGENCIES

If you use an agent—brick-and-mortar or virtual—you'll pay a fee for the service. And know that the service you get from some online agents isn't comprehensive. For example, neither Expedia nor Travelocity searches for prices on budget airlines like JetBlue, Southwest, and small foreign carriers. That said, some agents (online or not) *do* have access to fares that are difficult to find otherwise, and the savings can more than make up for any surcharge.

A knowledgeable brick-and-mortar travel agent can be a godsend if you're booking a cruise, a package trip that's not available to you directly, an air pass, or a complicated itinerary including several overseas flights. What's more, travel agents who specialize in a destination may have exclusive access to certain deals and insider information on things such as charter flights. Agents who specialize in types of travelers (senior citizens, gays and lesbians, naturists) or types of trips (cruises, luxury travel, safaris) can also be invaluable.

A top-notch agent planning your trip to Russia will make sure you get the correct visa application and complete it on time; the one booking your cruise may get you a cabin upgrade or arrange to have bottle of champagne chilling in your cabin when you embark. And complain about the surcharges all you like, but when things don't work out the way you'd hoped, it's nice to have an agent to put things right.

Agent Resources American Society of Travel Agents ☎ 703/739−2782 ⊕ www.travelsense.org. **Online Agents Expedia** ⊕ www.expedia.com. **Onetravel.com** ⊕ www.onetravel.com. **Orbitz** ⊕ www.orbitz.com. **Priceline.com** ⊕ www.priceline.com. **Travelocity** ⊕ www.travelocity.com.

VISITOR INFORMATION

L.A. Inc./The Convention and Visitors Bureau (CVB) publishes an annually updated general information packet with suggestions for entertainment, lodging, dining, and a list of special events. There are two L.A. visitor information centers, on Figueroa downtown and on Hollywood Boulevard in Hollywood. The Santa Monica CVB runs two drop-in visitor information centers, one in the Santa Monica Place Shopping Center and another in Palisades Park; both are open daily 10–4.

🚹 **Tourist Information Beverly Hills Conference and Visitors Bureau** ☎ 310/248-1000 or 800/345-2210 ⊕ www.beverlyhillsbehere.com. **California Office of Tourism** ☎ 916/444-4429 or 800/862-2543 ⊕ gocalif.ca.gov. **Glendale Chamber of Commerce** ☎ 818/240-7870 ⊕ www.glendalechamber.com. **Hollywood Chamber of Commerce Info Center** ☎ 323/469-8311 ⊕ www.hollywoodchamber.net. **L.A. Inc./The Convention and Visitors Bureau** ☎ 213/624-7300 or 800/228-2452 ⊕ www.lacvb. com. **Long Beach Area Convention and Visitors Bureau** ☎ 562/436-3645 ⊕ www.visitlongbeach. com. **Pasadena Convention & Visitors Bureau** ☎ 626/795-9311 ⊕ www.pasadenacal.com. **Redondo Beach Visitors Bureau** ☎ 310/374-2171 or 800/282-0333 ⊕ www.visitredondo.com. **Santa Monica Convention & Visitors Bureau** ☎ 310/319-6263 or 800/544-5319 ⊕ www.santamonica.com. **Santa Monica Visitor Centers** ☎ 310/393-7593. **West Hollywood Convention and Visitors Bureau** ☎ 310/289-2525 or 800/368-6020 ⊕ www. visitwesthollywood.com.

WEB SITES

We're really proud of our Web site: Fodors.com is a great place to begin any journey. Scan Travel Wire for suggested itineraries, travel deals, restaurant and hotel openings, and other up-to-the-minute info. Check out Booking to research prices and book plane tickets, hotel rooms, rental cars, and vacation packages. Head to Talk for on-the-ground pointers from travelers who frequent our message boards. You can also link to loads of other travel-related resources.

After your trip, be sure to rate the places you visited and share your experiences and travel tips with us and other Fodor-

ites in Travel Ratings and Talk on www. fodors.com.

LAVoice.org (⊕ www.lavoice.org) is an independent blog with news, observations, and unscripted rants about all things L.A. Check out **www.la.com** for insiders' guides to bars, restaurants, concerts, and other forms of entertainment. An editor's blog opines on everything from new billboards to movie premieres.

L.A. Observed (⊕ www.laobserved.com) is a must-read for many Angelenos, who want its daily media and political updates. It's also good for L.A. history references and links to other local media sites.

TV personality **Huell Howser's Web site** (⊕ www.kcet.com/programsa-z/huells) revisits unusual L.A. places he has covered on his show, from a *menudo* (tripe stew) factory to a museum for African-American firefighters. For L.A.-centric gossip, check out **Defamer** (⊕ www.defamer.com), which tracks movie deals, celebrity sightings, and the activities of A-list stars with snarky honesty. **Curbed L.A.** (⊕ la.curbed.com) is a straight-talking source for news on local lifestyle news, real estate (learn how much J.Lo is asking for her Sunset Strip mansion), and links to other L.A. sites.

The **city of Los Angeles** government site (⊕ www.lacity.org) has various entertainment and cultural links. The **Central Library's Web site** (⊕ www.lapl.org) has sections on books set in L.A. and regional history resources. There are several community Web sites that will give you a closer look at particular neighborhoods and often include events listings; a few of the best include **Echopark.net** (⊕ www. echopark.net), **Venicebeach.com** (⊕ www. venicebeach.com), and Santa Monica's **LookOut** newsletter site (⊕ www. surfsantamonica.com).

The **Los Angeles Conservancy** site (⊕ www.laconservancy.org) includes info on the preservation of local historic buildings, as well as the latest on its walking tours. For information on festivals, exhibitions, performances, and special events, visit the **Los Angeles Cultural Affairs Department** site (⊕ www.culturela.org). The city's **Department of Recreation and Parks**

(⊕ www.laparks.com) posts info on all kinds of sports facilities, parks, and even dog runs. Through **Gallery Guide.org** (⊕ www.galleryguide.org) you can check on upcoming openings, shows, and events in the city's fine-arts community. The **Academy of Motion Pictures Arts and Sciences** rolls out scads of Academy Awards info at ⊕ www.oscars.org, plus details on other Academy events. Get more celebrity scoop on where stars shop, dine, and play at ⊕ www.seeing-stars.com.

🛈 **Time Zones** Timeanddate.com ⊕ www.timeanddate.com/worldclock can help you figure out the correct time anywhere in the world.

🛈 **Weather** Accuweather.com ⊕ www.accuweather.com is an independent weather-forecasting service with especially good coverage of hurricanes. **Weather.com** ⊕ www.weather.com is the Web site for the Weather Channel.

INDEX

PHOTO CREDITS

NOTES

NOTES

NOTES

NOTES

NOTES

ABOUT OUR WRITERS

Matthew Flynn, a screenwriter and television producer, found that updating the Exploring chapter was the next best thing to showing you his beloved city himself. When not traveling, this native Angeleno scours L.A. for the ultimate chocolate cake and iced tea (they haven't been found). His favorite city view is from the roof of The Grove shopping center.

Journalist and gal about town, **Kastle Waserman** has been covering LA for the past decade for such publications as the *Los Angeles Times, Launch,* the *New York Post,* and *New Times.* Currently writing a regular column on L.A. for the Cool Grrrls Web site, she's always up for trying a signature drink at a new hot spot.

For the past decade, dining writer **Roger J. Grody** has been eating his way through the streets of Los Angeles, from nondescript taco stands to opulent dining rooms. Along the way he's recorded his discoveries for publications such as *Where–Los Angeles, Westways,* the Gault Millau guides, and the *Los Angeles Times* Web site.

Finding the unexpected is **Kathy A. McDonald's** favorite assignment. A writer with peripatetic beats who often writes about the film business, she covered our lodging chapter. An advocate for historic preservation (yes, L.A. has buildings worth saving!), she is a volunteer at Frank Lloyd Wright's Hollyhock House in Barnsdall Art Park as well as for the Los Angeles Conservancy, a local preservation organization.

Lina Lecaro, a born-and-raised Angeleno, covers our nightlife and arts beats. She has written for *LA Weekly* for nearly a decade and also regularly contributes to the *L.A. Times* calendar section and Sunday magazine. Her writing has been published in *Soma, Detour, Flaunt, Performer, Nightclub & Bar,* and Rollingstone.com.

Laura Randall has lived in L.A. since 1999; for this edition she updated our Sports & the Outdoors and Smart Travel Tips chapters. A film junkie, she served as the West Coast business editor of the *Hollywood Reporter* until 2001. She now writes regularly on travel, entertainment, and other topics for the *Los Angeles Times, Sunset Magazine,* the *New York Times,* and the *Philadelphia Daily News.* Her favorite L.A. flicks are *Chinatown* and *L.A. Story.*

Kristina Brooks, our shopping expert, lived in New York, Berkeley, Atlanta, and Philadelphia before eventually finding herself in the L.A. area. While at Berkeley, she became the managing editor of the Berkeley travel guides. She now works as freelance writer and at Scripps College.

Orange County expert **Kathy Bryant,** a freelance writer based in Huntington Beach, has been writing about art, antiques, design, and travel for nearly 30 years. She's been an art critic for the *Orange County Register,* editor-in-chief of *California Homes* magazine, and had a weekly design column in the *Los Angeles Times.* She is currently the Los Angeles correspondent for *Art & Antiques* and also writes for the *Los Angeles Times, California Homes,* and *TravelAge West,* among others.